The Naturalist and his 'Beautiful Islands'
Charles Morris Woodford in the Western Pacific

David Russell Lawrence

The Naturalist and his 'Beautiful Islands'
Charles Morris Woodford in the Western Pacific

David Russell Lawrence

PRESS

Published by ANU Press
The Australian National University
Canberra ACT 0200, Australia
Email: anupress@anu.edu.au
This title is also available online at http://press.anu.edu.au

National Library of Australia Cataloguing-in-Publication entry

Author: Lawrence, David (David Russell), author.

Title: The naturalist and his 'beautiful islands' : Charles Morris Woodford in the Western Pacific / David Russell Lawrence.

ISBN: 9781925022032 (paperback) 9781925022025 (ebook)

Subjects: Woodford, C. M., 1852-1927.
Great Britain. Colonial Office--Officials and employees--Biography.
Ethnology--Solomon Islands.
Natural history--Solomon Islands.
Colonial administrators--Solomon Islands--Biography.
Solomon Islands--Description and travel.

Dewey Number: 577.099593

All rights reserved. No part of this publication may be reproduced, stored in a retrieval system or transmitted in any form or by any means, electronic, mechanical, photocopying or otherwise, without the prior permission of the publisher.

Cover image: Woodford and men at Aola on return from Natalava (PMBPhoto56-021; Woodford 1890: 144).

Cover design and layout by ANU Press

This edition © 2014 ANU Press

Contents

Acknowledgments xi

Note on the text xiii

Introduction 1

1. Charles Morris Woodford: Early life and education 9
2. Pacific journeys 25
3. Commerce, trade and labour 35
4. A naturalist in the Solomon Islands 63
5. Liberalism, Imperialism and colonial expansion 139
6. The British Solomon Islands Protectorate: Colonialism without capital 169
7. Expansion of the Protectorate 1898–1900 197
8. The new social order 217
9. The plantation economy 243
10. The critical question of labour 287
11. Woodford and the Western Pacific High Commission 309

Conclusion 343

Bibliography 351

Woodford in London, 1885.

Source: PMBPhoto56-137.

This book is dedicated to my Solomon Islands colleagues and friends who have worked with me on numerous social science research projects in the islands since 2005. I have been fortunate to be involved with many Solomon Islanders in my work and to be able to travel widely within the 'these beautiful islands'. My special thanks goes to Solomon Rakei Seimoana, my long-term research assistant, guide, friend and, during some difficult times, my protector. His family from Tikopia, especially his brother John Foimua and sister-in-law Karen from Malaita, have been the secure and trustworthy foundation on which my work has been based.

My hope is that the Solomon Islands will emerge from this difficult period a much happier and more confident place. The beautiful islands—the shining place—that I remember from my childhood.

Acknowledgments

A very warm and special thanks goes to Joan and Keith Presswell for their friendship and for their generosity in depositing the Woodford archive at The Australian National University (ANU). My thanks also goes to Kylie Moloney at the Pacific Manuscripts Bureau and to Karina Taylor, formerly with the Pacific Research Archive at ANU, who sadly died during the writing of this book. Both archives contain wonderful resources for the Pacific historians and anthropologists, and these collections are world class. It is a fine thing to know that these institutions have now taken on the trust and care of the historically and culturally significant Woodford collection. Nicola Tubbs, Customer Service Assistant at the Gravesend Library, was exceptionally helpful and found the missing newspaper article written by a school colleague of Woodford that is referred to in this work. Mike Howlett, also of Gravesend and, like Woodford, an authority on birdwing butterflies—six degrees of separation—was kind enough to take a photograph of 146 Milton Road, Gravesend. I would also like to thank Herbie Whitmore of the West Grinstead Local History Group for his information and photographs of Grinstead House Farm and St Peter's Cowfold. All contacts were secured through the power of the internet.

I also wish to acknowledge the assistance of Dr Jari Kupiainen from the Centre for Creative Industries of the Karelia University of Applied Sciences in Joensuu, Finland, who spent much time enhancing and cleaning the historic images. I would also like to thank the staff of the Archives and Records section of the Australian Museum in Sydney, in particular Vanessa Finney, for giving me access to archives and the Capell/Lucas album, and to Dr Brian Lassig, the Assistant Director, Research and Collections at the Museum for facilitating that access. The staff of the Noel Butlin Archives Centre at ANU has given access to Burns, Philp & Co records. Staff at the Pictures Collection and the Microfilm sections of the National Library of Australia and the State Library of New South Wales have also been extremely kind and considerate. I am especially grateful for the assistance and support of Julian Ghonigolo, Mike Floyd Puhara, Louisa Laekemi and Kari James at the National Archives Solomon Islands (NASI). I hope we can work together to strengthen the ties between ANU and the NASI in preserving the heritage of the Solomon Islands. Dr Aoife O'Brien and Dr Ian Heath have been generous in allowing me access to their unpublished theses. Rhys Richards sent me a copy of his new book *Head Hunters Black and White* when I requested a copy. Dr Stewart Firth and the Pacific Editorial Board at ANU have been most encouraging.

Note on the text

Where necessary for clarity I have included relative values of the English pound. The figures, taken from www.measuringworth.com, include a range of comparative values. I have chosen to present the relative worth of the pound using average earnings. The following table illustrates that the value of average earnings declined during the period 1880–1915. The declining earnings are indicative of the economic downturn at the end of the 19th century.

Table 1. Comparative value of the pound sterling.

Original date	Value	Current date	Comparative value
1880	£1	2010	£421
1885	£1	2010	£423
1890	£1	2010	£416
1895	£1	2010	£376
1900	£1	2010	£346
1905	£1	2010	£337
1910	£1	2010	£331
1915	£1	2010	£287

Source: http://www.measuringworth.com.

Research into contemporary newspaper sources from the late-19th and early-20th centuries is now possible through the *Trove Digitised Newspaper* database maintained by the National Library of Australia and *Papers Past* online from the National Library of New Zealand. Both are wonderful research sources and I have made extensive use of them. Much important information was reported in newspapers and I consider those sources to be primary research tools that cross-reference and date many obscure historical notes. Newspaper accounts also report speeches and interviews with prominent people in some considerable detail. These are now accessible, at no cost in Australia, due to the excellent online library databases.

The spelling and names of people and places, particularly villages, in the Solomon Islands have changed significantly in recent years. Ingava, the prominent chief of Rubiana is now known as Hiqava of Roviana, Guadalcanar is now only known as Guadalcanal, Santa Ysabel is now called Santa Isabel or Isabel for short, San Christoval/San Cristobal is more commonly called Makira, Tucopia is now more famously known as Tikopia. Since independence on 7 July 1978, the Solomon Islands as a nation is now formally called 'Solomon Islands' without the definite article—as in the 'Government of Solomon Islands'. I have attempted to use the common spelling of the time for the sake of clarity but, where necessary, I have included both names.

David Lawrence

2014

Introduction

In January 1890 the account of three visits to the Solomon Islands made between 1886 and 1889 by the young English naturalist, Charles Morris Woodford, was published in London, to some critical acclaim, by George Philip and Sons. With a typical late-Victorian eye for romance in the exotic, and an appeal to the vogue for tales of adventure and daring, his publisher called the book *A Naturalist Among the Head-hunters* (Woodford 1890b). In that same year it was published in three editions, one in London, one in Melbourne, and one in New York. For a young traveller's account and first published book, it is well written, sympathetic to the social and economic conditions of the Solomon Islanders of that time and, even now, is very evocative for anyone familiar with the islands and the people. Publication of the book further emphasised the practical value of scientific observation from the field. Arguments about the relationship between observations made in the field and the scientific theorising made in the study and the museum were endemic in the world of 19th century natural history (Driver 1998: 24). Knowledge from the field was not always to be trusted. For the author, the authority of his exploration depended substantially on the writing of a well-accepted narrative of travel.

Woodford, then 38, listed his professional associations as Fellow of the Royal Geographical Society, Corresponding Fellow of the Zoological Society, Fellow of the Royal Geographical Society of Australia, and Fellow of the Linnaean Society of New South Wales. During the course of his travels and work in the Solomon Islands over the next 25 years, Woodford would make collections of over 20,000 natural history specimens for the British Museum of Natural History and give more than 500 ethnological specimens to the British Museum and other major collections (O'Brien 2011). He also left us a substantial archival collection of reports, press cuttings, personal diaries and photographs (Woodford papers PMB 1290 & PMB 1381, PMB Photo 56 & Photo 58). His contribution to the natural history and ethnology of the Solomon Islands is significant and the collections remain unequalled in size and diversity (Tennant 1999: 426). Unfortunately, his botanical, zoological and ethnological contributions to Pacific research remain largely unrecognised.

By the time Woodford published his main book, two descriptive reports of his three trips had been published in the *Proceedings of the Royal Geographical Society* (Woodford 1888a and 1890c). A short article with six images had been published in the *Illustrated London News*, the world's first illustrated weekly newspaper (Anon 1889b). A second article with four of those images had been published in the *Popular Science Monthly* (Woodford 1889) a successful American magazine founded by Edward Youmans to disseminate scientific knowledge to the educated nonprofessional. These papers focussed on the results of the first and second expeditions. The idea that men of science, amateur or professional, should also publish in popular literature was well accepted by the educated public of the late-Victorian period. Publishers with explicit religious credentials or sober academic values, like John Murray, competed with those whose literature was secular, even radical, such as John Chapman and his *Westminster Review*. Woodford's book was published at an opportune time. In fact, the Solomon Islands had just been the subject of two long articles in the *Westminster Review* (Anon 1888a and 1888b). To be taken as an authority on the Solomon Islands, Woodford had laid his ground soundly.

Reviews of his book were numerous. Alfred Russel Wallace, the naturalist considered to be the 19th century's leading expert on the geographical distribution of animal species, reviewed the book for *Nature*. While praising Woodford's writing style in a slightly condescending tone as perhaps a little humorous Wallace did say '[t]he book is well got up, well illustrated, and very pleasantly written. It is full of information regards the natives, the scenery, and the natural history of these little-known but very interesting islands, and can therefore be confidently recommended to all who care for books of travel in little-known countries' (Wallace 1890). In Australia the book was reviewed extensively in the *Sydney Morning Herald* (19 November 1890), in the *Australian Town and Country Journal* (26 April 1890: 27), and in the *Queenslander* (19 April 1890: 757). In England reviews appeared in the *Observer* (9 May 1890), in the *News of the World* (24 August 1890) and a number of other regional papers (Woodford papers PMB 1290 Items 9/28 & 9/28/1). Woodford also received a personal letter from Sir William MacGregor from Government House, Port Moresby in late October 1890 complimenting him on the quality and historical importance of his Solomon Islands book (Woodford papers PMB 1381/016b).

Woodford himself wrote '[t]hat the Solomon Islands will one day be of great importance to the Australian Colonies I have not the slightest doubt', and '[t]he object of my visit to the islands was neither political nor commercial, but the following pages, while giving some account of the islands, will enable the outside world to form an idea of the state of affairs now existing' (Woodford 1890b: preface). His natural history collecting gave him an opportunity to travel throughout the islands and this was to lead to an important career as the first Resident Commissioner of the British Solomon Islands Protectorate. He was to remain in that post from 1897 to 1915. Woodford almost single-handedly established the Protectorate, with very little financial or even political support from the British Colonial Office. As one writer has put it, the British Protectorate of the Solomon Islands was established with '[o]ne man and sixpence' (Coates 1970: 220–239). Woodford's contribution to the establishment of the British Solomon Islands Protectorate is therefore significant. At that time in the establishment of protectorates, Imperial agents like Woodford were key intermediaries between the colonial authorities and local peoples and settlers. These officials were brokers between two alien worlds. As mediators with local factions and as interpreters of local social and political groupings, they could be wayward, sometimes hard to control, sometimes tactful or blunt implementers of Imperial intentions (Newbury 2010: 1).

As Resident Commissioner, Woodford was in a difficult position. He was both a client of and a broker between the Colonial Office in London and the Western Pacific High Commission in Suva. His personal and professional relationships with senior officials in both agencies often led to difficulties and personal conflicts. Many of these conflicts have been discussed in other work that has considered Woodford's role as a colonial administrator (Bennett 1987; Heath 1974a and 1978). These studies have been assessments of Woodford's role in pacification campaigns in the New Georgia Islands and in the controversial waste lands regulations that alienated large areas of land for plantation use with little reference to customary owners and their rights. Colonial government was the politics of compromise. As Newbury (2010: 7) has shown in his careful re-examination of the career of Arthur Hamilton Gordon, Crown Colonies, such as Fiji and the Gilbert and Ellice Islands, and Protectorates, like the Solomon Islands, were managed as forms of benevolent tutelage often established following not-so-benevolent military intervention. The Solomon Islands were not occupied by military force in 1893 but in the four decades before annexation the coastal districts of many islands were bombarded by vessels of the Royal Navy Australia Station in reprisal for attacks on white traders and settlers. These 'acts of war' were indiscriminate, often careless and while it is difficult to know if many villagers were killed in these actions, much property was destroyed. To local people, the arrival of the Royal Navy was a signal to retreat into the deep jungle. It was also incomprehensible.

Few men have so prophetically determined their future as Woodford, who wrote: 'I know of no place where firm and paternal government would sooner produce beneficial results than in the Solomons. The numerous small tribes into which the population is split up would render any organised resistance to properly constituted authority quite futile, while I believe that the natives themselves would not be slow to recognise the advantages of increased security to life and property. Here is an object worthy indeed the devotion of one's life' (Woodford 1890b: 23fn). In truth, the 'natives' did not easily submit to colonial authority. There was long standing resistance to imposed law and order in New Georgia and on Malaita, but despite this, and some justifiable criticism of Woodford's pacification and land policies, he truly did devote himself to the islands. However, Woodford's career extended beyond the boundaries of the Solomon Islands. He collected natural history specimens in Fiji and the Gilbert and Ellice Islands (Kiribati and Tuvalu). He worked briefly with the Western Pacific High Commission and Treasury in Suva and was, for one short trip, a Government Agent on a labour vessel returning indentured workers back to their homes in the Gilbert Islands. He even collected moths on Peel Island in Moreton Bay during an enforced stay when quarantined there during a cholera scare. He lived and worked in the Western Pacific from 1882 to 1915. It was a long, often arduous, career.

Charles Morris Woodford was a product of his time, his class and his background. He was a strong believer in his work and his role in developing a peaceful Solomon Islands within the wider British colonial system. Formal colonialism was a paternalistic system. Both missionaries and colonial officials carried their cultures and perceptions, and by inference their biases, with them. Thomas (1990: 148) wisely wrote that 'both historians and anthropologists have written as though colonisers had no culture', for overgeneralising that all Europeans in the Pacific were racist invaders hardly enables one to evaluate the colonial experience faced by local peoples. This book seeks to explain why a man who wrote such a powerful phrase as 'the devotion of one's life' in the margins of a footnote of a book and then spent all his life in fulfilment of that duty. With the passage of time it is possible to see how Woodford lived his years in Tulagi on the periphery of British colonial developments. In the Solomon Islands he lived not only out of place but largely within a different mode of time. Fortunately, Charles Morris Woodford left us a large and valuable archive of papers, diaries and letters. Reading the actual written pages of the diaries is a thought-provoking experience. These have been available for research for some time (Woodford papers PMB 1290) but only recently have the original archival documents been made more accessible and new material gifted to The Australian National University by the descendants of the Woodford family (Woodford papers PMB 1381 and PMB Photo 56 & Photo 58). It seems a good time to revisit Charles Morris Woodford and his record.

Charles Morris Woodford—the man

What sort of man was Charles Morris Woodford? From the diaries of his early expeditions as a naturalist he appears strong, confident, assured of his place and comfortable in his role as an explorer/adventurer. He was a product of a particular class and society that trained men to see themselves as leaders, as men of authority and position. They were confident of their place in the world. Woodford's views of the Solomon Islanders would not have been greatly different from his opinions of working-class English or, for that matter, colonial Australians. It matters not now about our opinion of that class of English for in early times this view was unquestioned.

His relationship with his family was formal. At that time, this too was unquestioned. Woodford was the legal and assumed head of his family. He lived apart from his wife and sons for many years, but social convention did not see this as strange. His wife stayed at home in England or Australia, his sons went to boarding school. This was the pattern of normal upper-middle-class family life in the late-Victorian and Edwardian periods. The lack of available documentation between Woodford and his family makes it difficult to know more of the personal man but his marriage was long and comfortable and his sons respected their father.

As an administrator he assumed the role as head of his colonial officers. He was in a benevolent and paternalistic position over the local people—and the white traders, merchants, missionaries and beachcombers—who lived in the islands. He wrestled with the formalities of the bureaucracy and, given the burden of the Western Pacific High Commission and then the Colonial Office above that, it is easy to see why he sometimes rebelled. The British colonial structure was both pedantic and parsimonious. Some official correspondence is wonderfully insightful of people and place but much of it is mundane and tedious. Woodford's health began to fail after 1907 and some of his tendencies to antagonise his superiors date from after that. Woodford was seen by the white settler population as a good administrator. How local people viewed him and his decisions is not recorded.

Those colonial days are now past. We are fortunate to have much of Woodford's documents and photographs to add to the story of colonial life in the Solomon Islands before the First World War. Charles Morris Woodford gave his working life to the Solomon Islands, just as he said he would when he wrote that there was no other place where firm and paternal government would produce beneficial results as in the islands. He firmly believed that his mission was to bring security of life and property to the peoples of the islands. Having written '[h]ere is an object worthy indeed the devotion of one's life', he then tried to see his dream achieved. He deserves our respect for trying.

Solomon Islands today

There is, however, a more pressing need than simply academic research. The Solomon Islands are beautiful and dramatic. As an anthropologist I have been fortunate to have been working there since 2005 on various social science research projects, mainly large-scale surveys of social needs assessment. The Solomon Islands, as a nation, is in a difficult rebuilding stage. In late 1998, Guadalcanal freedom fighters, first called the Guadalcanal Revolutionary Army and then the Isatabu Freedom Movement, forced the evacuation of more than

35,000 migrant settlers, mostly Malaitans, living in the Honiara area. In response, a rival Malaitan Eagle Force emerged in mid-1999 and staged a coup d'état after combining with elements from the national police. The open conflict between these groups became known as the Tensions. In July 2003 intervention forces, called RAMSI (Regional Assistance Mission to Solomon Islands) composed of military and police from Australia, New Zealand and other Pacific nations, re-established law and order (Allen and Dinnen 2010). RAMSI has now been in the country for more than a decade and this policing component will be there for some time to come. There have been some excellent examinations of the crisis and the intervention, but they are not the focus of this book. The reader interested in the Tensions and RAMSI's role in the reconstruction is referred to Allen (2005, 2009 and 2011), Dinnen (2002), Allen and Dinnen (2010), Dinnen and Firth (2008), Fraenkel (2004), and Braithwaite *et al*. (2010). The reports of the Truth and Reconciliation Commission, recently made available despite the government embargo, contain much important information on the nature and extent of the civil unrest, its aftermath and the need to confront the truth as an act of healing (Solomon Islands Government. Truth and Reconciliation Commission 2012).

The civil unrest had strong historical roots despite being labelled 'ethnic violence' in the media. In fact internal conflicts are often the culmination of actions precipitated by a social environment structured in the past (Solomon Islands Government. Truth and Reconciliation Commission 2012: 27). The fighting between Malaitan and Guadalcanal groups was exacerbated by economic disparities that bred social and economic deprivation, especially in rural areas. The many-layered social and cultural context in which Melanesian land and resource use are constructed are entangled in 'historical articulations of resistance against a foreign state that is perceived as lacking local legitimacy' (Allen and Dinnen 2010: 308). This resistance is especially true in Malaita. Internal migration to the largest town, Honiara, by people seeking a better life led to the growth of large squatter settlements and illegal buying and selling of customary land. In-migration is inherently destabilising and has led to personal violence and anger between different cultural groups. The result was collapse of political legitimacy and virtual bankruptcy of the state. Restoration of law and order is only part of a larger picture. State building is centred on three pillars: law and justice, economic governance, and machinery of government. These are worthy goals but once again the West is seen to be imposing neo-liberal ideas of development, law enforcement and procedural justice and economic restructuring that assumes that 'Western-derived notions of "best practice" are inherently superior to any others' (Allen and Dinnen 2010: 318). Liberal peace serves to divorce conflicts, especially those in developing countries with a multiplicity of cultural and social subgroups, from the social context of the disharmony and deprivation.

This island-based deprivation was partly a result of resource availability, or lack thereof, and the suitability of land that could be used for plantation development. This disparity had its foundation in the early colonial period when the people of the Solomon Islands became divided into the 'haves' and the 'have-nots'. Those from the west, particularly Guadalcanal and New Georgia, were able to grow produce on their lands and sell it to traders and planters. They were the 'haves'. Those people from the east, notably from Malaita but also from other outer islands, had little choice but to sell their labour, firstly to recruiters who took men to the sugarcane fields of Queensland and Fiji, and then to planters in the west. These men, mostly Malaitans, became the principal wage labourers (Allen 2009). They became the 'have-nots'. This created elements of class tension among peoples and led to distrust, enmity and struggle by some Malaitans. They actively rejected pacification by the colonial administration and Christianity brought in by missionaries before the arrival of colonial rule. The act of British colonialisation imposed laws and values that were alien to the fragmented, culturally diverse peoples of the islands. At the time of colonialisation in 1893 the British Protectorate would have had only about 100,000 people speaking over 65 languages. Figures published by the Special Lands Commission in 1957 note that in 1930 Hogbin reported more than 20 dialects on Guadalcanal alone and the population figure quoted by the commissioners of 106,309 people was collated from local records not a formal census (Allan 1957: 12–17). Even today there are only a little over 500,000 people in the nation. Communities are generally coastal, small and physically isolated. There are more than 6,000 rural communities of varying sizes in the country (Lawrence, Allen *et al*. 2006–2007). This is a multifaceted society made up of many cultural and language groups. In the small villages, people continue to operate a subsistence economy, there is a substantial wage-earning agricultural working class on oil palm plantations and in the fishing industry, the government bureaucracy is inefficient but modernising, and in the main town, Honiara, there is now a sizable local middle class. The cost of living is high and wages are low. The ordinary wage earner is finding it hard to support his or her family. Support for the extended family is becoming a burden for many. Government services in rural regions are poor, education and health systems are not providing Solomon Islanders with quality of life and many of the underlying causes of the Tensions remain unresolved. The youth are particularly disaffected.

This book is a study of the life and work of the man who set up the framework of the first colonial state, the British Solomon Islands Protectorate, between 1897 and 1915. This was a time when a particularly British mix of idealism and pragmatism characterised Imperialism. Woodford's values, beliefs and directions are important to understand in the light of modern Solomon Islands history. Woodford's very genuine and firmly held belief that this particular group of islands would benefit from 'firm and paternal government' was visionary but not without its critics. In recent years the nation has been called Australia's 'failing neighbour' (Wainwright 2003). This discourse has become prominent in international relations following the breakdown of state-centred law and order in places such as Somalia, Bosnia, Kosovo and Afghanistan, leading to the policies of co-operative intervention (Wesley-Smith 2007: 39). Woodford would be sorely grieved to see his 'beautiful islands' reduced to such a parlous state (Woodford 1890b: 188). The problem with the small Melanesian states is not that they are prone to fall apart but that they were imperfectly assembled in the first place. Structures were rudimentary, resources—both manpower and financial—were limited. Opportunities to diversify an economy reliant on tropical product extraction remain limited, the territorial reach of the government incomplete. Western institutional implants exist uneasily alongside the indigenous institutions that have persisted throughout the colonial and post-colonial eras (Wesley-Smith 2007). The creation of a state is a complex task. This book attempts to explain how Solomon Islands, as a colonial state, came into existence through the eyes of its creator—Charles Morris Woodford.

1. Early life and education

Charles Morris Woodford was born in Milton next Gravesend in Kent on 30 October 1852, the eldest son of five children—three sons and two daughters—of Henry Pack Woodford and his wife Mary. The Woodfords lived at 91 Milton Road opposite a large park and the Gravesend Grammar School. Gravesend is a large and economically important town on the southern banks of the Thames Estuary with a long history as a trading and commercial centre dating back to Roman occupation. Both Gravesend and Milton are recorded in the Domesday Book, that great rural survey made under command of William the Conqueror and completed in 1068. Both appear as parishes within the Manor of Gravesham (Cruden 1843: 9–10). Gravesend absorbed Milton in 1914. Henry Pack Woodford was a prosperous wine and spirit merchant with premises at 146 Milton Road (Kelly Directories Ltd 1903). The building still stands. Henry Pack Woodford had assumed ownership of the family firm after the co-partnership with his father, Edward William Woodford, was dissolved in 1841 (*The London Gazette*, issue 20021, 24 September 1841: 2381).

Figure 1. 146 Milton Rd Gravesend: premises of Henry Pack Woodford, wine and spirit merchant.

Source: Photo courtesy of Mike Howlett, 2013.

Edward Woodford, Charles Woodford's grandfather who subsequently retired to Jersey, was formerly innkeeper of *The Falcon* in East Street Gravesend—now Royal Pier Road—at a time when an inn was not a tavern or public house but more like a hotel that also sold wine and spirits. He, in turn, was the son of William Woodford who established the family hotel business in 1785 in Gravesend, having moved from Northamptonshire (Woodford papers PMB 1381/005el). William was most certainly a joint owner of *The Falcon* in 1793. According to family traditions, he walked the distance to London with £4,000 in his boots. Henry Pack Woodford was a man of some importance to the commercial life of Gravesend. In addition to being an Alderman on the Town Council, he was a Governor of the Gravesend Hospital and director of the local gas company. He was an executor of the sale of settled estates and was appointed to a Committee of Inspection authorising him to act as an advisor and superintendent to the trustee of bankrupt estates (*The London Gazette* issue 23263, 14 June 1867: 3384 and issue 25616, 13 August 1886: 3992). When he died on 31 May 1889, his estate passed to his wife Mary and was probated in August (*The London Gazette* issue 25982, 11 October 1889: 5389; Woodford papers PMB 1381/034c). The estate, which included the Gravesend building, its stock and fittings, and a business in Wye, was valued at over £9,000 (£3,750,000 in current values). Mary Woodford died in June 1899 (*The Gravesend Reporter* 3 June 1899, Woodford papers PMB 1381/034c). The family was solid, well-established, and upper middle class at a time when London was the commercial centre of the British Empire.

Tonbridge School

The three sons of Henry Pack and Mary Woodford were Charles, Henry and Edward. They were all educated at Tonbridge School, also in Kent. Charles attended as a boarder from age 12 in 1864 and completed sixth form in 1871. Tonbridge, then a small but exclusive boys' grammar school located not far from Gravesend, was founded in 1553 on an endowment from The Skinners' Company, one of the oldest guild companies in England with power to control the lucrative fur trade. The school was established for the sons of local gentry and country families. In the early period, boys were expected to write in English and Latin for admission and as a grammar school, under its formal meaning, it was a requirement that Latin, Greek and Hebrew should be offered to students. Like a number of other public schools in England, Tonbridge began to grow when the demand for administrators and soldiers to serve the British Empire began in the early 19th century.

Other notable Tonbridgians who would become important to Woodford in the Solomon Islands were William Halse Rivers Rivers, the ethnologist and early psychologist, who was later to join with Alfred Cort Haddon and other academics in the Cambridge Anthropological Expedition to Torres Straits in 1898 (Haddon 19011935), the first multi-disciplinary ethnological expedition to Melanesia. Rivers would later visit the Solomon Islands as part of the Percy Sladen Trust Expedition in 1907 and 1908. Woodford would also contribute to a significant study Rivers made into the question of population decline in the Pacific following European contact (Rivers 1922). Another former student was Cecil Wilson who would become Bishop of Melanesia and a leader in the Melanesian Mission (Hughes-Hughes 1886). Wilson was a senior figure in the Anglican mission and would be a regular visitor to the administrative headquarters on Tulagi after the establishment of the British Solomon Island Protectorate. This formal link to the Anglican Church was to be an important one for the development of the Solomon Islands. The late-Victorian age was one bound by ties of family and friends, by links between schools and universities and by the constraints imposed by class. In the colonial outposts of the Empire these connections created bonds that provided the principal means of patronage and promotion before a centralised system of recruitment was created controlled by officers from the metropolitan capital, London (Hyam 2002: 308).

The attraction of Tonbridge was its growing academic credentials, its location and the construction of a large, comfortable new school building in 1864 and a chapel that had opened in 1859. The Head, Rev Dr James Ind Welldon, was a confirmed classicist. Latin prayers were heard three times a day. The curriculum was traditional. Science as a subject was not added to the curriculum until after his tenure in 1875. Apparently, he did recognise the talents of Charles Woodford who was excused from 'fagging' or 'calling over' so that he could indulge his hobby of butterfly collecting. Fagging at Tonbridge, contrary to popular ideas, was not the Dickensian idea of young boys performing menial servant duties for older boys. It meant taking turns fielding and fetching cricket balls and footballs for senior students. For small boys this could involve long periods on the playing fields in all weathers. It could be excused with a 'leave off' certificate signed by parents or teachers. Welldon abolished football fagging early in 1864 (Orchard 1991).

Educating the administrators and soldiers of the Empire

This particular period in the expansion of education for middle class boys was not matched by the expansion of employment considered suitable for the middle classes (Musgrove 1959). The middle class of the Victorian era in Britain has been variously defined. However, professional men, well-to-do clergy, the lesser gentry, as well as industrial managers constituted a group that earned a salary of between £200 (£120,000 in current values) and £1,000 (£600,000 in current values) per year at that time. In the middle of the 19th century maintenance of a suitable house, domestic servants, the necessary standards of dress and a fee-paying education for the children could not be obtained on less than £200 a year (Feinstein 1990a and 1990b). However, the public school education so admired by Victorian parents was really only suitable for those who had personal fortunes, estates to inherit or who could gain access to purchased commissions in the army or navy. Positions in the Anglican Church could also be obtained by patronage. Elite, gentlemanly education in late-Victorian England posed public service as a moral status symbol that stressed leadership, loyalty, casual assurance and a light touch in command well suited to the amateur ideal. Specialisation in any form was seen as narrowing one's talents. Effective leadership was seen to depend on qualities of mind, morals and manners, not expertise (Wilkinson 1963). The amateur idea of the well-rounded man stressed moderation and compromise, social harmony and the conservative notion that social inequality, and social class, was in accordance with the laws of nature. Elite education became a means by which members of the well-to-do middle class could be absorbed into the upper class of public officials, government and the established Church.

However, a higher class clerk in the War Office in 1887 began on only £100 a year and would not reach £200 until he was 30 years old. There was uncertainty and anxiety among the growing middle class, especially those who had risen to wealth by trade and commerce, that there was no access to the higher professions for their sons (Musgrove 1959: 108). Although London was the centre of political and economic life for the British Empire, prospects for a young man were even more depressing in the city. While the population was rising the number of career positions open to the well-educated was not expanding. There were few careers open to those with talent in the business houses. Conditions appeared to be worsening for 'the upward path of the penniless adventurer in the City, how great soever his aptitude and ability has become very much more arduous' (Musgrove 1959: 110, quoting from *The Cornhill Magazine*, 13 (1902): 764–775). Such a man could hope, at the best, for a salary in a clerical post of some £300 per annum at the end of his career. Later Woodford would attempt to establish a brief career in the city that would be unsuccessful. For young men like Charles Woodford, the prospects for useful and interesting employment in Britain during the 1870s were poor. The colonies of South Africa, Australia and the Pacific held more promise.

1. Early life and education

An obscure newspaper article

The only note documenting Woodford's talents as natural history collector at school is in an obscure article written for the local newspaper, the *Gravesend Journal, Dartford Observer and County Intelligencer*, dated 1888, written by an ex-student who signed his name as 'Ignotus Lybia Deserta, Drakensberg Mountains, South Africa' (Heath 1974a: 9; Woodford papers PMB 1290 Item 9/7/1). There is little to identify the author although there are some hints in Woodford's archives and school records. The signature title is part of a speech in the *Aeneid* (Book 1: 381–386) by Virgil (Publius Vergilius Maro) telling of the time when, having fled Troy, Aeneas arrives at Carthage on the shores of Africa after wandering the Mediterranean for seven years (Clay 1988: 200). Here in Carthage he finds himself destitute and unknown but soon discovers that the land is inhabited by the traces of an ancient civilisation. Among the Carthaginians he finds evidence of humanity and sees the growing glory of the city (Clay 1988: 195, 198). The full quote follows:

> 'Bis dēnīs Phrygium cōnscendī nāvibus aequor,
> mātre deā mōnstrante viam, data fāta secūtus;
> vix septem convolsae undīs Eurōque supersunt.
> Ipse ignōtus, egēns, Libyae dēserta peragrō,
> Eurōpā atque Asiā pulsus.'

Nec plūra querentem passa Venus mediō sīc interfāta dolōre est:

> 'I embarked on the Phrygian sea with twice ten ships,
> my goddess mother showing the way, I followed what the fates had given scarcely seven remain shattered by the waves and the Eastwind.
> I myself am unknown, and needy, I travel through the desert of Libya, having been driven from Europe and from Asia.'
> Venus did not endure him complaining more and thus she interrupted him in the middle of his sorrow:
> (Fairclough and Brown 1920: 16; Clay 1988: 195; Conington 1903: 30–31)

The subtext is that the heroes of the *Aeneid* encountered exile, struggle, defeat and success before their eventual return home in triumph. It is little wonder that many old boys from the school would also have sought fame and some fortune in South Africa during the commercial expansion of the Cape Colony in the 1870s and 1880s, the Anglo-Zulu War of 1879 and the subsequent Boer War of 1899–1902. The author of the article, then living in South Africa, had been sent a copy of the local newspaper dated 7 April 1888. This reported on a lecture given by Woodford in the Gravesend Town Hall on the evening of Wednesday 4 April 1888 (*The Gravesend Journal, Dartford Observer and County Intelligencer* 7 April 1888: 8). The well-attended lecture by Woodford that presented the

13

results of his successful two trips to the Solomon Islands between 1886 and 1888 was illustrated by lantern slides, maps, displays of natural history specimens and artefacts.

The author of the article highlighted Woodford's skills as a natural history collector and noted that Woodford informed his audience he had made over 17,000 specimens and brought back a number of cultural artefacts for the British Museum. The author had been a colleague at school. He had been excused from fagging at Tonbridge because of poor health and so spent much time with Woodford collecting in the fields and forests of Kent. The author wrote that he and Woodford had spent time before the departure for the Solomon Islands preparing 'the necessary goods and trinkets, so essential as a substitute for cash, among the raw savage natives of isles almost lost to human knowledge'. Expressions like 'raw savage natives' and 'lost to human knowledge' were common expressions in British magazines and newspapers of that day. The possession of a large, alien Empire meant that the British saw themselves as distinct and special, superior in their laws and political system, their standard of living, in their treatment of women and 'above all, their collective power against societies that they only imperfectly understood but usually perceived as far less developed' (Colley 1992: 324).

Woodford's skill as an amateur natural history collector while at school was not unusual for that time. Local natural history societies were a significant part of civil society in 19th century Britain. They provided a mediating layer of civil social activity between the state and the nation for the sedentary naturalist in the major museums and the many local fieldworkers in their natural history societies were closely linked. It has been estimated that there could have been close to 1,000 local scientific societies in Britain by the late-Victorian era, each conducting fieldtrips, engaging in discussions and lectures and many publishing their findings in reports and papers (Withers and Finnegan 2003). Fieldwork for the Victorian middle classes had a moral as well as a recreational value. The romantic vision of a peaceful rural England, a countryside of many villages linked in social harmony under the paternalistic rule of the local squire had faded in the post-Industrial period. Many towns and villages had been subsumed in the advancing path of industrial growth and the rural labourers had been transformed into the industrial poor. Time spent in the rural landscape was considered to be morally justified.

This intense interest in collecting and classifying spanned class and gender divisions and grew out of the influence of Darwinism in the 1870s and 1880s. The pursuit of science even entered into late-Victorian novels. In *Middlemarch*, written in 1872 but set in 1832, George Eliot placed two forms of scientific knowledge in opposition to each other: the amateur naturalist, the Reverend Farebrother with his study full of drawers of moths and blue-bottles, and the forward looking medical practitioner, Dr Tertius Lydgate, with his new professional views of disease and cleanliness obtained from training in Europe (Eliot 1872: 182–183). The Linnaean system for the classification of plants and animals democratised scientific endeavours and provided both amateurs and professionals with an internationally acceptable language. But the key to connecting locally-based amateurs with a potentially global community of professionals lay in mastering Latin and the binomial nomenclature (Coriale 2008). This explosion of scientific interest took a long time to filter down into the public school education system that continued to favour classical education, traditional social and religious values and conservative politics.

The unnamed author of the article noted that at Tonbridge the Headmaster Welldon had encouraged students with 'glowing accounts of Australia and New Zealand, then at the zenith of their prosperity and lusty youth', and boys read the tales of 'Captain' Thomas Mayne Reid and his adventure books for boys set in South Africa, the American west, Mexico, the Himalayas, and Jamaica. Welldon, at his own initiative and expense, had given an annual prize for entomology and Charles Woodford had won this prize on numerous occasions for his collections of butterflies and the skill in which he had displayed them. It was of little wonder to the author that Woodford should have ventured to the Pacific on collecting expeditions and that these travels had been so successful.

Exploration, adventure and the Empire

The later part of the 19th century saw a change in the way people interpreted colonial expansion, commercial growth and the role of the British Empire with its messages of commerce, civilisation and Christianity. During a century of imperialism—from 1815, the end of the Napoleonic Wars, to 1914, the start of the First World War—Britain extended its economic and cultural power to all parts of the world. Domestic growth was rising but with it came an increase in the population and a need to boost exports to cater for industrial investment and employment. But free trade and Imperialism were consequences of Britain's failure to maintain her position among her main European competitors (Cain and Hopkins 1980: 476). Social unrest was acute in the period 1815–1850. Much interest was shown in opening the supposedly empty lands of Canada, Australia and South Africa—empty of settlers that is. The presence of local Aboriginal and Indian peoples was not considered part of this development strategy. Lord Carnarvon, the Secretary of State for the Colonies, stated in 1874 that the 'waste lands of the earth were being filled up and there were few outlying properties left' (Cooper 1983: 32). The urge to travel and explore was a strong part of the Victorian character that naturally led to a fashion of sending an increasing number of young men abroad for personal, political, scientific and military reasons. For young men of wealth, leisure and talent, England was simply too small (Middleton 1972: 211).

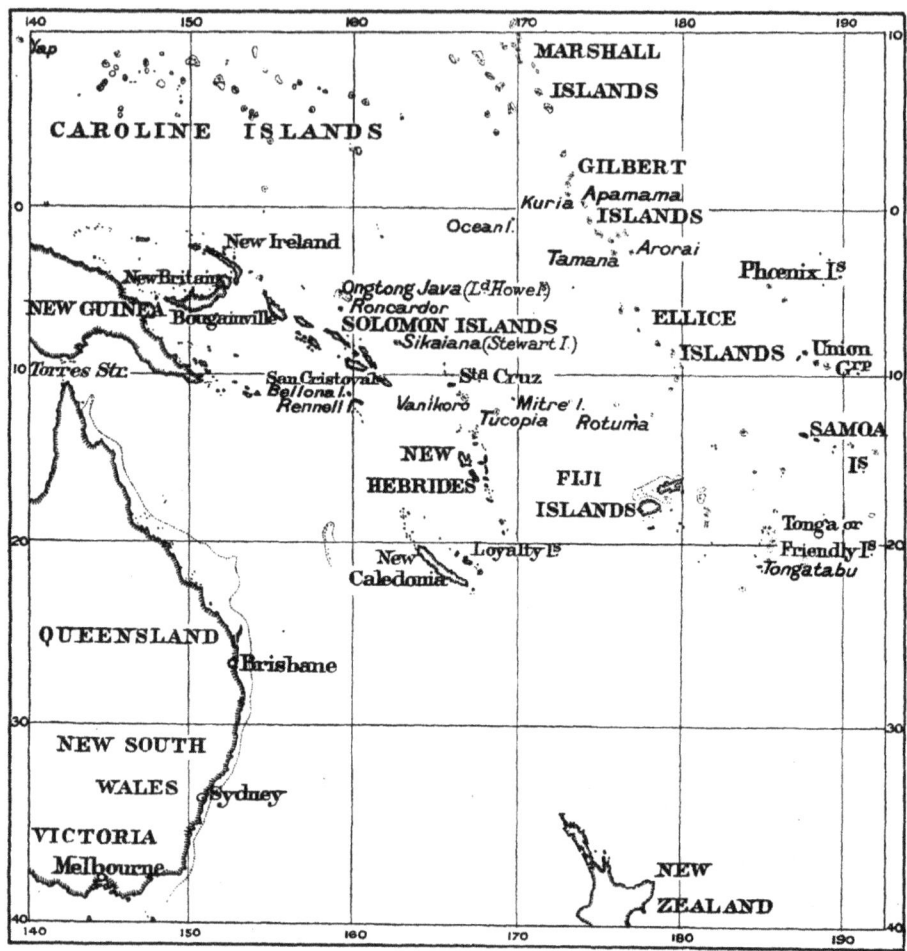

Map 1. Western Pacific Islands.

Source: (Woodford 1916: 29).

To a meeting of the Manchester Geographical Society in 1885, Henry Morton Stanley described 'the world as a huge market-place, its ports just "so many stalls", its people "so many vendors and buyers"'. In this world, the prime function of geographical knowledge was to clear the path for British enterprise and endeavour (Driver 1991: 138). But the acquisition of colonial territories after 1880 was an object of direct interest for all European powers. Interest focussed on the wealth of southern and eastern Africa that could command the attention of London merchants and notables but, apart from the white dominions of

Australia and New Zealand, the small islands of the Pacific held little promise. In Melanesia, the powers most attracted to the islands of the Western Pacific would be France and Germany. Britain was only reluctantly drawn into colonial annexation of lands with seemingly little wealth and few resources that were inhabited by bellicose peoples.

Tonbridge and the African connections

The anonymous author of the letter to the *Gravesend Journal* of 1888 was familiar with the West African expeditions of Sir Andrew Judd, a founder of Tonbridge School, and he noted that Major-General Charles Gordon, Gordon of Khartoum, had lived in Fort House in Gravesend during the construction of the Thames forts at New Tavern, Shornemead and Coalhouse, built between 1865 and 1871 when Woodford and the author were schoolboys. All this, the author of the letter stated, was evidence that 'England has been built up by adventurers'. There are a number of clues in the letter that identify the anonymous author as Arthur Joseph Todd Pattisson, one of 16 children of the lawyer Jacob Pattisson. Arthur Pattisson entered Tonbridge in 1862. Following his time at school he studied art at the Royal College of Art in Kensington Gore then travelled to Rome and Florence between 1872 and 1879. Pattisson never practised as an artist for he went to South Africa in 1879 where he joined the Colonial Commissariat, the official store for the Cape Colony (*Kaapkolonie*) that provided officials and armed forces with food, goods, general equipment and clothing (Hughes-Hughes 1893: 136). The Cape Colony had been founded by the Dutch East India Company (*Vereenigde Oostindische Compagnie*) in the 17th Century, but when Holland was occupied by the French revolutionary army in 1795, Britain occupied the colony. It was an important supply base and harbour for ships travelling to India and the Far East and Britain needed to keep the sea-lanes open. During the Napoleonic Wars, Holland was again occupied by the French and so Britain retained control of the Cape Colony. The Dutch eventually ceded the colony to Britain in 1814 and in 1872 it would become a Crown Colony with responsible government, a Parliament and an appointed Governor. By this time the original Dutch settlers had become an Afrikaans-speaking people. Following dissatisfaction with English control they began to move away from Cape Town into the savannah lands of the north. These migrant pastoralists, the Trekboeren, were better known to the English as the Boers. Their values and attitudes put them in opposition to the British settlers and Cape governments (Oliver and Atmore 2001: 226–7; see also Voigt 1900 for a Boer interpretation).

When diamonds were found in the Kimberley and De Beers mines in the 1870s it led to an expansion of the British commercial interest sponsored by entrepreneurs like Cecil Rhodes. South Africa entered a more prosperous phase based on mining and this economic expansion moved north into the pastoral lands now occupied by the Boers. The northern push by both the Boer farmers and the British settlers led to conflicts with the numerous local tribes living on the plateau and specifically with the Zulu peoples. Zulu tribes east of the Drakensberg amalgamated under Shaka (Chaka) into a highly disciplined fighting force in response to a breakdown of social, economic and political stability driven largely by internal agency within the various African peoples north of the Cape settlements. This was a period of severe and prolonged drought that led to great unrest among the tribal peoples of the whole region from the Drakensberg Mountains to the Kalahari Desert. The period is known as the Mfecane (in Zulu: the crushing) or the Difaqane (in SeSotho: the scattering) (Ballard 1986; Lye 1967: 130; Etherington 2004). Guns and ammunition were traded across the Drakensberg Mountains from Natal and from the southern Cape to the Orange and Vaal River regions (Atmore and Sanders 1971: 538). Much unrest was exacerbated by this trade, and by the illegal slavery that resulted from the capture of the remnants of smaller tribes on the Highveld (Eldridge 1992: 15–25). Large areas of land were then occupied by the northern Ndebele (Matabele) and later the Boers when they arrived in the Transvaal. Many tribal peoples also sought refuge in the Cape Colony where they were recruited into indentured labour as migrant workers, miners and domestics.

The Basotho, the SeSotho speakers, under their chief Moshweshwe, then took refuge in the Highveld of Basutoland (the land of the Basotho, now Lesotho) between present day Free State and KwaZulu-Natal. Moshweshwe and his warriors fought a series of wars with both the British and the Boers until he signed a treaty in 1868 that made Basutoland a British protectorate (Eldridge 1992). In this conflict the Basotho lost a considerable amount of land on the western lowlands occupied by Boer farmers. After Moshweshwe's death in 1871, the Cape Colony government annexed Basutoland and in the south another chief, Moirosi, rose in revolt. He stationed his forces in the Highveld at Moorosi's (Moirosi) Mountain where utilising guerrilla tactics and because of the rugged topography the warriors were able to hold the British in stalemate. During a night raid on 20 November 1879, Moirosi was killed and the rebellion crushed (Atmore and Sanders 1971: 542). While this was presented in the newspapers as a victory for the Cape Colony forces, the 800 troopers and 1,500 African soldiers had actually been kept at bay for eight months by only 300 local Phuthi-speaking tribesmen. In the end only 40 Phuthi were killed (Atmore and Sanders 1971: 542–543). Arthur Pattisson, then employed in the Colonial Commissariat, was present at the conflict on the mountain and he used his artistic skills to sketch Moorosi's Mountain and the night attack. These were subsequently published as engravings in the October, November and December 1879 issues of the *Graphic* an influential illustrated weekly newspaper that covered local and international news from the British Empire. A 30-page letter from Pattisson

1. Early life and education

dated 21 November 1879 and containing his sketches was auctionedin 1995 by Christie's London for £368. This is a more complete version of his report to the *Graphic*.

When the British attempted to disarm all the Basotho this again led to further insurrections. The Basuto Gun War of 1880–1881 occurred in response to proposals by the Cape Colony government to disarm all Basotho warriors and to make land in Basutoland available for settlement by white farmers. Basotho warriors again held the British at bay. In the meantime, Pattisson had settled in Basutoland near the Natal border and worked as a trader. He would have found his experiences in South Africa and serving with the Colonial Commissariat useful in this new career. It was from here that he wrote in the letter to the *Gravesend Journal* c.1888, with his Drakensberg Mountains address, that he had experience trading with 'natives' who were familiar only with trinkets and other goods used 'as a substitute for cash, among the raw savage natives of isles almost lost to human knowledge'. Following his experiences in South Africa, Pattisson joined the Pioneer Column in 1890 (Hole 1936). This was a force of white colonialists and armed police under the direction of Cecil Rhodes that occupied Matabeland (land of the Ndabele) and Mashonalands (land of the Shona) in the north (currently Zimbabwe). Rhodes formed the British South Africa Company (BSAC) and using the pretext that he held a royal grant he signed a treaty in 1888 with local Zulu/Ndabele chief, Lobengula, who ruled over both Matabeland and Mashonaland. But the Royal Grant that permitted the British South Africa Company to administer the northern protectorate from the Limpopo River to Lake Tanganyika was not formally approved by Queen Victoria until 1889. Rhodes had plans to expand his economic interest from diamonds at Kimberley and gold at Witwatersrand to include possible gold mining in Matabeleland. Eventually Mashonaland and Matabeleland became Southern Rhodesia (Phimister 1974). The British South Africa Company was a chartered company created under a Royal Grant. This was seen by many investors and developers as an ideal model for resource exploitation in the colonies and protectorates.

The planned Pioneer Column of 1890 consisted of an advance column of 180 civilian colonialists, 62 wagons of supplies, and 200 volunteers who later made up the corps of the British South Africa Police Force. This was followed by a rear column of 110 men, 16 supply wagons, 250 cattle, and 130 horses. In South Africa, Rhodes advertised for men but selected those from wealthy families for he calculated that if the columns were imperilled by local tribesmen the British government in London would be forced by pressure from wealthy, connected families to send in reinforcements. Each man was promised 3,000 acres (1,200 hectares) in the northern protectorate along with 15 mining claims (approximately 20 acres or 8 hectares each). Arthur Pattisson was an original member of the Pioneer Column and his skills in the commissariat would have been particularly useful in organising supplies for the troops. The Pioneer Column crossed into Bechuanaland (the land of the Tswana, now Botswana) in June 1890 and by 12 September they had occupied the hill, Harare Kopje (Neharwa Kopje). They raised the British flag over Metebeland and Mashonaland on 13 September 1890; this day was known as Pioneer Day in Southern Rhodesia. The fort constructed at Harare Kopje was renamed Fort Salisbury. This became Salisbury, the capital of Southern Rhodesia, and is now Harare, the capital of Zimbabwe. Each man in the column was allocated his land and mining claims and Pattisson settled in the Mazoe Valley in northern Rhodesia where he called his land Tonbridge Farm. Like other members of the Pioneers, he was awarded the British South Africa Company Medal of 1890 (Hughes-Hughes 1893: 136).

Photography was also used to effect in the wars of Southern Africa. The Pioneer Column also had an official photographer, William Fry, whose images were used to portray the idea that the white hunter and adventurer represented the ideal type of energetic, pioneering young man upon whom the British Empire depended (Ryan 1997: 107). These ideals of innate Anglo-Saxon racial characteristics were used to justify the occupation of Matabeleland and other colonial outposts. But in the early years the settlers faced many hardships, especially in a land-locked region remote from supplies and services in the Cape Colony, and malaria was a major health risk (Hole 1936: 45). Pattisson died young, aged 39, in 1891.

The draw of adventure and some fame in the colonies was strong in Victorian England. Another school colleague also went to Africa. Charles Woodford's younger brother Edward attended Tonbridge from 1867 to 1874. He would later study at Oxford and become an officer in the York and Lancashire Regiment, and he served in Egypt in 1882. One of his school colleagues was Arthur Jermy Mounteney Jephson (Hughes-Hughes 1893: 145, 157, 166). In 1886 Jephson paid £1,000 (about £450,000) given by his cousin, the Comtesse de Noailles, to join Henry Morton Stanley on the Emin Pasha Relief Expedition to Equatoria (the South Sudanese states of Central, Western and Eastern Equatoria). Stanley at first considered Jephson unsuitable and 'too high class', but took him largely because of the financial subscription (Jephson 1969: 3; Smith 1972: 87). The Relief Expedition was a highly promoted and expensively funded expedition that cost more than £33,000 in 1887 (about £13 million) (Jephson 1969: 427–428). It was planned to rescue the Emin Pasha (Mehmed Emin Pasha) from a Mahdist revolt in the upper Nile. The Emin Pasha was baptised Eduard Carl Oscar Theodor Schnitzer in Silesia, then part of Prussia but now part of Poland. He changed his name during service as a medical officer in the Ottoman Empire and became Governor of Equatoria on the death of General Charles Gordon in 1878 (Jephson 1969).

In 1885, the Emin Pasha and his government were isolated at Wadelai near Lake Albert by an uprising that aroused considerable indignation and resentment in Europe and Britain. Because Stanley was officially an employee of King Léopold of Belgium, and had assisted the Belgians to establish the so-called 'Free State' of the Congo, the expedition accessed East Africa by travelling up the Congo River (Stanley 1885; Driver 1991: 138). This was a major tactical error. At the start of the Emin Pasha Relief Expedition, Stanley arranged for a former contact in Zanzibar, Tippu Tib (Hamed bin Mohammed bin Juma bin Rajab el Murjebi) to travel with him to the Congo to find porters and assist with the movement of the large caravan of men and equipment up the Congo. Tippu Tib's past reputation as a slaver marred the status of the Emin Pasha Relief Expedition, especially at a time when the British and Foreign Anti-Slavery Society and the Aborigines Protection Society were stressing the sanctity of the universal principles of freedom, humanity and justice (Driver 1991: 155, 162). Between 1839 and 1909 these societies functioned as centres of national concern about colonialism, imperialism and economic expansionism in Africa and the Pacific. The Relief Expedition travelled up the Congo to Leopoldville and towards the Stanley Falls. It then separated into an advance column and a rear column. The advance group met with the Emin in Equatoria but he was not interested in leaving the territory, contrary to Stanley's goals of 'rescuing' him. In fact, the Emin was only interested in acquiring ammunition and other supplies to strengthen his position. The rear column meanwhile had disintegrated into chaos with great loss of life. When Stanley arrived near Lake Albert he received news that the Emin Pasha and Jephson were being held under house arrest by the Emin's officers at the Pasha Bey's fort at Dufile. This lasted from August to November 1888 (Jephson 1890). Finally, the relief expedition, with the Emin Pasha, arrived at Bagamoyo in German East Africa (Tanzania) in 1889 (Jephson 1890 and 1969). The expedition was a shambles but those British members who survived were feted in Britain and received medals from the Royal Geographic Society and honorary degrees.

Woodford followed the expedition to Central Africa and its political and scientific outcomes with some interest. There is a copy of the expedition map, showing the route taken from the mouth of the Aruwimi River to Bagamoyo, and an invitation to attend the Royal Geographical Society Stanley Reception Meeting, held in the Royal Albert Hall on 5 May 1890, in the Woodford archive (Woodford papers PMB 1290 Item 11/10). At this meeting, attended by over 6,000 people, all surviving English members of the expedition were awarded medals by the Prince of Wales. Stanley received a gold medal, and Jephson and others received bronze medals (Stanley 1890; Butlin 2009: 261–262; Jephson 1890 and 1969). As Charles Woodford was in England at that time, while his book on the Solomon Islands was being published, we may conclude that he was present at the reception meeting. At the annual meeting of the Royal

Geographical Society held in London in June 1890 Woodford was awarded the Gill Memorial medal for his explorations in the Solomon Islands and at that same meeting the Emin Pasha, in absentia, was awarded the Patron's Medal in 'recognition of the great services rendered by him to geography and the allied sciences by his explorations and researches in the countries east, west and south of the Upper Nile during his 12 years' administration of the Equatorial Province of Egypt' (*The Daily News* 19 June 1890; *The Telegraph* 17 June 1890 and *The Yorkshire Post* n.d., 1890; Woodford papers PMB 1290 Item 9/29).

The Zoological Society of London also received a large zoological collection made during the relief expedition that was noted and described in the Proceedings of the Zoological Society in 1888 by Oldfield Thomas, Arthur Butler, Dr A. Günther, the Keeper of Zoology, and others interested in the natural history of Equatorial Africa (Zoological Society of London 1888: 3–88). Thomas and Butler were also to describe the substantial collections presented to the British Museum by Woodford in that same issue of the Proceedings and Woodford would later correspond with Günther for many years. The *Gravesend Journal* of 7 June 1890 also carried a long article describing a public lecture given by Jephson at Tonbridge School that was well attended by local dignitaries (Woodford papers PMB 1290 Item 9/29). During the lecture Jephson described the difficulties faced by the expedition and hinted at the clash of personalities between himself, the Emin Pasha and Stanley. At that meeting Woodford was cited by the Headmaster as a fine example of an old boy of the school who had risked his death in the Solomon Islands 'in his enthusiasm for discovery'. In phraseology common to that time the Head went on to describe exploration as a means by which 'light was cast into all the dark corners of the earth', and it was of considerable 'pride that it was Englishmen who did these deeds', for '[w]e were set to govern the world'. These values were firmly held by Europeans well into the 20th century. Exploration, scientific discoveries and ethnographic collecting were combined in the one expedition. It was part of the process of bringing the unknown home, of opening up the world.

Work in the family wine business

The stories of Arthur Joseph Todd Pattisson and Arthur Jermy Mounteney Jephson are important to this examination of the explorations of Charles Morris Woodford. All three were products of an education and cultural system that was increasingly expansive and where the role of young men was to serve the needs of Empire. In such an environment of travel and exploration, and with British colonial expansion at its peak, the seeds were sown for Charles Woodford's wanderlust. But he was caught in a difficult social and economic position. He had prosperous, but not wealthy parents, and was without the excellent social connections needed at a time when patronage was a key to high office. On leaving school in 1871 Woodford had few options but to join his father's wine and spirit firm in Gravesend. After two years working with his father he joined the firm of Richard Harper and Sons in London. Then in 1874 he worked with C. Meynoie and Coy in Bordeaux. This was the normal way for a young man, soon perhaps to be head of the firm, to extend his personal contacts and learn the wine and spirits business firsthand (Heath 1974a: 10). From France he settled back in Gravesend in 1875. In 1880 the *London Gazette* listed his name, address and occupation as 'Charles Morris Woodford, Gravesend, wine merchant' and noted him as a customer of the London and Provincial Bank Ltd (Supplement to *The London Gazette*, issue 24685, 26 February 1879: 1573 and issue 24816, 25 February 1880: 1457). In 1874 he took out a commission in the 1st Kent Volunteer Artillery and he remained attached to the Volunteers until 1888 (Heath 1974a: 10–11; Woodford papers PMB 1381/008a-c). His second brother, Henry Gorham Woodford, had also joined the wine trade after only one year—1865—at Tonbridge (Hughes-Hughes 1893). After Henry Pack Woodford died in 1889 another son, Henry Gorham, was to expand the family business with offices in St Margaret's Street, Canterbury, as well as the main offices at 146 Milton Road, Gravesend. By 1917 Woodford and Co had been taken over by Russell's Gravesend Brewery and Henry and his wife had emigrated to Canada. Henry at least had been in a position to take over family responsibilities in England while Charles could nurture his dreams elsewhere.

2. Pacific journeys

Fiji

In 1881 Woodford abruptly left Gravesend and the family business and took a boat to Suva in Fiji to try to establish himself as a collector of natural history specimens that he might sell to museums and collectors back in England. Heath (1974a: 10) finds the decision that brought Woodford to the Pacific to be somewhat of a puzzle and questions why a young man with a possible career in the family business would begin a wandering rootless life in the South Seas. The stories of Pattisson and Jephson only serve to illustrate that the decisions made by young men to seek opportunities abroad were well grounded in their upbringing and their education. Undoubtedly, from Woodford's diaries, his book and his early journal articles, it was scientific collecting, ethnographic observation and, to some extent, adventure, that were primary motivating factors in his desire to escape the constraints of late-Victorian English life. Indeed it was true that 'the driving force behind empire-building was rather the export of surplus energy: that the expansion of Britain was the overspill of restless people. For a young man, life in Victorian Britain might seem intolerably dull' (Hyam 2002: 280). The chance to go overseas, free of family and social ties, could lead to adventure, an opportunity to make money and to see something of the world.

Woodford arrived in Fiji sometime in March 1882 and spent the first year in the islands collecting natural history specimens (Heath 1974a: 11). The colony of Fiji was annexed in 1874 following submission of a report by Commodore James Goodenough and Consul Edgar Layard (Great Britain. House of Commons. Parliamentary Reports 1874a). The first Governor of the Crown Colony of Fiji was Sir Arthur Gordon (later Lord Stanmore) (Newbury 2010: 85–118). The Colonial Office directions to Gordon were that the annexation of Fiji was to be at no cost to the British taxpayer and that he had to make the colony self-sufficient (Sohmer 1984). Under Gordon the colonial government of Fiji set about the preservation of traditional laws and customs and the maintenance of the authority of local chiefs as a way of utilising local communal organisations for the preservation of law and order. The aim was to make alienation of native land by European planters as difficult as possible (Heath 1974b: 85; Newbury 2010: 103). Gordon's purpose was 'the more the native polity is retained, native agency employed, and changes avoided until naturally and spontaneously called for' the less likely it was that the Fijian people would suffer from contact with Europeans. Gordon's objective was to stabilise a situation of land alienation by European settlement and acculturation that had quickly got out of hand. But this basic doctrine of ruling through indigenous political structures and elites was itself an artificial structure that implied 'if one was to rule well, one should not do too much with one's rule' (Cooper and Stoler 1989: 616; Heath 1974b: 86). It was adopted in Fiji in order to shelter indigenous society but it was really just rule by compromise for it allowed for a few European officers to command the lives of many local peoples (Newbury 2010: 179–180). Gordon was pompous, theatrical and liked to present himself as 'chief-like' (Scarr 1967a: 53). One of his first duties was to have himself installed as a paramount chief by the *Bose Vakaturaga*, the Great Council of Chiefs (Newbury 2010: 90). He famously wrote: 'I feel an excessive desire to be eminent ... I still most earnestly desire greatness and power' (Sohmer 1984: 143 quoting from Chapman 1964: 6). Gordon established colonial government by fiefdom where status was paramount. In the Western Pacific the scale of traditional politics was different from Africa. There were no concepts of statehood, not even at local levels, and the alien construction of depersonalised systems of administration, taxation and justice could not be grafted onto the customary body politic. Here British colonialism had no foundation upon which it could build (Macdonald 2001: 93).

Within this rather alien social and political environment, Woodford's Fijian collecting experiences did not go unnoticed. Details of this first collection of butterflies, presented to the British Museum of Natural History, were reported in the *Annals and Magazine of Natural History* in 1884 (Butler 1884) and, subsequently, the Zoological Society of London published a fuller account of *Lepidoptera*, sub-order *Heterocera* (the larger moths) of Fiji that Woodford had collected on Viti Levu (Druce 1888a; see Woodford papers PMB 1290 Item 4/10). Publication of the details of his natural history collections in the *Annals and Magazine of Natural History* and the *Proceedings* and the *Transactions of the Zoological Society of London* added to the prestige of Woodford's collecting. The *Annals and Magazine of Natural History* had first published in 1855 the important findings written in Sarawak by Alfred Russel Wallace about species diversity. These journals were seen as official organs of the Natural History Museum in London. The Zoological Society contained important members and Albert Günther, the Keeper of Zoology at the British Museum, received collections from all over the British Empire. The fact that the Woodford collections were well prepared, carefully packed and transported, and came with precise and detailed documentation made them exceedingly valuable. Woodford's collecting expeditions at Tonbridge School were returning a handsome dividend.

But after a little more than a year of active collecting and travelling throughout Fiji, Woodford found his finances running low and so, in April 1883, he sought a position as a junior clerk in the colonial Treasury under William MacGregor, then the Receiver General and Chief Medical Officer for Fiji who became Administrator of British New Guinea in 1888. Woodford was not happy at the

Treasury, nor it seems was the Treasury particularly impressed with Woodford (Heath 1974a: 12). Life as a 'grubbing' clerk in an isolated colonial outpost, even if it were Suva and the headquarters of the Western Pacific High Commission, would have been a tedious routine for someone eager for an outdoors life in the tropics. Seeking paid employment and some adventure away from the confines of colonial Suva, Woodford secured a temporary position as a Government Agent on the labour vessel returning Gilbertese workers back to their homelands.

The Gilbert and Ellice Islands

In Woodford's archive there is a long and detailed account of the trip he made to the Gilbert (Kiribati) and Ellice Islands (Tuvalu) between 4 March and 22 June 1884 (Woodford papers PMB 1290 Item 1/1). On the trip to the Gilbert and Ellice Islands he acted as Government Agent on the *Patience*, a 40-ton ketch chartered to return home 45 Gilbertese labourers stranded in Fiji. It was also a chance to see more of the Pacific and possibly do some collecting at the same time. This particular group of labourers had been returning from German-owned plantations in Samoa after completing their period of indenture when they were offloaded, on the shores of Malekula in the New Hebrides (Vanuatu), on the pretext of a need for urgent repairs. Their safety as strangers on a foreign shore was seriously compromised so they quickly signed on again as indentured labourers when seen by a passing Fiji bound labour vessel. The colonial administration in Suva refused to accept their new indentures for longer than 18 months so they were returned to the Gilbert Islands from Suva. Under the Moorsom system of marine measurement, one ton multiplied by 100 cubic feet per ton equalled the storage capacity, in cubic feet, of a sailing vessel. The 40-ton *Patience* was a small and crowded boat for such a long cruise in open ocean. In a maximum of 4,000 cubic feet were loaded the 45 labourers and their belongings, the food and belongings for all members of the crew, and the sailing gear. Woodford's job was to see to the care, accommodation and food of the men—his diary entry notes that he took charge of '56 lbs rice and 6 lbs [tinned] beef and some cocoanuts' for the trip. He was responsible for them on board the vessel and had to make sure that the islanders were landed at their correct home communities (Woodford papers PMB 1290 Item 1/1 Diary 4 March–22 June 1884). The journey took three and a half months to reach the Gilbert Islands more than 1,000 miles (1,600 kilometres) North-northwest of Fiji.

Woodford was keenly observant, perhaps even scientifically so, and his duties on board do not seem to have been onerous. But once in the islands he noted the internecine squabbles between the various island leaders and the mission politics that seemed to dominate Gilbertese life. Interdenominational disputes remained a source of conflict between the missions during the colonial period in the Gilbert Islands. This was especially so when the power of the *unimane*, the old men with control over customary power, clashed with the power of the local religious leaders and the central colonial administration (Macdonald 1972: 137). The *unimane* operated through the *maneaba*, the meeting house that was the focus of communal social life, a rest house for visitors and a seat of local customary law and justice. However, with missionisation and colonial administration other structures, such as the church and the district office, challenged the power of the meeting house (Macdonald 1972; Maude and Maude 1932: 275, 292). This combination made for a potent mix in a time of great change.

Woodford found the London Missionary Society pastors in control of much of the economic as well as spiritual life of the local people and noted particularly that one 'despotic' missionary fined locals for misdemeanours at the exorbitant cost of ten bags of copra priced at £2 (£850 in current values) per misdemeanour. A white trader was similarly fined 900 sticks of tobacco (about 35 pounds weight or 16 kg) by the same missionary for supplying 20 chickens to a passing ship with ill crew (1 pound weight of stick tobacco, that is 26 sticks, cost 2 shillings a pound, the total cost of the fine being £3/10/- or £1,500 in current values). In Woodford's diary he details the saga of the missionary from Nukunau (Nikunau) who had a weatherboard church built with contributions from the local people using timber imported from Auckland. The church was then demolished and a coral and lime church built in its place. The lumber was then appropriated by the missionary who had canoes built that he rented out to fishermen. The missionary had three houses full of copra that he wanted to trade with the captain of the *Patience* but Woodford would not agree to the deal (Woodford papers PMB 1290 Item 1/1 Diary 28 April 1884). Woodford had a little respect for local pastors and wrote:

> The people have blind faith in them [the pastors] and whatever they tell them they think must be right and the promise of eternal punishment if their commands are disobeyed, is the means by which they work upon the feelings of the people to blindly follow all they are told to do. I have seen now islands wholly christianised semi-christianised and in a state of darkness and all in the same group. The latter are in a very undesirable state. The two former might be very much better off than they are. The [London Missionary] Society say they cannot afford to keep white missionaries here but I think more rigid inspection and more definite instructions to the native teachers would conduce to the benefit of the people. The power of the missionaries here is as absolute as that of any chief in the old days.

(Woodford papers PMB 1290 Items 3/3, 3/4, 3/7, 3/3/1, 1/1 excluding 1/9, 1/1/3).

Missionaries were also able to impose traditional forms of punishment, such as community isolation, to enforce their power. All other islanders were forbidden to have contact with offenders. They and their extended families would have no access to copra buyers, would be excluded from the village cooperative society, and would be denied recruitment in overseas labour migration (Macdonald 1972: 142). Contact with European traders had seen local disputes and warfare become more serious with the introduction of firearms. Traditional occupations like coconut oil production, and more recently copra production, were extended to become the foundation for a cash economy. Plantation labourers repatriated from Fiji and Samoa had brought in new goods, new ideas and with that new religions (Macdonald 1972: 138). And so to voice his opinions Woodford began the first of a series of long detailed letters to his mentor in Fiji, John (later Sir John) Bates Thurston, then the Assistant High Commissioner for the Western Pacific. The first letter, dated 30 June 1884, detailed the fights between the people of Kuria and Apamama (Abemama) in the central islands and those from Nonuti (Nonouti) and Onoatoa (Onotoa) in the southern islands as well as the possible slavery of islanders from Apaiang (Abaiang) and Tarawa in the northern islands. This personal report to Thurston was detailed and perceptive and Thurston had a keen interest in the Gilbert Islands having visited there in the 1860s during his brief experiences as a first mate on a sailing ship.

The Gilbert Islands formally became a British protectorate in 1892 when Captain Edward Davis of the corvette HMS *Royalist* raised the British flag on the islands. The Ellice Islands were declared a British protectorate later the same year by Capt HWS Gibson of the frigate HMS *Curaçoa*. In 1893 Thurston travelled to the islands on HMS *Rapid* to appoint local tax collectors. The *Queenslander* (30 December 1893: 1253) reported that where 'no white trader's services were available some influential nigger was duly installed chief tax-gatherer' to collect the one dollar per adult male that was meant to support British administration in the islands. In a paper published in *The Geographical Journal* much later in 1895, following the declaration of a British Protectorate over the islands in 1892 and during a time when he was recognised authority of the Solomon Islands, Woodford put his notes and research into the Gilbert Islands into print. Much of the paper consists of detailed examination of the history of contact and the naming of the islands by passing ships' captains and comparing the local name with the name given by passing explorers and traders. Woodford repeats his opinion that 'the natives of the islands under the influence of the London Missionary Society are more liable to err from an excessive insistence upon matters of small importance than from a lack of religious zeal, and it seemed to me that there was a demand for more frequent supervision by a white missionary to mould the ideas of the natives in the right direction', and that 'the combined direction of the Government and the missions' would give the islands a 'bright and prosperous future' (Woodford 1895: 341–342). In the meantime, Woodford wrote of his ideas about population decrease following European contact and important notes about material culture. He also came to the conclusion that the Gilbertese islanders were entirely unsuited for indentured plantation labour and this opinion would come to affect his dealings with workers and employers when posted to Samoa as Acting Consul and Deputy Commissioner in 1895. He concluded his paper to the Royal Geographical Society with a detailed natural history examination listing the flora and fauna he observed there in his trip on the *Patience* making special note of the *Coleoptera* (beetles and weevils) and the *Lepidoptera* (moths) he collected and presented to the British Museum of Natural History (Woodford 1895: 345–349; Woodford papers PMB 1290 Items 4/4, 7/20/3, 6/1; Butler 1885; Woodford 1885).

The Trader's Yarn

Following the publication of the long scholarly paper on the Gilbert Islands, Woodford submitted a draft of a novella to the firm of AP Watt and Son of Hasting House, Norfolk Street, The Strand, London, originally titled *The Captain's Yarn: A tale of the South Sea*. The title was later crossed out and the work renamed *The Trader's Yarn* (Woodford papers PMB 1381/036). The draft was subsequently returned to his sister Mary Jane Woodford in March 1897 having been rejected for publication. Woodford had informed AP Watt and Son that he was the author of *The Naturalist Among the Head-hunters* but requested in his handwriting on the cover page that his name not be used if the draft were accepted for publication. It is understandable that he would not want to be identified with the novella: it is poorly constructed, has little real direct voice, and the reader would have little sympathy with the hero of the story, a young man who worked as a clerk for a merchant house in Auckland and who sought adventure by signing on as supercargo on a small trading vessel going north to the Gilbert and Ellice Islands. While the novella was not a success, it is interesting for its historic details and its connection with Woodford. In 1897, when the manuscript was returned to his sister Mary Jane Woodford, Charles Woodford had just been appointed to a permanent position as Resident Commissioner of the Solomon Islands. Woodford had obviously remained interested in the Gilbert Islands long after his first visit on the ketch *Patience* but the draft does not inform the reader of the diverse natural or cultural environment of the islands that would have given the novella some needed colour. The story has some interesting aspects that could have been expanded and embellished but Woodford appears to have rejected any further attempts at writing fiction.

In the short story, the unnamed young trader is accompanied by an Irish first mate, a Scots captain, two Tongan crewmen, and two Portuguese sailors who had deserted from an American whaler. They set sail from Auckland for the Gilberts where they plan to buy coconut oil for sale back in New Zealand. When they arrive at Onoatoa and Tepetewea in the Gilberts they find the northern islands at war with the southern islands, but at Apamama they find the king ready to trade in coconut oil. As there is not enough oil to buy, the king orders 20 or 30 people be taken to Kuria to make oil there. The captain at first refuses. The trade winds at that time of year were unpredictable and he was anxious about being able to return to Apamama. Eventually 33 men and 12 women are chosen or ordered by the king to go on the trading vessel and it sets off for the island. At Kuria the tender capsises and the captain is injured. The mate then takes a small canoe ashore to assist the captain and to repair the tender. During this time the main trading schooner drifts out to sea. The young trader, who had never been to sea before and has been left in charge of the vessel, has with him four crew and the Chinese cook as well as 22 men and 10 women from Apamama. The rest of the story concerns the trials of this young man as he attempts to find land again. The 'natives' of course mutiny, raid the stores and drink all the water. They bind the trader, the cook and the Portuguese sailors. The Tongans, being 'natives', naturally side with the Gilbertese. After the men gradually run out of food they catch a shark and eat it raw and, as the local men die of thirst one by one, the rest cannibalise the bodies. The trader remarks: 'then ensured the first of those scenes of horror, over which I will draw a veil'. Eventually the vessel is wrecked on the reef of Nonouti but all have died apart from the young trader, the cook, and four natives—three men and one woman. From Nonouti the Gilbertese take the survivors on a large trading canoe to Aranuka, sailing at night guided by signal bonfires. There they find the captain alive. Quickly they find another trading vessel that takes them back to Sydney.

The framework of the novella is obviously based on some personal experiences, but the detail is lacking. It could be expanded into a decent novel of the Pacific, not in the class of Stevenson or Conrad, but acceptable nonetheless. For the audience back in England the horrors that Woodford declined to describe were the very things that would have attracted the reader. Perhaps wisely he relegated the draft to the storage trunk. The value of the story is that it is interesting to read the ideas that were in Woodford's mind at the time and especially his interest in the Gilbert and Ellice Islands.

'These beautiful islands'

On his return to Fiji from the Gilbert Islands Woodford did not stay long in the colony. With his first collections of butterflies well received in London and seeing few opportunities for advancement in the colonial service, or perhaps more accurately understanding that his relationship with his superiors was discouraging, he could see a possible career opening as an expert natural history collector in the Western Pacific. At that time this was a well-tried path to recognition in the natural history world in England. But this time he would focus on a region only briefly visited and largely untouched by science—the Solomon Islands.

In 1885 when Charles Woodford left London on his first expedition to the Solomon Islands, little was then known of the double chain of six main continental islands, 20 smaller ones and over 900 small islets and coral reefs located east of the main island of New Guinea, south of Bougainville and north of the New Hebrides. These islands are located between latitudes 5°–12°S and longitudes 152°–170°E. The total land surface is little more than 27,990 square kilometres (2,799,000 ha). The climate is monsoonal tropical with an average temperature of 26°C and a mean rainfall of 3,000–5,000 mm per year. The heaviest rainfall season is between December and March.

The archaeological record in the islands is complex. Evidence of human use has been found from Pleistocene sites from Island Melanesia: New Britain, New Ireland and Buka in the northern Solomons. The Kilu Cave site on Buka contains deposits of shellfish remains, fishbone and worked shell that have been dated from 32,000 BP to 29,000 BP (Sheppard 2011: 801; Wickler 2001). Taro was used by people who lived in Kilu. It is assumed that parts of the Solomons south of Buka were colonised during the Pleistocene period. From 3,500 BP the Lapita cultural complex, identified by its distinctive elaborate pottery, skilled seamanship, long-distance movement of obsidian and proliferation of the Austronesian languages, appeared in the Bismarck Archipelago. The southern extension of this movement reached through New Ireland, Bougainville and onto the Solomon Islands as far as Santa Ana off Makira (Sheppard 2011: 799–840). At present we know that the northern and western Solomon Islands were settled by Austronesian-speaking and ceramic-producing peoples in the Late Lapita period around 2,600 BP (Sheppard and Walter 2006: 48; Sheppard 2011). There are numerous Lapita sites in the culturally important Roviana and Marovo Lagoons in the New Georgia region where the abundance of resource rich lagoons and large islands facilitated coastal settlement. The more remote south-east Solomon Islands were colonised in the Late Lapita period by peoples who moved from the resource rich Reef and Santa Cruz islands. These outer islands were settled by Lapita colonists who bypassed the main central islands of Malaita and Guadalcanal although the record is still incomplete and the subject of much debate. This suggests that there were direct, long-distance trading relationships between peoples in the Reef and Santa Cruz Islands and the Bougainville Archipelago to the north (Sheppard and Walter 2006: 59). The boundary between these converging movements of people, between Guadalcanal, Malaita and Isabel, is marked by a linguistic division called the Tryon-Hackman Line (Sheppard and Walter 2006: 54).

The 347 inhabited islands are home to a mixture of Melanesian and Polynesian peoples who speak some 67 languages, 44 dialects and one *lingua franca*, Solomons Pijin (Waite and Conru 2008: 13). Today Melanesians constitute 94.5 per cent of the population, with Polynesians at only 3 per cent. In addition there is now a small Micronesian group resettled from Kiribati that forms only 1.2 per cent of the population. The rural population, more than 80 per cent of the people, rely on fishing and subsistence agriculture for food (Solomon Islands Government. National Statistics Office 2011). The main crops grown are sweet potato, cassava, banana, taro, yams, and *pana*.

3. Commerce, trade and labour

Understanding the history of European contact with the Solomon Islands and the nature of the local peoples' social, cultural and economic lives is important if we are to appreciate the challenges that faced Charles Woodford, first as a young self-funded naturalist, and later as a colonial administrator. This was a complex, often challenging environment for any outsider.

The Solomon Islands were first sighted by European explorers when Alvaro de Mendaña de Neira and his company in two ships, the flagship *Los Reyes* (the *Capitana*) and the secondary ship *Todos Santos* (the *Almiranta*), sighted Santa Ysabel (Isabel) Island in February 1568. Mendaña was then a young man of 25; his second in command was Pedro Sarimento de Gamboa. The man who had promoted the idea of a voyage of discovery seeking the *Terra Australis Incognita*—the Unknown Land of the South—was Hernán Gallego whose journal became the most important record of the voyage. Gallego was the chief pilot. At Santa Ysabel de la Estrella the Spaniards built a light brigantine and with 30 men Mendaña explored the coasts of Ysabel (Isabel), Guadalcanal, Malaita and San Christoval (Makira) islands. On the east coast of Isabel they named a bay Estrella Bay (Port of the Star: Ghehe Bay) and on the northern coast of Guadalcanal named Port la Cruz (Port of the Cross: Point Cruz, now part of central Honiara). It has been said that the Spaniards also found small traces of gold at the mouth of the Mataniko River on Guadalcanal (Woodford 1890b: 1–8; Guppy 1887a: 192–256, 272–279 for comments on geographical names; Bennett 1987: 19–20). This led to the naming of the islands, Islas Salomon, the Solomon Islands. Mendaña and his crew then returned to Peru on in September 1596 intending to return in six months. Mendaña went to Spain to plead the case for more exploration of the Pacific but the wars between England and Spain intervened.

It was not until April 1595 that Mendaña again set out from Callao in Peru, this time with four ships, the *San Gerónimo* (the *Capitana*), the *Santa Ysabel* (the *Almiranta*), the smaller frigate *Santa Catalina* and the galiot *San Felipe*. The plans were to settle in the Solomon Islands. The chief pilot this time was a Portuguese-born navigator, Pedro Fernandes de Queirós (Lewis 1977). Instead of landing at Isabel and other known islands the ships reached Santa Cruz Island in the southern end of the island chain. Here they attempted to settle at Graciosa Bay but this was soon abandoned due to climate, attacks by local warriors and illness (see Yen 1973 for a report on the ethnobotany reported by Mendaña and de Queirós). Mendaña died at Ndeni (Nendö) on Santa Cruz and the group of ships headed north for the Philippines. In 1606, 11 years later, de Queirós, now the leader of a new voyage of discovery, sighted Taumako and Tikopia, even further south than Santa Cruz. The island of Espíritu Santo (Vanuatu) was also discovered by de Queirós. His second in command, Luis Vaez de Torres, sailed through the Torres Strait between Australia and Papua in 1607 on his way home to Spain via the Philippines. The ships of de Queirós and Torres had become separated and de Queirós sought safety by sailing home to Calleo via the north Pacific and Acapulco. The Spanish then lost interest in the region and further discovery of the Solomon Islands was abandoned. With the deaths of Mendaña and then de Quirós in 1615, Spanish interest in the fabled riches of the Solomons faded (Jack-Hinton 1962; Amherst and Thomson 1901). All knowledge of the Solomon Islands passed from European history for the journals of discovery remained unpublished deposits in the archives in Madrid and Manila.

In the 18 century few ships touched the shores of the Solomon Islands. In 1767 Captain Philip Carteret of the Royal Navy anchored off Santa Cruz in the HMS *Swallow* and then sailed close to Malaita and Buka in the northern Solomons above Bougainville Island. Carteret named New Britain, New Island and the Duke of York Islands. Carteret is also credited with the 'rediscovery' of the Solomon Islands. Captain John Shortland sailing on HMS *Alexander*, one of the supply ships for the newly established colony at Botany Bay, passed south of Bougainville Island and sighted and named the Treasury Islands (Mono) and Shortland Islands (Alu and Fauro) in 1788. Shortland urged the Admiralty to chart the east coast of Australia more closely and subsequently Matthew Flinders was dispatched in the HMS *Investigator* to circumnavigate the Australian continent.

French interests also focussed on the Pacific after Jean-Francois de Galaup, the Comte de la Pérouse, was appointed to lead a voyage of discovery around the world in 1785. The main objectives were scientific, geographic, ethnological and economic, but political interests and the possible establishment of French colonies in the Pacific were also underscored. After the ships rounded Cape Horn, la Pérouse headed for Chile and Hawai'i, then on to Alaska, California, Macau and the Philippines, Japan, and Kamchatka in Russia. He was ordered to investigate the establishment of the colony at Botany Bay in January 1788. Fortunately la Pérouse took the opportunity of contact with the Royal Navy in Botany Bay to send some of his journals and charts back to Britain on the HMS *Sirius*, one of the supply ships that had formed part of the First Fleet. After leaving Botany Bay the ships of la Pérouse headed north and were never sighted again. In 1793, while searching for the lost ships of la Pérouse that had been wrecked on the island of Vanikoro, the French explorer Bruni d'Entrecasteaux, who was also unsuccessful in sighting the main Solomon Islands group, sighted Vanikoro but was unable to land because of the dangerous fringing reefs. It was only in 1826 that Captain Peter Dillon was shown a French sword on Tikopia and told it came from Vanikoro that evidence of the wrecks was found. Dillon later discovered cannon balls and anchors from the wreckage at Vanikoro. A memorial to la Pérouse was erected there in 1828 by Captain Jules Dumont d'Urville during another French voyage of discovery. It was not until 1964 that the wreck of la Pérouse's ship, *La Boussole* (The Compass), was found off the coast of the island (Ballantyne 2004; Jack-Hinton 1962).

After the Spanish interest in the Solomon Islands declined, attention focussed on the Australian mainland to the south. British interests centred on the establishment of the colony in Botany Bay and Captain Arthur Phillip was instructed by the Home Office in London to use the resources of the Pacific Islands to supplement those available at the new colony. The first move was to Norfolk Island where flax, useful for sails, rope and clothing could be obtained. After 1800 there was evidence of declining stability in the Pacific Islands resulting from the depravity of beachcombers, sandalwood collectors, escaped convicts from New South Wales, whalers and traders. This was causing violence and dissent among the local peoples. In response to concerns about the actions of itinerant traders and beachcombers, the Rev Samuel Marsden formed the New South Wales Society for Affording Protection to the Natives of the South Sea Islands in 1813. The Imperial government in London then passed the first Act to deal with crimes committed on the high seas by British subjects (*The Offences at Sea Act* 1806, 46 Geo III c54) and subsequent legislation to allow for trial of murders committed abroad (*The Murders Abroad Act* 1817, 57 Geo III c53). However, these Acts were only implemented by the Crown to avert scandal to the British name (Ward 1948: 40–41). In reality, a policy of minimum intervention into the affairs of the Pacific still held sway. There was little mercantile interest in the Western Pacific, for trade and commerce needed little official protection. Missionary activity was only beginning and it was opposed to direct colonialisation in the Pacific islands. The Colonial Office shared these views. Apart from the colonies in Australia and New Zealand, official policy was to avoid any interference in the state of affairs of islands in the region. The British government spent over £15 million quelling the various Māori Wars in New Zealand and had little taste for colonising the rest of the Pacific (O'Brien 2009: 97). But it was the growth of plantation economies in Queensland, Fiji and Samoa and the resulting expansion of the Pacific labour trade that strained the minimum intervention policy (Ward 1994: 8).

Contact with the Solomon Islands and the islanders became more regular with the rise of Pacific sperm whaling in the 1830s. When winter closed the waters around Japan and the northern Pacific, American whaling ships moved south. Around February was a popular time for vessels to hunt in the warmer waters off the eastern Australian coast and along the eastern shores of Malaita, Isabel and Choiseul Islands. In the Solomon Islands, the Bougainville Strait between the Shortland Islands and Choiseul was a target area for migrating sperm whales

(McKinnon 1975: 291). These whaling vessels were at sea for long periods, often years, and began to call in at isolated communities in the islands to resupply with timber, water, and trade for local produce. At first, relationships were generally peaceful for the whalers rarely stayed long and the villagers had yet to learn of the importance of iron and guns. Before long, however, a trade developed in hoop iron from wooden barrels, nails, and gimlets—boring tools with wooden handles used by seamen. Coastal communities became trading localities and the supply of iron, axes and nails passing through these villages meant that the people along the coasts were in a stronger economic position than their bush neighbours who had only traditional stone tools.

Andrew Cheyne, a sea captain from Northmavine in the Shetland Islands, was a successful bêche-de-mer and sandalwood trader who wrote of his extensive voyages throughout the Western Pacific between 1841 and 1844 (Cheyne 1852; Shineberg 1971). His schooner, the *Naiad*, was one of the first regular trading vessels to ply the coasts of the islands. His opinion of the Solomon Islanders was one commonly held at that time: 'The whole of Solomon's Archipelago requires to be surveyed, as the charts in use at present are very erroneous. Merchant ships passing through this Archipelago should hold no intercourse with the natives, as they are not to be trusted' (Cheyne 1852: 31). Further to this he added:

> ... on no account should landing be made without a particular object, and then well armed. I allude chiefly to the Solomon Islands. You may perhaps pull in and go ashore without seeing a soul, but no sooner have you got a short distance from the boat, than they rush out from the thickets in hundreds. This has happened to one or two vessels at New Georgia, and the crews have with difficulty regained the boats with some mortality, and other severely wounded (Cheyne 1852: 71).

With the arrival of the 'ship men' (*tinoni vaka*: Roviana), some knowledge of 'whitemen', new technology and new diseases permeated the coastal, 'saltwater' communities in the Solomon Islands (Bennett 1987: 21). Communities inland, the 'bush' villages, remained largely isolated. This was the start of the island-based disparities. People with produce ready for sale to passing ships entered the commercial economy while those in the hills, especially on the large islands such as Malaita and Guadalcanal with a reputation for aggression, were pushed to the periphery. The people of these bush villages then became prey for the coastal people who had gained access to modern European weapons.

Meanwhile, between 1860 and 1900, the economy of the Australian colonies expanded rapidly. Trade, the influx of overseas capital for the growth of regional centres, the gold rush and the development of agriculture led to a boom economy. A booming economy needed a large labour force and immigration from Britain and Ireland only partly accommodated that need. Soon good markets in China opened up for bêche-de-mer and sandalwood, and in Europe for turtle shell and marine shells, particularly pearl shell. These became important items used in the manufacture of women's buttons. In the Solomon Islands the demand for turtle shell meant that traders needed local men to go on long-distance turtle hunts, especially for hawksbill turtles (*Eretmochelys imbricata*). The number of turtles in the early part of the 19th century was high but intensive hunting was to deplete the populations in the New Georgia lagoons. As demand continued local men began to travel to the turtle grounds of the Manning Strait between Choiseul and Isabel. The high demand by traders meant that local people began to insist on payment in long handled tomahawks that could be used to cut timber, clear forest and manufacture fine quality canoes. People in the islands learnt quickly that they could manipulate the traders by controlling access to scarce resources.

Early traders, like Andrew Cheyne, were prepared to pay for bêche-de-mer and shell with old 'Brown Bess' muskets but the humidity, problems with loading and unreliability of cartridges meant that soon there was a demand for breech-loading rifles (McKinnon 1975: 303). The introduction of iron, taken from trade or from shipwrecked passing boats, changed forever the traditional economy. Iron tools reduced men's labour and made canoe-making and forest clearing easier. Women's labour was largely unchanged as they continued to use traditional gardening techniques like the wooden digging stick. Men therefore had increased time to spend on the production of shell ornaments and valuables and 'politicking, ceremonials, legal disputes and fighting' (Bennett 1987: 35, quoting Salisbury 1970: 10). Power became concentrated in the hands of the few men with access to iron and access to traders. Demand for produce by visiting traders and ships' crews and demand for iron, tomahawks and then guns by local men resulted in an interlocking cycle. The coastal trader was tied to his local Big-man who had built up skills as a negotiator and regular supplier of produce. By manipulating indigenous culture, communal ties and ambition this Big-man could establish a power base that could be exploited for economic and political gain. This power base was much localised although powerful leaders from nearby regions could unite in time of warfare, ceremony or feasting. While the Big-man could exploit his connections he was tied to the trader who was the supplier of the material benefits of contact with the outside world of commerce (McKinnon 1975: 296). These relationships were inherently risky. They were created and maintained by volatile and constantly changeable personal power.

Blackbirding: The early kidnapping phase

In the early days, the few shore stations established by individual traders were not well protected and the trader had limited access to land. Usually they established a post on a small off-shore island. Some whitemen had tried to settle in the islands but the results were not successful. Benjamin Boyd, formerly a wealthy landowner, but by this time somewhat reduced in circumstances, attempted to establish a colony in 1851 called his 'Papuan Republic or Confederation' at Wanderer Bay on the Weather Coast of Guadalcanal. He disappeared while travelling inland. The bay is named after his schooner, the *Wanderer*. Boyd had been one of the first to recruit Pacific Islanders to work as shepherds on his sheep stations in the Riverina in 1847 but the men were unable to cope with the rigors of the winter climate. Under the *Masters and Servants Acts* 1845 (NSW) (9 Vic no 27) and 1847 (11 Vic no 9) they were free to leave their employment if they so desired and the New South Wales government, reacting to public concerns, released them from their indentures. This action has been acknowledged as the start of the 'blackbirding' or Pacific labour trade. The first group of South Sea Islanders brought in to Queensland came at the instigation of Robert Towns to work on the experimental cotton plantations he was developing at 'Townsvale' on the Logan River south of Brisbane. The outbreak of the American Civil War in 1861 had depleted supplies of cotton to the English mills and cotton prices soared. For a while it looked as if cotton would be an important local industry but the use of British immigrants, many from city backgrounds, to clear scrub, plant the cotton and then harvest it, was doomed from the start.

When faced with a persistent labour problem, Towns hired the *Don Juan* and sent it to collect Pacific Islanders to be field labourers. The first shipment of 67 men arrived in 1863 under an arrangement of engagement for only one year but by 1866 Towns had imported more than 360 labourers from the New Hebrides alone (Moore 1985: 167; Beck 2009: 35). When the American Civil War ended in 1865, and better quality American cotton was once more available, the Australian cotton local market collapsed. Captain Louis Hope in the meantime established, in 1864, an experimental sugar cane farm at Ormiston near Cleveland that was worked by the indentured labourers brought in on the *Don Juan*. This was successful. By 1869 most cotton plantations on the Logan River had been converted into sugar farms. It soon became apparent that the first small independent sugar farms were inefficient at all levels of production (Graves 1993: 24). The only economically viable operation was large-scale plantation production but this required considerable capital outlay and a regulated labour force to clear fields, plant cane, harvest, and then mill the cane on site. As mills operated all day during harvesting, and cane cutting was labour intensive, a resident labour population was needed. Plantation owners looked to the Melanesian islands to fill that labour need. These were the beginnings of the labour trade that was to last, at least in Queensland, until 1908.

The Pacific labour trade

In the 1860s stories of the kidnapping of local islanders who were taken to work the plantation fields of Fiji and Samoa and then Queensland began to circulate widely. The push by missionaries into the Solomon Islands, before establishment of colonial rule, meant that the British public was informed of regional affairs through a strong, politically astute, interlocking network of missionary, anti-slavery and naval interests. The naval officers who surveyed the islands came from a largely upper-middle class background and were strong promoters of 'Christian humanity'. They were not just 'floating policemen' (Samson 2003b: 283). The naval ships came from the Australian Division of the East Indies Station formed in 1848 and were stationed in Sydney. Its role was to protect the Australian colonies and patrol the Western Pacific. In 1859 the Admiralty established an independent command, the Australia Station, partly to reflect the growing strategic concerns in the Western Pacific and in part due to the prosperity of the Australian colonies. The Australia Station was located in Sydney. The initial success of the naval presence in patrolling the activities of the Pacific labour trade was due to the use of small corvettes and frigates that were able to navigate the still mostly unsurveyed tropical waters of the Pacific.

Regulating the labour trade

The early excesses of the labour trade raised public attention to the lack of regulation. Henry Ross Lewin, formerly the recruiter on the *Don Juan* sent by Robert Towns in 1863, had by now purchased his own boat, the *Daphne*, licensed to carry only 50 recruits. In 1869, the sloop HMS *Rosario* under the command of Commander George Palmer and with the Acting Consul John Thurston on board intercepted it off Levuka in Fiji with a load of 108 Islanders. The *Daphne*, licenced to ship the workers west to Brisbane, was apprehended far to the east instead (Mortensen 2000: 5). Palmer and Thurston found the *Daphne* fitted up precisely like an African slaver 'minus the irons' (Morrell 1960: 177). Under the Imperial *Offences at Sea Act* 1806 (46 Geo III c54), and the equipment clause in the *Slave Trade Acts* 1806 (46 Geo III c52), 1807 (47 Geo III Session 1 c36), the consolidation of the Acts in 1824 (5 Geo IV c113) and the *Slave Trade Suppression Acts* 1839 (2&3 Vict c57 & c73) and 1843 (6&7 Vict c98), a ship could be detained and condemned by the Royal Navy if it were equipped with the signs of slaving, such as open gratings rather than closed hatches, extra bulkheads and large planks that could serve as benches and beds, increased supplies of water, food and matting, and the presence of any irons and shackles (Mortensen 2000: 4).

Acting on this, Palmer sent the *Daphne* with a prize crew to Sydney under charges of slave trading. His lawyers in Sydney thought that the equipment clause would be sufficient to prosecute. Palmer's 'obsession with slaving' led to political and personal disaster (Samson 2003b: 288). The Vice Admiralty Court in New South Wales dismissed the charges on the grounds that the slave trade suppression Acts did not apply to the Western Pacific although the *Daphne* had been violating colonial merchant marine legislation. Palmer was subsequently sued by the ship's owners although he was later assisted with payment of his debt by the Admiralty. Palmer published his account of the cruise of the *Rosario* (Palmer 1871). The case, the publicity and the clear observations by Palmer that were 'unequivocal, emotive and publically accessible' (Samson 2003b: 288) gave much support to the naval position which was strongly anti-blackbirding. The case was reported widely in the press of the day (*The Sydney Morning Herald* 24 September 1869, 8 October 1869).

Political pressure on the Queensland colonial government to regulate the importation of Melanesian labourers who were being brought in to work the growing number of Queensland sugar plantations led to the passing of the *Polynesian Labourers Act* 1868 (Qld) (31 Vic no 47). The term 'Polynesian' was used as a generic name for any non-white Pacific Islander at that time. Albert Hastings Markham (1872: 230) in his review of exploration of the New Hebrides and Santa Cruz groups wrote: 'But it [the Queensland legislation] is said to be of little use in ameliorating the condition of the unfortunate islanders, and the labour trade, with its attendant kidnapping, continues in full vigour'. The Queensland legislation did permit the introduction of a licensing system that meant that masters of labour vessels had to execute a recruiting bond of £500 and produce a certificate for each recruit signed by a consul, missionary or known person that the labourers had engaged voluntarily and with full understanding of the nature and conditions of their agreements. Scales of rations, clothing and a minimum wage of £6 a year were set for employment in Queensland. Sugar planters, especially the larger plantations where many workers were needed, had to pay labour agents between £5 and £7/10/- per worker at the start of plantation expansion. By 1876 the agent fee had risen to between £10 and £16 a recruit and then to around £20 in the early 1880s. This passage money led to a sharp increase in the additional costs associated with recruitment and transportation. Once employed on a plantation, the recruit had to be fed, clothed, and provided with accommodation and medical services. New contract recruits were paid the minimum wage of £6 a year but time-expired workers who re-engaged knew of the opportunities open to them and used their bargaining skills to secure annual payments of between £6 to £8, rising later to £12 (Shlomowitz 1981:78). Employers had to post a £10 return passage fee with the Office for Pacific Island Immigration and after 1871, when the labour trade was more tightly regulated, pay a capitation tax of 10 shillings per recruit. This increased to 30 shillings (£1/10/-) per man in 1880 and then to £3 per man in 1885 (Shlomowitz: 1981: 71).

Subsequently the Queensland government passed legislation to revise the *Polynesian Labourers Act* 1868. The *Pacific Island Labourers Act* 1880 (44 Vic no 17) specified the number of recruits permitted on board vessels and further added employment controls and conditions (Moore 2013b: 3). It was again amended in 1884 (*Pacific Island Labourers Act* 1884 (Qld) (47 Vic no 12). Of importance was the creation of a Pacific Islanders' Fund, under an amendment to legislation in 1885 (*Pacific Island Labourers Act* 1880 *Amendment Act* 1885 (49 Vic no 17). This Treasury fund was established to administer the employment bonds, to supervise the wages of deceased labourers and to hold hospital capitation funds. Pacific islanders were induced to deposit their wages in a trust account with the Queensland Government Savings Bank. Clive Moore (2013b) presents a comprehensive assessment of misappropriation of these moneys—especially the wages of deceased labourers and the unexpended return passage money of dead workers—held by the Queensland government in the Pacific Islanders' Fund. The Queensland and the Commonwealth governments used this money to finance the administration of the labour trade, pay wages and expenses of Inspectors of Pacific Islanders and Government Agents aboard the labour vessels. Among other operational costs they later used the money to pay for the final repatriation of labourers in 1907 and 1908 (Moore 2013b: 6)

Internal structure of the labour trade

Irvine (2004) presents an excellent account of the costs of running a large central mill like the Colonial Sugar Refining Company's Goondi Estate near Innisfail, north Queensland. It was estimated that it cost £25–£35 to bring a labourer from the islands and £26 a year to keep each man. Pay was set at £6 per man with rations, blankets, clothing, provisions, housing and medical treatment provided. Provisions were set by government regulations and included meat, bread, flour, sugar and rice as well as sweet potatoes and bananas. Men were provided weekly with tobacco, salt, soap and yearly with three shirts, four pairs of trousers, a hat, shoes, pipes, matches and knives. In return they had to work 10-hour days and were confined to 'field work' under the *Pacific Island Labourers Act* 1880 *Amendment Act* (Qld) 1884 (Irvine 2004: 16).

However, conditions varied and in times of economic depression, in order to cut costs, planters reduced the quality of food, clothing and accommodation and stopped paying for access to medical care (Graves 1993: 29). In the early days, before regulation, the labour trade was open to abuse. At that time labour, certainly non-white indentured labour, was regarded as an 'impersonal asset and access to labour supplies was a frequent bargaining point in diplomatic negotiations between the Great Powers', especially when those great powers were Germany and Britain (Munro, McCreery and Firth 2004: 155). In Fiji the labour trade began in 1864 but diversified in the mid-1880s when planters changed from sea island cotton to copra production and then to the more profitable sugarcane. Islanders were preferred on the copra plantations but increasingly Indian indentured labourers were used on sugarcane plantations (Shlomowitz 1986: 110). The labour trade in Fiji was not formally regulated until 1877. Yearly rates of pay were set at only £3 with food, shelter, clothes and medical care supplied by the employers. It has been estimated that between 1870 and 1911 more than 17,000 Solomon Islanders were recruited for the Queensland plantations and over 7,000 sent to Fiji (Price and Baker 1976: 110–111; Moore 2007: 217). Although recruiting for Fiji ended in 1911 some labourers remained indentured until 1914. In a further examination of the *General Register of Polynesian Labourers Introduced to Fiji* in the National Archives of Fiji, Siegel (1985: 46) found that of the 27,000 Pacific Islanders indentured there between 1865 and 1911, over 8,000 were from the Solomons.

Even well-connected gentry from England were among the many sugar plantation owners and investors. Included in the first volume of Amherst and Thomson's *The Discovery of the Solomon Islands by Alvaro de Mendaña in 1568* (1901, 1: lxxviii) is a photograph of a group of Guadalcanal and Malaitan men working on Foulden Plantation, the Queensland sugar cane farm on the Pioneer River near Mackay. The plantation had been owned by Francis Tyssen Amherst, the brother of Lord Amherst of Hackney, the editor of the Mendaña volumes. Francis Amherst and his partner, a cousin, had purchased Foulden in 1870 along with other selections and Amherst named it after his birthplace in Norfolk. Foulden Mill was built in 1872 and by 1877 the plantation was worth £20,000 and Amherst's house was considered one of the grandest in the district (Moore 1985: 201). He represented Mackay in the colonial parliament and later bought neighbouring Farleigh selection in 1873. Francis Amherst died at sea on the way to England in 1881 and, following settlement of the estate, the two plantations were merged into the Farleigh Sugar Plantations Limited under Sir John Bennet Lawes, the inventor of chemical fertiliser.

Indentured labour on the Queensland, Samoan or Fijian plantations became the most important, regular means by which prized trade goods, fire arms, ammunition and metal tools were introduced into the local communities in the Solomon Islands. The continuous employment of indentured labourers for more than 40 years 'reinforced and considerably extended patterns of proletarianisation initiated in the region by whalers, sealers, sandalwood gatherers, bêche-de-mer fishermen, missionaries and settlers' (Graves 1993: 219). The vast amount of European-made commodities that were brought back by labourers, as well as the beach payments made upon recruitment, were all rapidly incorporated into the Melanesian system of customary exchange. The trade box, and its contents purchased in the sugar towns, became essential markers of a young man's success overseas. The goods distributed within the traditional systems of reciprocity enabled young men, in a culture dominated by old men, to gain status and prestige. Other social and cultural issues explain why young men signed up for indentured labour. These young men were at an intermediate age when they were often excluded from important religious and ceremonial roles. When bride-price was expensive and controlled by the older men, young men found that the status goods added to their chance to gain a wife. Some men were escaping from punishment for offences committed in their communities and others, especially later in the trade, were keen to learn about Christianity or seek medical care in plantation communities (Laracy, Alasia *et al.* 1989: 115).

An opponent of the Pacific labour trade, the Russian-born scientist and ethnologist Nicholas Miklouho-Maclay, wrote a strong letter to Commodore Wilson of the Royal Navy Australia Station condemning the trade and followed this with a comprehensive account of his observations in the Western Pacific. Miklouho-Maclay was a respected figure in 19th century science in Australia. His letter of 8 April 1881 was published with little additional comment in some Australian newspapers (*The Sydney Morning Herald* 21 April 1881: 7; *The Maitland Mercury & Hunter River General Advertiser* 21 April 1881: 3). However, while the letter to Wilson was published by the papers in 1881, the official account, *Kidnapping and Slavery in the Western Pacific*, was not published by the House of Commons until 1883 (Great Britain. House of Commons. Parliamentary Papers 1883a: 82-85). It contains important information on the internal dynamics of the labour trade. Miklouho-Maclay made some direct observations on why islanders recruited or were forced to recruit for plantation labour when he wrote: 'About 15% are taken by means of different artifices and lying promises', 'about 15% are sold by relatives and Chiefs', 'about 10% are obliged to leave their islands, being pressed by various enemies', 'about 25% are returning labourers, who, having convinced themselves that their property was stolen by their own people, prefer to go away', 'about 25% inquisitive, mostly young people, anxious to travel, or wishing to get arms, powder, &c, &c', 'about 5% pressed by want of food, after a hurricane, repeated dry seasons &c, &c', and 'about 5% by force'.

Because pay was deferred to the end of a labourer's contract, the time-expired worker had about £18 (£7,000 in current values). Those who re-engaged could argue for higher wages on the ground that they were experienced. Towards the end of the labour trade these men could ask for annual wages of between £26 and £32 (*The Queenslander*, Saturday 19 October 1895: 741–743). Workers were encouraged, even pressured, to spend their deferred pay in shops, known as Kanaka stores, directly or indirectly linked to the plantation. This system of deferred pay, credit and purchase arrangements called 'truck' was a means of controlling and stabilising the labour force (Graves 1993: 185 fn7). Although those working on estates located near towns could avoid the exploitative aspects of plantation trading by shopping in the town stores even these communities were largely controlled by merchants with economic and political connections to plantation owners. Itinerant, often Chinese, hawkers set up stalls near the labour lines to cater for the Melanesian labourers.

During their employment workers added to their trade box. This was a pine or deal-framed chest about 3 feet (approx. 1 metre) long with an 18 inch (approx. 0.5 metre) square end with handles and a lockable lid (Wawn and Corris 1973: 81, 123; Docker 1970: facing 260; Ivens 1918: 225). A sub-enclosure in the comprehensive list of papers to and from the Imperial government concerning the labour trade gives some idea of the trade items contained in one man's box at the end of three years employment (Great Britain. House of Commons. Parliamentary Papers 1873: 247, 248). In the early days, men returned home with one musket, one fathom of Turkey Red material—a hard-wearing fabric dyed red using the root of the madder herb that would not fade or bleach in the sun, commonly made into shirts and shawls—24 yards of navy blue serge, one white sheet, one axe, a 12-inch knife, a 10-inch knife, a six-inch knife, a belt and sheath, a pair of scissors and a comb, a mirror, four tins of powder—presumably skin powder—3/4 lbs of beads, pipes, rings and four Jew's harps, two lbs of lead shot, one box of firing caps, two yards of grey calico, needles and thread, two lbs of tobacco, one 'mission' hatchet, matches, soap and scented oil, one blanket, one pair of trousers, and one shirt. Men were keen to purchase playing cards, musical instruments like mouth organs and concertinas, and in addition to the tomahawks, files, knives and gimlets they brought saws, nails and hammers, fishing lines and nets, cooking equipment, mirrors, razors, and matches (Graves 1983; *The Brisbane Courier* 9 December 1892: 5–6; *Examiner*, 12 February 1907: 7). These personal trade items were not considered a problem for Queensland customs officials. However after a ban on trading firearms and ammunition to islanders was put in place in 1884 officials kept a keen eye for Snider-Enfield rifles that flooded the arms trade after 1870.

The Snider-Enfield was a converted muzzle-loading Enfield that had been fitted with a breech block mechanism. It was invented by the American Jacob Snider in 1869. The conversion increased the capabilities of the rifle. They were widely used by the British Army during the Māori Wars in New Zealand that lasted until 1872. The army then replaced the Snider-Enfield with the more accurate Martini-Henry guns (D'Arcy 1987: 57–58; Beck 2009: 135). As a result, large numbers of obsolete rifles flooded the international arms market. There was a ready trade in old guns in the Pacific and little attempt at regulation despite the concern in official circles (Great Britain. House of Commons. Parliamentary Papers 1887a). While British subjects were banned from dealing in the arms trade, the illegal sale of firearms continued (Graves 1983: 94–95). After 1884, in place of banned guns, men returned from plantation labour with cash and bought firearms from French and German traders who could still legally deal in arms (Foreign Office to Colonial Office 16 October 1893 CO 225 44 17601). This led to numerous incidents in the Solomon Islands when attempts were made to stop non-British traders trading arms and ammunition (Beck 2009: 50). Guns did not change the function of warfare in traditional society—it remained a means of maintaining individual and group prestige that required all deaths to be avenged even those accidental deaths that occurred in the faraway cane plantations—but the form of warfare was modified to accommodate the use of firearms, ammunition and tomahawks.

European trade items became part of gift-giving that was in accordance with custom and tradition. The whole moral, economic, social and political structure of Melanesian society was built around exchange and reciprocity, and the failure of both settlers and administrators to understand this came to be a principal reason for the many and varied land disputes. For the young men to acquire status, access to law and knowledge, and eventually access to women, they had to distribute their prestige goods. As more young men went to the plantations, and more returned, the migratory network evidenced a marked rise in the composition of social gift-giving. When returnees were landed back near their home communities, these young men were seen by ships' captains and crews to hand over their boxes to relatives and to chiefs without complaint, for immediate redistribution. This was evident on Malaita where the traditional cultural systems were the least impacted by European settlement (Graves 1983: 103). The trade box system brought about major changes in the social and economic structure of customary exchange but did not undermine it. In fact the returned workers and their trade boxes reinforced the long-standing relationships in traditional society (Graves 1983: 123–124).

Regulating the Queensland labour trade

The Queensland government, stung by the poor publicity surrounding the labour trade and the actions of Queensland vessels in the New Hebrides and the Solomon Islands, appointed Government Agents on all labour vessels from 1872. The Queensland government could only legislate for the actions of the trade within the colony and on Queensland ships not in the islands outside its jurisdiction. By this time the jurisdiction of the Australia Station had been widened to include the Solomon Islands and the Gilbert and Ellice Islands. The kidnapping phase had ended and largely voluntary recruitment was occurring despite condemnation by humanitarian groups and mission activists. Of course, voluntary recruitment had many shades of meaning in theory and practice, determined by the conduct of captains and crew on board labour vessels. The quality of the men appointed as Government Agents and vessel masters was fundamental to the regulation of the trade, but men of quality and substance did not sign on to be labour vessel crew. Government Agents were issued with instructions and copies of the legislation but as shown in the log of James Lane, Government Agent on the *Lizzie* that sailed to Joannet Harbour and Sudest Island between December 1883 and July 1884 under the command of William Wawn, the record provides almost no information on the recruiting practices undertaken or on the conditions aboard (Queensland State Archives Item ID7866).

In 1880 a labour vessel master could receive £16–£20 a month and a recruiter £9 a month while at sea. £1 was allocated for the beach payment for each man recruited. In the early days, the Government Agent was paid £10 a month while at sea but later, in order to attract a better type of applicant, six permanent positions were created with a salary of £200 a year (Giles and Scarr 1968: 10). By 1890 these prices had risen to £35 a month for the captain, £13–£15 a month for the agent and the beach payment risen to £5 for each man. This was usually paid to the family or to the 'passage master'—or 'beach captain'—often a local chief who was responsible for signing the men on (Graves 1993: 29). 'Passage' came to be the term used to describe the place of recruitment (Giles and Scarr 1968: 15). Passage money was mostly paid in trade goods, or a combination of cash and trade. Costs for recruiting were rising and there was open competition from recruiters from Fijian and Samoan plantations as well. In Queensland, medical attention for indentured labourers was not made compulsory until 1880 when provision was made for the construction of Pacific Islander Hospitals, but these were located apart from the general public hospitals that serviced the white population (Saunders 1976). Planters and the government were jointly responsible for the financing of these hospitals as both were loath to spend money on labourers at the expense of the general white public. The 'Kanaka' hospitals were an abject failure. In less than six years, the four hospitals at Maryborough, Mackay, Ingham and Geraldton (Innisfail) were deemed a financial failure. By 1890 all were closed (Saunders 1976: 49).

The labour trade was complex and constantly changeable, subject to the rise and fall of the sugar industry. Attitudes to the presence of Pacific Islanders in the mainland towns in north Queensland varied. The growing labour unions in the Australian colonies were strongly against the recruitment of South Seas Islander labour but their concerns were for the future of white labour. The actions of the Australia Station in dealing with 'outrages by natives on British subject' in New Guinea and the Solomon Islands were reported annually to the Admiralty and presented to the House of Commons. Still, Royal Navy officers saw their role as suppressing the trade and their humanitarian message carried far (Great Britain. House of Commons Parliamentary Papers 1872, 1881 and 1887a; Royal Navy (1886–1896); Woodford papers PMB 1290 Items 8/21/1–8/21/12). Apart from its contact with the Royal Navy, itinerant traders, labour recruiters and members of the Melanesian Mission, the Solomon Islands was little known to the general public either in Australia, or even less, in England.

The fabled riches of the Solomons

As contacts increased, ideas about the supposed resource riches of the Pacific also increased. Travellers like Walter Coote (1882, 1883: xiv–xv) wrote that the position of the Australian continent made it a natural outpost for annexation of the chain of islands that 'are the Solomon Islands, an archipelago of great resources, which, although at present practically unknown except by reason of the dark tragedies so often enacted around its coasts, will quite certainly, before long, be regarded as among the most valuable and important of all the South Sea groups'. The idea that the Solomon Islands were a source of fabled riches took a long time to die. However, in the eyes of the officials in the Colonial Office, Southern Africa had productive land and rich minerals. It also had a large resident, albeit coerced, labour force and indigenous chiefly structures that could be manipulated. The Solomon Islands was the very antithesis. The British government was slow to bring any legal or administrative control over the isolated islands in the Solomons group or the Gilbert and Ellice Islands north-east of the Solomons. The growing impression was that any expansion of interests into the Western Pacific was the province of the Australian or New Zealand colonies. The economic expansion of the Australian colonies made New South Wales, and the main port of Sydney, a secure base for regional trade and the expansion of mission activity into the Pacific. This primacy of economic influence was not turned into political ascendancy by the British government until it was forced to act.

Trade and traders

Colonial culture was profoundly materialistic. White people, predominantly men, went to the Pacific for trade, investment or to establish plantations (O'Hanlon 2000: 24). Local peoples saw Europeans in terms of the economic and political benefits that could accrue from trade and labour. While this trade structured social relationships, these were inherently fragile. Life for European traders in the Solomon Islands was fraught with difficulty, if not with physical danger. Collecting turtle shell and pearl shell was susceptible to market fluctuations; sandalwood and bêche de mer collecting declined in the 1860s, while in the 1870s the demand for coconut oil used in soaps, chemicals and explosives increased. Theodor Weber, the Samoa-based agent for Hamburg traders *Johann Caesar Godeffroy und Sohn*, had perfected the use of kiln-dried copra by 1869. This resulted in a virtual monopoly of export copra for Godeffroy. As a result, the poor quality, locally-produced coconut oil and the beach trade in badly treated sun-dried copra were supplanted by large-scale shipments of high quality kiln-dried copra to Europe. It was estimated that about 250 coconuts, the product of three trees, could produce between 20 and 30 quarts of oil (Anon 1888b: 476). Once the production of oil could be made more profitably and cleanly from dried copra, the small-scale native produced coconut oil export was doomed (Maude and Leeson 1965: 433). In Samoa, Weber established the first large-scale commercial copra plantations in order to reduce the level of dependence upon the irregular supply of locally harvested produce (Kennedy 1972: 263). Large-scale plantations under company control meant that Godeffroy could manage both the supply and the demand for coconut oil and the by-products of processing. But in the Solomon Islands small-scale coastal trading in copra was still the norm. Some pearl shell was available and the use of ivory nut (*Metroxylon salomomense*) increased the diversity of products. Ivory nut was not to be a successful export product. The nuts contained a considerable volume of water and could deteriorate if badly treated. The main market was Germany, where they were used as wheels on roller skates and cheaper buttons, but this market was small, fickle and the product from the Pacific was considered second-rate. Better quality material could be sourced from South America.

For physical protection from attack and from malaria, most early traders in the Solomons based themselves on islands in sheltered lagoons, such as in Roviana Lagoon, or off the coast, like Mbara off Aola and Uki ni Masi off Makira. These areas were defensible or places to which traders could easily retreat if necessary. White men could not easily travel inland for fear of attack from the bush tribes and small trading vessels could be raided from coastal communities (Heath 1974a: 22). Generally the trader was backed by a Sydney-based merchant who provided financial loans for the purchase of a small schooner or cutter, and trade goods. The debt was reduced when the backer was provided with product.

Others hired a trader who owned a small coastal vessel and the backer was the sole buyer of product. In the early days, the profit margin for the trader was high but as the number of traders increased margins fell. The on-selling profit was of distinct advantage to the backer. In either case, the trader was both physically and economically exposed while the Sydney-based backer had control over demand and supply. The sort of trade goods demanded by local people were practical implements, fishing gear, coloured calico, clay pipes and twist tobacco. Hatchets and tomahawks could be readily adapted into working tools and weapons but the main trade currency was tobacco. Because the demand for it was high, the profit and loss for the trader was largely determined by the market price in Sydney (Bennett 1987: 53). American twist tobacco was especially popular as it was soaked in molasses or rum, with each piece wound into two overlapping halves that could be easily divided and cut with a sharp knife (Hays 1991: 94). Right through the 1880s, the price for stick tobacco in Sydney remained reasonable at about 2 shillings a pound. Cheap twist tobacco was so poor that it was known as 'sheepwash' and Sydney traders were prepared to sell it to white men for as little as 1 shilling a pound (Maude and Lesson 1965: 429). In 1887 a trader could buy 26 sticks of tobacco to one pound weight and so could purchase about 260 sticks for £1 (20 shillings equals £1). At the same time, one ton of copra (approx. 1,000 dried copra kernels) cost £3. In effect, local villagers could expect to receive about 700–800 sticks of tobacco for one ton of copra (Bennett 1987: 53–55). Prices of course fluctuated, as did quality. Traders and local people bargained for better prices when copra was scarce. Because the trader was dependent on the supply of native produced copra it was in the interests of local people to keep supplies low and the price high. One ton of copra cost traders about 25 tomahawks or 700 to 800 sticks of tobacco depending on quality. At the same time, in 1887, 2 dozen Hurd's tomahawks at 30 shillings [£1/10/-] a dozen cost £3 from Hoffnung & Co, a large wholesale store in Charlotte Street, Brisbane (British New Guinea. Annual report 1887: *Correspondence and Report of Special Commissioner, New Guinea, Respecting the Return of Louisiade Islanders to Their Native Islands:* 4). Local people would have been quick to understand the dynamics of beach trading.

When traditional culture was still strong, European trade goods and the labour trade stimulated the development of a dual economy—the cash economy was beginning to intersect with the subsistence economy—traders occasionally dealt with dogs' teeth, porpoise teeth and shell arm rings, and foreign trade goods circulated within the customary exchange system (Bennett 1987: 54). In German New Guinea traders introduced ceramic arm rings made in Europe especially for this complex mix of traditional and non-traditional exchange (Beck 2009). In the early days, many trading stations were only manned for part of the year and some traders had a ring of trading locations where tropical product was collected. These stations were visited periodically on the annual trading voyages by white men who lived almost permanently aboard small sailing schooners.

The number of permanent or semi-permanent coastal traders was always small. Carl Ribbe, a German naturalist, wrote that when he visited the Solomon Islands in 1893 he knew of only about 20 stations and as many traders (Ribbe 1903: 76; Bennett 1987: 59). Ribbe's visit was made following the German annexation of the northern Solomon Islands in 1886. Although non-German traders suspected him of being an agent of the *Deutsche Neu-Guinea Kompanie*, the Commander in Chief of the Royal Navy Australia Station was requested to provide him with assistance in his travels (Admiralty to Colonial Office 23 December 1893 CO 225 44 21629 & 1 January 1894 CO 225 46 186). He must have been well-connected. From his home in Radebeul near Dresden in Germany, Ribbe later issued a comprehensive printed catalogue of *Lepidoptera* collected from the Bismarck Archipelago and Solomon Islands (Woodford papers PMB 1290 Item 7/38). For example, in 1896 he listed for sale a male *Ornithoptera victoriae regis* [Rothschild 1895] possibly collected on Bougainville for 25 marks or approximately £12/10/- (current value about £4,500). Obviously from Ribbe's catalogue a good natural history collector could make a reasonable income from privately funded expeditions to the Pacific.

The traders mentioned by Ribbe, however, were a cosmopolitan lot; mostly drifters, beachcombers and remittance men. Prominent coastal traders around this time were Fred Howard, a German, based at Uki ni Masi between 1877 and 1890; J. C. Macdonald, a Canadian, who was established at Santa Ana in 1881 but who soon moved via Aola to Siniasoro on Fauro in the Shortland Islands in 1885; and Lars Nielsen, a Dane, based at Savo in 1877, Mbara Island off Aola in 1887 and then at Gavutu (Ghavutu) off Nggela in 1891. Frank Wickham ran away from home in Somerset and after being shipwrecked in the Bougainville Strait settled in the Roviana Lagoon (Bennett 1987: 58–60). Jean Porret, a Frenchman, was based at Kau Kau (Kaoka) plantation in 1896, and Peter Edmund Pratt (known by a number of names such as French Peter and Edmunds Peter Pratt) and his brother Jean Pascal Pratt (or Jean Pierre Pratt), both French, were based on Simbo Island and at Hombuhombu, a small island off the Munda coast and close to Roviana Island, from 1896 to 1900 (Ribbe 1903: 268 shows Peter Edmund Pratt collecting copra from local people protected by an armed escort). Pratt had also purchased land at Mbilua on Vella Lavella. The cost was £33/18/- paid in Snider rifles and ammunition (Woodford to Thurston 17 July 1896, WPHC 4/IV 284/1896). Oscar and Theodore Svensen and partners bought Crawford Island (Tavanipupu) in Marau Sound in 1896 and paid £10 in trade (Woodford to Thurston 26 November 1896, WPHC 4/IV 475/1896). They established a large and profitable trading station on Crawford Island (Tavanipupu) in Marau Sound, sheltered from the south-east trades by Marapa Island. From here in 1892 Svensen expanded into copra plantations (Marau Co to Woodford 10 July 1896 CO 225 50 21650). He subsequently became known as 'Kapitan Marau' by the local people. He made friends with the islanders as well as European traders and the crews of labour vessels (Bennett 1981: 175). Because he was Norwegian, Svensen was not subject to the regulations prohibiting the trade in arms and ammunition and despite his genuine friendship with Woodford firearms were later brought into the protectorate on his company steamers, *Kurrara* and *Aldinga* (Foreign Office to Colonial Office 21 February 1893 CO 225 44 2995). Another foreign citizen was Frank (Franz Emil) Nyberg, identified as a Russian Finn by both Woodford and Captain Edward Davis of the HMS *Royalist* (Woodford papers PMB 1290 Item 1/2 Diary 11 May 1886; PMB 1290 Item 8/21/6: 1891). This is essentially correct, for all Finns born before 1917 were citizens of the Russian Grand Duchy of Finland. Nyberg had been a seaman on the labour vessel the *Venture* before settling at Santa Ana as a trader (*The Sydney Morning Herald* 21 June 1889: 8; Jari Kupiainen pers. comm. 2014). These foreigners could circumvent the regulations that prohibited British subjects from selling arms and ammunition to natives and this was a major flaw in the regulations.

Alexander Ferguson, who like many of the local traders married a local woman, was a close friend of Gorai the chief of Alu (Shortland) Island who named his nephew Ferguson. Ferguson, a partner with the Cowlishaw Brothers, bought tropical product for sale in Sydney. Many traders like Theodore Svensen and William Hamilton had also been involved in the labour trade (Bennett 1987: 56–57; Johnston 1980). Even those who lived for some time in the islands were still at risk. Fred Howard was killed in January 1891 by Malaitans looking for guns and 'blood' money paid by the Uki ni Masi people. J. C. Macdonald's boat crew were killed and his boat seized in Marau Sound in 1879. Lars Nielsen was attacked collecting copra off the beach at Rendova in New Georgia in 1889 and two Malaitan men working for Peter Pratt were killed at Rendova in 1888 (Bennett 1987: Appendix 6). Some traders or their workers were killed in retaliation for the deaths of labourers who had died in Fiji or Queensland but others were attacked in revenge for the desecration of graves and shrines (Bennett 1987: Appendix 6: 390–396). Motives were complex and often unclear at the time.

Traders occasionally acted as intermediaries in cases when the Royal Navy was seeking to punish local men for attacks on ships' crews. Undoubtedly they did so for personal advantage. Naval action could do little long-term damage and could only destroy villages accessible from the shore. The withdrawal of trading facilities was more effective, at least in the early days, but when the number of traders increased the threat of trade removal ceased to be effective. The threat of naval action could suppress disquiet over shady business transactions but both traders and later missionaries could be seen as agents of retribution. The complex relationship between traders and their producers was open and volatile: Norman Wheatley, then based at Nusa Zonga off the Munda area in Roviana Lagoon, was known to give arms to Hiqava, the *banara* of the Kekehe polity centred on the chiefly village of Sisiata in Munda, who used them in head hunting raids to Choiseul and Isabel. Long handled tomahawks and firearms made coastal communities formidable, and while not the only reason for the increase in activity, certainly gave New Georgia men an advantage in raiding. In the volatile area in the north-west islands, at the intersection of trade, warfare and ritual was predatory head hunting.

Head hunting in the northern islands

In an economic analysis of the increase in head hunting in the late-19th century McKinnon (1975: 300) reports that

> to trade big-men had to obtain shell and centralise its collection. The shell turtle had to be hunted in competition with others who were anxious to enter trade with Europeans. Although raiding and head hunting were most probably features of this inflationary or expansive period of New Georgia societies, it is also clear that head hunting and turtle hunting were not mutually exclusive.

As the turtle population was depleted around New Georgia, raiding parties hunted further afield and spread to Choiseul and Isabel Islands. The larger the raiding party the greater the status of the organiser and the greater the economic gains. It was in this atmosphere that the status and reputation of Big-men like Gorai (Koroi: Parkinson 1999: 214–215) of the Shortland Islands, Ingava (Hiqava) of Roviana, Muke of Simbo and Bera and his son Soga of Bugotu (Bughotu, Mbughotu) on Isabel grew (McKinnon 1975: 303; Jackson 1975). While it is indisputable that head hunting expanded in the late-19th century there is some difference of opinion over the reasons why it did so. After having been shown inside a men's house at Oneavesi (Honiavasa) in Roviana Lagoon Charles Woodford was to write: 'it is from New Georgia and the adjacent islands that head hunting is carried on to its fullest extent. Among these natives it appears to be a perfect passion' (Woodford 1888a: 360, 375). Head hunting also had a special season. The peak time for raiding, and trading, was determined by the availability of the *Canarium indicum* (*ngali*) nut during the north-westerlies that blow between October and March but most especially during calm weather in November and December before the onslaught of the wet season (Aswani 2000: 60; Hocart 1931: 303). This was also the peak turtle hunting season and so both events were ritually coordinated. This growing season was the best time for bonito, the fish that served as a major focus of ritual activity and economic activity, and a complex seasonal calendar was built around these social, economic and ritual activities (Burman 1981: 255). The *banara* was responsible for the coordination and timing of activities relating to gardening, feast-giving, warfare, head hunting and trading, and they and their ritual priests held the knowledge of the ceremonial cycles.

Recent ethnographical and archaeological evidence suggests other motives apart from ideas that it encapsulated the people's spirituality and was an expression of economic rationality (Dureau 2000: 7). Certainly, endemic warfare as a result of wealth acquired by trading with Europeans was noticed by traders, missionaries and naval officers. The early view that the introduction of iron, guns and metal axes led to the intensification of head hunting downplays the historical complexity of predatory head hunting that emerged from the expanding and contracting regional polities and changing indigenous ideological entanglements. These began well before the 19th century (Aswani 2000: 39). It is most probable that head hunting had been practiced by the maritime dwelling people of Roviana Lagoon for several generations, perhaps even centuries, before the arrival of Europeans. Aswani and Sheppard (2003: S53), in a comprehensive and finely crafted paper, suggest that a considerable shift in local social and political economies and in religious structures resulted in a major shift in settlement patterns and political centralisation in Roviana. This occurred as early as the 16th century. In the pre-colonial period the rise of powerful chiefs resulted in the 'burgeoning ritual, economic, and political activities including predatory head hunting and inter-island trade' (Aswani and Sheppard 2003: S69). In the pre-colonial period Roviana and Simbo war parties were allied and raided, and traded, with people in Vella Lavella, Ranongga (Ranoga), Kolombangara (Kolobangara/Nduke), and the Marovo Lagoon. Raiding, trading and turtle hunting later extended to Choiseul, Isabel, the Russell Islands (Parvuvu and Mbanika), and north-west Guadalcanal.

The people living on islands in the wider New Georgia region mixed, intermarried and traded both ceremonial valuables like clam shell ornaments (*poata*, white clam shell rings), *bakiha* (fossilised calm shell rings favoured for its reddish/yellow tinges), and shields (*lave*), as well as important food stuffs, like taro, *ngali* nuts and betel nut (*Areca catechu*) (Miller 1978: 289–292; see also Aswani and Sheppard 2003: S66 Fig 5: Young Roviana man with shell decorations, photograph taken by Walter H Lucas in 1899; Brunt and Thomas 2012: 240). An extensive trade network extended from Vella Lavella to Simbo, Ranongga, Kolombangara and on to Roviana Lagoon. But when European traders entered this region, first Simbo and then Roviana became the centres of customary trade and the local chiefs (*banara*) became wealthy (Schneider 1996: 82). Like systems in other Melanesian areas, customary trade across the islands was a successful, functioning, integrated system with its own internal dynamism. It was not static but changed with population movements, absorbed new technologies and goods, was interrupted by warfare and feuds, and was subject to the changing fortunes of groups of people and individuals (Hughes 1978: 310). Some groups were in a more advantageous position than others due to their location to traditional resources. Later, their proximity to distribution centres of trade goods enhanced their economic and political power.

Trading expeditions (*qalo*), turtle hunting and bonito fishing (*valusa*) could facilitate raiding expeditions (*qeto minate*) especially as head hunting intensified (Schneider 1996; Nagaoka 2011: 23). With the growth of Austronesian-speaking communities in the Marovo and Roviana Lagoons, the pre-historic long-distance trading networks retracted. These were replaced by more intensive local systems. This inter-island trading was made possible by use of specialised trading canoes (*gopu*) (Aswani and Sheppard 2003: S56, S57). Intricately carved and decorated war canoes (*tomoko* (Roviana), *magoru* (Marovo), *niabara* (Vella Lavella)) were between 12 and 18 metres in length, took more than 2 to 3 years to build, using traditional stone and shell tools. The large war canoes were estimated to be able to carry up to 50 warriors (Zelenietz 1983: 95 quoting from Somerville 1897 and Woodford 1888a). They were kept in canoe houses (*paele*) that measured 20 metres by 10 metres by 10 metres in height that also served as repositories for human heads taken on raids. *Tomoko* were well-crafted, long, narrow, blackened canoes that had raised prows and sterns decorated with cowrie shells, nautilus and pearl shell with identifying figureheads (*nuzunuzu*: Roviana; *toto isu*: Marovo) carved to represent the spirit figure *Tiola*. *Tiola*, meaning 'man go to fight', appeared in physical form as a dog and was the main oracle, the ancestral spirit, in Roviana mythology (Nagaoka 2011: 87). A stone statue of *Tiola*, placed in the principal shrine, was said to turn in the direction of attacking foes. He was said to originated in Nduke (Kolombangara) and then flew to Nusa Roviana where he taught people the art of building *tomoko* and *paele*, both shaped after his form (Thomas, Sheppard and Walter 2001: 566).

Archaeological excavations of the hill-fort (*toa or toqere*: hill) on Nusa Roviana and at Saikile on nearby Ndora Island indicate that large-scale aggregation and centralisation of political power began more than 300 years ago in the Roviana Lagoon area. Nagaoka (2011: 292) dates the occupation of Bao—a site inland from present day Munda—to 700–400 BP and the occupation of Nusa Roviana to 400–100 BP. This indicates that people from Bao, inland from the present day settlement of Munda, moved to the barrier reef islands around 400 BP. Here intensified head hunting, new political and economic structures, new rituals and ideology, alliance trading, and the manufacture of shell valuables emerged in a setting of shifting demographics and tribal interactions (Sheppard, Walter, Nagaoka 2000: 10; Nagaoka 2011). Production of valuables intensified

3. Commerce, trade and labour

with the use of European tools that were made by skilled craftsmen, *matazoṉa*, who were often captives taken on raiding expeditions. When European traders began using traditional shell ornaments in transactions with local people this led to inflationary pressure that expanded social and political networks. With customary trade networks intersecting with European trade it became important for chiefs to have a resident trader within their vicinity. In coastal districts more than one baṉara vied for the support of their followers. These associates could be from kinship or alliance groups but had to be recruited in a domain of active competition. For this reason large-scale organisation and alliances for head hunting under the control of one powerful chief were dynamic and volatile (Nagaoka 2011: 328).

Research in Roviana, based on archaeological investigations and oral history, confirms that the migration of the people of Bao to Nusa Roviana under the direction of the chiefly ancestors, *Luturu-Baṉara* and *Ididu-Baṉara*, was undertaken in the mid-17th and early-18th centuries (Thomas, Sheppard and Walter 2001; Nagaoka 2000 reports it to be 13–15 generations ago). On the island of Nusa Roviana three villages and three social divisions were established: Kokorapa (middle) on the headland facing the lagoon and the mainland, Kalikoqu (lagoon side) on the beach facing into the lagoon proper, and Vuragare (ocean side) facing towards Blanche Channel. Above the three villages was a large hill-fort (Thomas, Sheppard and Walter 2001: 550–551). In order to attain and keep political power semi-hereditary chiefs (*baṉara*) and paramount chiefs (*baṉara tuti baṉara*) required sanction from dead ancestors (*mateana*) from whom spiritual power was derived. Priests (*hiama*) mediated between the spirit world and the *butubutu*, the local land owning group. The acquisition of heads became the material form by which *mana* (efficacy) or *minana* (potency) was bestowed by these ancestors. To be *mana* was to be potent, efficacious, true and successful (Keesing 1984: 138). Success in human efforts resulted from the responsiveness of the spirits and the use of ritual charms (Schneider 1996: 82). This efficacy guided human actions, for *baṉara* required spiritual sanction to finance and lead head hunting raids (Hocart 1931: 309). In the communities of the lagoon, valued ancestor skulls were placed in separate shrines (*hope*) or skull houses of chiefs (*oru*) with the trophy skulls of the denigrated enemies displayed in the communal canoe houses (*paele*) (Sheppard, Walter and Nagaoka 2000; Nagaoka 2011: 64; see Brunt and Thomas 2012: 172 for a photograph of chief's skull decorated with shell valuables).

Head hunting was a way of denying enemies access to their ancestral *mana*. The captured head was displayed or transformed into *kibo*, over-modelled human likenesses (Wright 2005: 239). Like skull shrines, canoe houses and other ritual houses (*zelepade*) were places of *mana* where the worlds of the living and the dead met (Walter and Sheppard 2000: 305). *Zelepade* were small ornamented buildings about one fathom long (6 feet, 2 metres), one fathom wide and two fathoms high (12 feet, 4 metres) that contained ritual objects for fighting weapons. It was the temporary resting place for the body of a dead chief (Nagaoka 2011: 69). The local chiefs consummated their power with the control of local shrines, ancestor skulls and sacred artefacts, including war canoes. Human heads of an enemy and the abduction of captives both served to ritually nurture the ancestor spirits (Hocart 1931: 303; Aswani 2000: 57; Nagaoka 2000: 13). The completion of new *tomoko* and the construction of *paele* and *zelapade* were celebrated with a communal feast and with the sacrifice of the blood of head hunting victims.

Highly ritualised warfare structured local village relationships. Along with this came the rise and fall of Big-men and changes in regional economies (Dureau 2000: 77–78). Warfare also altered demographic patterns. People on Isabel, Choiseul and other islands were forced to move further away from the accessible coasts and retreat inland to safer regions. Ritual was involved in removing pollution on warriors, in calling on the ancestors for blessings, and in gathering the supernatural power of the warring spirits. Ritual cleanliness was especially important for the long-distance raiding parties as the raiding party could be lost at sea if an unclean person were to be included (Aswani 2000: 59). Roviana elites—the chiefly and priestly families—gained ancestral efficacy and political legitimacy by presenting offerings to ancestral shrines. Their power and wealth gave them control over the means of production, most notably of shell valuables, taro and *ngali* nuts used in ceremonial feasting. Only chiefs could amass the power and wealth to command the construction of war canoes, to fund rituals and organise head hunting expeditions (Aswani and Sheppard 2003: S61). The greater the power to control the forces of nature and man, the greater the social, political and economic status.

Political power was demonstrated by the accumulation of this wealth, by increases in feasting and gift-giving, formation of strong patron-client relationships, the establishment of larger gardens and houses, sponsoring the construction of canoe houses and ritual war-houses, and the building of larger canoes. Expansion of economic activities meant that more captives (*pinausu*) were acquired to support these activities. Captives taken by abduction would either be adopted into families or used as servants by the Big-men. In the New Georgia region these captives were obtained during warfare or purchased from other areas. This rise in powerful leaders in turn led to the attraction of more young men eager to serve Big-men and share in the gains of trade and warfare. Undoubtedly, the introduction of European technology made the construction of canoes, canoe houses and men's houses easier but the need to dedicate these houses to the *mateana* represented by natural phenomena such as meteors, shooting starts and rainbows led to the rise in head hunting observed by local traders, missionaries and naval officers patrolling the waters of the Solomon Islands (Nagaoka 2000).

The need for human heads fulfilled two important desires: 'First: the general belief that a man's greatness is in proportion to the number of human victims whom he has slain', and 'Second: the prevalent belief that on a great occasion, such as that of building of a tambu-house … and especially that of launching a canoe, a human head is essential to propitiate the spiritual powers' (Guppy 1887b: 16; Penny 1888: 46–47; Anon 1888a: 563). Taking captives and heads weakened one group, the victims, and strengthened the other group, the victors (Dureau 2000: 83). The heads of enemies, stripped of their *mana*, were placed in the communal men's houses where they symbolised the power of the leader and warriors. In their own country, the beheaded spirit became a malign spirit that could roam the forests killing anyone it came upon (Dureau 2000: 80). Conversely, the heads of kin and family were placed in ancestral shrines where their power served to strengthen the community (Dureau 2000). The skulls of ancestors were venerated at shrines while the skulls of enemies, detached from the bodies and removed from their home became 'metaphorically converted into animals and detachable objects' (Aswani 2000: 62).

Control of kin, the accumulation of human skulls and the shell valuables of the localised kin group, as well as command over sacred paraphernalia, afforded the chiefs control of the means of production to organise and finance raiding and trading expeditions and to control 'the means to bring into fruition the supernatural powers of *mateana*' (Aswani 2000: 49). The intensification of head hunting was a result of this complex polarising of political and economic power stimulated by interaction with traders and labour recruiters. It was also brought about by the shifting alliances, migrations and territorial displacement of peoples in the wider region. Warfare and disease reduced local populations. Local groups fought among themselves and were subject to retaliation measures by the Royal Navy when white traders and their workers were murdered in retribution over shady business deals, in attempts to secure valuable goods or for use of their heads for ritual and ceremony (Hviding 1996: 109).

Certainly, the introduction of European tools and weapons gave elite groups the power over gift and commodity production that afforded them access to wider political alliances, larger raiding parties and subsequently more slaves to manufacture shell valuables and foodstuffs. The pre-contact period saw the construction of massive coastal fortifications on the barrier islands and large, densely occupied coastal settlements. Chiefs gained control of the wetland taro production and food surpluses sustained feastings and the redistribution of valuables that could be used to finance raids, pay compensation for the use of other warriors and chiefs, and pay for ritual killings and assassinations.

Woodford, later writing about causes of depopulation in the Solomon Islands, noted that the depopulation of Isabel, the Russell Islands and the west end of Guadalcanal 'had been going on for at least three or four centuries, owing to the head hunting and slave raids carried on in those islands by the natives of New Georgia and adjacent islands' (Woodford 1922b: 69; Aswani 2000: 53). Head hunting raids were part of a ritual ceremonial cycle and warriors from New Georgia raided and traded with people on the Russell Islands, the Visale area on Guadalcanal, Zabana and Bugotu on Islander and Lauru on Choiseul. This was not one sided. Warriors from Roviana, Vella Lavella, Simbo, Ranongga and Rendova in the north also raided coastal communities around Marovo Lagoon in the south (Hviding 1996: 89, 92). Raids on neighbouring groups were mainly for revenge, assassinations or enmity killings but the distant islands were raided for trophy-heads and slaves (Aswani 2008: 185). Failure in raiding or the death of a chief was attributed to lack of efficacy and to appease the ancestor spirits a child (*vaela*) was sacrificed to restore social order (Schneider 1996: 87–88, Wright 2005: 239). Woodford (1890b: 155–157) described one such ritual conducted by the chief of Kalikoqu, Nona (Nono), that was witnessed by the trader John Macdonald in 1883 (Woodford papers PMB 1290 Item 1/4 Diary 1 September 1886; Nagaoka 2011: 64).

The New Georgia region was socially dynamic with groups of people aggregating to Roviana Lagoon, which indeed became the centre of head hunting. But chiefs in the Marovo Lagoon tried to secure a monopoly over the trade in clamshell valuables. Fossilised clam shells, quarried from the east side of Mount Kela on Ranongga, were intricately carved into large fretwork plaques. These *barava* are believed to be important land title deeds owned by clan groups (Richards and Roga 2004). Other valuable shell rings came from fossilised giant clams found in the interiors of low-lying rocky barrier islands. The secondary level valuables, made from cone shell or clam shells, were found in the water barriers between the offshore islands and beaches facing the coastal lagoons. It was important for the local leaders to control access to these areas in order to monopolise the manufacture of shell rings as the ownership of these rings was a statement of power, wealth and efficacy (Hviding 1996: 95).

In the meantime, raiding from New Georgia across to Choiseul spread south. With the rise in the number of guns available, head hunting spread beyond Bughotu in southern Isabel to Savo, northern Guadalcanal and northern areas of Malaita (Jackson 1975). What followed was the movement of more people into the hills and into protected settlements. It was the sight of apparent empty villages on the coast and deserted fishing camps that evoked the idea of apparent depopulation in the islands. The idea firmly held by missionaries, administrators and ethnologists was that the 'natives' were a dying race (Rivers 1922). Warfare and long-distance raiding certainly led to a significant number of people being killed or relocating in Choiseul and Isabel but the progressive depopulation of coastal areas in New Georgia, subject to local raiding, assassinations and internal feuds, commenced much earlier than the 1880s (Aswani 2000: 61–62). The intensification of head hunting intersected with the arrival of traders, labour recruiters and settlers. It created an unstable political and economic environment and began to impinge on the growth of commerce and trade (Sheppard, Walter and Nagaoka 2000: 9–10).

4. A naturalist in the Solomon Islands

It was into this complex, rather dangerous, but undeniably exciting region that Charles Morris Woodford ventured in 1885. He was intent on making a comprehensive collection of zoological and entomological specimens for possible sale to the British Museum of Natural History. On 23 October 1885, armed with collecting equipment, personal gear including a rifle and revolver, and survey instruments lent from the Royal Geographical Society, which included a 6 inch sextant (RGS no 970), a George's artificial horizon (RGS no 66), a prismatic compass (RGS no 13), a hydrometrical apparatus and two thermometers (RGS nos 8039, 8121 and 2154), an aneroid barometer (RGS no 841) and an ordinary thermometer (RGS no 12), he left Gravesend on the RMS *Dorunda* in the company of 23 other saloon passengers and 283 steerage adult emigrants bound for Queensland (Woodford papers PMB 1381/022 Diary 20 October 1885–8 April 1886; *The Brisbane Courier* 15 December 1885; *The Brisbane Telegraph* 15 December 1885). The Royal Geographic Society in London regularly lent exploration equipment to members but no doubt they expected to get their carefully numbered and itemised equipment back in good condition regardless of the place in which the explorer travelled.

Woodford had to be prepared to use arsenic, the standard taxidermic process in the 19th century, when treating animal skins and dead birds. There were practical health problems associated with using strong chemicals in village environments. The sago and bamboo huts and shelters are highly combustible, and floors have gaps for air. Liquids spilt on the floor above can drip on to people seated below. The floors are covered with pandanus mats that are used for seating and sleeping. Mats are valuable and damage to them means considerable work for the women who must repair or renew them. Woodford often found himself assigned to a small, discarded shelter or house well away from the main village area without quite knowing why. He occasionally commented in his diaries that he was allocated small, disused houses at a considerable cost in trade goods without realising the practicality of the decision-making from the villagers' perspective. Not only was he a white man and a stranger, surrounded with many trade goods and equipment, but he was keen to pay people to collect animals that they either ignored or hunted for food. He then dried the skins and stored them or, even worse, did not eat the food animals that he paid for. His behaviour would have been considered most peculiar. But these challenges, as well as the use of arsenic and photographic acid, were not the only dangers that a young explorer had to face. On the trip to Australia the passengers on the *Dorunda* were exposed to cholera.

Cholera and quarantine at Peel Island

The *Dorunda* stopped briefly at Batavia (Jakarta) on its way to Australia, then entered the Torres Strait and anchored at Thursday Island on 6 December 1885. Woodford immediately went for a walk in the bush collecting moths. By the time the ship reached Townsville several steerage passengers had come down with cholera, which was probably contracted in Batavia when the ship docked there for fresh food (*The Brisbane Courier* 17 and 19 December 1885; Woodford papers PMB 1381/022 Diary 20 October 1885–8 April 1886; *The Queenslander* 16 January 1886). This is the only time cholera is known to have reached Australia. When the ship reached Brisbane the entire ship's company was quarantined on Peel Island in Moreton Bay. Accompanying Woodford in first class was Augustus Spry, a prominent apiarist from Brisbane, together with his valuable collection of Liguarian, Italian, Syrian and Palestinian bees that were being imported to form a viable honey industry in Queensland. Nervous quarantine officials fumigated the bees. It appears, from newspaper reports, that the bees all died.

Woodford's diary details the boredom of his enforced stay on Peel Island during his quarantine there. Saloon passengers were accommodated in the largest buildings built on the Bluff in the south-eastern corner of the island. The ship's officers, the doctor, and female steerage passengers with children had separate quarters, as did married people with families, but the ship's crew and male steerage passengers slept in tents (Ludlow 2009). The single women 'under Miss Chase, the matron, [were] surrounded by a fence six feet high' (Woodford papers PMB 1381/022 Diary 20 October 1885–8 April 1886). Following discharge from Peel Island, while staying at Lennon's Hotel he visited the Brisbane Botanic Gardens in the city and the Museum, then located on Gregory Terrace, Bowen Hills, and wrote: 'The former is very pretty the latter indifferent'. Woodford also took the opportunity to meet with Hugh Hastings Romilly, the Deputy Commissioner for British New Guinea, on 18 January 1886. Romilly offered to take him to Papua but Woodford declined. He displayed some of his photographs of Peel Island in the window of Hislop's furniture store to aid the *Dorunda* Relief Fund that the Queensland government established to raise money for needy families of the 20 or more passengers who had died on the voyage. The cholera case was closely monitored by newspapers of the day though Woodford wrote in his diary that '[t]he people in Brisbane appear to have gone wild with funk' over the scare (*The Queenslander* 16 January 1886; Woodford papers PMB 1381/022 Diary 15 December 1885).

In late-January 1886 Woodford left for Sydney where he attended a lecture on Captain Henry Charles Everill's New Guinea expedition, which was sponsored by the Royal Geographical Society of Australasia. He sat next to the missionary, the Rev William Wyatt Gill, who agreed with him that the expedition was a fraud. The expedition led by Everill left Sydney in June 1885 with the intention of navigating the Fly River in Papua as far as the mountain foothills. Instructions from the Royal Geographical Society were highly detailed. The party was to make Aird Hills their base of exploration and to survey the flora, fauna, geology and climate of the Gulf region. They were instructed to make detailed notes and drawings and take photographs of the country between the coast and the highlands. They were given orders to avoid conflict with the local people and to survey local languages, habits and customs (*The Sydney Morning Herald* 15 June 1885: 5). Everill's party attempted to access the Central Highlands via the Aird River in the Gulf district but the country defeated them. They retreated and decided to travel along the Fly as far as the Strickland River. Assuming the Strickland would be navigable to the highlands they went about 200 miles until their vessel, the *Bonito*, stuck fast on the mud. After eight weeks the boat was re-floated on a flood tide and the expedition returned south. The *Townsville Bulletin* reported that 'if the party had explored the Aird instead of the Fly River, the net scientific results would have been greater' (*The Morning Bulletin* [Rockhampton] reporting from *The Townsville Bulletin* Friday 4 December 1885: 6). Woodford and Gill's opinions of the Everill expedition may have been severe but scientifically and ethnographically they were correct: nothing had been achieved (Everill 1886). Woodford wrote in his diary of 7 December 1885, 'I am told they [the expedition members] fired away a large part of their ammunition shooting at bottles between Sydney and Thursday Island. I do not believe in exploring by the aid of dynamite' (Woodford papers PMB 1381/022 Diary 7 December 1885). It is hoped that Woodford gained more from a discussion with Gill, a member of the London Missionary Society who had assisted A. W. Murray with the development of the first LMS mission station at Mawatta near Daru in 1872. In 1884, before the Everill expedition, he had taken the second group of Rarotongan pastors to Papua. He was an author of some standing whose writings had done much to improve the missionary image among scientific circles in Australia and England. Woodford no doubt hoped that his privately funded expeditions, without sponsorship from the Royal Geographical Society, would amount to something more significant.

Return to Fiji

Woodford finally arrived back in Suva on 17 February 1886 and took rooms above the offices of the *Suva Times*. He wrote in his diary: 'Suva looks much the same but very dull' (Woodford papers PMB 1381/022 Diary 20 October 1885–8 April 1886). Fiji was not the place for him. He was obviously attracted to the unexplored Solomon Islands. In Suva he attended a dance by Solomon Islanders at Dr Corney's plantation where he photographed the men in Meke costume. Woodford would later meet with the leader of this dance group on his return home to north-west Malaita. The *Suva Times* of 24 February 1886 reported that Woodford had 'come out on behalf of the British Museum, and will proceed by the first opportunity to the Solomon Islands for the purpose of collecting the reptiles and rare insects to be found in that group'. Woodford had made a small collection of natural history objects, mainly *Lepidoptera*, on his previous trip to the Gilbert and Ellice Islands in 1884 and some short papers had resulted from this collection (Butler 1885; Woodford 1885). His Fijian collections had attracted the notice of Dr Albert Günther, Keeper of Zoology at the British Museum of Natural History (Heath 1974a: 20) and Arthur Butler, a prominent taxonomist and Assistant Keeper of Zoology, had also praised them (Butler 1884). As a result of this previous work both the Royal Geographical Society and the British Museum of Natural History gave Woodford formal letters of introduction to the then Governor of Fiji, Sir John Bates Thurston (*The Gravesend Journal, Dartford Observer, and County Intelligencer* 7 April 1888: 8). Woodford had obviously known Thurston before for he had reported to him on conditions in the Gilbert and Ellice Islands during the trip there in 1884. It is curious to know why he needed a formal statement of intent but Thurston had to give official permission to travel to the Solomon Islands and the letters of introduction would have secured that request. Woodford was now recognised as a natural history collector not a minor clerk in the colonial service. Like many other young men of this period he was keen to make his mark. If the collection were of quality then he could legitimately sell it to an institution like the British Museum. Commercial artefact and natural history dealers in London were eager to receive new specimens from unexplored places in the Western Pacific. Having made a good start in Fiji, Woodford could now look elsewhere (see Barrow 2000 for an excellent study of the natural history trade in the United States in the late-Victorian period).

The Solomon Islands were a good choice. They were volcanic rather than coral atolls and would therefore show a range of biological diversity from the more common coastal species to endemic inland and mountain species. The islands were on the eastern extremity of the Melanesian chain. Here the people were predominately Melanesian. In the southern islands however they were predominately Polynesian. A small trading vessel could sail around the islands easily and Woodford was obviously confident enough to allay any fears that he would be in physical danger living with the people. Alfred Russel Wallace had recently published a sequel to his famous study of the geographical distribution of animals. In the new book, *Island Life* (1880), Wallace classified islands into three groups: oceanic islands, and two types of continental islands. The main Solomon Islands would fit the oceanic islands category well. Having been formed in mid-ocean and never part of a large continent, they would therefore be characterised by a lack of terrestrial mammals and amphibians, and their zoological inhabitants would be the result of accidental colonialisation and subsequent evolution. Consequently, there should be a large range of endemic species in the islands that would be a valuable case study as little comprehensive collecting had been done in the region.

Scientific rationalism of late-Victorian England

Exploration of the New World by young amateur scientists and travellers greatly expanded the understanding of the biological world and this biological reasoning underwrote the early scientific classification of human species. The late-Victorian era was a time of scientific rationalism. The static religious determinism that saw natural history as the work of God had been replaced by a constantly changing view based on the principles of evolution and adaptation stimulated by the writings on the origin of the species by Charles Darwin (1859). Taxonomy, and the classification of species, was essential to this scientific view of the world. Alfred Russel Wallace (1853 and 1869) had undertaken groundbreaking work in South America between 1848 and 1850 and in the Malay Archipelago between 1854 and 1862. This led to Wallace's theoretical classification of the world into biogeographic regions, which convinced him of the reality of evolution due to natural selection. His book, *The Geographical Distribution of Animals* (1876) would remain a definitive study of zoogeography for the next 80 years. The much examined crisis of faith of the late Victorians, triggered by the growth of science, was really a feature of the intellectual elite. The middle and working classes retained much of their religious conservatism well into the 20th century.

The naval officers and naturalists attached to Royal Navy ships from the Australia Station led the way in the biological discoveries in the Western Pacific. William Milne was attached to the survey ship HMS *Herald* as a botanist and collected 200 species of plants from Makira and Guadalcanal for the Royal Botanic Gardens at Kew in 1854, although William Hemsley, Principal Assistant at Kew Herbarium, wrote disparagingly that 'they were mostly common things from the coast region' (Hemsley 1891: 501 and 1895: 163). John MacGillivray, also on the *Herald*, is credited with capturing the first specimen of the large birdwing butterfly, *Ornithoptera victoriae* [Gray 1856] at Wanderer Bay. Here the crew from the *Herald* were investigating the disappearance of Benjamin Boyd (Macgillivray 1852–1854; Tennant 1997). The commonly reported story of the capture is that MacGillivray could not catch the butterfly in a net because it was flying so high that he had to shoot it down from the top of the tree and consequently this holotype female specimen is peppered with holes (Tennant

1997: illustration on 164). In fact, the truth behind the capture is a little more prosaic. As MacGillivray had no insect net at all he could only resort to shooting the insect—but it was most certainly caught at Wanderer Bay.

The first holotype male specimen would be captured by Woodford on Malaita quite some time later (Woodford 1890b: 66–68). Julius Brenchley (1873) who sailed on the HMS *Curaçoa* in 1865 made many scientific discoveries in the Solomons, as did Alexander Morton from the Australian Museum who travelled on the HMS *Cormorant* in 1881 (Morton 1883; *The Sydney Morning Herald* 12 September 1881: 5 and 26 September 1881: 7, 8). Morton reported that local people had discarded stone implements by this time in favour of traders' axes and that two forms of imported tools were used. One, an elongated cone flattened towards the base with a rounded cutting edge, was used as an adze while the other, conical in shape but with a wide flattened cutting edge ground sharp on both sides, was used as a ordinary axe or tomahawk (Morton 1883: 63). He had difficulties in collecting ethnological specimens apart from stone tomahawks, presumably those discarded in favour of metal axes, but noted: 'I secured, however, an interesting series of human skulls, and the head of a native from the Lord Howe's Group [Ontong Java] in spirits' (Morton 1883: 64). These he brought back to Sydney. He returned to the Australian Museum with 200 bird specimens, representing 50 species, 20 species of fishes, two species of crustaceans, four species of reptiles, 28 species of land snails and over 20 species of freshwater shells (Morton 1883). Morton was an expert natural history collector who had previously been part of an expedition to south-eastern New Guinea (Papua) in 1877. He accompanied Andrew Goldie who was working on behalf of a private natural history collector and seller R. B. Williams of Holloway Place in London (Ramsay 1879a, 1879b, 1880a and 1880b; see also Mullins, Bellamy and Moore 2012). This resulted in a large and important collection of mammals and birds from Papua that are now housed in the Australian Museum in Sydney.

Captain John Moresby (1876) on the HMS *Basilisk* made significant ethnographic observations during the cruise to New Guinea, parts of Polynesia and the pearling stations of the Torres Strait between 1871 and 1874 and Captain Cyprian Bridge (1886), like a number of naval officers, read a paper on his travels though Melanesia, Polynesia and to New Guinea during 1882 and 1885 before the Royal Geographical Society in London. Small collections from the Solomon Islands were made by naval officers like Lt Richards of the HMS *Renard* who visited the islands on their annual tours of inspection (Ramsay 1882a: 176–180, 1882b: 718–726, 1882c: 833–834). Private collectors also travelled on trading vessels. James Cockerell visited the Solomon Islands on the schooner *Ariel* owned by Captain Brodie and made a collection of 50 mammals and 350 bird skins that he sold to the Australian Museum (Ramsay 1880b: 65–84). The details of these collections were published in well-respected journals such as the *Proceedings of the Linnaean Society of New South Wales*. This scientific knowledge was then widely disseminated throughout the influential, intellectual elite of the Empire.

Scientific manuals of enquiry

Officers of the Royal Navy Australia Station published many short examinations of the physical or ethnological features of the islands and even published accounts in the Australian newspapers. Most data were collected using standardised sets of guidelines roughly equivalent to questionnaires which commenced with general facts and figures and then led to more detailed examinations of cultures and customs for those with more time at their disposal. The Admiralty's *Manual of Scientific Enquiry*, published in five editions between 1849 to 1886, was planned as a guide for naval officers but could be used by 'travellers in general' (Great Britain. Admiralty 1871). It was more scientific than the *Notes and Queries on Anthropology* first published in 1874 which was designed specifically for collecting information on both anthropology—described as the anatomical and physiological features of mankind—and ethnology—defined as the customs, history, religions, languages and arts of native peoples. *Notes and Queries on Anthropology* was published in six editions between 1874 and 1951 (Garson and Read 1892).

The questions on anthropology and ethnology in the first edition had been quickly drawn up in 1873 by Augustus Lane-Fox Pitt Rivers and a committee from the British Association for the Advancement of Science at the request of the organisers of the expedition sent to find Dr David Livingstone (Petch 2007). These expeditions had multiple roles. Members of the expedition sent back artefacts and natural history specimens, as well as reports on populations and cultures they encountered. Along with detailed survey maps and notes on geology and botany these were based on the guidelines set by *Notes and Queries*. The ethnology section in the first edition published in 1874 was written by E. B. Tylor, the prominent cultural evolutionist who later became the Keeper of the Oxford University Museum of Natural History.

In addition to these guides, J. G. Frazer at Cambridge privately printed his own set called *Questions on the Manners, Customs, Religion, Superstitions, &c, of Uncivilized or Semi-Civilized Peoples* in 1887 (Frazer and Holmes 1889). This edition was followed by two more in 1889 and 1907. Copies of the first edition and the third edition are contained in Woodford's papers so it is clear that he used this reference material (Woodford papers PMB 1290 Item 7/3 and 7/56). Certainly during his first and second expeditions to the islands Woodford collected social and cultural information that he later published. But it is clear that his real aim was collecting natural not cultural history. In addition, the Royal Geographical Society in London published its own set of questions called *Hints to Travellers* (Galton 1878, Driver 1998). This was widely used in the late-19th and early-20th centuries and went through 11 editions between 1865 and 1935. The fourth edition contained one of the first comprehensive accounts of the problems and prospects of field photography for explorers that would have been useful in the Solomon Islands (Galton 1878: 47–53). Both the fourth and fifth editions would have been available to Woodford. *Hints to Travellers* was an attempt by the Royal Geographical Society to reconcile different forms of knowledge: the theoretical and the empirical, the amateur and the professional, the global and the local, and the particular and the universal. The Royal Geographical Society was an important organisation at the forefront of colonial exploration. It occupied a pivotal position between the scientific establishment, the Imperial government and its elite world of political concerns, and the wider educated public (Ryan 1997: 22). The Royal Geographical Society was 'part social club, part learned society, part imperial information exchange and part platform for the promotion of sensational feats of exploration' (Driver 1998: 29). Knowledge was actively debated and contested within the Society. Issues of race, the 'civilizing mission', the process of modernisation and even esoteric knowledge were discussed at meetings. While the Society was not openly political its members were often staff of the Colonial Office, the India Office, the Admiralty and other organs of state. It was both influential and prestigious. Displaying the letters Fellowship of the Royal Geographical Society (FRGS) after one's name was a sign of important associations. Woodford became a Fellow of the Royal Geographical Society in 1885.

Of all of these important instructional manuals, the Admiralty manuals were the most encompassing and the most scientifically orientated. They were divided into four parts: part one xwas on astronomy and hydrography; part two was on meteorology and terrestrial magnetism; part three covered questions on geography, medical statistics and ethnology; and part four was on geology, zoology and botany. The chapter on ethnology, originally written by J. C. Pritchard, was revised by E. B. Taylor for the fourth edition. Travellers were recommended to report on 'all that relates to human beings, whether regarded as individuals, or as members of families or communities' (Great Britain. Admiralty 1871: 233). Anthropological science was advancing as a separate intellectual discipline, especially following the publication of the more comprehensive second edition of *Notes and Queries on Anthropology* in 1892 (Petch 2007). Boyle Somerville, a Lieutenant on the surveying ship HMS *Penguin*, spent more than eight months camped in the Marovo Lagoon area between 1893 and 1894 and, using the guidelines in *Notes and Queries*, he made many important ethnographic notes on New Georgia peoples later published by the Anthropological Institute (Somerville 1897). Somerville's notes are particularly detailed for a causal visitor at that time. He was one of the first to make some estimates of the comparative value of shell rings (*poata*), which he valued at about 1 shilling and 3 pence apiece. He valued whale's teeth much higher at £1 each and, for comparison, a stick of trade tobacco cost one halfpenny (Somerville 1897: 405). These practical manuals of information collecting were part of the expansion of intellectual enquiry in late-Victorian England. Much of the information, and most of the specimens, being taken back to the museums and scientific societies of the metropole was collected by amateurs not professionals.

Henry Brougham Guppy

It was Henry Brougham Guppy who was to contribute most of the social and economic information on the Solomon Islands before the expeditions of Woodford. Guppy was a naval surgeon trained in Edinburgh who wrote about the geology and geography of the islands, their potential as a British colony, and some well-considered comments on the lifestyles and culture of the local peoples (Guppy 1887a, 1887b and 1903–1906). Guppy was a perceptive observer, writer, amateur naturalist and scientist. He travelled widely and had been to the Far East before serving in the Pacific. Between 1881 and 1884 he served as a medical officer on the sailing schooner and survey vessel HMS *Lark*, engaged in the waters around the Solomon Islands and the Western Pacific at a time when trade between the Australian colonies and Asia and India was expanding. The tropical waters north of the Australian colonies were not well known and the Royal Navy sent many survey and patrol vessels to chart the islands, oceans and coral reefs. In 1887 Guppy published probably the first comprehensive study of the natural history, geology and botany of the Solomons (Guppy 1887a). His botanical collection, much of it collected on Fauro, Alu and the Mono Islands, was donated to the Royal Botanic Gardens at Kew (Hemsley 1895: 163). Guppy also investigated head hunting, ritual, material culture, physical anthropology, and languages, and he included one of the first translated versions of the journal of Hernán Gallego in his book. Guppy is credited with being the first serious scientist to investigate the cultural and natural history of the islands, although again Hemsley at Kew Herbarium was patronising in his gratitude for the specimens when he wrote: 'Dr Guppy had had no previous experience in selecting specimens of plants, and many unmistakable novelties were insufficient for description'. Despite this the preliminary findings by Hemsley (1891) established the fact that there were two distinct features in the composition of flora in the Solomon Islands: the first was a group of distinct endemic generic species, often found on higher altitudes and associated with rare Malayan and Polynesian types, the second was a group of shore plants of very wide general distribution in the tropics. During his time in Alu in the Shortland Islands, Guppy made the acquaintance of Gorai, the chief at Morgusaiai Island off the main Alu Island. This was to be a fortuitous meeting. Guppy (1903–1906) later published a two volume work of the observations of a naturalist in the Pacific that included studies in Fiji. Despite his short stay in the region, Guppy certainly established a foundation upon which scientific and cultural research could be based.

Henry Guppy presumably advised Woodford to some degree because the latter carried a recommendation to Gorai. The Solomon Islands seemed ideal for a young man with ambition. Exploration in the 19th century came to have a number of contested meanings. Science, literature, commerce, the Empire and even religion were all motivations driving the need to comprehend the world. But the explorer of the period was characteristically a white, middle class male, not wealthy but of some independent means, with an eccentric, even idiosyncratic, personality. These mostly young men were 'loath to be tied to any broader institutional system' and were a disquieting figure to the sedentary, conservative, metropole-based scientist (Butlin 2009: 226–228). They were often unknown men with little or no scientific training; risk-takers in a staid, conservative world bound by convention. Exploration tied science and Empire together and became one of the strengths of British colonial expansionism.

Science and Empire

During the 19th century scientific knowledge expanded, both within and outside the universities, as new scientific institutions like the British Museum, the British Museum of Natural History and the Royal Botanic Gardens at Kew grew in status. Kew became the nerve centre for all British colonial botanic gardens. Plants were received from all over the world and acclimatisation gardens were established in the colonial dominions and dependencies (see Mullins, Bellamy and Moore 2012). English botanic gardens operated in service of British colonial expansion and through the exercise of their scientific knowledge they increased the comparative commercial advantage of Western core powers over the rest of the world (Brockway 1979). The Victorian era accorded prestige and influence to eminent scientists.

The Royal Navy that was reconstructed after the Napoleonic Wars became a peacetime institution of high regard and some status, promoting British Imperial economic and political security. It also saw itself as the upholder of British social and cultural values. The naval officers who formed a network of enlightened, educated men with keen interest in science were instructed in drawing and mapping. Many became keen photographers. All this material added to the knowledge of the world. The British Museum benefited greatly from the ethnographic materials collected during voyages of discovery by the

Royal Navy ships (Owen 2006). The natural history collections sent to gardens at Kew and the Natural History Museum in Kensington were then studied and the results published. The Admiralty supported this work. Ethnographic materials, however, did not attract the same scientific attention. If they were displayed at all they were often poorly labelled and marked as exotic curiosities. Objects from the Pacific represented difference: the heathen black juxtaposed against the Christian white. They defined European identity through contrast rather than enhanced understanding. Ethnographic collections sent to Britain and Australia at this time illustrated the dichotomy between the savage and the civilised, between the morally superior and the benighted inferior. Ideas of intellectual and cultural superiority were inculcated into young men at an early age. At the reception and lecture at Tonbridge School lauding the expedition to Central Africa under Stanley and the participation of A. J. Mounteney Jepson, the Headmaster T. B. Rowe stated it 'was one of the great characteristics of the English race that it governs, civilizes and moulds the world at large, and extends throughout it a beneficent and civilizing influence … It was our lot under Providence to have an Empire … Patience, intrepidity, courage, obedience to constructed authority, the capabilities of self-government, sagacity and perseverance—these are the qualities which gave us our proud portion as a nation' (*The Gravesend Journal, Dartford Observer and County Intelligencer* 7 June 1890; Woodford papers PMB 1290 Item 9/2 Press cuttings 1886-1911).

But science was also a recognised avenue for social mobility at a moment of unprecedented change. Many scientists rose from the unglamorous beginnings as provincial amateur naturalists. Linnaean taxonomy transformed both botany and zoology and it was systematics—the classification of species, their description and preservation in museum collections, and the investigation into their evolutionary history and environmental adaptation—that underwrote evolutionary theorising (Raffles 2001: 525). But there remained the clear distinction between the place of the self-educated enthusiast and the professional. It was important for an ambitious natural history collector with talent to gain cultural capital and penetrate the elite. Members of institutions like the Royal Geographical Society were often members of the Royal Colonial Institute and the Linnaean and Zoological Societies. Membership of these associations allowed colonial officials and travellers an avenue for the presentation of their colonial encounters to their fellows. Even casual observations that mixed fact with prejudice were discussed, but membership of these learned societies remained largely the province of middle class males. This was a time of debate between the supporters of monogenesis, the belief that all humans have a common origin compatible with Christian teachings, and the supporters of polygenesis, the racialist position that placed emphasis on different racial and ethnic characteristics and classified peoples on a scale as either savage, barbarous or civilised (Lorimer 1988: 405). The basic assumption that the subject races were doomed to extinction following contact with supposedly superior stock from the Anglo-European world arose at this time. It grew to importance when the ethnologist Augustus Lane-Fox Pitt Rivers spoke openly of the eventual extermination of the subject races following sustained cultural contact (Lorimer 1988: 409, 420).

For a young man like Charles Woodford, the authority of the explorer depended substantially on the writing of a narrative that combined travel, science and adventure in an unexplored corner of the world. Alfred Russel Wallace, R. H. Codrington and Rev George Brown, believers in monogenesis philosophy, argued for a common origin and closer linguistic connections between Papuans and Polynesians (Lorimer 1988: 414). To cross the barrier between the unknown man of talent and the recognised man of science the amateur had to seek new ground and obtain first-hand experience of the region. For Woodford, the Solomon Islands and the Western Pacific in general, was the location of this scientific knowledge. Tropical nature and its manifold variety of plants, animals and peoples was perceived as a thing of wonder (Raffles 2001: 519). The key nodes of professionalism were Kew Gardens and the British Museum of Natural History. Only through sponsorship from these institutions, or by a self-funded expedition that led to official recognition, was it possible to attract the attention of the higher echelons of the metropolitan natural history circles. Woodford had chosen the second option, a self-funded expedition. This was the most difficult and most financially risky method of attracting attention, but men like Alfred Russel Wallace had done it and achieved success.

The tasks of collecting, cataloguing and describing nature's forms demanded a range of skills and experience but most of all it required considerable resources of time and money. The amateur had to know not only what to look for, but how to observe, and for this the numerous explorers' and travellers' manuals were essential (Driver 2004: 8, 853). An impressive natural history cabinet was a sign of some recognised social capital with significant exchange value. It would elevate the owner into the ranks of the learned scientific establishment that was inevitably filled by men with Oxbridge credentials (Raffles 2001: 525, 537). Victorians also looked to the work of Richard Hakluyt, 'the moving intellect of early British transoceanic expansion'. Hakluyt's achievements had been in the construction of exploration as a broad field of nation-making through the assembly and publication of the most important travel writings of the day (Raffles 2001: 523). Woodford's third and last expedition to the Solomon Islands was underwritten by the influential Hakluyt Society's need for detailed identification of the places visited in the Solomon Islands by the Spanish explorers under Mendaña.

The Imperial scientific network was a rich and powerful one. In the history of scientific exploration the spatial language of centre and periphery—'home and abroad, the cabinet and the field, the metropolis and the frontier'—long held sway (Driver 2004: 81). Scientific discoveries and new technologies formed a central part of the British colonial heritage. From this came the quest to order and categorise, to define nature and revise concepts of space and history, and to transform the resources of exploration into raw material for markets at home and the new museums that advertised this conquest and control over nature (Macleod 1993: 119). This quest for social and natural order rationalised colonialism and the expansion of the British Empire. Science brought with it views of nature and race that sustained much racial and cultural prejudice. Science became a colonising ideology even as it was being promoted as a means of improving and uplifting humankind from ignorance and superstition.

The best known of all the early scientists, Alfred Russel Wallace and Charles Darwin, had both begun their careers as amateur specimen collectors. Wallace began as a financially constrained sole collector in the Amazon and the Malay Archipelago, Darwin as a well-connected, gentleman companion and natural history savant on the HMS *Beagle* (Fagan 2007). Woodford had more in common with Wallace. Both were financially self-supporting, both lived largely alone with local villagers, and both had to rely on the assistance of porters and guides. Both men worked in difficult physical environments and followed routines organised around collecting and capture of specimens in the morning and early afternoon and the preparation of the samples late in the day and early evening. Both used the services of paid local hunters and collectors. Like Wallace, Woodford was collecting beetles and butterflies and more rarely shot birds and mammals. Both kept small live menageries. Wallace tailored his collecting according to what would sell: tropical birds, brightly coloured butterflies and beetles. Woodford's expeditions in the Solomon Islands yielded 20,000 specimens (Tennant 1997). By comparison, Wallace who spent much longer in the field, collected over 125,000 specimens in the Malay Archipelago alone. His Amazon collections, not counting almost the entire first collection lost at sea, amounted to a further 10,000 specimens (Fagan 2007: 617). Like Woodford, Wallace's field notes are complete detailed summaries with species counts collected at given localities. For a first-time collector and author it would have been daunting for Woodford to receive a review of his book in *Nature* (24 April 1890: 582–583) written by Wallace, but it would have been encouraging to know that his collection was well received at the British Museum. Like other adventurer/explorers, Woodford had to rely on hospitality trails of European settlers and traders, networks of planters, merchants and officials all arranged casually through letters of introduction or contacts made in the field. Living in local communities, both men were dependent upon the goodwill of the people and the availability of guides and porters. As an isolated explorer-scientist Woodford was exposed and vulnerable, probably more vulnerable than he really knew at the time.

Map 2. Solomon Islands and Guadalcanal showing locations visited by Woodford on the first and second expeditions.

Source: Woodford 1888: following 376.

First expedition

Woodford arrived back in Fiji in February 1886 hoping to catch an early boat going north to the Solomon Islands, but none was available. As it would have been the wet season in the north it can be assumed that boats were delayed by the weather. Having secured permission from Thurston all he could do was spend the time collecting insects and animals on Viti Levu. He also called on Ratu Tomoci, the son of Cakobau, who lived at Bau. After waiting two long months he finally secured passage on the *Christine*, a small topsail schooner of 97 tons that was taking 120 returnees back to their home communities in the

New Hebrides, the Solomon Islands and the Lord Howe's Group (Leueneuwa: Ontong Java). The *Christine*, like many vessels in the labour trade, had been previously used for other work, in this case the timber trade, and had been wrecked off Uki ni Masi. It had been subsequently re-floated and repaired in Auckland at a cost of £200 (Woodford papers PMB 1290 Item 1/2. Diary 16 April–5 June 1886). The *Christine* also had a licence to recruit 46 male labourers for Fiji and travelled with a Government Agent to supervise the repatriation and recruitment processes (Woodford 1888a: 354). The boat spent the latter part of April and early May in the New Hebrides recruiting for new labourers. Woodford detailed the manner in which young men were engaged for work:

> When ships are seen by the natives of their coast they make a smoke ashore if they want to communicate. The two boats [from the *Christine*] were then lowered, fully armed in case of accidents, with four rowers in each, one in charge of the recruiter and the other in charge of the Government Agent. The former backed in on to the beach, throwing a small anchor out of the bows, so as to be able to pull off in case of attack; the crew at the same time sit ready at the oars. The recruiter stands up in the stern of the boat, while the natives crowd round him, and he conducts the trading for yams or other food or tries to persuade boys to engage. The other boat, with the Government agent, keeps afloat, and acts as a covering boat to the other in case of attack. In some instances we only used one boat, and then the recruiter and Government agent went together; but wherever the natives were mistrusted we always made use of two boats (Woodford 1888a: 355; see also The Vagabond 1886 for details of similar recruiting procedures and an excellent photograph by J. W. Lindt in Brunt and Thomas 2012: 220 of recruiting vessel, two boats—one offshore—and men being recruited at Pangkumu in Malekula, New Hebrides in 1890).

On 10 May 1886 Woodford wrote in his diary: 'Position at noon 11°44'S 163°12'E 120 miles. At two o'clock we sighted land. This was the northeast end of San Christoval [Makira] and my first view of the Solomons Group'. Next day the *Christine* was becalmed off Santa Ana and men from the island came out in canoes without outriggers, ingeniously carved and decorated. The men had spears and wore white cowrie frontlets and white discs in their ears. The trader at Santa Ana, Frank Nyberg, told Woodford that he knew Gorai of Alu and 'says that I shall be quite safe with him' (Woodford papers PMB 1290 Item 1/2 Diary 11 May 1886). Like earlier explorers Woodford was impressed by the beauty and grace of the canoes of the Solomon Islanders. While later he thought those of the New Georgia people the best of all, on 11 May 1886 he wrote in his diary of his delight:

The Solomon Island canoes as I afterward found out are most certainly things of beauty. In fact I have never seen canoes that sit so gracefully upon the water. The long graceful sweeping curves of their bows and sterns must inevitably impress a stranger seeing them for the first time, while upon closer inspection the ingenious way in which the planking is fitted together and the seams caulked with vegetable putty compel admiration for the ingenuity and labour expended upon them (Woodford papers PMB 1290 Item 1/5 Revised Diary 11 May 1886).

On 12 May, Woodford was out early after insects and was delighted at his success. He felt that the beauty and variety of the flora and fauna, even on this his first island, augured well for the long-term success of his field work.

The *Young Dick* attack

From Santa Ana the boat sailed to Kahua on Makira, on to Ugi, and then crossed to Sa'a at the bottom of Maramasike (Small Malaita). Here it met with the Melanesian Mission vessel *Southern Cross*. On board the *Southern Cross* Woodford was told that the corvette HMS *Opal* had just been to punish the Kwaio people of central Malaita for their attack on the labour vessel, the *Young Dick*. According to oral history recorded by Roger Keesing (1986) a Kwaio fighting leader, Maeasuaa, from Uru Harbour had attacked and killed many crew members, and then plundered and burnt the labour vessels the *Borealis* in 1880 (*The Brisbane Courier*, 8 January 1881: 4) and the *Janet Stewart* in 1882 (*The Brisbane Courier*, 2 May 1882: 3). Retaliation by the Royal Navy had been ineffective. In fact the success of the attacks made Maeasuaa respected and raised his status. This made other men eager to attack labour vessels in the hope of raising their status in their communities. On 20 May 1886 the *Young Dick* was attempting to recruit for Queensland when it was attacked in Sinalagu (Sinalanggu) Harbour, south of Uru. The motive was cultural revenge. A man, Taafana'au, was in mourning over his son Boosui whom it was assumed had been kidnapped by a labour boat. He offered blood money to any man who could kill a white man from another labour vessel (Keesing 1986: 277). One man, 'Arumae, heard of the blood debt and so planned to attack the *Young Dick* that was then anchored offshore. Although all the purification rituals that he and his associates performed were rejected by the ancestral spirits they still planned to go ahead with the attack (Keesing 1986: 282–283). This was the second attack on the *Young Dick* in a matter of days and it too was unsuccessful, although a number of the crew including the Government Agent, the carpenter, the cook, one sailor, and a recruit were killed. The Kwaio warriors were eventually repelled by other men on board the boat.

In all, the crew of the *Young Dick* were attacked three times in their attempts to recruit along the east coast of Malaita that May. More than any other attack on a recruiting ship, the *Young Dick* raids earned the people of Malaita the reputation for the most savage in the islands (Boutilier 1983: 48). At a subsequent coroner's inquiry held in Maryborough on 5 June 1886 detailed evidence was given by the European crew and verbatim evidence in Pijin by Melanesian crew members. The testimony was often confusing. For instance, the Mate, Charles Marr, on 'being called, is [sic] too drunk to give evidence' (Great Britain. House of Commons. Parliamentary Papers 1887b). As a result it was recommended that part of the Malaita coast be closed to recruiting. The instigator of the revenge attack, Taafana'au, was then killed by the survivors of the raid in revenge for the deaths of their kinsmen. The son, Boosui, reportedly kidnapped, had been a voluntary recruit and he later returned from Fiji where he had been working on plantations (Keesing 1986: 285). Not long after, in July 1886, the *Young Dick* was lost off the coast of Queensland with around 130 to 140 labourers on board thus opening another deep wound in relations between Malaitans and recruiters. It was clear that both sides misunderstood each other. Woodford was sailing into a complex world where his values and attitudes would be seriously challenged.

Collecting on Malaita

Woodford's vessel, the *Christine*, anchored in Uru Harbour and then in North West Bay (Sinalanggu), both locations of previous attacks. It remained there from 26 May to 2 June 1886. During that time Woodford went ashore and collected insects, clearly untroubled by the recent violence, although he wrote: 'I always carry my revolver and then I have all the time my gun in one hand and net in the other and the natives would not venture to attack anyone unless they can get them at a dis-advantage' (Woodford papers PMB 1290 Item 1/2 Diary 28 May 1886). At Sinalanggu he also caught eight female and two male bird-winged butterfly (*Ornithoptera victoriae*) and wrote: 'The male, distinguished for the brilliant metallic green and gold colour of its wings, has never previously been discovered, although the much larger though more sombre-coloured female has been known for many years, from a single specimen captured during the visit to this group [Wanderer Bay on Guadalcanal by John MacGillivray] of H.M.S. Herald in 1854' (Woodford 1888a: 357; 1890b: 64). Woodford had been supplied with a tracing of the female specimen by Arthur Butler at the British Museum so the capture of male specimens would have been especially rewarding. The birdwing butterflies, *Ornithoptera priamus urvilleanus* and *O. victoriae*, endemic to the central Solomon Islands, lay their eggs on the host plant, *Aristolochia tagala* (Indian birthwort or Dutchman's pipe), commonly found along sandy beaches and in the undergrowth of old coconut plantations (Straatman 1969).

It appears Woodford, like MacGillvray earlier, was obliged to shoot at least two female butterflies with dust shot although he was pleased that he could capture a male in 'grand condition' (Woodford 1890b: 66–68; Tennant 1997: 170; Woodford papers PMB 1290 Item 1/5 Revised Diary 26 May 1886). Woodford's capture of the butterflies has not entered natural history folklore but as Tennant describes it, perhaps it should be there. Tennant wrote: 'It is odd that the story of a stark-naked future Resident Commissioner dashing along the beach with a butterfly net, and falling head over heels, watched by 100 "boys" [men on the recruiting vessel] and a lookout in the crow's nest, has not entered the folklore in the same way as MacGillivray's story—which is surely tame by comparison' (Tennant 1997: 171). However, this interpretation of the day's collecting may be rather anecdotal for Woodford's diary entries are more restrained. There are no entries describing a naked run on the beach. He did note with amazement the size and beauty of the butterflies on the east coast of Malaita and reported that the first one seen was at least eight inches in wingspan. Woodford wrote: 'The sight of these insects on the wing is very fine as they fly along among the tree tops with a lazy flapping flight and occasionally sailing with outspread wings' (Woodford papers PMB 1290 Item 1/2 Diary 27 May 1886). In his revised diary these events are expanded in more detail and Woodford documents the history of the discovery and the range of the species on Guadalcanal and Malaita.

Woodford's travels to Alu, where he planned to stay, were to take him first to Malu'u, at the northern end of Malaita, then to Coleridge Bay (Fauabu) just north of Cape Ritter on the north-east coast of Malaita. This was the home of the men who had danced at Dr Corney's plantation in Suva. He recorded in his diary that labourers in Fiji get paid £6 for the first two years—£3 a year—but only in trade, not money, and that the payment of £12 for the third year is given in cash: a total of £6 in trade and £12 in cash. The problem was that the trade goods were chosen for the men by the plantation owners. This differed from the situation in Queensland where men were paid £6 a year in cash and not goods. The leader of the Meke dance in Suva was landed back in Coleridge Bay all dressed in 'bright red flannel shirt, turkey red Sulu and a woollen "Tam O'Shanter" cap in which the colours yellow green red & blue are absolutely dazzling to the eye'. On 6 June the *Christine* anchored at Gera (Mbara) island, off the village of Aola on Guadalcanal, where Lars Nielsen had built a trading station. Nielsen had been at Mbara since 1885 and Woodford wrote: 'The natives here have a much better character than those of Malayta [Malaita] and I believe this would not be at all a bad place to stay at, with the idea of making an excursion into the interior and up the high peaks of the island' (Woodford papers PMB 1290 Item 1/2 Diary 6 June 1886). The mountains and long rivers behind Aola fascinated Woodford from the beginning and he was later to spend some time in the area. It was during this visit that he decided to base himself at Aola in his future expeditions, for he 'formed such a favourable estimate of the capabilities of the locality as a collecting ground and also was as favourability impressed with the natives' (Woodford papers PMB 1290 Item 1/5 Revised Diary 7 June 1886).

He took numerous photographs of the region and wrote: 'I saw some cycads growing straight up to a height of fifty feet and the stems of them thicker than most cocoa-nut palms'. These tall forests of sago palm are commonly found in the lower river mouths along the south-east coast of Guadalcanal. On 12 June 1886 the *Christine* called in to Marau Sound where 'the natives of this place speak the same language as is spoken on the S.E. coast of Malayta and the canoes constantly pass to & fro'. In Marau the people from south Malaita resettled on the coastal atolls and islets many centuries ago. They remain culturally distinct from the mainland dwelling people of Guadalcanal. Here was the profitable trading station of Oscar Svensen. Woodford also noted that 10s was equal to 100 sticks of tobacco, 100 clay pipes and a little calico. This is comparable with the values for trade goods sold wholesale by Hoffnung & Co with a small margin of profit for the trader. From Marau Sound the *Christine* continued its way along the dangerous Weather Coast of Guadalcanal. Here Woodford wrote in his diary: 'It is a very bad coast to be caught upon as the water is deep right up to the shore and there is no anchorage or protection of any kind', apart from Wanderer Bay which he considered a 'capital anchorage and well protected from prevailing winds' (Woodford papers PMB 1290 Item 1/5 Revised Diary 15 June 1886). More returnees were then landed at Tangarere north of Wanderer Bay. On June 19 Woodford sighted Rendova, Simbo and Ranongga off New Georgia.

Collecting at Alu and his host, Gorai

Charles Woodford arrived at Alu in the Shortland Islands off Bougainville on 23 June 1886. Here he met Gorai dressed 'in a red flannel shirt and pair of trousers, and an old sun helmet on his head' (Woodford 1888a: 358). In his diary he wrote 'The traders gave him [Gorai] a very bad character, the officers of the Men O' War on the other hand speak very well of him' (Woodford papers PMB 1290 Item 1/2. Diary 23 June 1886). Gorai was descended from a grandfather who had come from Bougainville to the north. This warrior leader subsequently installed himself as chief of the Mono and Alu islands after defeating the local people there (Woodford papers PMB 1290 Item 1/2 Diary 9 July 1886). Gorai may have appeared to a visiting European to be strangely dressed but he was a shrewd businessman and drove a good bargain. When Woodford requested a separate house for himself and all his field equipment the price was: '1 axe, 4 knives, 3 necklaces of beads, 3 fathoms of cloth, 20 sticks of tobacco, 1 flannel shirt' (Woodford 1888a: 358). A conservative estimate based on prices at that time would value this at £1 10s (£600 in current values). With the house came two women to cook and clean and a regular supply of garden food. Woodford was put ashore on 24 June and wrote: 'At daylight having taken leave of all on board the captain brought me ashore and left me taking on board with him two natives to pilot the ship to Fauro. At seven o'clock the ship sailed and I was left alone with the natives' (Woodford papers PMB 1290 Item 1/5. Revised Diary 24 June 1886). He was to remain there from 24 June to 7 August 1886 and during this time he made a large collection of 'Lepidoptera and Coleoptera as well as the birds, mammals, reptiles and batrachians (frogs &c) of the locality' (Woodford 1888a: 358). Both Woodford and Gorai would have been pleased with the outcomes of the arrangement, for in addition to payment for the house, which would have been shared with the owner who may or may not have been Gorai, the chief also received 1 axe, 1 knife, some cloth, some tobacco, an umbrella and some sugar (Woodford papers PMB 1290 Item 1/2 Diary 24 June 1886).

Gorai had his village Taoai/Maleai (Irwin 1973: 228, 238) on Magusaiai Island close by and Woodford was left alone with the local people on a small coral island off the coast. The large island, generally called Shortland Island, is known locally as Alu, and the three smaller islands off the south-east of the main island are Morgusaiai, Pirumeri and Poporang. It is most likely that Woodford lived on Pirumeri Island where the old village, called Paramata, had a population in 1894 of about 300 people (Irwin 1973: 231). All these islands were a short canoe trip to Gorai's village that consisted of about 300 huts with a population of around 1,500 and Guppy noted that around the village was almost a mile of continuous cultivation (Irwin 1973: 239 quoting Guppy 1887b: 81). Gorai's house was quite substantial. Guppy measured it as being 40 feet by 20 feet and near it was a house for his wives that measured 60 feet by 30 feet and was 20 feet in height (Anon 1888a: 559). Woodford's host and protector, Gorai, had built up considerable wealth from his position as chief. He had a house with 'thirty pairs of sash windows … A room set apart for entertaining foreign visitors contained "a small ship's cannon, a dozen rifles of all types, a picture of the Queen of England, a variety of wall clocks, some large mirrors"'. His dining room was well lighted with kerosene lamps imported from Sydney (Bennett 1987: 96; Sack 2005: 340; Johnston 1980: 58). Gorai had built this wealth by acting as a 'passage master' for men like Captain William Hamilton who, when promised 120 men for plantation work, had to provide weapons, knives and building materials including the window sashes noted above (Johnston 1980: 58).

Woodford photographed this house with Gorai and some of his wives in front. Gorai's brother was the chief of the Mono (Treasury Islands), but on Alu the main village probably Haleta, belonged to a son, Kupanne who, it was said in German accounts did not like whites (Sack 2005: 343 quoting from Parkinson 1887–1888). Woodford never seemed to be in any difficulty during his stay in the area although he had some reservations at first. He wrote: 'the "Christine" sailed away and left me; nor will I conceal the fact that I had some slight feelings of regret as I saw the last link connecting me with civilisation disappear below the horizon' (Woodford 1890b: 18). This was indeed the reason for his success both as a collector and a man living in the islands unprotected. He was prepared to take the risk and live alone with the people. Most especially he lived his daily life in front of them and not apart. He ate their food and entertained them as he must have done by his strange collecting and hunting habits. He also showed that he was not afraid of the people. Unlike the traders, he did not isolate himself on an offshore island and travel in his own trading vessel. He took an especial interest in the daily activities of village life and made numerous comments on what was happening around him. His diaries are full of surprised asides starting with 'I forgot to mention' as if he were writing to himself in absentia calling up the experiences of the day. He found some of those experiences humorous and some strange but all of them interesting. Most of all he did not drink and did not abuse the people, especially the women. He was polite.

Figure 2. Gorai's house at Alu with Gorai and family in front.

Source: PMB Photo 56–067.

Woodford took the opportunity of the departure of the *Christine* to forward a letter to Thurston in Fiji informing him of his safe arrival in Alu. He would not have another chance of reporting back to Thurston until much later in the year. In the meantime he collected each day and prepared and skinned his animals at night. His efforts at photography were unsuccessful at first as the developing water was invariably poor. Although collecting proceeded well in Alu and the nearby islands by 1 July he was feeling his first attack of malaria. It was at this time that he met the trader John Champion Macdonald based on nearby Fauro. Macdonald had paid Gorai £10 in cash and £10 in trade for the entire island (£4,000 in cash and another £4,000 in trade goods in current values) and Gorai arranged a marriage between a daughter, from one of his supposedly 100 wives, to John Macdonald, John Champion Macdonald's son (Bennett 1987: 60). This was yet another way of cementing his relationships with white traders and planters.

Figure 3. Woodford's house at Alu.

Source: PMB Photo 56–065.

German annexation of the northern Solomon Islands

While at Alu, Woodford found out that the German government made claim to the northern Solomon Islands of Choiseul, Isabel and the Shortland Islands and on 15 November 1886 the German flag was hoisted on all the islands by Captain von Wietersheim of the German gunboat the SMS *Adler* (Sack 2005: 344). The Anglo-German Demarcation agreement signed in Berlin on 6 April

1886 defined the English and German spheres of influence in the Western Pacific (see *The Queenslander* 3 July 1886 for a full copy of the Declaration of 6 April 1886; *Evening Post* [New Zealand] Vol. 31, Issue 104, 5 May 1886: 2; see also Scholefield 1919: 320–321; Woodford papers PMB 1381/035). As a result of the demarcation, Germany was free to establish protectorates north and west of the line while Britain could annex territory to the south and east, except for Tonga, Samoa and Niue, which were to remain neutral (Great Britain. Admiralty, Naval Intelligence Bureau (1943–1945): 324). The separation of the Solomon Islands into a German northern group and a British southern group was to remain in place for another 14 years.

Under the agreement German firms could continue to recruit indentured labourers in the southern Solomon Islands, which now belonged to Britain, but British planters could not recruit in the northern German islands. The cost of labour recruiting had grown in a tight labour market. Payments to beach captains and to relatives of recruits had increased as recruiters had tried to gain the advantage over each other. British labour vessels were prohibited from trading in guns and ammunition but German and French vessels were not restricted. Colonial governments were attempting to reserve special areas of operation for their vessels and the only way to do this was by direct annexation of islands. The trading firm *Godeffroy und Sohn* was declared bankrupt in 1879 as the result of poor investments in Europe following speculation on the German money markets. Its Pacific interests were then taken over by the newly created *Detusche Handels-und Plantagen Gesellschaft der Südsee-Isleln zu Hamburg* (DHPG) (Bollard 1981: 16). DHPG became a major political player in Samoa. Although the size of the labour needed for the plantations was small compared with Queensland and Fiji, the company was anxious to restrict Queensland and Fijian labour boats access to the Bismarck Archipelago, Buka and Bougainville.

The development of the German colonial empire was, more than anything, a commercial venture (Henderson 1938). Germany suffered a severe economic depression between 1882 and 1886 and the Imperial government in Berlin thought colonial expansion using the chartered company model would help solve the social and economic woes of the Reich (Kennedy 1972: 262). It was believed that colonies would keep emigrating Germans within the confines of the German Empire and 'divert the masses from the appeal of social revolution by providing them with an alternative Utopia' (Firth 1972: 361). The colonies were seen as reservoirs of raw materials for German industry and as the future markets for the manufactured products of German factories. In the late 1880s a number of powerful political lobby groups that promoted the establishment of colonies were created, among them the *Kolonialverein*, established in 1882, and the *Gesellschaft für Deutsche Kolonisation*, formed in 1884. They combined into a single powerful association in 1887, *Die Deutsche Kolonialgesellschaft*. These influential and well-connected societies pressured Bismarck to establish a formal colonial policy for the German empire and Bismarck skilfully used the economic imperative as a way of arousing chauvinistic patriotism in Germany against threatening encroachments from Britain.

At first, German policy was to annex territories by grants of charter to private commercial companies rather than by direct Imperial annexation (Townsend 1921). These companies were then responsible for funding administration, thus relieving the Imperial government of the costs of colonial rule. The German New Guinea Company (*Neu-Guinea Compagnie*), financially backed with a capital of £375,000 by one of the largest banks in Germany, *Disconto Gesellschaft*, was given a charter by Bismarck in 1885 with rights over the northern New Guinea mainland and the Bismarck Archipelago. By declaring a protectorate (*Das Schutzgebiet der Neu-Guinea Compagnie*) over northern New Guinea (*Kaiser Wilhelmsland*), New Britain (*Neu Pommern*) and New Ireland (*Neu Mecklenburg*) and the valuable trading posts on Duke of York Islands (*Neu Lauenburggruppe*), the German government was able to have the establishment and administrative costs of the colony borne by the *Neu-Guinea Compagnie*. This haphazard experiment, administered from headquarters at Herbertshöhe (Kokopo) was costly in both economic terms and in terms of human life. In 1899 the German government was forced to assume control of the territory although it continued to be developed as an economic enterprise (Ohff 2008).

However, the Protectorate of the New Guinea Company in *Kaiser Wilhemsland* was largely a commercial failure. Only large plantations on the Gazelle Peninsula around Kokopo and the Duke of York Islands were commercially viable. Mainland plantations, apart from some around Madang (*Friedrich Wilhelmshafen*), were abandoned in the face of malaria, a shortage of willing labour, attacks by landowners and simple lack of understanding of the nature of the land and climate. The *Neu-Guinea Compagnie* relinquished control to the German government in 1899 after considerable debate in the Reichstag, the *Budgetkommission* and the *Kolonialrat*, all of whom criticised the *Neu-Guinea Compagnie* for its mismanagement of the protectorate. In the end, the people of German New Guinea remained largely unaffected by attempts at force, the inducement of trade goods or the assumed benefits of long-term plantation labour (Firth 1972: 377). German protectorates in the Western Pacific were disappointing from a commercial view as they had little capacity to absorb manufactured goods. Apart from copra, tropical products found a limited market in Europe and freight charges, despite the concessions, made it almost impossible for German merchants in the Pacific to compete with Australian and American rivals (Henderson 1938: 13–14). The lonely islands of the Pacific were, for the most part, poor territories with few natural resources.

In 1885 Buka and Bougainville Islands were added to the territory of the New Guinea Company. Germany also annexed the Marshall Islands in 1885 but the cost for administration were born by Jaluit-Gesellschaft, the combined trading interests of Robertson and Hernsheim and DHPG (Firth 1973: 24). The northern Solomon Islands of Choiseul, Isabel and the Shortland Islands were later added to German territory in 1886. Thus DHPG was able to retain access to labour for German plantations both inside German New Guinea and for German plantations in Samoa, notably from the Gilbert Islands (Munro and Firth 1987 and 1990). When DHPG was threatened by a lack of indentured labourers in Samoa in 1882 it refused to repatriate time-expired workers and consequently lost even more workers who chose to go to the Queensland cane fields rather than to Samoa (Kennedy 1972: 266). Working expenses were kept low and labour cheap and the steamers of the Norddeutscher-Lloyd shipping company transported produce to Europe at favourable terms (Overlack 1973: 131).

The northern Solomon Islands were a source of contention between the British and the Germans. Initially seen as a rich area of labour recruitment early in the Anglo-German talks it had been marked out early as a territory for annexation by Germany (Munro and Firth 1990: 93). In fact, few labourers came from there, for German companies found New Guinea islanders more amenable to recruitment. In 1885 DHPG anticipated the conclusion of the negotiations by buying land and harbours in Buka, Bougainville, the Shortland Islands and along the southern coast of Isabel. Shortland Harbour just north of Poporang Island was planned to be a major recruiting area. Woodford was based nearby. DHPG came to an 'agreement with a passage master named Gorai, who regularly supplied labourers to recruiters from Queensland and Fiji' (Munro and Firth 1990: 93). Woodford came one day to Gorai's village and found the old man counting knots on a piece of string. It appeared that it recorded the time away from the village of an indentured labourer: one knot for each day and one loop of knots for one month. When Woodford counted the loops he found it almost equalled three years (Woodford papers PMB 1290 Item 1/3 Diary 17 July 1886).

Peter Edmund Pratt, the trader, travelled as an interpreter and pilot for the German expedition that surveyed the islands. He provided Woodford with a copy of the deed by which the Germans were buying land from local people. A copy of the deed was attached to his report to Thurston (Woodford papers PMB 1290 Item 12/6, PMB 1381/020, see also PMB 1381/022b). The agreement is complex and convoluted but in essence gave DHPG access to 'the foreshores and adjacent Reefs and Isles to a distance recognized by International Law together with all trees and plants and together with all and singular the hereditaments and appurtenances belonging or in anywise appertaining thereto'. The agreement was written in complex legalistic Hochdeutsch unfathomable to local people. The promise of trade goods and other supplies would have been sufficient reason for someone like Gorai, in a complex web of obligations and responsibilities, and supposedly having 100 wives, to sign such an agreement. As for the annexation of the northern Solomons by the Germans, Woodford wrote: 'the whole thing may be traced to Lord Derby and Mr Gladstone who refused to sanction the annexation of New Guinea by the Queensland Govt.' (Woodford papers PMB 1290 Item 1/3 Diary 1 August 1886).

With the signing of the Anglo-German demarcation agreement DHPG was free to recruit anywhere in the northern Solomons and payments were made in axes, guns and tobacco. This was a major destabilising factor in local, social and political relationships, especially after Gorai died. Sack (2005: 345 fn31) writes that this probably occurred in 1891 but Graham Officer (1901– MS 9321), reporting that J. C. Macdonald from Fauro had witnessed the death, stated it was most likely in 1899. Parkinson (1999: 214) wrote in 1907 that Gorai (called Korai by Parkinson) was 'the deceased chief', and his death, along with that of the other warrior chiefs in the western and north-western islands between 1900 and 1906, signalled the end of the inter-island raiding, and large-scale trading expeditions. This was also a time when widespread epidemics of influenza and dysentery were killing off many people, especially the elderly. Certainly, guns and ammunition from the northern islands made their way into southern Solomons. Moore (1985: 79) records that: 'In 1893 SM Smith, Government Agent on the "Helena", had the problem stated to him bluntly in Olomburi [Malaita]: "No sniders, no boys"' (Moore 1985: 79; Munro and Firth 1990: 96). The German position was that guns and alcohol were the items most coveted by Islanders and that prohibiting the traffic in them would seriously damage German commercial interests.

As a result of this international political theatre being played out around him, Woodford found himself working in German territory. Woodford was no friend of the Germans. In his later career in Samoa he saw German intervention in action and when he came to plant the English flag on these northern islands in 1900 he took some delight in doing so. Woodford later wrote in a revised version of his diary of early 1886 that he 'never had cause to regret the confidence that I placed in Gorai and his people when I landed a perfect stranger among them'. He 'left with feelings of regret and a certainty that I should meet with a cordial welcome if I ever had occasion to visit the island again' (Woodford papers PMB 1290 Item 1/5 Revised Diary 24 June 1886). Having finished his work in Alu and the Shortland Islands, and now with malaria, he moved to Fauro Islands where he remained until 17 September 1886 in the company of Macdonald and his family. Macdonald had established a large plantation there and his brother had settled on a nearby island. On 14 August 1886 Woodford wrote:

> Today I have an attack of fever and it is an effort to drag one leg before another. Nevertheless I spent all day in the bush and cleared a space

to take a photograph of a large ficus which I propose doing tomorrow morning. I was not successful in collecting, getting only a few of the usual type, nothing new. I shot a 'Tigeno' [lizard] which I skinned in the evening. Just as I was going to shoot I had a fit of cold shakes which lasted some hours (Woodford papers PMB 1290 Item 1/4 Diary 14 August 1886. See also Woodford papers PMB 1381/022 for copy).

Woodford's health did not improve, and so when the steamer the *Ripple* arrived at Fauro he moved across to Rubiana [Roviana] in New Georgia. He arrived there on 24 September 1886 and was to remain for two weeks.

Figure 4. Woodford's house at Fauro, located on the Macdonald plantation at Siniasoro Bay.

Source: PMB Photo 56–110.

Roviana and meeting with Hiqava

Roviana was one of the most complex and confusing parts of the Solomon Islands at that time. A range of domestic and foreign factors, social, cultural and economic, had led to the expansion of the coastal communities. The completion of a new men's house, new canoe houses and the construction of larger war canoes meant an increase in the need for human heads for use in ritual inauguration by village priests. More than any other area of the Solomons, the New Georgia region was highly destabilised. It was a highly dangerous place for an independent natural history collector. Woodford wrote: 'It may be considered the centre of the head hunting district, for the natives of this and the adjacent islands are the most notorious head-hunters and cannibals' (Woodford 1888a: 360). He spent most of the time in the Roviana Lagoon visiting the coastal and island communities. Despite the dangers, a few small trading stations had been established around the Roviana Lagoon and Woodford stayed with a local trader, probably William Harland or Thomas Woodhouse, at Nusa Zonga a small island off Munda. Woodhouse lived on Nusa Zonga when not captaining his steamship the *Ripple* and it was the head station of the traders T. G. Kelly and J. Williams of Sydney (Bennett 1987: Appendix 5; Woodford papers PMB 1290 Item 1/4 Diary 3 October 1886). Munda had become the centre of European commerce in the New Georgia region but it had also been one of the main centres for head hunting. The two occupations were not incompatible. The traders supplied the tools and weapons that assisted ritual building and warfare and in return local people provided the trading stations with the products needed for sale, especially turtle shell and copra.

Figure 5. Nusa Zonga. The Kelly and William's trading station, Roviana.

Source: PMB Photo 56–108.

In Roviana, accompanied by a trader referred to as 'Peter' and 'French Peter'— most definitely Peter Edmund Pratt—and Robert Cable the master of the *Lizzie,* Woodford travelled around the lagoon on a copra buying expedition. He remarked: 'at every place we landed we were careful to take our loaded revolvers with us' (Woodford papers PMB 1290 Item 1/4 Diary 28 September

1886). The first call was at Nusa Roviana where Frank Wickham and Pratt had local trading partners. Wickham bought the island of Hombupeka in 1875 and Pratt purchased Hombuhombu in 1886 but they also had copra depots on Nusa Roviana. Woodford photographed the interiors of men's houses and canoe houses and recorded: 'At the principal canoe-house in another village we visited there [Sisiata now part of Munda] were five large head hunting canoes, profusely ornamented and inlaid with pearl shell' (Woodford 1888a: 360; Woodford papers PMB 1290 Item 1/4 Diary 26 September 1886). The war canoes had high prows and sterns decorated with cowrie shells and carvings, in particular the ubiquitous *nuzunuzu* (Roviana) (*toto isu* Marovo). This figure attached low on the canoe's prow served to protect the canoe from malevolent spirits of the water for its eyes were always open (Hess *et al.* 2009). War canoes were also used in bonito fishing (Barraud 1972).

Woodford was at Sisiata when he saw a canoe house (*paele*) that was about 80 feet long, with a high pitched roof and with the front end closed in except for two long narrow slits left for the high prows of canoes to pass through. This was the *paele* of Ingava (Hiqava) the warrior chief (*banara warane*). Hiqava later paid Woodford a visit on Nusa Zonga. Hiqava said that if the people of Sydney saw a photograph of the *tomoko* that Woodford had just taken they would want to take the canoe away. At Sisiata Woodford also noted the many stone jetties: 'about eighty to a hundred yards long built out into the sea and on the shore are tanks fenced with stones for keeping turtles and fish' (Woodford papers PMB 1290 Item 1/4 Diary 26 September 1886). Coastal villages were aggregating along the shore. This consolidation gave the impression that large numbers of people, and war canoes, were concentrated in the lagoons. Massive war fleets of 1,000 to 1,500 canoes were supposedly seen in 1880 by Captain Ferguson departing from New Georgia but this was most likely an exaggeration (McKinnon 1975: 303). Dureau estimates that if large canoes could hold between 15 and 30 men then each these war parties would have contained from 15,000 to 30,000 men. She has some justifiable reservations about the actual number of canoes sighted (Dureau 1998:207). Schneider (1996: 114–115, 117) dismisses the idea that massive fleets of war canoes could be assembled in the Roviana Lagoon area. He estimates that the combined population of the Nusa Roviana villages would have been 400 people and, of that, the population of adult males would have been only about 100–150 men. Sisiata would also have contained about 400 people and the whole coastal Munda region, Kekehe, supported about 1,200 people. Of that the adult male population would have been about 300. He estimates that one good sized *tomoko* would have held between 15 and 20 men. Schneider (1996: 117) calculates that 1,000 *tomoko* would need a population of 20,000 adult men and the entire region a clearly unsustainable population of more than 40,000 people. Indeed Graham Officer was later told by local men at Roviana that fleets of 30 or 40 canoes had regularly departed on head hunting raids and this tends to disprove the idea that fleets of 1,000 or more canoes could have been dispatched from the region (Officer 1901- MS 9321 Box 4332/5).

Certainly, the area was still volatile. Woodford wrote in his diary:

> October 5. Tuesday. Early this morning a large *tomoko* and Wange's boat [Wange was Hiqava's ritual specialist, *hiamo*, see Woodford 1890b: 150–152] called at the station on their way from Sisieta to Isabel on a turtle-hunting & head hunting expedition. Wange also came in a small canoe but is not going with them. He told me they might be away for two months. Wange, Ingava and some others had come to see some photographs I took of them the other day and appear to be amused with them especially with that of the one legged and one armed boy (Woodford papers PMB 1290 Item 1/4 Diary 5 October 1886).

This boy was photographed earlier, not because of his deformities, but because he was wearing a particularly interesting ear decoration of palm leaf bent in a circle. Woodford wrote: 'they will not give up the idea that I am a missionary although I repeatedly assured them to the contrary' (Woodford papers PMB 1290 Item 1/4 Diary 3 October 1886). He gave up wearing a large Indian pith helmet (shola topee) and changed to wearing a Panama hat so as not to be confused with the missionaries. He then crossed the lagoon to Honiavasa Island where he photographed the interior of a men's house with posts carved in the shape of crocodiles and 'along the rafters was a row of heads', and took a now famous photograph of an old man standing in front of a *beku*, a carved pole representing a dead ancestor (Woodford 1888a: 360; Woodford papers PMB 1290 Item 1/4 Diary 28 September 1886). He had to develop his own photographs at Frank Wickham's station and fitted up a darkroom. Some of these are his best images.

But he could not get rid of his malaria, so he went to Aola on Guadalcanal on the *Ripple* stopping at various places in the islands on the way. In his diary he wrote: 'I also hear a good account of Nielsen the trader at Aola on Guadalcanar, both from McD[onald] and McLiver of the *Christine*. [John] Stevens of Uji [Uki ni Masi] I formed an unfavourable opinion of on our visit there and I have heard he bears an unenviable character for sharp practice' (Woodford papers PMB 1290 Item 1/4 Diary 1 September 1886). He made up his mind quickly about basing himself at Aola on Guadalcanal for the start of his second expedition. It was wise for an independent young collector to have a resident trader living nearby. From Aola he took the schooner *Lizzie* to Sydney. The *Lizzie* was a 230-ton barquentine built in Maine that had been a coastal trader before Robert Towns bought her in 1882 and refitted the vessel for the Pacific labour trade. It had been captained by William Wawn between 1883 and 1884 (Wawn and Corriss 1973; Wawn 1893; Stevens 1950: 391; The Vagabond [Julian Thomas] 1886;

Queensland State Archives ID7866). Since 1884 the *Lizzie* had been owned by the trading firm TG Kelly & J Williams, used on the Australia to Solomon Islands run. The *Lizzie* was to be Woodford's regular means of transport to and from the islands until it was wrecked in December 1888. While on board, travelling between the Solomon Islands and Sydney, he wrote yet another long letter, dated November 1886, to Thurston in Fiji on his observations and opinions of life and conditions in the Solomon Islands. In this letter he reported on the German presence in the northern islands and the way in which the German traders had offered Gorai £100 and a new cutter boat in exchange for the small islands off Alu and for rights to half the big island as well. Peter Edmund Pratt had been open about the German purchases. He reported to Woodford that most of the coast of Isabel had been bought for two large knives, six fathoms of calico, 100 sticks of tobacco, a few pipes, machetes, one tomahawk, and two or three Jew's harps, and the Germans were actively recruiting for Samoa in exchange for Snider rifles and ammunition. The trade in firearms was also carried on illegally by the English traders in the Solomon Islands and in order to keep communities bonded a trader would make advance payments of goods and guns, thus making people indebted to him. Woodford estimated that Gorai was in debt to the extent of 120,000 copra kernels, about 20 ton, or approximately £200 worth of trade goods (£85,000 in current values). This of course made the people who were indebted to Gorai tied even more tightly to Gorai's chieftainship and may explain why the old man was reported to have 100 wives (Woodford papers PMB 1290 Item 1/4 Diary attachment: Letter to J. B. Thurston dated November 1886).

Figure 6. The schooner *Lizzie*, Woodford's regular transport to and from Sydney.

Source: PMB Photo 56–111.

Figure 7. Communal canoe house (*paele*) at Sisiata, Roviana.

Source: PMB Photo 56–114.

Note: Another photograph of this *paele* (see Woodford 1890: 159) was modified with the removal of the large coconut tree in front of the *tomoko* and published in *The Illustrated London News* 23 February 1889, *Popular Science Monthly* 1889: 479 fig 2, and Brunt and Thomas 2012: 13).

Figure 8. Gemu standing in front of a *tomoko*, Sisiata, Roviana.

Source: ANUA 481 G.

Figure 9. Sisiata village, Roviana.

Source: PMB Photo 56–112.

Figure 10. Ceremonial food trough (*hao*), Sisiata, Roviana.

Source: PMB Photo 56–119.

Figure 11. Roviana warrior with trade tomahawk and shell decorations.

Source: PMB Photo 56–122.

Woodford's greatest personal concern was a moral one, and it would concern him for much of the first decade after the establishment of the protectorate. It was the 'extent to which the horrible practice [of head hunting] is carried [out]' in Roviana. He reported to Thurston that between 25 September and 4 October men from the village of Kokorapa, the central village on Nusa Roviana, from Sisieta on the mainland of New Georgia, and other villages in Roviana Lagoon had taken 24 heads and five captives (Woodford papers PMB 1290 Item 1/4 Diary attachment: Letter to J. B. Thurston dated November 1886). In addition to the murders of local people, the killing of European traders was discussed in some detail with his suggestion that the practice of head hunting might be suppressed by the destruction of all large *tomoko* in the area or the permanent presence of 15 to 20 armed police, presumably from Fiji.

The destruction of *tomoko* would be both a physical and a moral confrontation, for the war canoe was the physical embodiment of cosmological beliefs and a visual representation of the wealth, power and status of the chiefs. The destruction was also a challenge to the power of the ritual priests who rendered the canoe sacred through ritual and human sacrifice. This, Woodford believed, would be the most effective way to eliminate head hunting and would also eliminate the need for the Royal Navy action that was so ineffective. The *modus operandi* later developed by Woodford and his assistant Arthur Mahaffy during the early stages of the establishment of the protectorate was swift retribution for head hunting and the destruction of the war canoes used in raids. His justification for the presence of armed and mobile police was that: 'The native character being cowardly in the extreme they will only attack white men and even other natives when they can take them at a disadvantage or even surprise them by a coup de main' (Woodford papers PMB 1290 Item 1/4 Diary attachment: Letter to J. B. Thurston dated November 1886). Woodford and Mahaffy made the suppression of head hunting their first priority. The aim was to secure a stable and permanent peace for mission and plantation expansion. His plan for the destruction of *tomoko* has been widely criticised but it was a plan submitted to Thurston in 1886 long before the formal establishment of the British Solomon Island Protectorate in 1897. As a policy it may well be seen that 'the government compensated for what it lacked in consistent and balanced administration by massive overkill' (Bennett 1987: 109). Certainly there would be well-documented incidences of poor leadership and wanton destruction of villages and gardens during the pacification campaigns, but the destruction of *tomoko* was to be the final act in the suppression of head hunting and the power of the old *baṉara*. O'Brien (2011: 46) makes a considered judgement that the policy introduced by Woodford, and practiced by Mahaffy, of destroying all *tomoko* and burning other canoes had a significant and disruptive impact on interisland trade. However, many *tomoko* were successfully hidden from punitive expeditions and they were not the common trading canoe used by people from the New Georgia area. By the end of the 19th century, the dynamics of inter-island trade had also changed. Resident traders and copra buyers had made inroads into customary trading systems. People now desired imported goods and had substituted many trade goods for local produce. The many European whaleboats bought in from Australia became a logical and practical replacement for locally made canoes.

Second expedition

Woodford arrived in Sydney on the *Lizzie* in November 1886 and remained in New South Wales for two and a half months. During this time he travelled the state 'having been given a free pass by the Railway Department' (Woodford papers PMB 1290 Item 1/6 Diary 24 January–5 June 1887). Fortunately, the *Lizzie* was once again in Sydney Harbour and he was able to leave on 22 January 1887, almost immediately after arriving back in the city. After a stormy passage he arrived at Nusa Zonga in Roviana in February 1887. Thomas Woodhouse had by now become a partner in the trading firm—now Kelly, Williams and Woodhouse—that bought the island in 1881. Woodford's friend Lars Nielsen had also bought Banga (Mbanga) Island in the Diamond Narrows in 1882. Despite its reputation as the most dangerous place in the Solomon Islands, the Roviana Lagoon was also the centre of commercial transactions between European traders and islanders. It would have been an exciting place for a young adventurer. He later wrote about Hiqava's *paele* at Sisiata:

> It is about seventy feet long and thirty wide. It is covered entirely in sago-thatch, the ridge of the steeply sloping roof being perhaps thirty feet from the ground. The ends are closed with screens made of sago-leaves, and the seaward-facing end [this was the entrance for men, women could only enter from the back] two singular-looking slits are left to allow the high-pointed ends of the *tomakos* or large head hunting canoes, to be carried in and out (Woodford 1890b: 152; Woodford papers PMB 1290 Item 1/4 Diary 26 September 1886).

At this time, Sisiata had five *tomoko*, some English-built whaleboats and a 'large arsenal' (Jackson 1978: 96).

Woodford spent a fortnight in Roviana revisiting Sisiata village that had about 24 houses where he saw and photographed the inauguration of a large trough (*hao*) for use in preparation of ceremonial food composed of yams, taro and *ngali* nuts (*Canarium indicum*). This trough was about 30 feet long and was carved to represent a crocodile. As it was too dark in the canoe house to be photographed Woodford arranged for the food trough to be moved outside into the light the next day. According to Woodford, 22 men could sit on each side. He wrote: 'the big trough was in the centre of the house with the end representing the crocodile head with a carved human head in the jaw facing toward the seaward entrance', and '[a]bove were the grinning heads on the rafters, eight of them, besides turtles' heads & the heads of frigate birds'. To demonstrate to Woodford and the others, an old man, possibly the *hiama*, wearing full ceremonial 'fighting rig', and then Hiqava himself came from the ceremonial house nearby and made a speech to the men seated around the *hao*. At a signal the men then began to pound the taro and *ngali* nuts in the trough (Woodford papers PMB 1290 Item 1/6 Diary 10 March 1887; Waite 2000: 119–122). Woodford was then asked to leave but not without taking more photographs. Later James Edge-Partington (1903) was to report details of a large food trough removed from Roviana by the crew of the HMS *Royalist* that he presumed was the one seen and photographed by Woodford. In fact, the food trough taken by Captain Edward Davis and presented to the British Museum had been removed from Kalikoqu, the inland village on Nusa Roviana. The one seen and photographed by Woodford was located at Hiqava's village of Sisiata on the mainland. The earlier statement by Edge-Partington was later qualified by Woodford and Thomas Edge-Partington

(Edge-Partington 1906: 121; Wright 2009: 231 fn13). The food trough taken by Davis was kept as personal property and he attempted to sell it in England before it was placed in the British Museum. Davis falsely claimed that it was used to cook the bodies of captives (Brunt and Thomas 2012: 230–231).

Woodford wrote that the men of the Roviana area had recently brought back six heads from Bugotu on the south of Isabel island and one of the heads belonged to the native teacher from the Melanesian Mission station there (Woodford 1888a: 361). The Melanesian Mission had established a base in southern Isabel. The local people there were also a maritime culture who lived around Thousand Islands Bay, a fine natural harbour. However, the consequences of head hunting by men from Roviana had destabilised the entire southern end of Isabel and this continued for some time (Woodford to O'Brien 17 April 1897 WPHC 4/IV 8/1898). The mid-east coastal people, the A'ara, moved inland to fortified villages or went to safety at the southern end under the protection of Big-men like Bera and Soga. Dr Henry Welchman, known as Dokita (Doctor), was successful in converting many people from the southern end who saw the mission as a way of securing peace, release from the victimisation of the head hunting raiders, and a means for achieving economic prosperity and a new worldly status as Christians (White 1983: 123). Peace for the Big-men established new alliances and brought in trade goods to the local people. This increased chiefly *mana* that was further enhanced by the presence of the mission in the area controlled by the chief. The church had ritual and symbolism that filled the void left by the old moral order and while Bera remained pagan, his son Soga converted with his wife and 70 followers. 'Soga was undoubtedly a remarkable character who perceived mission teaching as a way of building prestige and influence' (White 1983: 127). The population of the entire south-eastern end of Isabel converted to Anglicanism. Soga even led armed groups to Nggela and Savo to negotiate peace but his prestige was such that he sailed there on the old war canoes. Peace, significantly, was marked by feasting and oratory. Soga was an able leader who could transfer his Big-man status, derived from warfare, wealth and prestige, into a Europeanised form of civil, judicial and administrative control, encompassing all Mbughotu (Jackson 1975: 73). But men like Soga, and Hiqava at Roviana, took advantage of the rivalry between missions and traders to gain bargaining power. As a result the Melanesian Mission, and not the protectorate government, was the real face of the administration in Isabel, and after Soga died the power and authority of political leadership passed to the church.

In his diary during his second expedition, Woodford also noted that Thomas Woodhouse had purchased large tracks of land on the north-east end of Guadalcanal—presumably near the present day Visale mission—in exchange for muskets, Snider rifles, cartridges and ammunition. Woodford wrote: 'This end of Guadalcanar has the appearance from a distance like an English countryside as there are large patches of grass interspersed with belts of wood in the gullies'. Woodhouse was one of the more successful traders of the early period. But even successful traders had runs of bad luck. His boat, the *Ripple*, was later lost off the coast of Isabel but without loss of life. Woodhouse and his business partners were bankrupt by 1896 (Bennett 1987: 55 and Appendix 5). Thomas Woodhouse, the 'Old Commodore', ended his life as a crippled old man on Uji ni Masi off Makira and his estate was valued at just £12 (Bennett 1987: 55).

Settlement and work at Aola

On 30 March 1887, the *Lizzie*, Woodford's regular means of transport, arrived at Roviana to take him to Aola on the northern coast of Guadalcanal where he was to remain for six months. He had visited the village before on his way south after his first expedition to the islands. Aola was recommended as a safe location by Lars Nielsen who had a small trading station on Gera (Mbara) Island just off the coast and within easy contact of the village. The location was logistically sound. Trading boats passed Aola on the way to Oscar Svensen's station at Marau Sound. It was healthy, with a large river behind the village and an open, wide bay in front. It appeared to be a good base for collecting in the mountains of Guadalcanal that arose from the hinterland behind the village. From Aola, Woodford thought it would be possible to reach Mount Lammas (6,791 feet or 2,070 metres) via the Bokokimbo (Mbokokimbo) River nearby.

Figure 12. Aola village, Guadalcanal.

Source: PMB Photo 56–017. See also Woodford 1890: 92. Original photograph is PMB Photo 56–041.

Figure 13. Brodie with a dead hornbill.

Source: PMB Photo 56–024 and PMB Photo 56–126; Woodford 1890b: frontispiece and front engraving. Caption reads: 'Boy, native of Aola, Guadalcanar, one of my best hunters, with dead hornbill'. Photograph also sent to Lord Ripon 7 September 1893.

Just before the *Lizzie* left for Sydney, Woodford wrote yet another long letter, dated 3 April 1887, to Thurston in Fiji, this time detailing the lack of regulation in the firearms trade and its disruptive effects on Solomon Islands society. These personal and confidential letters to Thurston indicate that the two men had a close relationship of trust, for the letters describe the business dealings of many resident traders. This bond did not continue with other High Commissioners and Woodford's career as an administrator was often marked by years of conflict with officials in Suva. In this personal letter he told Thurston that the majority of British traders obeyed the laws but the major culprit breaking the regulations was a trader named Farrell sailing the schooner *Eudora* under the American flag based out of New Britain in the Protectorate of the German New Guinea Company. However, despite being warned and fined by the captain of HMS *Diamond*, J. Hawkins of the *Fairlie* also continued to supply Snider rifles to traders in Roviana in exchange for turtle shell (Woodford papers PMB 1290 Item 1/6 Letter to Thurston 3 April 1887). The campaign against the gun trade eventually forced Hawkins out of business but he sold his stock to Peter Pratt, an even more unscrupulous dealer (Bennett 1987: 55). Another issue worrying Woodford was the casual disregard that captains of labour vessels had for dropping off returning labourers at any part of the island from which they originated. The case he spelt out for Thurston described one man who had been landed at Savo and was immediately robbed and then killed on the beach by fellow islanders. In the letter to Thurston, Woodford enclosed another letter he addressed to the Agent-General of Polynesian Immigration in Brisbane highlighting this continuing practice (Woodford papers PMB 1290 Item 1/6 Attachment to letter to J. B. Thurston dated 3 April 1887). In fact the practice was well known and little was done to stop it, so it continued until the end of the Pacific labour trade (Woodford to Salisbury 20 August 1895 CO225 49 18609).

Figure 14. Woodford and men at Aola.

Source: PMB Photo 56–010.

In Aola the old chief Ululu arranged for the sale of a disused house for which Woodford paid 20 sticks of tobacco. This price was considerably less than the profitable rent gained by Gorai in Alu. At that time 25 sticks of tobacco constituted about one pound in weight and cost two shillings (Bennett 1987: 81). As part of the arrangement the villagers in Aola built Woodford a new kitchen and he engaged the services of a local boy, Hogarè, to cook and clean for him. Hogarè was from Buka, to the north, and had worked as a plantation labourer in Fiji but was now working for one of the traders so was presumably living on the nearby island occupied by Nielsen. Nielsen was also trading in partnership with John Champion Macdonald from Fauro in the Shortland Islands. Woodford was sensibly using his growing network of associates and friends in facilitating his life in the islands. It appears that other people in Aola who worked either for Nielsen or for Macdonald also spoke some Fijian so they too would have been returned workers from the plantations there. Hogarè and his family may have been willing to remain at Aola rather than return home to Buka, that had now become part of the German territories.

Figure 15. Aola 'My daily afternoon visitors bringing birds, insects, etc'.

Source: PMB Photo 56–011 and PMB Photo 56–133; Woodford 1890b: 116. Caption in book reads: 'My house and kitchen, Aola, Guadalcanar. Daily reception of natives'.

Woodford felt perfectly safe in the Aola community although he reported that in the first weeks after his arrival the men from Aola and Ruavatu nearby had killed a number of bush men in recent raids inland. His photographs from that period show him completely at ease among the people. By mixing with the young men and talking regularly with the elders he would have come to be accepted by the women who would have been nervous with a white man living near them. They would certainly have found his habits and work amusing for he wrote: 'They were of course inquisitive as to my occupation and the things that were being brought to me created great merriment. I shewed them the skinned parrot and the snakes in spirits and explained to them what they were for, one boy then said he had been in the Museum in Sydney and understood me'. Later he saw, and the men captured, a large crocodile that had been seen swimming past. This he measured and photographed. He would later skin it as well. On April 14 he wrote: 'Bye & bye however Yoni arrived with a large Hornbill that he had shot with bow and arrow and another boy known as Brodie had a very pretty new flycatcher with black breast spotted with white. This Brodie is a very bright intelligent boy and I took his photo with his bow and arrows and Hornbill in the foreground' (Woodford papers PMB 1290 Item 1/6 Diary 13 April 1887). Woodford subsequently used this image in the frontispiece of his book (Woodford 1890b) and an engraving of the image was used on the leather binding of all three editions. It is a striking portrait and was obviously one of his favourite images.

Attempts to climb Mount Lammas

From Aola, Woodford planned three inland trips hoping to climb Mount Lammas, located on the Weather Coast side of Guadalcanal. The mountain was named by Lt John Shortland in 1788 in honour of the 'Loaf Mass', the harvest festival celebrated on the first day of August, when he passed through the islands on the *Alexander* returning to England from Botany Bay. Woodford's plan to access the mountain via the Mbokokimbo River on the northern side was ambitious, perhaps too ambitious as it turned out. To gain access to the river he needed support and approval from the Ruavatu people, further along the coast. Fortunately they were allies of the Aola people. Woodford took his camera with him and photographed the mouth of the river near Ruavatu and described the vegetation as 'most luxuriant, and composed of large ficus and other large forest trees with occasional clumps of sago and areca palms, but few coco-nuts'. Woodford's mission, explained to other inland people by his two guides, was: 'I was buying butterflies, birds, snakes and stone-axes and measuring the water' (Woodford 1888a: 362). It would have been totally incomprehensible to bush peoples that a white man was buying the uneatable animals, useless stone axes now superseded by valuable iron tomahawks, and measuring water. At Reko village along the Mbokokimbo River the guides refused to travel further and so the party was forced to return to the coast. This was his first unsuccessful attempt.

The second trip inland was equally unsuccessful. Woodford and his party went inland along the Kobua River behind Aola where they came upon a group of men returning from a raid on villages along the exploration path. Woodford wrote: 'It is these constant raids of the coast natives upon the bushmen and retaliatory ones on the part of the bushmen upon the coast natives that render it difficult and dangerous to penetrate any distance into the interior'. He convinced a bushman, Turapara, to take him inland as far as Mount Vatupusau. At 4,360 feet (1,329 metres) Vatupusau was lower than Lammas but still visible from the coast. For this trip Woodford took along his gun, ammunition and revolver as well as a prismatic compass, aneroid, standard and boiling thermometers, a blanket, three boxes of sardines, one dozen biscuits, a tea billy, 200 sticks of tobacco, a dozen pipes, three knives, matches, and 'nothing else' (Woodford papers PMB 1290 Item 1/7 Diary 19 July 1887). To stop his boots from flooding when crossing streams he cut open the heel and back seams and tied the legs with laces and added a strap that buckled over the instep. With such a complicated arrangement he had to take his wash with his boots on, as they took so long to put on and off. After arriving at the lower slopes of Vatupusau and overnighting in Natalava village on the Nggurambusu River—marked as the Kombua River (Woodford 1888a)—his guides sensibly demanded that he return to the coast. On the way he made some collections and noted that the inland heights of Guadalcanal may be good for planting tea.

Figure 16. Trader and house. Possibly Lars Nielsen at Gavutu.

Source: PMB Photo 56–054.

The third and final trip from the northern coast left on 20 August 1887 when Woodford, a larger party of 11 men including one man, Beta, from the slopes of Vatupusau, made yet another attempt to climb the interior mountains. They reached Beta's village, Valemenga, located at 800 feet and remained there the night. Woodford's gift to the community was one axe, one knife, some clay pipes, matches and the necessary tobacco. These were all items difficult for bush people to obtain. There were again sensible reasons for not climbing the mountains for 'they were afraid of the devil and of bushmen', and '[n]o one had ever been there, there was no road' (Woodford 1888a: 367). In local communities people were afraid of spirits. Attacks by bush men could occur at any time. In truth it was probable that no one had ever been there before, for there was no reason to go, and there were most definitely no roads, tracks or paths. The journey itself opened up a new world to the explorer. 'Every bend of the stream disclosed some fresh beauty, and I regretted that I had no one with me whose pen could better describe the lovely nature of the scenery through which I was passing' (Woodford 1888a: 368). His long attachment to the Solomon Islands was beginning to take root. However, the brutal nature of intertribal fighting was evident when Woodford learnt that only four days later the village of Valemenga was attacked and of the 40 people who entertained him earlier, only 11 survived. Woodford would have to wait until much later before he could gain access to the inhospitable mountains of Guadalcanal.

While stationed at Aola, Woodford made a visit to Nggela, presumably on the boat owned by Lars Nielsen who claimed ownership of the island of Gavutu near Tulagi. Nielsen later registered three claims to the islands of Gavutu, Tanambogo and Gaomi off Tulagi for which he paid local Nggela chiefs £20 in trade goods (Woodford to Thurston 27 July 1896, WPHC 4/IV 288/1896). Nielsen and Woodford had by now become friends and Nielsen was by all accounts a sensible and well-liked man. Rev Turnbull from the Melanesian Mission lived in a split bamboo house and church of similar construction at the nearby village of Honggo on the Mboli Passsage and the Melanesian Mission had established yet another mission at Gaeta village on the eastern coast of Nggela. It was here that Woodford heard the story of the HMS *Sandfly* massacre on Mandoliana Island and the assistance given by Bishop Selwyn in the arrest of the killers by the Royal Navy (Woodford papers PMB 1290 Item 1/2 Diary 12–13 June 1887).

Results of the first and second expeditions

Just before he left to return to England, Woodford received mail from home and he wrote in his diary: 'My collections sent from Alu safely received and making a splash. What will they say to the present one!'. He also wrote

> My menagerie [at Aola] is increasing and at present they are all doing well. The Hornbill is most voracious and so is the pigeon. The Parrot not so savage. The three cuscus who sleep all day make up for it at night and the crocodile has slept all the time. After dinner skinned a small green parrot and read the newspapers brought by the 'Lizzie' (Woodford papers PMB 1290 Item 1/7 Diary 5 and 9 August 1887).

However, before leaving he had to deal with a major medical incident at Nielsen's trading station on Mbara when one of the workers, Pewa, a man from Lord Howe (Ontong Java), injured himself while dynamite fishing off the reef. He held the dynamite in his left hand and a fire stick in the right and failed to release the lit dynamite stick in time. When the dynamite exploded it shattered his right hand, which was left hanging from the wrist. The right cheek was laid open, the jawbone broken in two places, the right eye damaged and a hole about the size of a half crown piece (32 mm) was blown in the left breast. The skin around the throat and breast was also torn. Woodford cleaned and dressed the wounds and visited the man over the next few days. After his return from his third expedition to the mountains he again travelled to the offshore island to treat the wound. Pewa continued to live on despite his injuries but on 23 August Woodford wrote in his diary that the sight of the darkening wounds was one of the most sickening things he had ever seen. Pewa did not die until 26 August, ten days after the accident (Woodford papers PMB 1290 Item 1/7 Diary 16-26 August 1887). It was probably with relief that Woodford spent the next few days soldering up his large metal collection trunk that contained the bird skins, the insect collections and his documentation. Packing and making up boxes took up most of the next few weeks for the *Lizzie* did not arrive at Aola until 15 September. On 18 September he heard that William Macdonald, brother of his host at Fauro, John Champion Macdonald, had killed himself while dynamite fishing.

After saying goodbye to his friends at Aola, Woodford left for Sydney on 25 September 1887 and arrived there on 23 October. After a fortnight in the city he left quickly for England on the SS *Austral* and arrived in Plymouth on 22 December 1887. From the first and second expeditions he amassed 17,000 specimens that included three new genera, eight new species of mammals, 15 new species of birds, six new species of reptiles, and 100 new species of *Lepidoptera*. His collecting expeditions had been remarkable successes (Tennant 1999: 425, Lever 1974). On 4 April 1888 Woodford, now a newly returned naturalist and explorer, gave a public lecture in the Town Hall at his home of Gravesend and called it *A Naturalist's Exploration in the Solomon Islands*. The Mayor, supported by Henry Pack Woodford and other dignitaries, opened the evening and the press reported that the hall was packed with local people. Woodford's lecture was very comprehensive and reported in considerable detail by the *Gravesend Journal, Dartford Observer and County Intelligencer* of 7 April 1888 (Woodford papers PMB 1290 Item 9/7/1). Woodford was a young man of the town who had done exciting things in a faraway, rather obscure part of the Empire. This lecture summarised his travels and experiences during the trips made in 1886 and 1887 and Woodford was able to advertise his collecting successes with displays of some of the 17,000 specimens brought back to England. The lecture was illustrated by 'views from negatives taken by Mr Woodford during his explorations, several of the places having never previously been visited by a white man', and a 'collection of native weapons, stone axes, ornaments, together with several cases containing remarkably fine specimens of butterflies and birds also added to the interest of the lecture'. It was this lecture and the report in the Gravesend newspaper that attracted the attention of his former school friend,

Arthur Pattison, then living in the Drakensburg Mountains of South Africa. He was obviously a subscriber to the local town papers (Woodford papers PMB 1290 Item 9/7/1).

The scientific collections, mostly butterflies, moths, bats and mammals made by Woodford, would occupy the time of the curators at the British Museum of Natural History for several years. O'Brien (2011: 128–129) rather critically assessed Woodford's collecting style as 'running and grabbing' but this neglects the scale and size of his natural history collection—and this, not artefact collecting, was his primary objective—the care and documentation that went into making the collection, the physical dangers faced in the field as a lone, self-funded operator, and the irregular, unpredictable nature of travel arrangements in the islands. The *Annals and Magazine of Natural History* contains the results of collecting in six papers published in 1887 and five in 1888 (Thomas 1887a, 1887b, 1888a and 1888b; Butler 1887a, 1887b, 1887c, 1887d, 18887e; Godman and Salvin 1888a and 1888b; Gahan 1888). Another paper published by Hamilton H. Druce (Druce 1890) may be assumed to be the description of an item given or sold to Herbert Druce, a collector who also wrote a paper on the large moths that Woodford collected at Suva (Druce 1888a). Woodford's collection was all the more important in that few substantial collections of natural history had been made in the Solomon Islands by that time. It was of considerable use to scientists back in London. William Hemsley from the Kew Herbarium later wrote that he used Guppy's book *The Solomon Islands and their Natives* (1887b), and Woodford's article published in the *Proceedings of the Royal Geographical Society* (1890c) to identify the many specimens of plants later donated to the Royal Botanic Gardens (Hemsley 1891: 502).

In 1887, the *Transactions of the Zoological Society of London* published details of the collection of butterflies made by Gervase Mathew, a Staff Paymaster on board the HMS *Espiègle* that had been part of Royal Navy patrols between 1882 and 1883. The fact that the Mathew collection was made in the Shortland Islands also served to make Woodford's well-documented collections valuable. It was not until 1890 that the *Transactions of the Zoological Society* published details of Henry Guppy's collections of reptiles and frogs made between 1883 and 1884, for although Guppy had given his collections from San Cristobal (Makira), Santa Ana, Ugi (Uki ni Masi) and the Shortland Islands to the British Museum in 1883, they had not been reported on until Woodford's collections had been received (Boulenger 1890a and 1890b). The results of Woodford's collections were presented in three papers of the *Proceedings of the Zoological Society* in 1887, seven in 1888, and one in 1890 (Thomas 1887a, 1887b, 1888a and 1888b; Ogilvie-Grant 1887 and 1888; Boulenger 1887, 1888 and 1890; Salvin 1888; Sharpe 1888; Woodford 1888b; Druce 1888a and 1888b). The collections were obviously considered important by natural history scientists in London at the time although Tennant (1999) considers Woodford a 'forgotten Solomon Islands naturalist'.

Other collectors and agencies were becoming interested in Solomon Islands natural history during this important phase. Much of this interest was stimulated by Woodford's collecting. The *Entomologist's Monthly Magazine* published a description of some of the new butterflies collected in the Solomon Islands by Woodford (Grose Smith 1888–1889) and the *Records of the Australian Museum*, Sydney contain a description of a small zoological collection from Howla Island (also called Howlah) obtained by purchase from a collector then resident in the Shortland Islands group (Ramsay and Ogilby 1890). Howlah is the local pronunciation of Aola and was used by traders to refer to the wider Aola district on Guadalcanal. Howla or Aola Island was also known as Mbara Island. The name of the collector is not given in the published records but archival papers show that it was purchased from Mrs Macdonald on 16 July 1890 for 6 pounds and 5 shillings, the money collected on her behalf by Robert Cable, formerly master of the schooner *Lizzie*. John Champion Macdonald, his wife Melinda and family were then resident at Siniasoro Bay on Fauro. Woodford had been a guest living in a house on the beach near their newly developed plantation and trading station. Melinda Macdonald was obviously a keen amateur collector who may have been encouraged by Woodford during his stay. The Macdonalds had been traders at Santa Ana and at Aola before they established the Fauro plantation. In 1890 Melinda Macdonald and her daughter had to seek safety at Aola during trouble at Fauro. It would have been possible to make a small natural history collection at Aola as Woodford had done the groundwork there and local people would have been willing to assist in collecting. Melinda Macdonald had also been a passenger on the *Lizzie* when it was struck by a cyclone off San Cristobal (Makira) in November 1888 on its way back to the Solomon Islands from Sydney. The ship was badly damaged during the storm but managed to reach Guadalcanal. It was subsequently condemned and allowed to sink off Howlah (Mbara) Island on 1 December 1888 (*Te Aroha News* VI (334) 16 January 1889: 6; *The Sydney Morning Herald* 3 January 1889: 8).

By 1890 Woodford had established a creditable reputation in London as an explorer, photographer and scientist during his expeditions to Fiji, the Gilbert Islands and now the Solomon Islands. He had also established a useful network of contacts both among the rather rough and ready trading community in the Solomon Islands as well as among the urbane scientific elite of London. On 26 March, Woodford gave a paper to the evening meeting of the Royal Geographical Society in London on the same topic, *A Naturalist's Exploration in the Solomon Islands*, but more detailed and better suited to his more academic and distinguished audience (Woodford papers PMB 1290 Item 9/7/2). In the paper he outlined his collecting experiences and successes but gave more emphasis to social, economic and cultural issues in the Solomon Islands at that time. The paper describing the first and second expeditions was subsequently published in the *Proceedings of the Royal Geographical Society* (Woodford 1888a). This was the first serious study of the Solomon Islands that Woodford was to publish in his long working career. At the end of his lecture and published paper he presented some general, and for the time fairly accurate, ethnographic notes under the title *The Natives and their Customs*, in which he wrote of the problem caused by the unregulated trade in firearms and his particular dislike of head hunting and cannibalism (Woodford 1888a: 371). Woodford also expressed his dismay at the use of 'Commodore Justice' and told his audience that the people simply fade into the bush at the sight of the men-of-war and that shelling the villages caused little if any inconvenience to coastal people who simply rebuilt their houses and replanted their trees.

Woodford was by now an accomplished photographer and would have had shared a common interest in photography with Thurston in Fiji. Much later, when Woodford was Resident Commissioner of the Solomon Islands and based in Tulagi, he published the first of two *Handbooks of the British Solomon Islands Protectorate* (British Solomon Islands Protectorate 1911; Woodford papers PMB 1290 Item 8/5) in which he had the opportunity to present details of the fauna and flora of the islands in condensed form. He wrote that the only large mammals in the islands were the native pig and the wild dog. The wild dogs in the mountains of Guadalcanal, he said, were known to hunt in packs and were capable of running down and killing a man. Later Woodford and Svensen on their successful climb to Mount Popomanaseu in 1898 would come upon evidence of these dogs in the high ranges. Guadalcanal also had large bush rats that were 'as large as rabbits'. Domestic rats, commonly carried across the world in ships, were found around trading stations where cargo was stored. The common cuscus occurred on most islands with the exception of Makira and the southern Santa Cruz group. There were many species of bats peculiar to the islands. Whales and porpoises were common. Woodford noted the 'teeth of the latter [porpoises] are highly prized as currency by the natives. At certain seasons of the year the natives of parts of Malaita organize hunting parties, and drive the porpoises into shallow water, where they smother themselves in the mud. As many as four hundred have been known to have been taken at a single drive' (British Solomon Islands Protectorate 1911: 28). Dugongs were also plentiful in the waters around the islands.

Although there were a great many birds and 'some of them are of great beauty', the Bird of Paradise, common to Papua and New Guinea, did not exist in the Solomons. Mostly the birds consisted of cockatoos, parrots, lorikeets, pigmy parrots and kingfishers. There were also many ducks, eagles, ospreys, hawks and buzzards and hornbills, but the most common bird was the large fruit-eating pigeon. In some cases many thousands of these exist on small islands off the coast. On Savo, off Guadalcanal, the most interesting bird was the Megapode. This relative of the brush turkey was about the size of a large pigeon and laid an egg the size of a duck's egg that was buried in a mound and left to hatch in the warm volcanic sand in laying yards apportioned to particular owners who had rights to collect the eggs (British Solomon Islands Protectorate 1911: 28–29). There were many reptiles. Crocodiles were found especially along the coast of Guadalcanal and many large monitor lizards existed in the islands. There were also many smaller lizards and geckos. There were numerous snakes and frogs and although sea turtles, both green turtles and hawksbill turtles were common, there were no land turtles. Commercially the hawksbill turtle was important for its shell—it was collected during head hunting raids—but the green turtle was used for food. The large leather-backed turtle was only rarely seen in the waters around the Nggela islands. Woodford was very keen on insects and his collection of *Lepidoptera* was very comprehensive and he noted his success in collecting the large bird-winged butterflies, *Ornithoptera victoriae* and *Ornithoptera D'Urvilleana* in the Handbook, during his first and second expeditions (British Solomon Islands Protectorate 1911: 30–31).

The first male holotype of the large birdwing butterfly, *O. victoriae*, had been collected at Sinalanggu on Malaita in 1886. This was subsequently named *Aethoptera victoriae reginae* (Salvin 1888) (syn. *A. victoriae* [Salvin and Godman 1887] & *A. buinensis* [Grose Smith 1887]). *Aethoptera* is a sub-genus of *Ornithoptera*. This species of large birdwing butterfly, obviously named after Queen Victoria, is restricted to the Solomon Islands. The *Ornithoptera D'Urvilleana*, now known as *Ornithoptera priamus urvillianus*, was first described by Félix Guérin-Méneville in 1838, although the specimen collected by Woodford carries the synonym *O. durvilliana* (Woodford 1888b). The butterfly is named after its first collector, Jules Sébastien César Dumont D'Urville, the French explorer, botanist and cartographer who found the wreckage of la Pérouse's ship at Vanikoro (see www.nagypal.net/images/zzpriamu.htm#urvillianus). Much of this material on butterflies has been published in the authorised papers of the British Museum of Natural History and the Zoological Society of London (see Godman and Salvin 1888a and 1888b; Druce 1888a and 1888b and Druce 1890) and has been recently described by Tennant (1997 and 1999). Over the years many papers relating to the collection and identification of butterflies and insects from the Pacific and the Solomon Islands in particular were sent to Woodford by correspondents in various museums and botanic gardens across the world (see Woodford papers PMB 1381/021, 1381/028 and 1381/031s).

Photographing the Solomon Islanders

Victorian colonial photography, from travel images and landscapes to natural history and ethnography, was broadly about geography and difference (Ryan 1997: 24). In 1889 Charles Woodford published a summary of the first and second expeditions—with four photographs—in a paper published in the May-October edition of *Popular Science Monthly* (Woodford 1889). The rather grainy sketches taken from original photographs were those of the Roviana man wearing a plaited coconut-leaf sun-shade (*toropae*) with a sacred image (*beku*) of a dead ancestor or chief that was considered to be the 'seat' of the ancestor (Wright 2005: 221), a head hunting canoe (*tomoko*) and canoe house (*paele*) also at Roviana, sago palms and trees on the Mbokokimbo River on Guadalcanal and a photograph of the Aola villagers, possibly with the chief, Ululu, in the background behind a dead crocodile (see also Amherst and Thomson 1901, Vol. 2: 372). This was a good promotional opportunity where a young collector of promise could display the success of his work. The same photographs, with two others—a clump of coconuts at the Aola River and a canoe house with a large group of villagers—had previously been published in February 1889 as a single page montage in the *Illustrated London News* (Anon 1889b: 246–247).

Missing from the family albums (Woodford papers PMB Photo 56) are the original images of the *Illustrated London News* sketches, except for a copy of 'Sacred image at the village of Oneavesi, Rubiana Lagoon' (Woodford 1890b: 150) and 'Sago palms on the Bokokimbo River' (Woodford 1890b: 128). The original of the famous photograph, 'Head hunting canoe and canoe-house. Village of Sisieta, Rubiana Lagoon' (see Woodford 1890b: 159) was modified for publication in the montage with the removal of the large coconut palm in front of the *paele* and *tomoko*. The process of retouching or removing extraneous material from images was a common practice done for publication and in some cases the entire image was retouched and enhanced (see Ryan 1997: 220 for an excellent example of this form of visualisation). This image is also missing from the family albums, although a copy exists in the British Museum photographic archives. Another image of Gemu standing in front of a *tomoko* at Sisiata held in the British Museum has been found in a series of framed photographs (A ANUA 481/g). Once again in these articles, Solomon Islanders were depicted as inveterate head hunters and cannibals, although Woodford's moral justification for this was the people's exasperation at 'the wanton outrages of European kidnappers and the licentious crews of whaling-vessels accustomed to visit this region'. In Victorian eyes these photographs and short articles enabled the reader not only to familiarise themselves with foreign regions but also to symbolically travel through, explore and even possess, those alien spaces without leaving the comforts of the metropole (Ryan 1997: 214). These articles in the popular, scientific, human interest magazines then much in vogue among late-Victorian society would have helped to make Woodford's name as a young explorer. Nevertheless, breaching the gap between gifted amateur and well-known professional was a difficult step.

Figure 17. *The Illustrated London News*, 23 February 1889.

Source: *The Illustrated London News*, 23 February 1889.

Figure 18. Old man wearing plaited sun shade (*toropae*) with *beku* (chief's grave marker) at Honiavasa.

Source: PMB Photo 56–036; Woodford 1890b: 150. Caption reads: 'Sacred image at the village of Oneavesi, Rubiana Lagoon'; see also *Popular Science Monthly* 1889: 478 fig 1, Lord Amherst of Hackney and Thomson 1901, Volume 2: 248.

In addition to the itemised field equipment from the Royal Geographical Society, Woodford had to transport his own dry plates for photography along with stock of developing solution, which included pyrogallic acid, methyl-alcohol, and glycerine, that had to be mixed together. The pyrogallic acid could also be mixed with citric acid and water if the other materials were not available, but the resulting solution was inferior in quality. A second developing solution that was commercially available used potassium bromide, distilled water and ammonia. The advertisement by B. J. Edwards and Co of London states: 'The above [solutions] will keep good, if well corked, for months' (Woodford papers PMB 1381/022 Diary 20 October 1885–8 April 1886). In a good environment, with access to clean water, no humidity and no insect problems and stored in an airy cool room perhaps the advertisements may have been correct, but in the Solomon Islands, where travel was difficult and dangerous, and the climate continuously wet, hot and humid, the problems associated with taking photographs were enormous.

Figure 19. Sago palms on Mbokokimbo River, Guadalcanal.

Source: PMB Photo 56–020; Woodford 1890b:128; see also *Popular Science Monthly* 1889: 481 fig 3.

The Woodford descendants in Australia have two cameras owned by Charles Morris Woodford during his time in the Solomon Islands. The oldest is a No. 4 Folding Kodak Box Camera, c.1890, with a Bausch and Lomb Optical Co shutter, dated 6 January 1891. The Bausch and Lomb shutter was considered one of the finest lenses of its time and the camera could use either 4 inch or 5 inch glass plates. It could be updated to take rollfilm that produced 48 exposures. At that time, the camera could be fitted with an Eastman-Walker roll holder that used gelatin paper dry plates but as the roll film had a tendency to produce grainy images it is likely that Woodford used glass plates and developed his photographs himself. It is possible that this camera was the one used by Woodford in some of his early expeditions but was later modified. As the camera was expensive for its time (US$50 in 1890 or US$1,250 in current values) modifying it was a rational economic option. The second camera is a No. 3 Folding Pocket Kodak Model

F. The Folding Pocket camera was produced with a number of modifications between 1900 and 1914. The camera had a flat rectangular front door and a covered lens board concealing the rotary shutter. The camera used Kodak No. 118 rollfilm and the exposure format was 3 1/4 inch by 4 1/4 inch. It was one of the most popular and most successful cameras made by Eastman Kodak and its popularity made the firm one of the most prominent camera makers in the world. It too was relatively expensive for its day. In a deluxe version in 1914 it cost US$75 (US$1,250 in current values) and in a standard version it cost US$68 (US$1,150 in current values). It is also possible that Woodford had a much earlier camera as well as these but the quality of the extant cameras does indicate that he was a keen photographer who purchased good equipment.

In the late-19th century, natural history and ethnography were part of an intellectual continuum. Woodford began his career in the Solomon Islands as a natural history collector before becoming a colonial administrator. William MacGregor, formerly a medical doctor, became both Receiver General and Chief Medical Officer for Fiji, then Administrator of British New Guinea. Rev George Brown of the Methodist Mission was formerly an ornithologist in Samoa, and Alfred Cort Haddon, who became the most important ethnologist of his time, was a Professor of Zoology. These men also made substantial collections of photographs and artefacts. MacGregor's artefact collection formed the basis for the Papuan collection at the Queensland Museum, although much has been repatriated to the National Museum in Port Moresby (Quinnell 2000: 81–102). George Brown's extensive collection of 1,287 albumen photographs is held by the Mitchell Library, Sydney (PXA 435). In addition to photography, Brown made an extensive collection of 3,000 objects that were, at first, located in Brown's home town in north England but then sold to the Osaka Museum of Ethnology (Gardner 2006: 150–154; Reeson 2013). The Haddon archive and collection of Torres Strait material culture at the University of Cambridge is the foremost collection in the world (Davis 2004; Herle and Rouse 1998). The underlying aim of photography and collecting, both natural history and cultural history, was the purposeful determination to collect 'before it has become too late' (Quinnell 2000: 81–83).

Photography had been used extensively by Alfred Cort Haddon during his first expedition to the Torres Strait in 1888 (Philp 2004: 90). His primary purpose for this trip was to record the fauna, structure and the growth of coral reefs in the region. He was drawn to ethnology because of the way in which he felt Torres Strait Islanders were perceived by Europeans living on Thursday Island and by his interest in salvage ethnology: the documenting, recording, collecting and photographing the cultural knowledge of the people before the past disappeared (Philp 2004: 91). Salvage ethnology—now subject of much obloquy—was vogue in the late Victorian period, and photographing native communities and collecting artefacts both had important roles to play in this methodology (O'Hanlon 2000: 1). Salvage ethnology was predicated on the view that living conditions among indigenous peoples were unsustainable and while their cultures were doomed, it was the duty of European scientists to understand this as part of human evolution. This disappearance was a 'vexing moral issue' (Bell 2009: 151). The images became an aide-mémoire for Haddon's research when he returned to his post in Dublin and he used them as a form of exchange between colleagues. Photographs of native peoples and the display of their artefacts acted as a 'kind of moral if exotic tourism brought to European audiences through photographs and objects for public consumption' (Philp 2004: 99). Middle class Victorian society was eager for education and improvement, and moral uplift, and the rise of Christian humanism with the rise of the Aboriginal Protection Society and the Anti-Slavery Society that highlighted concern with the relationship between the so-called 'Uncivilised Tribes', especially in the British colonies, and the colonisers. The photographic construction of the Empire was undertaken on a number of levels: exploration, survey, art, witness to change, progress, acceptance of Christianity, political domination as well as for personal means (Ryan 1997: 224).

In 1898 Haddon returned to the Torres Strait—this time with six fellow academics, William McDougall, William Halse Rivers Rivers, Charles Seligman, Sidney Ray and Charles Myers, and junior assistant and photographer Anthony Wilkin—members of the Cambridge Anthropological Expedition to Torres Straits (Haddon 1901/03–1935; Herle and Rouse 1998). This expedition was instrumental in many ways. It was the first multi-disciplinary field expedition to Melanesia by British ethnologists and the first ethnographic motion picture, shot in five sequences on Murray Islands between 1–6 September 1898. It records a short sequence in the Malo-Bomai dance, secular dances and fire-making (National Film and Sound Archive, Canberra Film number 8879; Lawrence 2010b). Some still frames of this dance were also included in the Reports of the Expedition (Haddon 1908 Volume 6: Plates 25–27, 29–30). The Cambridge Museum holds over 2,000 objects from the Torres Strait region.

At the same time, photography was used in Australia as an exercise in attracting settlers and securing ownership of the vast alien continent. Between 1886 and 1888 a collection of engravings and photographs were published by Andrew Garran in subscription format under the title, *The Picturesque Atlas of Australasia*. This also played a role in developing a sense of nationalism in late-19th century (Garran 1886-1888; Hughes-d'Aeth 2001). John William Lindt, one of the most important figures in early colonial photography, published a series of illustrations titled *Picturesque New Guinea* that was part of a group of photographic studies of Pacific island communities that supported Australian sub-colonial expansionism in the Pacific (Lindt 1887). His photographs were a means of opening up landscapes where 'even in savage New Guinea the blessed light of the word of God is gradually dispelling the darkness of barbarism and cannibalism' (Lindt 1887: 30; Ryan 1997: 72). The use of the term 'picturesque' in the titles gives some indication of the style, and orientation, of these publications but underlying the subtlety of the term was the message that through photography it was possible to open up these alien landscapes and their inhabitants to colonial improvement and the order of civilisation.

The political and social power of the image was beginning to be recognised early in the life of ethnographic photography. Following his period as Governor of Fiji and High Commissioner for the Western Pacific, Everard im Thurn was very influential in anthropological circles in England and published an important paper on the anthropological use of the camera in 1893 (im Thurn 1893: 184–203). His paper on the anthropological uses of the camera contains a great deal about im Thurn and his approach to colonial questions but very little on the actual uses of a camera to ethnology apart from his philosophy that imagery should be naturalistic not posed or stylised (im Thurn 1893; Ryan 1997: 181; Dalziell 2007: 97–116). Certainly im Thurn disapproved of the use of static anthropological studio photography and promoted realistic, naturalistic images shot on location. He acknowledged a debit to 'that useful little book, "Hints to Travellers", published by the Royal Geographical Society' and wrote of his own personal hints on the need for portability of camera equipment and his recommendations on the best lens to use. He also had comments about the problem of excessive light in the tropics that made changing glass plates a difficulty. He recommended that the photographer use a smaller still camera using quarter plates rather than the rollfilms then available (im Thurn 1893: 200–203).

To his credit, im Thurn was one of the first to actually describe and recommend photographic material to travellers and ethnologists. For his earlier work in British Guiana (Guyana) he used both a smaller hand-held camera for immediate photographs and a larger fixed view camera. He wrote that the small hand cameras of that time 'are an abomination and are really much more difficult to work with [for] satisfactory results than are fixed cameras' (im Thurn 1893: 201). The view camera of the period consisted of a front standard that held the lens plate, the shutter and the lens joined to a back standard by means of a bellows, and a flexible, accordion-pleated box that had the ability to accommodate the movement of the two standards. The rear standard held the film plate. This rear standard was a frame that held a ground glass used for focussing and composing the image before exposure. The whole apparatus could be collapsed for transportation but required the solid support of a fixed base. Quarter plate stand cameras were still in use in 1914 but required considerable expertise, especially in the isolated tropics (Bell 2009: 155). Im Thurn recommended the use of tele-photographic, concentric lenses, and although film substitutes based on xylonite (celluloid) were becoming available, he preferred the use of the heavy glass-plate mainly because the lighter films of that time did not keep their condition in tropical regions. His recommendation was: 'On the whole it seems best at present to take a certain number of good glass plates for the special work' (im Thurn 1893: 201). It was then necessary to have a dark room or darkened tent and a changing bag to keep the plates after exposure. Dry developing chemicals, such as amidol, a colourless crystalline compound, were also available. But in addition to this cumbersome equipment and clean water and chemicals, it was essential to have good ventilation to counter the effects of heat, damp and insects. All these discussions were current when Woodford commenced his field expeditions in the Solomon Islands.

Whether posed or naturalistic, photography as a field research tool was also a technology that allowed for objectivity combined with commonly held evolutionist values. 'Native' or 'primitive' peoples were photographed in various performances, actions, dances or rituals to illustrate the hierarchy of human evolution. The positivist assumption was that if culture was something that could be seen to be happening it would be embedded in observable gestures, ceremonies and artefacts that could be recorded. Early ethnologists and scientists sought out subjects that followed a taxonomic classification inherited from the natural sciences. Images of physical types and facial structures of local people were keenly sought and social customs, rituals and performances were important subjects that were recorded either as they happened or were ordered to be performed for the photographer's benefit. The other major subject was material culture of all types such as clothing, body decoration, house and building styles, weaponry and means of transport. These photographs could then act as a 'transparent method of visual note-taking' (Young 1998: 4). The idea that photographs could form neutral, transparent and objective data—a documentary mode of interpretation—ignored the social role of the subject and the inherent power of the ethnocentrism of the photographer (Ruby 1996; Quanchi 2007: 11). What the camera sees depends on who is using it. Photographs need to be examined for forensic evidence of the history behind the image, its importance to local people, how, when and where the image was made—a reflective mode of interpretation (Eves 2006).

Photographs recorded visual facts for later use in lectures, publications and magazine articles. Photography was seen to be able to deliver pure facts as part of broad scientific knowledge. The Royal Geographic Society, positioned at the nexus of science, journalism and colonial officialdom, was an important venue for the display of photographs and evening meetings at Burlington Gardens, the theatre of the University of London. These events were rarely held without the use of lantern slides (Ryan 1997: 22). Woodford's presentation at the evening meeting on 26 March 1888 was accompanied by a display of photographs and Guppy, then present, remarked that Woodford's 'collection of photographs was certainly the best ever obtained in the islands, and perhaps in the Western Pacific. His [Guppy's] own experiences in photography were not very successful' (Woodford 1888a: 375; Woodford papers PMB Photo 56 and Photo 58). These lectures and photographic shows allowed the Royal Geographic Society to consolidate itself as the national centre of geographic science and endow exploration and geography with an aura of national usefulness: the understanding and mapping of the vast resources of Empire (Ryan 1997: 31).

Photographic techniques used by Woodford varied. Wide framed images of people in groups situated in the middle distance recorded their place within their natural environment. This positioning in the optimal distance meant that the image contained both the subject and enough situational background for the observer to read the social and cultural context of the image. It was in effect a 'methodologically driven style' rather than a sign of reticence or modesty (Young 1998: 17). The aim was to produce a natural relationship between people, action and place. There are numerous portraits of men, women and children whom Woodford obviously knew but few are personally identified. These proximate images are personal and empathetic. Likewise Woodford took many photographs of places that he visited, where he stayed and even of the sailing ships he used. Images taken at a distance naturally present a detached point of view; in the case of landscapes, the intention is deliberate. All photographs show the entanglement of traditional societies with the traders and the encroaching colonial world. They are not primitivist images that seek to remove the western materials, clothing, hats, guns or other traded goods from view. They illustrate many cross-cultural encounters. These photographs required the active participation of the local people, but once removed from the islands the images circulated in many ways.

Haddon used his images of the Torres Strait Islanders as a sort of currency for the exchange of information between institutions (Philp 2004: 99). Images from the colonial periphery moved to become the visual information of the metropole in the same way that artefacts collected in the field became the objects of interpretation in London. Natural history objects collected in the field also became the objects of research and interpretation in the centre of colonial power. Woodford similarly exchanged his images with other writers and institutions as can be seen by the extensive use of his images in the Hakluyt Society publication of the Spanish journals of discovery (Amherst and Thomson 1901), newspaper articles and papers submitted to scholarly journals. Photographs, as evidenced in the use of images by the *Popular Science Monthly* and the *Illustrated London News*, also have social biographies. They were projected into different spaces and performed different roles, moving between the place of production and their place of viewing, exchange, ownership and public consumption (Edwards 2012: 222–223). Photographs document a fleeting moment in time that becomes a fixed event: 'possibly no other historical form except oral histories has that fluidity' (Edwards 1998: 109). Haddon, in the Torres Strait work of the Cambridge Expedition, used photography like scientific drawing. It became a visual representation of scientific data and a means of 'virtual witnessing' that could be used not just as images of things but as something to think with—active entities in the making and unmaking of histories and science (Edwards 1998: 134). For this reason it will be important later in this book to consider the fine photographs taken by Walter Henry Lucas, Island Manager for Burns, Philp & Co, within the context of Woodford's photographic collection for they are frequently taken at the same place and time.

Touristic photographs of native types, of marginal areas and indigenous material culture became scientific through order, archiving and display. Photographs are the products of the vision and preoccupations of the photographer. This is important to acknowledge when using historic images. By examining the documentary content and context of the image we can understand the history and condition of the Solomon Islander peoples at a particular point in time (Edwards 2012: 231; Gardner and Philp 2006: 189–190; Eves 2006: 743). Images contain both an intended meaning, established by the subject matter, composition or framing at the site of taking the photograph and an unintended meaning, that is, the one discerned by the reader at the site of use or exhibition of the image (Quanchi 2007: 21, 85, basing his interpretation of historical photographs on the theory developed by Roland Barthes 1981). According to this interpretation, photography undertaken by colonial officials, missionaries and early anthropologists served as a metaphor for colonialism that is predatory, acquisitive, presumptuous and sought to objectify the subject. Certainly, photographs expose the privileged field of view of the European photographer (Poignant 1992: 65). Colonised peoples were often presented bound within their natural world and this served to distance the wild savage from the civilised coloniser (Ryan 1997: 139).

Woodford took his photographs from a position of power. Despite the warmth and friendliness of the villages where he stayed, especially in Aola, Alu and Fauro, he was a white man working in a pre-colonial society where his subjects, black men and women, were not in a position to challenge his privileged place and purpose in their communities. His sense of humanity in the diaries of the first two expeditions to the islands between 1886 and 1888 shows that he was a man of perception, humour and decency. Some images are posed but not contrived. The images taken at Aola, where he is surrounded by village men who have just returned with him from the mountains, show him as a strong Anglo-Saxon white male at the peak of his physical, intellectual and moral development. This would not be denied by Woodford nor does it denigrate the people of Aola. His other photography was experimental, as his notes report. There are landscapes, vertical as well as horizontally framed images, portraits, some posed groups of people and a few images of Woodford relaxing or in the company of young men. There are some dramatic, powerful images. All images are now historically important to the Solomon Islander people. They are socially constructed artefacts that tell us not only about Solomon Islands societies and their contact with the West at a time of change but they also tell us much about the society and culture of the photographer. There is a great deal of information on the subjects of the images that can only now be discerned with better access to sites, our greater ease and ability to communicate with people in the region and with over a century of documented history.

Third expedition

Woodford would be very busy in London for the next five months displaying his collections and talking to meetings of learned societies. Then on 8 June 1888 he left for Sydney on the *Ormuz*, a modern 6,000-ton steamship built in Glasgow for the Orient Steam Navigation Company's United Kingdom–Australia run (C. B. 1889). On this trip he was not only returning as a successful natural history collector, and by now a known face in the Solomon Islands, but he was to meet his future wife, Florence Palmer of Bathurst, returning to Australia from a long holiday in London. Not long after the *Ormuz* landed in Sydney on 23 July 1888 Woodford secured passage on the schooner *Marshall S* owned by G. J. Waterhouse. The boat left for the Solomon Islands on 6 August. On 16 August, Woodford wrote in his diary: 'I was glad to see once more the familiar green of the tropical bush and to hear the sound of the waves breaking on the coral reef' (Woodford papers PMB 129. Item 1/8 Diary 16 August 1888). Next day the *Marshall S* met with other schooners, the *Lizzie* captained by Robert Cable, the *Emma Fisher* owned by Thomas Woodhouse, and the *Minnie Mack*. All were anchored off the trading station on Nusa Zonga.

There was still no effective enforcement of British law and order in the Solomon Islands. Life remained precarious for local people. In his diary, and later in his main book on the Solomon Islands, Woodford (1890b: 150–152) described the torture and killing of a woman accused by Hiqava of putting illness upon him. With the woman's death, following her gruesome punishment and the return of a small quantity of hidden tobacco, Hiqava was somehow miraculously cured. Woodford also wrote that head hunting appeared to be worse than ever in the Roviana Lagoon and despite their power and position even chiefs did not survive head hunting raids. Paravo, a chief from Marovo Lagoon, led a head hunting raid to the Russell Islands and the north-western tip of Guadalcanal but on the return journey the raiders were caught by bad weather and forced to seek shelter on Murray Island (Mborokua) in the often dangerous seas between the Russell Island group and Nggatokae Island. Paravo died here and the men, short of food, ate his body and buried his head. Frank Wickham, in a calculated move to gain reciprocity and support from the local communities, sailed to Mborokua, retrieved the head and returned it to Paravo's people (Woodford papers PMB 1290 Item 1/8 Diary 20 August 1888; Woodford 1890c: 393–394).

At Nusa Zonga, Woodford secured the services of another servant boy, Barakosa, originally from Treasury Island (Mono) part of the Shortland group (see Woodford 1890b: 101 for photo of Barakosa in forest). Barakosa was about 10 years old but had been kidnapped from his home island by four men—presumably returning indentured labourers—from the Dobeli (Ndovele) village on north Vella Lavella. They had been left stranded at Mono by a returning German labour ship. When the men fled back to Vella Lavella they took Barakosa with them. Frank Wickham called into Ndovele on a trading trip and Barakosa hid on board Wickham's vessel. He was taken to Nusa Zonga where, presumably, he was working as a servant. Woodford wrote: 'He wishes to go with me and I shall send him home if I get the opportunity by a man of war or otherwise. He is a bright little fellow' (Woodford papers. PMB 1290 Item 1/8 Diary 30 August 1888). Barakosa was also pleased that Woodford could speak some of his Mono/Alu language and he in turn could speak a 'good many words of English'.

The Spanish explorations

Instead of returning to natural history collecting, Woodford spent this third expedition plotting the voyages of Mendaña and other Spanish explorers using translations of the journals supplied by Lord Amherst (Woodford papers PMB 1290 Item 5/12). At the end of August the *Marshall S* left Woodford and Barakosa at Lars Nielsen's station on Gavutu. Accompanied by Nielsen and his crew in the trading boat, Woodford commenced a survey of the east coast of Isabel searching for the locations of Mendaña's settlements starting at Estrella Bay (Ghehe Bay) (Amherst and Thomson 1901, Vol. 1: end piece shows Woodford's photograph of Estrella Bay). They surveyed about 60 miles of Isabel's east coast and then travelled across to Guadalcanal and Savo. At Savo Woodford, Nielsen and some of his men climbed the 1,800 foot (600 metre) volcano and examined the many megapode nests. Recent research indicates that these megapode fields on the north coast of Savo were probably formed around 1560–1570 AD (Petterson *et al.* 2003) and that people living on the island have been forced to relocate a number of times due to volcanic activity. In his paper on his third expedition, Woodford mentions his interest in the geological formations around the crater of Savo Mountain and he apparently took photographs of the landslips of huge blocks of stone. Some unnamed photographs in his albums show landslips and stone cliffs and they may be from Savo (Woodford papers PMB Photo 56/39, 40 & 41). He also made a sketch of Savo for Amherst and Thomson so that they could compare the island's shape with that of Sesagar, an island off the Spanish coast (Amherst and Thomson 1901, Vol. 1: 30, sketches by Woodford and Lady William Cecil, daughter of Lord Amherst). It was Mendaña who had originally named Savo, Sesagar.

Basing their findings on oral testimony and sound geological research, scientists have recently determined that there have been three eruptions of the Savo volcano (Petterson *et al.* 2003). A cataclysmic eruption, called the Toghavitu, meaning either 7,000 or 1,007—being the number of deaths reported—forced the complete evacuation of Savo in the late 1500s. In 1568 Mendaña observed volcanic plumes and ash clouds coming from Savo but he also reported that the island was then well inhabited because his brigantine was visited by 16 canoes containing approximately 100 men (Guppy 1887b; Amherst and Thomson 1901, Vol. 1: 30–31, 49). This would date the first major eruption to post-1570. Another eruption occurred between 1600 and 1700 according to block-and-ash flow fan association (Patterson *et al.* 2000: 168). Guppy (1887b) reported that another sustained period of volcanic disturbance occurred between 1830 and 1840 (*The Queenslander* 26 January 1907: 7). A more recent period of mudflows following heavy rains occurred in 1953 (Petterson *et al.* 2000: 169). All these disturbances added to the size of the island. The long oral history of volcanic activity on the island means that the nervousness of Woodford's guides, who declined to climb into the volcano's crater, is now understandable. From the diaries it is not possible to determine how much information Woodford had of Savo's history. Certainly the island, when dormant, looks innocent enough and Guppy's reporting was largely anecdotal. No doubt, to a young adventurer, Savo looked like a good climb and he was always keen to collect endemic species from mountain regions to send back to London. Most likely the success of the climb stimulated the desire, once more, to attempt to scale Mount Lammas.

Further attempts to climb Mount Lammas

Woodford based himself at Gavutu utilising Nielsen's house and access to boats and stores. He took Barakosa to church at Halavo on the mainland of Nggela on Sunday 23 September and remarked that the boy behaved well, 'but was, I think, a little overawed' by the service conducted in Gela language by local pastor Alfred Lombu (Woodford papers PMB 1290 Item 1/8 Diary 23 September 1888; Hilliard 1978: 94, 95). He also crossed back to Aola to do more natural history collecting while Nielsen and his traders gathered cargo from villagers. In Aola his main collector, Pengoa, assisted with the supply of material. By

15 October he had undertaken enough collecting. Woodford, accompanied by Lars Nielsen, who would have been well known to local people, once more set out for Mount Lammas by ascending the Mberande River from Tasimboko and then crossing the Mbalisuna River. After travelling about 30 miles inland the party ascended the hills from which they could see to Pari Island and Mount Vatupusau in the south. Woodford wrote: 'Nielsen was, of course, described as the trader from Gavotu [Gavutu], while I was said to be the man who previously lived at Aola and ate snakes' (Woodford 1890c: 399). Woodford later reported to the Royal Geographical Society, incorrectly in fact, that his friend Lars Nielsen and his men were killed and eaten (Woodford 1890b: 21 fn1). It was Carl Nielsen (or Nelson) the second mate on the schooner *Enterprise* who was killed at Lokokongo on Rendova in September 1889, not Lars Nielsen (*The Sydney Morning Herald* 5 November 1889: 8).

The party was aiming for Mount Lammas again, or at any rate heading for the mountainous range that contained the Lion's Head and Mount Popomanaseu. At 7,661 feet (2,335 metres), Popomanaseu, the highest mountain on Guadalcanal, is a saddle plateau and the home of endemic and restricted high range species. It would have been an ideal place for Woodford to continue his collecting for it was the unusual animals and plants of the tropical mountains that were of interest to the specialists in the British Museum of Natural History rather than the well-known coastal species. The mountain is also of significant cultural importance to local people and his guides would have been at some risk in taking him there even if the material rewards appeared beneficial. The distance inland along the Mbalisuna River and difficulty of climbing the hinterland again thwarted plans for a successful climb. His longed for goal to ascend Mount Lammas would have to wait for a time chosen by the local people. The party returned to the coast on 19 October and then crossed back to Gavutu on Nielsen's vessel. The time was not wasted for Woodford had undertaken a successful survey of the Guadalcanal coast from Visale to Tandai (Point Cruz) and the Lungga River region (also known as the Tuumbuto River). At Point Cruz, the site later chosen to be Honiara, Woodford wrote: 'As to Point Cruz I cannot call it a good harbour and the bottom is uneven. We had 7 fathoms just ahead of us and 15 just astern … Still it was better than an anchorage on an open coast'. He also discovered that Aola, his previous home, had been visited by the Mendaña and although the Spaniards noted, with their usual exaggeration, that the local population was 3,000, Woodford was pleased to write: 'It is a matter of considerable satisfaction to me to find that, upon the three occasions that the Spaniards communicated with the natives of Aola, they were enabled to do so on a friendly footing' (Woodford 1890b: 411).

Figure 20. Senior man with shell decorations and trade tomahawk, Ulawa.

Source: PMB Photo 56–049; Lord Amherst of Hackney and Thomson 1901, Volume 2 frontispiece. Photograph also sent to Lord Ripon, 7 September 1893.

Return to Aola

At the end of his third expedition he wrote in his diary:

> Reading this evening in Thackeray's Paris Sketch Book (Page 109 Pocket edition) about the ignorance of Englishmen of French Society even after a residence in France of many years (unless for the purpose of making a book then 3 weeks are sufficient). This is very true and equally applicable to our knowledge of the natives of Fiji and other parts of the Western Pacific. It is only after years of residence among them that one finds how little one really knows (Woodford papers PMB 1290 Item 1/ Diary 29 October 1888).

This was another prophetic note in the margins of his papers. On 21 November 1888 Woodford once again crossed to Aola. Here he found the old chief Ululu in fading health and wrote in his diary: 'He had been a good friend to me'. He stayed for one month in his old house while waiting for transport back south. It was here that he received news that the *Lizzie* had lost its main mast in a cyclone not far from the village and so he had to wait until the *Renard* arrived on 13 December to take him away via Sa'a on Malaita, then Ulawa and Santa Ana. He reached Sydney on 3 January 1889.

Marriage

From Sydney, Woodford had personal business to attend to before he returned to London. He married Florence Margaret Palmer, the second child of grazier John Palmer and his wife Margaret Yates Beatty, at the All Saints Cathedral, Bathurst on 2 March 1889 (NSW Marriage Certificate 1889/003725). The Palmers lived in 'Moreauvia', a large Victorian country house located at 135 Lagoon Road in Orton Park, south of Bathurst, designed by Benjamin Backhouse. Margaret Yates Beatty's mother was from the Moreau family and it was from this association that the house was named (Woodford papers PMB 1381/005b). The Palmers were a prominent Bathurst family and the house, built for Palmer in 1876 on a Crown grant of 320 acres of good agricultural and grazing country, was a two-story filigree mansion with verandahs on three sides with cast iron columns, balustrade and frieze. The house, in its heyday, would have been a substantial mansion surrounded by mature gardens and trees. It was a local showpiece and a visible indication of wealth and confidence presented by the squatters of the Western Plains. Severely damaged by fire in the 1980s it is now in ruins. But when John Palmer died in 1884 he left a widow who was mother to 12 children (NSW Death Certificate 1884/006762). It would appear that following John Palmer's death, Florence Palmer travelled to Britain with her mother in order to visit family. Subsequently, 'Moreauvia' was advertised for sale and sold in early 1891 (*The Australian Town and Country Journal* 27 December 1890: 4, 3 January 1891: 4).

Woodford had married well, but for someone who had just spent two years as an adventurer-collector-explorer, living with tribal groups and making one of the largest collections of natural history of the Solomon Islands, it is curious that he gave his profession on his marriage certificate as 'wine merchant' resident in 'Sydney' (New South Wales, Marriage Certificate, 1889/003725). The next year was to be another busy one for Woodford for he was not only a newly married man, an established natural history collector and a published author of some well-received articles, but he was also writing a book of his experiences in the Solomon Islands. Woodford and his new wife returned to London in August

1889. He had been elected to the Royal Geographical Society in 1885 and became a Fellow of the Linnaean Society of New South Wales in 1887. He was listed as a gentleman of independent means (Heath 1974a: 31).

Results of the third expedition

At the conclusion of his third expedition to the Solomon Islands, Woodford was once again invited to present a lecture to the members of the Royal Geographical Society in London. This was given at an evening meeting on 24 February 1890 (Woodford 1890c). He told the attending members that the 'principal object in visiting the islands mentioned above [in the lecture] was for the purpose of endeavouring to identify the places visited by the Spanish expedition, under Mendaña, that discovered the Solomon Islands in the year 1568. In this I think I may say I have been entirely successful' (Woodford 1890c: 397). It was also obvious that he found the islands beautiful. His words describing sailing though the Hathorn Sound between Kohinggo and New Georgia are pure romance:

> The trees tower on either side high above the ship's masts, overhanging and dropping their ripe fruit and blossoms into the water. Cockatoos scream defiance from the trees at the invaders of their solitudes, and startled fruit-pigeons take flight with a great clatter of wings as the unwonted appearance of the ship disturbs them from their repast among the nutmegs. Crimson lories in flocks of half a dozen fly across high in the air with ear-piercing screech on their way to a honeyed feast from the bright crimson blossoms of the coral-tree (*Erythrina* sp.), a conspicuous object among the uniform green of the surrounding forest, rivalling in brilliance of colouring the plumage of the lories themselves (Woodford 1890c: 394).

In almost the same spot, Boyle Somerville (1897: 359–360) on the survey vessel HMS *Penguin* later wrote: 'to look down upon the lagoon from the summit of any of the hills of the large islands is to have spread before one the strangest and most picturesque scene imaginable … The middle distance is filled with the lagoon itself, dark blue in the deeps, pale blue in the shallows, light brown over the labyrinthine reefs—a feast of colour'.

Woodford was also invited to make a short presentation to a meeting of the Zoological Society of London where he spoke about the fauna he had collected for the British Museum and displayed many of his photographs (Woodford 1890a). Another address, this one also accompanied by lantern slides and an exhibition of artefacts, was again presented to the people of Gravesend in the Town Hall, but this was a charity lecture given in aid of the Gravesend Hospital. It was comprehensively reported in the *Gravesend Journal, Dartford Observer and County Intelligencer* and in the other local paper *The Gravesend and Dartford Reporter* on 15 March 1890 (Woodford papers PMB 1290 Item 9/29 Press cuttings 1886–1911). His work was highly praised and his natural history collecting the subject of much comment.

The results of the third expedition, published as a substantial paper with map by the Royal Geographical Society, appeared around the same time as his new book (Woodford 1890c). The paper details much of Woodford's expedition in search of the Spanish discoveries and the places and names visited by Mendaña and his men. Among those in attendance at the meeting of the Society was Lord Amherst who was naturally interested in the results of the third expedition for he was preparing the Spanish manuscripts for publication by the Hakluyt Society. Amherst was a curious choice for this work. He was a wealthy collector of incunabula and rare books and a Conservative Member of Parliament, and although he had serious financial difficulties and was forced to sell most of his collection, he was an important ally in the world of status and class that bound English society together. However, he was a tardy worker. Much to the annoyance of Sir Clements Markham, President of the Royal Geographical Society in 1893, the two volumes would take Amherst and Thomson another 11 years to produce. As Markham was also President of the Hakluyt Society his opinion was an important one. When the books were finally published much of Woodford's work had been incorporated into the text along with many photographs by Woodford, Thurston and Walter Henry Lucas included as illustrations but with little reference to their origin. At the Society meeting, Sir Mountstuart Grant Duff, the then President of the Royal Geographical Society, complimented Lord Amherst for having contributed to the success of Woodford's expedition by lending him copies of the translations of the Spanish manuscripts when in fact Woodford had used the translation of the Gallego journal previously published by Henry Guppy (1887b). Only a copy of the journal written by Gomez Catoira, the chief purser of Mendaña's fleet, was provided by Amherst (Woodford 1890c: 401). It appears that Guppy and Woodford subsequently had a falling out over the use of these Spanish journals (O'Brien 2011: 132, quoting from Royal Geographical Society archives RGS/CB7/Guppy). The importance of the work, besides the obvious value of the Spanish translations, is that it is possible to identify many of Woodford's photographs and compare them with those illustrations available in his archives (Woodford papers PMB Photo 56).

Henry Guppy, *The Westminster Review* and *Littell's Living Age*

The late-Victorian era was one of intellectual and cultural vigour stimulated by new scientific and commercial discoveries. The intellectual vigour of naturalists, navigators, explorers and collectors extended the reach of British power and knowledge across the globe and the knowledge gained supported expansionist ideals. One particular quarterly publication, the *Westminster Review*, began in 1823 and continued to be important to the intellectual elite of the British Empire right through the late-Victorian era until it ceased in 1914. The journal was closely associated with the philosophical views of John Stuart Mill. In 1851 it was acquired by the publisher and editor John Chapman and based in his home and office at 142 Strand, London. This became known as the most radical address in Victorian London (Ashton 2006).

Chapman was to remain owner and publisher until his death in 1895 when it was acquired by his wife who continued to publish the review until its demise in 1914 (VanArsdel 1968). The *Westminster Review* was the pre-eminent periodical of radical opinion in British journalism in the 19th century (Turner 2000: 273). Articles in the review promoted liberalism, scientific naturalism over theology, and the extension of suffrage for working class men and women. It also supported movements for national independence in Europe and demands for reform in education and government. In a conservative era it supported theories of evolution following publication of Darwin's *On the Origin of Species* in 1859 (Rosenberg 2000: 225). Thomas Huxley contributed to the *Westminster Review* and he first used the term 'Darwinism' in an 1860 issue.

Two substantial articles on the Solomon Islands were published in 1888. Both articles summarise the two volumes published by Henry Brougham Guppy in 1887 on the cultures and customs of the Solomon Islanders and the general physical features of the islands and their suitability for colonisation (Guppy 1887a and 1887b). The articles present Guppy's opinions rather in the fashion of a condensed book. For the general public such articles saved the cost of purchase of the large expensive tomes and offered much of the information in easy-to-read sections. The fact that the books were chosen indicates that Guppy's status as a botanist, geologist, ethnologist and author was high. It also shows that the Solomon Islands, and presumably the many articles on head hunting, were common topics in newspapers at the time. Guppy's works were well received back in London (W. H. H. 1888 and Anon 1888). He was later awarded a gold medal by the Linnaean Society in 1917 for his botanical studies and was elected to the Royal Society in 1918. Guppy had also received instructions on collecting by Günther at the British Museum and it was through Günther that he had received £150 (£60,000 in current values) from the Royal Society to pay for exploration into the interior of Guadalcanal (Guppy 1887b). Guppy would have encouraged Woodford to attempt the assent of the mountainous ridges of Guadalcanal to collect montane plant species because he was prevented by a serious illness, possibly malaria, from achieving that aim and so would have been particularly pleased to be Woodford's mentor and advisor. He would later attend Woodford's formal presentation to the Royal Geographical Society and no doubt influenced the Society in its presentation of the Gill Memorial to Woodford. Guppy was a useful contact in London.

The articles in the *Westminster Review* were called 'The Discovery of the Solomon Islands' and 'The Natives of the Solomon Islands' (Anon 1888a and 1888b). 'The Natives of the Solomon Islands' article also included information taken from *Ten Years in Melanesia* by Alfred Penny of the Melanesian Mission (1888) and the *Jottings during the cruise of HMS Curaçoa among the South Sea Islands in 1865* by Julius Brenchley (1873). The anonymous author of the articles wrote:

> Descriptions of newly discovered countries and their inhabitants are extremely attractive to almost every one who is not exclusively preoccupied with his own affairs, or those immediately around him. But of all the habitable parts of our little globe few now remain to be described, and still fewer to be discovered. Among those of which the public know next to nothing, and concerning which geographers and ethnologists knew but little until recently, are the Solomon Islands (Anon 1888b: 457).

The writer remarked that the considering public must thank Dr Henry Guppy for the little information then available.

These articles are significant for they were published at the same time Woodford was returning to England with substantial collections of zoological material and was writing detailed papers on his explorations. Woodford's book, *A Naturalist Among the Head-hunters* (1890b) was just about to be published. It was an opportune time both for Woodford and for the Solomon Islands. Interest in the Solomon Islands was spreading beyond the confines of intellectual circles in London. In the United States, the Littell family of Boston commenced the publication of a general magazine containing selections from English and American magazines, journal and newspapers in 1844. It was designed for general American interest, rather like the *Popular Science Monthly* that was published in New York. Unlike the *Westminster Review*, *Littell's Living Age* was not a magazine appealing to the intellectual or radical elite but for general readership. In May 1888, the magazine reprinted the entire article 'The Discovery of the Solomon Islands' taken from the *Westminster Review* (Anon 1888c). The second article on the Solomon Islanders and their culture was not reprinted. It would appear that in America there was interest in the details of the Spanish discoveries of the islands but little interest in the 'native' peoples who lived there. The poaching of articles from other journals when there were no international copyright laws was standard practice, especially between popular magazines. Woodford would have his main book published by three separate publishers on three continents to avoid this problem.

Publication of *The Naturalist Among the Head-hunters*

Charles Woodford's narrative of his expeditions to the Solomon Islands was published simultaneously in Australia, England and the United States in 1890. The first edition was published by Edward Petherick & Co in Melbourne, the second edition, the one commonly available from rare book dealers at present, was published in London by George Philip & Sons of 32 Fleet Street, one of the oldest publishers in Britain and a specialist in exploration maps, atlases and textbooks. An American edition published in 1890 by Longmans in New York also became available at the same time. The Petherick edition is extremely rare but two copies are held in the general collection at the National Library of Australia. Edward Petherick had been the London-based agent for the successful Australian publisher, George Robertson & Company, in the late 1880s and he and Robertson built up a solid reputation as agents for British publishers wishing to sell their books and journals to colonial audiences (Rukavina 2010). In 1887 Petherick left Robertson's employment. Still based in London he opened his own firm trading as the Colonial Booksellers' Agency in Paternoster Row with a capital of £800 and additional stock in lieu and loans from other publishers of more than £2,500.

The Colonial Booksellers' Agency opened branches in Melbourne and Sydney in 1889 and in Adelaide in 1891. Petherick acted as an intermediary. He purchased stock from other publishers, shipped it to the colonies and then paid his accounts when the books sold. The problem with this was that the lack of swift money transfers from the colonies and the delays in clearance of cheques made cash flow extremely tight unless the agent had substantial capital reserves. In 1889 Petherick ambitiously started his own imprint, EA Petherick & Co, and at the same time published a substantial catalogue *Petherick's Collection of Favourite and Approved Authors for Circulation in the Colonies Only* (Rukavina 2010: 111). Of course this stimulated demand for the books, but once again substantial capital was needed. Petherick's titles of Australiana were published with distinctive covers embossed with animals: a kangaroo for Australia for example. Woodford's book has dark green covers, with the image of Brodie and the Hornbill engraved on the front cover and used as the frontispiece with the title 'Boy, Native of Aola, Guadalcanar, one of my best hunters, with dead Hornbill'. On the spine is a black etching of a young Roviana man with extended ear lobes. The map in the back of the book shows all four expeditions undertaken by Woodford in the Pacific: three to the Solomon Islands and one to the Gilbert and Ellice Islands.

Reading in the Victorian era was central to English society and a major social and leisure activity; the possession of books and a home library was seen as a sign of respectability and social rank (Rukavina 2010: 106). There was much enthusiasm for novels that depicted the Australian experience and a keen desire to comprehend the world, but in strictly European terms. Mapping, museology, archaeology, and ethnography were all becoming democratised. The written form that most suited the urban middle classes was travel writing for '[i]n the case of ethnographic writing, the reader was the traveller' (McDougall 2007: 49). In principle, Woodford had chosen a good publishing firm to produce his first book but this was also a time of economic depression in the Australian colonies. His book was retailed at the Petherick bookstore at 333 George Street Sydney for 8/6 (*The Australian Town and Country Journal* 12 April 1890: 46). This was expensive for the small local market. By late 1891 Edward Petherick was bankrupt. He had borrowed large sums of money from various creditors including the failed Federal Bank of Australia and when the Official Receiver realised on his assets he had debts of more than £50,000 with assets of only £20,000 (*South Australian Register* 5 January 1895: 6). Petherick was a widely read man, a life member of the Royal Geographical Society, a member of the Hakluyt Society and the Linnaean Society as well as the Royal Colonial Institute. He had a keen interest in the exploration of the Pacific. Woodford's work in the Solomons would have appealed to him and they would have moved in the same social circles for a time. In 1893 Petherick wrote to a colleague interested in collecting historical accounts of exploration and explained the difficulties in marketing Woodford's book:

> I was particularly interested, as you know, in Mr Woodford's volume on the Solomon Islands having purchased 250 [copies] and [for] the Australian market. That liberal order induced others to order and the Publishers to supply more to Australia, and the 1st ed, it was soon dispersed. And, the London publisher's representative forgetting another condition I had made, printed a second edition without consulting me & I had a lot left unsold and he too. Result, loss to all of us.
>
> Yours very truly, Edw A. Petherick
>
> (Woodford papers PMB 1290 Item 2/303 EA Petherick to Silver 9 December 1893).

Fortunately, the editions published by George Philip in London and by Longmans in the United States sold well.

In the late-19th century travel, exploration and knowledge of the periphery was opening up the wider world to the general public of the metropolis. Woodford was only one of many men, and a few women, combining the goals of scientific exploration with adventurous travel and making the boundaries merge between the sober and the sensational, and between the analytical and the aesthetic. However, the sensationalist exploits of men like Henry Morton Stanley in Central Africa caused deep concerns about social change and the impact of European civilisation on local peoples. In his descriptions of the natural environment, botany and biology of the Solomon Islands, Woodford also commented on the impact of traders, missionaries and labour recruiters on islander life. Publication of travels and scientific findings was also important for Woodford in establishing himself as a writer and a collector (Driver 2004). It was essential to publish quickly and to present his findings to scientific bodies back in London where the raw material of nature was imaginatively synthesised and transformed into true knowledge (Driver 2004: 82). Science was still characterised by patronage and little government support, and there were limited employment opportunities in the major cultural institutions.

Employment in the City of London

In the meantime, Woodford had to find an occupation that would support his new wife and the child they were expecting in early 1890. He subsequently joined a firm in the City of London trading on the London Stock Exchange (Heath 1974a: 32). Industrial capitalism reached its peak in England by the late 1870s but was followed by a short economic crisis between 1873 and 1876. The outstanding feature of the period of transition following this crisis was the growth of 'capitalist overseas empires' when the major industrial nations of Europe completed the seizure of the small countries and islands in places like the Pacific to use as markets for manufactured goods and as suppliers of raw materials (Eckstein 1991: 308). This expansion needed to be financed. As a result of this dynamic growth London and the south-east of England changed from a production to a financial service centre and grew to be the most important commercial region in the world. From this developed 'gentlemanly capitalism' that suited men whose entry into the City of London was facilitated by meritocratic selection from the best schools and universities (Cain and Hopkins 1987: 2). In this way the intelligent sons of the middle classes were able to push through the social barriers imposed by aristocratic patronage. But despite their wealth and its economic power the great mercantile families still suffered under the disapprobation 'trade'. There remained a marked social and class distinction between those in 'trade' and the landed gentry. Two-thirds of the £6 billion raised on the London financial markets between 1865 and

1912 went into enterprises in foreign countries or those of the British Empire. The majority of the investors were from wealthy landed families or were from 'service', that being from financial backgrounds. Gradually the educated elite mixed and married into the aristocratic elite and created a new affluent moneyed class based in the home counties.

The growth of the City of London trading centre established the importance of London as a global banking centre (McGowan and Kordan 1981: 56; Cain and Hopkins 1987: 3). Free trade made the city a world market place and the spread of sterling, upon which the city depended, was possible through the use of the gold standard. But the Imperial government needed to keep expenditure low and budgets balanced. Budgetary policy was not made in the city but in the Bank of England and the Treasury but the officials in both institutions were from the same class and background as those of the city merchants. This gave the city enormous prestige and influence. Britain's ability to control international finance increased her global influence. Through substantial loans and credit, and the very real threat of credit suspension, the City of London manipulated the economic power that fed Britain's political power (Cain and Hopkins 1980: 486; McGowan and Kordan 1981: 58).

For Woodford, accustomed to the freedom of travel and with a keen interest in the Western Pacific, the four years he spent in the city did not appeal. By 1893 he was looking for a way to return to the Pacific as a collector, colonial official or both. While his expeditions to the Solomon Islands had earned him credit there was little financial reward in scientific collecting and authorship of one book of travel experiences. Woodford approached Sir Robert Henry Meade, the Under Secretary of State in the Colonial Office, with a request that he be considered for the post of Resident or Deputy Commissioner of the newly declared protectorate of the southern Solomon Islands (Woodford to Meade 8 August 1893 CO 225 44 13694). He reported to Meade that Sir William MacGregor in British New Guinea had said in a letter dated 19 October 1892 that Woodford was as well suited as anyone for the post. Then again MacGregor may have been merely obtuse, for that comment could be read two ways. In his letter to the Colonial Office Woodford nominated Captain Wharton of the Royal Navy, the Council of the Royal Geographical Society and Lord Amherst as referees. He enclosed copies of his papers published by the Royal Geographical Society and referred Meade to his newly written account of life in the islands. It would appear the Colonial Office requested a supporting statement from the Royal Geographical Society for the new President, Sir Clements Markham, wrote back to Lord Ripon, the Secretary of State for the Colonies, to say that Woodford was 'one of our best explorers' (Markham to Ripon 10 August 1893 CO 225 44 13694).

Enquiries were then made about Woodford's employment in Fiji but the note states only that 'he held a small appointment in the Treasury which is not noticed in the Blue Books of the time'. Woodford's letter was subsequently copied to Thurston in Suva while the Colonial Office annotated the file with: 'The islands were protected on the understanding that they should cost nothing & it may be long before any understanding with the chiefs can be arrived at' (Fuller to Fairfield 10 August 1893 CO 225 44 13694). Woodford was informed personally that his application for appointment was premature but undismayed he wrote to Lord Ripon from his home 'Rubiana' at Epsom. This time his approach was made through a long descriptive account of the islands, their exports and imports, the climate, the natural products and his opinion of the natives (Woodford to Ripon 7 September 1893 CO 225 44 15492). To this statement, he wisely attached copies of some photographs taken during his three expeditions. These at least appear to have reached Lord Ripon for they are appended to the file. Colonial Office officials annotated the file with the remark: 'The natives seem (generally) to wear at least what decency requires, & the children take to smoking pretty early' (Fuller to Bramston 13 September 1893 CO 225 44 15492). Woodford's comments on the Solomon Islander people not only reflect attitudes of the time but also reflect the personal values that were to guide his work in Tulagi. He wrote that although the Malaitans were 'physically the finest [they] bear perhaps the worst character of any natives in the group', and that the Solomon Islanders are 'as a race highly intelligent, fairly industrious and certainly capable of great improvement', for 'they can be led but not driven', and when 'left to do things their own way their work is characterized by a faithfulness & thoroughness that begets admiration'. Woodford wrote honestly that he sought to improve conditions in the islands in order to get people to live peacefully among themselves and their neighbours (Woodford to Ripon 7 September 1893 CO 225 44 15492).

Woodford also made a personal approach to Thurston in Fiji requesting appointment to the Solomon Islands in an official position that Woodford would fund privately. Thurston declined the offer (Heath 1974a: 33–34). Thurston obviously had some respect for Woodford as a person but rather doubted his seriousness as a colonial administrator. He wrote back to the Colonial Office to say that he did not know if Woodford possessed any legal training or any administrative abilities though he 'is by no means wanting in capacity, when he chooses to exercise it'. Thurston privately thought Woodford was seeking an excuse to return to the islands to continue his work as a naturalist (Thurston to Ripon 30 March 1894 CO 225 45 9079). At that same time Thurston was preparing for a tour of inspection of the Solomon Islands and took a copy of Woodford's book *A Naturalist Smong the Head-hunters* with him on the HMS *Ringdove* when he left Suva on 8 September 1894 (Scarr 1973: 276). In the meantime, Woodford approached the Royal Geographical Society with a request for official assistance for a scientific expedition to Dutch New Guinea (West Papua). The proposal was to equip a 150-ton schooner and steam launch in England and to sail via Christmas Island and the Malay Archipelago to Seram, Kei and the Aru Islands north of Australia. The aim was to explore the coastal regions of Dutch New Guinea around Etna Bay, Bintuni Bay and Gelvink Bay. The purpose was to collect zoological and ethnological specimens presumably for sale back in London. The Malay Archipelago was the area in which Alfred Russel Wallace had explored between 1854 and 1862 and for a recognised natural history collector it would have been an ideal place to continue that investigation. The ambitious project failed when sufficient financial backing was not forthcoming (Heath 1974a: 34). Once again Woodford approached Lord Ripon directly canvassing, but to no avail, the possibility that a position as Resident Commissioner was available in the Solomon Islands (Woodford to Ripon 11 January 1894 CO 225 46 746).

5. Liberalism, Imperialism and colonial expansion

Of all the colonies in the Pacific Ocean, only Fiji, where the labour trade was also active, was seen to be of much interest to the Imperial government (Ward 1948: 261). This had not always been so. In 1855, Seru Ebenezer Cakobau, warrior chief (*Vunivalu*) of Bau, had been held responsible by the United States Government for the payment of compensation to the government totalling US$45,000 as a result of a fire that had begun by accident. Cakobau was seen by the Americans to be the 'King of Fiji' and as a result of this demand he turned to the British Consul for assistance. In 1858 he petitioned Great Britain to accept his offer of ceding the whole of Fiji to the Crown. The Colonial Office declined. Lord Carnarvon reported that Fiji 'would be a troublesome and unprofitable addition to the empire' (Drus 1950: 87). There was also some disquiet in London about Cakobau's claims to be paramount chief and his right to cede all islands to a foreign power (Robson 1995: 173).

The Colonial Office was strongly influenced in this decision by Sir William Denison, the Governor of New South Wales, who become alarmed by unrest in New Zealand as a result of the influx of white settlers there. So strongly was the Colonial Office against annexation of the islands that they requested the Foreign Office to formally rebuke Consul William Pritchard who had promoted the idea. Pritchard was later dismissed from the service after a very dubious commission of inquiry and a campaign against him by the Wesleyan missionaries (Robson 1995: 175; Drus 1950: 90). The excuses London gave were to echo throughout colonial history in the Pacific: the cost of administration would be too great, it would involve Britain in native wars, and it would create disputes with other civilised countries, notably Germany and France. However, settlers from Australia began moving into Fiji in the late 1860s and indentured labourers from other islands were imported to work the settler plantations. The general impression in London was that New South Wales might be willing to administer the Fijian islands but the idea of sub-Imperialism was not practical.

Eventually, in reply to a request from Fiji, the British government sent a commission of inquiry to consider the situation with regard to succession. In 1874 Commodore James Goodenough of the Royal Navy Australia Station and Edgar L. Layard, then the new British Consul for Fiji and Tonga, were commissioned to report on the possibility of annexing Fiji to the territories of the British Crown. Personal instructions from Prime Minister Gladstone were that annexation was to be the last resort. The Colonial Office expressed a preference for a protectorate rather than a colony. However, Goodenough and Layard reported back to Parliament that same year with a long report recommending formal annexation of the Fijian islands and stating that as a 'Crown Colony, we think that Fiji would certainly become a prosperous Settlement' (Great Britain. Parliament. House of Commons 1874a and 1874b; Scholefield 1919: 90). The two men had spent more than five months investigating the prospects of Fiji but when the comprehensive report came to be discussed in Parliament, Gladstone was no longer in office. He publically declined to support annexation. The new Conservative Party government which subsequently annexed Fiji was able to have the *Pacific Islanders Protection Act* 1875 (38 & 39 Vic c51) passed containing a clause giving jurisdiction over British subjects in the Pacific (see Whittaker *et al.* 1975: Document D38). Cakobau, chosen by the British government to be High Chief, was never fully recognised as paramount chief of all the islands. The annexation was in response to concerns that the white settlers of Fiji, keen to develop a plantation economy in the islands, were threatening communal landowners with dispossession and exploitation; but more than this, Britain was without a naval base between Australia and America. There was no intention of embarking on an expansive policy of widespread annexation of islands in the Pacific. Despite this, the annexation of Fiji was the start of the breakdown of the 'jealously guarded ramparts of the minimum intervention policy'. From this time British influence in the Pacific widened (Drus 1950: 109; Ward 1948: 265).

Western Pacific High Commission

Annexation did not solve the many problems of trade, politics and European settlement in the Western Pacific. It would not be until 1877 that the complete and complex Western Pacific Order In Council would be formulated to manage the engagement of indentured labourers and to control the excess of British subjects in the Western Pacific beyond the jurisdiction of British and colonial Australian laws (see Whittaker *et. al* 1975: Document D39; Great Britain. Laws etc 1877–1893; Hertslet 1880 and 1885). With the order in council the Colonial Office in London proposed the establishment of a Commission of the Governor of Fiji that would give the Governor authority over persons and acts in the islands south of the equator (Morrell 1960: 181). The original document of 321 articles specified that the Governor, as High Commissioner and Consul-General, had four important functions: to communicate with local representatives of the foreign powers, to conduct diplomatic relations specifically with the Polynesian governments of Samoa and Tonga, to regulate the Pacific labour trade where it was conducted by British subjects only, and to maintain law and order among British subjects in the Pacific islands where there were no recognised governments, such as in Melanesia.

The power to enter into relations with native states and tribes was effective only in the southern Polynesian islands where chieftainship was hereditary and a formal hierarchy of responsibility rested with the chiefly class. This power was ineffective in Melanesia where local leaders, known as either Big-men or Chiefs, held power only over the immediate village or group of villages. Their power was not hereditary but open and volatile, subject to allegiances of kinsmen and personal followers. Here the idea of negotiating the concept of a broad encompassing 'statehood' was irrelevant. The Western Pacific Order in Council was designed to be 'an ingeniously worked out experiment, an attempt to make the new Crown Colony of Fiji a centre from which law and order might be disused throughout the unannexed islands of the Pacific' (Morrell 1960: 185). But the 321 articles dealt mostly with the appointment of officials and their powers, and matters of procedure of the High Commissioner's Court that sat in Suva. The Chief Justice of Fiji was also the Judicial Commissioner for the Western Pacific. Only six articles related to the actual duties of the High Commissioner. The most important of these gave the High Commissioner significant powers to make regulations for the government of British subjects in the Western Pacific (Art 24), to prohibit any person dangerous to peace and good order from living in any part of the Pacific (Art 25), and if necessary to remove that person from any island in which he is living (Art 26). These powers could be delegated to Deputy Commissioners. For these tasks the Colonial Office allocated annual funds of £5,000 (Scarr 1967a: 34). The Foreign Office and the Colonial Office were in constant disagreement over legal and administrative roles and responsibilities but between 1877 and the early 1900s the office of High Commissioner of the Western Pacific was to gain executive powers over a wide area of the Western Pacific.

The Western Pacific Order in Council was reviewed by a commission of inquiry in 1883 (Great Britain. House of Commons. Parliamentary Papers 1884b; Newbury 2010: 108). This commission noted the complexity of the code and the sheer physical difficulty in applying the principles of the orders in such a scattered area as the Western Pacific. Subsequently a consolidation was prepared in 1888 and a revised Order in Council in 1893 gave Resident Commissioners wider autonomy (Great Britain. High Commissioner for Western Pacific Islands 1893; Great Britain. House of Commons. Parliamentary Papers 1893; Great Britain. Laws etc 1877–1893; Scarr 1967a: 252). Initially, underlying these principles was the desire of both the Colonial and Foreign Offices to avoid the financial and political complications associated with making new annexations in an area considered so economically worthless as the Pacific. The administrative agency, the Western Pacific High Commission, despite its influence in the Pacific region for more than 80 years, 'should be seen as a rather weak experiment in providing order and jurisdiction without assuming sovereignty' (Hyam 2002: 209).

Christianity and the Melanesian Mission

By the end of the 19th century, Britain had become a 'proselytizing nation' where mission influence and prestige stood high in political life (Ward 1948: 328). The policy of minimum intervention was overturned by the expansion of the other colonial powers, Germany and France, into the Pacific. The Australian colonies were becoming richer and more economically important after the gold rushes and missionary activity centred in the colonies was spreading outwards and into the Pacific. But the first missionaries to try to establish a base in the Solomon Islands were members of the Roman Catholic Society of Mary. The party of 11 Marist Fathers landed at Astrolabe Bay on Isabel in 1845 but the leader, Bishop Jean-Baptiste Epalle, was killed at Pinhudi with one of his own trade axes and buried at Haili on the island of San Jorge (St George Island) (Laracy 1976: 17–18; see Whittaker *et al*. 1975: Document C15). The rest of the party then relocated to the south and lived for 20 months at Makira Bay on San Cristobal. Here, again, mistrust between the local people and the priests grew and fever, dysentery and attacks from the bush people killed off three more. This mission was abandoned in September 1847. They were not to return until 1898.

After George Augustus Selwyn, the Anglican Bishop of New Zealand, formed the Australasian Board of Missions in 1850, the idea of a Melanesian Mission in the Western Pacific began and the role of a missionary bishop was fostered within the Anglican Churches in the colonies (Davidson 2000: 9–10). It was the Anglican Church under Selwyn, and not the British government, that made the first direct move into the Western Pacific. Each year after 1847 Selwyn, based in New Zealand, made a long missionary tour through the Samoan and Cook Islands, into New Hebrides and on into the Melanesian islands. In 1854, Selwyn secured a new mission schooner, the *Southern Cross*, and enlisted the aid of John Coleridge Patteson. The Melanesian Mission established a centre at Mota Island in the Banks Group (now the Torba Province of Vanuatu) and Mota became the lingua franca of the mission. In 1861, Bishop Patteson was consecrated as 'Missionary Bishop among the Western Islands of the South Pacific Ocean' and he began regular voyages around the Melanesian islands (Davidson 2000: 19). These continued until his death in Nukapu in 1871. The Melanesian Mission supported Britain's pacification and civilising influences and enhanced its power and status in London with the appointment in London of prominent men to positions of Vice-President of the English Committee of the church. These men had close and direct ties with the even more powerful Colonial Office. Ties of class and friendship were powerful factors behind the strength of the colonial state and Anglican missions.

The Protestant churches—the London Missionary Society, the Methodists, the Presbyterians, and the Melanesian Mission—carved out spheres of influence for themselves in the Western Pacific. At first, Selwyn declared that there was no rivalry between the denominations and this comity principle was to form the basis of future agreements in the Solomon Islands. But the arrival of the evangelists, the members of the Queensland Kanaka Mission, the Seventh-day Adventists and other sects would be another matter (Davidson 2000: 20). The London Missionary Society first settled in Samoa and part of New Caledonia before moving on to the Torres Strait and mainland Papua, the Methodists took responsibility for Fiji and Tonga, the Presbyterians had taken over the southern parts of New Hebrides, while the Melanesian Mission secured the northern islands of New Hebrides and the Solomon Islands. In Polynesia, the Methodists and the London Missionary Society had the advantage of commonalities between eastern and western Polynesian languages and Māori and some degree of social hierarchy and formal structure. These indigenous characteristics enabled the hierarchical nature of church leadership to gain adherents within the islands.

Missionary activities in Melanesia would face much more complex local factors. In particular, there were numerous small groups of people with no formal social hierarchy visible to Europeans and with many hundreds of separate, mutually unintelligible languages (Davidson 2000: 12). In addition, the early attitudes of people to Christianity would confuse. Many local people saw the teachings of the church as another set of commodities that could be blended into the customary social and economic systems. Prayers and rituals took the place of sorcery and magic. Both could be taught to followers or traded to allies. To overcome these obstacles, Selwyn planned to take young men from their home communities to a central location and train them for future evangelising on their return. This began in 1851 after the first group of islander men arrived at Auckland on the Melanesian Mission boat *Border Maid* having been brought south by the HMS *Havannah*. Their early experiences in New Zealand were not a success. Many young men, removed from the tropical climate to Kohimarama near Auckland, could not adjust to the climate and illnesses. In 1867, the Mission established St Banabas College, a church and training centre on Norfolk Island. Here the public school model was adopted and Mota language, adopted from the mission based in the New Hebrides, was used as a lingua franca for education and worship. Christian ideas of marriage and the formality of European society were taken as a guide for relationships between men and women and English church rituals were transplanted along with the use of the Book of Common Prayer (Davidson 2000: 22). But a growing paternalism meant the increased reliance on English staff delayed the achievement of an independent indigenous church.

Removing young men from the islands for their Christian training was not entirely an original idea of the Melanesian Mission. It stemmed from the problems faced by the Presbyterian missions in the New Hebrides. The Rev John Inglis of the Reformed Presbyterian Church had written a detailed report for the Governor of New Zealand, Sir George Grey, describing a three-month missionary tour to the New Hebrides, the southern Solomon Islands and New Caledonia made on HMS *Havannah* in 1851. Grey was particularly concerned with possible French expansion in the Pacific and the settlement of English Protestant missionaries in New Hebrides was supported as a counter to French colonialism and the inroads made by Catholic missionaries (Sinclair 2011). Inglis was a careful observer of the local people and the problems faced by missions establishing themselves in the remote islands. He suggested in his report that young men be removed to New Zealand for training and this report was subsequently printed in the New Zealand government gazette and in full in a leading Sydney newspaper ('Missionary tour' *The Sydney Morning Herald* 30 May 1851: 3–4). In the end, Inglis and his wife accepted John Geddie's invitation to assist in the Presbyterian mission on Aneityum in the south of the New Hebrides where they were to remain for the next 24 years (Parsonson 2010). These English missionaries in the Pacific were not the conscious agents of British colonialism, although they certainly advanced British Protestant ideals (Hilliard 1974: 94). While they actively sought the overarching protection of English law and order they did not demand annexation of the islands as a means for achieving this protection. Still, they were identifiably Imperialist in association. The Melanesian Mission was regarded as High Church Anglican founded on Christian Humanism. It was, however, a 'well-bred mission' for many of the clergy came from well-to-do, educated upper-middle class, well-connected families (Hilliard 1978: 145). They brought with them ideas of paternalism and hierarchy that was sympathetic to the aims of colonial administration.

Cecil Wilson, the third missionary Anglican Bishop of Melanesia between 1894 to 1911, was, like Charles Woodford, educated at Tonbridge. Wilson graduated from Jesus College, Cambridge, and served in several parishes in England before his consecration. The Melanesian Mission was led by Oxford and Cambridge graduates who, like Wilson, were imbued with Victorian intellectual ideas and who were fascinated with studies of local languages, ethnology and cultural practices. While they remained fascinated by native culture it was seen only as an intellectual study for they consciously sought to change people's beliefs and practices in their everyday lives. Hilliard (1966: 139) comments that 'Wilson was a conscientious but uninspiring missionary; humourless and, his bishop observed, "quick to see wrong or faulty doing"'.

In order to service their stations, the Melanesian Mission acquired the first of a number of ships to be called *Southern Cross*. The first *Southern Cross* was built to replace the *Undine*, a small 21-ton schooner used from 1849 to 1857. It was a 100-ton schooner that served from 1855 to 1860 when it was wrecked off the coast of

New Zealand. The second *Southern Cross* served from 1863 to 1873. It was a 93-ton brigantine built in Southampton and was the vessel involved in the Nukapu incident when John Coleridge Patteson and his assistants were murdered. The killing of Patteson raised the anger of the British public not only because a senior member of the Anglican clergy was murdered but also by the evidence presented to Parliament by Albert Markham: 'It has been the custom of some of these [labour] vessels to visit the different islands which the late Bishop Patteson used to frequent, and inform the natives that they were sent by him, and on some occasions these unprincipled men have actually walked about on deck in surplices, so as to represent the bishop' (Great Britain. House of Commons. Parliamentary Papers 1872: 8). Markham reported that some labour vessels traded in captured heads and exchanged them for the equivalent number of live men (Great Britain. House of Commons. Parliamentary Papers 1872: 9). The third *Southern Cross* was a larger topsail schooner of 180-tons with an auxiliary steam engine that saw service in the Solomon Islands from 1874 to 1892. This vessel was built in Auckland at the cost of £5,000. It would be of considerable importance to Charles Woodford during his early work as a naturalist from 1886 to 1889 for he met with the mission ship at a number of places during his travels. The fourth *Southern Cross* was a 240-ton three-masted schooner built in Essex in England at the cost of £9,000 which was contributed by Bishop John Selwyn and others. It saw service from 1892 to 1902. The fifth *Southern Cross* was a steel, three-masted schooner with an auxiliary steam engine launched by Bishop Cecil Wilson. It was in service from 1903 to the early 1930s (Beattie 1906; Sinker 1907; Wilson 1932).

The Melanesian Mission, along with the Pacific labour trade and the few coastal traders, preceded the establishment of colonial administration in the Solomon Islands by more than 40 years. Most of these mission stations were isolated, vulnerable and dependant on the generosity of local villagers during an unstable social and political time. Stability and amity were required between the missions and the local people. To understand the power relations that existed in communities, missionaries were often the first to learn local language. An understanding of local language required some cultural knowledge and so the missionaries often became the earliest interlockers between tradition and change. But even the missions depended on the visits by the Royal Naval men-of-war that patrolled the islands between May and October each year. This was the only time that British law was enforced. Even the intervention of the navy was seasonal, as was the annual voyage of the *Southern Cross*.

Missionaries saw themselves as pursuing a political agenda that filled the gap between fervent British colonialism and neutrality. The local people, however, saw the missionaries, the traders, the labour recruiters and later the government officials as representing one group: foreigners with power, technology and unlimited resources. Missionaries certainly saw themselves as a social and moral group much superior to traders and labour recruiters. All white men were seen by the local people as agents of change regardless of their moral and philosophical character (Hilliard 1974: 97). The success of the Christian missions was dependant on political and social stability; societies in a perpetual state of war and victimisation could not be converted peacefully. Although George Selwyn wrote that the Melanesian frontier could not be pacified by annexation or naval bombardment, his faith in 'moral influence and good example' would not be sufficient to calm troubled peoples. While adverse to annexation by the Crown, the Melanesian Mission did not object to the formation of a protectorate. Under international law a protectorate was not regarded as a separate state. It was presumed to have a strong colonial 'protector' assisting and guiding the rule of a native state. In a protectorate, indigenous forms of governance were supposed to be available for use by the protecting state. The administration was overseen by a Commissioner or High Commissioner, not a Governor. In the case of the Solomon Islands, as in other parts of Melanesia where there were no pre-existing native states to grant Britain power and jurisdiction by treaty, grant or other law, the protectorate would be in effect a colony without formal annexation. Legally British protectorates existed outside the Territorial Dominions of the Crown. In Melanesia, where they were not obtained by treaty, jurisdiction was limited to rule over British subjects (Hookey 1971: 233). Together with the *Pacific Islanders Protection Act* 1875, the *Foreign Jurisdiction Act* 1890 (53 & 54 Vic c.37) gave the Crown jurisdiction within any islands and places in the Pacific Ocean not being within the dominions of the Crown nor within the jurisdiction of any civilised, by definition European, power. The implications of this vague legal status would be important for colonial policing, the trade in arms and ammunition, the prosecution of non-British subjects and the alienation of land. Although the Germans had made a distinction in theory between colonies (*Kolonien*) and protectorates (*Schutzgebieten*) in practice they were governed alike (Munro, McCreery and Firth 2004: 146). It was not until the passing of the consolidation of the foreign jurisdiction legislation in 1890 that Britain brought its theory into line with continental practice. From then on British colonial protectorates were administered as if they were formal colonies. By the mid-1890s British legal jurisdiction in the Western Pacific was extended over British subjects, foreigners and 'natives' alike. This would have important implications when the Gilbert and Ellice Islands came under British control in 1893 and the southern Solomon Islands came under Woodford's administration in 1897.

Commodore Justice

It was the death of John Coleridge Patteson, the newly consecrated Bishop of Melanesia, in September 1871 at Nukapu in the Solomon Islands that increased efforts to regulate the Pacific labour trade. It was widely believed that Patteson was killed because young men being taken away from the islands by labour recruiters did not return. Another version of the death was that the missionaries failed to understand the complexities of reciprocity. Patteson had given the Nukapu chief a considerable gift, but then gave a smaller gift to the chief of Santa Cruz who considered himself of higher status. To avenge the honour of the chief the people of Santa Cruz travelled to Nukapu and killed Patteson there (Scarr 1973: 277). A more complex interpretation is that Patteson, by repeated and increasingly unwelcome visits to Nukapu, ignored the message that the people did not want their young men taken away. Perhaps Patteson's interactions with women on the island, contrary to strict Polynesian custom, served to undermine the political and cosmological equilibrium (Kolshus and Hovdhaugen 2010: 351–355). Patteson thus became the 'martyr bishop' of the Melanesian Mission (Hilliard 1966: 58).

Albert Markham, commander of the HMS *Rosario*, had been commissioned to board and inspect all vessels suspected of being involved in the labour trade off the New Hebrides and the Santa Cruz Islands. At Norfolk Island he learned of the murder of Patteson and proceeded to Nukapu with instructions to punish the murderers. There, at Nukapu, the *Rosario* fired a broadside of shells from the man-of-war towards the small coral island that would have done considerable damage (Great Britain. House of Commons. Parliamentary Papers 1873: 15). Later, Markham's superior, Commodore Stirling, wrote to the Admiralty that he was 'totally adverse to any indiscriminate firing upon the South Sea Islanders; the wrongs which they have suffered and are suffering at the hands of white people are well known' (Bach 1968: 19). Markham felt that there was a need 'to shield and protect the Islanders' from what he saw as 'the nefarious system of kidnapping [that] is practised to a most inconceivable extent' throughout the islands (Samson 2003b: 290). It was his opinion that the 'consequent retaliations on the part of the islanders' were solely due to the lawless acts perpetuated by labour recruiters and vessel captains (Markham 1872: 231).

Markham subsequently wrote detailed accounts of the cruise of the *Rosario* in 1871 and 1872, and the topic became the subject of much debate in London (Markham 1872 and 1871–1872; Great Britain. House of Commons. Parliamentary Papers 1872). The navy was forced into a position where it was subject to increasing pressure to take punitive action against islanders involved in retaliatory action. There was little satisfaction to be found in navigating coral waters to 'throw a handful of shot into grass huts and palm trees' (Bach 1968:

13). Despite Markham's belief that in many cases the local people were justified in taking retaliatory action against labour vessels, the action of the *Rosario* could hardly be dismissed with simply throwing 'a handful of shot into grass huts'. The *Rosario* shelled the small coral atoll with 100 rounds from a RML 7 inch $6\frac{1}{2}$ ton gun and an Armstrong RBL 40 pounder fired at broadside. Both guns were heavy defence naval guns used in shore installations and on naval frigates ('The *Rosario* and the murderers of Bishop Patteson', *The Argus* 15 February 1872: 7). The *Argus* strongly condemned the action it had just reported. In the same paper it stated: 'It is merely repeating a trite maxim to affirm that to prevent the commission of a crime is a much more rational proceeding than to wait until it has been perpetrated, and then to punish the culprit' (*The Argus*, 15 February 1872: 4 and 5).

This naval action became known as 'Commodore Justice' (Ward 1948: 58; Healy 1967: 19) or 'Government by Commodore' (Scholefield 191: 63). The two types of naval visits—the expeditions sent to administer justice against outrages committed by natives and the routine visits of inspection and survey—merged into one (Ward 1948: 60). The administration of 'Commodore Justice' was also used as part of the early attempts at establishing a protectorate in British New Guinea. When missionaries, traders and miners became attracted to south-western New Guinea after the 1870s, the Royal Navy sent ships to the coast to monitor British interests 'and occasionally bombarded recalcitrant villages to show them how to keep the peace' (Quinnell 2000: 82). These arbitrary and informal sanctions applied by the Royal Navy in the Western Pacific were designed solely to protect or avenge the lives of Europeans in order to open up the territory to white settlement, plantation development, and in the case of British New Guinea, to gold mining (Healy 1967: 20–21). In order for the Royal Navy to perform such tasks the action was officially declared an 'act of war' and in the early period the Royal Navy was at its own discretion in administering retribution (Ward 1948: 277). For local people the arrival of the men-of-war was a signal to flee the area. It was obvious that the navy was clearly unsuited for such broad and difficult policing tasks that required local understanding, cross-cultural communication and some measure of diplomacy. The navy misrepresented the power of local Big-men, failed to understand local ideas of justice, retribution and conflict resolution and the complexities of compensation.

This stimulated anti-slavery and humanitarian groups in Britain to lobby the government and subsequently the *Pacific Islanders Protection Act* 1872 (35 & 36 Vict c19) was passed (Scholefield 1919: 60, WPHC 10/V Item 185). The act is also known as the *Kidnapping Act* of 1872 although the full title, *Act of the British Parliament for the Prevention of Criminal Charges upon Natives of the Islands in the Pacific Ocean (Kidnapping)*, provides the clue to the purpose, intent and limitations of the legislation. The Kidnapping Act was seen by the Imperial government in London as a means for addressing a slave trade in the Pacific, but having been found wanting in the *Daphne* case, all references to slavery in the legislation were removed. In future, any prosecutions for illegal actions by blackbirders had to avoid the use of the term slavery in the courts (Mortensen 2000: 13). Under the now failing policy of minimum intervention the Imperial government in London declined to interfere markedly in affairs in the Pacific, apart from direct action by the Royal Navy Australia Station. But naval action could hardly be called minimum intervention. The activities of the labour recruiters in the Solomon Islands also drew comment from American writers in the years following the American Civil War of 1860–1865 and Markham's book was used as the basis of a long article published in the *Harper's New Monthly Magazine* that was full of pious hope for the Christianisation of the 'natives'—described in racist terms of social degradation and inhumanity—while deploring the activities of the Pacific labour traders (Rideing 1874). The Pacific labour trade did not pass unnoticed in other parts of the world.

Punitive action in the Solomon Islands

The Melanesian Mission and the Royal Navy became inextricably linked into ties of dependency and cooperation long before the formation of the British Solomon Islands Protectorate in 1893. One such case was the search for the murderers of the boat crew from the HMS schooner *Sandfly* at Nggela (Florida Islands), the islands between Guadalcanal and Malaita. Lieutenant-Commander Bower and five crew men from the *Sandfly* had gone in October 1880 from Tasimboko on Guadalcanal by small boat to survey Nggela but when they were reported overdue an expedition was mounted. Eventually the bodies of four headless men were found on the beach on the small Mandoleana (Mandoliana) Island off Nggela Pile (Small Nggela). They had been attacked by men from Gaeta village whose chief was Kalekona.

One man had drowned in an escape attempt but another sailor, Francis Savage, swam to nearby Honggo village on Nggela Pile. He was then handed over to the *Sandfly* crew by these friendly villagers. The remaining crew of the *Sandfly* then burned a village at Raita Bay (Mboli) (*The Nelson Evening Mail*, 15 (250), 13 December 1880: 4) in retaliation for the murders. In December 1880 the corvette HMS *Emerald* under Captain William Maxwell was ordered by Commodore Wilson to find the murderers of the *Sandfly* crew and 'pursuing them even into the interior of their country "inflict" on them the severe punishment they so well deserve. This is a case where the prestige of the Navy is deeply concerned, and one by which if the murderers are not severely chastised, its power for good, and as a deterrent to crime amongst the islands, will receive a great shock'

(Great Britain. House of Commons. Parliamentary Papers 1881; Scholefield 1919: 65). Maxwell landed with a party of 60 men but 'notwithstanding all my [Maxwell's] precautions, and though my orders were executed with exactness, and the party landed before dawn of day, the natives [of the hill villages] had all decamped, and no one was to be seen'. The marines then proceeded to Raita (Mboli) in Mboli Passage and once again set a village alight and destroyed more than 270 coconut trees. The crew of the *Emerald* shelled other coastal villages before sailing to Malaita to investigate attacks on other vessels. The 'whole district was in ashes' wrote Bishop John Selwyn (Hilliard 1978: 91, 116 fn11). On this second attempt, the murderers of Bower and his men were not found. Subsequently, these proceedings were the subject of questions in the House of Commons when the Secretary of the Admiralty was forced to defend punitive action in the islands (Great Britain. House of Commons. Parliamentary Papers, Commons sitting of Monday 18 July 1881).

In May 1881 yet another expedition was sent to Nggela. The naval sloop HMS *Cormorant* was despatched from Sydney to find the murderers and execute them. The *Cormorant* rendezvoused with the mission vessel *Southern Cross* at Uji and Bishop Selwyn 'had an interview with Commander Bruce [of the *Cormorant*] and represented that he had discovered the whole story of the massacre, and that if Commander Bruce should use coercion and take time the murderers of Lieutenant Bower would be given up' (*Maitland Mercury and Hunter River General Advertiser* 7 July 1881: 7, quoting from *The Sydney Morning Herald*). Selwyn joined this second expedition in the role of mediator. He convinced Kalekona, referred to as the chief of Nggela, to turn Queen's evidence on receipt of a pardon and to surrender the men responsible for the murders (Guppy 1887b: 17). Vurea, Kalekona's son, who had been involved in the attack on Bower, was held as hostage until the men were apprehended. Commander Bruce submitted a full report to the Western Pacific High Commission on the action taken in the *Sandfly* case but the Royal Navy's version differs considerably from local understanding.

Three men caught were subsequently executed: Honambosa, the leader, was hanged over Bower's grave on Mandoliana, Illomali was killed at Mboli, and a third man Tafou was taken to Uji and shot there (Woodford papers PMB 1290. Item 1/4 Diary 25 August 1886). Vurea, the chief's son, was held as a hostage until all men were surrendered and then sent to Uji to work for nine months with the trader John Stephens. He was then released (*The Sydney Morning Herald*, 12 September 1881: 5 and 26 September 1881: 7–8). Selwyn's reasoning for using his influence was that the 'whole island was threatened with war if the men were not surrendered. The justice of the demand was fully acknowledged by themselves. The lesson was needed, and has been most salutary, and will under God, put a stop to such attempts for the future' (Hilliard 1974: 99 quoting the Report of the Melanesian Mission for the year 1881). Selwyn also referred to this incident in his Christmas report on the work of the Melanesian Mission in 1896 (Selwyn 1896: 10). Much later, during his travels to the islands, Woodford would hear that Tafou, the young man executed in place of Vurea, was a Malaitan slave boy offered up in place of the chief's son. The trader at Fauro, J. C. Macdonald, would later tell Woodford that Selwyn had participated in 'a grievous miscarriage of justice'. The likely story of the substitution of a slave boy was not confirmed by the Rev Alfred Penny in his account of the naval actions. Penny reported that a fourth man, Puko, escaped capture and fled to another part of Nggela (Penny 1888). He was never caught.

The reason for the murder of Bower and his men was that Kalekona had lost some shell money and felt himself spiritually rebuked. He believed only the taking of a man's head would resolve the trouble. In his pastoral paper Selwyn wrote that the women of the village taunted the men and told them they were afraid to kill white men and that this was sufficient reason for the men taking action to murder the sailors. In fact, little attempt was made to fully understand the motives behind the killings and even less attempt was made to find out the status of the men who were executed. Kalekona's relationship with the three executed was also an important factor in the entire episode. This too was never examined. For local people, the action by Selwyn was evidence that the mission and the navy worked together. Rev Penny referred to this incident in his book not only to justify the men-of-war actions in the islands but also to emphasise that the navy had to exercise caution in its punishment of the people and in the destruction of their homes and crops. He felt justified in chastising the local people and believed that they needed to learn caution. The moral was that retribution, like the actions of the Christian God, could be swift and fatal. Kalekona had yet another view on the incident for he boasted that he had once arranged to kill white men and used to say 'White man all same picaninny' (Woodford papers PMB 1290 Item 1/4 Diary 25 August 1886).

During the early stage of colonial contact in the Solomon Islands the white presence was maintained by the changing crews of labour vessels, a few missionaries and some traders living precariously on small islands or at isolated trading stations. Hugh Hastings Romilly (1882 and 1889), Deputy Commissioner for the Western Pacific between 1881 and 1883 and later Deputy Commissioner and Consul for the New Hebrides and the Solomon Islands from 1887 to 1889, a man well known for his heavy drinking and for being largely unsympathetic about Pacific Islanders in general, prophetically wrote: 'The civilizing process which the Solomon Islanders have received at the hands of white men since that time [the 1850s] has made terrible savages of them' (Romilly 1886: 65). Romilly came to the conclusion that it 'was obvious that a deputy commissioner who commanded a warship would obtain obedience more readily than one who lived on the hospitality of traders and travelled in labour ships' (Scarr 1967a: 128). Accompanying General Sir Peter Scratchley, the Special Commissioner in charge of the Protectorate of British New Guinea, on a tour of inspection of the eastern and north-eastern coasts of Papua in 1885, Romilly wrote:

We have been burning towns [villages] and smashing canoes, and other police work. We all hate it, and feel very mean while we are doing it. The natives have sworn to kill every white man, and they have killed a good many. They say they were stolen by Queensland ships and half their men died in Queensland, and they must have revenge ... It will take years before we have friendly intercourse with the natives of all these groups of islands. At present they hate us, and I think with justice (Whittaker *et al*. 1975: Document D40, 502–503; Healy 1967: 20).

Disillusioned with employment in the Colonial Office, and his work in the Western Pacific despite his good credentials and connections, Romilly went prospecting in Mashonaland in Southern Africa in 1891 and died there of fever aged 36 (Romilly 1893). He was another restless young man who found life in Victorian England stifling.

The voyage of HMS *Royalist* under Captain Edward Davis

In the Western Pacific, the inability of the High Commission to deal with offences committed by Islanders meant that the ships from the Royal Navy Australia Station, manned by men with strong humanitarian traditions like George Palmer and Albert Hastings Markham, were sent with increasing frequency to isolated islands with orders to pursue the murderers of white men. As commerce and Christianity spread into the islands, naval ships sought redress for crimes against Europeans who, in almost all cases, had voluntarily chosen to live there. Often the white foreigner was the guilty party responsible for breaking cultural prohibitions or insulting or physically assaulting local people. Trading stations were also places where coveted goods were seen to be hoarded or hidden. One consequence of the punitive campaigns was criticism from Britain where the opinion was that 'a naval officer was little more than an épauletted and power conscious bully, roving the ocean and terrorising harmless native communities at the expense of the English taxpayer' (Bach 1968: 13). The practice of shelling the villages where it was assumed offenders lived, proved to be arbitrary, unpredictable, often completely unfair and lastly, irrelevant.

Figure 21. HMS *Royalist*, 1883.

Source: Australian War Memorial (www.awm.gov.au/collection/302264).

The 1891 voyage of the HMS *Royalist* to the Solomon Islands is a good example of the exercise of naval power in administering collective punishment. A letter by Peter Edmund Pratt to the *Sydney Morning Herald* (29 March 1889: 5) listed a number of murders of traders dating far back to 1867 that he said had not been adequately dealt with by the Royal Navy. Pratt considered the naval actions in the Solomon Islands to be lenient to the locals to such an extent that the men of Roviana were boasting of the powerlessness of the Royal Navy. He listed five murders in particular: the 1867 murders of 12 men from the *Marion Rennie* killed at Banietta on Rendova; the deaths of McIntosh and Jaffery from the *Esperanza* at Kolombangara in 1879; the murder of James Howie and crew from the *Elibank Castle* in May 1885 also at Banietta; the death of a John Childe (or Childers) at Simbo in September 1885; and the murders of two men from a vessel he called the Prospect at Dogby on Piandova—most likely the murder of two men from the *Progress* that occurred at Hughli on Rendova in 1887 (Bennett 1987: Appendix 6). These murders had a long history of over 20 years. Frank Wickham wrote to Rear Admiral George Tryon concerning these murders and reported the natives to be 'snider-on-the-brain' for they only had a few old rifles and were anxious to gain more Snider rifles (Great Britain. House of Commons.

Parliamentary Papers 1886: 13–14). But Pratt was especially angered over three raids on his trading station at Hombuhombu between October 1888 and June 1889. In these attacks he lost over £200 of trade goods in the early raids by men from Banietta and in late 1889 all the windows, doors and furniture of his house on the island were stolen. Even his kitchen garden was uprooted (*The Sydney Morning Herald* 29 March 1889: 5; Wright 2005: 280–281; Royal Navy (1886–1896), see Woodford papers PMB 1290 Item 8/21/6: 1891). During the 20 June 1889 raid, while Pratt was away, men from Mbilua on Vella Lavella killed the manager, William Dabelle, and three workmen (Wright 2005: 275).

A second report in the paper (*The Sydney Morning Herald* 10 September 1889: 5) by Robert Cable, now master of the Maroon, detailed the growing insecurity felt by whites in the islands. It was this instability that forced Melinda Macdonald and her daughter from their Siniasoro Bay plantation on Fauro to the safety of their former trading station at Howla (Aola) on the north coast of Guadalcanal (Woodford to Thurston 10 January 1897 WPHC 4/IV 20/1897). Cable was working for Kelly and Williams, trading competitors of Peter Edmund Pratt, and Cable's report contains veiled criticisms of Pratt, who was known to have a poor business reputation. Captain George Hand, commander of the HMS *Royalist*, was then dispatched to the islands to investigate these murders (Woodford papers PMB 1290 Item 8/21/4: 1889). Pratt would not accompany the ship on its cruise for fear his presence on board the naval gunboat would damage his trade there but Hand bombarded Narovo on Simbo after hearing that the men who made the first attack were hiding in this location. Hand then took the *Royalist* to Anuta on another matter. There he arrested the chief, Sono (Jackson) there for the murder of Thomas Dabelle, brother of William Dabelle, on the grounds that Dabelle's belongings were found in Sono's possession. Sono was taken to Suva for investigation but was later released after the Rev Richard Comins of the Melanesian Mission and the trader Fred Howard wrote in support of his case (Woodford papers PMB 1290 Item 8/21/5, 1890: 14). Subsequently Sono was returned to Hada Bay with trade goods to the value of £5 and an assurance from local chiefs that they could better capture the murderers than the Royal Navy. Testimony against Sono had been given by Sam Keating and Thomas Woodhouse both of whom worked for Kelly and Williams. Sono, on the other hand, was trading for business rival G. J. Waterhouse (Bennett 1987: 55–56; *The Sydney Morning Herald* 5 November 1889: 8). It was clear that traders were interfering in local politics and using the power of the navy to settle scores. The Royal Navy could not find the murderers of Thomas Dabelle and, after much expense; the case was closed (Woodford papers PMB 1290 Item 8/21/6, 1891: 31). The new corvette, the HMS *Cordelia*, relocated to Australia from the China Station, was then sent to the islands to exact retribution. The command of the Australia Station was sensitive to criticism at that stage and so the *Cordelia* under Captain Harry Grenfell was ordered straight to the islands without first going to Sydney.

5. Liberalism, Imperialism and colonial expansion

On Rendova, the village of Lokokongo was burnt, at Simbo arms were seized and villages shelled, at Waisisi on Malaita where the schooner *Savo* had been attacked the village and canoes were destroyed. As the *Cordelia* had ten 6-inch breech loading guns the firepower would have been considerable (*The Sydney Morning Herald* 28 October 1890: 6).

Following all this destruction, the *Royalist* under Captain Edward Davis was sent to the Solomon Islands in May 1891 to avenge a number of murders committed in previous years (*The Queenslander* 19 December 1891: 1158–1159; *The Brisbane Courier* 15 December 1891: 6; Woodford papers PMB 1290 Item 9/13). The details of the voyage were described to the newspapers by Thomas Woodhouse. Villages in the Maramasike Passage in south Malaita were shelled to punish Malaitans for the murder of Fred Howard, the German trader who had lived for years in the islands. Howard was killed for blood money in Uki ni Masi off the northern coast of Makira. Coastal communities in Makira were then shelled in response to the murder of Sam Craig of the schooner *Sandfly* who had been killed at Anuta in retribution for the deaths of some Makiran labourers in Fiji. A local man Tamahine (Taiemi) was executed at the same spot that Craig was killed (Woodford papers PMB 1290 Item 8/21/6, 1891: 12). Then on Vella Lavella, the *Royalist* shelled the hill village of Ndovele because four crewmen of a trading vessel were killed for their heads by Tono, a local chief. Tono was later found dead in the village. Tono's war canoes, the construction and dedication of which were the purpose for taking the heads, were then burnt.

But it was the destruction wrought on the coastal communities of the Roviana Lagoon that was to cause the most sustained impact. The *Royalist* was anchored in Hathorn Sound between Kohinggo and New Georgia. Davis and his men in the ship's boats then proceeded to Roviana Lagoon but Davis could not secure the apprehension of the seven men from Mbilua on Vella Lavella wanted for the murders of William Dabelle, and the men from the *Marshall S*. Hiqava and his priest Wange were implicated in hiding the accused, so Davis assembled all the local *baṉara* on the evening of 24 September and warned them that their homes and villages would all be burnt if the men were not found. Davis and his men, including over 80 from the *Royalist* and the *Ringdove,* camped at Kokorapa on Nusa Roviana. When the wanted men were not handed over in time Davis landed at Munda. 'All the villages were destroyed, and it is to be hoped that these savages, the noted Rubiana head-hunters, who have depopulated all the surrounding islands by their cruel practices, will not soon forget their well-merited punishment', reported the *Sydney Morning Herald* (10 December 1891: 4). Davis later wrote in his report to the Admiralty that '400 houses, 150 canoes, and 1,000 heads were destroyed. In one house I found twenty-four heads ranged along one side, but it was too dark to see the rest of the house', but the marines could not find all the *tomoko* for the 'big canoes had been removed into the shallow lagoons, where, with the small force at my disposal, it was quite impossible to get at them' (Wright 2005: 288 and 2009: 230; *The Sydney Morning Herald* 10 December 1891: 4; Royal Navy (1886–1896), see Woodford papers PMB 1290 Item 8/21/6, 1891: 11). Sisiata, Hiqava's village in Kekehe district, was not damaged because he was on an apparently innocent fishing expedition.

Schneider (1996: 114–115), who undertook research along the Munda coast, doubts that the crew of the *Royalist* could have destroyed all the villages in the area and burnt the coastal village of Kalikoqu on the lagoon side of Nusa Roviana as well. He also casts doubt on the figures quoted by Davis and repeated by Jackson (1978: 101) that the men of the *Royalist* were able to burn such a large number of houses and canoes and were able to smash 1,000 skulls in the time they spent in the Roviana area. But Davis did destroy ancestral shrines, burnt canoe houses and ritual houses and removed a number of artefacts including one intact skull-house, a ritual food trough and a *tomoko*. Photographs of the action show smoke from burning huts among coconut groves and troops parading in front from canoe and dwelling houses, but not the widespread destruction reported by Davis (Macleay Museum, University of Sydney. Photographs from an original album from the Fiji Museum, Suva. HP87.14 images 11, 13, 21, 22 and 24). The artefacts taken by Davis are now in the British Museum, the Auckland Museum and in Germany (Wright 2005: 290).

Hiqava was supported by Norman Wheatley, a rival of fellow trader Frank Wickham. Wheatley supplied firearms to Hiqava and other chiefs at the same time other traders, like Kelly, Williams and Woodhouse, attempted to cultivate Hiqava's favour (Bennett 1987: 61). The interference in local politics by traders changed the balance of power in the region. However, it was indigenous adjustment that brought about the most profound changes to the local social structures. People on Nusa Roviana fled to safety on the mainland and the impact of this destruction was that the main centre of local polity at Kokorapa moved to the coastal communities around Kekehe. The actions of the *Royalist* certainly improved the political position of Hiqava relative to other local *banara* but his survival, in political and economic terms, was attributed to his having ancestral efficacy (Wright 2005: 291). These changes did not occur quickly. Suppression of head hunting, the aim of the *Royalist* expedition, was only temporary. Not long after the naval visit to Roviana, Hiqava was able to muster 500 men, 22 *tomoko* and two English built boats along with 300-400 rifles and 5,000 rounds of ammunition for a raid on Choiseul in 1894 (Bennett 1987: 91; Wright 2005: 291). Destruction of the power of the other *banara* meant that warriors coalesced to Hiqava and he emerged wealthy and powerful. Thus, when Woodford and Mahaffy began the final acts of pacification of the western Solomons after 1896, the centre of power had moved to the chiefly community of Sisiata and the power of the *banara* on Nusa Roviana had waned. But the Dabelle cases remained unsolved. Despite the long voyages, the cost of ship time, the cost of coal—30 shillings a ton, with men-of-war generally commanding 120 tons at a time—the murderers of William Dabelle and his brother were never captured (Woodford papers PMB 1290 Item 8/21/6, 1891: 19–23).

The *Royalist* then continued its six months cruise of the islands, in the meantime arresting the crew of the *Emma Fisher* for recruiting labourers without a licence (*The Australian Town and Country Journal* 2 January 1892: 45). The shipmaster, Thomas Woodhouse, had an expired licence but was in Sydney at the time. The temporary master of the ship was Robert Cable, now officially master of the schooner *Nautilus*, who had no licence to recruit at all. The *Emma Fisher* was towed to Suva and under the *Pacific Islanders Protection Acts* 1872 and 1875 the vessel, cargo and effects were condemned, or forfeited to the Crown by the Vice Admiralty Court (*The Queenslander* 19 December 1891: 1158–1159). The ship and its effects were sold for £400 (Woodford papers PMB 1290 Item 8/21/6, 1891: 48-61 and 8/21/7, 1891: 1–17). The cost of this action to the Royal Navy, and the bureaucratic time and expense incurred by the High Commission in Suva, while justified in law, was incalculable. The significance of this case is that the very people who had reported the killing of William Dabelle and who had complained about Royal Navy inaction the year before were deliberately and consciously breaking the labour recruitment laws at the same time. Peter Pratt's relations with the men of Mbilua, where he had damaged a *tomoko* in 1890, and with those in the Roviana Lagoon, whom he had cheated in copra buying deals, were primary reasons for the attacks on his station. Pratt was taken to Sydney by Captain Grenfell of the *Cordelia* to answer charges for his 'reprehensible conduct' where he was bound over to keep the peace for 12 months with a surety of £200 (Wright 2005: 283–284; *The Sydney Morning Herald* 28 October 1890: 6).

Not all Australian newspapers supported the Royal Navy's version of 'Commodore Justice'. The *Brisbane Courier* (16 December 1891: 4) compared the impact of the naval shelling of villages with the supposedly enlightened administration of Sir William MacGregor in British New Guinea. The paper stated that in British New Guinea 'it is possible to make friends of foes, even when they are ignorant, bloodthirsty savages, and by what methods it may be accomplished have been marvellously illustrated in the administration of Sir William MacGregor in New Guinea'. The only arms destroyed, according to the paper, were 'the arms of the turbulent,' and the supremacy of the administration has been achieved without loss of life. By comparison, Captain Davis on the *Royalist* almost without exception inflicted punishment on the guilty and the innocent by destroying villages and plantations. The revenge was also inflicted more than three years after the actual murders. The lack of concurrence between crime committed and punishment inflicted only accentuated the incomprehensibility of British law and order. It was, according to the *Brisbane Courier* (16 December 1891: 4), 'inconsistent with the patience necessary to find individual culprits and impress the natives with the scrupulosity of British justice'.

Return to the Pacific

In 1894 Charles Woodford made the decision to return to Fiji with the hope that he could secure an official position by being on the spot in Suva. Britain had declared a protectorate in 1893 over the southern Solomon Islands, excluding Choiseul, Isabel and the Shortland Islands which were German territory, but this political move was not made to secure the islands for commercial reasons nor to protect the local people. It was a strategic move designed to thwart possible French and German intervention into the Western Pacific. The Germans had secured the northern Choiseul, Isabel and the Shortland Islands. To the south, New Caledonia had been annexed by France in 1853 along with the Loyalty Islands of Maré, Lifou and Ouvéa. Wallis (Uvea), Fortuna and Alofi were then annexed between 1887 and 1888. Britain saw these moves as a challenge to their interests in Fiji, Samoa, Tonga and the New Hebrides. Although the idea of the appointment of a British resident had been discussed in the Australian press as early as 1888 (*The South Australian Advertiser* 11 January 1888: 5) and 1894 (*The Argus* 13 December 1894: 5) no officials were appointed to administer the British sector. Sir William MacGregor, Administrator of British New Guinea, urged Lord Ripon to transfer jurisdiction over the Solomon Islands to him so that he would then be able to control the Pacific labour trade but Australian newspapers reported: 'The expense involved in this appointment of resident magistrates on the islands, however, hinders the consent of the [Imperial] Government being granted to this proposal' (*The Queenslander* 23 February 1895: 352). MacGregor's proposal was never acted upon by London. The Colonial Office knew that a resident Deputy Commissioner was required to watch over labour recruiting and to stop the trade in firearms that were being shipped from Sydney in boxes labelled hollowware, but they prevaricated. Criticism by Bishop John Richardson Selwyn in a speech to the Royal Colonial Institute that the office of the High Commission in Suva had failed to protect both local people and missionaries in the islands embarrassed the officials (Selwyn 1894; Scarr 1973: 275). This, from a senior bishop of the established church before influential members of the institute, carried considerable weight in London.

Festetics de Tolna and the search for the exotic

Not all visitors to the Western Pacific were scientists, naval officers or missionaries. The Solomon Islands was becoming a popular tourist destination even at that time—at least for wealthy aristocrats. Comte Rodolphe Festetics de Tolna, an Austro-Hungarian born in Paris and married to a wealthy California heiress, began an eight-year voyage around the world in 1893 on his 76-ton yacht *Le Tolna*. After visiting Sydney they headed for the Solomon Islands and visited Santa Cruz, Santa Ana, Choiseul, New Georgia and the Shortland Islands (Festetics de Tolna 1903). De Tolna's visit to the islands is more than an interesting appendage to history. He made a considerable collection of artefacts from the Western Pacific that he took back to France and made some of the earliest photographic images of the islands and the islanders.

However, the Royal Navy was so concerned for the safety of the Count's vessel, which looked very much like a labour recruiting ship, that they had the *Le Tolna* follow them around the islands (Woodford papers PMB 1290 Item 8/21/11, 1895: 5–6). As he did not appear to be a man of much tact or diplomacy, or even good common sense, this probably gave de Tolna more protection than he realised. In the long Pacific adventure de Tolna took more than 400 photographs and obtained a large collection of artefacts. The exact number is not known but it exceeded 1,400. When the *Le Tolna* was wrecked, looted and burnt in the Maldives much of the contents of the ship were destroyed but a substantial amount of documentation survived (Boulay 2007). De Tolna's book is a mix of fact and fiction typical of that period. He called it *Chez les Cannibals* to appeal to an audience that could not get enough gruesome stories of the Pacific. In Roviana he met Jean Pascal Pratt whom he called 'le fameux pirate français qui écumait ces mers depuis plusieurs années, faisant la traite et des commerces prohibés': the famous French pirate who scoured these seas for many years, trafficking in prohibited goods. Hiqava was 'le fameux chasseur de têtes, vint solennellement render homage à la femme du chef blanc et déposer ses armes devant elle': the famous head hunter, who solemnly rendered homage to the white female chief—most likely reference to Queen Victoria—and laid his arms before her (Festetics de Tolna 1903: 347, 349). Actually, it was Peter Edmund Pratt who was the principal trafficker in prohibited goods, although his brother was implicated and it is doubtful if Hiqava ever solemnly pledged homage to anyone, let alone Queen Victoria. While on Choiseul, de Tolna joined a head hunting expedition and after a few days returned 'more than a little distressed' (Boulay 2007: 12). Wealthy travellers like de Tolna were slowly adding to an understanding of the islands although often from a perspective coloured by racial bias, a quest for only finding the exotic and strange and in almost complete ignorance of the cultures they were describing. The *Australian Town and Country Journal* (12 October 1895: 21) published an article on island massacres in the Solomons accompanied by a series of five photographs taken in Roviana that date from this period and may be associated with de Tolna and his travels in the region. The journal article refers briefly to Woodford, who was then Consul in Samoa, and his valuable book on 'native life and character not ascertainable by the ordinary trader or missionary'.

The Samoan imbroglio

When Woodford arrived in Fiji in October 1894 it was at a critical time in the relationships between Germany, England and the United States over control of Samoa, where international diplomacy and local chiefly rights had culminated in two civil wars. The Samoan situation led to some of the most intense diplomatic negotiations in Pacific history. Britain established a consular post in Apia in 1847, the United States in 1853, and Germany in 1861, but by the end of the 19th century commercial rivalry grew between the three powers. The key issue was the copra trade. Godeffroy und Sohn had established early trading posts in a number of Pacific islands after expanding from the original Valparaiso agency. The trading post in Samoa became the jewel in the crown of German commercial enterprise in the Western Pacific and Apia became an entrepôt for trade in coconut oil, turtle shell and pearl shell. Theodor Weber and other agents expanded the commercial operations with the purchase of plantation land, but it was Weber's invention of kiln dried coconut kernel that retained the essential coconut oils that led to widespread plantation expansion.

The dried copra was exported to Europe for use in soap and candles, and the residue was turned into cattle feed. This made operations semi-industrialised and more commercially viable than relying on native produced sun-dried copra which was poor in quality and unreliable in quantity. Godeffroy agents demonstrated the superior kiln drying techniques and encouraged islanders to use this method. This was part of Weber's commercial success. The German plantation economy, largely controlled by the Godeffroy firm, assumed as much as 70 per cent of commerce in the South Pacific (Kennedy 1972: 263). Godeffroy agents also sent artefacts from around the Pacific back to the Hamburg headquarters and these formed part of the famous Godeffroy Museum. When the firm later collapsed many of the 3,000 objects in the museum were sold off to other institutions in Germany and Europe, including the Museum of Ethnography in Leipzig. A collection of Australian and Pacific insects was obtained by the Museum of Victoria in Melbourne (Scheps 2005). The Godeffroy museum director, Johann Schmeltz, was a keen collector of human skulls from the Pacific and these were sold at profit to scientific institutions and museums across the world at a time when anthropometry was a major study (Buschmann 2000: 59). Even while dealing in the trade of artefacts and natural history, Godeffroy made it clear in business, and in his dealings over cultural and natural history, that the company was in the region for commercial gain and not moral justification (Bollard 1981: 5). The firm was willing to offer more credit to islanders than the inefficient, capital starved British traders, and although they charged higher rates of interest, they took land as security. The Godeffroy trade stores were also prepared to sell islanders arms and ammunition, alcohol and virtually anything else profitable.

Rapidly, independent agencies operating under the Godeffroy name were established throughout Samoa, Tonga, the Gilbert and Ellice Islands and in time extended as far as New Britain, New Ireland, and the Duke of York Islands (Bollard 1981: 4). Another profitable concern involved currency manipulation. Before the establishment of the gold standard and widespread use of the English pound sterling, Godeffroy und Sohn imported debased silver coin, mostly Spanish dollars brought cheaply in Valparasio. This was used as currency in many Pacific communities with the flow of money controlled by the Godeffroy head office. Currency bought at discounted value in South America purchased copra from islanders. When the islanders went into Godeffroy trade stores to buy goods they were then charged at the nominal face value of the coin with a resulting profit to the firm (Bollard 1981: 10–11). After Britain annexed Fiji in 1874 and subjected previous land transactions by early German settlers to close scrutiny, German commercial interests in the Pacific were seen by Berlin as under threat from British political moves. German traders looked anxiously at the situation in Samoa and Weber petitioned Bismarck, the German Chancellor, to claim Samoa as a German protectorate. Bismarck refused on the grounds that administering a colony in the Pacific would be expensive. Bismarck wrote on Weber's scheme: 'It all costs money' (Kennedy 1972: 265).

The severe economic depression that followed the Franco-Prussian War of 1870–1871 caused the financial collapse of Godeffroy und Sohn when the company speculated on the volatile German currency market (Bollard 1981: 16). The new trading company, Deutsche Handels-und Plantagen-Gesellschaft der Südsee-Inseln zu Hamberg (DHPG) formed in 1878 and assumed management of the profitable Samoan interests. The main threats to German commercial interests in Samoa were seen to be annexation of the islands by a foreign power such as England, irregular or curtailed labour recruitment for the Samoan plantations, and the unsatisfactory government of Susuga Malietoa Laupepa, the Samoan King. The problem for both the Germans and the British was that while Laupepa was pro-English, the Vice-King, Tupua Tamasese Titimaea, was pro-German. In 1883 and again in 1884, Laupepa petitioned Queen Victoria to make Samoa a British protectorate but these offers were refuted by the Colonial Office. In 1885, to force the abdication of Laupepa, German marines from the man-of-war SMS *Albatos* landed in Apia and proclaimed Titimaea the Samoan King. The action of the marines and Weber's involvement in Samoan politics were of considerable embarrassment to Bismarck at a time when Germany and Britain were in the middle of sensitive diplomatic negotiations over the question of spheres of influence in New Guinea. While Thurston, the chief British negotiator, privately supported German administration of the Samoan islands it was officially opposed by the British government (Kennedy 1972: 270, 274).

The political situation rapidly deteriorated. In 1887 Laupepa was exiled to the German occupied Marshall Islands and replaced by Titimaea with German military backing and support from his aristocratic Sa Tupua followers. Titiamaea insulted Samoan cultural protocols and this sparked opposition from the aristocratic Sa Malietoa families. The next year, Malietoa Laupepa's kinsman, Tupua Malietoa To'oa Mata'afa Iosefo, assembled a force of rebels and commenced military action against the German settlers and plantation owners. Iosefo was supported by the Scottish writer, Robert Louis Stevenson, then resident at Vailima on 'Upolu, and this further angered Thurston in Suva who had a particular dislike for Stevenson and his Pacific romanticism. During this rebellion the German consul and the German naval commander in Apia declared martial law.

During this Samoan debacle, Germany and Britain signed the 1886 accord which partitioned eastern New Guinea into British New Guinea and German New Guinea (Woodford papers PMB 1381/035a; see Whittaker *et al.* 1975: Documents D26–D36). German New Guinea included the northern Solomon Islands, but the most important gain for Germany was Bougainville and the neighbouring island of Buka. It was with this agreement that Britain reluctantly and unenthusiastically gained the right to declare a protectorate over the southern Solomon Islands. DHPG profitably gained access to the rich labour recruiting grounds of the Bismarck Archipelago and the northern Solomons, no doubt with much cheering among the powerful colonialist lobby groups in Berlin (Great Britain. Parliament. House of Commons 1886a). Not only were the islands seen as good recruiting grounds but Germany also gained access to the fine Shortland Harbour at Alu and much plantation land as well. Because the German traders were not constrained by the British firearms prohibition of 1887 that regulated sale of guns and dynamite, firearms and ammunition were dispersed widely through customary trading linkages from the northern into the southern Solomon islands (Great Britain. House of Commons. Parliamentary Papers 1887a).

By 1890 much of the Western Pacific had been carved up among the major European powers. Nevertheless, after 1888 the situation in Samoa again deteriorated. An attack on German sailors by Mata'afa Iosefo's forces led to his defeat, although this action was one of the catalysts for the negotiations leading to the Berlin Treaty of 1889. Few countries in the Pacific, in relative proportion to size and economic importance, generated as much inter-governmental correspondence as the affairs of Samoa at this time (Great Britain. Parliament. House of Commons 1889). At a conference in Berlin, Germany renounced any exclusive rights to Samoa based on commercial predominance and recognised the equality of rights of Britain and the United States that had by now built a naval base in Pago Pago after signing a bilateral treaty with the Tutuila chiefs (Kennedy 1972: 281). The three colonial contenders established the tripartite administration of Samoa under the Final Act of the Berlin Samoan Conference of 1889. This treaty was ratified in 1890 (Great Britain. Parliament. House of Commons 1890; Bevans 1968: 116–128). The condominium arrangements in place between 1890 and 1899 were attempts at remedying the crisis-prone imbalance of power existing between German, British and American interests. However, the arrangements lacked coercive powers and moral authority to succeed. The competing European interest groups only exacerbated the internal divisions in Samoan society for they nominated kings unacceptable to the strongest Samoan factions of the time (Campbell 2005: 67). The colonial governments lacked legitimacy. They were constituted by non-Samoans with little understanding of the internal dynamics of local communities and the condominium government itself was eroded by poor relations between Britain and Germany after the Jameson Raid in the Transvaal and by suspicions between the United States and Germany over strategic competition (Ellison 1939: 263). German colonial aspirations in Samoa were commercial. The United States saw its presence in Pago Pago as a defence position that would secure the neutralisation of the South Pacific in the same way that the military presence in Hawai'i neutralised the northern Pacific (Ide 1899). The American concept of neutralisation really meant maintaining the security of trade routes between the west coast of the United States, the Asian markets then recently opened to trade and the Australian colonies at a time of rapid growth during and after the Australian and Californian gold rushes (Anderson 1978: 45).

The condominium arrangements created administrative chaos. The Berlin Act established a municipality of Apia governed by a council of six non-Samoan members elected by the taxpayers and a President nominated by the three powers but appointed by the Samoan government. The Supreme Court was presided over by a Chief Justice and a three member Lands Commission was created. But the three consuls, German, English and American, could advise the President independent of the Apia council. The Samoan government, headed by the King, was officially autonomous but had little real power and no financial control (Heath 1974a: 39–41). The settler-controlled governments operated behind a Samoan façade. Again, the state of affairs in Samoa continued to be the subject of much diplomatic correspondence during this time (Great Britain.

Parliament. House of Commons 1893–1894). Henry Clay Ide, the American appointed to the post of Chief Justice between 1893 and 1897, would later write scathingly of German involvement in Samoan affairs while neglecting to comment on British involvement. He re-emphasised the fundamental purpose of the American presence in the islands as both strategic and, for Ide at least, moral. He wrote: 'Every other important group in the South Seas has been seized and appropriated by some foreign Government. Samoa was the only foothold open to us'. Furthermore, he stated: 'we cannot afford to make the slightest relaxation of the rights in Samoa that have been secured to us by the Berlin Treaty. "The white man's burden" in Samoa rests as heavily upon German shoulders as upon those of England and America' (Ide 1899: 686; Anderson 1978). Ide was certainly promoting America's Pacific destiny but he at least had the sense to call his paper 'The Imbroglio in Samoa', for indeed the political situation was a confused and muddied mess (Ide 1899).

Woodford's role in Samoan politics

Between 1890 and 1899 Samoa remained the victim of international rivalry that only further exacerbated the internal factionalism of Samoan chiefs. Mata'afa Iosefo was detained and exiled to the German Marshall Islands in 1893 following further civil unrest (Woodford papers PMB 1290 Item 7/60 and PMB 1381/019ix). A new rebel group then emerged in the rural areas loyal to Tupua Tamasese Lealofi-o-a'ana, the son of Titimaea. Thurston in Fiji was in a difficult administrative position at this critical time. The wife of the British Consul at Apia, Thomas Cusack-Smith, had recently died and Cusack-Smith himself was in poor health and requested leave (Foreign Office to Colonial Office 28 November 1894 CO 225 46 20667). Thurston needed to appoint an acting Consul. Despite the rather unfavourable opinion held by senior colonial officials of him during his brief employment in the Fijian service in 1883 and 1884, Woodford was the only man available in Suva. Both the Foreign Office and the Colonial Office considered the Municipal Magistrate of Apia, Mr Cooper, the only other local replacement, as unacceptable to the various factions. An officer from Fiji was requested (Foreign Office to Colonial Office 12 December 1894 CO 225 46 21621 and telegram 8 December 1894 CO 225 46 21332). Woodford believed that he would be offered the Resident Commissioner's position in the Solomon Islands on completion of satisfactory service in Apia and readily accepted (Heath 1974a: 37–38). As a result, Woodford was appointed as Acting British Consul and Deputy Commissioner in Apia on 24 December 1894 in a letter from Thurston with a certificate of appointment signed by Wilfred Collet following on 29 December (Woodford papers PMB 1381/008e–f).

His position was not well defined either by the Colonial Office in London nor by Thurston in Fiji although both aimed to secure peace and avoid unfavourable criticism by maintaining the status quo. But even the status quo was hard to define. In fact Woodford was advised by letter to 'do as little as possible during your temporary tenure' and not to be hurried into precipitous actions (Woodford papers PMB 1381/008e). Thurston advised Woodford that he would receive no consular salary while in Apia apart from his pay as an Acting Deputy Commissioner although his expenses, presumably including housing and allowances, would be covered from the consulate funds. The rules of engagement were vague. Thurston was opposed to any expansionism from New Zealand and wanted to avoid any quarrels with the Australian colonies but both Australia and New Zealand were uneasy over German politics in the Pacific. Most concern was expressed over German economic moves into the region for the government in Berlin was actively supporting the commercial aspirations of DHPG. The Americans were formulating their own version of a Pacific destiny by meddling in local affairs (Anderson 1978).

Woodford was keen for Samoa to be annexed by Great Britain. One of his first actions after arriving in Apia was to confiscate a shipment of 120 rifles hidden in hollowware and 25,000 cartridges of ammunition in paint tins destined for forces in Samoa loyal to the Germans (Woodford to Thurston 28 January 1895, WPHC 4/IV 30/1895; 20 February 1895 WPHC 4/IV 76/1895; Heath 1974a: 42–43). The arms and ammunition was seized, shipped to Sydney and then dumped off Sydney Heads (Thurston to Ripon 12 February 1895 enclosing Woodford to Thurston 28 January 1895 CO 225 47 5561). These weapons most likely originated in Australia. Sydney was the main source of supply for munitions illegally shipped across the Western Pacific on private and chartered vessels (Thurston to Duff, Governor of New South Wales, 28 February 1895 and Thurston to Ripon 12 February 1895 CO 225 47 5562). The problem was compounded by arms brought into Samoa by men returning from Fiji, but this was more difficult to control (Woodford to Thurston 22 March 1895 WPHC 4/IV 104/1895).

The petty internecine disputes between the colonial officials in Apia were the subject of Woodford's detailed monthly reports to Thurston and the Foreign Office but Woodford had a serious falling out with the American Consul, J. A. Mulligan, over American support for the rebel groups of Tupua Tamasese Lealofi-o-a'ana. When Laupepa, who had returned from exile in 1889, again offered to cede Samoa to Britain, it appeared that Woodford had achieved his goal but Laupepa did not speak for all Samoans. Woodford then arranged a reconciliation meeting between Laupepa and Lealofi-o-a'ana in 1895 (see Woodford papers PMB 1290 Item 8/23 draft speech to Samoan chiefs concerning peace negotiations). This was reported in the Australian and Samoan newspapers although the

Samoa Times (7 September 1895) was not especially complimentary about Woodford's actions, primarily because the editor considered Lealofi-o-a'ana a rebel who should not have been accorded any privileges (Woodford papers PMB 1381/019vi, 1381/019x and PMB 1290 Items 9/37 & 9/37/11). The editor assumed, sarcastically, that Woodford was no doubt driven by 'public good and not for personal aggrandisement only'. The *Brisbane Courier* (12 September 1895: 5) also speculated, '[w]hat effect the event will have on the political situation in Samoa can only be conjectured. In some quarters the reconciliation is believed to be merely a hollow pretence'. The rapprochement between the two Samoan chiefs was resented by Consul Mulligan and it was, in the light of future events, politically insignificant. German commercial activity in Samoa continued. German labour boats retained access to the recruiting grounds in the Gilbert Islands and the northern Solomons. In less than five years Britain would renounce any claims over Samoa in exchange for these northern Solomon Islands.

DHPG reorganised its Pacific operations in 1890s and reduced its number of trading agencies. The profitable ones in Tonga and the Bismarck Archipelago remained and in Samoa German plantations totalled 7,800 acres with 7,000 planted for copra. These commercial plantations in Samoa produced more than 2,000 tons of copra a year, a further 1,000 tons came from native plantations. Woodford remained convinced that 'Polynesian natives (using the word in its true sense and not as generally applied in Fiji) of these low coral islands are unsuited for the hard plantation work demanded of them … they rapidly fall away and die' (Heath 1974a: 47). He inspected a German plantation where Gilbertese workers had gone on strike but found their conditions satisfactory. He conversed with them in Fijian and their complaints concerning a preference for salt beef over fresh beef were resolved. The Gilbertese, called 'lazy, sulky, and subject to occasional outbursts of passion', were not considered good workers by the Germans (Woodford to Thurston 11 July 1895, WPHC 4/IV 235/1895; Woodford to Salisbury 8 August 1895 CO 225 49 17053 and Woodford to Berkeley 11 July 1895 CO 225 49 18391). He was also opposed to the capitation tax equivalent to 4 shillings per head per year imposed on all Samoans that had to be paid in copra not cash. On the other hand DHPG paid a capitation tax of 8 shillings per head in cash on the indentured labourers brought in to work their plantations. The capitation tax was designed to force native copra production.

In April 1895, Woodford wrote the annual Consular report on trade and finance of Samoa for 1894 that was submitted to Lord Kimberley at the Foreign Office (Woodford papers PMB 1290 Items 8/6 copies at 8/12 & 8/22). In this he wrote that the unrest in the islands was fermented by the small European population that consisted of only 400 people in a community of 30,000 Samoans. Trade had been impacted 'in consequence of the wretchedly unsettled state of the country' and as a consequence of this London was informed that local Samoans had neglected their communal gardens 'and steal from anyone who happens to be the fortunate, or unfortunate, possessor of anything eatable' (Great Britain. Foreign Office 1895: 14). The civil unrest had seen government revenues decline. Because the gardens were unproductive local people had to buy imported foods and consequently both imports of foodstuffs and exports of plantation copra had shown a marked rise. The increased trade figures therefore were indirectly due to the unsatisfactory state of local politics. The domestic disturbances as well as a regular steamer service to Sydney had made it possible for Australian traders to sell goods to Apia stores.

Despite the turmoil, tourism was adding to the local economy. Woodford noted that Samoans made money from posing for photographs and the sale of 'native curiosities' (Great Britain. Foreign Office 1895: 2; Woodford papers PMB 1290 Item 8/6). In fact, at this time many studio photographs of half-dressed Polynesian women with exotic captions were circulating in the islands and these were collected, reprinted and republished extensively (see Burnett 1911; Thomas 1992: 369). His report was surprisingly comprehensive for an Acting Consul with limited experience. Undoubtedly his time in Samoa was a probationary period but he appears to have passed with satisfactory reports both from some members of the press and from the Foreign Office in London. H. Perry Anderson of the Foreign Office wrote a personal note to Woodford to say he had been directed by the Marquess of Salisbury—the Prime Minister and Foreign Secretary—following a report by Consul Cusack-Smith, to convey 'his entire approval of your proceedings while in charge of Her Majesty's Consulate in Apia' (Woodford papers PMB 1381/016h). A personal letter directed by the Prime Minister, who was also the Foreign Secretary, to a temporary official in the Western Pacific was a significant gesture. But when Woodford returned to Suva in September 1895 he was forced to accept a clerical position in the Western Pacific High Commission. While disappointed he was at least in Suva and not in London. In the meantime he was appointed as Stipendiary Magistrate of Nadroga province in the Sigatoka district of Viti Levu (Woodford papers PMB 1381/008g). Woodford's eyes were on the prize: the Solomon Islands. First he had to convince the Colonial Office of the need to finance the position of Resident Commissioner.

In Samoa, the situation declined further following the deaths of Titimaea in 1891 and Laupepa in 1898. The second Samoan civil war and the siege of Apia resulted in the return to Samoa of the exiled Mata'afa Iosefo, but another candidate for the position of King appeared, the son of Malietoa Laupepa, Susuga Malietoa Tanumafili I. Samoan forces loyal to Mata'afa Iosefo ambushed British and American naval men and decapitated the slain sailors (Ellison 1939: 267). Reaction to the murders was bitter. Newspapers in the United States, England

and Germany denounced the actions of the great powers in Samoa as interfering, threatening and blustering, calling it the 'Samoan fiasco' (Chambers to Foreign Office 18 February 1899 CO 225 57 1480 Report by William Lea Chambers, Chief Justice of Samoa). At the height of the civil unrest in Apia the Kaiser wrote an impolite letter to Queen Victoria, his grandmother, informing her that the British bombardment of Apia 'may in the end lead to bad blood' (Ellison 1939: 276). This led to bitterness at the very top of the social establishment in both London and Berlin.

After years of intrigue and haggling, Britain, Germany and the United States announced a settlement to the Samoan question but Britain and Germany were set on separate paths of diplomacy and colonialism. These paths were to cross over other areas away from the Pacific, notably in South Africa. The Samoan debacle was resolved when the Tripartite Convention, signed on 14 November 1899 and again in Washington on 2 December, resulted in the formal partition of Samoa into a German colony and a United States territory (Scholefield 1919: 176 and see 324–326 for copies of the agreement; see also WPHC 4/IV, 218/1900; Foreign Office to Colonial Office 20 November 1899 CO 225 58 32244). Germany received 'Upolu and Savai'i and the United States took Tutuila and later the Manu'a Group. German newspapers proclaimed a great victory for Germany that had secured 'the cradle of her colonization in the Pacific' (Ellison 1939: 273; Great Britain. Parliament. House of Commons 1900; Bevans 1968: 273–277). The German Kaiser, Wilhelm II, was then proclaimed *Tupu Sili o Samoa* (Paramount Chief of Samoa) and Britain surrendered all rights in Samoa in return for the transfer of Tonga, considered a better site for a naval and coaling station. Most importantly for Charles Woodford, who was by then the Resident Commissioner of the Solomon Islands, Britain received the northern Solomon Islands of Choiseul, Isabel and the Shortland Islands. Woodford, on the HMS *Torch*, was then able to raise the British flag on all the northern islands that came under his control. The flag ceremony was held on Isabel, Gower (Dai Is off Malaita), at Ontong Java and Nukumanu, at Fauro, at the Shortland Islands, on Choiseul at Kondakanimboko Island in Choiseul Bay and possibly at Oema Island (*The Brisbane Courier* 14 November 1900: 6; *The Advertiser* [Adelaide] 26 October 1900: 5; *The Sydney Morning Herald* 27 January 1881: 8). The Tripartite Convention was to remain in place for only 14 years. At the outbreak of the First World War in 1914, New Zealand forces, assisted by Australian troops, occupied German Samoa. At the same time, Australian troops occupied German New Guinea. With that the German empire in the Western Pacific ended.

6. The British Solomon Islands Protectorate: Colonialism without capital

Thurston made a visit of inspection to Tonga, Samoa and the Gilbert Islands in 1893 on the corvette HMS *Rapid*. On 17 September, Wilfred Collet, Secretary to the High Commissioner, formally announced that the provisions of the High Commissioner's court and the consolidated Pacific Orders in Council were extended over the southern Solomon Islands (The Pacific Order, no. 78, 1893; Woodford papers PMB 1290 Item 8/4/1, *The Queenslander* 30 December 1893: 1253). The southern Solomons, while officially a protectorate since June, still had no administrative staff to enforce British law and order (WPHC 8/III Items 27 & 28). Thurston reported that it was not possible to establish a protectorate on so satisfactory a basis as existed in the Gilbert and Ellice Islands as no treaties could be made with local authorities and no local revenue could be expected to finance British administration in the islands (Scarr 1967a: 258–259). In fact Thurston had simply visited each island group in the Gilberts and appointed a tax collector to collect one dollar's worth of copra per year per adult man to offset the cost of colonial administration. This could hardly be called mutual agreement by treaty. Enforcement of the Pacific Order in Council was impossible in such a circumstance. In fact, British protectorate status in the southern Solomons only extended over New Georgia, Malaita, Guadalcanal, the central Nggela Islands and present day Makira and surrounding smaller islands. At that time, the protectorate did not extend over Rennell, Bellona, the Santa Cruz Islands, and the Polynesian islands south to Tikopia. These would not be added to the protectorate until 1898 and 1899.

The proclamation declaring the establishment of the protectorate was reported in the *Brisbane Courier* of 10 August 1893 and in the *Argus* and the *Sydney Morning Herald* in 22 August 1893. In May HMS *Curaçoa* and the HMS *Goldfinch* had left Australia charged with secret orders to raise the Union Jack in the southern Solomon Islands (Woodford papers PMB 1290 Item 8/21/9, 1893: 3–4; PMB 1290 Item 9/2/3; see PMB 1290 Item 9/24 for copies of the proclamations). The crews were to raise 30 flags starting at Mono Island in the north, continuing throughout the western islands and the on to the main southern islands. The *Argus* also reported an incident when the *Curaçoa* inflicted 'Commodore Justice' on the village of Abona (Ubuna) for the murder of a crew member of the recruiting vessel *Helena*. And so, during the formal ceremonies of gun salutes and flag raising, the Royal Navy continued its fine tradition of bombarding coastal villages. In Britain the newspapers also announced that the 'Solomon Island which have long been within the British sphere of influence have been placed under the protectorate of Great Britain' (*The Manchester Guardian* 29 July 1893). Almost simultaneously the *Manchester Guardian* (21 September 1893) reported that the HMS *Curaçoa* had both formally raised the flag in the islands and bombarded a village, location not given, and destroyed the principal huts. This was the same Ubuna village on the north coast of Makira mentioned in the *Argus*. To the local people British justice was both complex and contradictory (Woodford papers PMB 1290 Item 8/21/9, 1893: 14). In fact, there was some justification for the attack on the crew members from the *Helena* for they had been desecrating graves on the island (Bennett 1987: appendix 6). The rest of Ubuna area was then torched by a landing party after which the crew of HMS *Curaçoa* fired a 21-gun salute when the British flag was raised and '[m]any of the natives were so scared at the booming of the guns that they took to their heels and hid themselves in the bush'. The reporter for the *Manchester Guardian* reinforced British opinion of the inherent savagery of the local people by finishing the article: 'Tribal wars are very frequent in the islands, and about the time of the annexation one canoe passed nearly filled with the heads of natives who had fallen in the fight, and whose heads were cut off and carried away as trophies of victory'. These articles were a combination of fact and pure fiction but they fed popular imagination of the lawlessness and brutality of the islanders. At the same time the Melanesian Mission at Siota on Nggela Sule could proudly proclaim that it had 3,000 Christian converts (*The Sydney Morning Herald* 22 August 1893: 5).

Figure 22. Group of village people Uji (Uki ni Masi).

Source: PMB Photo 56–048.

Figure 23. Small canoe house Uji.

Source: PMB Photo 56–051.

The Solomon Islanders were often in the news for all the wrong reasons. The *Daily Graphic* (2 August 1893), a popular illustrated newspaper in competition with the *Illustrated London News*, reported on the establishment of the protectorate in a long article that paraphrased much of Henry Guppy's material with some poorly sketched illustrations of Gorai, his wife and son, Suenna village on Uji and some village houses from Fauro. The article declared: 'The British Protectorate which has just been proclaimed over the Solomon Islands, in the Western Pacific, is part of a slowly-developed scheme, the broad lines of which were settled ten years ago'. This was a reference to Australian colonial concerns about the expansion into the Pacific of the Germany trading companies and the aborted claim over British New Guinea attempted by the Queensland government in 1883. The article contained veiled criticisms of 'the tedious negotiations between the Imperial and Colonial authorities' to annex the north-eastern corner of New Guinea and the Bismarck Archipelago. This rendered the delimitation agreement with Germany necessary. The article in the *Daily Graphic* named Woodford as the source of an interesting shark cult on Savo but made no reference to his recently published book on the Solomon Islands.

The *Australian Town and Country Journal* of 12 October 1895 also ran a long article, this time illustrated with some excellent photographs of Roviana villages and people taken by William Lodder, an engineer on the steamer *Kelloe*. While the article began by saying that the purpose of the report was not to describe the numerous and brutal murders of white men by natives of the islands, and in particular those from Roviana Lagoon, 'the inhabitants of which are noted as the most fearless and warlike race in the Solomons', it went on to describe these murders in much detail. The purpose of the article was to highlight the 'extraordinarily beautiful appearance, magnificent fertility, and potentialities for future settlement' of the islands. The *Australian Town and Country Journal* was a well-respected newspaper published in Sydney that featured colonial issues, parliamentary reports and rural affairs. Obviously Woodford had been collecting articles about the Solomon Islands at that time for a large number of these cuttings and articles may be found in his archive (Woodford papers PMB 1290 See Item 9/38/2).

Woodford's commission of 1896

There was some confusion about the appointment of Woodford to the position of Resident Commissioner in 1896. Thurston wrote to Sir Henry Berkeley, the Assistant High Commissioner, about the possible appointment and Berkeley, assuming that establishment funds were available, appointed Woodford as Resident Commissioner in April 1896. However, the Colonial Office in London did not confirm this. Berkeley was notified that an appointment as Acting Deputy Commissioner for six months was acceptable but was not renewable. This direction was later repeated in a telegram from the Colonial Office forwarded by the Governor of New South Wales confirming that Woodford's appointment was for six months only (Governor of NSW to Thurston 2 October 1896, WPHC 4/IV 399/1896; Thurston to Chamberlain 20 October 1896 CO 225 50 26148). The Colonial Office was definite that Woodford, with instructions from Berkeley to inspect the southern Solomon Islands as a newly appointed Acting Deputy Commissioner, was to report local conditions only and not establish a permanent post in the islands (Heath 1974a: 50; WPHC 4/IV 115/1896).

Woodford left Suva on the HMS *Pylades* on 20 May 1896 and arrived in Santa Ana on 30 May (Rear Admiral Bridge to Berkeley 6 May 1896 WPHC 4/IV 146/1896). The *Pylades* then took him on a tour of inspection of all islands, expect Mono, in the north and Vella Lavella in the west, arriving back at Gavutu on 24 July (Woodford papers PMB 1290 Item 1/9 Diary of tour of duty aboard the *Pylades* 30 May to 10 August 1896). In June, Woodford reported to Thurston on the activities of traders in the islands and sent the letter to Fiji via the Burns Philp steamer *Titus* that he met in Marau Sound (Woodford to Thurston 6 June 1896 CO 225 50 17325). For a time Woodford even considered Marau a possible place for a government station. Accompanying the letter to Thurston was a draft regulation prohibiting any future freehold land purchases in the islands unless approved by the High Commission in Suva (Woodford to Thurston 6 June 1896, WPHC 4/IV 199/1896; Woodford to Thurston 26 June 1896 and Thurston to Colonial Office 21 August 1896 CO 225 50 21667). For some time traders and planters had been buying land from local people in exchange for cash and trade goods. There were few formal records of these land sales and those that existed were legally dubious. The tour of the islands was not without incident. In August, Woodford was distracted from his mission.

Figure 24. HMS *Pylades*, 1884.

Source: Australian War Memorial (www.awm.gov.au/collection/302246).

International attention: The murder of Baron von Norbeck

In his brief diary written during the *Pylades* voyage Woodford noted that he met with the captain of the Austrian survey ship SMS *Albatros* at anchor off Guadalcanal and was informed that a party of 30 men were planning an expedition to the Lion's Head in the interior of Guadalcanal (Woodford papers PMB 1290 Item 1/9 Diary 8 August 1896). Little further mention was made in the diary of this expedition of Austrian marines and naturalists but the results would create international exposure. The leader was Baron Heinrich Foullon von Norbeck, a geologist and Director of the Imperial and Royal Geological Society in Vienna during the Austro-Hungarian Empire. Described as about 50 years old, short, stout and not unlike the Prince of Wales (later Edward VII) von Norbeck was commissioned to search the New Hebrides and the Solomon Islands for nickel. Apparently the idea was that if deposits were found the Austro-Hungarian Empire would annex the islands as a colony. Von Norbeck left

Europe in late 1895 and at Sydney connected with the steam-frigate *Saida*. He was in charge of exploration parties and more than 30 surveys were undertaken in the New Hebrides without incident (Horthy 2000). No deposits of nickel were found but von Norbeck returned to the Pacific the following year to continue his investigations, this time on the *Albatros,* a barque-rigged wooden screw steamer of about 600 tons that had been converted to a surveying ship in 1888 and was based in the Pacific (Schaller 2005; *The Sydney Morning Herald* 19 September 1896). The *Albatros* also undertook detailed hydrogeological surveys of the waters between New Hebrides and the Solomon Islands. At Marau Sound, Oscar Svensen and the crew of his ketch, *Siskin*, were contracted to provide supplies to the main vessel and to the various landing parties (Veperdi n.d.).

On 3 August 1896, von Norbeck and a large, well-equipped exploration party landed near Tetere village on the north coast of Guadalcanal. Here three local chiefs, Saki, Billi and Jonny Parramatta—a man who had served on trading vessels to Sydney—set out for the Lion's Head along a route between the Mbalisuna and Mberande Rivers. Apart from the four local guides the party had no previous experience of the country inland from the Guadalcanal coast. The eight officers and petty officers and 16 sailors were heavily armed with either Manlicher rifles or with revolvers. At night, the well-provisioned party camped on the side of Mount Tatuve. On 10 August the parties separated on von Norbeck's orders despite concerns from the military leader. One group remained guarding the camp and stores while von Norbeck and the rest of the team continued to climb towards Mount Lammas. This group was attacked that day and the rear party was simultaneously attacked at the camp. Foullon von Norbeck had his skull crushed and four others died, including a young midshipman, Armand de Beaufort. Their bodies were left behind under cover when the exploration party retreated. Word was sent back to the *Albatros* and a relief party set off to find the wounded sailors still on Mount Tatuve.

Woodford at that time was in the middle of his tour of inspection of the islands. From Gavutu he sailed in Lars Nielsen's schooner, *Narovo*, and met up with the *Albatros* off Guadalcanal. Woodford first reported to Captain Josef Ritter von Mauler von Elisenau and then cabled the news of the massacre to Admiral Cyprian Bridge, Commander of the Royal Navy Australia Station, on the day that the international news broke (Woodford to Bridge 22 August 1896 CO 225 51 22666; Commander in Chief Australia to Admiralty 18 September 1896 CO 225 51 19711; Franks and Forrestier Smith 2001; *The Sydney Morning Herald* 18 September 1896). Woodford joined the relief team sent to retrieve the wounded. He then took part in a second, but unsuccessful, attempt to recover the bodies of the dead. This time he was accompanied by Fred Ericson, another trader from Gavutu. They found the bodies had been removed and were not retrieved at the time. Much later the remains were found on Tatuve by Dr Northcote

Deck from the South Seas Evangelical Mission when on an overland crossing of Guadalcanal (Woodford papers PMB 1290 Items 2/501, 9/25 and 7/36; *Daily Telegraph* 21 October 1910; *The Sydney Morning Herald* 12 August 1911: 5; *Advocate* [Burnie] 10 April 1936: 11).

Woodford was highly commended by the captain of the *Albatros* for his assistance and sympathies. Being on hand at the time and bearing his official title as Deputy Commissioner he appears to have smoothed over a rather unpleasant diplomatic incident (*The Sydney Morning Herald* 13 October 1896; Woodford papers PMB 1381/012). Woodford was not uncritical of the Austrian expedition and in his report stated: 'The Baron doubtless was an able scientist and a most estimable man, but something more is needed than this when leading an expedition into the forest clad mountains of perhaps the most ferocious people in the South Seas' (Thurston to Colonial Office 3 October 1896 CO 225 50 22808). Certainly the expedition was a disaster—the result of carelessness, inexperience and a lack of planning. Later the Austrian Emperor sent Woodford a jewelled box as a token of gratitude. A monument to the expedition was erected near Tetere village and Count Deym, the Austro-Hungarian Ambassador in London subsequently wrote to the Foreign Office thanking Woodford for his assistance with the erection of this memorial (Schaller 2005, Woodford to Jackson 26 March 1903 enclosing letter from Austro Hungarian Embassy London dated 23 October 1902 and report Woodford to Thurston 25 August 1896 WPHC 4/IV 351/1896; Deym to Lansdowne 20 May 1901 CO 225 61 18461).

The incident made the papers right across the region, not only because it raised diplomatic issues at a difficult time in relations between the British and the German governments, but also because many of the Austrians involved were gentry (*The Brisbane Courier* 18 September 1896: 5; *The Age* 18 and 28 September 1896; *The Advertiser* 18 September 1896: 5; *The Sydney Morning Herald* 18 September 1896: 5 and 19 September 1896: 9, 13 October 1896: 5; *The Queenslander* 26 September 1896: 581; *The Australian Town and Country Journal* 26 September 1896: 20, *The Argus* 28 September 1896: 5; see also Woodford papers PMB 1290 Item 9/31). Nevertheless, not all the papers were sympathetic to the plight of the Austrians despite their high social status. The *South Australian Register* (21 September 1896: 4-5) reported: 'This massacre will doubtless lead to more 'justice' and probably to further revenge, so that the danger to life [of white men] increases rather than decreases. The Austrians must have known what they had to face, and it is greatly to be regretted that they should have rashly incurred the risk of so lamentable a disaster'. Later in October, Woodford met with Captain von Mauler von Elisenau in Melbourne who informed him that the blame for the attack was placed upon Midshipman de Beaufort, who had been killed. De Beaufort had been asleep during guard duties on the night of 9 August when the party were camped at the base of the

Lion's Head and in the morning had ordered the men to pile their weapons but stand guard without them. For this, he would have been court marshalled and shot (Woodford to Thurston 30 October 1896, WHPC 4/IV 459/1896; Woodford to Thurston 30 October 1896 and Thurston to Chamberlain 9 December 1896 CO 225 50 1848).

The *Albatros* continued its survey work in German New Guinea and the northern Solomon Islands for another year (*The Sydney Morning Herald* 6 July 1897). During that time two fine harbours were located, one on Isabel Island and another on Choiseul. While Bougainville and Buka were the favoured recruiting grounds for German traders, the northern Solomons was seen as attractive for its harbours, labourers and potential plantation areas. Later Woodford protested at a proposal by the captain of the *Albatros* to make a second expedition to the Solomons. He made sure that the HMS *Rapid* was in Guadalcanal waters before the arrival of the German warship and that no shore expeditions would be permitted (Admiralty to Colonial Offie 28 April 1897 enclosing confidential report by Rear Admiral Bridge 20 March 1897 CO 225 53 9142; Woodford to High Commissioner 27 March 1897, WPHC 4/IV 144/1897).

The report to Joseph Chamberlain

On 14 September 1896 Woodford met with the *Pylades* at Ugi and was taken back to Gauvtu. During this time he again reported back to Thurston in Suva on regular intervals. Subsequently he sailed on the *Titus*, to Sydney on 4 October arriving on 16 October. In the meantime, Woodford had crafted his report to Thurston while on the *Pylades* and delivered it to him on 25 November (Woodford to Thurston 5 July 1896, WPHC 4/IV 292/1896; Berkeley to Chamberlain 21 April 1896 CO 225 50 12714). This report was then forwarded on 8 December 1896 to Joseph Chamberlain, the Secretary of State for the Colonies. The Colonial Office appeared impressed with the extent and content of Woodford's report for Chamberlain wrote: 'All these papers show that Mr Woodford is an energetic and sensible man who w[oul]d make a good resident [commissioner]' (Heath 1974a: 53).

Woodford's report was indeed a comprehensive and detailed document (Great Britain. House of Commons. Parliamentary Papers 1897b). He noted that there were 48 Europeans resident in the Solomon Islands including four missionaries but by the time the report had been published at least two traders had been killed. The nationalities of the resident traders varied: British, French, Norwegian, German and Swedish were mentioned. There were 21 trading vessels of various sizes. The exact number of traders and trading vessels was important for they were to be a source of taxation revenue. The question of

6. The British Solomon Islands Protectorate

finance was the most important one in the minds of the officials at the Colonial Office. Woodford recommended a capitation, or poll, tax of £5 per head for any European man aged between 16 and 60. Missionaries were exempt. Each trading station was to be taxed at £10 per station and ship licences for vessels operating within the protectorate were to be charged at the rate of £1 per ton to the maximum rate of £100 (Thurston to Chamberlain 8 December 1896 CO 225 50 1846). Vessels operating to and from the protectorate were to be taxed at the rate of £100 per vessel. Basing his figures on this Woodford arrived an ambitious estimated revenue of £1,245 a year (Great Britain. House of Commons. Parliamentary Papers 1897b: 20). When these new taxation regulations were published in the Australian newspapers they incited considerable criticism from traders and merchants both in Australia and in the islands (*The Queenslander* 7 August 1897: 253).

Woodford quickly realised that this revenue estimate was unreliable, certainly in the first years of establishment. He therefore submitted a revised set of figures below the original estimates. The anticipated poll tax revenue was reduced to £120, calculated at £5 per man based on a permanent resident white population of 22, the trading station tax was reduced to £120 based on £10 per station with 12 permanent trading stations and the 21 trading vessels of various sizes would earn around £350 a year. As there were only four trading vessels operating to and from the protectorate they were to be charge £50 per ship, earning only £200. Optimistically he also assumed that additional fees and fines would bring in about £30 a year. Total revenue would now be only £800. The four vessels operating to and from the Solomon Islands were the *Titus,* a 760-ton steamer built in 1878 and purchased in 1896 by Burns Philp based in Sydney, the *Chittoor*, a schooner, and the *Kurrara*, a steamer, both owned by G. J. Waterhouse, and the *Lark*, a schooner owned by J. Hawkins also from Sydney. Woodford believed that with increased fees the two sailing vessels would prove to be unprofitable and the two steamers would take over most of the traffic. The *Titus* began making between four and seven round trips from Sydney to the Solomon Islands from January 1896 (Burns Philp & Co 1883–1983 AU NBAC N115/72).

The Solomons (Revenue) Regulation of 1897 (Queen's Regulation no 3 of 1897) was published in the *Victoria Government Gazette* (no 52 Friday April 30, 1897) with full details of the head tax and the various fees listed. The title of the regulation, 'To provide for the raising of a local revenue in the British Solomon Islands', only partly described the reason for the imposition of taxation in the islands. By imposing a head tax and a trading station tax Woodford hoped that traders would increase the prices of shop goods and this in turn would force the local people to increase the production of cash crops, especially copra. It would also help to reduce the 'wild competition now existing' in local trade and force out 'the beachcombing class and their loss would not be matter for regret' (Great Britain. House of Commons. Parliamentary Papers 1897b: 20–21). When he returned to Fiji, Woodford again refined his revenue estimates. He proposed that the protectorate would earn only £120 from capitation taxes, £5 each from a population of only 22 permanent traders, and that the trading stations tax would be eliminated in favour of a ship licence fee of £10 per vessel that would include the trading station licence. This would hopefully earn the administration £550 a year. In addition, the estimated revenue from fees, fines and registrations would remain at £30. Total revenue was now to be £700.

In his covering letter to Joseph Chamberlain, Thurston yet again revised the scheme of taxation proposed for the protectorate. He submitted estimates of revenue based on a £5 capitation tax on adult non-native males, not being ministers of religion, a trading station tax of £10 and a trading vessel fee of £1 per ton. Open boats also would be charged at £1 per ton based on carrying capacity. Thurston believed revenue would now amount to £820 a year. All the figures indicate that the internal trading system was highly unstable and market driven. In 1898 the revenue regulation was amended slightly to correct any anomalies in fees imposed on recruiting and returning labour vessels (Queen's Regulation no 1 of 1898; 1 J. Soc. Comp. Legis. Ns 475 1899). There were no accurate figures for beach trading at this stage and movements of traders and their vessels, in and out of the protectorate, had not been recorded except privately. Few traders knew the details of their neighbour's business operations. In March 1897 Joseph Chamberlain wrote on Woodford's report: 'This really is a most excellent report and I think we should express our appreciation. Mr Woodford must be a clever and practical man and might I think be very useful in any Tropical possession which we want to develop. He should be kept in mind'. All things considered this was a most favourable report from the Secretary of State for the Colonies.

In the middle of his tour of investigation Woodford was caught up in a murder case that attracted newspaper attention. A trader on Uji, Edward Hamilton Wright, was murdered by local men apparently at the request of the local chief Rora (Woodford to High Commissioner 3 October 1898 WPHC 4/IV 343/1898). Woodford could come to no conclusion as to culpability despite interviewing local men including a native policeman who had returned to Uji. Rora was well known to visiting ship crews. He would often dress up in cast-off naval uniforms with strange decorations (Bennett 1987: 99; Festetics de Tolna 1903: 303). According to Bennett (1987: 98), Woodford confiscated these clothes from a recalcitrant Rora because he could not tolerate this aping of British authority. The report by Woodford to the High Commissioner does not mention this. He certainly found evidence of stealing on the island and Thomas Woodhouse, the 'Old Commodore' was now living there in fear of his life from Malaitans who came to trade copra. Woodhouse was by now a cripple having broken both thighs, the bones in one leg and his knee cap. He complained to Woodford that the Uji villagers were stealing his pigs and chickens. Woodford was spending an enforced stay at Uji as his cutter, his only transport, was being repaired. He found that the Eti-Eti villagers were implicated in the thefts and so with the sailors from the HMS *Goldfinch* he raided the village, shot 12 pigs and took away some food troughs and wooden drums. Valuables in the houses of the chiefs, Rora, Tomani and Tahio were also confiscated. Among these were Rora's uniforms and medals. Woodford reported: 'The chief Rora has indeed been quite a pet among the crews of warships visiting Uji and has been in the habit of appearing in complete naval full dress uniform covered with medals and orders of various kinds. The uniform I found in his deserted house and as I thought he would probably have no further use for it at present I removed it, leaving it with Mr Woodhouse to be returned to Rora in case of his future good behaviour' (Woodford to O'Brien 3 October 1898 WPHC 4/IV 343/1898). Presumably Rora receive his uniforms and medals later. There is no mention of anger at the aping of British formality.

Tulagi: Purchased in anticipation

In the meantime, and in anticipation of a positive response to his request for establishment of the British Solomon Islands Protectorate, on 29 September 1896 Woodford purchased the island of Tulagi, off Gavutu, for £42 (£15,600 in current values) (Woodford to Thurston 25 November 1896, WPHC 4/IV 474/1896). The deed of purchase was signed by Woodford and 32 local men representing land owners from nearby Nggela. Tulagi was ideally situated for a small government station. It was hilly, well covered in forest, had some good springs of fresh water, a high annual rainfall of nearly 120 inches (3,000 mm), faced the cooler trade winds, and had a well-protected harbour. Apart from some pockets of good soil in the small valleys, it did not have good gardening land but would soon be converted into coconut plantations and attractive domestic gardens. The payment, in gold, was divided between a local chief Tambokoro and his sons, who received £12 (£4,500 in current values), the village of Matanibana that had used Tulagi for garden lands was given £10, Haleta villagers were given £10, and Tugumata village was given £10 (£3,700 each in current values) (*The Manchester Guardian* 9 June 1897; Moore 2009b: 6). The £12 given to Tambokoro and his sons was the equivalent of three years' hard work for one adult male labourer in the Queensland sugar fields. Woodford's friend, Lars Nielsen, acted as a broker between Woodford and the Nggela communities who owned the island (Heath 1979: 79).

Tulagi Island was also a convenient three miles from Gavutu, the island owned by Nielsen. In all the island was about three miles in length by half a mile in width and about 800 acres in area (4 square kilometres or about 400 ha). Woodford reported that the island was hilly and a 'healthy site for a residence with extensive view is to be found at the east end of the island with an elevation of about 200 feet' (Great Britain. House of Commons. Parliamentary Papers 1897b: 24). He had obviously made a quick decision to buy the island when he was at Gavutu because Woodford wrote: 'I trust that in going beyond my instructions in the matter if purchase I have your Excellency's approval'. The decision could not be rescinded. The 32 local people who had signed the land sale had already been paid and the cash distributed (Woodford to Thurston 25 November 1896 WPHC 4/IV 474/1896). Woodford's Tulagi was set to become the headquarters for the British Solomon Islands Protectorate until the Japanese invasion on 1 May 1942.

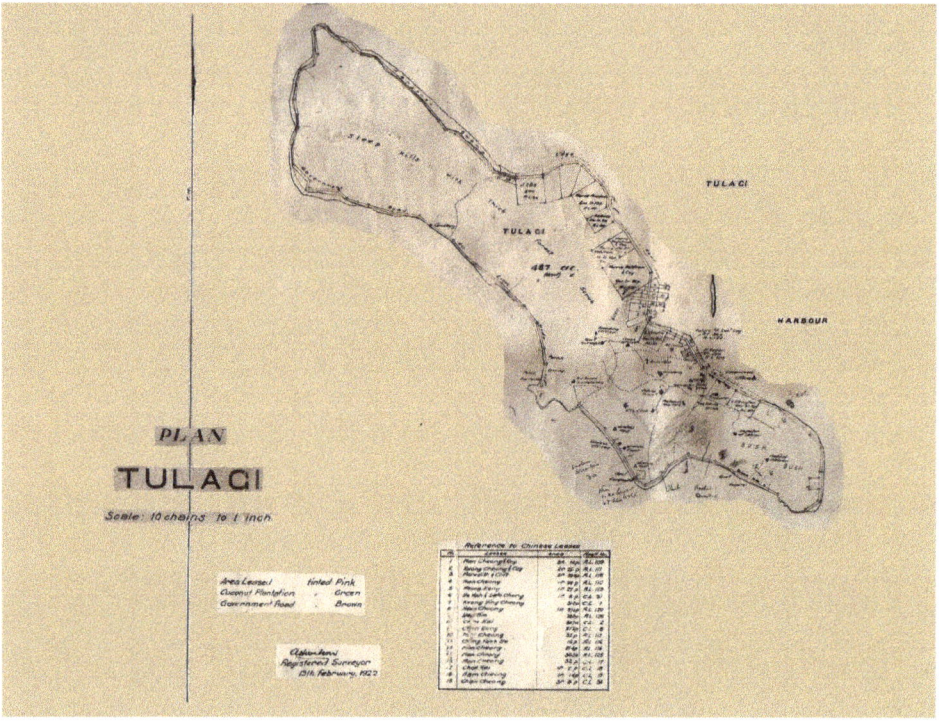

Map 3. Drawn 19 February 1922.

Source: Courtesy of Hugh Laracy.

Laws and regulations

Although Woodford informed the Colonial Office that, to the best of his knowledge, the sale of arms and ammunition had been discontinued, at least by the British traders, the transhipment of arms and ammunition was still a problem. On board the *Titus* returning to Sydney Woodford received an anonymous letter, posted to him from Port Douglas in Queensland, that stated: 'Sir-A Winchester carbine was sold at Sisipi [village on] Savo in June last year and paid for with turtle shell. Ammunition in large quantities [is] still sold, especially in places where men-of-war are not likely to call, for example, Tawatauna and Ubuna [both villages on] Makira-(Sd) Fairplay' (Great Britain. House of Commons. Parliamentary Papers 1897b: 25). Early in 1893 two regulations, *The Arms (Amendment) Regulation of 1893* (Queen's Regulation no 3 of 1893) and *The Liquor Regulation of 1893* (Queen's Regulation no 4 of 1893) were imposed to restrict the sale of arms, ammunition and explosives to 'natives of the Western Pacific' and restrict the sale of intoxicating liquors. Both were unenforceable. Woodford proposed that the administration offer a £10 reward for information leading to the successful conviction of anyone found trading in arms, ammunition, alcohol and dynamite. A regulation specifically addressing the issue of the sale of arms and ammunition in the Solomon Islands, *The Solomons (Arms) Regulation of 1897* (Queen's Regulation no 4 of 1897; 1 J. Soc. Comp. Legis. Ns 102 1899), was also published in the *Victoria Government Gazette* (no 52 April 30, 1897). Woodford and the High Commission in Fiji were certain that much of the arms, ammunition, dynamite and alcohol being sold to local people in the islands—like the Samoan case—originated in the Australian colonies. A later amendment would allow an employer to give a shotgun to a 'servant for a day to shoot birds, etc' but that too would have been practically unenforceable (12 J. Soc. Comp. Legis. Ns 388 1911).

Locally, Woodford's most urgent concern during this inspection was the possible introduction of cholera and smallpox from German New Guinea where it was causing deaths both among the native population and the German settlers (Woodford to Collet 10 January 1897, WPHC 4/IV 16/1897). Quarantine regulations (*The Solomons (Quarantine) Regulation no I of 1897* (Queen's Regulation no 1 of 1897); 1 J. Soc. Comp. Legis. Ns 102 1899) designed to prevent the introduction of contagious diseases such as cholera, smallpox, yellow fever and measles from the northern Solomons into the southern islands. This meant that all vessels were required to go to the 'seat of government [Tulagi] and perform quarantine till pratique is granted'. This included all vessels from German Pacific colonies and applied to trading ships, such as those of Burns Philp that entered the protectorate through German New Guinea.

While Woodford and Thurston had reasonably well grounded ideas about the possible taxation potential of a small island protectorate, the estimates for export potential and agricultural opportunities were rather unrealistic. In 1895 Woodford's estimates for export of produce from the Solomon Islands were 1,200 tons of copra, 585 tons of ivory nuts, 6.5 tons of pearl shell, 891 pounds of turtle shell and 8 tons of bêche de mer. Freight to Sydney by steamer was 35 shillings (£1 15s) a ton. In 1896 the figures were similar, and not spectacular: 1,400 tons of copra, 600 tons of ivory nuts, 9 tons of pearl shell, 1,400 pounds of turtle shell, and 4 tons of bêche de mer. Clearly the protectorate, with a maximum of 40 traders buying from local sellers where no productive plantations had been established, had limited economic potential. In addition the copra was smoke-dried, dirty and of poor quality. By comparison, the copra from the large German plantations in Samoa was sun dried, or kiln dried, and commanded a higher price. Local people sold dried copra to beach traders by the string: 10 full kernels or 20 half kernels threaded onto a string made from bush rope *(Hibiscus tiliaceus)* generally about 6 feet in length. This was purchased for one stick of tobacco at a cost to the trader of only one halfpenny. The profit was about £2 a ton.

People were honest in the dealings and advances of trade goods would eventually be repaid, but the concept of credit was unknown and could be abused by traders. Tobacco was the universal currency. Beside the trade in imported goods from Australia, many white traders also dealt in local currencies like dogs' teeth, porpoise teeth, whales' teeth, shell armlets and shell money from Malaita. A *Native Contract Regulation of 1896* (Queen's Regulation no 2 of 1896) designed to protect 'aboriginal natives of the Pacific' who entered into contracts with 'non-native persons' was in place. In essence the regulation meant that no native person could be sued in the High Commissioner's court in Suva but that natives could sue non-natives when in disagreement over money paid, labour undertaken, or goods supplied. While this regulation protected local people to some extent it also meant that they would not be able to secure credit. Traders would not lend money to any person who defaulted and who could not be forced by law to repay the loan. It was not until 1907 that the definition of a native was established in law. Under the *Definition (Native) Regulation of 1907* (King's Regulation no 3 of 1907) a native was defined, without much real clarification, as 'any aboriginal native of any island in the Pacific Ocean'. But any person of mixed descent, on the application of a parent or guardian, and 'who has abandoned native ways of life and speaks one European language' was considered a European.

Despite the potential few commercial plantations had been developed. The only plantings had been made at Gera (Mbara) Island off Aola, a small plantation of 30 acres near Aola and one at Marau Sound, all by Oscar Svensen. Svensen paid only £1 for the Aola plantation previously owned by the now bankrupt firm of Kelly, Williams and Woodhouse (Woodford to O'Brien 15 December 1898– 18 February 1900 WPHC 4/IV 48/1899). Lars Nielsen had a small plantation of 15 acres on Gavutu. 10,000 acres of land had been purchased by the Marau Company, Oscar Svensen again, between the Kaoka and Singgalia Rivers in east

Guadalcanal. Here the aim was to plant coffee, cocoa and bananas. There had been numerous speculative land purchases before the protectorate had been declared. Kelly, Williams and Woodhouse bought 50–60 square miles at Lungga on the north coast of Guadalcanal in 1886 for £60 paid in trade goods (Heath 1979: 82). Louis Nixon bought two islands off Nggela for £30 in 1881 but died that same year. John Stephens, the trader at Uji ni Masi, was also dead. He owned several thousand acres of land that was now left idle. In 1891 a company called Messrs Carpenter and Young bought land at Wanderer Bay on Guadalcanal but their aim was gold prospecting. Large tracts of land on the Guadalcanal plains had been bought by Joseph Vos, the former blackbirder and captain of the *Hopeful* and *William Manson* (Moore 1985: 43, 45; Wawn and Corris 1973: 295). This land between the Taivo and Mbalisuna Rivers on north Guadalcanal included the entire village of Tasimboko. These areas were never developed by Vos (Great Britain. House of Commons Parliamentary Papers 1897b: 8–9). The people of Tasimboko had been driven off their lands by raids from the inland bushmen in 1893 but after investigation Woodford found in favour of the remnants of the Tasimboko people and Vos's land claim was disallowed (Woodford to O'Brien 9 November 1898 WPHC 4/IV 12/1899).

As a result of these speculative deals, the first regulation relating to land acquisition was also drawn up. *Queen's Regulation no 4 of 1896* was designed to restrict the further alienation of lands in the British Solomon Islands (Woodford to Thurston 6 June 1896 WPHC 4/IV 199/1896; Butterworth and others 1897: 203; *Victoria Government Gazette* no. 115, Friday 20 November 1896). The regulation specified that land could be purchased from local people, leased from them or leased from the government but only after formal approval by the High Commissioner in Suva (Allen 1957: 35). However, the largest land speculator was Oscar Svensen who, between 1890 and 1907, bought 51,000 acres either from local people outright or from other Europeans who had failed in their plantation and trading ventures and who wanted to leave the islands (Bennett 1987: 143). Svensen would later capitalise on these purchases. DHPG also laid claim to areas of land on Kolombangara, Gizo, the Shortland Islands and at Tangarere, north of Wanderer Bay on Guadalcanal. When the company presented Woodford with a deed of sale for this land he saw it as a 'notorious and gigantic land grab' (Heath 1979: 86; Woodford to High Commissioner 3 July 1900 WPHC 4/IV 91/1898).

Copra was to be the only sustainable plantation crop in the islands. Ivory nuts (*Metroxylon salomonense*), a subspecies of the *Arecaceae* sago palm family and endemic to the Solomon Islands were, for a short time, used in Germany for buttons and as wheels for roller skates. The price in Sydney was only £5 a ton. Pearl shell was known to occur at Port Purvis south-east of Tulagi in the Nggela Islands and in the Manning Straits between Choiseul and Isabel Islands. At a time when pearl shell was becoming scarce in the Torres Strait it was felt that the

Solomon Islands would offer new collecting grounds. Turtle shell obtained from the villagers in the New Georgia islands was brought into the British protectorate after head hunting raids that ventured into German territory. Before firearm regulation, turtle shell was traded for weapons. The price: three turtle shells for one Snider rifle. At a time when the cost of one rifle was about £5 or the equivalent of 10,000 dried coconut shells (about 83 days of work) access to the Manning Straits was contested by rival chiefs in the western islands (Bennett 1987: Table 2, 81). Bêche de mer, also subject to market demand from Chinese traders, was collected in the Roviana Lagoon close to Frank Wickham's trading station. But the badly cured sun-dried product fetched poor prices.

Woodford supplied the High Commissioner with a detailed list of possible agricultural products that the protectorate could supply (Great Britain. House of Commons Parliamentary Papers 1897b). In addition to copra, the main market crop, Woodford felt that Para rubber would be a suitable product. However, local rubber production would never compete with the high-grade product secured from the commercially successful Malayan plantations. He also considered that sago produced from local palms would also be marketable in Sydney, but local production was mostly confined to the Shortland Islands, then part of German territory. It was also made by washing the pulp with seawater and putting beach almonds into the mix. While this may have been palatable to local villagers it would not meet domestic market tastes in Sydney. Quality sago sold at £8 to £10 a ton in Sydney but this was mostly used in the production of paper and some adhesives. It was unrealistic to think that a local produce could be transported and sold to a domestic market that had little use for the material other than as a thickening agent. Manila canes were also found throughout the islands and used for the manufacture of strong baskets but cane could be sourced elsewhere. Sandalwood was not available in the Solomon Islands and there was little accessible timber apart from trees found along the coastal strand. Sponges were considered a possible product but those collected by local people would only fetch one shilling a pound. There was no incentive to collect, process and then try to market such a commodity. The possibility of minerals, in particular gold, was also considered by Woodford. He felt that Makira and Guadalcanal had the potential to be good locations for gold prospecting and so he recommended that the protectorate have a set of mining regulations in place in case of possible exploration activity.

Establishment of the Protectorate

Following presentation of his report Woodford returned to Fiji to await the decisions of the Colonial Office about a permanent appointment. In February 1897 he wrote to Wilfred Collet, Secretary to the High Commissioner, complaining of the delay. He asked Collet: was he to be sent to establish a protectorate and then see it abandoned, was he to do the rough work at a labourer's wages and then hand over to another man, and did the Colonial Office object to him personally? All reasonable questions to a man impatient to begin and who wrote 'whoever they get I can safely say they will get not one who takes a greater interest in the place of more anxious to make it a success than I am' (Heath 1974a: 54). In the meantime Woodford moved with his family to Sydney and rented 'Trevenna' at 21 Billyard Avenue in Elizabeth Bay. From there he again wrote to Joseph Chamberlain at the Colonial Office requesting a permanent position as Resident Commissioner in the Solomon Islands. Chamberlain's reply only stated that his application had been read and noted (Woodford to Chamberlain 7 February 1897 CO 225 54 6068).

The Colonial Office remained ambivalent about establishing a post in the Solomons. In Suva local salary savings from the High Commission vote were used to pay Woodford's first year in Tulagi and 'Downing Street gave in to the excellence of his [Woodford's] reports' (Scarr 1980: 313). This argument over salary payments continued well into 1897 (Thurston to Chamberlain 12 December 1896 CO 225 50 1850). A coded telegram from the Lieutenant-Governor of NSW to the Acting High Commissioner on 15 February 1897 clearly stated that Treasury had made no authorisation for payment of Woodford's salary from the 1896 estimates (Lt. Gov of New South Wales to High Commissioner 15 February 1897 WPHC 4/IV 65/1897). In fact a grant-in-aid of £1,200 (£400,000 in current values) had been made by Treasury for the establishment of the protectorate but this had to include the physical construction of the offices and residency on Tulagi, salaries for employees for one year, including the six policemen recruited from Fiji, and the cost of a whaleboat (Coates 1970: 229). Scarr (1967a: 263) has estimated that with all expenses removed from the grant Woodford would have been left with just 6d to spend (Coates 1970: 220–239). Finally, on 17 February 1897 Woodford was formally appointed Resident Commissioner and he acknowledged his appointment in March (Woodford papers PMB 1381/008h copy of appointment signed by Berkeley 17 February 1897; Woodford to Berkeley 3 March 1897 WPHC 4/IV 83/1897). At the same time the separate Governors of the Australian colonies wrote to Berkeley acknowledging Woodford's appointment as Resident Commissioner in the Solomon Islands (WPHC 4/IV 93/1897, 112/1897, 123/1897; Woodford papers PMB 1381/008h). His duties were clear. As Resident Commissioner he was required to watch over the Pacific labour trade operating in Solomon Island waters and to stop the illegal trade in firearms that was destabilising the islands (Scarr 1980: 275). The mandate of the colonial state was consolidation of the boundaries, the protection of the people, their life and property, and the creation of a prosperous economic future. Apart from this fine moral philosophy the Colonial Office was only concerned that the Solomon Island protectorate be self-sufficient.

The Naturalist and his 'Beautiful Islands': Charles Morris Woodford in the Western Pacific

In March 1897 Woodford left Suva with his police and a 27-foot open whaleboat on HMS *Rapid*, her last patrol duty of a 12-year attachment to the Australia Station. This was to be her 'most exciting cruise' (*The Sydney Morning Herald* 20 September 1897: 5). On board Woodford had a whaleboat specially made for him in Sydney at the cost of £39, the 20 Martini-Henry rifles, 6,000 rounds of ammunition, a further 2,000 rounds of blanks, 2 aiming tubes and 2,000 rounds of aiming tube ammunition all purchased from the Sydney Naval Yards for £125/16/6- (Woodford to Berkeley 8 February 1897 WPHC 4/IV 42/1897 see also 38/1897 and 41/1897). The arms and ammunition that accompanied Woodford and the police was almost double that specified on the supply listing sent by Rear Admiral Bridge to the Admiralty in London. The Naval Yards in Sydney also charged almost four times the original estimates (Admiralty to Colonial Office 22 July 1897 CO 225 53 16013). Food and provisions to feed him, his police and any local workers cost £28/13/6- out of the financial allocation (Woodford to Berkeley 20 March 1897 WPHC 4/IV 133/1897). The *Rapid* took Woodford to Gavutu and then, accompanied by Woodford, made the annual visit of a British man-of-war to the Solomon Islands where the sailors avenged the deaths of traders at Rendova, New Georgia, Nggatokae and Vella Lavella. The warship then met with the Burns Philp steamer, the *Titus,* at Gavutu. The group of Fijian police—most likely Solomon Islanders trained as police in Fiji— arrived later on the HMS *Torch*. But even company steamers needed checking. The *Titus* was found to be carrying arms and ammunition for Peter Edmund Pratt who was cautioned by Woodford (Woodford to Berkeley 8 February 1897 WPHC 4/IV 43/1897). Also on board were whaleboats that traders were now selling to local people to replace *tomoko*. The crew of the *Rapid* also took away a large wooden carving said to be 'a hideous wooden god with shining and monstrous eyes', most likely a *beku* carving of an ancestor or chief, and a war canoe seized from Vella Lavella. Both were given to the British Museum (*The Sydney Morning Herald* 20 September 1897: 5). British colonialism had arrived.

A journalist reports on the establishment

On its regular calls to trading stations in Papua, the Bismarck Archipelago and the Solomon Islands, the *Titus* now called at Gavutu. A passenger on the May, June and July cruise in 1897 was a special correspondent from the *North Queensland Register* (21 July 1897: 12–13) in Townsville who later filed a long and rather poetic report on the Solomon Islands. Passing through the Hathorn Sound and the Diamond Narrows separating Kohinggo and Vonavona (Parara) from the main island of New Georgia, on the way south towards Rendova, the reporter, like Woodford and Somerville before him, wrote eloquently: 'On both sides [of the passage] the bare coral reef could be discerned projecting into the water and dropping off perpendicularly to many fathoms in depth, creating the impression as of artificial walls'. Entering the Roviana Lagoon he reported: 'What appeared a continuous stretch of land ahead dissolved into hundreds of picturesque islands'. These are the outer barrier islands of the long lagoon that stretches from Nusa Roviana and Honiavasa to Rereghana, Ndora and Petani Islands. Along the shore of both the islands and on the mainland were numerous settlements but most were concentrated along the Munda shoreline.

The Titus was making the circular voyage profitable for Burns Philp for under the new regulations enforced by Woodford the cost of £100 a year for a ship licence was forcing the smaller and slower schooner trade out of business. Steamers had the ability to carry more cargo and passengers and were charged the same ship licence as other vessels. The *Titus* called at the trading stations of Norman Wheatley Frank Wickham in the Roviana Lagoon. The schooner, *Chittoor*, belonging to G. J. Waterhouse was also anchored off Nusa Zonga. The new fees imposed by the administration included the ships' licence for trading vessels from Sydney, plus a fee of £3 per passenger and £5 for each small boat carried on the schooner or steamer. For local traders a fee of £1 a ton based on carrying capacity of the vessel applied. Each station had to pay £10 for a trading licence and there was a head tax of £5 for each permanent non-native resident. Vessels like the *Titus* coming south from German New Guinea were quarantined for three weeks at Gavutu or had to pass back to Australia via German New Guinea. This was causing some disquiet among the old traders who, it was noted by the *Morning Post* (29 July 1897) from Cairns, now had to submit to strictly imposed regulations—the once free and easy days had finished.

When the *Titus* arrived at Gavutu on 8 June 1897 the reporter found the HMS *Rapid* at anchor in the harbour. By then Lars Nielsen on Gavutu had a well-established property, a fine house in a fenced paddock surrounded by coconut trees with the island connected to nearby Tanambogo by a stone causeway. He had a comfortable house, copra sheds, small plantation and a trading boat. It was at Tulagi where the 'newly appointed Deputy Commissioner Mr C. M. Woodford intends to reside. At present his headquarters are Gavutu. He is a comparatively young man, but his experience on the islands has been a large one from 1886–89. He is the author of a valuable contribution to the entomological knowledge of the Pacific, called "A Naturalist among the Headhunters" but the ominous title covers excursions rather among bugs and butterflies than encounters with ferocious natives'. Woodford, the reporter continued, 'is gifted with that talent one cannot acquire, the ability to get on with the natives'. 'At present', the reporter continued, 'the entire Government staff consists of Mr Woodford, but by the cruiser "Torch" that comes to relieve the "Rapid" (the latter is going to Cairns), a secretary is coming up, and a troop of Solomon policeboys from Fiji'. The journalist's impression was that: 'Mr Woodford, [is] a quiet and unobtrusive man, with an iron will and a constitution of the same material ... he is of course handicapped, as his actions are controlled from Fiji'. The writer had little regard for Thurston whom he said represented the majesty of the law so well that local people looked upon him as 'Government incarnate'. When Thurston died in 1897 it was reported that the view of the people was that Government died with him (see also obituary in *South Australian Register* [Adelaide] 9 February 1897: 6 and list of appointments in *The Australian Town and Country Journal* 15 May 1880: 17). Thurston had the same complaint as Sir William MacGregor, according to the reports, and this was 'an overwhelming prejudice in favour of the natives'. Apparently, Thurston had the Roviana men make him a *tomoko* that was elaborately carved and decorated with shell but as Thurston was dead by this stage the canoe remained rotting on the beach at Frank Wickham's trading station on Hombupeka. The Special Correspondent was probably expressing local trader gossip when he remarked that the massacre of Foullon von Norbeck and party was muddled, a mystery and most likely due to their own foolhardiness (*The North Queensland Register* 21 July 1897: 12–13). Some of these comments were reasonably perceptive. They give a good description of the social, economic and political position of the southern Solomon Islands from the point of view of a causal visitor. The overall impression is that warfare in the Roviana Lagoon was coming to an end, that beach trading was the mainstay of the cash economy and that the administration was constrained by control from Suva and a lack of resources. His description of Woodford was accurate and his opinion of the ineptness of the Austrian exploration party was justified.

Building Tulagi

One constant theme underlying British colonial expansion in the Pacific is the reluctance of the Colonial Office and the Foreign Office to support further annexation of small island groups with few economic attractions (Overlack 1998: 133). Apart from the comprehensive report written to Chamberlain, Woodford's own impression of the establishment of the protectorate comes from the first, second and third annual reports for British Solomon Islands for the years 1897–1898, 1898–1899 and 1899–1900 (Great Britain. House of Commons. Parliamentary Papers 1898, 1899 and 1901; see Woodford papers PMB 1290 Item 8/7 and 8/13 for copies of reports from 1896 to 1904/05 & 1913). It is clear he was busy. The most important task was the physical establishment of a government headquarters at Tulagi. Woodford employed local villagers from the Nggela villages across the harbour, to cut timber and clear pathways on the island. Sites for the residency, to be located on top of the main hill, and police quarters were selected. During May and June 1897 Woodford and five prisoners and three local men lived in huts on the beach near the landing place. Each Saturday

Woodford and his prisoners, for there was no jail, travelled back to Gavutu for the weekend (*The Sydney Mail* 8 March 1911 shows a photograph of the bush material hut Woodford used as his first government residence; Woodford papers PMB 1290 9/24; Woodford to O'Brien 21 June 1897 WPHC 4/IV 305/1897). In June 1897 the eight police had arrived but they too had to live at Gavutu at the end of the working week.

The *Titus* from Sydney brought in a supply of cut timber and a carpenter on 5 August 1897 (Thomson 1899: 511 shows photograph of Woodford, the carpenter and local men unloading timber). The carpenter was employed to build the residency and jail. By the end of August the police, at least, were living in bush material huts on Tulagi (Woodford to O'Brien 10 June 1897 WPHC 4/IV 302/1897). Woodford reported to the High Commissioner on the slow progress of cutting trails, removing large trees and unloading timber. To this report he attached some photographs of the work that he developed himself, some taken by Walter Henry Lucas from Burns, Philp & Co who arrived on the *Titus* (Woodford to O'Brien 25 September 1897 WPHC 4/IV 507/1897). He was able to move across to his newly constructed house in November—this was built at the site of the first temporary hut—and at the same time the jail was finished and a permanent water supply for washing was installed (Woodford to O'Brien 24 November 1897 WPHC 4/IV 3/1898; *The Sydney Morning Herald* 23 December 1897: 5; Moore 2009b: 7). Malaria was a problem. The police and the carpenter all fell ill during the clearing work.

Figure 25. The Melanesian Mission vessel *Southern Cross* and the Burns Philp steamer SS *Titus*, Gavutu Harbour, 1897.

Source: Noel Butlin Archives Centre, The Australian National University, Burns Philp collection, N115–503–1.

Figure 26. Woodford's arrival at Gavutu, 1897, with SS *Titus* in background. Painting by Brett Hilder.

Source: Noel Butlin Archives Centre, The Australian National University, Burns Philp collection, N115–503–2.

Figure 27. 'Seats of Government in the Solomons'. Source: *The Sydney Mail*, 8 March 1911.

Figure 28. 'The First Government House'.

Source: WPHC 4/IV 507/1897. Photograph possibly by Walter H. Lucas but developed by Woodford.

Figure 29. 'Unloading timber for Govt. Residence and Lock up at Tulagi. Photographed by Mr Lucas SS 'Titus'. a. Resident Commissioner. b. The Carpenter'.

Source: WPHC 4/IV 507/1897. Photo developed by Woodford.

Pressing administrative matters intervened. Woodford wrote to O'Brien about the continuing illegal trade in arms and ammunition and the distressing accounts of dynamite fatalities that occurred when men used old explosives for reef fishing. At a meeting of all the traders of the newly established protectorate held on Gavutu, it was agreed that they would discontinue the practice of giving out trade in credit and to insist that 100 coconuts would equal 10 sticks of tobacco—an agreed currency of sorts. All trading disputes would from that time be handled by the new Resident Commissioner and as from 31 March 1898 all traders in the area would agree to pay their trade store, shipping and boat licences (*The Sydney Morning Herald* 23 December 1897: 5). By 1898 Tulagi was, more or less, the established site of colonial government in the protectorate (Great Britain. House of Commons. Parliamentary Papers 1899a: 12–13).

A boathouse and landing stage were built and some of the swampy north-east foreshore was partially drained and planted with coconuts. A garden of about 7 acres was established in the 30 acres of cleared land and a wide variety of food plants and ornamental plants were being grown there. This would be increased each year. By now local villagers from Nggela were bringing fruit and vegetables for sale to the small community. This compensated for the lack of good gardening land on the island. In the next annual report Woodford also announced that a house for an Assistant Commissioner had been started (Great Britain, House of Commons. Parliamentary Papers 1899a: 14–15). Woodford's first annual report concluded with a request for more police but Sir George O'Brien, the High Commissioner in Suva, in his covering letter to Joseph Chamberlain, rebutted that request by stating: 'Mr Woodford at the end of his Report refers to the desirability of increasing his police force, and of his being provided with a small steamer to facilitate his visiting the distant parts of the group; but as you are doubtless aware, the revenue of the Protectorate is at present barely sufficient to balance the existing expenditure' (Great Britain. House of Commons. Parliamentary Papers 1899a: 3).

The Imperial treasury grant-in-aid of £1,200 for 1897 was spent by March 1898 although the new protectorate had a balance of £460 in the Bank of New Zealand in Sydney (Woodford to O'Brien 7 August 1897 WPHC 4/IV 378/1897). This balance was not from savings made during the year but simply unexpended monies. Licence fees and capitation taxes would not generate sufficient resources to enable the protectorate to expand without Treasury grants (O'Brien to Chamberlain 5 February 1898 CO 225 55 3275). Judging from the annual figures the export potential of the colony was poor. In the 1897–1898 year only 1,600 tons of copra was exported. This would not improve until March 1900. Ivory nuts were unsaleable due to the poor quality of the product and competition from better quality supply in South America. The market fell from around 600 tons in 1897 to a mere 20 tons in 1900. Pearl shell rose due to better collecting methods, the use of diving suits—using white divers—and the rise in the value of gold lipped shell. Exports rose from a little over 8 tons in 1897 to more than around 16 tons in 1900. Turtle shell also showed a marked rise. About 400 lbs had been collected from locals in the western islands in 1895, but this rose to more than 3,000 lbs in the 1900 figures. It seems incongruous that as the demand for turtle shell rose, the administration was exerting a protracted pacification campaign against head hunters from the western islands, and head hunting raids were performed as part of turtle hunting expeditions.

The market in bêche de mer remained steady with a little more than 5 tons a year exported to Chinese markets. In 1900 a market for green snail opened up. The shell, like pearl shell, was used in the manufacture of buttons and jewellery. In the first year of exporting more than 31 tons were shipped overseas. This was not a stable commodity and, like the market in rattan cane, it soon fell away. The sale of plants—mostly orchids—fluctuated. Some indication of the volatility of the market for tropical products can be seen in the export of palm seeds. In 1897 seven bags were exported, in 1900 only one box was sent away (Great Britain.

House of Commons. Parliamentary Papers 1899a: 6, 1899:8 and 1901: 8). The figures would not have excited the attention of the bureaucrats in the Colonial Office or the Treasury in London. Plantation development was beginning. *Queen's Regulation no 4 of 1898* (1 J. Soc. Comp. Legis. Ns 102 1899 and Ns 475 1899) allowed for men to be removed from the Solomon Islands to work on foreign vessels but only with a permit from the High Commissioner in Suva. *The Solomons (Labour) Regulation of 1897* (Queen's Regulation 7 of 1897; 1 J. Soc. Comp. Legis. Ns. 102 1899) was designed to regulate the recruiting of labourers within the protectorate, and their employment both in the islands and outside. Labour ships had to be licenced and regulations were made for the inspection, feeding, wages and hours worked, treatment and repatriation of the labourers employed on plantations. While Woodford considered that most labourers were well treated and that conditions on labour vessels, and on plantations, were better than the 'sordid conditions' that existed in most villages, it was clear that this regulation did not give the administration sufficient powers to control abuses against workers. It would have to be repealed in 1912 and new, tighter, regulation implemented (Bennett 1987: 153).

Niels Peter Sorensen and the quest for gold

Speculators, beachcombers and miscreants still made trouble in the islands. In September 1897 the *Sophia Sutherland*, a former Canadian sealer under the command of Alexander McLean, left San Francisco on a trading and exploration cruise to the Solomon Islands (Laracy 2001). The attempt by this group of prospectors to search for minerals was a failure in large part due to the false hopes provided to the Americans by 'a man of notorious character' (Great Britain. House of Commons. Parliamentary Papers 1899a: 8; *The Sydney Morning Herald* 23 December 1897: 5). It was a spectacular misadventure. The unnamed man was Niels Peter Sorensen. He had convinced 14 Americans to finance a trip to search for copper at Rennell and Bellona, and for gold on Guadalcanal (Woodford to O'Brien 27 January 1898 WPHC 4/IV 84/1898). The scheme had been promoted to financial backers in the United States by the disreputable Sorensen who claimed to have purchased Mono Island from chief Mulekupa, a relative of Gorai of Alu. This was despite Mono being a coaling station for British men-of-war since 1884 and the fact that DHPG had purchased land there in 1886 (Laracy 2000). The term coaling station sounds grander than it really was. Essentially, it was just a pile of coal on a beach, hopefully covered from the sun and rain, and left in charge of a resident trader or chief. Likewise, DHPG had never invested time or money into plantation development on Mono. Regardless of the legality of the situation, Sorensen claimed ownership of the island for most of his rather pathetic life.

Sorensen had a criminal record in Queensland. He had been released from St Helena prison in Moreton Bay after serving a sentence for crimes of violence and robbery committed while running a pearling station in southern Isabel. Among other notorious dealings he was reported to have killed one local man and flogged another at the station. Captain McLean, warned about Sorensen by Woodford, was nevertheless issued with temporary prospecting licenses. The mineral quest came to nothing (*The Sydney Morning Herald* 16 February 1898: 4). To avoid the failed mineral explorers from lynching Sorensen in anger, McLean put him ashore on Gavutu leaving Woodford £5 for the fare to Sydney. Sorensen was living in a 'native hut on the mainland opposite Tulagi' and Woodford made sure a daily report on his activities was sent across from local villagers (Woodford to O'Brien 27 February 1898 enclosed with O'Brien to Chamberlain 2 March 1898 CO 225 55 8659). The malaria ridden crew of the *Sophia Sutherland* returned empty handed to San Francisco. The *Sophia Sutherland* had another brief claim to fame. Jack London, the American author, sailed on it in 1893 on a long Pacific seal hunting voyage that became, in part, the basis of his 1904 novel *The Sea Wolf* (Laracy 2000: 156; 2001). Later Jack London and his wife Charmain Kittredge London visited Tulagi and corresponded with Woodford over a number of years after they returned to the United States (Woodford papers PMB 1381/004a-d). London set his novel *Adventure* in the Solomon Islands (London 1911). But Woodford unfortunately was not finished with Sorensen. In June 1913 he again turned up at Tulagi reclaiming his rights to Mono. In order to get rid of him, once and for all, he was declared a person dangerous to peace and good order and deported (Laracy 2000: 161). He was a more notable example of the troublesome, beachcombing confidence trickster found in the Western Pacific at that time.

Massacre at Kaoka and retaliation campaigns

Meanwhile, Oscar Svensen had established a coffee plantation at Kaukau (Kaoka) near Marau but his plans for rubber had not met with success. For the land between the Kaoka and Singgalia Rivers he had paid porpoise teeth and trade goods to the value of £35 (Woodford to Thurston 5 September 1896, WPHC 4/IV 414/1896). But life in the islands was still precarious for isolated white men. Svensen's manager, Jean Pouret (Porret), a Swiss national who had been in New Caledonia, and two local men were murdered at Kaoka in 1896. Woodford, with six police and ten traders went to the area to arrest the killers (Woodford to O'Brien 25 September 1897 WPHC 4/IV 508/1897). Newspapers reported that three local men were shot and two were arrested. These men were sent to Fiji via Sydney for trial where they were imprisoned for ten years (*The Brisbane Courier* 21 October 1897; *The Queenslander* 13 November 1897: 960). Actually the traders shot two local men and by mistake almost shot police sergeant William Buruka who was accompanying Woodford. This was the start of the questionable practice of using local traders to support police, militia and government officers in punitive raids. Many of these police actions turned to ill-disciplined rabble with junior and inexperienced officials trying to manage aggressive, often drunken, traders and planters. Captain John Williams of the *Titus* was reported as stating 'the natives not only on Guadalcanar but everywhere pretty well are too insolent; they are not by any means the poor, benighted, suppliant creatures they are represented to be, but tricky, treacherous, eminently untrustworthy and dishonest and withal as cheeky as they make them' (*The Queenslander* 12 November 1897: 960). This sort of language would be used to describe local people right through the colonial period. This latent racism led to exploitation by traders, plantation labour abuses and, as a consequence, Solomon Islanders retaliated (see O'Brien 2009 for a discussion of similar attitudes in Papua).

Their retaliation then led to punitive campaigns that caused much death, widespread destruction and considerable enmity. One example of this is the search for Zito Latavaki after the attack on Jean Pascal Pratt. Pratt, also known as Jean Pierre Prat and Pascal Jean Pratt, in 1897 purchased land at Narovo on Simbo to build a trading station (Woodford to O'Brien 21 April 1897, WPHC 4/IV 185/1897). He was the brother of Peter Edmund Pratt. Late in December 1897 Jean Pratt was wounded when his schooner *Eclipse* was raided at Vella Lavella (Woodford to O'Brien December 1897 WPHC 4/IV 8/1898). Woodford only had a whaleboat for his official duties at that time and as the distance was far from Gavutu he did not attend to the case (*The Sydney Morning Herald* 23 December 1897: 5). Pratt was the victim of a failed trading agreement involving illegal arms and ammunition between his brother and Zito (Sito) Latavaki, a local *warane*. Jean Pratt was taken by his islander crew to Gavutu for treatment. He was treated by Dr Henry Welchman of the Melanesian Mission, the most qualified medical missionary based in the islands, in the small hospital at Siota on Nggela where many accident cases were treated (Wilson 1935). Pratt later died from a seizure, the result of the severe wound to his head. The hunt for Zito, the man considered responsible for the attack, would then become a major part of the work of Gizo District Magistrates.

7. Expansion of the Protectorate 1898–1900

In the early colonial period, economic and social disparities became apparent even if colonial rule brought some measure of peace and security to troubled areas. The 'lack of economic and educational opportunities, the alien and sometimes repressive nature of British administration and the failure of both government, and the Melanesian Mission, as the dominant mission of the area, despite taxes and church collections, to give them [the people] in return the means of achieving the economic, political and social equality with Europeans which they had been encouraged to expect' served to accentuate social inequality and island based disparities (Hilliard 1974: 114). This constant theme was to run right through Solomon Islander social, economic and political life into the contemporary period. The traders and missionaries were powerful agents for change in pre-colonial life in the Solomon Islands. But most of all it was the influence of large-scale labour migrations to the plantations of Queensland, Fiji and Samoa that generated, in the minds of Malaitans in particular, ideas of difference, disparity and discord. It was capitalism that created rich and poor Solomon Islanders.

In the meantime, the southern islands of Rennell, Bellona, Sikiana the Santa Cruz group and Reef Islands and Tikopia were proclaimed part of the Solomon Islands protectorate in 1898 and 1899 (1 J. Soc. Comp. Legis. Ns 475 1899; Woodford papers PMB 1290 Items 8/19/1; Woodford to O'Brien 17 & 18 June 1898 WPHC 4/IV 233/1898). The British flag was hoisted on the various islands by the HMS *Goldfinch* and the HMS *Mohawk* from the Royal Navy Australia Station (*The Sydney Morning Herald* 5 September 1898: 6; *The Australian Town and Country Journal* 8 October 1898: 30–31 shows photographs of the ceremony on Tikopia). When the HMS *Mohawk* was proclaiming Utupua as part of the British Solomon Islands Protectorate a young boy sought protection saying that he was being held there after a raid on a visiting cutter in which three traders were killed and the cutter burnt. The sailors from the *Mohawk* found the bodies of three white men in the bush and, in retaliation, torched a village (*The Australian Town and Country Journal* 9 July 1898: 7). Behind the pomp and circumstance of the proclamation of the protectorate, the ineffective and unsatisfactory process of 'Commodore Justice' continued. This southern expansion incorporated all the islands south to the New Hebrides—all far beyond the reach of the one man in Tulagi.

In 1899, following on from the tortuous negotiations over Samoa, the northern Solomon Islands of Choiseul, Isabel, the Shortland Islands, Fauro and Ontong Java (Leueneuwa) became part of the British Solomon Islands Protectorate

(Woodford papers PMB 1290 Items 8/19/2 & 8/19/3). With this proclamation in October 1900 Woodford finally had all 'those splendid islands' under his administration (*The Advertiser* 26 October 1900; *The Sydney Daily Telegraph* 26 October 1900; *The Manawatu* [New Zealand] *Herald* 21 November 1899: 2). The proclamation that the islands were now British was also announced in the Sydney press in an article by Walter Henry Lucas from Burns Philp illustrated with a photomontage of 12 images, 11 by Lucas and one of the ship's company raising of the British flag taken by or belonging to Woodford. The article states: 'In August last year Mr Charles M. Woodford, Resident Commissioner of the Western Pacific [sic] was commissioned by the Home Government to take formal possession of the new territory [the northern Solomon Islands]. In company with Mr A. Mahaffy, Deputy Commissioner, he proceeded in HMS "Torch" to Lord Howe Island, and there read the proclamation of annexation to the natives assembled, hoisted the British flag, the ship simultaneously fired a salute of 21 guns, and then three cheers were given for the Queen' ((*The Sydney Mail & New South Wales Advertiser* 3 November 1900: 1040 and 1051). Lucas also used this montage of his photographs and the associated article to promote the work of Burns Philp, the advantages of a steamer connection between Sydney and the islands and the benefits of the extension of the annexation over the former German territory. No doubt Lucas also wrote the final section that stated: 'It is of vital importance that these islands should eventually come under the control of the Commonwealth, and every advantage now gained by another nation in the Western Pacific is a menace to the future welfare of Australia'.

Arthur William Mahaffy

Smallpox in German New Guinea was introduced to the region by Malay plantation labourers from the Straits Settlements and spread quickly among the local people on the mainland and then across to New Britain. The Sacred Heart Mission priests condemned the *Neu-Guinea Compagnie* administration for their inability to stop the spread of the disease. When it spread to the Raluana Mission near Herbertshöhe (Kokopo) where the Wesleyan mission had established a base it made news in Australia (*The Sydney Morning Herald* 22 February 1897: 5). The introduction of quarantine regulations in the Solomon Islands meant that trading vessels from Sydney could not enter the protectorate from the German territory but the northern Solomons was open and unprotected. Woodford was located in the central Solomons and the attack on Jean Pratt at Simbo illustrated the inability of the one-man administration with only a whaleboat to respond to crises without assistance. Mahaffy, appointed as Deputy Commissioner, arrived in the islands in January 1898 and spent the first year at Tulagi and in travelling around the region (Woodford to O'Brien 30 January 1898 WPHC 4/IV 85/1898).

7. Expansion of the Protectorate 1898–1900

Figure 30. Government Residency, 1909.

Source: PMB Photo 56–12; see also National Archives of Australia NAA: R32, Sundry 1/12, 1909.

Figure 31. Sketch of Woodford's office on Tulagi.

Source: Woodford papers PMB 1290 Item 11/4.

Figure 32. Tulagi waterfront.

Source: Noel Butlin Archives Centre, The Australian National University, CSR Collection, N115–513–4.

He was an unusual man for policing work in such an out-of-the-way place as the Solomon Islands. The son of John Pentland Mahaffy, Provost of Trinity College Dublin, a well-known teacher of Oscar Wilde (Foster 1893: 397), Mahaffy was a very different character to Woodford although they appear to have worked well together. He had been educated at Marlborough and graduated as a classics scholar from Magdalen College, Oxford and then studied briefly at Trinity College, Dublin. He then joined the Royal Munster Fusiliers as a 2nd Lieutenant (O'Brien 2011). Prior to his appointment to the Solomon Islands, where he served from 1898 to 1904, he spent two years as District Officer in the Gilbert and Ellice Islands (1896–1898).

Woodford and Mahaffy began to recruit police from Malaita, Savo and from Isabel. They did not recruit from Nggela. It is assumed that he felt the people there were too much under the influence of the Melanesian Mission which had established a large training school and small bush hospital at Siota at the end of the Mboli Passage. However, the decision may have been largely personal. Woodford and Welchman had a disagreement over treatment of a young Roviana man who passed on an epidemic of dysentery that killed a number of students at St Luke's College (Hilliard 1978: 131). As a result, Welchman closed his small hospital and gave Woodford a dressing down that caused some bitterness between the two men (Wilson 1935). Mahaffy's reports to Woodford were detailed and descriptive although he only wrote one published piece on the Solomon Islands (Mahaffy 1902). However, before this he was to be Woodford's chief assistant based in Gizo with the primary task of suppressing head hunting in New Georgia and neighbouring islands (Scarr 1967a: 267, Golden 1993: 236–237). He would serve under Woodford for only six years.

7. Expansion of the Protectorate 1898–1900

Figure 33. 'Solomon Islands'.

Source: *The Sydney Mail*, 3 November 1900.

In the Solomon Islands the process of pacification began with retribution meted out to villagers during the annual visits of the Royal Navy men-of-war but local people had learnt to deal with this by retreating inland away from the coast and the shipping channels. 'Commodore Justice' as an exercise in power, had little real impact on local people. Much coastal property was destroyed but few people were killed in these actions. It was apparent that this official 'act of war' was both unsatisfactory in practice and improper in itself. But this was a point of view more frequently promoted by Royal Navy officers than by the High Commissioner for the Western Pacific (Scarr 1967a: 73). This type of pacification was enforced when European interests, trade or mission, were threatened. The Royal Navy took little active interest in the internal conflicts between warring groups. As most plantation development was now set to take place on the accessible coastal regions of Guadalcanal and New Georgia it was there that police action was concentrated. The presence of district magistrates supported by police changed the face of justice (Bennett 1987: 106–107).

Woodford and Mahaffy could not rely on the annual visits of the Royal Navy to take them around the islands. In 1899 a second grant-in-aid of £2,500 allowed the administration to build a second station at Gizo and buy the ketch-rigged yacht the *Lahloo* but the problems of using a sailing vessel in a region known for its gales and long periods of calm hot weather soon became apparent (O'Brien to Colonial Office 9 January 1900 CO 225 59 5939). The Gizo station was finished in January 1900 although clearing the site and cutting timber for buildings took time (Great Britain. House of Commons. Parliamentary Papers 1901: 13-15; O'Brien to Colonial Office 21 April CO 225 57 14091 and Treasury to Colonial Office 22 February 1899 CO225 57 4609). Mahaffy's salary was £400 a year. A further £400 was allocated for wages and allowances for extra police needed to maintain law and order in the northern sector of the protectorate (O'Brien to Colonial Office 20 April 1899 CO225 57 14089 and 30 September 1899 CO225 57 32175). The Solomon Islands, with a population of 60 whites in 1900 and with an uncounted but overestimated number of 150,000 local people, was a poor sister to more established tropical colonies like Fiji, Samoa, New Hebrides and Queensland. In economic terms, British New Guinea, undergoing an internal struggle for power following the departure of Sir William MacGregor, fared little better (Gibbney 1966; O'Brien 2009). To create an environment conducive to investment and economic development, the western islands had first to be pacified.

Mahaffy and his canoe-borne police force were quick to respond to incidents in the New Georgia area and '[s]o effective was this mobile force that by 1900 they had stopped head hunting from Roviana, Simbo and Mbilua and enforced peace among adjacent peoples' (Bennett 1987: 107). Mahaffy's long and detailed reports on his actions against head hunters in the western islands are included, with copies in Woodford's handwriting, in the archive of the Western Pacific High Commission (WPHC 4/IV 295/1898). They are sober reading. Not only for the details of head hunting activities but also for the direct and often ruthless means used by Mahaffy and his police in suppression of the activity. Much of the content of the reports was repeated in submissions to the High Commission and to the Colonial Office as part of the concerted efforts to secure funds for a steam launch for use by policing patrols (O'Brien to Colonial Office enclosing despatch by Woodford dated 27 August 1898 and report by Mahaffy dated 1 August 1898 CO225 55 25981).

By 1902 the Roviana and Marovo Lagoons, and the islands of Simbo, Valla Lavella and Ranongga had been largely pacified and so, after three years in the New Georgia district, Mahaffy requested six months leave. In September 1902 he also published his only examination of Solomon Islander life and culture in *The Empire Review* (Mahaffy 1902; Woodford papers PMB 1290 Item 7/18). Mahaffy continued to call the islanders 'treacherous', 'blood-thirsty', 'primitive savages, cannibals and head-hunters', although he did give them some credit for the 'black race make long journeys, as far as two hundred miles, in their great war canoes, which hold from twenty to thirty men, and are probably the most splendid purely native-built vessels in the world' (Mahaffy 1902: 192). Mahaffy advocated the importation of Chinese or Indian labourers for he considered the local labour force was unable to meet the demands of the assumed prosperous plantation economy then being established in the islands. His position on Christian conversion was conservative and presumably followed the official line. Mahaffy gave support to the Melanesian Mission approach of education first and conversion to follow. He did not consider the evangelical churches' position that faith and conversion should precede education as an effective solution for 'really primitive savages I believe that religion must follow, and follow slowly, the education of the people to a state of mind in which the truths of Christianity can be understood' (Mahaffy 1902: 195).

It is unlikely that Mahaffy's article would have made much of a splash in London. *The Empire Review* was a rather dreary magazine devoted to Imperialism and the promotion of the British Empire. Correspondents tended to be titled conservatives, many of them colleagues or friends of the editor Clement (late Sir Clement) Kinloch-Cooke. In Australia it was considered pompous and scathingly described as a monthly magazine 'founded to foster unity and provide a platform for the discussion of Imperial matters', but that 'most of the contributors are bigwigs with handles to their names, who have nothing particular to say and say it in ponderous platitudes' (*The Advertiser* [Adelaide] 16 March 1901: 8). After describing the islands in general and their poor climate for white men, Mahaffy wrote that the people 'have been known as the most treacherous and blood-thirsty savages in the Pacific; their ancient custom of head hunting has disposed of a large number of traders', without mentioning that head hunting had disposed of an even greater number of islanders as well.

Mahaffy noted that the war canoe he had confiscated from Kolokongo (Kolikongo or Kalikoqu) on Nusa Roviana in 1900, and used successfully in policing raids, could cover 12 miles in two hours with a crew of about 16 men (*The Morning Bulletin* [Rockhampton] 22 February 1900: 5, 3 March 1900: 6). The raid of Kalikoqu was undertaken on 21 January 1900 (WPHC 4/IV 56/1900). Mahaffy, Woodford and the police in two whaleboats left Hathorn Sound under cover of darkness. After stopping at Frank Wickham's trading station on Hombupeka they raided Kalikoqu village on the lagoon side of Nusa Roviana. Here they found the canoe that had been used in the Bugotu attack and confiscated it. The police were again permitted to remove any valuables they found. Following this raid Mahaffy and the police paddled back to Gizo in four hours (Woodford to O'Brien 22 January 1900 WPHC 4/IV 58/1900). Generally, *tomoko* carried a crew of between 15 and 20 men although some special ones were larger (see photograph McMahon 1918: 157). Mahaffy's canoe was 48 feet in length and once covered 90 miles in 24 hours with only two breaks (Mahaffy 1902: 192). This *tomoko* was then decorated by the police with white cockatoo feathers on the bow and stern, and blue and white calico was hung on decorated cross bars. Also on board the canoe was Mahaffy's dog Jack and when on policing patrols a flag with 'P.O. Jack' [Police Officer Jack] was flown (Officer 1901– MS 9321 Diary 17 April 1901). Graham Officer, when visiting Mahaffy in 1901, wrote: 'A native of Rubiana [Roviana] told me that these "extra" decorations were not usual because the rain & spray from the waves destroyed the appearance of the feathers" (Officer 1901– MS 9321 Box 4332/5). It was undoubtedly a local showpiece. The *Queenslander* (5 January 1907: 25) ran a full illustrated page of scenes from the western Solomon Islands that included images of Thomas Edge-Partington, Arthur Mahaffy and his dog Jack under the headline '"Repatriating" in the Solomons'. It was a report on the final repatriation of labourers from Queensland cane fields. The illustrations were a little out-of-date as Mahaffy was in Fiji by that date.

Mahaffy was not impressed with the use of the 'grotesque and hideous Pigeon-English' but no doubt he used the language for Gizo station had been built up by 1902 into a base for the District Magistrate and about 30 policemen (Woodford to O'Brien 14 January 1900 WPHC 4/IV 56/1900). Local people from other islands then began moving there to be close to a police centre, a trading post and other services. Most likely many of these people were from the groups of original owners who had been chased away during head hunting raids. Mahaffy acknowledged that 'head hunting has been largely diminished, if unfortunately, not quite stamped out' (Mahaffy 1902: 193). Certainly, the police actions were effective at the end of the intensive head hunting period. Schneider (1996: 109) notes: 'I regard the end of headhunting as the result of economic and cultural factors, in which Europeans and New Georgians played their different parts as agents of change. The coercive means used by the British Administration in the suppression of headhunting activities were not decisive factors'. Men did not give up head hunting until traditional enemies on Choiseul and Isabel began to retaliate against raids by New Georgians. Then within the lagoonal areas around New Georgia, and between groups in the offshore islands, like Vella Lavella and Simbo, internal conflict led to a spiral of violence in which people preyed on each other. The island of Tetepare off New Georgia was almost depopulated by the mid-1800s by raids from Marovo, Roviana and Rendova warriors, sorcery attacks and epidemics and the remaining people sought shelter in other communities on the mainland nearby (Hviding 1996: 109). Gizo people had likewise abandoned the island around 1830–1840 and the small island of

Mbava, off Vella Lavella, was deserted in the 1850s because the people were too few and too vulnerable to resist attack (Nagaoka 2011: 301). The loss of warriors who could not be replaced was also taken as a failure of spiritual support and a loss of *mana*—the loss of efficacy, success or potency. The link between politics and religion was broken and head hunting as an activity, and the power of the chiefs, declined (Schneider 1996: 116). Christianity undermined the power of the pagan chiefs and priests and broke down the traditional cycles of agriculture, feasting, prestation and warfare. The period of unrest and warfare prior to 1901 is known as *taem befo Lotu* (the time before Christianity) and the time after 1902, *taem bihaen Lotu* (the time after the coming of Christianity) (Wright 2005: 273fn). The year 1902 is a crucial date in the history of the western Solomons for many reasons.

Mahaffy trained his police recruits in military fashion—using his British Army experience—and selected men from islands like Malaita, Savo and Isabel that had felt the impact of head hunting. In this way they 'relished the opportunity to avenge their own people with Government approval and support' (Golden 1993: 236). At the turn of the 20th century, while newspapers in Australia continued to report attacks on white residents in the islands, the reports began to focus more on policing actions that suppressed raiding. The *Bathurst Free Press and Mining Journal* (14 February 1900: 2), a newspaper no doubt read by the family of Woodford's wife, reported: 'Head-hunting is still the favourite occupation of the Solomon Islander'. The paper reported that the 'abominable business is being put down by the Resident Commissioner, Mr Woodford, with a firm hand, and I [G. J. Wilson, a trader] venture to say that by the end of the year head hunting will be less congenial pastime with the Solomon Islander than it has been for so many years past'. Woodford, it reported, was 'the right man in the right place'. It was reported that during a raid by Roviana people on Isabel a number of young boys and a missionary catechist had been murdered and in retaliation Woodford and the police raided villages in Roviana where a senior chief and his son were killed. The major factor in controlling rival killings was the physical presence of police at Gizo and the rapidity of their response (*The Advertiser* [Adelaide] 14 February 1900: 6; *The Morning Bulletin* [Rockhampton] 22 February 1900: 5). This rapid response by Mahaffy and the police was a fundamental part of the pacification campaign. Jackson (1978: 133) interviewed Pula, Hiqava's daughter, who confirmed that her father had ceased to raid because Mahaffy and his team, using a confiscated war canoe, could live off the land, chase the *tomokos* into the shallow waters and respond quickly to incidents. But there were also changes to the social order and the spiritual world that altered people's perceptions. The impact of Christianity was profound as were the effects of epidemics that caused loss of life among the older generation.

The moral world was changing. It was only then after 'the backbone not only of the chiefs, but also of native culture and tradition had been broken' that people submitted to the orders of the government (Thurnwald 1936: 352).

The final ascent of Mount Lammas

Before the islands were pacified Woodford had one last goal—the ascent of Mount Lammas on Guadalcanal. There is little in the annual report to indicate just why Woodford undertook an assent of the interior range on Guadalcanal apart from it being a long cherished ambition (Woodford 1888a, 1889, 1890b and 1890c). It was the sort of ambition held by a naturalist. Guppy had been thwarted by malaria before he reached Guadalcanal. The possible montane flora and fauna that had not been collected before would make made another 'splash' at the National History Museum and at Kew Gardens. All Woodford's previous attempts, and those of the disastrous Austrian attempt of 1896, had commenced from the northern coast and across the Guadalcanal plains using the main river systems. This time the party wisely left from the Weather Coast in November 1898 (Woodford to O'Brien 30 November 1898 WPHC 4/IV 15/1899). Woodford was accompanied by Oscar Svensen, two white crewmen from Svensen's boat the *Sikiana*, two policemen, five Malaitans who worked for Svensen at Marau, Pauro, a local chief, and one other local man. Woodford had some advantages being the Resident Commissioner and familiar with the area instead of being an independent naturalist whose travels were subject to irregular shipping and the goodwill of the local people. Starting from Wanderer Bay the men headed up Cape Hunter (Vaghato) and then followed the Itina River, the largest catchment area on the south coast. Climbing through areas of moss and fern they came to the Churimelanga River that flows from Mt Popomanaseu.

From Popomanaseu, Woodford collected seed and orchids he sent to the Botanic Gardens in Sydney and collected orchids for display at Tulagi (Woodford papers PMB 1290 Items 2/108 and 4/16). He reported on the presence of wild dogs and native rats in the mountains and was obviously pleased to be back working with natural history for a brief period. They then found that they were climbing a mountain he called Balumanau (Mt Makarakomburu, 7,422 feet or 2,262 metres) from which, above 6,000 feet, they could see over the ranges as far north and north-west as the Russell Islands (Pavuvu and Mbanika) and Savo. From that point they would also have been able to see the Nggela Islands and possibly as far as northern Malaita. At the point where the party rested the peak of Mt Popomanaseu was to the east and more than 300 feet higher. After one week they returned to Wanderer Bay. Woodford reported that Mt Lammas, sighted and named by Captains Denham and Shortland, was known locally as Mt Tatuve (Great Britain. Parliamentary Papers 1899: 18–30). The peak he called Lammas is in fact known as Mt Toghatogha, one of the highest peaks in Guadalcanal (6,791 feet or 2,070 metres), and it is the Lion's Head, a much lower mountain, that is known locally as Mt Tatuve (4,931 feet or 1,503 metres). The long and comprehensive report of the expedition concluded with a letter to the Admiralty correcting map coordinates.

The climb appears not to have been widely reported (*The Mercury* [Hobart] 28 December 1898; *The Scotsman* 9 November 1899: 6). It was not until 1965 that further scientific research on the mountain areas of the high islands in the region was undertaken. Between July and December 1965, a group of 10 botanists and zoologists from the United Kingdom, Australia and New Zealand went to the Solomon Islands on what was called the 'largest and logistically most complex biological expedition' mounted by the Royal Society in the second half of the 20th century (Hemmen 2010). The aim of Royal Society Expedition to the British Solomon Islands Protectorate was to concentrate on limited areas of the unknown mountainous interiors and to collect specimens at various altitudinal variations. A small party climbed Popomanaseu and collected seed-plants from above 1,300 metres (4,265 feet). These were then identified at the Royal Botanic Gardens at Kew. Among the many species collected were rare montane orchids. Woodford, Svensen and their party collected flora and fauna samples from higher altitudes: among them rare orchids and Araucaria species (Corner 1969b). The finding of the Royal Society expedition was that there were significant botanical and zoological differences between the flora and fauna of the mountainous regions of the Solomon Islands and Vanuatu further south (Hemman 2010: S92).

'The true conception of our Empire'

At the end of the 19th century British colonialism was at its apogee. It was the Secretary of State for the Colonies, Joseph Chamberlain, who laid out the formal basis for British colonialism in a short, but important, speech given to the annual dinner of the Royal Colonial Institute in London in March 1897 (Chamberlain 1897: 228–239; *The Nelson Evening Mail* 31 (78), 2 April 1897: 3; Bennett 1962: 317–320; Bell 2007). Chamberlain made the Colonial Office one of the most powerful institutions in the British government and there was no greater champion of this Imperial expansionism than Chamberlain. The British, he stated, had a national mission to be 'a great governing race'. He spoke of the three chapters in colonial development: the first was when colonies were valued for their direct profit to Britain; the second was when dependencies were thought to be expendable and made to separate from the Mother Country; and the third, the 'true conception of our Empire', was when a sense of possession gave way to a sense of obligation. That obligation came with responsibilities, or as Chamberlain famously expressed it: 'You cannot have omelettes without breaking eggs; you cannot destroy the practices of barbarism, of slavery, of superstition ... without the use of force'. Thus, pacification was justified, for 'when these [colonial] conquests have been made there has been bloodshed, there has been loss of life among the native populations, loss of still more precious lives among those who have been sent out to bring them into order and peaceable habits'. While Chamberlain was speaking specifically about West and East Africa he could just as well have been describing pacification in the Solomon Islands or British New Guinea. The speech was greeted with enthusiasm by many papers of the day (see for example *The Queenslander* 10 April 1897: 772).

Journalists and public opinion

After years of negative publicity that focussed on fatal accidents or the latest murder the administration needed some good news stories. These would be provided by Ernest Favenc, a popular journalist and historian of that period who contributed to the Sydney newspapers, notably the *Evening News* and the *Sydney Morning Herald*. After an early career as an explorer in northern Australia he became a writer of local histories. In 1901 he made a circuit tour of the Solomon Islands on the *Titus* in which he visited all the main islands of the group. While the articles, titled 'To the Happy and the Unhappy Isles', were written in Favenc's melodramatic and florid style they provide a useful look at the developments that had taken place in the establishment years of the Protectorate (Favenc and Taylor 1997). His first point of contact with the Solomons was Svensen's trading station at Marau Sound that he called 'only a copra-house on the shore of Guadalcanar' and he soon tired of the coconut trees which he found boring and monotonous. As he had only just touched the shores of the islands he was not off to a good start. At Rua Sura Island off Aola he noted the development of the Marist Mission station and the small school that had been established there in 1899. He described a second trading station there, presumably a reference to Mbara Island. By then Gavutu was a prosperous trading station and coaling base for Royal Navy steamers.

Tulagi, Favenc noted, was the headquarters of the Resident Commissioner who joined the voyage. The *Titus* then hoisted the British Ensign with R. C. (Resident Commissioner) emblazoned upon it. The journey took Favenc to Savo, Marovo Lagoon and through Roviana Lagoon without incident. The area was so quiet that a prospective copper mine was being established on Rendova Island, pearling was showing signs of profitability and an unnamed entomologist who wished to search for insects in the jungles of New Georgia Island was set down at Roviana. The Shortland Islands had been handed over to the British Protectorate and plantations were operating on Poporang and Faisi Islands as well as at Siniasoro Bay on Fauro where he noted there 'is one of the oldest stations in this group, and a great deal of land has been cleared and planted with coconut trees' (*The Sydney Morning Herald* 11 June 1901: 8). The plantation at Siniasoro Bay was the home of John Champion Macdonald and his wife Melinda who had earlier contributed a collection of natural history specimens to the Australian Museum.

Favenc then paid a visit to Vella Lavella, notorious, he said, as 'the headquarters of the head-hunters who have nearly depopulated Choiseul Island', although he appeared disappointed that things were so quiet on shore. Much to Favenc's dismay the Roviana Lagoon had been pacified by mid-1901. The articles were now designed to be read by prospective settlers and planters rather than by people scandalised by the exploits of head hunters. Reflecting on the opinions of those settlers, Favenc made critical comments about the process of leasing land when he said: 'At present the control [of land in the Solomon Islands] is not altogether satisfactory. The Resident Commissioner is responsible to the High Commissioner at Fiji. More power should be invested in the Resident Commissioner, especially with regard to the granting of leases of land … the local Commissioner, who practically knows all about it, there seems no reason why this application should not be dealt with on the spot' (*The Sydney Morning Herald* 4 July 1901: 9). Now the allocation of land for plantation development and not pacification would be the most contentious issue between the administration, the planters and the local people.

Graham Officer from the Museum of Victoria

The Solomon Islands had been attracting the attention of journalists for some time but now it became the turn of artefact collectors. Graham Officer, a curator at the Museum of Victoria and a geologist by training, made an eight-month tour of the islands collecting 'curios' for the museum. Officer collected over 700 objects for the Museum of Victoria and also made a collection of butterflies, snakes, lizards and other natural history specimens including a number of large frogs. Baldwin Spencer, the Director of the Museum of Victoria, gave Officer £150 (about £12,000 in current values) to purchase artefacts and specimens. In addition to this, Officer took with him to the islands a well-documented list of trade goods that he purchased for £21/15/- (about £1,840) in Melbourne. The list provides an excellent example of the type of goods traded and their economic value at that time. He took 100 pounds (45 kg) weight of tobacco, one gross (144) of clay pipes, 2 gross boxes of matches, two dozen knives, one box of ¾ axes, 2 dozen small zinc mirrors, 2 gross of Jew's Harps, 120 yards of calico, one dozen shirts, two dozen undershirts (singlets), 20 handkerchiefs, and 4 pieces (about 60 yards each) of Turkey Red calico (Officer 1901– MS 9321). Considering the return steamer fare to the islands was £25 (£2,000 in current values) the money given to Officer to purchase objects was substantial (Vanderwal 2001: 109–110). On his return to Australia in August 1901 the press reporting on Officer's visit described the Solomon Islands as 'a happy hunting ground for the museum collector for most of the islanders are savage, nearly all of them cannibals and many of them insatiable head-hunters' (*The Register* [Adelaide] 5 September 1901: 6; *The Mercury* [Hobart] 2 October 1901: 6).

Officer was an elected member of the Royal Society of Victoria and a science graduate from the University of Melbourne. He had published a number of papers on the glacial geology of the Bacchus Marsh region in Victoria and on the geology of Lake St Clair in Tasmania but it is not clear why a geologist was sent to collect ethnological artefacts (Officer 1901– MS 9321 Box 4332/6). It was certainly life-changing. He noted in his manuscript on canoe manufacture: 'I spent 6 months in the group through the kindness & courtesy of Mr Woodford Commissioner, & Mr Mahaffy, Deputy Commissioner, I was enabled to enjoy experiences which seldom fall to the lot of the visitor' (Officer 1901– MS 9321 Box 4332/5).

Officer left Australia on the SS *Ysabel* on 1 January 1901, the day of Federation, and arrived in the Solomons in mid-January having been to Port Vila and New Caledonia. His primary goal was the New Georgia area but bad weather during the wet season forced the vessel to avoid Simbo and the Shortland Islands and to take protection at Roviana. Here Officer described the large canoe houses and grave shrines of the local people whom he referred to, in the common language of that time, as 'niggers' (Officer 1901– MS 9321 Diary 25 January). The *Ysabel* returned to Gavutu where Officer was surprised to find a splendid harbour with good wharves, store sheds and a fine house on the island. His first meeting with Woodford was cordial although he was disappointed to find his plans had to be changed: 'Mr Woodford came on board. Found Mahaffy had not arrived ... Woodford asked me to his residency on Tulagi next day. Says I will do no good at Gizo & Govt Yacht "Lalu" [*Lahloo*] is laid up having lost all her sails in a recent gale ... I am in a bit of a hole' (Office 1901– MS 9321 Diary 27 January). Like Woodford on his expeditions between 1886 and 1889, Officer was to find transport between the various islands his greatest hindrance. Inexplicably, he chose to go to the tropics at the very worst time of year: the wet season. Officer was impressed with the site of the residency on Tulagi and wrote in his diary: 'House on top of a knoll sev[eral]. hundred ft. above sea built as usual on piles 8 ft. high. Garden laid out—A most beautiful spot'. The residency garden contained a large range of both ornamental and commercial and must have been both extensive and impressive (Bennett 2000a: 386; Great Britain. House of Commons. Parliamentary Papers 1899a).

Woodford recommended that Officer visit Aola and start by making a collection of natural history objects for the museum. Officer's description of Woodford is well considered: 'Wdfd [Woodford] is a lithe thin man with finely cut features, slight moustache, firmly compressed rather thin lips, short incisive way of speaking, very uncommunicative but a man who is I think "not of words but of actions", was very kind to me & I feel confidence in his advice—'. On Woodford's recommendation Officer went to Lungga where Oscar Svensen owned a plantation of about 15,000 acres, then to the Catholic mission on Rua Sura under the management of Father Chatelet and two sisters from the Third Order of Mary. Finally, he moved in to Svensen's house at the Aola plantation and almost immediately he was supplied with insects, butterflies, snakes, and some cuscus. To Officer's dismay he was only supplied with these objects and he had difficulty in explaining that he was keen to collect artefacts as well. His local assistant was Pengoa, a man recommended by Woodford, whom Officer said 'seems [a] decent nigger'. It was obvious that the local people thought another white man, seeking the inedible and the no longer useful, was collecting insects and animals, especially if he came with a recommendation from the Resident Commissioner.

For most of early February, Officer's diary documents his tentative natural history collecting. But he soon found his specimens were eaten by rats and his cardboard boxes became mouldy in the rainy weather. Finally he sought out Woodford on Tulagi and received some immediate advice about collecting zoological specimens in the tropics. All February was spent at Aola and eventually Officer did collect some cultural artefacts from the region as well. In fact his diary of 16 March reports that he had collected over 30 stone axes from the Aola region alone. Eventually the *Titus* arrived off the coast. On board was Albert Meek collecting birds for Lord Lionel Rothschild's collection at Tring Park in Hertfordshire and three men—Johnson, Hardy and Martel—sent by Norman Wheatley to prospect for copper at Rendova Island (see Richards 2012: 154, 158). These were the prospectors referred to by Favenc. It would appear that Favenc, Meek, Officer and the prospectors were all aboard the *Titus* for the trip to New Georgia. As both Officer and Meek were collecting natural history specimens at Aola either man may have been the entomologist referred to by Favenc.

At Gizo, Officer caught up with Mahaffy who 'came off [in his canoe] with a crew of fine stalwart boys with lavalava and red turbans looking very picturesque' (Officer 1901– MS 9321 Diary 1 April). His impression of Gizo was even more effusive than his description of Tulagi. He wrote in his diary: 'This is the most picturesque spot I've seen yet in the Solomons. The view from the verandah [of Mahaffy's house] is exquisite. House situated on a steep knoll with gaol & boys' quarters surrounded by palisade & entrenchments in front'. Mahaffy was well protected against attack from any war party and it appears that the threat of attack was ever present. Local information concerned the exploits of Peter Edmund Pratt who was expelled from the Protectorate and fined £100 for trading guns and ammunitions to the locals and bound over with a surety of another £100 for good behaviour. Pratt did not leave the Protectorate impoverished. The sale of his property and ship to Norman Wheatley netted him £1,000, but he left his wife and children destitute. Woodford's comment was: 'The Protectorate is to be congratulated upon being at last rid of this most undesirable resident' (Woodford to O'Brien 7 April 1901. WPHC 4/IV 74/1901). Pratt may have been an unsavoury character but he had survived, even prospered, in an unstable environment for more than 16 years.

When Graham Officer arrived at Gizo, Mahaffy had just returned from policing work at Simbo. Officer then sailed with Mahaffy in his confiscated *tomoko* to Roviana to 'see what we can get in the way of native gear'. To bargain for artefacts Officer took along his trade box full of tobacco, calico and other items that he had listed in his notebook. The sight of the *tomoko* was not welcome. Peace was still only fragile. When they entered the Roviana Lagoon many of the villagers along the shore bolted into the bush but Mahaffy had the canoe pull into Sisiata where they met with Hiqava. Officer wrote: 'He seemed a decent old chap [and] was very friendly' (Officer 1901– MS 9321 Diary 17 April). When Hiqava died on 12 August 1906 during an influenza epidemic his obituary was published in *Man* (Edge-Partington 1907) and in the *Sydney Morning Herald* (13 September 1906: 6). He was called '[o]ne of the most determined head-hunters' whose prestige was dealt a great blow by the attack of the *Royalist* in 1891 but he was also known to be a 'friend to the white man, especially to traders'. Hiqava was a shrewd manipulator of traders, planters and then the missionaries and had made himself and his community wealthy by encouraging them to concentrate their efforts into the Munda area. Hiqava and Gemu, another chief, removed their skull shrine from Sisiata and took it to Kundu Hite Island in nearby Vonavona Lagoon (see photograph Aswani 2008: 184). There it was safe from souvenir collectors and well away from the Methodists (Schneider 1996: 52 appendix V; Wright 2005; Waite 2000: 126 see figures 1–4).

On this trip Officer bought a small canoe, newly made, that he said was beautifully made and inlaid with shell, for 10 feet of calico, 100 sticks of tobacco and a large knife. He appears to have sold this canoe to Martel, one of the three prospectors sent to Rendova (Richards 2012: 154, 158 and 161). The prospectors on Rendova were finding their expedition a waste of time. As a geologist Officer commented ruefully: 'A little geolog[ical] knowledge w[oul]d help these prospectors greatly' (Officer 1901– MS 9321 Diary 23 April). The new canoe sold to Martel may have been one taken from a police raid on Honiavasa in March 1901. Mahaffy's report states that it was paddled back to Gizo by a crew of eight men and so it would have been only half the size of a large *tomoko* (Mahaffy to Woodford 11 March 1901 WPHC 4/IV 156/1901). On Gizo, Mahaffy's police and canoe men were touching up Mahaffy's canoe and this gave Officer a chance to describe the process of making the charcoal and breadfruit paste used to blacken the hulls of *tomoko*. The canoe was made watertight with a caulking made from fruit of the *tita* tree (*Parinarium laurinum* syn. *Parinari glaberrima*) crushed with a stone (Officer 1901– MS 9321 Diary 29 April). Officer's archive also contains a long handwritten and unpublished paper on the manufacture and use of canoes in the Solomon Islands (Officer 1901– MS 9321 Box 4332/5).

Officer certainly experienced excitement during his brief stay in New Georgia. Accompanied by Mahaffy he travelled in the confiscated police *tomoko* to Kolombangara where they planned to climb to the crater of the volcano, a height of about 6,000 feet. Woodford and a party of 14 local men had managed to climb to 3,000 feet, half way to the top in 1900 but this time Mahaffy, Officer and 14 men estimated that they had made it to about 5,000 feet. The final section to the peak was considered too steep and difficult (Officer 1901– MS 9321 Diary 3–7 May; *Wanganui Herald* 19 September 1901). In late May, the *Lahloo* arrived but it was not there to cruise the islands. Mahaffy was planning another raid on villages on Ranongga where the men had recently returned from Choiseul with nine heads. The Ranongga men had allies in the war party with men from Vella Lavella who had already been disciplined for their part in the exercise. Officer joined the raid and on 10 June the party of 18 police and boat crew, Mahaffy and others left Gizo for 'KumbuKotta' (Kumbokota: Pienuna) at the north-western end of Ranongga (Officer 1901– MS 9321 Diary 11 June). They approached the village in two boats early in the morning but found that all the people had fled to the bush, having been warned in advance, leaving behind some large and some small canoes. Mahaffy had the boats broken up. Further along the coast they came to another larger village where they found two large *tomoko* on the beach. Officer took an ornamented head from a skull shire even though Mahaffy was much against it. This ornamented skull is now housed in Museum Victoria. Inland from the villages the gardens were damaged, coconut trees cut down and fruit trees cut and burnt. Later in July at Gizo, when he was packing to leave the region, Officer was approached by a man called Panangatta who requested the return of the skull from Kumbokota that he said belonged to his father, once the most powerful chief on Ranongga. Officer refused the request and packed the head into a box that he hid in Mahaffy's house and later shipped to Melbourne (Officer 1901– MS 9321 Diary 30 July; Vanderwal 2001: 110).

Officer obtained a large canoe from Mahaffy and later transported it to the Museum of Victoria. Rhys Richards (2012: 207–211) has traced the provenance of the canoe to Kumbokota where the canoe's name was *Mbatu-mbatu* (Head of the head or the pinnacle of success or sacredness). It was made by a renowned carver named Bilikei. The canoe measures 43'7" in length, 3'6" in the beam, has a bow height of 8'5" and a stern height of 10'5". It supported a crew of 18 men although it could carry 24 (Richards 2012: 212). This canoe, housed in Museum Victoria, is older than the one housed in the British Museum that was originally commissioned by Ralph Brodhurst-Hill around 1910 (West 1992: 277–278). Brodhurst-Hill was then stationed at Gizo and, being interested in the war canoes, had one made for him by Jiosi Angele from Vella Lavella. The canoe, some 11.3 metres in length with 11 ribs cut from a single piece of wood, may have been originally called *Lotu* (Christianity). William Lever paid £75 for the canoe and it was shipped to the Lady Lever Gallery at Port Sunlight in 1913. It has recently undergone 3D digital scanning and documentation and virtual restoration (Hess *et al*. 2009).

Following the raid on Ranongga, Officer made visits to Simbo and to the Shortland Islands where he stayed with the Atkinson family at Awa, the small island off Fauro, where they had a trading station and coconut plantation. By early August 1901, Officer was ready to leave the Solomons and had his large canoe taken off to the *Titus* but first the stern terminal piece had to be removed (Vanderwal 2001: 110). The pieces have since been joined back together. The *Titus* called in again at the Shortland Islands and Officer described the approach to Macdonald's plantation at Siniasoro Bay in some detail. Entrance Bay (Haliuna) was a '[n]arrow entrance into a good harbour surrounded by high hills. Very hot. Went ashore & found an extensive settlement in among fine coconut trees ... There are very few natives in Fauro altho' a large island. Disease (venereal) killed them off years ago' (Officer 1901– MS 9321 Diary 4 August). After a final meeting with Woodford on board the steamer, and a short stop at Marau where he met Oscar Svensen, Officer departed the islands on 13 August.

The *Australian Town and Country Journal* (7 September 1901: 38) published an illustrated description of a war canoe that Officer had obtained for the museum collection. The article reported: 'The Government have [sic] now prohibited their manufacture, and wherever they are found they are confiscated'. Head hunting was being suppressed by the destruction of war canoes and local people were buying whaleboats imported from Sydney. These whaleboats were now the government approved sea transport. Reporting on Officer's successful trip to the Solomon Islands The *Mercury* [Hobart] (2 October 1901: 6) noted that a large feast was being prepared in Roviana Lagoon at the time of the tour of the group and local informants had stated that it was 'to celebrate the "giving up" of head hunting in Rubiana [Roviana] Lagoon'. Arthur Mahaffy too was interviewed by the *Sydney Morning* Herald (24 December 1901: 6) on a trip to Australia and he took pains to report on the current stability of the islands, the economic prospects of the proposed plantation economy and the availability of local men for employment once the Queensland labour trade had ended. The newspapers in Australia were now turning their attention to the bright economic future that had been brought about by *Pax Britannica*.

Your new-caught, sullen peoples,

Half-devil and half-child

Rudyard Kipling published his poem *The White Man's Burden* in 1899 in response to the occupation of the Philippines by the United States. It is emblematic both of European racism of the era and Imperialist aspiration to secure the dominance of the vast unsettled world. At a time of active evangelical Christianity and expanding colonial boundaries, the poem was a great success. It typified two characteristics of the supposed savage man: he was both half-devil and half-child. It was assumed that all native societies lived in a state of constant warfare—head hunting, raiding, tribal fighting—and these were seen as the sole objects of indigenous men's lives. The half-devil and half-child had to be pacified, controlled and contained. The pacification process had a threefold purpose. It was not only justified in bringing peace for political control, it paved the way for economic development, and it was seen as essential for the expansion of Christianity in the islands. Peace made the half-devil safe, and Christianity made the half-child a member of the church brotherhood. Peace and Christianity combined to make the half-devil/half-child a useful worker in the economic development of the islands. If the pacification process had three purposes, it also had three goals and they were political, religious and commercial. But the three modes of colonialism were different.

First, the islands had to be contained. Catholic mission expansion on Guadalcanal had been hindered by raids on missions and in October 1900 it was reported that a priest had been burnt to death by a raiding party led by Sulukavo a 'warrior, cum bounty hunter or *malaghai*' (Bennett 1987: 108–109; *Sydney Daily Telegraph* 26 October 1900; *The Advertiser* [Adelaide] 26 October 1900). As a *malaghai* Sulukavo was paid by other Big-men to kill those accused of breaking social mores but he had been operating unchecked since the 1880s. In retaliation for the attack on the mission, Woodford and a party of 15 men, mostly from Savo, raided the deserted village of Tasule, inland from Marovovo on the north-west coast of Guadalcanal, and burnt down several houses. Attacks on missions on the north-west coast ceased. Later Sulukavo sold the area called Lavuro, near Marovovo, to a consortium based in Brisbane for a substantial price of '£20, 2,000 porpoise teeth, 200 dog teeth, 1 case of tobacco, 1 case of pipes, 2 gross of matches, 1 piece of calico, 2 knives, and 2 axes' (Bennett 1987: 117, 140–141). The Catholic mission at Visale on the tip of Guadalcanal then developed in peace. The Melanesian Mission built a hospital on 500 acres of land at Hautabu near Marovovo in 1911 and a theological college at Marovovo in 1916 (Boutilier

1974: 21, 52). However, the proximity of the Anglicans and the Catholics made the western end of Guadalcanal a 'scene of intense religious rivalry as each mission raced the other to secure the allegiance of confused and uncommitted villagers' (Hilliard 1978: 139).

The pacification process in the western islands continued for some time. Following first contact, the speed by which pacification occurred surprised government officials and other commentators. It was not a sign of passive acceptance of imposed codes of law and behaviour. Most Melanesian societies impacted by punitive campaigns were quick to realise the overwhelming coercive power of European police and government and saw pacification as a pragmatic step in the desire to acquire new economic, social and religious benefits. The causes and consequences of pacification are unique to every situation and culture. Coastal areas, like the Guadalcanal plains and the New Georgia Islands, were pacified more quickly than mountainous regions. Lands seen as more economically significant were subject to intensive pacification actions while isolated areas where access was difficult were ignored. Acceptance of an imposed peace not only meant access to new economic, social and religious benefits but it also permitted people to move out of chiefly control over resource use towards individual ownership of resources and their use. Local people came to realise that '[b]ecause pacification represents a politically and economically dominant power's determination to deepen the linkages with an encapsulated society, failure to achieve immediate success is merely a tactical setback. The means used to achieve pacification may change, attempts to enforce peace may lapse temporarily, the attitudes of the people being pacified may alter greatly; but eventually pacification will be complete' (Rodman 1983: 22). This was especially true in the Solomon Islands. Even after the process of pacification was completed in the New Georgia area it continued in Malaita. There it was achieved, after much bloodshed, following the Bell massacre of 1927. In the pacified areas, the new structures of law, government and church entered customary exchange and spiritual systems and were rapidly indigenised.

8. The new social order

Colonial rule is often seen as both coherent and hegemonic but encounters between indigenous peoples and settlers, traders, planters, missionaries and police were marked not only by tension and struggle but also by mutual misrepresentation and misunderstanding. Colonial administration in the Solomon Islands, and in Papua to the west, attempted to impose law and order—through pacification—by using forms of violence adopted from the very societies it sought to transform (Maclean 1998). The process of civilisation was made imperfect by imperfect agents. Many settlers, traders and even many missionaries had only a superficial understanding of their own culture and civilisation. Indeed, history shows that many of these people were fleeing the constraints of their own European society. It was unlikely that they would have had a comprehensive understanding of the rules of civility, law and justice that they sought to transmit to colonised peoples. Imposition of a legal system that argued for a universalist moral obligation to all and impartial justice that emphasised the nature of the wrong rather than the relationship between the offended parties was indeed alien to the Melanesian villager (Maclean 1998: 80).

Policing the islands

The fact that justice was in the hands of inexperienced, often unknown, junior white district officers made it appear even more contradictory in the eyes of local people. Colonial rule may have been founded on English law but British justice was another matter. Violence, when it erupted, was considered a crisis that required immediate action. When local people resorted to violence it was seen as indigenous agency out of control, but from an indigenous perspective, retaliation, revenge, pay-back, sorcery and retribution were the logical constructs of local polity. As evidenced in stories of the actions of Hiqava of Roviana, his status as a chief and power as a war leader were constructed around his ability to utilise the very qualities that British justice sought to suppress. What was documented in reports and newspaper accounts are the confrontations between two specific forms of violence that had been experimenting with each other for some time (Maclean 1998). What appeared to be a systematic and pervasive penetration of colonial rule in the Solomon Islands was in fact a patchwork of controlled and uncontrolled areas and this patchwork remained in existence for most of the colonial period.

The colonial state was a superficial layer of calm and order. Pacification campaigns and punitive expeditions were the visible and violent responses to the breakdown between indigenous and non-indigenous groups. Violence was an ever present accompaniment to trade, exchange, labour recruiting, exploration and evangelisation. All these places of contact could become places of conflict. The history of the Solomon Islands is full of examples of contact situations that turned to violence. The imposition of colonial rule in all Melanesian countries followed similar paths: exploration, patrolling, mapping, reporting, regulation, law and punishment, and taxation. All were elements of control and suppression. The wonderment was that a small group of European officials with limited knowledge of the country could pacify the many disparate groups (Maclean 1998: 88). Fundamental to that pacification was a measure of voluntary submission to colonial rule. While the goal of colonial rule was to transform the uncivilised native into the civilised wage labourer, the strategy employed was conservative. Traditional lifestyles, values and attitudes were retained while the veneer was retouched from pagan to Christian, savage to civilised. But some colonial goals also conformed to village goals, for communal life was directed by a conservative gerontocracy that blended with the imposed conservatism of the new social and religious order.

The way to govern colonial dependencies was part of an ongoing debate about efficient and effective rule that sought to impose centralised control while incorporating structures of local society into a powerful hierarchical and racial form of authority with white officers at the top and local police as the agents of power (Lattas and Rio 2011: 3). In Polynesian societies, with inherent hierarchical structures of chiefly power and authority where taboos, traditions and a complex cosmology governed daily life, the use of local power structures by colonial governments was less complex. In Melanesian societies Big-man and semi-hereditary chiefly structures were unstable, even volatile, and local power structures could not be relied upon to support colonial administrations. In the Western Pacific the protectorates were de facto colonies where the colonial power established internal administrative structures and controlled external, territorial and financial affairs. European patrol officers were supported by indigenous police selected from areas other than those in which they served. This established a cost-effective system of policing, but the local police used a culture of fear as a way of managing crime. This was little different from the power of violence and physical threats that allowed warrior leaders and Big-men to maintain control over local people. Extrajudicial punishments frequently characterised police arrests and interrogations and this technique of governing Melanesia now has a long history. It was used in the early colonial periods as part of armed police action when confronted with villagers who resisted or who were considered too pig-headed or too stubborn to understand directions. It formed part of the 'primitivist constructions that underpinned colonial race-class relations and state power' that has not disappeared (Lattas and Rio 2011: 10).

Following punitive raids and the capture of war leaders the Australian press often ran pictorial features and long descriptive articles describing the process of 'civilization' in the islands. The *Queenslander* (13 August 1910: 8, 22, 27 August 1910: 8, 3 September 1910: 24, 17 September 1910: 24 and 1 October 1910: 7, 22) published articles by the author 'Sketcher' with illustrated supplements under the headline *The Mysterious Solomons* that were poorly disguised sales pitches for plantation investment (Perkins and Quanchi 2010; Quanchi 2003, 2004, 2006 and 2007). These articles give useful facts and figures taken from government reports and the illustrated full page supplements document many important people and places. The *Sydney Daily Telegraph* (April 1910, Woodford papers PMB 1290 Item 9/30) called the Solomon Islands the 'Richest in the Pacific'. The article called Tulagi a civilised centre but then described islands full of fever and head hunters in long swift war canoes. For those venturing to invest in the islands, the article detailed the current rates of pay for white labourers and white sailors and compared them, in favour of the whites, with the contracted plantation labourer's salary set by order at £6 a year, with keep. This had been the standard contract payment for labourers since the late 1880s. By 1910 experienced domestic servants and labourers with skills could ask for up to £12 a year.

Missionaries and traders became agents of government pacification on the frontier. Woodford and his administration have been condemned for their use of force and the resulting 'massive overkill' (Bennett 1987: 109) but clearly the government saw it as a necessity to pacify the islands before European settlement could be encouraged and a plantation economy started. 'Woodford clearly saw "pacification" as both an end in itself and a necessary pre-condition to the promotion of large-scale European development' (Heath 1979: 98). Following the first attempts at securing the killers of Burns the *Sydney Morning Herald* (3 October 1908: 14) ran an anonymous article replying to the criticisms of the Solomon Islands administration. Said to be an interview with a 'prominent authority on island questions, who is intimately acquainted with the position in the Solomons', it reads very much like an interview with Walter Lucas. Given that the article was a criticism of Faddy, and indirectly the Lever's workers in general, it would not be surprising if it were written by someone connected with Burns Philp. The article stated that the only effective method of securing control in the islands was the establishment of a native police force with white officers along the lines of the system operating in Papua. Woodford was described as

> a man well acquainted with the habits of the natives, for he has long resided in the group. Many years ago he spent a good deal of time in the Solomons as a naturalist before taking up his present official position. He is a quiet, resourceful, level-headed man who can be firm in action

without becoming hysterical or being led into errors of judgement. Given an effective police system he may be relied upon to establish a wholesome respect for law and order.

There was much discussion between the High Commission and the Colonial Office about the establishment of an effective Solomon Islands police force made up of recruits from Tanna in the New Hebrides, Fijians, Gurkhas or even Pathan tribesmen (Mahaffy to High Commission 26 April 1911 WPHC 4/IV 831/1908). None of this eventuated. Mahaffy did submit a memorandum on the development of a local force in which he clarified that the six men brought from Fiji in 1897 were indeed Solomon Islanders who spoke Fijian and had been trained in Fiji. These men also served as Woodford's boat crew in the early days. It was found that the crews of visiting naval ships, the 'Bluejackets', were not a success in land-based policing. The climate, hilly terrain and language difficulties meant the sailors could not penetrate far from the shore. When the *Lahloo* was purchased and Gizo established, Mahaffy recruited 25 men from Malaita, Savo, Isabel and Guadalcanal. They were trained to use the Martini Henry rifles. These men used the confiscated *tomoko* for transport, were highly mobile, easily fed and accustomed to local conditions. Six police were stationed at Tulagi. Later Edge-Partington trained another 25 police to work on Malaita. Heffernan recruited six to work on the Shortland Islands but also trained a militia of volunteers who carried tomahawks instead of guns. When punitive campaigns were mounted the district magistrates raised a levy of local men from the labourers employed by planters and traders. These militia groups were used, to little success and much antagonism, on Vella Lavella and Malaita (Mahaffy to High Commission [undated] 1910 WPHC 4/IV 831/1908).

Murder of Oliver Burns: The beginning of the end of the pacification campaigns

Two significant punitive actions signalled the end of the pacification period in New Georgia. The first followed the murder of Oliver Burns, a trading agent of Norman Wheatley, killed in Jae Passage in Marovo Lagoon in May 1908 in retaliation for the imprisonment of Ara the brother of Lela, a local chief (Jackson 1978: 175). Ara committed suicide in Tulagi jail and Lela sought the head of a white man in compensation. Burns was on his schooner, the *Heela*, when he was attacked and killed along with members of his crew. The murders were reported widely in the Australian newspapers especially as the first punitive expedition in July 1908 failed to secure the killers despite having logistical support from Lever Brothers and use of their schooner *Leueneuwa*. This was led by an acting government officer, Arthur Sykes, the Inspector of Labour, and consisted of traders and their labourers. The presence of the Methodist missionaries, Reginald Nicholson and Ernest Shackell, was believed to moderate the behaviour of the white traders although the punitive party destroyed or captured some war canoes and whaleboats (*The Advertiser* [Adelaide] 3 August 1908; *The Sydney Morning Herald* 23 June 1908: 7, 30 June 1908: 7, 8 September 1908: 7; *The Brisbane Courier* 3 August 1908: 5).

The administration then came under intense criticism for its failure to protect traders in the Marovo Lagoon. First, Walter Henry Lucas, having returned from a tour of inspection of the Solomon Islands Development Co. stated that the prosperity of the islands was imperilled by the 'defiant and menacing natives' (*The Brisbane Courier* 3 August 1908: 5). Burns, Philp & Co, under Lucas's direction, then made the steamer *Makambo* available to Woodford to transport a second punitive party to Marovo. C. B. Faddy, the Trade Department Manager of Lever's Pacific Plantations Ltd stationed in the Marovo Lagoon, also attacked the government stating that the 'administration is a disgrace to the whole country … I have had to carry a revolver in case of an attack by the natives, who might come at any moment' and he was reported to be carrying 'three years' pent-up disgust' at the way murderers of white traders had been allowed to escape justice (*The Sydney Morning Herald* 2 October 1908: 7). The Oliver Burns case was but one of a number of murders of whites then mentioned by Faddy. Woodford came under personal criticism for finding against a white resident who had shot a local man. Faddy considered it most inappropriate that this white resident was forbidden to hold a recruiting license, not permitted to recruit any local man for his plantation or to have any local man employed on any vessel that he owned. This white resident must have been connected to Lever's plantations for the incident in question occurred on their schooner *Leueneuwa*. According to Faddy, and this would have had support from Lever's management, the German administration's tough approach to labour discipline in the Bismarck Archipelago was the standard to follow. Faddy had a speech impediment that local warriors considered a sign of spiritual possession and so he was spared from attack. When he found out that he was a possible target for retribution, presumably the speech impediment no longer having any effect, he made his escape to Sydney (Burnett 1911: 107–110; Woodford papers PMB 1290 Item 9/29).

What followed in Marovo was a second, larger punitive expedition. Woodford and the crew of HMS *Cambrian* went to Marovo Lagoon to search for the murderers of Burns and the looters of his schooner. The *Cambrian* was on a regular patrol of the region. Everard im Thurn, the High Commissioner, had joined the ship in Suva and been taken to the New Hebrides to finalise the details of the Anglo-French Condominium so Woodford requested the ship be sent on to the islands (*Auckland Star* 15 September 1908: 5). The crew of the man-of-war first attempted to arrest the murderers of Captain Mackenzie who had been killed at Langa Langa Lagoon on the north-west coast of Malaita. When 75 marines and officers could not secure the murderers the ship shelled the crowd of men jeering the crew from the shore. The expedition of the *Cambrian* in Marovo Lagoon was also unsuccessful. Six of the ship's whaleboats cruised the lagoon in heavy rain and found that the local people 'being prepared for the visit left absolutely nothing that could be destroyed' (*The Sydney Morning Herald* 8 September 1908: 7).

When plantation stores were plundered by the killers of Burns some time later in December 1908, Woodford returned to Marovo. This time on the government steamer *Belama* with District Magistrates NS Heffernan and Thomas Edge-Partington, a Shortland Islander militia and the trader Norman Wheatley. They raided gardens, burnt houses and in Woodford's own words: 'The lesson inflicted ... has been a severe one' (Bennett 1987: 107 quoting Woodford to Major 11 January 1909 WPHC 4/IV 261/1908; Hviding 1996: 113, 119). The criminal statistics report for 1909 notes that a 'punitive expedition against the natives of Marovo Lagoon, for the murder of a white man and the subsequent plundering of a trading station, was undertaken in December 1908. Thirteen large canoes were destroyed and eight of the guilty party were killed' (British Solomon Islands Protectorate 1909: 23).

Despite Wheatley being party to the punitive expedition the people from Jae Passage fled to the safety of his trading station near Ramata Island in Querasi Lagoon north of the main lagoon. They only returned after 1912. The police later captured the men believed to be involved in the murder of Burns. One man had been a locally engaged crewmember of the HMS *Pegasus* and was called 'Launchy' by the other crew. His real name was Lanasi. While settler and trader opinion was that he was the killer of Burns it could have been yet another case of a surrogate handed to the administration in place of senior chiefs or war leaders. Another culprit in the murder was Ngatu, the son of a chief (*The Sydney Morning Herald* 5 March 1910: 10; Bennett 1987: 116). Norman Wheatley used his influence to secure the apprehension of Ngatu and another man, Kama Gora (Burnett 1911: 144). After a period in prison on Tulagi, and his release secured by Rev John Goldie, Ngatu converted to Christianity. Following baptism as Ishmael, Ngatu then became a senior elder in the Methodist church, a District Headman and chief. During the Second World War he was part of a group of local men who passed information about Japanese troop movements to Coastwatchers on New Georgia (Bennett 1987: 244 and 290; Hviding 1996: 113, 119).

The raid on Vella Lavella and the capture of Zito Latavaki

The capture of Zito Latavaki (Sito) was a case of overzealous, ill-disciplined police action. Jean Pascal Pratt had been attacked by the war chief, Zito, over a failed illegal arms deal in 1897 but he was not captured until 1909. Following the attack on Pratt, Zito had gone into hiding on the Mbilua coast of Vella Lavella but he continued to be a presence in the area. The first punitive operation that sought to capture Zito was led by Mahaffy in November 1901 (Mahaffy to Woodford 15 November 1901 WPHC 4/IV 41/1902 contains two hand drawn maps). This party consisted of Norman Wheatley, Thomas Woodhouse, Joseph Binskin and a new District Officer, William Hazelton. It also had a support group of 32 police and 14 volunteers mostly from Simbo, Kolombangara, Roviana, and some even from Vella Lavella itself. On the eastern coast they raided villages, burnt Zito's canoes and shot pigs. When they arrived at Mbilua, Zito's fortified village, the people had fled but all 20 houses were burnt. Mahaffy then led raids on the western coast villages. In all 10 villages were destroyed, 100 canoes burnt or confiscated and Zito driven from his Mbilua hideout.

Following this incident Joseph Binskin secured a lease over 1,000 acres on the north coast of Bagga (Mbava/Bagha) Island off the coast of Vella Lavella in 1901 (Woodford to O'Brien 25 December 1901 WPHC 4/IV 35a/1902). Binskin was well respected locally but he was implicated in the punitive expedition on Mbilua that had caused such destruction. A second raid on Mbilua was led by District Magistrate Thomas Edge-Partington in 1908. This consisted of a large party of 'undisciplined Malaitan militia', local traders and white officers who scoured Vella Lavella for two weeks searching for Zito's supporters (Dureau 1998: 211). The Malaitan militia raided sacred shrines and destroyed villages (Burnett 1911: 152). Zito's wife and daughter were killed in this attack. In a revenge attack, Zito sent his men to Bagga Island to kill Binskin's Malaiatan wife Unga and his two young daughters. Binskin was away from his trading station at the time. His unpublished diary records his many trading voyages around the New Georgia Islands but gives only brief details of the murder of his family and almost no information on the events that followed. The only direct remark was: 'I had to go & force the Government to come on this raid. [They] did not want to do it' (Binskin 1909; *The Advertiser* [Adelaide] 20 May 1910: 7; *The Mercury* [Hobart] 27 May 1910: 7)

An even larger expedition took place on the return of Woodford from leave in England in 1909. Wheatley, Binskin and a force of more than 200 volunteers, police, white officers and rival clansmen captured three of the ring-leaders—Tongava, Pakobatu and Pekumbessa—but only after local people assisted the police. Zito escaped to Kolombangara (*The Argus* 5 January 1910: 8; *The*

Advertiser [Adelaide] 5 January 1910: 10). He was handed over to Norman Wheatley who took him to Gizo police station. 17 people were killed in this punitive expedition and 12 arrested and jailed (*The Sydney Morning Herald* 5 March 1910: 10). Rev R. C. Nicholson of the Methodist Foreign Mission—he had by now established a mission on Vella Lavella—was critical of the police actions, in particular of the native militia raid of the Methodist mission stations and gardens. Rev John Goldie wrote to Woodford and complained of the damage done to the missions and as a result some of the police party were charged. As a result of the Zito campaign Goldie considered that the 'Methodist Mission stood between the people of the western Solomons and their exploitation, even destruction, at the hands of the traders and government officials' (Hilliard 1966: 326).

Briskin took charge of Zito's associates, Pakobatu and Pekumbessa, when they were captured but they were later found dead in the jail on Gizo. They had died from beatings inflicted by native police (Hilliard 1966: 270). Joseph Binskin was investigated for the deaths of the two men while in his custody, but following hearings on Mbava Island, he was not charged as an accessory. He remarried in 1910 and his second wife, Florence, was the daughter of Norman Wheatley and his Roviana-born wife Nautele (Bennett 1987: 180–181 Table 5 and 1987: 74: Photos 6 and 7). Florence married Binskin when she was only 17. They returned to Mbava where Florence remained, apart from some years in Sydney in the 1950s, for the rest of her life. Joseph Binskin died in 1941 and Florence in 1972 (Smith 1971; *The Australian Women's Weekly* 14 April 1971: 28; Boutilier 1975: 29).

The entire episode raised concerns about the value of the ongoing punitive actions. Bitter memories of Malaitan participation in the Zito affair surfaced long after when Malaitans and westerner islanders came into contact in Honiara (Dureau 1998: 211 and 215). Zito was tried for murder at Tulagi by Charles Major, the Chief Judicial Commissioner of the Western Pacific High Commission, who was taken to the Solomon Islands on the HMS *Pegasus* to hear these cases (WPHC 2/VI Item 4; *The Brisbane Courier* 28 May 1910: 4). However, both Zito and Tongava were acquitted for the only witness was the young Binskin child who had survived the attack and Major found the police evidence inconclusive. But Zito and Tongava were considered too important or too dangerous to release back into their communities and so they were sent to jail in Suva on other charges (*The Sydney Morning Herald* 16 June 1910: 8). It was later reported that Zito had died in jail (*Examiner* [Launceston] 27 December 1911: 2).

A second trial held by Chief Judicial Commissioner in Tulagi sentenced Lanasi to death for the murder of the trader Oliver Burns (*The Sydney Morning Herald* 16 June 1910: 8; *The Morning Bulletin* [Rockhampton] 21 June 1910: 5). Following the capture of Zito on Vella Lavella, the Binskin attacks and the murder of Oliver Burns, the High Commission in Suva was convinced that the Protectorate faced many difficulties without a Resident Judicial Officer. The Chief Judicial

Commissioner, located in Suva, was dependent on transport from the Royal Navy and this delayed his movements. Charles Major also had a poor opinion of Australian traders and planters in general and he strongly condemned the use of vigilante groups. He wrote to im Thurn: 'how very difficult it is to control this class of Australian, and if a gross miscarriage of justice should occur in the case of these murders it will be certain that we may except a crop of crimes on the part of the people who will take the law into their hands' (Boutilier 1983: 62 quoting Major to im Thurn 8 March 1910 WPHC 4/IV 1121/1909). In 1911 the Resident Commissioner was given judicial powers but Woodford, and the Protectorate administration in general, came under savage criticism for the handling of the Binskin case from Frank Burnett, a Canadian traveller, photographer and writer.

Through Polynesia and Papua

Burnett was an itinerant travel writer, photographer and amateur ethnographer who wrote four books on his travels in the Pacific. They are all examples of the common genre then fashionable for illustrated travel narratives (Thomas 1992: 369). While commonly regarded as peripheral, unreliable sources of information on social and cultural issues, Burnett's books provide a useful backdrop to the local politics in the islands at that time. His book, *Through Polynesia and Papua* (1911), contains more than 100 pages of action packed drama recording his time in the Solomon Islands. He stayed for nearly a year with Norman Wheatley at Lambete plantation on the Munda coast. It is obvious that most of the commentary provided by Burnett comes from Wheatley, for the book contains savage criticism of missionaries and the administration. At that time, 1909–1910, Wheatley was in open dispute with the Methodist missions and their expansion into plantation ownership, trading and local politics. Wheatley was a well-regarded trader with good local contacts but he did not like losing trade and influence to the industrial missions.

Burnett saw young Polynesian women with light skins and amorous, uninhibited ways as Island Belles. He emphasised the soft and pliant side of Polynesians and illustrated that with diffused images. Burnett's book contains numerous 'unambiguously sexualized' studio photographs of unnamed, Polynesian women positioned looking away from the viewer and shrouded by exotic foliage (Thomas 1992: 369). These images were of the type purchased from studios or sold to ships' passengers. On the other hand, aggressive Melanesian men were seen as Savages, characterised by their dark skins, confronting direct gaze and hostile manner (Burnett 1911, facing 52; Mayer 2006: 218, 234, 235, 236). They were photographed in their villages, in groups or in natural surroundings. The effect was to show that they were uncivilised and cruel, even somewhat inhuman. Melanesian women were described as socially degraded and portrayed as physically ugly in comparison with romanticised Polynesian beauties. Burnett's books are a mixture of fact and fiction (Mayer 2006: 237). Burnett (1911: 74–80) wrote: 'there is not much to admire in the Solomon islander ... he is, in fact, a ferocious, treacherous savage, whose principal and most congenial occupation in the past was head hunting'. In his opinion, their houses were dirty, their clothing was poor and they were devil worshippers. Indeed, the place was full of flies and mosquitoes. In common with the general attitudes of the day, Burnett believed that Pacific Islanders and their cultures were doomed to extinction with their customary ways endangered by colonial expansion and missionary conversion. The white traders and settlers were also condemned. They were, collectively, a group of malaria-infected alcoholics.

In Roviana and Marovo Lagoons, Burnett spent a large part of his time collecting artefacts and taking photographs. He bought, at low prices, over 300 objects obtained by some most unsavoury practices. In search of curios, he entered peoples' houses and wrote: 'After ransacking most of the principal houses [in a village off Ramata Island], and securing all the articles I could find that were of any interest to me, such as canoe-gods, spears, shields, and carved shell ornaments, I wandered up to a large "tambo" [*tabu*] house situated on a slight eminence behind the village'. Here he raided the sacred shrines (Burnett 1911: 91–92, 120).

But it is his open condemnation of missionaries and government officers that makes Burnett's book interesting. Burnett (1911: 127) included a photograph, not acknowledged, of a Marau family taken by Walter Henry Lucas that had been published in the Amherst and Thomson volumes (1901, Volume 2: facing 340). He obviously sourced his photographs from many people. His underlying message was that: 'distant islands of "Edenistic" wonder accommodated cannibals and headhunting as customary practice, and whose continued existence colonial expansion and missionary fervour endangered' (Mayer 2006: 223). He found cannibalism and head hunting more colourful than colonialism and Christianity. Of the Methodists in Roviana he stated: 'The mission is a concern apparently conducted as a copra-raising, property-acquiring, and commercial undertaking, incidentally ready to save the soul of any stray heathen who may "happen along", desirous of becoming a faithful worker in the Vineyard of the Lord, or—in other words—Mission Copra Plantation' (Burnett 1911: 95). Burnett was scathing in his criticism of the Binskin affair (Burnett 1911: 158–174).

Of the administration of the British Solomon Island Protectorate he was even more condemnatory:

> x am ashamed to say, a protectorate of Great Britain. The administration consists nominally of a Resident Commissioner—who is responsible to the High Commissioner for the Western Pacific at Fiji—a collector

of customs, who is also chief postmaster, a labour inspector, and three resident magistrates, two of whom, mere inexperienced youth, are deputy commissioners, by virtue of which latter appointments they are invested with almost unlimited powers, though devoid of any administrative knowledge of ability, and lamentably ignorant of law or legal procedure (Burnett 1911: 130).

Woodford was of course the Resident Commissioner named, and the three District Magistrates were Nesbit Seeley Heffernan, Thomas Edge-Partington and Ralph Brodhurst-Hill. The Labour Inspector at that time was Arthur Tasman Sykes, and the Collector of Customs, Chief Post-master and Health Officer was Frederick Joshua Barnett (Protectorate of British Solomon Islands 1909). After castigating Woodford and Mahaffy, Burnett wrote of N. S. Heffernan, then District Magistrate in the Shortland Islands based at Faisi: 'Embodied in the august person of the youth in charge of this extensive district, are the positions of Assistant Commissioner, District Magistrate, and Postmaster, not one of which—let alone all three—is he fitted to fill. His arrogance is colossal and equalled only by the ignorance he displays of all matters connected with administration' (Burnett 1911: 172). All these men, apart from Sykes, served for many years in the Solomon Islands despite Burnett's very public slander.

Woodford was aggrieved by the attacks on the administration that was called 'incompetent' and a 'disgrace to the British Empire' but was reassured by the High Commission in Suva that both Burnett and his comments could be ignored (Boutilier 1975: 35; Woodford to May 11 February 1912 and 31 May 1912 WPHC 4/IV 577/1912). The book was ridiculed by the Secretary of State for the Colonies who wrote that, while Burnett dedicated the book to his wife, it included 'indecent photographs which he claims to have made himself but which happen to be hawked for sale in Tahiti and Rarotonga' (Jackson 1978: 196). Burnett's book was not well reviewed. *The Field* (10 February 1912) reported the book to be neither well informed nor impartial and told readers that Burnett's 'special bugbear, however, is the missionary, whose faults pervade the book from preface to appendix' and that the illustrations appeared to be selected solely for the purpose of 'depicting natives in various stages of undress' (Woodford papers PMB 1381/009d).

Everard im Thurn: Colonial governor, explorer and photographer

Everard im Thurn, High Commissioner from 1904 to 1911, played an important role in the development of the British Solomon Islands Protectorate. But his poor personal relationship with Woodford has been seen as Woodford's failure to conform to the rules and dictates of the High Commissioner rather than any errors in judgement of im Thurn himself (Heath 1974a; Bennett 1987). Im Thurn, like Woodford, was a complex and contradictory character. Born in Sydenham, south of London, the son of a Swiss-German father and an English mother, he was from an established family but had a 'meandering career'. Chapelle (1976: 10) considered this to be an indication of impulsiveness and lack of purpose although he too may have been an adventurous young man bored in Victorian England. He was not quite at ease in authority. He was well educated, having studied at Oxford, Edinburgh and Sydney universities. When his father, a merchant banker in the City of London, went bankrupt he joined the colonial service as curator of the British Guiana (Guyana) Museum in Georgetown. He served with some distinction in that post from 1877 to 1882 and was then appointed regional magistrate from 1882 to 1891. He wrote a classic study of the culture of the Amerindians, *Among the Indians of Guiana*, in 1883 and then, following a successful ascent of Mount Roraima in 1884, published the details of the botany of the mountain areas in 1887 (im Thurn 1967 and 1887). He served as Government Agent in British Guiana between 1891 and 1899 and was awarded the CMG (Companion of the Order of St Michael and St George) in 1892. He had an interesting and diverse background and was successful in his South American work.

Im Thurn then returned to London where he became a 1st class clerk—the head of a department—at the Colonial Office before being appointed to Ceylon as Lieutenant Governor and Colonial Secretary. He was then cross-posted to Fiji as Governor and High Commissioner for the Western Pacific (Scarr 1967a: 117). General assessments of im Thurn's career have been varied. He was seen by mountaineers as the conqueror of Mount Roraima and as a sensitive and innovative photographer by visual anthropologists. He was a representative of

> that community of intellectually versatile and physically resilient British colonial administrators who turned their attention to the interconnections between the disciplines of ethnography, geography, botany, ornithology, administration, and economic and cultural development. As collectors, lecturers, and writers their output was extraordinarily extensive. As residents in often geographically remote British colonies they developed attachments and loyalties to the lands of their posting that often created tensions with their personal and professional ambitions and commitment to the imperial centre (Dalziell 2007: 102)

The same statement could be used to describe Woodford. Im Thurn was also a skilful botanist and sent many rare plants and ethno-botanical objects to the Kew gardens. He was a follower of the evolutionary anthropology of William Halse

Rivers Rivers and, as a follower of the theory that the Fijian people were a dying race, he contributed the preface to *Essays on the Depopulation of Melanesia*. Woodford also contributed an article (Rivers 1922; Woodford 1922b).

Although Scarr (1967a) covered much of im Thurn's administration in some detail in his study of the history of the Western Pacific High Commission, im Thurn's time in the Pacific has not been subject to the level of critical investigation given to the work of John Bates Thurston (Scarr 1973 and 1980). Important too was the role of Merton King, appointed as Secretary to the High Commissioner in 1898. Merton King came with some reluctance to the Pacific although he remained in Fiji until 1907 and then served as Resident Commissioner in the New Hebrides until 1924 (Heath 1974a: 95; Scarr 1967a: 117). As Governor of Fiji, im Thurn succeeded Sir Henry Moore Jackson. During his long tenure in office—1904 to 1911—he created some controversy by altering the land laws implemented by Sir Arthur Gordon (Lord Stanmore). Gordon had codified Fijian land ownership and prevented native Fijians from working outside their village economies and social structure. There was some internal labour migration but it was unofficial and open to bribery (Newbury 210: 105). This in turn formally identified people with defined geographical boundaries and set ordered social groupings in contrast to the more flexible social and economic structures that had existed before. Gordon's three keystones of native policy were the non-alienation of customary land, the creation of a permanent Council of Chiefs to direct native affairs and the payment of a head tax through produce rather than in cash. Gordon's purpose was to restrict sale of land to Europeans and provide an economic basis for the establishment of the colonial government. These were logical choices made at the time, but his essentialist ideals fixed Fijians to their land and social ties and allowed for little flexibility (Sohmer 1984: 153). To historians of the Pacific, Gordon understood very little of the true nature of Fijian laws and customs.

Im Thurn brought to Fiji many of the beliefs and attitudes he saw developed in Guiana and Ceylon. In Ceylon the Crown Lands Encroachment Ordinance of 1840 established the policy that all forests, and waste lands—those lands seen as unoccupied or uncultivated—should be declared Crown land. Although the ordinance was repealed in Ceylon in 1897 the basic principles remained in law (Chapelle 1976: 6). He believed that the same regulations should operate in Fiji despite the understanding that land use and land occupation came under such a variety of customary laws which differed from place to place that they defied codification (Chapelle 1976: 481). In order to stimulate the economy im Thurn opened up large tracks of native land for speculation by the Colonial Sugar Refining Company (CSR). Fijian land owners were pushed into the banana industry while the capital-intensive sugar industry was reserved for non-indigenous entrepreneurs and planters (*The West Australian* 17 November

1908: 3). The government's opinion was that '[t]here was no disinclination on the side of the natives to part with their lands. On the contrary, the fear was expressed that they might dispose of so much that the remainder would be insufficient for their future requirements' (*The Sydney Morning Herald* 22 August 1908: 18). When im Thurn did implement controversial land reforms in Fiji, between 1904 and 1908, they were attacked not only by members of the Fijian Legislative Council but also with some vengeance by Stanmore, then in the House of Lords (Chapelle 1976; Great Britain. Parliament. House of Lords. Debates, 16 July 1908: 192: cc998-1002). The introduced ordinances for land sale and leasing were complex. They assumed a blatant racist position that Fijians were incapable of appreciating the advantages or disadvantages of land transactions. The belief was that the 'colonial Government consequently stands in loco parentis' and this condescending attitude excused the declaration of large areas of native lands as waste property.

In Suva, im Thurn decided that Fijians had no prior claim to land and that the state should take it over and privatise it. He based this on the belief that the colonialising process was irreversible and that strong colonial economies could only develop based on individual enterprise. This served European interests but also served to support im Thurn's opinion that British colonial administration provided the best example in the rule of law and order. He failed to understand the complexities of the customary land traditions and the conflict between it and the growing economic exploitation created by the large-scale plantation system and its demand for imported coolie labour (Dalziell 2007: 105). The imported Indian labourers were subjected to harsh employment conditions, poor housing and remained on the social margins of Fijian life. The inevitable exploitation of Indian plantation labour intensified for '[t]here was always exploitation under the indenture system in the sense that indentured labour was paid less than the going free-market wage' (Knapman 1985: 59). In a paper presented to the Royal Geographical Society the year before he retired im Thurn (1909) spelt out his conservative attitudes to governing the many different colonies in the Western Pacific. He credited his time as High Commissioner with the suppression of the evils of the Pacific labour trade, even though recruiting for the labour trade from the Solomon Islands to Fiji continued until 1911, the year he retired from office (im Thurn 1909: 279). He also failed to acknowledge the impact of changing labour and economic conditions within the Queensland sugar industry, the impact of the White Australia Policy, and the strongly voiced social opinions from among church members in the Australian states. These were internal factors that led to the end of the Queensland labour trade. Recruitment of Indian labour to Fiji stopped in March 1917 by which time the Colonial Sugar Refining Company had secured a monopoly over sugar production in Fiji (Knapman 1985: 61). Im Thurn supported the development of the phosphate mines on Ocean Island that he called 'small, rocky and scrub-covered, and at the time that it came into

European ken had but few inhabitants' (im Thurn 1909: 284). He considered the conversion of this supposedly desolate piece of rock into a busy centre of industry a positive move for the 'few natives have prospered greatly under the employment thus afforded to them'. In this, he failed to see that the long-term result would be the dispossession and economic destitution of the Banaban people. The contradiction was that while arguing against Lord Stanmore over changing Fijian land laws he was supporting Stanmore's commercial activities as a director of Pacific Phosphate Company Ltd, the company profiting from the destruction of Banaba.

A new social order

In the Solomon Islands head hunting raids from the New Georgia group ceased around 1902 but isolated incidents of retribution and murder, like the Burns and Binskin cases, continued. Punitive campaigns against raiders by white officers and native police targeted the large war canoes. When a sufficient number of these *tomoko* were destroyed, raiding ceased. Not all *tomoko* were destroyed. But while this was a visible act in the cessation of head hunting, it did not cause it. There were many other factors involved. Destruction of canoes disrupted intergroup communication, as well as warfare, and broke the alliance, kinship and affinal linkages that facilitated many social and economic ties. Local leadership was discredited by defeat at the hands of the police and into that power vacuum came the Christian churches. Inter-island connections unravelled and relations between islanders and Europeans became dominated by trade based around copra making (Boutilier 1975: 32; Dureau 1998: 208).

The pacification of the Solomon Islands coincided with the early years of Federation in Australia, the passing of the *Pacific Island Labourers Act 1901* (Cth) (1 Edward VII 16 1901) designed to bring about the conclusion of the Queensland labour trade by 31 March 1904 and the final deportation of any remaining labourers by 31 December 1906. Paradoxically, the end of the labour trade that would see the end to the illegal smuggling of firearms and ammunition into the islands would also lead to a downturn in revenue. Labour ships no longer travelled to and from Queensland and no longer paid an annual £100 licence fee. The period of establishment leading up to 1901 saw the Protectorate poor and barely able to maintain its way (Great Britain. Parliament. House of Commons. Parliamentary Papers 1902a: 5). The new government station at Gizo had to be built with another grant-in-aid from the Imperial treasury of £500 (Woodford to O'Brien 14 January 1900 WPHC 4/IV 56/1900). The small white population of 76 people consisted mostly of traders (48) and missionaries (17). Even women and children outnumbered government officials. The government continued to estimate the local population at 150,000 but as no census was ever undertaken this lack of specificity contributed to the general assumptions about depopulation of Melanesia.

Pacification had a secondary impact on the export trade. Turtle hunting in the Manning Straits between Choiseul and Bougainville Islands was undertaken either before or after head hunting raids by men from the western islands. When head hunting was suppressed, trade in turtle shell declined (McKinnon 1975). Primary exports were still sales of copra, some ivory nuts and bêche de mer, but for the first time local people sold 15 cases of curios and there was a marked increase in pearling (Great Britain. House of Commons. Parliamentary Papers 1901). With the Manning Straits now pacified, commercial exploitation of pearls and pearl shell could continue. William Hamilton had secured a lease from the German administration and this was converted to a 99 year pearling lease in 1904 when the area became British territory. This was only two years after the area had been a favourite turtle hunting ground for Roviana head hunters (Bennett 1987: 132–133; Golden 1993: 225–226; AU NBAC N115/488).

Now head hunting no longer interfered with the management and the development of the plantations. Pacification, essential for the viability of the plantation economy, also allowed the missions to Christianise large areas of the western islands. This was completed, at least in the Methodist areas in Roviana, by 1902. This pacification made great changes to social and economic systems, but the administration itself was really of marginal importance to village life in missionised regions. It was the mission, not the administration, that assumed responsibilities for education, health and welfare programs. The missions became the media through which local people sought attention from the government (Dureau 1998: 213). Participation in Christianity became the new key to social mobility. Being Christian and wearing the cross in place of pagan charms was a new way of protecting oneself from attack, sickness and misfortune and a way of staying in harmony with the new spiritual world (White 1983: 135). The religious acts of blessing, anointing and baptising became 'weapons in the spiritual arsenal of indigenous Christians' and the churches became major political as well as social organisations (White 1991: 108).

The early period of the Protectorate, from 1896 to 1902, had been one of constant violence. Islanders quickly learned that the Europeans had stronger lasting power. The settler community saw pacification of the islands as essential for future development but so too did local people who realised that trade goods and services, like Christianity, would flow more evenly during times of peace. The missions and the government set about reordering local communities into nucleated villages along the coasts that had once been indefensible. People on islands like Isabel and Choiseul who had been subjected to head hunting now moved back to the coasts where communities clustered around the missions.

The position of Big-men had been marked by 'magical powers, gardening prowess, mastery of oratory style, perhaps bravery in war and feud' (Sahlins 1963). Their power was cemented in the distribution of goods but when these could be obtained by employment with the missions or on the plantations the status of the Big-man declined. Serious disputes now centred on land tenure. Establishing rights over communal land became partly economic to gain access to a productive resource like copra and then timber, and partly the pursuit of prestige and status validated by control of property (Scheffler 1964).

Feasting and the acceptance of peace and Christianity

The feast to celebrate the 'giving up' of head hunting witnessed by Graham Officer was not the only ritual performance of celebratory feasting used by local people to signal the start of a new social order. Rev George Brown of the Methodist Mission commenced evangelising work at Port Hunter in the Duke of York Islands, between New Britain and New Ireland, in August 1875. He secured land for his mission from two local Big-men, Waruwarum and To Pulu. During the early years he was especially reliant on the support and protection of these men (Gardner and Philp 2006). By being on their land, the Methodists were incorporated into the local trading bloc that extended across the region and, because they were the providers of new and valuable trade goods, the movements of the missionaries were constrained by the Big-men. The flow of trade, including the spiritual 'trade' of new prayers and hymns and the mission teachers, first moved out to allied villages. The people in these communities than accepted Christianity as part of the customary exchange network.

The complex web of reciprocity, missionisation and the changing dynamic of local power relations can be seen in the circumstances surrounding the great feast given by the Big-men when Brown departed from the Bismarck Archipelago in 1881. That feast, organised for New Year's Eve of December 1880, was viewed by the missionaries as a testament to the people's love of Brown and his work (Reeson 2013: 162). But for the more than 400–500 people who attended the celebration, it was an act of reciprocity. In repayment for the gifts of prayer, ritual and a new spiritual order, Brown was ceremonially feasted on his departure from their land. Beside Waruwarum and To Pulu, the Big-men from the affiliated villages attended. Brown was a keen photographer (Brown 1908 and 1910). Although mission texts record that the local men played a major part in the success of the evangelisation of the islands the images 'reveal that the relationship between the big-men and the mission, while essential to the success of the later, was based more on Duke of York economies and alliances than on Christian principles' (Gardner and Philp 2006: 180). The former 'pagan' moral order was subsumed by a new Christianised structure but that too was indigenised.

The Methodist mission to New Georgia

In 1902, Brown, Rev John Goldie, Rev Stephen Rabone Rooney, a party of four Fijian and three Samoan teachers and their wives set out from Sydney for the Solomon Islands (Hilliard 1966: 249). With the encouragement and logistical support of Frank Wickham and Norman Wheatley they headed for Roviana Lagoon (*The Sydney Morning Herald* 10 May 1902: 11, 39). The day they arrived, 23 May 1902, is now acknowledged as the first day of a new era of peace and Christianity. The Methodists first erected a mission house at Nusa Zonga on land purchased from the traders but then bought a larger property on the mainland of New Georgia at Kokeqolo, Munda Point (Woodford to O'Brien 29 July 1902 WPHC 4/IV 150/1902). The orthodox evangelist's view was that the native was a heathen, a pagan ripe for conversion. The past too was dark and savage, and only the present—with acceptance of Christianity—and the future were times of hope, brightness and light. In the Solomon Islands Christianity became infused with the concepts of *mana* and the supernatural, particularly as pacification arrived in the western islands at the same time as the church. With the end of head hunting and the arrival of the Methodists, the power of the *banara* faded. Hocart (1922: 79–80) reported that people complained 'the chiefs are dullards (*tuturu*) and like commoners (*tinoni homboro*) … No one is mighty now; they are all alike; they have no money, they cannot go headhunting, they all "stop nothing"'. The vacuum created in the power structure was replaced by the church. Just as political influence and respect were accorded those who possessed *mana*, so too was status and respect accorded to the Christian ministers and pastors (Burman 1981: 264–295). Inequalities of wealth and position were explained, and justified, by a lack of grace rather than lack of *mana*. Like the efficacy of *mana*, being in a state of grace was now defined by success in religious and secular activities. The savage was not accorded masculine or feminine characteristics but those of infancy. Christian literature was full of the trope of childhood. The native was to be taught faith and the notion of sin, given training and guidance, and brought into a new way of living. Missionary texts defined native peoples as children being led to salvation. God was the father, Jesus his son, missionaries were brothers and sisters, heathens were childlike, and converts, like domestic servants, were mission 'boys' and 'girls' who benefited from discipline and propriety (Thomas 1990: 150). The missions were structured on this familial order and hierarchy.

The Methodists were particularly successful in the western islands for they established industrial missions where men and women were taught skills as well as religion and so 'the mission was not simply a religious instrument but rather a total social fact' (Thomas 1992: 384). The mission controlled work, leisure, celebration and worship and became a new community with chiefly structures established through the church elders, both senior men and women, and the new 'macrofamilial institution' fitted into the Christianised social and moral order. The mission became a major local, social, economic and political entity but the response to this was not complete acceptance. Conflict between denominations and conflict between the churches, traders and the administration weakened the apparent hegemonic power of the colonisers in the eyes of the people. This plurality of forces left room for a dynamic indigenous response of accommodation and resistance (Thomas 1992: 388). Acceptance of the mission presence and the spread of Christianity was impossible without the support of local people. The people played a significant role in the process of conversion for the '[i]ndigenous interaction with and agency for new European-initiated religious missionary movements was a complex process' largely unseen and unknown to the white missionaries and administrators (Butlin 2009: 383). From the mission perspective, the permanent presence of the police and government officials at Gizo, the growing plantation economy, the economic power of traders and new polity established by the presence of administration headquarters at Tulagi, provided the Methodists with an environment in which they could establish their head station at Munda. The linkage between acceptance of Christianity and celebratory feasting was again apparent when Stephen Rooney and his wife attempted to establish a new mission on Choiseul. The village of Sasamungga (Sasamuqa) on the Mbambatana coast was chosen but a great Christmas feast in 1906 disposed many local people who had not accepted Christianity to turn in favour of the mission (Hilliard 1966: 258).

The great feast of honour

Mahaffy left Gizo on leave in February 1903. Before he went he held a great feast in honour of the coronation of King Edward VII (O'Brien 2011: 202–207). A date in November 1902, just after his article was published in *The Empire Review*, was chosen because it was the time of the best clear and calm weather before the wet, stormy end of the year. Mahaffy invited all the important *baṉara* and their followers from across the New Georgia region. These were the same men he had been fighting over the past two years in the suppression of head hunting. The feast to celebrate the end of head hunting witnessed by Graham Officer was held in Roviana on 27 July 1901 (Officer 1901– MS 9321; see Richards 2012). As reciprocal feasting and ceremonies were an integral part of the pre-Christian polity, the feast given by Mahaffy became another part of this ritual cycle (*The Mercury* [Hobart] 2 October 1901: 6; Zelenietz 1983: 101). A man's wealth and power was measured by the lavishness of the feasts he could sponsor and for his great feast Mahaffy planned for 1,000 guests (Burman 1981: 265). He had his police construct sleeping houses, feasting areas and a dancing ground (*pavasa*) and using the canoes confiscated during raids he sought food to feed this vast number of guests. The feast and the dancing were scheduled to last three days. In all 1,892 people attended and Mahaffy wrote that it was a 'picturesque sight to see the great canoes all decorated with streamers and each with its full complement of men, coming up the [Gizo] harbour at full speed' (O'Brien 2011: 204). It was obvious that Mahaffy and the police had not succeeded in destroying or confiscating all the great *tomoko*. Many had been well hidden during the police raids on villages. Now that peace had come to the islands, and the mission had been established on Hiqava's land at Munda, it was possible to display the canoes for they were no longer under threat of destruction.

Hiqava and the other chiefs had incorporated both the *Lotu* and the government into their own spheres of influence. Some idea of the importance of feasting as a sign of cementing new political relationships was becoming apparent to the administration. Woodford wrote to Sir George O'Brien following Mahaffy's raid on Mbilua and stated: 'Between the natives of Rubiana, Simbo and Narovo [central Simbo] and the Government the friendliest relations now subsist. Invitations to attend native feasts are now always sent to the Government Station at Gizo and pigs instead of human beings are sacrificed upon the inauguration of new canoes' (Woodford to O'Brien 15 September 1902 WPHC 4/IV 41/1902). Even Woodford was forced to admit that 'the punishment inflicted [upon suspected head hunters], which in reality only amounts to the loss of their head-hunting canoes, will appear a moderate one'.

But O'Brien (2011: 205) is correct in her general assessment of Mahaffy's great feast. Mahaffy did not fully understand the social, political and economic complexities of this very entangled part of the Solomon Islands. Financing ceremonial feasts was part of chiefly strategy to gain status, prestige and to consolidate power among followers and allies. Of all the local *banara* it was Hiqava who had emerged as powerful and influential. He was not the greatest chief in the region by any means but he was a great manipulator. Like the Big-men of the Duke of York Islands, he had contained the head station of the Methodist mission to his lands and now he was reaping the material, spiritual and social benefits of their presence there. At the great feast, Mahaffy gave management of the distribution of food to Hiqava. This in the eyes of the people attending would show that Hiqava was in charge of the feast and that he, not the government, was bringing the new moral order to the region. Mahaffy was but a temporary figure in the area. He left in early 1903 and did not return from this extended leave until May 1904. In September 1904 he was offered, and accepted, a senior post in the office of the High Commission in Suva (O'Brien 2011: 199, 202, 208).

South Seas Evangelical Mission

The foundation of one of the most influential and longest serving evangelical churches in the Solomon Islands, the South Seas Evangelical Mission (SSEM)—later the South Seas Evangelical Church (SSEC)—was laid at this time. The Queensland Kanaka Mission (QKM), the forerunner of the South Seas Evangelical Mission, was unusual. It was formed by a woman and started at the very heart of the plantation labour area. Established by lay-missionary Florence Young at Fairymead Plantation outside Bundaberg in 1886, the mission began after she had commenced preaching to planters' families in the region. Florence Young was described as 'a wealthy spinster and member of a prominent Plymouth Brethren family … a woman of determination and drive. Stout and bespectacled, with a buoyant Evangelical faith and overwhelming assurance of the will of God, she was a striking example of that army of emancipated Victorian women who found an outlet for the crusading instincts in religious causes, preferably those in which they themselves could occupy a commanding position' (Boutilier 1974: 45 quoting from Hilliard 1969: 42).

Fairymead, owned by her brothers, Arthur, Horace and Ernest, was a profitable sugar plantation and mill and their background and business acumen were also significant in the development of the mission. They owned two labour recruiting vessels, the *May* and the *Lochiel*. The Youngs began to recruit from the Gilbert Islands where conditions were safer for white men and the recruiting process conducted through the *unimame*, the Council of Elders (Munro 1992: 453–454). The *Lochiel*, like a number of labour vessels, was an old cargo boat converted to labour-carriage with the addition of two or three tiers of bunks in the hold. It had been the first labour schooner of William Hamilton who developed the pearling industry in the Solomon Islands. Its suitability for the labour trade was called into question by Woodford who complained that it was not fit to carry produce let alone human beings (Johnston 1980: 51 quoting Woodford to the Governor of Queensland 28 March 1904 QSA PRE/84). The Gilbertese did not remain long in the plantation economy. Most were repatriated by 1898 for they fought with the Melanesian labourers and by 1900, when phosphate was discovered on Ocean Island, Gilbertese became mine workers rather than agricultural labourers (Munro 1992: 459, 462).

When transported to Queensland, the vast majority of Pacific Island labourers were illiterate, could not understand spoken English and many had no idea of formalised Christianity. Any Christian teaching would have to start with these fundamental problems and build from there. The mainland churches, both Protestant and Catholic, were preoccupied with establishing themselves among the European population in the rapidly growing towns of north Queensland. Anglican missions to the Islander population encountered resistance and prejudice from settlers in northern Australia (Moore 2008a: 302). The Pacific mission churches, the London Missionary Society and the Melanesian Mission, declined to send pastors to Queensland to preach to the labourers. They remained island based and preferred to follow the pattern of using senior white missionaries and South Sea Islander pastors and teachers (Hilliard 1969: 41). The Melanesian Mission did not foster connections with Queensland Anglican dioceses until 1895.

The aim of the Queensland Kanaka Mission was to have the men reject 'heathen' customs and the habits of alcohol abuse, swearing, fighting and gambling that many had acquired. There was a sizable population of Melanesians in the Bundaberg region. One quarter of the 10,000 indentured labourers in Queensland were located there at that time (Hilliard 1969: 42). Of the more than 17,000 labourers brought to Queensland from the Solomon Islands more than 9,000 were from Malaita (Price and Baker 1976: 110–111, 115–116). This led to important implications for the mission that became predominantly Malaitan in its membership and its value system. When time came to establish an island-based mission the place chosen to settle was Onepusu on the south-western coast of Malaita. As an evangelical, non-denominational mission, the QKM preached 'salvation before education and civilization' (Moore 2013a: 3). The guiding conviction was that the Christian Gospel must be brought to those without it. No educational, medical or social work was to impede the message of salvation first and the primary aim was to prepare Melanesian men for their eventual repatriation back to the islands where they would spread the message of salvation. However, many labourers had a keen desire to learn to read and write and a high standard of moral conduct and verbal testimony was required before conversion. Drinking, swearing and gambling were expressly proscribed. This prohibition on alcohol and gambling, and the need to learn to read and write, were all part of the attraction of the QKM. Drinking and gambling had become major health and livelihood issues among the labourers and the deferred pay system was imposed as one way to exercise control over alcohol abuse. Alcohol, drugs and gambling were, in fact, important devices for social control. Drinking parties were incorporated into worker leisure activity and the giving and receiving of alcohol and money became part of a transplanted exchange system (Graves 1983: 118). The QKM activities were a way in which men could take control of their own lives and become more accepted within the European community. By breaking with these worker leisure activities and by forswearing alcohol and gambling, the men made the mission their social centre.

Following on from the China Inland Mission model, the QKM maintained a solid uncompromising stance based on a literal interpretation of the New Testament (Moore 2013a: 4). This fundamentalist approach to Biblical teaching then became the primary religious philosophy taken back to the Solomon Islands. Conflicting values surfaced in the islands where the pidgin-English fundamentalism taught by early QKM pastors had little affinity with the Melanesian Mission's formal liturgical Christianity (Hilliard 1966: 131). When the Queensland government proposed to end the labour trade in 1890 Florence Young went to work with the China Inland Mission, the body with which she most closely identified. The government reversed this decision in 1892 and the labour trade was extended for a further ten years. The QKM then re-engaged with the imported workers. During the Boxer Rebellion of 1900 Florence Young was forced to leave China and return to Queensland and so from that time she devoted her energies to the QKM that remained based in Queensland until 1906. It was renamed the South Sea Evangelical Mission (SSEM) and became fully island-based from 1907. After 1964 it was renamed the South Seas Evangelical Church (SSEC) (Moore 2009a).

The evangelical groundwork in the Solomon Islands was largely built on the efforts of returned workers rather than white missionaries. One man instrumental in establishing the mission on Malaita was Peter Abu'ofa who, after a faltering start at Lau Lagoon, eventually built a church and school at Malu'u in north Malaita (Moore 2013a: 5). Although this was his home area the establishment of the mission there was precarious for he faced hostility from local people and even from within his own family (Moore 2013a: 14; Moore 2009a). A man of some resolution Abu'ofa even accused Joseph Vos, the captain and part-owner of the labour vessel *William Man*son, of kidnapping in 1894. Vos had been accused of illegal recruiting practices before. As captain of the labour schooner the *Lizzie* in 1883 his recruiter Peter Dowell had taken a woman from Ambrym against the wishes of her people and then kidnapped a man who had come to take her back (Scarr 1967b: 19–20; The Vagabond [Julian Thomas] 1886; Johnston 1980). But this latest episode resulted from a complaint of kidnapping being made by Abu'ofa and other islanders who had been returned to Queensland rather than let off at their homes in north Malaita. Subsequently Vos, the Government Agent, the mate, the recruiter and three seamen of the 'William Manson' were arrested in Brisbane and charged under the *Pacific Island Labourers Act 1880* (44 Vict c.17) and the amendment acts of 1884, 1885 and 1886. Two long and highly publicised trials ensued, first in the City Police Court between November and December 1894, and then in the Supreme Court of Queensland in March 1895. The *William Manson* crew were found not guilty. Despite these findings, no doubt influenced by the judge's biased statement that 'a great number of the witnesses were South Sea Islanders, coloured men—uneducated men—men unacquainted with religion and other sanctions which bind white men to the truth', the Queensland Government barred all the accused from participation in the labour trade (Moore 2013a: 6–10; *The Sydney Morning Herald* 16 August 1894: 6; *The Queenslander* 30 March 1895: 614–615). The case was reported widely in Australian newspapers (*South Australian Chronicle* 24 November 1894: 10; *South Australian Register* 7 December 1894: 6; *The Brisbane Courier* 20 November 1894: 2). To that extent, the only legal case brought by a Pacific Islander to challenge the Queensland labour trade was a small victory for the prosecution.

By 1905 the QKM claimed over 2,000 converts in Queensland. Like Abu'ofa the repatriated teachers who returned to the islands, many to Malaita, faced a difficult time. When they could they formed small enclaves on the coast where they could continue to build churches and schools. Still they faced threats from other groups, especially the neighbouring bush communities. When the labour trade was abolished by an act of the Australian Federal Parliament in 1901, the QKM ceased to be necessary as a separate evangelising mission in Queensland (Hilliard 1969: 48). It had served its purpose. Now a need was obvious to establish the mission in the islands and to support the lay pastors there. Florence Young began visiting the Solomon Islands each year after 1904 and continued to do so until 1926. Her nephews, Northcote Deck and Norman Deck, subsequently took up duties in the Solomon Islands as resident missionaries. The SSEM retained an executive council of nine members resident in Sydney and Melbourne, and a headquarters based at Eldon Chambers, 92 Pitt Street Sydney, for the mission remained entirely dependent on unsolicited donations from supporters, mostly in Australia and New Zealand.

In a decidedly uncritical history of the SSEM written in 1951 by the then District Officer at Auki, possibly A. A. MacKeith (BSIP 1/III F23/9), the expansion into the plantation economy also had Christian meaning. Florence Young 'decided to look around for a company of "sympathetic Christian gentlemen" who might wish to render the mission a great service and at the same time find a safe investment in the Solomons'. These 'sympathetic Christian gentlemen' were her brothers from the Fairymead Plantation who formed the Malayta Company in 1908 with a strong capital base of £30,000. They established Baunani copra plantation along a 15 mile strip of coast (24 kilometres) that covered 10,000 acres (4,000 hectares) (Moore 2009a: 28). The plantation was located just 20 miles (32 kilometres) north of the mission headquarters at Onepusu, The land, previously owned by W. H. Pope, cost the Young family and their investors £35,000 (Boutilier 1983: 50). It was the largest and earliest alienation of plantation land on Malaita but, like other alienations of land in the islands, it was made without accurate survey. Here members of the mission could find work and attend evening education and scripture classes. The establishment of the plantation came after the formation of the SSEM but the commercial incentive to develop the plantation, with its large resident Christian workforce, mirrors the foundation of the mission at Fairymead Plantation in Bundaberg.

One of the most successful moves made by the SSEM was to hold services in Pijin or local language. The administration later had requested that the mission re-evaluate this language policy and use English as the medium of instruction. Many islanders later understood that the real key to power was good education, and not just literacy, and so the use of local languages in the church declined. Another successful move was to begin a nucleus of mission stations and schools around the coasts of Malaita, Guadalcanal and Makira. The size of Malaita, and the reputation of the people there, had limited the success of the Melanesian Mission and the other churches. By basing the mission on Malaita the impact of the SSEM on the established spheres of influence of the mainstream churches was limited. However Peter Abu'ofa's contribution to the pacification and formation of Christian communities in north Malaita was outstanding (Moore 2013a: 18). From 1895 Abu'ofa began building cooperation between inland villages and the new Christian coastal communities and he 'can be said to have established the foundations of modern society in north Malaita'. This cooperation began well before the British administration constructed a post at Auki in 1909.

Regrettably, the presence of the SSEM in Guadalcanal and Makira was different. There, it did raise concerns within the mainstream churches. The mission was referred to by one Anglican missionary as 'dissent in its barest and crudest form' (Hilliard 1969: 49 quoting from the Annual Report of the Melanesian Mission for 1908: 35). The SSEM made a strict distinction between the mission, whose aims were to instruct and preach, and the church, the national organisation of members who had been evangelised. The SSEM chose to remain ideologically removed from the administration. This was due to fundamental differences in philosophy and social position. Norman Deck, interviewed by Boutilier (1974: 59), reported that he had told the Resident Commissioner Jack Barley: 'God has sent us here primarily with a gospel to win these people to the Christian faith. We give them education because they don't know how to read until we teach them to read. And central was the scriptures. Our whole work is built upon the knowledge of the scriptures'. The aim of education Young had also stated was 'above all they [local people] learn to depend on GOD' (BSIP 1/III F23/9). The commitment to scripture based faith, the operations of the Malayta Company and the financial role of the Young brothers were to cause discontent between the mission and the administration (Hilliard 1969: 52). It was clear that Woodford had some dislike of the methods and philosophies of both the SSEM and the Methodists. They formed powerful factions. Both the Youngs and the Decks on Malaita and Goldie and his senior pastors at Roviana had direct and powerful contacts in the Colonial Office and the Western Pacific High

Commission. They were also prepared to use their connections and resources. But the main success of the SSEM was its ability to inculcate in the minds of local people, especially in Malaita, a belief in their own capabilities and to encourage a degree of autonomy at the local level which other missions found impossible to achieve. This congregational nature of local church government, administered by pastor-teachers and local elders, was readily adaptable to the local authority structures (Hilliard 1969: 60). Teaching was simple, based on a strict fundamentalist interpretation of the Bible. This scriptural authority was a convenient and final determination for many with both secular and religious authority.

9. The plantation economy

The State Library of Victoria holds a small but interesting archive of papers from W. Stawell—possibly William Stawell a prominent lawyer in Melbourne and senior partner in the firm Stawell and Nankivell (Stawell 1910, MS 9273). These papers provide some idea of the investment potential of plantations in the Solomon Islands in the first decade of the 20th century. Stawell made enquires of a stockbroker, John Goodall, with offices at 99 Queens Street in Melbourne. Stawell approached the firm with an enquiry about investing in plantation development in the Solomon Islands in 1910 when copra prices were high. From the correspondence, it is possible to deduce the costs of establishing a small-scale copra plantation in the islands and the profits to be expected. The firm wrote to Stawell that the population estimates on Guadalcanal and Malaita were between 100,000 and 150,000 each—misreading the figures in the annual reports of the Protectorate. They estimated that one Solomon Islander worker could look after 7–8 acres a year and that the cost of felling timbers and planting coconut palms was about £19 per acre. In 1910, with the copra price at £27/10/- a ton and production estimates at £15 a ton, the predicted profit was £12 a ton. No indication of the volatility of copra prices was given. The firm told Stawell that profit on an initial capital input of £7,754 was £3.360 or almost 45% on the investment after seven years. The company writing to Stawell provided a complete breakdown of costs on an annual basis and the need for an initial £7,000 capital investment figure was drawn from those estimates. Other costs included a salary of £300 a year for the white manager, with the basic contract wages of £6 a year per worker, an estimate of 10/- a month per person for food and a recruiting fee of £7 per person.

The plantation land under investigation by Stawell was located on the western side of Kolomgangara and south of the Lever's Pacific Plantations Ltd concession. The land between Wilson Cove (Hambere) and Ariel Cove (Meresu near Kukundu) that fronted Porpoise Bay (Vella Gulf) was about 4 square miles or 2,560 acres in area. This property was later purchased by Norman Wheatley in order to keep it out of the hands of investors. The chiefs proposed that Wheatley buy the land with a stipulation that local people could collect coconuts there (Burnett 1911: 136–137; Bennett 1987: 120). The land under consideration was presented to Stawell as flat and dry land that could be converted to plantation. In fact it was occupied, heavily forested, with steep hills intersected by many creeks and streams and had a high annual rainfall. The large Lever's concession covered almost two-thirds of the island and there were few planters located on the west side (Stawell 1910, MS 9273). The only other property owner on the south-west was shown to be Mr A. Fischer. Burnett (1911: 135) travelling on the *Makambo* with Arthur Mahaffy noted that one potential investor in land on Kolombangara was a close relative of Mahaffy and the other 'an alleged German-American tobacco planter'. Clearly, there were other investors besides the large companies interested in the plantation economy. The costs provided to Stawell gave no indication of the physical difficulties associated in developing a plantation in such an isolated location and the problems that would be encountered in dealing with local landowners and immigrant labour. There are no indications that Stawell ever invested in plantation land on Kolombangara. This can be compared with a proposal undertaken in 1905 by L. F. Giblin for Lord Stanmore. Giblin proposed that it would require an investment of £39,900 over seven years to provide a 10% profit of £3,910. In that time 3,960 acres of land would be planted with coconuts (WPHC 4/IV 70/1906). In comparison the proposal submitted to Stanwell by his Melbourne stockbroker was clearly unviable.

With the plantation economy developing, albeit at a slower pace than expected, the range of imports at this time expanded. The most highly sought after produce remained tobacco, still used in part as a currency, along with rice, calico, axes, knives, tinned meat, flour and kerosene. Beer and spirits were imported from Australia but the *Liquor Regulation of 1893* (Queen's Regulation no 4 of 1893) prohibited their sale to islanders. Construction materials such as timber and corrugated iron were imported along with numerous whaleboats. These whaleboats became an important commodity in communities and Woodford specifically noted in the annual report that 'natives continue to buy boats, and several arrive from Sydney by every steamer' (Great Britain. Parliament. House of Commons. Parliamentary Papers 1902: 6). Coastal people needed boats and with peace came a more permanent settlement of the littoral. The demand for the more acceptable whaleboats became a sign of the times, but in order to pay for the boats people needed to participate in the developing plantation economy. Tobacco remained part currency and part wage payment for some time. The annual expenditure report to the High Commission for the year 1913–1914 would record that the £12,000 allocated for the purchase of tobacco by the administration was overspent by more than £1,000 (BSIP 3/1/1).

Before the labour trade had finished, and before all indentured labourers were deported from Queensland, the last of the labour migrants were utilising the time to bring in arms hidden in sails, down the galley funnel, in water tanks and even fastened to fishing lines and dropped over the side. An inspection of all returning labour boats was undertaken at the departure port in Queensland and again in Tulagi harbour but many weapons escaped detection. The smuggling of firearms at the end of the labour trade was a problem for all. It was even reported to the *Brisbane Courier* (4 September 1908: 2) by Florence Young who stated that guns and ammunition were being bought in Papua and shipped on Burns Philp steamers to the Solomons via German New Guinea. This practice continued for some time for it was later confirmed by Thomas Edge-Partington, the District Magistrate at Auki, in his report to Woodford on 5 April 1911 (BSIP 14/40). Earlier Woodford had told the *Sydney Morning Herald* (30 June 1908: 7) that not only illegal importing of guns was a problem but that he estimated that on Malaita alone there could be as many as 4,000 to 5,000 Winchester repeating rifles. It was believed that 'should the recruiting of labourers for the Queensland plantations be stopped altogether by the Federal Australian Government as is probable, the effect would be to render available a larger supply of labourers for local requirements' but it was hoped it would also stop the importation of guns and ammunition from Australia, Papua or German New Guinea. The illegal supply of arms continued until after 1914 when indentured labourers in Fiji were returned to the islands. Arms and ammunition were also traded between Marau on Guadalcanal and Malaita during the regular movement of people across Indispensable Strait (BSIP 14/42).

The waste land regulations

The need to make the protectorate self-supporting led to a preoccupation with the establishment of a plantation economy in which the long-term interests of the islanders were relegated to the background (WPHC 8/III Items 31–40: Memos and Land Policy in the BSIP 1893–1914; Scarr 1967a: 291). Prior to the establishment of the Protectorate land could be secured by direct negotiation between landowners and white men but the system was flawed. Woodford wrote in his annual report: 'No attempt was made [by the purchasers] to enquire into the title of the native who was supposed to sell the land. The first native encountered on the beach was considered good enough to purchase from' (Great Britain. Parliament. House of Commons. Parliamentary Papers 1902: 13–14). Following formal declaration of the Protectorate the *Solomons (Land) Regulation of 1896* (Queen's Regulation no 4 of 1896) specified that every trading station and agricultural area secured by purchase or lease from traditional owners was only granted provisionally until ownership was approved by the High Commissioner in Fiji. Under the regulation, one-tenth of the land had to be planted with cultivated crops within five years or it would revert to its original owners. The regulation was implemented to restrict further freehold sale of land.

Subsequently a waste land regulation was implemented. Officially, protectorates lay outside the territorial dominion of the Crown. Protectorate status gave the administration rights to call any land Crown land provided it was first described as 'waste and unoccupied'. Under English law, the colonial government could not acquire radical title over this unoccupied or waste land and therefore was unable to grant proprietary rights to that land. It could only offer rights of occupation. Woodford believed that Solomon Islanders attached little value to land but viewed property rights under custom being conferred to the things planted on the land, and the fruits of the trees (Heath 1979: 120). He wrote: 'After the crops are taken off the land is allowed to relapse again to forest. When, however, a native plants coco-nuts his property appears to be in the trees themselves, apart altogether from any ownership in the land upon which they are planted' (Woodford 1890b: 33). He believed all people had open access to virgin forest and areas of secondary growth that could be used for gardens. This was a misreading of the diffuse and still uncertain rights to land recognised by custom. Some of this was also due to the repeated acts of some islanders misrepresenting themselves as landowners and selling the land. These sales were often conducted without consultation with other landowners for, under customary laws, any alienation of land must be negotiated with all claimants (Heath 1979: 76). Woodford believed that he could reverse any anomalies in land transactions when found later. This was unrealistic.

Confusing land tenure systems also operated in the islands: Malaita and Choiseul peoples followed patrilineal descent, Guadalcanal, Isabel and Makira peoples followed matrilineal descent lines. In the New Georgia region, as a result of the movement of migrations to the coast and intermarriage, people followed ambilineal descent lines. These descent constructs were 'diverse, flexible and contingently arranged' (Heath 1979: 46). If Woodford and his land officers realised that the ancient law of usufruct—the rights to enjoy the produce of the land—was closer to the nature of Melanesian land occupation then perhaps many mistakes could have been avoided. Usufruct in European civil law is a subordinate legal right to ownership. In Melanesian societies land is communally owned by the clan or tribe. The fact that much land appears unoccupied does not mean it is not owned nor does it mean the land is unmanaged. All land may be occupied but the use of certain plots is conditional upon negotiation and communal agreement. Melanesian custom does not permit permanent land alienation nor does it permit absentee land ownership.

The Solomon (Waste Land) Regulation of 1900 (Queen's Regulation no 3 of 1900) was later amended and consolidated in 1901 (King's Regulation. 1 of 1901) and again in 1904 (King's Regulation no 1 of 1904). This policy was an attempt to meet the conflicting and confusing requirements of cultural interaction and the diverse interpretations of the meaning of land ownership (Heath 1979: viii). The difficulty was not just a lack of understanding of the differences between European and Melanesian concepts of land ownership. The misunderstanding was accentuated by the complex authority structure in orthodox British colonialism with divided administrative responsibilities between the local British Solomon Islands administration in Tulagi, the Western Pacific High Commission in Suva, and the Colonial Office in London (Heath 1979: xi). It allowed the administration to issue Certificates of Occupation for any land declared 'not owned, cultivated, or occupied by any native or non-native person'. The term 'Certificate of Occupation' was introduced in a file note during internal discussions at the Colonial Office. It was considered an alternative to the term 'License to Occupy' that implied more definite ownership of land. In his letter to the Colonial Office, Sir George O'Brien in Suva stated that the lease of land 'consists of an endorsement of the application thereof, [and] covers the grant of fishing rights where the land borders the sea' (O'Brien to Colonial Office 15 January 1900 CO 225 59 5940). O'Brien's failure to clarify the legal position whether this meant exclusive rights to fish would cause considerable bureaucratic consternation later on.

Under this regulation it was hoped that large areas of supposedly unoccupied land could be made available for cultivation. The official position in London was:

> Having been informed by the Foreign Office that the natives of certain regions were 'practically savages without any proper conceptions of ownership of land', the Law Officers replied that the right of dealing with all waste and unoccupied land accrued to the Crown by virtue of its protectorate, since protectorates over territories occupied by savage tribes really involve the assumption of control over the lands unappropriated. Her Majesty might, if she is pleased, declare them to be Crown lands, or make grants of them to individuals in fee, or for any term (Heath 1979: 104 quoting Foreign Office to Law Officers 18 November 1899 and Law Office to Foreign Office 13 December 1899 FO 834/19).

The waste land regulation was enacted to encourage large-scale plantation development. The licence for coconut planting was 50 years but could be renewed and a Register of Claims was kept in Suva with a copy of the register in Tulagi. The transaction would incur an administrative fee payable by the claimant but '[i]t is hoped that no time will be lost in putting the whole question of outstanding land claims upon a more satisfactory footing, and of disposing, once and for all, of certain preposterous claims which have been lately advancing', for any plantation economy was then mostly at a standstill (Great Britain. Parliament. House of Commons. Parliamentary Papers 1902: 14). However the Crown policy of issuing only Certificates of Occupation, not leases, created a problem with finance for potential planters. The certificates only secured the rights of the holder to use of the lands to the exclusion of any other party. They were not accepted as collateral to secure development funding from banks. Only well capitalised, large-scale plantation developments could survive in this financial climate.

While tidying up the register of claims was fundamental to the management of land transactions, the administration did not see, or chose not to see, that the entire premise that the land was unoccupied, and therefore 'waste', was flawed.

The perceived absence of people did not mean that the land was not owned by a community. People shift their gardens continuously, and their villages and hamlets occasionally, but their sacred groves and their food trees are fixed (Miller 1980: 457). While Woodford has been strongly criticised for implementing this policy in the Solomon Islands, the concept of waste lands in colonial states was well entrenched in colonial law (Bennett 1987: 130). In the final analysis Jackson (1978: 240) wrote: 'His [Woodford's] passionate commitment to the commercial development of the island placed him at one with many of the demands of the planting community, but this support was modified by his frustration and disappointment at what he considered to be the slow pace of progress'. The Solomon Islands was not the only tropical protectorate struggling with uninspiring economic development.

After Hugh Hastings Romilly had raised the British flag at Port Moresby on 6 November 1884, Sir Peter Scratchley purchased land from Motuan leaders in 1885. After this initial purchase the economic development of British New Guinea faltered. When the Protectorate became a Crown Colony, and Sir William MacGregor became Administrator, *Land Regulation Ordinance 2 of 1888* was enacted to regulate the acquisition of Crown lands by the administration and to restrict further purchases of land made between local people and traders (British New Guinea 1888). Under this ordinance only the Administrator could acquire land from 'natives'. This would be held as Crown land. The annual report stated: 'Waste and vacant lands not used nor likely to be required by the natives may be taken possession of by the Crown as Crown land. In such acquisitions an attesting instrument is to be prepared, with a full description of the land, and to be recorded in the office of the Registrar-General' (Mair 1970: 135, British New Guinea 1892: v–vi). Subsequently MacGregor passed *Land Ordinance no 7 of 1890* to regulate the settlement of land claims that had occurred between the declaration of protectorate status on 6 November 1884 and the declaration of sovereignty made on 4 September 1888. Land for coconut planting was made available to be leased for a minimum of 60 years with an increasing rent as the plantation became established. The moves by MacGregor to register alienated land, to clean up irregular land purchases and to allocate land for plantation development were largely copied by Woodford in the Solomon Islands. In both cases, the justification for introducing such a policy was to hasten the economic development of the region. Out of a total of 442,965 acres alienated as Crown land in Papua by 1890, 326,400 acres had been acquired under the waste and vacant land legislation (Mair 1970: 136).

By the end of MacGregor's term in office in 1898 no coconut planting of any importance had been started in British New Guinea. MacGregor enacted *Native Board Regulation 2 of 1894* (known as the Planting Coconuts Regulation). This specified that all villagers must plant a certain number of coconut trees with the number being set by Resident Magistrates taking into account the nature of the land and the agricultural possibilities of growing coconuts in the area. The aim of this regulation was to assist the development of a copra industry based around native grown produce. Following the 1906 Royal Commission into the conditions of government in the colony, Hubert Murray, the Chief Judicial Officer, emerged unscathed from the political debacle (Australia. Parliament 1907; National Archives of Australia 1904–1907; Gibbney 1966; Lattas 1996; Lett 1949). He was installed as Acting Administrator until the new Papua Act was passed by the Australian Parliament in 1905 and, when it came into force on 1 September 1906, British New Guinea became Papua with Murray as Lieutenant Governor.

The Papua Act forbade the sale of freehold land and all leaseholds were then to be assessed on their unimproved value. Under *Land Ordinance no 5 of 1906*, Crown lands could only be disposed of as leases and a maximum term was 99 years with a right of renewal. All leases became subject to improvement conditions in order to prevent speculation or large land acquisitions (Papua 1906/07–1940/41). By 1910, Murray had secured more than one million acres of land as Crown lands under these waste lands provisions. But even with this large amount of Crown land at its disposal, the administration in Papua had trouble attracting investment (Mair 1970: 136–137). Commercial ineptness and government intervention maintained an undue administrative control over commercial development in Papua. Consequently the economy suffered (Ohff 2008). Copra was the main driver of the economy. This was the only tropical product that could not be grown in Australia. In Papua, other produce, pearl shell, turtle shell, trochus, bêche de mer and even gold mining boomed and then went bust. As in the Solomons where many similar regulations were implemented, perceptions of the fabled riches of the tropics faded.

Pacific Islands Company Ltd

The problems faced by the Pacific Islands Company in establishing viable coconut plantations illustrates the complexity of land negotiations in the Solomon Islands. John Thomas Arundel, a Sydney merchant, built up a diversified trading company that operated guano mines, coconut plantations and copra trading and shipping in the Pacific. The main Australian guano projects were small-scale and located on remote places like Raine Island and Lady Elliott Island on the Great Barrier Reef off Queensland. Coconut plantations were started in the Gilbert Islands. Arundel's company merged with a London based trading company to form the Pacific Islands Company in May 1897 with Lord Stanmore—formerly Sir Arthur Gordon, Governor of Fiji and the first High Commissioner for the Western Pacific—as its chairman (PMB 1205 MP1174/1/210 Pacific Islands

Company Memorandum and Articles of Association). Some of the powerful London-based directors had been in the Colonial Office and others had been prosperous merchants and traders (Pacific Islands Company Prospectus enclosed in CO 225 54 13747; PMB 1205 MP1174/1/248). Two directors had Colonial Office experience: Sir Robert Herbert had been permanent Under-Secretary of State for the Colonial Office and Sir John Bramston an Assistant Under Secretary of the Colonial Office. The power and influence of these men no doubt assisted them in securing an indenture between the Crown and the company for a license to occupy Ocean Island (Banaba) to mine its guano deposits (WPHC 10/IX Item 238).

Their proposal in the Solomon Islands was to develop large-scale plantations using the chartered company model of the British South Africa Company (BSAC) formed by Cecil Rhodes (Stanmore to Secretary of State for the Colonies 17 April 1898 BSIP 18/III Item 1). In fact Stanmore quoted substantially from the BSAC prospectus in his request to the Colonial Office, remarking that the model used in South Africa had clear implications for the Pacific Islands Company proposals in the Solomon Islands. The Pacific Islands Company actually sought a concession to secure all the 'unoccupied lands' in the islands but the chartered company structure was not favoured by the Colonial Office. This approach failed to come to fruition in part due to imprecise understanding of the rights of the Crown to alienate lands in a protectorate (Arundel to Woodford 25 February 1898 enclosed with O'Brien to Colonial Office 4 July 1898 CO 225 55 17972). Arundel also wrote directly to Woodford on this matter but Woodford stated in a reply that there was little possibility that the Pacific Islands Company request would be granted although Woodford did recommend a survey of Kolombangara and the New Georgia region (Arundel to Woodford 25 February 1898 and Woodford to Arundel 11 Aril 1898 BSIP 18/III Item 1). The company wanted to purchase its freehold land from the Crown, not from Solomon Islanders, for they were only interested in land that was not subject to traditional customary rights (Colonial Office to Stanmore 16 September 1899 BSIP 18/III Item 1). Stanmore pressed the Colonial Office for access to 200,000 acres of land and complained the 99-year lease was too short. Subsequently the request for 200,000 acres was granted by the Colonial Office although O'Brien, the High Commissioner, informed Woodford that the choice of lands must not lead to interference or molestation by natives and must be lands that local people would not later claim (Stanmore to Colonial Office 22 September 1899; Colonial Office to Stanmore 3 October 1899 and O'Brien to Woodford 24 November 1899 BSIP 18/III Item 1). Land developments occupied much of Woodford's time in 1899 and 1900. Under the headline *Important British Developments*, the *Sydney Daily Telegraph* (29 May 1900) reported that it 'transpires that the amount of land taken up by the Pacific Islands Company is 200,000 acres' and that the directors of a trading company had been for a survey tour of the islands accompanied by Woodford who was reported to say there 'is plenty of land for everybody … millions of acres in fact'. These reports served to encourage land speculators and concessionaries whose activities occupied much time for little gain.

One such concessionaire was Audley Coote, English born but for many years a resident in Tasmania. Coote became a member of the Tasmanian House of Assembly and was an active promoter of large-scale infrastructure projects, mostly rail and telegraph lines. They were notably unsuccessful (O'Neill 1969). Coote was an eminent failure. In 1901 he applied for 4,000 acres of plantation land on Guadalcanal. The area is now central Honiara behind Point Cruz (WPHC 4/IV 167/1901). Coote complained to Woodford about the development clause in the Certificate of Occupation agreement and the length of time the lease was granted. He then tried unsuccessfully to sell the certificate in Sydney. Woodford finally cancelled the license, but after much annoyance. Coote then claimed ownership of St George Island off Isabel. This Woodford reported as a 'pretended claim to the island in question [that] can therefore merit nothing but a summary refusal' (Woodford to O'Brien [undated 1901] WPHC 4/IV 209/1900). Coote's claims and counterclaims occupied much time and filled many pages of official correspondence. Woodford complained bitterly to the High Commissioner of the numerous speculators, 'company promoters and concessionaries' (Allan 1957: 39).

Subsequent to the correspondence between the Pacific Islands Company directors and the Colonial Office a tour of the islands was made in 1900 on the Adelaide Steamships Company steamer *Rob Roy* surveying possible sites for plantations (*The Brisbane Courier* 7 March 1900: 3). The SS *Rob Roy*, built in 1867, was a sizable steam launch of 309 tons that could carry 60 passengers on the Melbourne to Launceston run. It was sold to the Adelaide Steamships Company in 1883. On the Solomon Islands survey mission it was under the command of Capt F. J. Dillamore with Captain Wilson, the Harbour-Master of Fiji, as a pilot. The team sent by the Pacific Islands Company included Albert Ellis, P. Hantenstein and J. Grant from Hong Kong and, it appears from newspaper reports, Oscar Svensen was a member of the original party (*The Brisbane Courier* 7 March 1900: 3; *The Sydney Morning Herald* 28 May 1900: 3). Lt Frederick Lennox Langdale was sent to be the survey director. Langdale, a former Royal Navy officer, had settled in Fiji when he purchased the island of Wakaya off Levuka. He had also been member of the Legislative Council of Fiji. The *Rob Roy* left Sydney on 4 February 1900 and reached Tulagi on 13 March after some mechanical problems in Australia. At Tulagi, Woodford offered the *Lahloo* as a support vessel. The survey team then remained in the islands until 16 May and returned to Sydney on 25 May. Areas selected were on Gizo, Kolombangara, Wana Wana on the New Georgia coast, on Isabel, Choiseul and land on Guadalcanal (Heath 1974a: 75).

This survey expedition to find prospective plantation lands in the Solomons that involved Woodford and the Directors of the Pacific Islands Company cost the company £3,000.

Bennett (1987: 131) remarks that most of the *Rob Roy* survey was done from the foredeck of the ship and that apart from Kolombangara and Vaghena little ground survey was undertaken and that the apparent lack of people living along the areas investigated only added to the prevailing depopulation argument. Certainly, like most European observers, Woodford saw economic potential in what was perceived to be numberless, uninhabited, verdant, fertile islands (Bennett 1987: 146–147; Great Britain. House of Commons. Parliamentary Papers 1910). O'Brien's instructions to Woodford did not request a fully detailed land survey. He wrote: 'It will be necessary to roughly estimate the areas of the lands selected for the purpose of entry in the leases and the computation of rents to be paid (O'Brien to Woodford 22 November 1899 BSIP 18/III Item 1). However Langdale's report dated May 1900, copies of which are still extant in the archives in Honiara, show that the survey teams spent over two months in the western islands. 25 days were spent surveying Kolombangara and WanaWana alone (see BSIP 18/III Item 1, 18/I/22C and 18/I/22D). This was done by sea, certainly, but numerous shore parties investigated lands upriver and along the foreshores and an attempt was made to climb Kolombangara itself. Langdale clearly knew the cursory nature of his surveying when he wrote that 'we are quite unable to make more than a very superficial inspection of this immense area of land; to do so thoroughly would take years even if it could be done at all' (Langdale to H. E. Denson of Pacific Island Company 31 March 1900 BSIP 18/III Item 1 copies also in 18/I/22C and 22D). The original Langdale report of 70 pages included 14 sketch maps of the islands but only two survive in the Honiara archive collection (see PMB 1205 MP1174/1/306 for a full copy of the report). Kolombangara was strongly recommended as the location of the head station by Langdale. Langdale also paid careful attention to the nature, size and value of the estates of Oscar Svensen and Lars Nielsen and supplied the directors with detailed calculations of the current copra trade and the labour question. Dillmore also supplied a report on the trading stations in the islands and their access from a shipping perspective. He recommended the continued use of the *Rob Roy* as a first class sea boat although it appears its decks and topside were in poor condition and would need attention. The Colonial Office subsequently offered selections of up to 200,000 acres at a nominal rental. This was double Woodford's original suggestion for the company (Woodford to O'Brien 29 May 1900 WPHC 4/IV 91/1898; CO 225 60 42651 contains a précis of negotiations between the Pacific Islands Company and the Colonial Office). The High Commissioner in Suva 'obviously shared Woodford's enthusiasm for the concession because, despite the incredible vagueness of the boundaries, the lack of any survey, and the sheer perfunctoriness of the boundaries, or, more truly, neglect of the inquiry into who had interests in the land, he acquiesced in the transaction' (Bennett 1987: 131).

Although not happy with the amount of coastline that would be alienated, the size of the concession and the promises made by the company, it seemed to Woodford that the bright commercial future was a reality (Heath 1974a: 75–76). Woodford travelled back to Sydney on the *Rob Roy* and gave an encouraging interview to the *Sydney Morning Herald* (28 May 1900: 3). He reported that Langdale had selected lands, notably on Kolombangara, and stated the Pacific Islands Company had 'practically unlimited funds behind them', for even if 'they only bring half the area they have acquired under cultivation, it will mean and expenditure of millions'. Woodford was to be disappointed with the Pacific Islands Company. From the beginning Lord Stanmore was unimpressed with the conditions attached to Certificates of Occupation that would give the Pacific Islands Company only limited security of title. He wrote personally to the office of the Secretary of State for the Colonies complaining of procedures in the High Commission (Stanmore to Anderson 10 February 1901 CO 225 60 42651; Stanmore to Colonial Office 5 March 1901 BSIP 18/III Item 1). Stanmore's particular complaint was the condition in the certificates that prohibited subletting of leased lands to other parties. Obviously the Pacific Islands Company had no intention of managing all their chosen leases themselves. He was particularly critical of the obtuse comment from the Colonial Office that stated it had 'no prohibition of subletting in regard to certificates now being issued, but that in regard to [the] future complete liberty is reserved to insert such a prohibition if it should be considered desirable' (Colonial Office to Stanmore 15 March 1901 and Stanmore to Colonial Office 12 April 1901 BSIP 18/III Item 1). The decision was finally passed over to O'Brien, the High Commissioner in Suva.

The Pacific Islands Company even began negotiating rights to five islands on the Gizo Reef from Norman Wheatley who himself had only held title to the islands for a little over 6 months (Woodford to O'Brien 28 May 1900 WPHC 4/IV 54/1900). This then raised complaints from Peter Edmund Pratt who claimed ownership of Shelter Islands (Logha). In turn this was refuted by Hiqava and Wange and other *banara* from Roviana (Woodford to O'Brien 26 February 1902 WPHC 4/IV 55/1900). Actually, Wheatley had bought the Logha islands for only about £30 in trade in 1899. He later sold them to Lever's Pacific Plantations in 1911 for £12,000 (Bennett 1897: 143). Clearly everyone—traders, planters and even the local *banara*—were speculating in land. At the other end of the scale Woodford was reported as saying that it was possible for small capitalists with £4,000 or £5,000 to start a viable coconut plantation, but that it would take five to six years for the trees to reach maturity. The cost of clearing and planting the land was estimated to be £10,000. These figures were not dissimilar to those presented to Stawell by his stockbroker in Melbourne. No estimate for housing, wages to plantation workers, storage facilities or transportation to markets was given. The push to expand commercial plantations was also premised on the belief that local people lived in subsistence affluence for 'natives have so few wants that they won't make copra except to supply their limited requirements' (*The Sydney Daily Telegraph* 29 May 1900; see also Stawell 1910). This too was incorrect.

The Pacific Islands Company canvassed for 99-year leases over vast estates of declared waste land. The claim of 200,000 acres noted in newspaper articles was certainly the company objective in 1900 and 1901. However, when the German plantation and trading firm, DHPG, submitted a claim for title over large amounts of land that they had purchased in the northern islands, now part of the British protectorate the Pacific Islands Company was forced reconsider its position (Foreign Office to Colonial Office 3 October 1900 CO 225 60 32343 includes statement respecting claims on land ad translated copies of bills of purchase). Much of the land claimed by the German company comprised coastal property on Choiseul and Isabel and some on Guadalcanal. The company was not backed by the German government according to Colonial Office reports but they were making equal claims to land in Bougainville and lands now in the British territory in the south (Colonial Office to Pacific Islands Company 11 November 1901 and 12 February 1902 BSIP 18/III Item 1). The Colonial Office preferred the matter to be handled in the courts but political considerations were paramount. Woodford's arguments against respecting the German claims were dismissed despite his threat to tender his resignation if they were admitted. He wrote in confidence to John Arundel about the High Commissioner's actions but copies of the confidential letters—obviously passed on by Arundel—made their way onto the Colonial Office files (Woodford to Arundel 30 September 1900 CO 225 60 42651). Woodford was not pleased with the arrangement, and was angry with the High Commission in Fiji for even entertaining the validity of the German claims, but his complaints were considered 'childish' (Heath 1974a: 77; Woodford to O'Brien 3 July and 26 September 1900 WPHC 91/1898).

And so, in 1902, the directors of Pacific Islands Company were informed that, on surrender of the deeds to the land claimed by DHPG, the Colonial Office would grant the company rights to 200,000 acres and be paid £1,500. The Pacific Islands Company subsequently purchased the outstanding German claims, as certified by a notary public in Hamburg, for £2,000 and then sold them to the Crown (Heath 1974a: 77; Heath 1979: 102; Hookey 1971: 232). At first, the Colonial Office, notorious for its parsimony, offered the company £1,500 with a rent abatement of £1,000 for what the officials considered a 'considerable service to His Majesty's Government'. Stanmore and his fellow directors were not without position and influence. They counter-offered a sale of £2,000 with a rent abatement of £500 (Colonial Office to Stanmore 17 September 1902 BSIP 18/III Item 1; Stanmore to Colonial Office 11 August 1902 CO 225 64 33134). The transaction was designed to sell to the Crown full proprietorship of lands owned by DHPG. Subsequent to this the Pacific Islands Company was reconstructed into a paper company Pacific Islands Company (1902) Limited and it was this company that finalised the transaction with the Colonial Office (PMB 1205 MP1174/1/206 Pacific Islands Company (1902) Memorandum and Articles of Association). In December 1902 the Crown Agents for the Colonies, through the High Commissioner, paid Pacific Islands Company (1902) Ltd its £2,000 and the deeds were made over the Crown (Colonial Office to Pacific Islands Company 25 December 1902 BSIP 18/III Item 1; a file letter Pacific Islands Company to Colonial Office dated 30 December 1902 contains full details of the deeds). The company was then granted title to 193,490 acres of land in the islands on a 99 year lease (PMB 1205 MP1174/1/216 Certificate of Occupation states 189,400 acres). The largest component was 70,000 acres on Kolombangara. When the Protectorate was subsequently debited with an account for the £1,500 that had to be repaid within ten years at 3.5 per cent interest, Woodford's anger over the transactions was justified. It was also obvious that the company was not going to develop a plantation economy in the islands. The repayments to the High Commission over ten years at 3.5 per cent totalled £2,025. It was 'a debt Woodford never forgave the High Commission' (Heath 1979: 102).

The Pacific Islands Company, despite its prominent directors, was never capitalised successfully. The licences to remove guano or to plant coconuts on small isolated islands in the Pacific did not guarantee economic viability. The sheer size of the Western Pacific meant that managing small-scale operations in isolated areas was financially risky. When the company was dissolved in 1902 it owed £60,000 (Hookey 1971: 230). Woodford, quickly disenchanted with the Pacific Islands Company, soon abandoned any hopes that they would establish their large-scale plantations in the islands. Seeking economic development of the protectorate and freedom from dependency on the Imperial treasury funds, he approached Sir William Lever of Lever Brothers to invest in the islands. The directors of Pacific Islands Company tried unsuccessfully to sell off their Certificates of Occupation to Lever but he was only interested in freehold title over alienated lands (WPHC 10/IX Item 239). In 1906, Lever Brothers' Pacific subsidiary, Lever's Pacific Plantations Limited, was able to secure the remaining Pacific Islands Company concessions in the Solomon Islands for £5,000 (Heath 1979: 111; Bennett 1987: 128; Harcourt to Lever's Pacific Plantations Ltd 13 December 1911 WPHC 4/IV 61/1905). The Colonial Office tried unsuccessfully to claim half this transfer money. The Pacific Islands Company case, despite the high profile of its directors, had been a fiasco.

The question of land tenure was fundamental to the development of a plantation economy. The only successful plantations were those established on land acquired directly from the Solomon Islanders and not on leased land held under Certificates of Occupation. The Certificates of Occupation were not formal leases or sales of land by the Crown. They guaranteed and protected the holder's occupation rights under British law and, while not granting proprietary rights, prevented unauthorised occupation by another party. However, they prevented the land from being sub-leased to another party. The process was a matter of policing land use rather than land lease or sale (Hookey 1971: 232–233).

First decade of the new century

In the meantime, Tulagi was expanded as a government station. Gizo was cleared and a police house, boat house and landing wharf constructed. By 1902 Woodford was sending his annual report to Joseph Chamberlain, the Secretary of State for the Colonies, rather than through Suva. In the covering letter attached to the annual report for 1902/1903 Woodford wrote that the report was forwarded to London to 'avoid the delay of transmission via Fiji' (Great Britain. House of Commons. Parliamentary Papers. 1905: 3). There was obviously some internal disagreement over the content or the editing of the reports. There would be no annual reports for the period 1905/1906 to 1911/1912 with no explanation for the suspension of seven years. These corresponded with the years when Everard im Thurn was High Commissioner. Woodford and im Thurn had a poor working relationship exacerbated by the even worse relationship between Woodford and the Secretary of the High Commission, Merton King. No reports would be submitted for the three years from 1915/1916 to 1917/1918 although that coincided with the First World War and can be more easily explained. Administrative attention in London was far removed from the Solomon Islands.

By 1902 the white population of the islands had increased to 83. The passing of the *Pacific Island Labourers Act* 1901 (1 Edward VII 16 1901) on 17 December and the *Immigration Restriction Act* 1901 (1 Edward VII 17 1901) on 23 December signalled the formal ending of the recruitment of Pacific Islander labourers for Queensland sugar plantations. Active recruitment could continue until 31 March 1904 under the legislation but any labourers remaining in Queensland after 1906 would be deported to their homes (Moore 2000). Now fewer Queensland labour vessels were coming to the Solomons to recruit. This resulted in a decline in shipping licence fees. Again, expenditure exceeded revenue in the rather impoverished Protectorate that remained heavily dependent on export of copra, ivory nuts, pearl shell and turtle shell. In order to stress the need for a direct steamer service from Tulagi to Sydney, Woodford listed three and a half pages of imports, mostly obtained from Sydney, in his annual report. Among the usual products—beads, boxes, clothing, food stuffs, crockery, furniture, and hardware—was the continued reliance on tobacco (Great Britain. Parliament. House of Commons. Parliamentary Papers 1902: 11). But realistically speaking there was little need for a regular steamer service that would be uneconomical. Only a portion of land had been allocated to white settlers at this time. By 1902 less than 1,500 acres in total had been planted and the main plantation was 400 acres located at Lungga (Lungga Point) on the northern coast of Guadalcanal. Other areas were also on Guadalcanal at Aola (200 acres) and Kaukau (Kaoka) (100 acres). Oscar Svensen was a major partner in all these ventures and the only other substantial development was the Macdonald plantation at Fauro in the Shortland Islands where 300 acres had been planted with coconuts. Woodford agreed on 15 May 1903 to the sale of 2,000 acres of land between the Mberande and Mbalisuna Rivers on Guadalcanal between Oscar Svensen and the local people. The price was 3,000 porpoise teeth (valued at £16/10/-), five cases of tobacco, each case containing 200 pounds (value £50), £5 in cash and calico, cigarette paper and matches valued at £5. The total value was £76/10/- (AU NBAC Z385/434).

By 1903 the white population of the Solomon Islands had reached 91. There were only four government officials in control, presumably Woodford, Mahaffy and two assistants. Members of missions and government officials did not pay capitation tax and so the revenue from the fee only amounted to £256 for the entire year. Station licences earned a further £206. Again there was a sharp fall-off in shipping licences paid by vessels in the Queensland labour trade. Between 1901 and 1902, £960 was earned from vessel licenses. In the next financial year only £660 was earned, but in the year 1903–1904 only £440 was earned (Great Britain. Parliament. House of Commons. Parliamentary Papers 1903: 5). Clearly a move to a viable plantation economy was desperately needed to keep the fragile economy alive. Local labour was needed to develop a plantation economy but as long as men had the opportunity to travel to Queensland and Fiji, local plantations would suffer. It was essential that the labour trade to Fiji and Samoa be stopped for economic reasons not moral ones.

The final phase of the Pacific labour trade

Although legislation had been passed in Australia to formally end the Pacific labour trade, the Protectorate was still being destabilised by its fall-out. Samuel (later Sir Samuel) Griffith, the Lieutenant Governor of Queensland, forwarded to Woodford a letter from Robert (later Sir Robert) Philp regarding the continued smuggling of arms into the Solomon Islands by men employed on the labour vessels. These were not returning labourers but men who had signed on as crew in order to travel backwards and forwards to Queensland. The smuggling of arms had not been brought under control. Mahaffy reported that most Malaita men had guns because 'not a single labour vessel leaves Queensland without a quality of arms, ammunition, and dynamite concealed on board' (Great Britain. Parliament. House of Commons. Parliamentary Papers 1903: 15). The fine for concealing weapons of £25 was not an impediment for in many cases it was paid in cash at once.

Arms were being bought in Papua and German New Guinea and smuggled into the Solomons. Philp was the former partner of James Burns in the trading company Burns, Philp & Co and director of the company instrumental in establishing the labour trade. In his new position as Premier of Queensland he wrote to Woodford expressing his regret that no breaches of the arms trade regulations could be found by customs officers in Queensland ports. In Philp's opinion it would be necessary for the Protectorate to provide land for some returnees for in 'many cases it will be impossible for these unfortunates to return to the places whence they were recruited, as they left home in the first instance to escape the punishment of their own misdeeds'. Philp was being spurious. Not all men had run away from their past misdeeds, many had recruited to gain access to much needed trade goods, others had by now converted to Christianity and they were most certainly not 'unfortunates'. Philp also noted that Malaitans who had made up about two-thirds of labourers recruited for the sugar cane plantations could not enter the copra trade and so continued to have only their labour to sell. This correspondence was reprinted in the Protectorate's annual report (Great Britain. Parliament. House of Commons. Parliamentary Papers 1902: 12–14). The alienation of land for commercial plantations combined with the large, floating, population of Malaitan men with little to trade except their labour at first seemed to be the making of a viable plantation economy, but in fact it was continuing a cycle of disadvantage that would lead to even greater social and economic stress.

When recruiting for the sugar cane plantations ceased on 31 December 1903 it was estimated that about 9,500 Melanesian labourers remained in Queensland awaiting repatriation back to their island homes. This included about 4,000 Solomon Islanders. Options for the resettlement of returned labourers were canvassed. Woodford wrote to the High Commissioner to say that all men should first be sent to Tulagi where they could then be questioned on personal choices of settlement and occupation. Adherents of main Christian religions should be settled near mission stations where they could access education, health and religious services. In the case of the Melanesian Mission these stations had to be staffed by permanent white missionaries. Other men could be settled on 'waste lands' on the north coast of Guadalcanal. This assumed that the Guadalcanal people along the coast no longer claimed that land, or used it. Another historical fallacy with major repercussions (Woodford to Jackson 2 May 1903 WPHC 4/IV

153/1902). Both Mahaffy and Woodford used every opportunity to press home the need for a small steamer to replace the *Lahloo* that could be becalmed for weeks. The sailing vessel was also the victim of rough weather and considerably damaged on a voyage to Santa Cruz in October 1900 (Woodford to O'Brien 21 November 1900 and O'Brien to Colonial Office 2 January 1901 CO 225 61 6969). The request for a small steamer was a reasonable one. Policing the islands was difficult without adequate transport. Malaita was a good case in point.

The impact of the Pacific labour trade on Malaitan society was never addressed during the colonial period but the issues were well known. They included fighting between inland and coastal peoples, arms smuggling, the high number of guns on the island, and the lack of a permanent police and mission presence. The external labour movement was now to be replaced by internal labour migration (Woodford to im Thurn 21 February 1908 WPHC 4/IV 82/1898). This would create many complex problems. Malaitan society had been destabilised by the actions of labour recruiters and revenge attacks were not uncommon. Mahaffy made one unsuccessful attempt to pacify north Malaita in September 1902. A series of murders had taken place on the island. When a young man died in Queensland his father paid for the murder of a white man as compensation. Consequently, the recruiter on board the *Rhoderick Dhu*, James McCabe, was shot. The three other murders involved local people: Bauleni, the Fijian wife of one Malaitan man, was killed for her evangelising attempts; another man, Aimisia, who returned from labour indenture in Fiji, was murdered on the way to his gardens; and a Big-man from the northern Malu'u region killed a number of people on an island off Auki (Boutilier 1983: 52-53). Mahaffy on the HMS *Sparrow* went to Oru Island off Malu'u and the ship bombarded the island, destroying all the huts. The village pigs were also killed. These attempts at suppression of the Malaitan situation had little impact. Mahaffy reported to the Woodford and the Western Pacific High Commission that 'I am sure that eighty per cent of the men [of Malaita] are so [armed] and to hope for the pacification of a warlike and quarrelsome race under such circumstances is surely merest nonsense' (Boutilier 1983: 54 quoting Mahaffy to Woodford 1 October 1902; WPHC 4/IV 7/1903). He also believed that coastal people in Malaita, the saltwater people, sheltered behind a time-honoured tradition that bushmen were always the guilty party. Mahaffy considered that hardly any outrage was committed on the island without the assistance of the saltwater people (Mahaffy to Woodford 1 October 1902 CO 225 65 7462). Im Thurn considered it the duty of the Resident Commissioner to patrol the islands 'steadily and constantly'. This was unrealistic. It was properly the duty of a locally based patrol service, not a Resident Commissioner. It was quickly realised that on Malaita white men and government officials could not penetrate more than a few hundred metres from the shore (Boutilier 1983: 55).

Mahaffy and the High Commission

Mahaffy had a low opinion of the Solomon Islanders and, in racist terms that were normal for the time, he wrote they could be described as having 'manners none, customs beastly'. In dealing with the people he observed, with some perception, two strict rules: never fail to fulfil promises made whatever the cost or sacrifice, and be patient. Following his marriage in Melbourne on 16 March 1903 to Enid Boyd, daughter of Captain Theodore Boyd of the North Devon Regiment, he was appointed to the office of the High Commissioner in Suva (*The Argus* 28 March 1903; *The Australian Town and Country Journal* 25 March 1903: 42). As Colonial Secretary and Receiver-General in Fiji he replaced Merton King. After 1908 he became the personal assistant to im Thurn who accusing him of being 'pro native to an extent that was dangerous' (Golden 1993: 237 quoting from Scarr 1967a: 293; im Thurn to Colonial Office 20 December 1909 CO 225 87 3121). Mahaffy was often sent on long inspection tours of the Western Pacific and his recommendations generally ignored (Scarr 1967a: 287). His trip to the New Hebrides reported on French developments and his opinions on the depopulation of the islands. Im Thurn wrote to the Colonial Office requesting the return of Merton King whom he called 'an exceptionally highly trained administrator under the Crown Colony system and has an exceptional knowledge of the administrative requirements of the Pacific'. As Assistant to the High Commissioner im Thurn stated would be 'better than any man I know'. The implications being he was better in the position than Mahaffy (Mahaffy to im Thurn 13 November 1909 and im Thurn to Colonial Office 22 December 9109 CO 225 87 3121). Their long working relationship must have been strained at times. Merton King must have been a difficult man, even if he were a capable administrator. When James Burns wrote from his home, 'Gowan Brae' at North Parramatta, asking for information on Woodford's health he commented: 'I suppose you have heard Mr Merton King of Fiji has been appointed to take the place of Captain Rason [in the New Hebrides], who is retiring to go home to England. From all I hear Mr Merton King is not too popular, or has not been too popular in Fiji, as many of the actions which were blamed upon Im Thurn have been actually caused by him' (AU NBAC N115/488). Indeed, the news would not have been a surprise to Woodford.

Mahaffy was sent back to the Solomon Islands in 1908 to make a long report on the progress of the Protectorate. He wrote that 'the aboriginal population is dying off very fast indeed' and blamed this on the peace and prosperity now present. Like others Mahaffy believed that warfare 'kept the minds of the community alert and their bodies active'. His Anglo-Irish background came to the fore when describing plantation managers. He considered the average Australian to be a racist undesirable and considering many of the Lever's managers were Australian, this meant trouble. Mahaffy thought these men unfit for life in the tropics (Mahaffy to im Thurn 21 December 1908 WPHC 4/ IV 830/1908). Im Thurn would have agreed with these comments and at least understood the pompous language.

Mahaffy was sent back to the Gilbert Islands as Acting Resident Commissioner to prepare a report for the High Commission on social and economic changes on the Gilbert and Ellice Islands and on Ocean Island (Banaba) following the commencement of phosphate mining (Great Britain. House of Commons. Parliamentary Papers 1910; Macdonald 2001: 85). His report on the Gilbert and Ellice Islands is short but it is a useful summary of colonial attitudes to circumstances then developing in the Western Pacific (Great Britain. House of Commons. Parliamentary Papers 1910). The situation in the Gilbert Islands was very different from that of the Solomon Islands. By 1909 a native tax had been implemented and this funded the appointment of a High Chief, Magistrates, Scribes—in charge of village accounts and community records—the police and the *Kaubure*, a small group of advisers. Villages were clean, roads were well constructed and all islands had hospitals. Despite this order and good management Mahaffy found that the 'rapid decline of the simple arts and crafts among the natives is to be much regretted and tends to accentuate the extreme monotony of their lives' (Great Britain. House of Commons. Parliamentary Papers 1910: 4). He much regretted the change in diet from coconuts, pandanus and fish to the 'cultivated taste which demands rice, meat, sugar and biscuits' and the '[c]lothes of shocking shape and of atrocious colour have almost replaced the picturesque kilt of leaves or fine woven mat, and in their canoes, now no longer laboriously sewn together of small and narrow coconut planks, but constructed of American or Australian timbers'. This modernity was attributed to the economic influence of the phosphate mine on Ocean Island. Mahaffy too saw these islanders as doomed. He wrote that 'imported diseases, the wearing of unsuitable clothes, the alarming increase in phthisis, too close a system of intermarriage, monotony of life, poverty of the food supply, and, finally, the new feature of the disinclination of the women to bear more than a limited number of children and the increased and increasing number of sterile marriages—all these affect the population and accelerate its diminution' (Great Britain. House of Commons. Parliamentary Papers 1910: 4). The gradual fading away of the islanders would have one benefit. Those islands would make valuable coconut plantations and 'should prove veritable mines of wealth to their fortunate [white] possessors' (Great Britain. House of Commons. Parliamentary Papers 1910: 5). The poor Gilbertese, it seemed, could do nothing right.

Pacific Phosphate Company Ltd

The Pacific Islands Company, a failure as a plantation developer, branched out into more lucrative phosphate mining. In 1902 the Pacific Islands Company split to become Pacific Phosphate Company and Pacific Islands Company (1902) Ltd, a paper company whose only assets were the undeveloped concessions in the Solomon Islands (Heath 1974a: 78; PMB 1176 and PMB 1206). In 1905 Stanmore also announced his intention of forming a subsidiary company under his paper company, Pacific Islands Company (1902) Ltd. To promote this new Solomon Islands Syndicate he commissioned a report on plantation prospects by L. F. Giblin, an English tropical agriculture expert. Giblin was tasked with studying the prospects for the cultivation of coconuts, rubber, cotton, ramie, coffee and cocoa but quickly declared copra to be the only viable crop. He was also commissioned to find ways of subleasing excess lands and engaging in trading. At first he found Woodford hospitable and was provided with all facts and figures available but it was clear that Woodford, after the Pacific Islands Company debacle, had 'declared himself hostile to the purposes of the Syndicate'. Giblin was also told that a new syndicate had no legal right to claim the Pacific Islands Company concessions. Giblin, it seems, spent six weeks touring the islands making an accurate assessment of the local plantation economy, all for nothing. Stanmore could not raise £30,000 to save his company from bankruptcy and he would have known this when he sent Giblin to the islands. In hindsight Woodford's lack of support for Giblin is understandable but the file comment made in Suva reads: 'Mr Woodford's attitude as reported by Mr Giblin was unfortunate' (Giblin to Stanmore 21 July 1905 and Woodford to im Thurn 10 February 1906 WPHC 4/IV 70/1906). Perhaps it was, but chaos had been looming since 1900. The company was dissolved in June 1905 when the concessions were purchased by Lever's Pacific Plantations Ltd. Sir William Lever had purchased shares in Pacific Islands Company (1902) Ltd in order to give him a foothold in the copra trade at little cost. Those shares then gave him control of the Pacific Islands Company copra concessions (Bennett 1987: 128; Heath 1974a: 29).

Albert Ellis, an analyst and prospector for the Pacific Islands Company, had confirmed the presence of large deposits of guano on Ocean Island (Banaba) in 1899 (Shlomowitz and Munro 1992: 104). Phosphates had also been found on Nauru Island, at that time a German protectorate. In 1902 the phosphate interests of the Pacific Islands Company were taken over by a new company, Pacific Phosphate Company. John Arundel and Lord Stanmore then financed new mining projects on both islands in partnership with Jaluit Gesellschaft, a Hamburg based company. Mining guano on 'waste or unoccupied lands' could only be undertaken with a licence from the High Commissioner or the Resident Commissioner of the Gilbert Islands (3 J. Soc. Comp. Legis. Ns 329 1901). Under the *Gilbert and Ellice (Guano) Regulation no 2 of 1900* full rights to mine were given to the Pacific Phosphate Company. Woodford, angry over the acquiescence of the Western Pacific High Commission in relation to the DHPG land claims in the northern Solomons, was now angry about the share dealings between Jaluit Gesellschaft and the Pacific Phosphate Company (Heath 1978: 78). Under the agreement, Jaluit Gesellschaft received one-third of any profits (Firth 1973: 25). Woodford had reason to be concerned with the partnership. Jaluit Gesellschaft was a merger between DHPG and the Micronesian interests of Robertson and Hernsheim. The name Jaluit came from the atoll in the Marshall Islands where Hernsheim had a successful trading operation (Firth 1973: 13, 24). It was yet another business coup for DHPG.

The administration in the Solomon Islands may have been unrewarded by the commercial dealings with the Pacific Islands Company but the inhabitants of Banaba were to be treated even worse by the Pacific Phosphate Company. The indigenous Banabans were powerless to exact adequate compensation and royalty payments from large, well-capitalised, influential trading companies (Firth 1973: 26). An agreement was signed giving the Pacific Phosphate Company exclusive rights to mine for 999 years at a rental of only £50 a year in an arrangement that was to come under strong condemnation. The mining licence in effect became political annexation of the island by Britain. In understating the value of Ocean Island phosphate by half, Pacific Phosphate Company secured a low 6 pence per ton royalty payment to Banabans that only began in 1906. These terms of arrangement were specified in an agreement with the Western Pacific High Commission (WPHC 10/IX Item 242). The relationship between the Pacific Phosphate Company and the Colonial Office became the subject of much public comment. The connection between Stanmore, Herbert, Arundel and the Colonial Office was considered a minor scandal when the inequities of the leasing arrangement and royalty payments were made public knowledge late in 1908 (*The Fiji Times* October 1908 copied from *The New Age*, London, 10 October 1908; Woodford papers PMB 1290 Item 9/29). In particular, Stanmore's participation as chairman of the Pacific Phosphate Company was at 'variance with his established humanitarian concern for the rights of islanders after European settlement' (Newbury 2010: 178). The directors, all men with knowledge, influence, and experience of the Pacific, had little regard for the future of the Banaban people.

Few Banabans chose to work at the mines and, with overseas labour migration closed to Gilbertese from the mid-1890s, the only well paid employment open to men was on Ocean Island. This meant that the Gilbertese workers became another case where a colonial government created an exclusive recruiting zone. They reserved the labour supply within the protectorate for one particular industry. The wage in 1907 was 32 shillings (£1/12/-) a month for the first six months and then 40 shillings (£2) a month after that. At £21/12/- for the first year and then £24 a year for the following year it was considerably higher than the plantation wage of £12 a year but work at the mines was hard and dirty (Shlomowitz and Munro 1992: 113, 115). With the price of phosphate increasing and high profits to be made from mining, Stanmore wrote urgently to the Colonial Office requesting action on plans to import Japanese mine workers. He commented, patronisingly, that the Board of the company would 'at all times *prefer* to employ Polynesians, if their services can be procured. Their employment is less costly than that of the Japanese, and they are more docile and more easily controlled' (Stanmore to Colonial Office 31 December 1907 CO 225 80 440). When Japanese were introduced as semi-skilled contract labourers they proved to be less docile, as Stanmore ruefully predicted. Mining caused major damage to both land and water resources forcing the relocation of many residents. Commitments for compensation to Banabans were never realised. The mining operations were highly profitable for Pacific Phosphate Company, who saw profits of £1,750,000 between 1900 and 1913 while Banabans were paid less than £10,000 royalties (Macdonald 2001: 99). Compared with the paltry amount offered for rental this was one of the more despicable examples of environment vandalism in the Western Pacific. It was compounded by being countenanced by Lord Stanmore, a former High Commissioner of the Western Pacific.

Lever's Pacific Plantations Ltd

The Pacific Islands Company and the Pacific Phosphate Company were not the only industrial capitalists interested in the Solomon Islands. A major player in the plantation economy would be Lever's Pacific Plantations Ltd, a subsidiary of the large Lever Brothers. The firm was created by William Hesketh Lever, the son of a successful grocer in north England, who was educated within a strict Calvinist philosophy. He later remarked that the 'grocery trade has been a university training for me' (Church and Clark 2001: 531). As a junior partner of his family business in 1872 he expanded the operations throughout northern England. In the early stage the firm bought bar soaps wholesale and then retailed them under the name 'Sunlight'. The product, 'Sunlight Self-Washer Soap', was seen as innovative for its distinctive packaging and content, and proved immensely popular. Lever developed a soap made from a mixture of copra and pine kernel oils rather than from the old fashioned animal tallow. To protect it from the open air the soap bars were individually wrapped in imitation parchment, a practice adopted from American soap makers (Church and Clark 2001: 532).

Lever then expanded using £4,000 borrowed from his father. His company, Lever & Co, operated from a small business and factory in Warrington, with Lever as the manager and cashier, and a works manager in charge of the soap boiling.

Within three years 'Sunlight Soap' was the largest selling soap in Britain. Lever subsequently introduced the 'Lifebuoy Soap' brand and acquired the 'Pears' soap brand. Lever moved from Warrington to a new factory site located near Liverpool on the Mersey that he called Port Sunlight. Here on 50 acres, later expanded to 500 acres, he established one of the first purpose-built factory and worker housing estate with high standards in design, leisure amenities and other community services. It even had a literary and science society. Lever constructed a carefully managed positive image of himself and his company by fostering a strong corporate culture in response to the prevailing discourses of Imperialism, alienating industrialisation and the problems of economic decline in the late-19th century (Rowan 2003: 2). The firm, incorporated in England in 1890 as Lever Brothers Ltd, was reincorporated in Australia in 1894. By 1897 Lever Brothers Ltd had established an Australian factory at the western end of Balmain in Sydney adjacent to wharf facilities at White Bay. Here the factory extracted oil from imported copra. This purified oil was shipped back to the main firm at Port Sunlight. Lever Brothers became a limited liability company in 1890 with a capital of £300,000. Later it went public with more than £1.5 million in capital (£600 million in current values) (Rowan 2003: 6). Lever Brothers was one of the remarkable economic success stories of the late-19th century.

Lever was skilled at marketing and introducing new types of soap products. Many became famous brand names. 'Lux Flakes', for example, commenced production in 1900. Between 1910 and 1913 several more acquisitions widened Lever's range of products and reduced those of his competitors. By 1905 the Lever Brothers Ltd factory in Sydney was crushing 13,000 tons of copra yearly, all of it from Pacific plantations. Even the by-products of the crushing plant were profitable. Refuse was made into coconut cakes used as cattle feed and coconut oil was exported to Germany for use as butter fat (*The Brisbane Courier* 17 June 1905: 6). Having a factory in Australia was also an economic decision for it meant the company avoided import duties and Sydney became a base for further expansion into the Pacific. When merged with Margarie Unie in 1930 it became Unilever, the first modern multinational trading company. More than 500 subsidiary companies now come under the Unilever name.

William Lever (later Lord Leverhulme of the Western Isles) exemplified the Victorian doctrine that hard work, rather than genius, led to success. Calvinist ideals of self-culture, self-control and growth in knowledge and wisdom were the essential characteristics of a complete man. These conservative values fed neatly into the social and class-based paternalism of the late-19th and early-20th centuries (Rowan 2003: 11). This paternalism had deep roots in society at all levels of English society. Landowners, industrialists, civil servants workers and labourers were conditioned by the residual aristocratic culture that still permeated British consciousness. They were all constrained by the habits of deference. Paternalism held that society was based on hierarchy and that even in a pluralistic society each social sphere had its own hierarchy. This social paternalism mirrored the industrial paternalism of Lever's company. It was further mirrored in colonial paternalism and missionary humanitarianism that was evangelical paternalism thinly disguised. Within Lever Brothers and the subsidiary companies an effective corporate culture maintained employee loyalty and built familial identity. Lever was an industrial paternalist but it was clear that this structural relationship between employer and employee was applicable only within white Anglo-Saxon communities. In contrast Lever's Pacific Plantation Ltd would have a poor reputation in its dealings with Melanesian plantation workers in the Solomon Islands.

The company developed a thriving export trade throughout the world and the factories needed larger volumes of copra than could be provided from small-scale beach traders. Lever was astute and determined not to rely on other suppliers for raw materials. The most economical solution was ownership of land and for the company to control management of large-scale commercial copra plantations in the islands. It was also clear to the financially troubled administration in Tulagi that attracting Lever Brothers to the Solomon Islands would be a great economic advantage. Lever's Pacific Plantations Ltd (LPPL) was formed in 1902, and pointedly, at the same time William Lever was appointed to the board of the Pacific Phosphate Company. In 1905, Joseph Meek, Chairman of Lever Brothers Australia and Chairman of Directors for Lever's Pacific Plantations Ltd, began buying freehold land from islanders as well as from individual traders and the many unsuccessful small-scale planters. Meek and his family left Australia on the New South Wales government steamer the *Victoria* under charter to investigate prospective plantation lands in the Solomon Islands, German New Guinea, Singapore and Malaya. Lever's Pacific Plantations certainly had capital to invest. The tour of the *Victoria* alone cost the company £6,000. In 1903, Oscar Svensen had tried to sell his substantial land holdings along with three schooners, one ketch and three cutters, and other assets valued at £11,000 to Burns, Philp & Co for £10,000. At that stage Burns Philp considered themselves merchants and shipping agents, not planters, and so declined his offer. Svensen had also purchased Gavutu for £3,000 from Lars Nielsen who retired to Denmark in poor health after more than 20 years in the islands (Bennett 1981: 182). The Gavutu property contained a substantial house by this stage that was raised on piles with the lower floor enclosed to form part tradestore and part living room. The file note by Walter Henry Lucas states 'must risk Levers' (AU NBAC N115/589). Lucas, an aggressive dealer, lost this time. Svensen successfully negotiated the sale of his lands and islands to Levers for £6,500 as well as acted as agent for the sale of the remaining concessions owned by the Pacific Islands Company for £5,000 (Statement of Expenditure 15 January 1912 WPHC 4/IV 61/1915). By 1907 when Lever's Pacific Plantations Ltd began to develop properties in earnest, Svensen had sold the company more than 50,000 acres of land (Bennett 1987: 143). A wealthy man, Svensen retired to 'Norway', his large home at Galloway's Hill overlooking the Brisbane River. Both Nielsen and Svensen were able business men in a region where business failures were more common. When Svensen was earning between £2,000 and £6,000 (£690,000 to £2 million in current values) a year, Woodford as Resident Commissioner, was earning only £300 (£104,000 in current values) a year (Bennett 1981: 181; Golden 1993: 132).

Soon the *Brisbane Courier* (17 June 1905: 6) reported that Meek had secured nearly 80,000 acres in the Solomons: 51,000 acres from former traders and planters and 28,870 acres obtained by purchase from local people (Hookey 1971: 237). This was distributed on more than 14 islands. Some of the land obtained under Certificates of Occupation had the leases extended from 99 years to 999 years. In this way, in 1904 the company obtained some of the prime land on the Guadalcanal plains along the northern coast of the island in the areas of Tenaru, Lungga and Kukum. The Solomon Islands were favoured, according to Meek, because 'Lever Bros. preferred to only carry on business under the British flag'. Scarr (1967a: 284) stated that im Thurn looked with mixed feelings over Woodford's success in attracting such a prized development as Lever's Pacific Plantations Ltd to the Solomon Islands. In fact the involvement was welcomed by a High Commissioner anxious for the islands to become economically self-sufficient. Im Thurn wrote: 'I am strongly of the opinion that it is highly desirable if the Solomon Islands Protectorate is ever to be developed that Lever's Pacific Plantations should be encouraged to take up land there' (Heath 1974a: 81 quoting im Thurn to Colonial Office 9 May 1905 CO 225 69; see also WPHC 10/IX Item 240). The single most important reason for encouraging Lever's Pacific Plantations Ltd was the need to reduce the already overstretched budget of the protectorate. All this occurred at a time when Woodford's reputation at the High Commission in Suva was tarnished, both by his own rashness and inability to conform to rules set by his superiors, as much as by their inability to give him independence of action.

By 1911, having obtained much of Norman Wheatley's properties, Lever's Pacific Plantations Ltd had obtained 218,820 acres in the western and central Solomons under various tenures (Woodford to High Commissioner 2 February 1911 BSIP 18/I/22D). Once again, Woodford was to be disappointed. The company chose not to develop the leased lands until all the freehold lands were planted. The sheer size of the holdings, their scattered location on many islands, and the high establishment costs of infrastructure and employment were such that Lever's Pacific Plantations would never develop all their acquisitions (Hookey 1971: 237). By 1911, William Lever wanted to dispose of unsuitable lands and keep only productive coconut plantation areas but the Colonial Office declined to accept the proposal (McDowell, Secretary, Lever Brothers to Colonial Office 13

January 1911 BSIP 18/I/22D). Woodford was aware that alienation of customary land would be a major administrative mistake but the land regulations were not designed to clarify tenure, they were designed to raise funds for the administration. The earlier acquisition of freehold land by purchase from islanders gave the administration no revenue. Only an administrative fee was charged on transactions that gave planters Certificates of Occupation. To overcome these difficulties Woodford proposed that the government would buy land from the Solomon Islanders then lease it out to planters at a better return to the administration. The result was that 250,000 acres were alienated as leasehold land. The term was 99 years. Almost 170,000 acres had been purchased from islanders by Europeans. Land claimed to have been secured by purchase or trade before the commencement of records in 1896 totalled 80,000 acres some of which was never occupied. In addition to this, small parcels of land had been obtained by various missions and traders under agreements with local land owners. There are examples of when Woodford withdrew land from transfer to plantation owners when the original land owners were identified (Heath 1974a: 84). Stopping some sales of land, and insisting on strict conformity with the improvement clauses on leases, made Woodford increasingly unpopular with Lever's management. So much so that in 1909 Joseph Meek wrote directly to the Colonial Office: 'His [Woodford's] opposition to Lever's land purchases and his complaints against Lever's employees led to a company official [Meek] to approach the Colonial Office in 1909 requesting Woodford's retirement' (Heath 1974a: 82 quoting from McDowell to Colonial Office 15 March 1909 CO 225 89. Letter includes undated correspondence from Joseph Meek to LPPL advocating Woodford's removal).

Even though the waste land regulations were modified in 1901 and again in 1904 freehold land acquisition continued. A 1912 draft land regulation was considered that would prohibit the sale of any land from a native to a European. This draft regulation recommended three classifications of non-alienated land: native lands, vacant lands, and waste lands. This regulation did not proceed because the Protectorate became involved in contested claims by local people to lands that had already been alienated (Allan 1957: 45). The draft regulation was not approved by the Colonial Office. The waste land legislations were not repealed until 1914. The *Solomons (Land) Regulation of 1914* (King's Regulation no 3 of 1914) consolidated and amended the waste lands regulations by repealing the regulations of 1896, 1901 and 1904. With this act the extensive alienation of land formally ended and a leasehold system was instituted. It had become evident that the concept of 'waste lands' was obsolete. The 1914 land regulation specified that land would legally be one of three types: native lands; private land, being alienated freehold land and public lands; and other alienated leased land (Allen 1957: 41). In future Woodford declared that it would be more convenient to consider that vacant land in the Protectorate was 'practically non existent' (Jackson 1978: 262). Under the new regulation, the declaration of public lands and native lands—land owned by natives or subject to the exercise by natives of rights of occupation or cultivation—allowed for land *not* owned by natives or *not* cultivated or occupied to be declared public lands when sold to the government (Allan 1957: 40–41). Public lands could then be leased out to non-natives. Subsequently non-natives could hold land under one of three claims: freehold land purchased directly from local people; waste or unoccupied land held under existing Certificates of Occupation; and lands leased under the *Solomons (Land) Regulation of 1914*.

However, transactions between Europeans were not prohibited. Land that had previously been sold for little return to customary owners could be resold at a high market price, especially if the land had been partly developed. In this way Oscar Svensen capitalised on his land sales to Lever's Pacific Plantations Ltd. In most cases, the original owners were unaware of the commercial transfer. The land rights initially granted by Melanesians to their European buyers were 'personal, contingent, and indefinite. The rights increasingly assumed by Europeans [in transactions with other Europeans] were transferable, absolute, and permanent' (Lamour 1984: 4). This is perhaps the clearest description of the relationships with the land held by Melanesians and by Europeans. For the former, land use is open to negotiation based on personal relationships, for the latter, ownership of land is binding and permanent. It is a commercial rather than a personal transaction. The concept of land alienation with its dual and contradictory aims at protecting Melanesian owners and European purchasers was in fact one of the reasons for direct colonial intervention. The alienation of land in the Solomon Islands was not unique, nor were the actions taken by the Tulagi administrative considered insensitive at that time. Similar land alienation practices were happening throughout the Pacific. In Australia at this time there was no legal recognition of indigenous land at all and the expropriation of Aboriginal land under the legal fiction of *terra nullius* was simply a device to validate land acquisition. The basic premise in all cases was that local political organisations did not exist. This too was false. The dualism of the colonial period was a double bind that has parallels in the situation today. Writing about land management in independent Melanesian nations, Lamour (1984: 39) stated: 'on one hand they [governments] are supposed to be protecting the custom owners against alienation of their land, and on the other they are supposed to be promoting alienation in the interests of national development or at least the maintenance of government services'.

Burns Philp and the role of Walter Henry Lucas

Burns, Philp & Co long held off acquiring land in the Solomon Islands by concentrating on shipping and trading. Walter Henry Lucas, Island Manager in Sydney, had made a tentative move by securing 100 acres for a trading station at Danae Bay, on both sides of Jetty Point, in Marau Sound in 1898. The price paid was £10 in trade (Woodford to O'Brien 9 November 1898 WPHC 4/IV 10/1899). The area remained largely undeveloped. Lucas, a shrewd, aggressive dealer, was well connected in Australian political circles. He was a confidant of Atlee Hunt and regularly corresponded with James Burns. Lucas is not a minor figure in the colonial history of the Solomon Islands. As Island Manager for Burns Philp, Director of the Solomon Islands Development Company and, after 1914, being influential in the expropriation of German property in New Guinea, he would play a significant role in the economic development of the region. He was an excellent photographer, as the albums in the National Library (National Library of Australia PIC Album 783) and the Australian Museum archives illustrate (AM Archives Capell Collection Solomon Islands Photographs, this album of photographs is by Lucas but was donated to the Museum in 1944 by Dr Arthur Capell, Reader in Oceanic Studies at the University of Sydney). The photographs by Lucas are important social and cultural documents for they provide useful counterpoints to the images taken by Woodford. The Lucas album is a valuable document in the colonial history of the Solomon Islands. A photographic montage in the *Sydney Mail* (3 November 1900: 1051 with text at 1040) of 11 images, copies of those in the album, taken by Lucas surrounding one by Woodford raising the British flag at Kondakanimboko Island in Choiseul Bay brings the presence of Lucas to the fore.

In 1904, Burns Philp also began to move into the plantation economy in the Solomons (WPHC 10/IX Item 241). Lucas, through Atlee Hunt, secured a mail contract with the Australian Government worth £6,000 a year (£2 million a year in current values). The mail service and shipping remained the backbone of Burns Philp's business in the Western Pacific. Tourism was also developing, stimulated by brochures advertising exotic travel to Papua, the New Hebrides and the Solomon Islands, but tourists were just another commodity that filled the space on company steamers (Burns, Philp & Co 1911 and 1913; Douglas 1997: 58). With the former German islands now in the northern Solomons part of the Protectorate and under British control, the company moved to secure the plantations of the Tindal, Atkinson and Macdonald families in the Shortland Islands. These three families were related through the wives, who were sisters. Lucas negotiated the purchase of the Tindal estates at Faisi and Alu following the death of Nicholas Tindal and his wife, who left one daughter and three stepchildren—the Austen children—almost penniless. The trading stations and plantations of the Shortland Islands were the subject of a full-page supplement in the *Queenslander* (22 December 1906: 24) illustrating their productivity and development. The newspaper coverage was designed to attract the attention of prospective investors. Together with the 800 acres in the northern islands, and the mail contract, Burns, Philp & Co purchased the small island of Makambo in the Tulagi Harbour. This became a sizable trading station and cargo depot for the company in direct competition with Lever's operation on nearby Gavutu. Opposite these stations on Tulagi were the administrative headquarters and ancillary property such as the hospital, jail, hotel and clubhouse, and a small but growing Chinatown built on the drained swampland along the foreshore.

Figure 34. 'Portrait of man, Simbo' and 'Simbo woman'.

Source: AMS330/8 and AMS330/9, Capell Collection, The Australian Museum. Photographs by Walter H. Lucas circa. 1900. See also Amherst and Thomson 1901, Volume 1: 133. The hunchback was a respected young man with deep cultural knowledge.

Figure 35. 'Marau canoe' and 'Buying copra [at Oscar Svensen's trading station], Marau'.

Source: AMS330/44 and AMS330/45, Capell Collection, The Australian Museum. Photographs by Walter H. Lucas circa. 1900.

Figure 36. 'Two old headhunters' and 'Portrait of Rubiana [Roviana] man wearing body ornaments'.

Source: AMS330/20 and AMS330/21, Capell Collection, The Australian Museum. Photographs by Walter H. Lucas circa. 1900. *The Sydney Mail* caption for AMS330/20 is Chief, Simbo. See also Amherst and Thomson 1901, Volume 2: 352.

In his confidential reports to James Burns, Lucas advocated freehold purchase of land as his preferred option (AU NBAC N115/2). Lucas was also an active speculator in land. He arranged the purchase of Tetepare Island in November 1907 for £100 on behalf of Burns Philp. In April 1909 this was then sold to the Solomon Islands Development Co, a Burns Philp subsidiary, for £154/14/- (AU NBAC N115/589). Burns Philp also bought Neal Island (Valelua) off the coast of Guadalcanal and land at Mataniko for £600 in 1907. Along with the property came all labourers then under engagement. Burns Philp sought to buy freehold land on the open grasslands of northern Guadalcanal along the Ngalimbu River near Lungga Point. The Tetere property was chosen for its potential use as grazing land. Woodford wrote to James Burns on 16 July 1907 to say: 'I think I can get you a block of ten thousand acres of grass land upon Guadalcanar upon Occupation License as Waste Land' (AU NBAC N115/488). Burns certainly considered this suitable in his reply of 12 December. The subsidiary company, Solomon Islands Development Company (SIDC), capitalised in 1908 with £100,000 and with Lucas as its Australian director, then began direct negotiations with land owners (AU NBAC N115/487). It was clear that the land was occupied and used for gardens. The area under question totalled 10,000 acres. The Melanesian Mission had strong influence with the local people in the region and with mission encouragement the sale was rejected by the land owners. The Guadalcanal people of the plains were not keen to have an influx of Malaitan plantation workers, some of whom would have had experiences as indentured labourers in Queensland or Fiji, living near their communities (Bennett 1987: 135). Despite Woodford's apparent offer nothing eventuated. On 3 November 1908, Lucas complained to Adam Forsyth of the Sydney office that Woodford had done nothing to assist the Solomon Islands Development Company in gaining access to the grass lands they desired. Lucas continued to push for rights to this land in his 23-page report to Burns following a tour of inspection of properties that the Solomon Islands Development Company had obtained elsewhere (AU NBAC N115/488 contains copies of the Solomon Islands Development Company Certificates of Occupation). The claim to Tetere lands was refused by the Colonial Office and all the Solomon Islands Development Company managed to obtain was 650 acres on the coast that could be used as a trading station (AU NBAC N115/2). The Solomon Islands Development Company persisted in its search for plantation land and bought estates formerly owned by white settlers.

Certainly Woodford wrote encouragingly to Burns about possible plantation land on Guadalcanal but Bennett's findings (1987: 135–138) that Woodford was embarrassed when new land regulations were introduced in 1912 is a supposition. The letters to Burns dated 1907 and 1908 were followed by complaints from Lucas about Woodford. Lucas was a regular visitor to Tulagi but he was not an uncritical one. The 1912 land regulation was also a draft law that was not admitted by the Colonial Office. It was not until 1914 that new land regulation came into force. Woodford retired in 1914. He did make presentations to the Colonial Office on behalf of Burns, Philp & Co but then again he also approached them on behalf of Lever's Pacific Plantations Ltd and on other issues. It was not until 1917 that the Solomon Islands Development Company managed to obtain Certificates of Occupation on a considerable part of the coastal land near Lungga—the Muvia, Nalimbiu and Gavaga leases—on a 999 year lease (WPHC 10/IX Item 245). This area of 15,000 acres comprised most of the flat, coastal land between the Mataniko and Mbalisuna Rivers. These lands were confirmed only after a special regulation, the *Solomons (Certificate of Occupation Solomon Islands Development Co Ltd) Validation Regulation of 1918* (King's Regulation no 10 of 1918) was created under the *Solomons (Land) Regulation of 1914* (AU NBAC N115/489).

Figure 37. 'Rubiana "Tambu" Native Club House' [actually an ordinary canoe house, *vetu mola*] and 'War-canoe house [communal canoe house, *paele*] of Ingowar [Hiqava]'.

Source: AMS330/18 and AMS330/19, Capell Collection, The Australian Museum. Photographs by Walter H. Lucas circa. 1900.

Figure 38. 'Alu women carrying loads' and 'Trading station, Simbo'.

Source: AMS330/4 and AMS330/5, Capell Collection, The Australian Museum. Photographs by Walter H. Lucas circa. 1900. The Simbo trading station was owned by Peter Edmund Pratt.

In 1907, Lucas and a journalist from Sydney, Arthur Wilberforce Jose, wrote a series of letters to the *Sydney Morning Herald* under the anonymous name 'Melanesia' criticising the actions of the Colonial Office in the Western Pacific (*The Sydney Morning Herald* 30 October 1907: 8, 9, 31 October 1907: 10, 1 November 1907: 3, 2 November 1907: 6, 4 November 1907: 5). Lucas actively used his contacts with the newspapers, especially the *Sydney Morning Herald*, to promote

Australian interests in the Pacific. The articles were later collated and published as *British Mismanagement in the Pacific Islands* (Jose and Lucas 1907; Woodford papers PMB 1290 Item 7/28). They are a xenophobic diatribe against German and French commercial and political influence in the Western Pacific. The articles were a direct and very unsubtle attack on the Colonial Office and the Western Pacific High Commissioner in Suva. They are significant because a second series of articles was published in the same paper in 1915 just after Australian troops had occupied German New Guinea. Again they condemned the actions of the British government in the Pacific, only this time the articles and the pamphlet, *British Mismanagement in the Pacific Islands No. 2*, highlighted Burns Philp's land acquisition problems in the Solomon Islands (Bennett 1987: 137). Lucas and Jose advocated for an advisory council to assist the High Commissioner with land issues and recommended that the High Commissioner have greater autonomy from the Colonial Office. Lucas and Jose were constant advocates for the Western Pacific High Commission to be relocated to Australia (Bennett 1987: 137–138). The arguments against the location of the High Commission in Fiji were the poor communications with Australia, the fact that the High Commissioner was unaware of public opinion in the Commonwealth and the problems associated with the Royal Navy Australia Station and Admiralty being located in Sydney (*The Sydney Morning Herald* 6 November 1908: 6).

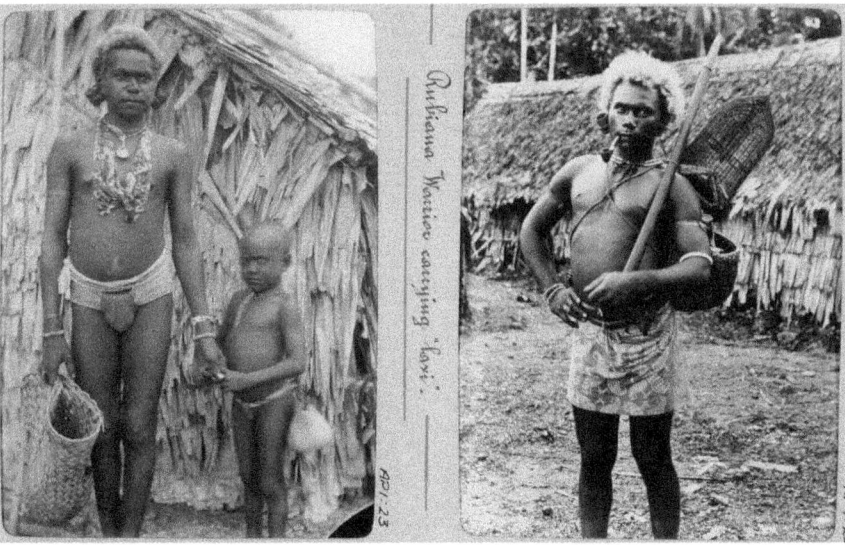

Figure 39. 'Rubiana boys in typical dress' and 'Rubiana warrior carrying "lavi [*lave*]" [shield]'.

Source: AMS330/22 and AMS330/23, Capell Collection, The Australian Museum. Photographs by Walter H. Lucas circa. 1900.

Lucas continued with this line in an interview with the *Sydney Morning Herald* (31 December 1910: 11) after he had arrived back in Australia from another tour of inspection of the Solomon Islands Development Company plantations. His main complaint was that the laws and regulations applicable in the islands were made by bureaucrats from the Colonial Office in London rather than by local officials who, he said, had the real knowledge and understanding of the area. This was especially noticeable in protectorates that did not have the status of Crown Colonies—a direct comment on the Solomon Islands. Lucas was angry over the decision to allow for only two-year recruitment contracts for indentured labourers rather than the three-year contracts of earlier days. Two-year contracts raised the costs of recruiting and repatriation of workers and Lucas was of course on the side of the planters. The labour regulations of 1910 and the amendments of 1911 and 1912 allowed for workers to be employed for 50 hours a week. The working period, from Monday to Friday, consisted of 9-hour days. Saturday was a 5-hour working day. Sunday was a rest day (*The Solomons (Labour) Regulation of 1910*, King's Regulation no 3 of 1910 and amendments King's Regulation no 9 of 1911 and no 8 of 1912). These labour regulations gave the administration increased powers to scrutinise activities of recruiters and greater access to plantations. It could fine any planter found making false statements in any workers' books and the labour officials could order a worker to hospital, or in case of bad treatment, could remove or repatriate any worker back to their home community. Worker living quarters could be inspected and ration books issued to each worker, which specified the range of food provided at the plantation, could be examined. This ration included yams, sweet potato, taro, bananas, rice, coconuts, bread, sugar, biscuits, meat, fish, salt, soap, and, of course, tobacco. Any labourer who sold or bartered his rations could be fined 10 shillings. If this was designed to stop the regular trade in tobacco it is difficult to see how one labour inspector could supervise more than 2,000 labourers in scattered plantations across numerous islands.

The number of labourers employed on all plantations, by companies and at the missions, including the 81 people employed by the government, was listed in the statistical report of 1909. Lever's Pacific Plantations Ltd employed 900, Burns, Philp & Co employed 120 and the Solomon Islands Development Company 160. W. H. Pope, who sold his plantation at Baunani, north of Onepusu, to the Malayta Company, employed 197 people and presumably they became workers on the mission company plantation (British Solomon Islands Protectorate 1909: 25). In total, only 2,300 people were employed on plantations, trading stations and local vessels within the Protectorate. The legislation gave the government access to pay books. Lucas, like other planters and traders, and the policy makers in the Colonial Office, saw the Solomon Islanders first as workers who could be 'improved' by regular work. Industrial training was permitted providing it fostered discipline and encouraged productive labour 'to utilise

[Islanders] in the material development of the wealth of these tropical islands' (Bennett 2000a: 46 quoting Walter Henry Lucas 1917). By 1914, Woodford had the labour regulations that he had taken considerable effort to produce, but their effectiveness could only be measured in their application.

Following his return to Sydney, Lucas wrote to Woodford in a letter dated 14 January 1911 marked 'Strictly private' that explained his position regarding the 'yell about the establishment of the High Commissioner in the [Australian] Commonwealth' (Woodford papers PMB 1290 Item 2/23 and 9/20). While Lucas wanted the office of the High Commissioner relocated to Australia, he still expected the Commissioner to be an 'Imperial Officer', in other words paid and supported from the Imperial rather than Australian treasury. Lucas believed that by relocating the High Commissioner to Australia he would somehow become immediately sympathetic to Australian interests. Newspaper articles pushed this line, no doubt with some influence from Lucas (*The Sydney Morning Herald* 4 January 1911). His move to separate the powers of the High Commissioner was in response to the 'indignation over [labour] regulations such as that re Solomon Labor being passed and becoming law without anybody having an opportunity to express an opinion'. Lucas was a man with a mission. His goal was the expansion of Anglo-Australian trade opportunities, and more specifically those of Burns, Philp & Co, in the Western Pacific. For Lucas the problem lay in the poor communications between Suva and the outlying colonies and protectorates. Everard im Thurn came under some criticism with the newspaper publicly stating: 'We have, for example, found Sir E. im Thurn rather dogmatic occasionally in the wrong direction'. The *Sydney Morning Herald* article of January 1911 reported that im Thurn's retirement would prove to be an excellent opportunity for an improvement in the relationship between Suva and Australia. As one would expect, the proposal for the separation of the powers was quickly rejected by the British government.

Lucas had a long history of conflict with German traders. He was supercargo on the *Titus* when he came into conflict with Norddeutscher-Lloyd Co over contracts for shipping that led to the exclusion of Burns Philp in German New Guinea. He was an influential man. He led a delegation of Federal members of Parliament on an inspection tour of Papua in 1911 (National Library of Australia PIC Album 783 and 782). 19 members of Parliament and their entourage visited Port Moresby, Yule Island, Samarai and Woodlark Island on the Burns Philp steamer *Matunga* (*The Brisbane Courier* 3 June 1911:4, 5 June 1911: 7). The company's collaboration in this exercise was of course organised by Lucas (National Archives of Australia A1, 1911/16361, 1911/3212, 1911/3213). The tour of inspection came at a time when there had been much speculation in plantation land in Papua following the passing of the Papuan Land Ordinance of 1906 and the amendments in 1908 that were part of Hubert Murray's scheme to build a profitable plantation economy in Papua. There was an initial rush to acquire land on 99-year leases with a right of renewal. However by the end of 1909 the vast majority of these leases were unoccupied (Mair 1970: 30, Lett 1944: 112, *The Advertiser* [Adelaide] 27 February 1911: 10). Despite the obvious lack of promise, the delegation enthusiastically reported through the newspapers that Papua was the healthiest tropical country anywhere in the world: 'The only trouble is malarial fever, and that is not so bad … Most people get it, but it is only like getting a touch of influenza' (*The Advertiser* [Adelaide] 18 July 1911: 10). Lucas also advanced this argument to James Burns in his report of September 1910 when he wrote that the Solomons had a 'less trying climate, better supply of labour, freehold titles to land and Imperial Control' (AU NBAC N115/195). According to one a member of the delegation Papua was the 'coming country' where '[t]he soil is magnificent … Native labour is so cheap that whites do not have to do any really hard work' (*The Advertiser* [Adelaide] 18 July 1911: 10). In fact the real productive plantation land was in the hands of the Germans to the north and Lucas kept his eye on that prize for many years. His chance was not long in coming.

Following the occupation of the German territory by Australian troops in 1914, Lucas, Atlee Hunt, now Permanent Secretary for the Commonwealth Department of Home and Territories, and Judge Hubert Murray of Papua were appointed to a three member Royal Commission on late German New Guinea. This commenced in 1919. Hunt and Lucas produced a majority report in 1920 that was not supported by Murray, the chairman (Bassett 1969: 15fn). Lucas was then appointed Technical Adviser for New Guinea and Chairman of the Expropriation Board responsible for the liquidation of all German financial interests in New Guinea. This was a fine example of greed and corruption on a large-scale. In fact, the whole occupation of German New Guinea was a clever business move by the astute and aggressive Lucas to benefit Burns Philp (Ohff 2008: 5). The expropriation of German property between 1920 and 1927 was entangled in appeals, alleged labour problems, incorrect land registrations and surveys as well as problems with the settlement of outstanding villager rights and nationality rights (Australia. Custodian of Expropriated Property 1925; Cahill 1997: 13). By using 'dummies' financed by the large trading companies both Burns Philp and Carpenters were able to consolidate their position as the principal plantation and trading companies in New Guinea. Both Lucas, whom Cahill (1997: 27) called a 'xenophobic nonentity', and Jose, a trenchant advocate of the Australian point-of-view, believed in the Imperialist philosophies of Joseph Chamberlain, in the White Australia Policy, and in special commercial advantages for Australian interests in the Western Pacific.

The young Australian traveller, Marnie Bassett, in letters from New Guinea written in 1921, described Lucas in almost libellous terms. She wrote home to her parents that 'Rabaul gossip from the inside [is]—chiefly about Mr Lucas of the Expropriation Board, whom they all hate and are ashamed of' (Bassett 1969: 15). Later Bassett and her companion sailed with Lucas on the steamer *Siar*, the former steamer of the *Neu-Guinea Compagnie* confiscated in 1914, and she found him to be 'one of those civilian fire-eaters who is plainly out for revenge, and he is seemingly a most objectionable type of man' (Bassett 1969: 38). She found him to be a terrifying person: 'I have never met a more revolting man—His personal and his business reputation are both said to be bad and there isn't a soul that doesn't hate him; and here he is, the biggest man in the territory, next to the Administrator' (Bassett 1969: 57). Lucas may have been objectionable to Bassett, and his business dealings questionable, but he was a prime example of the aggressive commercial entrepreneur with excellent political connections who used access to the newspapers to promote his opinions.

Promotional publications

In 1911 the first of two handbooks of the British Solomon Islands Protectorate was published. The reference book contained a brief description of the early European discoveries of the islands, the administrative structure, the climate, fauna and flora, and some brief details of agricultural potential. While the white population was given as 443, obviously counted, the local population estimate remained at 150,000, obviously uncounted (British Solomon Islands Protectorate 1911). This figure would not be qualified until the first census in 1931. The high estimated figure only added to the assumption that the Solomon Islanders were a dying race. Even John Macmillan Brown, the New Zealand scholar and academic who wrote a number of papers on Polynesian and Māori culture, considered the Solomon Islanders a dying race and stated to the press: 'It is not European diseases that are threatening their existence. It is luxury and idleness'. Macmillan Brown, returning from a long tour of the islands, anticipated the islanders would 'vanish within fifty years' (*The Sydney Morning Herald* 12 August 1911: 5). He also went on to say 'copra has so risen in price that their cocoanuts and cocoanut lands have made them primitive millionaires'. Such beliefs were common at that time.

In fact the expansion of plantation land was slow. Of the 9,500,000 acres of total land area, of which only a fraction consisted of potential plantation land, 164,640 acres had been purchased freehold from islanders and 228,000 acres were held under Certificates of Occupation. Only 18,000 acres had been planted out (British Solomon Islands Protectorate 1911: 42). In the Solomon Islands, three plantation companies dominated: Lever's Pacific Plantations Ltd, Solomon Islands Development Company, a subsidiary of Burns, Philp & Co, and the Malayta Company. Of the more than 400,000 acres in the Solomon Islands alienated by 1913, 231,000 acres would be held by Lever's Pacific Plantations Ltd, 48,000 by Solomon Islands Development Company and 9,000 acres by the Malayta Company (Allan 1957: 38–39; Heath 1974a: 82). The figure of 400,000 acres, imprecise and unreliable as it may have been, was virtually the extent of European land alienation in the islands (Heath 1979: 112, 119). To further encourage would-be planters, other guides to owning and managing copra plantations were well promoted. One such self-help manual was the famous *Coconuts: The consols of the East* which covered all topics thought to be of benefit to newcomers. It was given an encouraging foreword by none other than Sir William Lever (Smith and Pape 1917). It was only after Lever's Pacific Plantations commenced large-scale copra production that the British Solomon Islands Protectorate's finances turned from deficit to surplus. The reason for the surplus was that the debit in relation to the DHPG concessions had been paid out. It was paid out in full on the tenth year as required.

Spreading the administrative net

In Tulagi, the need for a government vessel for police work and transport was a constant concern for Woodford. The first government ketch, *Lahloo*, a 33-ton ketch purchased in 1899 for £1,435 was used extensively in supressing head hunting in the New Georgia group. The boat, built in Launceston, Tasmania, was purchased from E. L. McCaughan in Williamstown in Melbourne with the trader G. J. Waterhouse negotiating the sale for the administration (WPHC 4/IV 205/1898; *The Launceston Examiner* 6 September 1899: 4). General complaints were that the vessel was often becalmed in the narrow channels between the islands and could not respond quickly to policing requests. When Woodford finally got his longed for steamer, the *Belama*, this made holes in the 1908–1909 budget. The first *Belama*, a 100-ton steamer, built in Sydney by the Einarsen Bros of Balmain was designed specifically to be a steam yacht that could be used for rapid response in policing work (*The Sydney Morning Herald* 8 July 1908: 9). The name *Belama*—frigate bird—is not without significance. Woodford photographed a man with a frigate bird tattoo on his chest during his time in Aola. The frigate bird was carved into canoes and other decorations in the New Georgia area. It appears in stories, legends and songs across the Solomon Islands for it gathers above the sea when bonito are in a feeding frenzy on small baitfish. The sight of the frigate bird is important in all coastal islander cultures. At the same time Mahaffy, now based in Suva, purchased steamers for use by the British colonial administrations in the Gilbert and Ellice Islands and in the New Hebrides (*The Sydney Morning Herald* 16 November 1908: 6, 21 December 1908: 8; Woodford papers PMB 1290 Item 8/1). The transition from sail to steam was considered important for all government work across the Western Pacific territories. One of the first uses of the *Belama* was a policing campaign when it was sent to assist in the capture of Zito on Vella Lavella (*The Register* [Adelaide] 5 January 1910: 8). The *Lahloo* was wrecked in 1909 (see *The Queenslander* 1 October 1910: 7 and 22 for a photograph of the *Lahloo*). In February 1911 the first *Belama* was also wrecked when it struck an uncharted reef off Isabel (see *The Queenslander* 17 September 1910: 24 for a photograph of the *Belama*). As a result of the loss of the steamer the Protectorate was financially constrained. The boat was uninsured and had cost £7,000 to buy (Woodford papers PMB 1381/004 Letter to James Edge-Partington 8 April 1911). Woodford was left without any patrol vessel for some time.

Woodford purchased a new vessel, presumably using another Imperial grant. The second *Belama*, formerly the river steamer *Awittaka* from Hobart was built by Purdon and Featherstone Pty Ltd. Although popular with Tasmanian locals it was considered too expensive for use in the Derwent River (*The Examiner* [Launceston] 7 August 1911: 4). Renamed the *Belama*, it arrived at Tulagi in August 1911 (*The Sydney Morning Herald* 11 October 1911: 16). A steamer with 60 tons carrying capacity, it had a larger carrying capacity than the *Lahloo* but was smaller than the first *Belama*. The boat was 125 feet in length, with a beam of 22 feet and was capable of 13 knots per hour. It required a crew of 22 men apart from a captain, cook and chief engineer. 12 men were employed as firemen/stokers in the engine room, eight as general sailors and two as assistants to the Chinese cook (*The Brisbane Courier* 28 December 1912: 4). It also required 15 tons of coal. All this crew, and the need for maintenance and repairs as well as large amounts of coal, made the vessel effective in patrolling but a financial liability for a small colony. It was expensive to operate. Annual reports show it cost the administration £2,936 in 1910–1911, £3,596 in 1911–1912 and £4,339 in 1912–1913. This was double the annual public works expenditure and nearly three times that of district administration for 1912–1913. The second *Belama* served for ten years until it too was wrecked off Isabel in 1921 (*The Brisbane Courier* 25 July 1921: 6).

In the meantime, a new government station was opened at Auki when a site near the Quaibala River at Rarasu was purchased in October 1909 for £10 (BSIP 14/4). Thomas Edge-Partington was sent there to establish the patrol station and to recruit and train police. Edge-Partington was sent to Malaita partly as punishment for keeping a Simboese mistress while stationed in Gizo. He formally apologised to the administration and to the Colonial Office. Officially reprimanded by London he was recommended to get married as soon as possible (Edge-Partington to Barnett 20 September 1909 and im Thurn to Colonial Office 16 November 1909 CO 225 87 170; Mahaffy to High Commissioner 22 December 1908 and Woodford to Major 30 September 1910 WPHC 4/IV 836/1908). It was fortunate that his family had influence. 'Concubinage' with local women in the British colonial service was a dismissible offence. Edge-Partington's correspondence with Woodford during the foundation years of the police service in Malaita have fortunately survived as have the daily diaries of the station (BSIP 14/14/1–14/10 and BSIP 15/VIII 135/1911–139/1915). The daily life of an isolated District Magistrate at Auki was not comfortable—even replacing broken cane chairs required formal approval (BSIP 14/8). On Malaita other officials found local people's opinion to be that 'government is an institution to keep clear of' and Edge-Partington found people fled at the sight of him or the sight of his whaleboat coming along the coast. It would have been disheartening at times. As the jail on Tulagi was only a small lockup at this time, the Vella Lavella men implicated in the Zito escapades were sent to Auki to work as labourers. They were warned that if they escaped into the bush the Malaitans would kill them (BSIP 14/4).

Edge-Partington remained at Auki until January 1915 when he resigned from the service after his requests for transfer to East Africa were refused and he came into conflict with Frank Barnett, who replaced Woodford in 1914 (BSIP 14/9). He found police work on Malaita to be a 'special and dangerous service' and complained that the Fijian police officer sent to train constables was 'quite useless'. Edge-Partington recruited his police from the New Georgia area but this too had problems. He found them disrespectful and often rude (BSIP 14/5 and 14/42). No doubt they too knew that he had kept a mistress on Gizo, that he had been transferred as punishment, and treated him, a very young man, accordingly. Life for Europeans in tropical Pacific colonies was characterised by what was considered sound medical evidence proving the 'popular representations of white man's inevitable slide into a state of drunkenness and degeneracy precipitated by a life of idleness, boredom and too intimate contact with natives' (O'Brien 2009: 103). Tropical climates were thought to bring about indolence and excess, they stimulated the appetite for over-indulgence and alcoholism and led to physiological effects that caused sexual excess (Eves 2005: 308). A 'moral economy of climate' that proscribed the proper mode of living in the tropics meant that women and children were discouraged from settlement (Eves 2005: 320–321). Colonial cultures were not direct copies of European society translated to the tropics but 'homespun' creations with their own social and moral codes. The quality and intensity of the racial divide varied enormously according to the colonial context, the location and the historical moment. But colonial racism and class structures were measures of how people classified themselves. Contact with poor or impoverished whites, beachcombers or drifters was seen to be as socially stigmatising as an 'improper' contact with local people (Stoler 1989).

With the demand for local plantation labour increasing, police work on a dangerous island like Malaita was unattractive, and while Malaitan men made good police, if they served elsewhere, employing them to pacify their home island was fraught with a 'grave risk of disaster' (Boutilier 1983: 57–58 quoting from WPHC 4/IV 831/1908 and 2161/1911). When the South Seas Evangelical Mission missionary Frederick Daniels was murdered at Ngongosila, a small island off the east Kwara'ae coast, the *Belama* was sent there on police action. The Gua'ala cultural group who owned the island maintained trading links along much of the east coast and this made Ngongosila a useful base for a mission station (Moore 2010: 37). Daniels was killed while conducting an evening service. It was ostensibly in retaliation for the death of a labourer on plantation service but Rev Arthur Hopkins of the Melanesian Mission and Edge-Partington found that Daniels had given protection to a man who had seduced the daughter of a local Big-man. Daniels was murdered for being complicit in breaking strict Malaitan sexual codes (Hilliard 1969: 54; Bennett 1987: 109). Barnett was acting Resident Commissioner at the time and wrote on 24 June 1911 to Edge-Partington that little could be done for missionaries like Daniels who 'often stupidly persist in placing themselves in the front rank of danger' in their communities (BSIP 14/6). Barnett also warned of criticism from Florence Young but Edge-Partington, whose relationship with Barnett became increasingly acrimonious, considered her to be always 'sensible and nice' (BSIP 14/40). But the South Seas Evangelical Mission did request government intervention this time and so the HMS *Torch*, which was taking the High Commissioner Sir Francis May on an inspection tour, launched a punitive expedition against Uru Island. Here the village was burnt and all the fishing nets and pigs were confiscated (*The Sydney Morning Herald* 11 December 1911: 9). Following this expedition the Judicial Commissioner Sir Charles Major ruled that no punitive expedition could take place without official sanction of the High Commissioner. A second ruling was that the Resident Commissioner in Tulagi could pass the death sentence on a murderer but could not carry out punishment. It had to be done in Suva (BSIP 14/6 and 14/7). While the news of the punitive expedition silenced antagonism against the government in other parts of Malaita, in Ngongosila the mission suffered a serious setback. It was not reopened until 1923 and the effects were longstanding. Uru was a centre of Kwaio land and they had built up a fierce reputation for their attacks on recruiting boats. If the Kwaio could be 'humbled by the government then surely this was a force to be reckoned with' (Bennett 1987: 111). Retribution for the murders of Europeans was quick. At first it looked as if people on Malaita were prepared to accept British law and order but the ripple effect was wide. The Kwaio would not be humbled. They would seek revenge for many grievances in the murder of District Officer, William Bell, in October 1927.

10. The critical question of labour

Between 1863 and 1906 more than 60,000 Melanesian labourers were recruited for plantation labour in Queensland. Some 20,000 were recruited for work in Fiji between 1864 and 1914 and about 6,000 for work in Samoa between 1885 and 1913 (Newbury 1981: 6; Giles and Scarr 1968: 2). Of the 62,475 recruited for Queensland, 18,217 came from the southern and central Solomon Islands and Santa Cruz areas (Price and Baker 1976: 110–111 Table 1). The largest component of Solomon Islands recruitment was 17,033 from the southern islands of Malaita, some parts of Guadalcanal, the Florida Islands and Makira (Price and Baker 1976: 115–116 Table 2). Because of their reputation the men of New Georgia were avoided. Only recruitment from the northern islands of the New Hebrides exceeded this figure (Price and Baker 1976: 111, 115). Woodford's opposition to the external labour trade was based around a number of issues. Returnees smuggled guns, ammunition and dynamite back into the Protectorate, they destabilised the home areas with their manners and attitudes, some returned with leprosy and venereal disease, and perhaps more significantly, labourers sent overseas deprived local plantations of labour. The final reason for the cessation of labour trafficking was the belief that it contributed to the depopulation of the islands. It was believed that the men going overseas were not marrying and having children before they recruited or that they declined to have children when they returned.

Some of the first pieces of legislation passed by the newly formed Federal Parliament of Australia impacted directly on the Solomon Islands. The first, the *Pacific Island Labourers Act* 1901 (1 Edward VII 16 1901), set time limits for ending the labour trade and the deportation of any remaining Islander workers. The second, the *Immigration Restriction Act* 1901 (1 Edward VII 17 1901), was designed to exclude any non-European migrant to the new Commonwealth (Butterworth *et al*. 1902: 250, 258–261). The Act began the restrictive practice of the dictation test, in any prescribed language, for any non-European migrant to the country. A complementary piece of legislation was the *Postal and Telegraph Services Act* 1901 (1 Edward VII 12 1901). This specified that any ship carrying Australian mail to and from the country had to be crewed by white labour only. These pieces of legislation were based on racist sentiments well enshrined in the Australian nationalism of the 1880s and 1890s that moved to restrict non-European labour from entering the country. Institutionalised racism was a part of early Australian political developments.

Repatriation of labourers and expansion of mission control

In 1901 there were approximately 9,800 islander labourers in Queensland. It was estimated about 500 older men could choose to remain, for various reasons, in Queensland. These older men were classed as industrious men of good character, men who had white men as employees or those who had married white, Torres Strait Islander or Aboriginal women in Queensland. They were permitted to stay. The exact number of labourers to be deported by 1908 was determined by the commission into the question of labour for the sugar industry (Queensland. Sugar Industry Labour Commission 1906: lx–lxi; Moore 2000: 27). One factor that complicated the matter was that recruiting did not finish in 1901 for the *Pacific Islands Labourers Act* permitted the trade to taper off between 1902 and 1903 (Moore 1985: 287). According to Boutilier (1983: 49), who based his figures on those published by Corris (1973), there were 6,389 left in 1906. From that, 1,642 men were exempt from deportation on various grounds and the final figure was 4,747 (Moore 2000: 28 fn34).

Woodford, interviewed by the *Sydney Morning Herald* (22 December 1903: 3), stated that the last recruiting ship had to leave Queensland for the Solomon Islands before 31 December 1903 for it to be considered legal. He estimated, fairly accurately, that there were about 6,000 islanders to be repatriated in 1903. At the end of 1906, the legal time for deportation to commence, approximately 4,800 labourers from the Solomon Islands remained in Queensland; 2,500 of these were Malaitans (Boutiler 1983: 49). Of this number 265 men chose to go to work in Fiji rather than return home (Wright 1969: 13). The Governor-General Lord Northcote wrote to the High Commissioner in Suva reporting the number to be 5,000, mostly from the New Hebrides and the Solomon Islands. All arrangements for their housing, resettlement and reemployment were left to the Resident Commissioners in the protectorates (Northcote to im Thurn 11 May 1906 WPHC 4/IV 82/1898).

Officials in the islands, Woodford included, were not satisfied that the Queensland government was undertaking the repatriation with the well-being of the workers in mind. Concerns were raised that vessels were unseaworthy. In addition, and despite the supposed rigorous checking at the ports, the illegal supply of arms and ammunition continued. With the planned return of labourers from Queensland new legislation was passed to prevent the introduction of communicable diseases (*The Solomons (Quarantine) Regulation of 1907*, King's Regulation no 1 of 1907). Rev Arthur Hopkins of the Melanesian Mission had some misgivings about the nature of the men, especially Malaitans, repatriated after 1906 (Hopkins 1934). Hopkins stated that the presence of returned labourers had both good and bad effects on other islanders: good because the men often went back to their home villages and started schools or established new villages, bad for the jealousy that arose from local chiefs who felt that their power was being usurped. Hopkins also had concerns over the resentment and quarrels that followed when the contents of trade boxes were distributed, and the disruption that followed the return of men accused of old social and cultural offences.

In addition to his land deals Svensen negotiated with Walter Lucas in Burns Philp to participate in the repatriation of the remaining Solomon Islander indentured labourers in Queensland. Burns Philp was in a commanding position to secure this deal. Only Commonwealth subsidised steamers operating the Pacific trade could be used. The Queensland government paid the shipping company £8 a head to transport the men to Tulagi. Burns Philp paid Svenson £3 of this to transport the men to their homes within the Protectorate.

With more than £85,000 in unused passage money and £35,000 in unpaid wages belonging to deceased labourers, the Queensland and Commonwealth governments were more than able to finance the deportation (Moore 2013b: 5–7). Between them, Burns Philp and Svensen shared the more than £32,000 paid in transportation fees (Wright 1969: 13; Moore 2013b). For Arthur Hopkins the years 1905 to 1907 would be anxious (Great Britain. Parliament. House of Commons. Parliamentary Papers 1905: 25). It was first estimated that only 1,000 men were expected to be needed by local plantations. By 1905, only about 3,500 acres of land were planted and attempts at growing cotton, rubber, maize and commercial qualities of fruit, such as bananas, had all been unsuccessful. These small-scale plantations would not absorb the men returning to the islands if they sought further indentures.

Woodford requested that he personally supervise their returns home and that all deportations be concentrated through the selected Queensland ports of Brisbane, Cairns and Mackay. While Woodford was largely successful in having the men removed from the three ports specified, his request to supervise the repatriation was declined (Moore 1985: 288). Initially he clashed with im Thurn over the problem of labourers returning from Fiji with leprosy so he approached im Thurn in 1905 to end the Fijian trade completely (Heath 1974a: 89). Im Thurn was unwilling to do so because the Solomon Islander labourers were seen as a valuable labour source for Fiji before the importation of Indian labourers, and 'Im Thurn argued that the experience the Solomon Islanders gained in Queensland and Fiji was a civilizing one, an argument Woodford clearly rejected' (Heath 1974a: 90). Following the general theme then current, im Thurn was repeating the belief in a 'civilizing mission', meaning that indentured labour was necessary for indigenous peoples, who were inferior mentally and morally and lacked practical capacity when compared with white Europeans. For men like im Thurn, the experience in the cane fields was to be viewed as a process of cultural and social development and enhancement of practical skills. Evidence suggests that im Thurn favoured development in Fiji over that of other protectorates like the Solomon Islands (Scarr 1967a: 282).

Woodford, arguing against im Thurn's position, took his cause to the Colonial Office in 1905 and subsequently won. Labour trafficking from the Solomon Islands to Fiji ended in 1911 with the final group of labourers returned by 1914. Antipathy between Woodford and im Thurn lasted for most of the High Commissioner's long reign. To make his point that the plantations in the Solomon Islands needed labour, Woodford was interviewed by the *Sydney Morning Herald* (6 June 1911: 7) and confidently said: 'The place is going ahead so fast that unless our labour supply is supplemented from new sources we shall be in a serious fix within the next 12 months'. He reported that over 4,000 men were currently employed in the islands, a figure that was not verified. Woodford also reported that 'Malaita is still the principal island for recruiting. On some of the islands the natives will not touch plantation work at all'. While the recruitment of men from Malaita was seen as beneficial to the development of the plantation economy, there was little understanding of the growing problems that these internal migrants would face. Malaita was left undeveloped, a cheap labour pool for the rest of the islands. It remained a place for the 'have nots'. Meanwhile on New Georgia and in parts of Guadalcanal, where local people declined to work on the plantations, the regions occupied by the 'haves' developed. This was a strategy used by British, German and French colonial administrations. Certain cultural groups were seen as valuable labour pools—the Kiwai in Papua as police and boat crews, the Tolai in New Britain as plantation workers, the Gilbertese as boat crews and mine labourers on Banaba, and the Torres Strait Islanders as pearl divers. In this way these groups became wage labourers subject to the supply and demand of the market economy.

Internal labour migration

When the external labour trade creased or slowed, inter-island recruitment of labourers for plantations within the Pacific colonies continued. The major plantation economies of Papua, German New Guinea, New Hebrides and the Solomon Islands all recruited local workers from one district and transported them to plantations in other areas. Only Fiji imported labourers from India. In Papua native labour regulations limited the hours of work. The weight load of patrol carriers was regulated as was the distance they could be made to cover in one day. Housing on plantations, and for those in domestic service, was scheduled and a simple ration scale set down. These regulations required enforcement and the Papuan patrol staff was not large (Mair 1970: 166). As in the Solomon Islands the pay for indentured labour was set at 10 shillings a month

(£6 a year). By comparison, workers in the Torres Strait pearling industry, many of them Papuan from the Daru coast, could earn between £1 and £2 a month (£12–£24 a year) but these men were at sea for many months working long hours. This was a dangerous maritime industry comparable with the mine labourers' wage on Banaba. Recruitment in the pearling industry served to pacify tribal fighting along the Daru coast and became a new initiation period for young men with its seclusion from women, its struggle for status and the return home laden with goods (Lawrence 2010: 13). For the Kiwai, employment in the maritime industries was an important economic foundation for the home villages. Once the pearling industry declined the standard of living in the coastal Kiwai villages also declined and in the Torres Strait they became the poorest of the poor.

In the Solomon Islands new contracts of two years became common and men from Malaita, the Guadalcanal south-east and Weather Coast, and Makira were mainly selected (Shlomowitz and Bedford 1988: 77 Table 7 & 14). Shorter employment arrangements for casual work or for particular planting and weeding periods or for cutting copra were made with local communities. This was also common when people needed money to pay for church contributions or special occasions and ceremonies. The cost of employing labourers increased during the 1910s to the 1920s as the price of copra increased and the plantation economy grew. Conversely, when the cost of copra plummeted in the 1930s fewer men were recruited for work and labourers were sent back to the village. This fluctuation in employment and earnings caused many economic and social problems in the home villages. For plantation owners, employment costs consisted of a recruiting bonus or beach payment, the average annual wage paid, general recruiting fees and a repatriation fee paid at the end of the contract when the worker was returned home. In the Solomons, the recruiting bonus was paid to relatives of the recruit in the form of trade goods, such as tobacco, knives and calico but the cost of these trade goods increased in value from £1–£3 between 1909 and 1913 and from £3–£5 between 1915 and 1918. The average wage was officially set at £6 a year. This increased to £12 a year, rising to £24 and £36 a year in the 1920s but only in special cases when workers had experience and skills. No labourer could be recruited if he—the labourer were usually male—was under 16 years old. The recruiting fee in the Solomons was paid to the professional recruiters and varied according to the demand and the difficulty in obtaining recruits. A repatriation fee of between £1–£2 was charged to return time-expired recruits home (Shlomowitz and Bedford 1988: 68-69).

Solomon Islanders entered the internal labour trade for a variety of reasons. First was the desire to obtain trade goods; this was a major factor behind participation in the earlier Pacific labour trade. Secondly, when the poll tax was introduced in 1920 (King's Regulation no 10 of 1920) it levied a head tax on all adult males between 16 and 60. The tax varied according to the home islands. On Nggela it was £1 per head, on Guadalcanal 10 shillings, and on Malaita 5 shillings. Plantation workers were exempt—their tax was paid by the plantation company—but the men had to pay the tax for other family members. The tax was initially designed to raise revenue rather than stimulate recruitment but villagers did not see it that way (Shlomowitz and Bedford 1988: 64).

Hubert Murray was sent to report on the alleged labour shortage in the Solomon Islands in 1916 and he considered it important that regions be completely pacified before recruitment proceed. Planters and government officials disagreed. This difference in opinion was readily acknowledged by Murray in his report to the Western Pacific High Commission (Shlomowitz and Bedford 1988: 64 quoting from WPHC 4/IV 1779/1916; *The Brisbane Courier* 26 January 1916: 3). Murray considered that recruitment would be more successful in pacified areas of Guadalcanal and Malaita but he based that opinion on the Papuan situation where the country was, ostensibly, pacified before recruitment started. J. C. Barley, District Officer at Gizo in 1926, was strongly of the opinion that the process of pacification reduced the supply of recruits because men no longer fled tribal fighting and pay-back. In fact it was not possible to access the impact of pacification on levels of recruitment. Men from Malaita had been going to the overseas plantations for decades before any attempts were made to penetrate past the immediate coastal areas. Many who returned from overseas labour went home to areas declared unpacified. It was the price of copra that was a major factor in labour fluctuations. Quite simply, when prices were high, more men were recruited. When the prices fell the number of men required was reduced. Melanesians also chose their own time and place to work as wage labourers. When conditions were right, or people needed money, then they participated, otherwise they remained disinterested. Plantations with good conditions, and a good reputation for treatment of workers, rarely went short of willing workers. Reputation by word of mouth was far more important than esoteric ideas of the value of pacification.

One problem facing recruits was disease in the crowded and often unsanitary housing lines and transit camps. The annual death rate during the early colonial period in the Solomon Islands has been estimated at 15 persons per 1,000 (1.5 per cent). The most significant causes of death were bacillary dysentery, tuberculosis, pneumonia-influenza related respiratory illnesses, beriberi, and work accidents (Shlomowitz and Bedford 1988: 66–67 Tables 9–11). The widespread dysentery epidemic of 1914–1915 resulted in more than 100 of the annual count of 172 deaths in the Protectorate. The epidemic took serious toll of labourers in plantation lines then spread to the Lever's labour deport on Gavutu and to the Burns Philp depot on Makambo. Both were crowded places with poor levels of sanitation and hygiene, but they were located within Tulagi Harbour where supervision would have been easy. In all, it was estimated that 5 per cent of the total number of labourers died but on the large Lever's plantations it was closer to 10 per cent (Bennett 1987: 158). The young, newly recruited men who had not built resistance were the group most likely to succumb to dysentery and other communicable diseases. But workers had to overcome labour abuse as well as disease. Following a tour of inspection of plantations by Arthur Mahaffy in 1908 and a report on labour abuses (Mahaffy to High Commission 21 December 1908 WPHC 4/IV 1605/1912), Woodford managed to have the *Solomons (Labour) Regulation of 1910* (King's Regulation no 3 of 1910) implemented. He thought that power in the hands of ignorant and prejudiced persons constituted a real danger to workers (Bennett 1987: 157). Abuse of labour meant that fewer men offered for employment and the figures for 1913 show some indication of this trend. The new regulations specified conditions for employment and repatriation to home villages and listed daily rations and medical proceedures (Fairley, Rigby and Co Ltd 1912–1941 Item A.1972.0053, 4/14). In 1912 the labour regulation was amended to set 50 maximum working hours in a week, with Sunday a day of rest, but the amendment also set a penalty for neglect of work by the labourer (*The Solomons (Labour Amendment) Regulations of 1912*; King's Regulation no 8 of 1912; 14 J. Soc. Comp. Legis Ns 95 1914; Bennett 1987: 157). A new Inspector of Labour, William Bell, was employed in 1911 who found planters without copies of the regulations and labourers who had been signed on without the presence of a government officer. Records on estates were also poor. Bell's immediate complaint to Woodford was that he did not have a boat and could not conduct plantation inspections. Having regulations in place was one thing, but being able to supervise labour and inspect conditions was a near impossible task.

Concern with the external labour trade in the annual reports to 1905 would, by 1913, be replaced with concerns over the increasing demands for local labour. By this time 25,000 acres had been planted, not all productive, and copra continued to be of poor quality. In 1913 the amount of land claimed to have been purchased from local people by Europeans was estimated at almost 170,000 acres (Butterworth *et al.* 1897: 203). Land speculation between 1886 and 1896 had resulted in 80,000 acres alienated by purchase from local people, at least on paper (Heath 1979: 61–62). Waste land held on Certificates of Occupation was 240,000 acres and the amount of land purchased by the government that was to be leased to Europeans was 18,110 acres. Direct leases to Europeans, mostly land used for trading stations or missions, totalled only 980 acres (Great Britain. Parliament. House of Commons. Parliamentary Papers 1913: 13). The progress of the plantation economy was painfully slow. Copra was the main export produce that showed only an incremental rise in exports (British Solomon Islands Protectorate 1909: 19). From an initial quantity of 1,200 tons in 1895 the amount exported rose to less than 3,000 tons in 1903–1904 but only increased to 4,200 tons in 1912–1913. Oscar Svensen continued to invest in plantation development in the Solomons after his successful sales to Lever's Pacific Plantations Ltd. A consortium of directors, including Svensen, based in Brisbane and Sydney funded the purchase of 5,000 acres of freehold plantation land at Mamara, on the coast north-west of the present site of Honiara on Guadalcanal. The capital raised was £130,000 (Bennett 1987: 139, 140–141). The project was well advertised in the *Sun* [Sydney] newspaper under the banner *The Wealth of the Solomons* (6 August 1911: 24; Woodford papers PMB 1290 Item 9/2/1 and 9/21/2). The aim was to produce copra, rubber and cotton. The prospects were reported to be 'fascinating' and 'immense' and the estimated profits after 12 years were projected to be more than £200,000. This arrangement was put in place before the government imposed controls over the freehold sale of land. Svensen and partners also invested in Ndoma plantation further along the north-west coast of Guadalcanal.

The administration was now actively promoting its leasehold arrangements, declared in 1912, under which land would be leased for 99 years at a minimum rent of 3 pence per acre for the first five years, 6 pence per acre for the years 5 to 11, 3 shillings per acre for the years 11 to 20, and 6 shillings per acre for the years 21 to 33. Then the land rent would be calculated at 5 per cent of the unimproved value (Great Britain. Parliament. House of Commons. Parliamentary Papers 1913: 14). One-tenth of the land had to be cultivated within five years or it would be resumed. The annual report stated that 'considerable areas of land have recently been forfeited owing to non-compliance with the improvement conditions'. This covenant on planting within five years had never been particularly effective. When Stanley Knibbs was appointed Crown Surveyor in 1914 he found the area claimed by plantation owners often exceeded their legal right. Resumption of land was a drawn out legal process and even then the loss of uncultivated areas was not often contested.

However, the main problem with copra from the Solomon Islands was quality. It was so poor that it attracted very low prices. Smoke dried copra was still the standard and 'this slovenly way of preparation still prevails to a great extent' for only the larger plantations were beginning to use the more superior kiln-dried production. The Germans had been using this technique for decades. The Germans, under Weber, had been promoting effective kiln construction since the 1870s and before 1915 much of the world's copra and coconut oil production was shipped to Germany for use in the margarine and food industries (*The Brisbane Courier* 22 April 1915: 8). Fire-dried copra returned £1 to £2 a ton more than lesser quality produce. The annual report to the British government gave a lengthy description of improved coconut tree cultivation and the preparation of copra using a simple kiln made from corrugated iron, timber and fire bricks that could produce 1–2 tons of copra in 24 hours (Great Britain. Parliament. House of Commons. Parliamentary Papers 1913: 16-23). This could not rescue the Solomon Islands from having a reputation for producing copra considered the 'second worst in the world' (Boutilier 1974: 35; Kane to Advisory Council 20 November 1923 WPHC 4/IV 64/1924). Many kilns in the Solomon Islands were jerry-built affairs that only produced poor quality smoke-dried copra (see Smith 1971 for a photograph of the Binskin home-built kiln on Mbava Island).

Ivory nuts, collected from wild sago palms, were also poor quality. The Solomon Islands ivory nuts were coarse, hard to turn and polish and did not take a dye. At £12 10s per ton delivered to Sydney they were not profitable. The palm also took seven years to mature, gave only one very large crop and could not be cultivated as it grew in swampy, riverine areas (Smith and Pape 1917: 489). The sale of ivory nuts, in particular, was not assisted by a new regulation introduced in 1911 that controlled the sale of copra and nuts collected from native lands (King's Regulation no 12 of 1911). The trader had to agree to pay a £10 per centum (10 per cent of sales) to the administration as a fee and pay the local people for the nuts as well. For copra, this may have been economical, but for the fluctuating market in ivory nuts it meant its gradual demise.

Labour control

As a result, the economy remained heavily dependent on copra exports. At this stage, the main problem within the Protectorate continued to be labour, not land. Malaitans became internal labour migrants instead of external migrants. This would be the start of the long running tensions between cultural groups. In 1909 only 2,284 labourers were indentured, in 1911 the total number contracted was 3,940, but in 1912 only 3,713 had engaged. Woodford ended his report gloomily with: 'As recruiting for employment on plantations has never been carried on so vigorously as at present, it would appear that the limit of the available local supply has been reached, and the outlook is a most serious one. Applicants for fresh leasehold are in all cases warned of the difficulty in obtaining labourers, but it seems to have no effect upon the demand for land' (Great Britain. Parliament. House of Commons. Parliamentary Papers 1913: 15). As a result of this demand, wages rose from £6 a year to £10 a year or even £12 a year in some cases (Smith and Pape 1917: 495).

By 1919, Lever's Pacific Plantations Ltd had become the largest employer of local labour with 26 plantations although this is probably based on 1916 figures (Allen 1919: 255; see also WPHC 10/IX Item 243). With Lever's an active participant in the copra industry the Protectorate was now considered the envy of older Pacific colonies. But of the 290,000 acres of land alienated to Lever's by 1912 little more than 9,000 acres were planted. The second largest employer was the Malayta Company with seven plantations, followed by the Burns, Philp

& Co group of subsidiaries—the Solomon Islands Development Company, the Shortland Islands Plantation Ltd and Choiseul Plantations Ltd—which had seven plantations. More than 55 per cent of all labour worked for these three main companies and their subsidiaries. Lever's Pacific Plantations Ltd proposal to overcome potential labour shortages by importing Indian labour was refused by the India Office in London and the plans to bring in Javanese and Chinese plantation labourers were also unsuccessful. Even at this early stage, Lever's plantation overseers were beginning to get a reputation for rough treatment of local labour. Their largely Australian overseers were renowned for being men of poor character who were generally unsympathetic to local people (Heath 1974a: 91). The large plantations needed a large labour force and the desire for cheap labour often led to the argument that indigenous workers needed to be treated differently—with force—from those back in the metropole. Certainly, Lever's model factory town at Port Sunlight stood in stark contrast to the plantation lines in the Solomon Islands. Heath's comment on Woodford's approach to labour abuses was: 'He may have been willing to quite ruthlessly put down armed opposition to his administration, but he was not willing to see brutal methods used on islanders because they would not work' (Heath 1974a: 91).

Bennett (1987: 153) has divided the Protectorate's development into three phases when analysing labour control. In the first period, 1897–1913, abuse of labour was worse due to poor government regulatory control and a 'concomitant frontier mentality among many overseers and managers' of plantations. As a place of work and residence, the Solomon Islands offered little in the way of attraction to potential European employees. The larger companies just took the managers they could get. These men may have been 'abundant in hopes but deficient in experiences' and so they took their frustrations out on the labourers (Bennett 1987: 156). Government control of both labour and supervisors was weak due to the shortage of staff, inadequate inspection and poor regulation of labour. The second period, 1914–1923, saw better legislative powers available to the administration and the employment of an Inspector of Labour. During this period labour costs increased but copra prices were high. This began the period of closer supervision. Costs rose but so did profits and the employment atmosphere calmed. In the third period, 1923–1939, the system of indenture and regulation was more stable. However, during this period labour costs remained high when copra prices declined. As a result uneconomic plantations closed and workers were laid off.

In the early period the labour regulation (*The Solomons (Labour) Regulation no 7 of 1897*) and the native contracts regulations (*The Native Contracts Regulation no 2 of 1896*) were designed to manage the activities of small-scale traders and planters. To some extent they regulated the external labour trade. These rules and regulations were not designed to supervise a large-scale commercial plantation economy employing indentured workers from within the Protectorate. There was limited judicial authority and the chief justice was located far away in Suva. Many conflicts on the plantations did not get to court because no legal commissioner was based in Tulagi until 1914. Abuse of Solomon Islander workers by traders or planters was resolved by having the European removed from the islands using powers given to the Resident Commissioner under the Western Pacific Order in Council. To local people the different treatment of whites and non-whites was startlingly clear. If a native killed a local man or a white he would be shot or hanged, but a white man was ordered to leave the Protectorate (Bennett 1987: 155).

The case of the labour vessel, the *Rhoderick Dhu*, highlighted the need for regulation of the conditions on board recruiting vessels. The *Rhoderick Dhu* had a poor reputation. In 1898 it had been named as the labour vessel that had landed 50 rifles on the coast of Malaita contrary to the arms regulations (Woodford to O'Brien 12 January 1898 WPHC 4/IV 82/1898). In 1903, having collected men around the islands, the schooner arrived at Tulagi barely afloat. On board were over 100 labourers. Woodford cabled quickly to the Colonial Office that he prohibited any further recruiting to Queensland until he had fresh legislation to allow him to inspect vessels. He subsequently received power to force all labour ships to call into Tulagi harbour for inspection (King's Regulation no 3 of 1903; Heath 1974a: 87). Interviewed at length by the *Sydney Morning Herald* (22 December 1903: 3), Woodford explained his actions in temporarily stopping the labour trade. He had two objections: men were returning to the Solomons with hidden arms and ammunition that were not being detected by customs officials in Queensland, and the vessels, like the *Rhoderick Dhu*, were substandard and should not be permitted to recruit in the islands. The men were subsequently transferred to the *Lady Norman* and sent to Queensland. Woodford had his inspection regulations.

With the opening up of larger areas of commercial plantations after 1914, it became necessary to strengthen the powers of the administration with regard to conditions on the labour lines. Underlying much of this development was also the belief, common at that time, that the islanders were a declining race with little future. Woodford (1922b) also wrote on this constant question of depopulation, although his sympathy with the inevitable extinction of the people did not allow him to be derelict in his duty to protect them from abuse of their person or their livelihood (Heath 1974a: 83). The rapid growth in plantations meant that by 1908 conditions on some estates were 'sordid in the extreme' (Bennett 1987: 153). Government documents of the period paint a dismal picture of employment conditions in all areas. Woodford was able to send staff to inspect plantations located near government centres but those in more isolated areas were not inspected. Native hospitals were non-existent and plantation clinics were shoddy. Lever's managers, in particular, did not appreciate inspection of their properties by government officials. Following court action and direct criticism of Sir William Lever by the Colonial Office in London, some attention was finally paid to the issue of labour management. This occurred at a time when Lever was trying to convince the Colonial Office of his company's care for coolie labour in other colonies. The personal admonishment by the Colonial Office resulted in quick action taken to replace notorious plantation management staff. Regulations were tightened, labourers had to sign on in front of a government officer, their health was monitored, their pay was checked, and new government stations opened at Auki on Malaita in 1909, Aola on Guadalcanal in 1914, and at Kirikira on Makira in 1918. Labour rights were better protected, but so too were the rights of the employers. Employers were able to exploit the regulations by imposing a daily task instead of a number of hours worked. The conventionally expected rate was 450 pounds of copra per day per man. This was unstipulated but generally accepted. The Malayta Company employees were expected to produce 510 pounds of copra a day and this imposed hard labour conditions (Bennett 1987: 160).

The Percy Sladen Trust Expedition to Melanesia

In 1907, W. H. R. Rivers, Arthur M. Hocart and C. Gerald Wheeler travelled from Cambridge University to the Solomon Islands to undertake joint ethnographic research. The Percy Sladen expedition is relevant to an examination of this period in Solomon Islands colonial history. It was the first ethnological survey of the islands by English academics and it was an attempt to follow the model used for the 1898 Cambridge Anthropological Expedition to the Torres Strait under Alfred Cort Haddon. The Torres Strait expedition was the first multidisciplinary anthropological expedition to Melanesia (Haddon 1901–1935, see particularly Volume 5 (1904), Volume 8 (1908) and Volume 4 (1912)). It was innovative for its day and set many standards for the development of anthropology as a discipline. Rivers was a notable member of the Torres Strait expedition and between 1898 and 1907 he transformed himself from a medical practitioner to a neurophysiologist and an experimental psychologist. But he retained a lifelong interest in ethnology. Rivers was an influential man who promoted a number of controversial theories of his day. Now discredited, they had a significant impact on academic thinking and colonial policy in the early-20th century.

When the Percy Sladen expedition members reached the Solomon Islands, instead of remaining as a team, they separated. Gerard Wheeler went north to the Shortland Islands to work on the language and folklore of the Mono and Alu islanders (Wheeler 1926; see also Woodford papers PMB 1381/021k). Rivers and Hocart concentrated on three months intensive work of population studies and genealogical work on Simbo, as known as Eddystone Island (Hocart 1922 and 1931: see also Scheffler 1962). Following this, they undertook rapid survey work on Vella Lavella, Kolombangara, and in the Roviana Lagoon, all areas of intensive head hunting less than a decade earlier. They followed this genealogical and survey work with shorter visits to Savo, Guadalcanal and Malaita. Although Hocart and Rivers travelled together they really only cooperated rather than collaborated with each other (Kuklick 1996: 632; Richards 2012).

In the Solomon Islands, Rivers and his partners made use of the Melanesian Mission vessel, the *Southern Cross*, for Rivers came from a family with strong Anglican sympathies. Rivers wrote to Woodford for guidance about travel and locations for anthropological work but it was clear that Rivers had not done much planning even by mid-1907 (Woodford papers PMB 1290 Item 2/59 Letter from WHR Rivers to Woodford dated 10 July 1907). The main publication that arose from this work was *The History of Melanesian Society* (Rivers 1914). While important, this work does not compare with the richness of the material gathered in the Torres Strait with its strong links to people and place (Lawrence 1994; Welsch 1996). The information contained in the study of Melanesian society is complex but somewhat confusing. The aim of the expedition was to explain the then current belief that there was a natural transition from maternal to paternal descent among indigenous people. As a result, the first volume contains a mass of data relating to kinship terminologies in many of the societies visited. The second volume is a theoretical analysis of systems of relationships. The conclusion was that these systems reflect social organisation in particular states of marriage. The finding was that a definite correlation existed between relatives designated by certain kinship terms and certain social functions. Reviews of the massive tomes complimented Rivers on his intellectual achievement but then found critical voice in stating: 'It must suffice here to point out that the sweeping use made by the author of the principle of diffusion of culture is methodologically altogether unjustifiable and must of necessity lead to the gravest errors in historical reconstruction' (Goldenweiser 1916: 336–339). Other reviews followed a similar vein (Lowie 1915: 588–591). During the Percy Sladen expedition, Rivers and Hocart believed that they could make confident statements from genealogical research about the size of families, the number of childless marriages, and the rate of child mortality. Rivers based his work on a speculative evolutionary approach that set out to establish the importance of matrilineal descent in Melanesian communities. However, the development of bilaterial or cognatic descent patterns evidenced in the Roviana Lagoon and elsewhere in the New Georgia region was not examined (Schneider 1996; Nagaoka 2011).

During their genealogical research Rivers and Hocart found evidence of a dramatic decline in fertility on Simbo since the 1850s (Bayliss-Smtith 2006: 28–30). In fact the population increased in the years following the establishment of the Protectorate, the abolition of head hunting and raiding and the consolidation of the Methodist church on the island after 1904 (Groenewegen 1970: 122; Burman 1981: 252). Rivers remained convinced that a 'psychological factor' explained the depopulation of Melanesian islands. The explanation given was that women in Melanesia were too apathetic to conceive or to give birth or even nurture healthy children. This lacked any foundation for it was based on a synchronic analysis of the community at a time of great change. It was also dismissive of the introduction of alien diseases, such as venereal diseases, and the long-term impact they had on population growth and fertility. Rivers saw in the Solomon Islands a people traumatised by the impacts of colonialism and this contributed to the then current theories regarding a supposed lack of vitality among the Melanesian peoples.

Rivers had great insight but his examination of the psychological factor in the depopulation of Melanesia was not supported by concrete evidence. The dominant discourse at that time was that the native races of Melanesia were vanishing as a regrettable but inevitable consequence of contact with a 'higher civilisation' from the West. This was a theory also promoted by Dr Thorold Qualfe, a medical officer with Lever's Pacific Plantations Ltd, who believed that mental apathy, laziness, improvidence and lack of ambition were the prime reasons for the 'decadence of the native races'. He considered peace and good administration had weakened peoples' resolve and that 'savage warfare had made the people alert, active, wary, and provident' (*The Sydney Morning Herald* 23 January 1913: 9; Woodford papers PMB 1290 Item 9/46). Qualfe was reported as saying that as soon as Malaita was settled and fighting stopped the people would start to die out. He did not go so far as to say people should be allowed to start fighting again so that populations would, somehow, grow and prosper. Qualfe's position with Lever's also puts his theory into perspective for the company was actively promoting its case for the introduction of Asian labour at that time.

At the time, these ideas were not considered strange or irrational. Rivers had also become deeply involved in the diffusionism of Grafton Elliot Smith (1911) that held that Europe was the cradle of humanity and human civilisation. The heliocentric views of William Perry (1923), a colleague, considered Egypt to be the source of all cultural innovation. This theory of diffusion from one source, or hyperdiffusion, became widely accepted. Volume two of *The History of Melanesian Society* (Rivers 1914) contains a section on prevailing ideas of sun and moon cults and the spread of megalithic stone structures in Oceania. Rivers later developed this into a journal article (Rivers 1915: 431–445). In his critical review Goldenweiser (1916: 336–339) recognised the complex and intricate analysis and compilation of facts made by Rivers but then stated: 'in the minds of many assent to the author's position will no doubt be prompted by the arduousness of the task of refutation'. Hardly an encouraging and supporting statement. The theory of diffusion assisted colonialism and gave credence to European economic and social expansionism in places like the Pacific where the 'superior' cultures of the West could introduce new technologies and new social structures to advance the 'savage natives'. At the time of Rivers' death in 1922 these views were widely held and praised. They later tarnished his contribution to ethnology, especially when Malinowski and his theory of functionalism began to excite students and ethnologists (Bartlett 1923: 2–14). The importance of the Percy Sladen Trust Expedition to the Solomon Islands lies more in the ties that bound class and Empire. Rivers and Woodford were both educated at Tonbridge and both had strong ties to the established church. The access to the *Southern Cross* was not just chance. Another ex-Tonbridgian was Bishop Cecil Wilson of the Melanesian Mission.

The question of depopulation

The depopulation of Melanesia was taken for granted in both the 19th and the early-20th centuries. The most influential document of the period was the *Report of the Commission Appointed to Inquire into the Decrease of the Native Population in Fiji* (Colony of Fiji 1896). Figures collected for the census of population in Fiji from 1881 seemed to confirm the gradual decrease in the native Fijian (iTaukei) people. A figure of 114,748 people indicated that native Fijians comprised 90 per cent of the population in 1881. In 1891 the figure had decreased to 105,800 or 87.3 per cent, and in 1901 to 94,397 or 78.6 per cent. By 1911 the figure was considered alarming at 87,096 or 62.4 per cent (Colony of Fiji 1896; http://www.statsfiji.gov.fj/index.php/component/content/article/9-social-statistics/social-general/113-population-and-demography21). But the Fijian population had also been impacted by alien diseases and epidemics and the influx of migrant workers statistically reduced the overall percentage of native Fijians in the population. The reason given for the decrease in the early years was that Islander populations were declining because they no longer found life exciting and so had lost their zest for life. This had to be reinvigorated (O'Brien 2009: 110). It was assumed that contact with the West had weakened the resolve of Melanesian people to produce, to survive and to prosper. Their fate, it was assumed, was to be annihilated.

Rivers subsequently published a collection of papers on depopulation in Melanesia that provides a standard reference for understanding the views of missionaries and colonial officials on the theory of depopulation in the early-20th century (Rivers 1922). With a preface by Sir Everard im Thurn the book presented a conservative opinion of a former high official. Im Thurn's introduction was full of paternalistic concern for the fate of the 'folk' over whom British colonialism had assumed control. He was full of 'sympathy' for the 'natives' but his main finding was that the 'most potent cause of the decay of the race is the loss of interest in life' brought about by changes in their material and spiritual condition (im Thurn 1922: vii). The main paper that had stimulated this depopulation debate came from Dr Felix Speiser, a Swiss chemist turned ethnologist who had spent 18 months in the New Hebrides. His paper, 'Decadence and Preservation in the New Hebrides' (Speiser 1922: 25–61), was written in 1912 based on research undertaken in 1910 (Speiser 1913; Adam 1950/1951: 66). The English language version, published by Rivers, was translated from the German by Rev Arthur Hopkins from the Melanesian Mission. Speiser was principally interested in genetics and the movements of cultural groups across the Pacific. His theoretical ideas were based on *Siedlungsgechichte* (settlement history), evolution and the diffusion of cultural traits. Speiser repeated the commonly held views that 'the natives of the New Hebrides are rapidly decreasing in number' and that '[t]his is to be regretted both from a humanitarian and a commercial standpoint'. Speiser's role in this publication places much of the treatise in its true perspective. He was a strong advocate of the megalithic culture thesis that considered the presence of monumental stonework in Melanesia to be a sign of contact with higher cultures from outside the region (Speiser 1913). The theory, supported by Rivers but now much rejected, held sway for a considerable time at the turn of the 20th century (Riesenfeld 1950).

River's depopulation ideas were mirrored in missionary paternalism. The paper by Rev Walter Durrad from the Melanesian Mission concentrated on problems in the Banks and Torres Islands in the New Hebrides (Durrad 1922: 3–24). William O'Ferrall, another Anglican missionary, was more considered when he wrote that the depopulation of the Santa Cruz and Reef Islands was due to diseases like influenza and dysentery introduced by traders (O'Ferrall 1922: 67–68). Influenza and pneumonia were major health issues at that time (Groenewegen 1970: 9-10). The worldwide influenza pandemic of 1918–1920 killed 5.5 per cent of the Fijian population and 24 per cent of the Samoan population. In many colonial states inconsistent under-reporting meant that accurate figures were not available (Johnson and Mueller 2002; Wilson *et al.* 2005: 347). Arthur Hopkins, who worked for many years on Malaita and became principal of the Theological College at Siota in 1919, wrote about depopulation on Malaita. He suggested that the causes of population decline were the decrease in the size of families, the postponement of marriage to a later age, a move towards monogamy, the securing of abortions using tree bark concoctions, and sexually transmitted disease. Hopkins also listed 'dysentery', 'pulmonary diseases', 'infant mortality' and 'plantation life' (Hopkins 1922: 62–66). But despite the evidence suggesting the impact of diseases was significant, Rivers declared that depopulation was due to a 'psychological factor' and that many societies disrupted by European intervention suffered from a 'loss of interest in life' that resulted in fewer births and more deaths (Rivers 1922: 93–97; Patterson 1975: 233).

Rivers' (1922) book on depopulation in Melanesia was taken as scientific evidence that the peoples of the Western Pacific were in terminal decline. Woodford had previously written that 'nothing in the way of the most paternal legislation or fostered care, carried out at any expense whatever, can prevent the eventual extinction of the Melanesian race in the Pacific. This I look upon as a fundamental fact and as certain as the rising and setting of the sun' (Hilliard 1978: 157, 162 fn91; Scarr 1967a: 293–297). Some time later he qualified this by noting that, in the absence of any guide in the nature of a census, it was impossible to state categorically that the population of the Solomon Islands had declined since the arrival of white men. He also stated that, 'in particular localities thirty years ago [1880s] compared with the number observed in 1914 is that there has been a considerable decrease' and that this was most noticeable on Isabel, the Russell Islands and the north-western end of Guadalcanal. This decrease, he stated, was due to slave raiding and head hunting that had been going on for three to four centuries. Woodford was of the opinion that recruitment of men from Guadalcanal, Makira and Malaita had been responsible for a decrease in population in those areas but his main argument focussed on two causes. The first was the impact of Europeans who have changed the conditions of 'native life, among which I give preference to the injudicious use of unsuitable clothing'. This he considered advanced the spread of mostly pulmonary disease. Suitable clothing for men meant the wearing of a *lava-lava* or *lap-lap*. The second cause was the introduction of new diseases, such as dysentery, influenza and yaws, caused by a bacterium that produced weeping sores. Yaws was transmitted by skin to skin contact with an infected lesion but was more prevalent among the coastal people than the inland dwelling bush peoples (Woodford 1922b: 69; Boutilier 1974: 30).

Woodford recommended that the government undertake a census of the population, prevent the use of unnecessary European clothing, and impose regulations for village sanitation and clean water supply. While many of his recommendations are simple practical steps, his suggestion that the government should form industrial settlements populated by nuclear families removed from their traditional cultural ties is the voice of a colonial administrator looking on the success of the industrial missions of the Methodists and the Seventh-day Adventists (Woodford 1922b: 69–77). Depopulation had become a keystone of British colonial policy in the Pacific by this time. Officials and settlers in the Solomon Islands 'drew what they imagined to be the only conclusion and set themselves to attract investment of capital to secure for the group a prosperous future, but one in which the Solomon Islanders would have no permanent place' (Scarr 1967a: 297).

Population estimates for the Solomon Islands

The early narratives of the Spanish explorers who landed on Isabel in 1568 tell of large populations of people in coastal regions and sizable numbers of men appearing armed for potential fights against the Spanish. In his journal, Mendaña lists wildly exaggerated estimates of the numbers of people on various islands visited. Hernan Gallego wrote that 'we saw more than one hundred Indians approaching with their bows and arrows and clubs' at Isabel, and later at Nggela wrote that '[t]here would be more than seven hundred Indians', and still later on the return journey to Isabel passed St George Island (San Jorge: Veru) and noted that '[i]n the Island of Veru, which has more than 300 huts, the Indians received us peacefully'. San Jorge, Mendaña wrote, was also thickly populated as at one place more than 100 canoes were drawn up on the shore. In conclusion, Mendaña estimated that 30,000 fighting men could be raised from Isabel and 10,000 from San Jorge. The annotation by Woodford noted that in 1888 no village was left on St George Island because the inhabitants and the settlement were 'swept away some years ago by head-hunters from New Georgia' (Amherst and Thomson 1901, Volume 1: 24, 28, 33).

At Guadalcanal, Gallego also reported that the 'whole coast seemed full of villages' and noted 'more than six hundred warriors' assembled for battle (Amherst and Thomson 1901, Volume 1: 41). He estimated that more than 300,000 men could be gathered from Guadalcanal and from the Nggela islands another 50,000. On Nggela, Mendaña reported that the 'island is thickly populated: all the people are well-grown and good-looking', and that their canoes were large and each contained 30 men (Amherst and Thomson 1901, Volume 1: 146, 147). From Santiago (Uki ni Masi) more than 100,000 men could be obtained and the same from San Christoval (Makira) (Amherst and Thomson 1901, Volume 1: 180–181). The figures are of course astounding. Mendaña was looking for the fabled Isles of Solomon and, if he found riches, he had to convince the Spanish authorities that a colony could be established there. Large numbers of 'indians' were also potential slaves. The annotation to the reports by Woodford acknowledges the exaggerations, 'but it is evident that the population in 1567 was at least four times greater than it is now. Head hunting and epidemics are the most probable causes of the decrease'. These annotations are consistent with and taken from the notes made by Woodford during his third expedition to the islands in 1888. In his published paper Woodford also noted that the Spanish sailors estimated the population of Aola village at 3,000 people (Woodford 1888a: 411). Such figures only added to the later belief that Solomon Islanders had suffered a catastrophic decline in the 300 years between about 1600 and 1900.

The widely believed depopulation of the islands should be treated with suspicion for factors such as internecine warfare, labour recruitment and infectious diseases did not act continuously or uniformly over the whole area (Groenewegen 1970: 1). But Groenewegen, who noted the gross over-estimations made by Mendaña in the Spanish journals, wrote that in '1911 the first British Resident Commissioner in the Solomon Islands, Mr. C. M. Woodford, who was considered to have great knowledge of the area but was not in a position actually to count the population, gave an estimate of 150,000'. The same figure was still used as an estimate of the Solomon Islander population in the 1921 census (WPHC 4/IV 2991/1922). When island populations were counted and the figure revealed a total much lower than the accepted number, this was interpreted as evidence of depopulation. Numerous examples of such depopulation have been enshrined in the theory that Pacific peoples were becoming extinct in the face of Western civilization. It was apparent from evidence that some islander populations did suffer notable declines, and most certainly in the last half of the 19th century and the early-20th century each area must be considered on a case by case basis. The often quoted reasons for the decline were the increased scale and effects of warfare following the introduction of firearms, the rapid abandonment of social customs that led to the 'psychological factor' or the loss of the will to live, and the third reason, the introduction of foreign diseases that led to increased mortality of the young and those of reproductive age (Roberts 1927 quoted in Bayliss-Smith 2006: 21–22).

In 1913, Arthur Mahaffy was quoted by the *Sydney Morning Herald* (24 May 1913: 19) as saying:

> The dark-skinned island peoples are slowly melting away. In nearly every group [in the Pacific] the native race is enfeebled, riven by disease, with no prospect ahead than annihilation … Mr Mahaffy said that various causes were producing decay, and one of the chief of these was idleness … They are dying fast from phthisis [pulmonary consumption] mainly, which is making great ravages in all the islands. The introduction of clothes and other habits had been responsible for this.

Mahaffy was primarily concerned about the impact poor health and the inability of men to work would have on the plantation labour problem. He too advocated the introduction of Indian collie labour into the Solomon Islands as had been done in Fiji. Mahaffy's opinions were part of the accepted view of islander populations and their future.

Rev Walter Ivens (1918; *The Argus* 10 October 1925: 6, 1930) from the Melanesian Mission was a careful linguist and ethnologist based on Malaita. He divided the depopulation question into three phases. The first was the period from the 1860s to the 1890s that coincided with the growth of the Pacific labour trade. Many men did not return, some by choice, and some died, but some of those who did return either delayed their marriage or did not marry at all. The second phase was the period of escalating warfare between the 1870s and the 1890s when traders and blackbirders introduced firearms into the islands as payment for island produce and as part of the 'beach payment' for indentured labourers. Returning labourers also brought back weapons smuggled in their trade boxes. This period of warfare also advanced but did not entirely cause an increase in head hunting in the New Georgia region. As a result of warfare many villages along the coast of Vella Lavella, parts of New Georgia and Maramasike passage on southern Malaita were abandoned by people escaping raiders and the possible return of the Royal Navy's men-of-war bringing their annual display of 'Commodore Justice' (Scarr 1967a: 174).

In the New Georgia group the depopulation was indeed severe. It is estimated that in parts of New Georgia a population decline of 70 per cent was likely between 1850 and 1930 (Bayliss-Smith, Hviding and Whitmore 2003: 351). Indeed, the population of Simbo in 1908 was thought to be only 400 people (Hocart 1922: 74, Scheffler 1962: 137). The final period of population decline was the most devastating and widespread. Between the 1880s and the 1920s epidemic diseases spread throughout the islands. Diseases spread quickly through nucleated villages and the plantation labour lines. People moved between the villages and the plantations carrying dysentery, influenza, measles and whooping cough. Malaria and yaws were already known on the islands but ironically spread among people brought together in an effort to change living standards, to improve hygiene and to control pigs, garbage and effluent. The other major cause of population decline was the spread of malaria. It was not until 1897 that the mosquito was found to be the key vector in the transmission of the disease. Apart from causing death, a severe impact of malaria may cause foetal and infant mortality as well as miscarriages, premature births and stillbirths in women (Bayliss-Smith 2006: 41).

It was generally assumed that the population of the Solomon Islands for the period 1912–1913 was between 100,000 and 150,000 (Bennett 1987: 151 quoting British Solomon Islands Protectorate Annual report 1912–1913; Bayliss-Smith 2006: 27). Certainly, the colonial administration had been using the larger figure for some time (Great Britain. House of Commons. Parliamentary Papers 1905: 5; British Solomon Islands Protectorate 1911: 45). This was repeated throughout the early years of the 20th century (*The Register* [Adelaide] 19 February 1906: 4; *The Daily News* [Perth] 17 January 1916: 4; Scholefield 1919: 241). It was apparent that plantation companies were using the declining population thesis to support the case for the introduction of Asian labour (*The Brisbane Courier* 11 June 1927: 20).

Basing his data on a number of sources, Moore (2009a: 15–16) gives a more accurate population figure for Malaita circa 1900 as 50,000, for Nggela 5,000, and for Isabel a population of 4,000 in the 1890s. An extrapolation from these data would give an estimated population of the islands as 90,000 at the end of the 19th century. This would be a more accurate figure at the end of the sustained contact period when the effects of epidemic disease, local warfare and population movements had taken their toll. This is largely confirmed by the population figures of 93,415 from the 1931 census, although this was largely a head count carried out by District Officers who relied on figures provided by District Headmen. Based on these figures, it is most likely that the pre-contact population of the Solomon Islands—one of the many demographic unknowns of the Pacific—was about 100,000 people and that about 10 per cent were affected by internecine warfare, epidemic diseases or the resulting fertility and mortality issues of the later quarter of the 19th century. Quoting the title of Jarred Diamond's book *Guns, Germs and Steel*, Bayliss-Smith (2006: 47) summarised the issue of depopulation in Melanesia as: 'Guns and steel were important aspects of colonialism, but the role of Germs is more subtle than is usually assumed'. It was clear that colonial planning was based on bias with a poor understanding of epidemiology and was most certainly confused on the depopulation discourse.

11. Woodford and the Western Pacific High Commission

In his 18 years as Resident Commissioner, Woodford served under six High Commissioners and three acting High Commissioners (Heath 1974a: 94). These relationships were mostly cordial. Given the distance from Suva and the inadequate communication of the day, he was largely left to manage the Protectorate independently. But the Western Pacific High Commission was a complex political institution and distant Resident Commissioners had to maintain good relations not only with the High Commissioner but also with his official Secretary. Woodford had trouble with two senior officials who served at the same time and who both served in their powerful positions for considerable periods. His relationships with Everard im Thurn, High Commissioner from 1904 to 1910, and Merton King, Secretary from 1898 to 1907, were far from cordial. King subsequently became British Resident Commissioner in the New Hebrides from 1907 to 1924, a long service of 17 years. King and Woodford did not agree and, considering the length of service each man would serve in the Pacific, this mutual dislike would be long lasting.

When Woodford first came to Suva seeking a position in the Solomon Islands, John Bates Thurston was Governor of Fiji and High Commissioner for the Western Pacific. The Secretary under Thurston was Wilfred Collet. A man of some ability, training and expertise in colonial affairs, Collet appointed Woodford to a temporary position in the High Commission between November 1896 and January 1897. Collet approached Thurston with a proposal to pay Woodford out of surplus votes in the judicial and travelling accounts while Woodford was drafting new land regulations for the southern Solomon Islands Protectorate (Collet to Thurston 30 November 1896 WPHC 4/IV 478/1896). Collet also offered to go without extra salary, presumably allowance payments, if Woodford could be retained in Suva while the High Commissioner negotiated with the Treasury to fund a position at Tulagi (Collet to High Commissioner 30 November 1896 WPHC 4/IV 478/1896; Heath 1974a: 94). Fortunately, Woodford's relationship with Thurston appears to have been warm and he supplied a number of personal accounts to the High Commissioner during the trip to the Gilbert Islands and the three scientific expeditions to the Solomons. Woodford carefully made copies of these reports and inserted them into his personal diaries. Thurston was not from an elite background. He had been a first mate on the sailing ship *James* and a sheep farmer in Australia and was interested in the botany of the Pacific. His father-in-law, John Barry of Albury in New South Wales, was appointed to the Survey Department of the Fiji government in 1877 and rose to be Commissioner of Land, Works and Surveys. Thurston, by now well connected to colonial gentry, settled at Thornbury on Viti Levu and a property, 'St Helier's', on Taviuni Island. He established the Suva Botanical Gardens, now the Thurston Gardens, and published a small booklet on the plants and shrubs that could be acclimatised to grow in the islands (Thurston 1886; Woodford papers PMB 1290 Item 7/37). He was an important mentor for Woodford.

Thurston was the fourth High Commissioner for the Western Pacific and served from 1888 to his death on 7 February 1897. During Woodford's not so successful period of employment in Suva in 1883 he had been a minor clerk under Sir William MacGregor. Under Thurston and Collet he had been given a certain amount of freedom to act independently in Tulagi but Thurston's death came at a time when Collet too left Suva. Thurston was replaced by Sir George O'Brien and Collet by Merton King. Under these two men the working relation deteriorated. O'Brien had been Colonial Secretary in Hong Kong and was Governor of Fiji from 1897 to 1901. This was a time when the pacification of the Solomon Islands was being intensified, the Treasury parsimonious with grants-in-aid, and officials in Tulagi still trying to establish a physical presence in the Protectorate. While O'Brien was punctilious and found constant errors in the financial accounts sent from Tulagi, King was pedantic and the combination of the two only served to aggravate Woodford. Woodford appears to have little tolerance for people he disliked and his 'methods were rarely painstakingly or carefully thought out, he acted (and re-acted) quickly and decisively, an ideal man-on-the-spot for a demanding task, but a poor subordinate' (Heath 1974a: 96). For Woodford, the greater problem was the sarcasm and petty comments made by Secretary Merton King.

Under Sir Henry Moore Jackson, who followed O'Brien, relations improved although at this stage Merton King was still official Secretary. Woodford believed the limited freedom given to him by Sir Henry was a sign of Jackson's beliefs in the development of the islands but ironically they stemmed from Jackson's complete indifference to the future of the Solomons (Heath 1974a: 97). Woodford clashed with Jackson over a mistaken belief that Certificates of Occupation gave the holders exclusive fishing rights in waters along the boundaries of their properties. Woodford took up the cause of native fishing rights but it would appear to have been a misinterpretation of the licensees' rights in the first place. The terms of the Certificate state the 'Occupier [has] a Certificate of Occupation in respect of the unoccupied pieces of land … together with the right to fish the produce of the waters marching with the coast boundary (if any) of such land' (Pacific Islands Company Certificate of Occupation enclosed in WPHC 4/IV 91/1898). The meaning is unclear but it certainly does not state the lessee has exclusive rights. The minor debate over fishing rights lasted for some time (Allardyce to Colonial Office 4 June 1902 CO 225 63 30786). Finally the discussion was meant to be resolved by the *Solomons (Fisheries) Regulation of*

1902 (King's Regulation No 2 of 1902) but the matter of exclusive rights claimed by holders of Certificates of Occupation, the rights of owners of vessel licenses and the rights of local people to artisanal fishing in coastal waters only became more muddied (Woodford to Colonial Office 28 February 1903 CO 225 65 20094).

If relations had been cool under some previous High Commissioners things would turn for the worst with the appointment of Everard im Thurn. Both im Thurn and Merton King were not happy to be appointed to the Pacific. In a private letter to the Director of the Royal Botanic Gardens at Kew im Thurn even went so far as to write 'I am *not* pleased at having been sent here—but have made up my mind to bear my exile with equanimity' (Heath 1974a: 98). He was most certainly a complex character. One would have thought a man with his experience in British Guiana, where he had been curator of the museum, who was the author of a number of scientific books and papers on botan,y and who had a reputation as an amateur anthropologist—he was to be the President of the Royal Anthropological Institute in 1919 and 1920—would have had more in common with Woodford. Both men came to their positions as administrators after long experience in the field. Im Thurn, like Sir Arthur Gordon, had his own high self-regard as a champion and protector of the 'loyal Native subjects of the British Crown' (Heath 1974a: 98). When Mahaffy was transferred to Suva in 1904 he too would find im Thurn difficult. Mahaffy's antipathy to im Thurn, like that between Woodford and im Thurn, 'seems rather to have been that the High Commissioner himself—an able, vigorous man with literary powers and some evident self-satisfaction in his own abilities—preferred to surround himself with comparative cyphers, rather than men capable of meeting him on equal terms' (Scarr 1967a: 287). Both Mahaffy and Woodford found im Thurn unpredictable. Commenting on im Thurn's administrative style in dealing with developments in the Gilbert and Ellice islands, Macdonald (2001: 125) wrote: 'For a time, while im Thurn remained High Commissioner, it seemed that reforms might be implemented but when changes did take place, it was seldom in the manner expected'. At least for Woodford, im Thurn's appointment came at a time when some small signs were showing of economic growth in the Solomon Islands.

The two men met for the first time more than seven months after im Thurn's appointment. At this meeting in Suva in April 1905 they found little to agree upon. Woodford was on his way to London for long leave and im Thurn forwarded a long critical memorandum to the Colonial Office at the same time. In the confidential memo to London, im Thurn wrote that Woodford had a habit of thought that 'was almost excessively philoprogressivist [implying Woodford had strong ideas about the direction of social and economic change]; *his* work is the only good work (and it really is *good* work) and *his* islands are almost the only part of the British Empire worth preserving' (Heath 1974a: 100 quoting im Thurn with original emphasis). When im Thrun had occasion to criticise Woodford for what was called 'grave disobedience of orders given', Woodford's reply was 'that the laws of the Medes and Persians were not for him and that if the Government did not want his work they must do without it' (Heath 1974a: 100 quoting im Thurn). The quote, no doubt well known to im Thurn, implying that the laws of the High Commissioner were rigid and unbending, comes from Daniel 6:8: 'Now, O king...sign the writing, that it be not changed, according to the law of the Medes and Persians which altereth not'. Being called unbending and rigid like a Persian king would be guaranteed to rile a person like im Thurn with a very high opinion of himself. At this time 21 leading white citizens of the Protectorate presented Woodford with an illustrated testimonial of esteem and respect. This was a well intentioned, but undoubtledly political, statement of support.

Figure 40. Illustrated testimonial presented to Charles Morris Woodford in March 1905 by 21 leading white settlers in the Solomon Islands.

Source: ANUA 481 D.

The Oliphant affair

Woodford took long leave in 1905. He left in early March and met with im Thurn in Suva in April on the way to London. A poor choice of temporary replacement for his position was made that further alienated Suva from Tulagi. Mahaffy, who would have been the logical choice of Acting Resident Commissioner, had gone to Fiji by then and the only other officers in the islands were newcomers. On the recommendations of Edmund Barton and Alfred Deakin, who both should have known better, Arthur Oliphant from South Australia was appointed. Soon after he and his family arrived in April 1905 they were installed in the residency (Oliphant to im Thurn 1 April 1905 WPHC 4/IV 243/1899 and 9 June 1905 WPHC 4/IV 26/1905). Oliphant, in his short time in Tulagi, managed to make a mess of the administration and involved the Protectorate in small scandals and bad publicity that eventually resulted in legal liability. For Woodford the scandal and financial liability would have been sufficient to cause acute anger at a time when his status with Suva was low.

In what the newspaper reports call a romance worthy of Robert Louis Stevenson the full account of Oliphant's pomposity becomes evident. Upon arrival in the Protectorate Oliphant went to the Shortland Islands to investigate the death of a Mr McConville who had disappeared on Bougainville (Oliphant to im Thurn 24 July 1905 WPHC 4/IV 122/1905). While at Faisi he charged Alfred Hearnes, a business partner of William Hazelton, with supplying alcohol to the natives. Hearnes was fined £20 with a surety of £100 on two breaches of the Liquor Regulation of 1893. Hearnes could not pay and immediately left the islands. Contrary to regulations Oliphant returned some of the fine to finance his exit to Australia (Oliphant to im Thurn 24 July 1905 WPHC 4/IV 131/1905). Hazelton, who had previously joined Mahaffy in police operations in the New Georgia area, had since left the colonial service and gone into trading. He was also trying to secure the purchase of 1,400 acres of land in Marovo Lagoon but he was believed to be acting as an agent for Lever's Pacific Plantations Ltd (Woodford to im Thurn 27 October 1906 WPHC 4/IV 134/1899). Following the deportation of his business partner it was apparent he was about to rile Oliphant.

On 15 June, at Gavutu, convinced that the boat contained contraband firearms, Oliphant attempted to board Hazelton's schooner *Lindsay*. When he made to board the vessel he was pushed back into the government launch by Hazelton who told him he would throw him overboard if he were to come on the yacht. Oliphant found Hazelton flying a skull and cross bones flag apparently 'in a sportive spirit' but Oliphant considered this an official breach of the peace (*The Mercury* [Hobart] 11 July 1905: 3; *The Sydney Morning Herald* 6 July 1905: 3). Subsequent to this farce, Oliphant served Hazelton with a warrant for his arrest, found him guilty of assault and insult and fined him £10. This was later increased to £30. Hazelton was eventually sentenced to be deported to Suva and imprisoned for three months. Oliphant, however, had been both the judge of the case as well as the magistrate who signed the warrant and appointed court assessors, as he had in the Hearnes case, who were ordered not to have anything to say during the court proceedings. The amount of the fine was reduced to £4/15/- when Hazelton signed a formal apology to King Edward VII for insulting one of His Majesty's officers and another apology to the High Commissioner in Suva (*The Sydney Morning Herald* 13 July 1905: 6). After Hazelton signed these documents he was still deported to Suva for imprisonment. Both Oliphant and Hazelton then sailed together for Suva via Brisbane and Sydney. On the voyage both men were seen drinking heavily, presumably in each other's company according to many press reports, but Oliphant in an inebriated state dictated a new, second, warrant for the arrest of Hazelton while the ship was in Brisbane (*The Brisbane Courier* 14 July 1905: 3). Hazelton's solicitor in Sydney issued an application of habeas corpus and at a hearing before Justice Cohen, Hazelton was released from custody because the warrant, signed on board the ship, had been issued outside the jurisdiction of the Protectorate. This was just the 'decadent white men in the tropics' story that newspapers loved. Confidential memos following the affair also pointed out, snobbishly but no doubt accurately, that Oliphant was a weak character much dominated by his wife (Heath 1974a: 108). In the middle of this low drama Oliphant wrote to im Thurn requesting that he not be called 'Acting' Resident Commissioner as no one would take his advice seriously while Woodford was on leave. The file is clearly marked: 'there will be no necessity to reply to this despatch' (Oliphant to im Thurn 3 May 1905 WPHC 4/IV 119/1905). The Oliphant fiasco even became the subject of some mention in the Burns Philp records at the time (AU NBAC N115/589). Oliphant was subsequently removed from office and replaced by Thomas Edge-Partington.

Relations with Suva would have been further strained by the aftermath of the affair. In October 1905 im Thurn was forced to travel to Tulagi on HMS *Torch* to give Hazelton a written apology that stated:

> As High Commissioner and in virtue of the power given me under the Pacific Order-in-Council 1882, section III (9), I hereby remit any order of deportation from the Solomon Islands that may have been made by Arthur Oliphant, lately Deputy Commissioner and Acting Resident Commissioner for the British Solomon Islands Protectorate against William Henry Hazelton.
>
> (Signed) Everard im Thurn, Gavutu, 24th August 1905 (The Sydney Morning Herald 18 October 1905: 9).

Hazelton not only won a case of wrongful arrest but he received his letter of apology from im Thurn in person. This would have insulted the most high dignity of im Thurn even more. Not only did im Thurn have to make the official apology but he chose, deliberately, to go to Tulagi while Woodford was on leave. Consequently, im Thurn and Woodford's relationship did not improve. In June 1906, Hazelton was granted damages for the wrongful arrest. Although he initially sued the Inspector of Police in Tulagi for £1,000 he was awarded £229. Woodford returned from leave in January 1906 in the middle of this embarrassing mess. For a man with strong opinions of Australia and Australians in general, despite having an Australian wife, he would not have been amused to read the minor island scandal that was printed, and reprinted, with some amusement in the 'colonial' press.

Postal services in the Solomon Islands

While this minor charade was being acted out in Tulagi, Woodford had been advancing the case for Levers in the Solomons in London and importantly, and often not recognised, laid the foundation for the first postal service in the Solomon Islands using stamps that he had himself designed (Woodford papers PMB 1381/007). There is much available on the subject of the postal history and the design of the stamps of the early British Solomon Islands Protectorate. The best papers are by R. P. Croom-Johnson (1928), Harold Gisburn (1956) and a series of articles by Don Franks (2000a and 2000b). Some of these articles have been summarised, and illustrated, by Roland Klinger (www.ro-klinger.de/tulagi).

The postal service had humble beginnings. In the early years on Tulagi, Woodford sent letters with a personal cheque for the cost of the stamps on the regular steamers operated by Burns Philp to Sydney. The letters and parcels were stamped—British Solomon Islands Paid—and in the Sydney GPO were stamped and franked with Australian postage stamps. Later Woodford kept a stock of Australian postage stamps at Tulagi but as the Protectorate was outside Australia, the stamps were not defaced. That was done in Sydney. Many of the covers sighted by Gisburn (1956: 25) are in Woodford's own handwriting. Woodford introduced the first locally identified stamps in 1907 and this coincided with the establishment of the first post offices in the islands. In addition to the office on Tulagi, post offices were located in the district headquarters at Aola on Guadalcanal, Gizo in the New Georgia group, Faisi at Shortland Harbour in the north and at the trading station of Gavutu off Tulagi. Gizo and Shortland Harbour were important trading areas. Most of these post offices were operational by 1908. They were declared ports of entry in 1907 to facilitate trade through German New Guinea (WPHC 10/V Item 131; British Solomon Islands Protectorate 1909: 21). This however was another source of contention between Tulagi and Suva. Gavutu was declared a port of entry rather than Tulagi and it took Merton King another six months to correct the minor but financially important mistake (Woodford to im Thurn 15 April 1907 WPHC 4/IV 75/1905; WPHC 4/IV 73/1906)

Woodford wrote later, in what appears to be correspondence with Gisburn (1956: 27) on the subject of the stamp design: 'The postal work had so much increased that in my estimates for the year 1906–07 I had asked [the High Commission in Suva] for an issue of postage stamps, and had estimated a revenue of £600 to be received from the sale. This estimate [said to be only £300 according to Croom-Johnson (1928: 7)] was subsequently reduced to £100 by the office of the High Commissioner'. While waiting for the response from Suva, Woodford ordered the first stamps in 1906 but they were badly printed on poor quality paper by W. E. Smith of Sydney. Although W. E. Smith was a general printing firm with no expertise in postal stamp design they advertised themselves as high-class stationers and printers. The choice of this firm was perhaps governed by convenience and reputation. They were located at 30 Bridge Street, not far from the Sydney headquarters of Burns Philp at 5–11 Bridge Street. The Burns Philp Building, one of the notable city constructions built in a grandiose, richly carved and decorated Romanesque style, was a major meeting place and business centre for traders and planters from the Western Pacific. Woodford wrote that he could not wait for the decision of im Thurn, for 'if I had waited for the High Commissioner to order the stamps I should have had to wait certainly another two years, but by forcing his hand he was bound to get the stamps recognised' (Gisburn 1956: 28).

The first set of stamps designed by Woodford is known by philatelists as the 'Large Canoe' series. These stamps show a composite image of the Tulagi in the background, coconut palms on either side in the foreground and in the middle distance, a New Georgia *tomoko*. This series of stamps was printed in denominations of $\frac{1}{2}$d (ultramarine), 1d (rose-carmine), 2d (indigo), $2\frac{1}{2}$d (orange-yellow), 5d (emerald-green), 6d (chocolate), and one shilling (bright purple) in order to conform with the postage rates used in Australia (Howard-White 1972). The problem with the stamps was twofold. Not only was the paper course white stock and the stamps printed by lithography, but the glue backing was not suitable for the tropics and caused constant problems. Woodford wrote that the stamps were 'very poor workmanship' and constant type errors occurred due to the use of printing transfers (Gisburn 1956: 32). The stocks were rather large for such a small population: 60,000 stamps of each denomination between $\frac{1}{2}$d and $2\frac{1}{2}$d, and 30,000 stamps of each denomination between 5d and one shilling were printed. These went on sale at Tulagi on 14 February 1907 (Croom-Johnson 1928: 6). This series remained in use until 1 November 1908 when all remaining stamps, carefully itemised by Woodford, were destroyed in front of witnesses. As postage stamps are a form of taxation paid to facilitate the transportation of mail, unused stamps are in effect equivalent to their face value. Any attempt to forge stamps, print them illegally or steal them is a criminal offence. The process of demonetisation of postage or revenue stamps that rendered them no longer valid is a rare event.

When the remaining stocks were destroyed Woodford specified that all printing plates should be defaced and no reprints made. Apparently this was not done and some unauthorised reprints were made by a confidential employee and sold to a London stamps dealer (Gisburn 1956: 35). W. E. Smith sold his printing business in Sydney in 1910 and the Company Secretary of the new firm found the original printing stones that had not been cleaned off. It was this person referred to as a 'confidential employee' who had new sheets of the old stamps printed and passed them onto London dealers (Croom-Johnson 1928: 8). Woodford took legal action and had the illegal stamps seized and destroyed. There was considerable correspondence between Woodford and notable stamps dealers, such as Fred Hagen of Sydney, Stanley Gibbons in London and Oswald Marsh in Norwood, London at this time. It may have been Marsh who was the dealer referred to above (Franks and Forrestier Smith 2001: 61). Howard-White (1972: 218) also reports that correspondence between Woodford and a collector in London refers to another dealer, W. H. Peckitt of 47 Strand London, but the date, 1912, is much later. It is unlikely that Peckitt was involved in the illegal trading.

When the British Solomon Islands Protectorate was accepted as part of the Universal Postal Union (UPU) on 3 September 1907 the Colonial Office gave permission for a second series of stamps to be issued. As a member of the Union, the new stamps had to conform to agreed style and colour schemes. The General Post Office in London wrote to the Colonial Office specifying, in some detail, the formalities and requirements of the Protectorate in now adhering to the UPU conditions. As the British postal service now assumed responsibility for all postal transactions in the Solomon Islands the Protectorate post offices had to adopt British postal rates and services (General Post Office to Colonial Office 24 December 1907 CO 225 80 44799). New stamps had to be officially approved by the Office of the Crown Agents in London and then printed and designed by Thomas De La Rue and Co, the official printers of postage stamps in England.

Although postal historians agree that the British Solomon Islands Protectorate was admitted to the postal union in 1907 it appears that the formalities were not completed by the High Commissioner's office in Suva (Croom-Johnson 1928: 6). Writing to the Secretary of the General Post Office, then based in Melbourne, the office of the High Commissioner deferred the settlement of various questions relating to the postal service pending Woodford's return from leave in 1909

(NAA Secretary of High Commissioner to Secretary of General Post Office 11 October 1909 A1, 1911/2030). Subsequent to his return, and in reply to the High Commissioner, Woodford wrote:

> ... upon the subject of Postal matters in this Protectorate, I have the honour to observe that my views had already been stated as to the expediency of the Protectorate being admitted to the Postal Union. I believe that at the time the new emission of postage stamps [1908] was issued a certain number of specimens were retained by the Postmaster General in London for distribution to the countries constituting the Postal Union, with a view to the Protectorate's early admission. 2. If therefore the necessary formalities are still incomplete, I would ask you to take the steps requisite for the inclusion of the Protectorate among the list of countries adhering to the Postal Union as soon as possible (NAA Woodford to High Commissioner 10 June 1910 A1, 1911/2030).

The High Commissioner's excuse for the delay in clarifying the date of admission was that the Postmaster General in London suggested the Gilbert and Ellice Islands Protectorate should be admitted to the UPU at the same time. He then passed the decision-making over to the Australian Postmaster-General (NAA High Commissioner to Secretary of Department of External Affairs 28 July 1910 A1, 1911/2030).

The design and printing of what is called the 'Small Canoe' series was approved by the Crown Agents on 31 March 1908 and the Protectorate would certainly have been admitted to the UPU by then. The role of the Office of the Crown Agents is important in considering the internal management of British protectorates and colonies. The office was the sole official commercial and financial agent for the Protectorates and Crown colonies. Prior to 1833 colonial governors and administrators had appointed private individuals to act as their agents in London. Following creation of the sole office much of the new capital raised by the Crown Agents came from floating loans on the London securities market. These transactions were not underwritten by government guarantees. After 1880, the Colonial Office enforced a policy that all official purchases and financial transactions had to be approved by the Office of the Crown Agents. From that time the agency held a virtual monopoly over government retail supply. It was the only route for capital investment in the British territories and the agents held the grants made to the colonies by the Treasury. The agency also recruited some staff for the colonies, and purchased general government supplies. It was a powerful financial and commercial entity that acted as a broker between the Treasury and the colonial financial institutions. For these reasons, the Office of the Crown Agents became the official intermediary in the printing and design of the future stamps of the Protectorate. One of the main impediments to economic growth in the Protectorate was the separation of powers between the official brokers. The Western Pacific High Commissioner facilitated access to and from the Colonial Office and the Office of Crown Agents facilitated access to and from the Treasury. Imperial policy makers could agree on the major points of interest—peace, prosperity and Imperial power—but could rarely agree on process.

The second series of stamps was printed on paper supplied to the Crown Agents by Roughway Mills from Tonbridge in Kent and the stamps printed under license. When these reached Tulagi in 1908 they came in a much larger supply: 100,000 stamps of denominations ½d, 1d, 2d and 2½d, 30,000 stamps of denominations 5d, 6d and one shilling, and later stamps of denominations 4d, two shillings, two shillings and sixpence, and five shillings were printed. These stamps also conformed with Australian postal charges (Gisburn 1956: 42–43). Writing in praise of the composition of the 'Small Canoe' series, Gisburn (1956: 44) stated: 'In summary, this issue, both in design and printing, may be said to have been one of the neatest and most satisfactory series ever to have emanated from the House of De La Rue'. The 'Small Canoe' remained in circulation for only five years. The remaining stock was demonetised in July and August 1914 and replaced by less picturesque but more economical stamps with the image of King George V. Croom-Johnson (1928: 12) comments: 'It would be hard to find a cleaner country from a stamp man's point of view … All the fascinations of philately are to be found over a period of eighteen years, with the added certainty that the total possible supply of stamps is known and quite small'. To commemorate the opening of the new post office in central Honiara in 1970 a first day cover was issued that featured a portrait of Charles Morris Woodford and a copy of the a 2d 'Large Canoe' stamp with the words: 'British Solomon Islands 14c'. Woodford's role in the postal history of the Solomon Islands is an important and interesting annex to his story.

Education and health services in the early years

During the establishment period, social services received little attention from the administration. Pacification, police patrols, routine administrative duties, and attempts to secure economic stability based on copra plantations absorbed the attention of the small staff. The first obvious social service needed was medical care. Mahaffy had been appointed to help deal with problems associated with a smallpox outbreak in German New Guinea. The problem for the northern Solomons was that people crossed between Bougainville and the Shortland Islands, then part of German territory. If guns and ammunition could flow openly south, then so could epidemics. Medical problems in the islands were 'stupendous' (Boutilier 1974: 5). Malaria was endemic, even in Tulagi, and amoebic dysentery, beri-beri, blackwater fever, hookworm and yaws were all common. In the New Georgia area people had a long history of building leprosy shrines during the pre-contact period so this disease too may have been common throughout the islands (see Nagaoka 2011: 33). The shipping services, and the Labour Trade, introduced foreign diseases like influenza, venereal diseases and polio into the islands. The first regulation (Queen's Regulation no 1 of 1897) was a quarantine law but this was ineffective against the spread of disease coming from the north. A new regulation implemented in 1907 (*The Solomons (Quarantine) Regulation of 1907*; King's Regulation no 1 of 1907) that repealed the first one was designed to prevent the introduction of disease by making all vessels perform pratique at Gavutu. In some cases this meant pratique took more than two weeks.

The climate was considered hard on white people. Woodford was so ill with malaria in 1900 that he had to be helped on board the vessel taking him to Sydney for treatment. Requests for leave had to be approved by the High Commissioner in Suva. Hazelton threatened to resign if his leave were not granted. In the end he resigned anyway. Woodford, Mahaffy and Hazelton all suffered from the side effects of large doses of quinine. Eczema on the body, face and hands, insomnia and partial deafness were only a few of the health problems encountered in such a hot, humid environment (Woodford to O'Brien 28 December 1901 WPHC 243/1899). The greatest danger was to young unmarried men stationed on Tulagi whose diet was poor and who no doubt drank heavily. Medical attention was first devoted to keeping administration staff on Tulagi healthy. The need for a hospital at Tulagi was raised as early as 1897. At a meeting held on Gavutu to discuss the imposition of ships' license fees in late November a subscription of £14 guineas was raised from traders. This was given to Dr Henry Welchman who used it to construct a small clinic at Siota attached to St Luke's College. Welchman had been undertaking most of the emergency medical work at Siota and he cared for Jean Pratt there after he was attacked by Zito. For this Pratt had given the mission a new boat and a contribution to the hospital fund (*The Sydney Morning Herald* 16 February 1898: 4). The distance from Tulagi to Siota, 12 miles along Mboli Passage, was a problem for emergency cases. It was agreed that a hospital should be built on Tulagi at government expense because Siota would not always be served by a medical missionary. Welchman himself preferred to work at Bugotu on southern Isabel.

As with other social services, the progress of hospital construction either by missions or by the government was slow. The first hospital building was a leaf-hut construction that was found to be inadequate. Then two wooden buildings were built on the beachfront a few hundred metres from the south-east end of the main Tulagi wharf (Boutilier 1974: 11). One building contained a large, 18-bed ward for native male patients, an isolation ward, a ward for native female patients and a ward of four beds for the 'better class' natives and Chinese

(Boutilier 1974: 11). These 'native' wards were for local people on Tulagi who worked for whites as domestics or office staff, or men sent there by Department of Labour inspectors (Bennett 1987: 210; Moore 2009b: 9). The other building constructed was the main hospital to serve the needs of the white community with separate wards for men and women. There was also a Medical Officer's office, an operating theatre and nurses' quarters. Some doctors sent to Tulagi were found to be unsuitable. During the early years of the First World War Dr O'Sullivan was considered to have 'qualities inherent in the Irish peasant' but his real problem was a wife with ardent Sinn Fein associations. The longest serving Doctor-in-Charge was Dr Nathaniel Crichlow, a part-Chinese, part-Scottish doctor who served as Government Medical Officer from 1914–1923 and as District Medical Officer from 1923–1942 (Boutilier 1974: 14; Moore 2009b: 22).

For local people in the villages and on outer islands the nearest medical attention was at clinics belonging to plantations or at mission stations. Although the Methodists established one of the first rural hospitals at Sasamungga (Sasamuqa) on Choiseul in 1906, most mission stations did not construct suitable hospital facilities for local people until well into the 1920s (Boutilier 1974). The Melanesian Mission opened the Welchman Memorial Hospital in 1912 at Hautabu, near Marovovo at the north-western end of Guadalcanal, under the direction of Dr Russell Marshall. Patients paid for their medicine in-kind. When they were discharged they were required to work at the hospital plantation for two weeks cutting copra for the hospital fund (Boutilier 1974: 21; *Waiapu Church Gazette* Volume 3 (9), 1 March 1913: 131; Anon 1926). However the hospital closed in 1916 when the doctor married the matron and went off to the First World War. In the early years the administration relied on the missions to provide essential services because money was scarce, distances were great, and staffing was limited. But while the missions often had qualified people and good organisational structures that reached into the small villages, there was a fatal flaw in this relationship. Reliance on the missions to deliver services became institutionalised and was an excuse for not tackling the major health issues on the islands.

The situation regarding the provision of education services in those early days mirrors that of health. Again, education was left to the missions but the guiding principle behind the religious institutions was the development of Industrial Missions. The major preoccupation for the Catholics, Anglicans and evangelical churches was conversion, not education. Even though local people were keen for education in English, it conflicted with mission policy. As a result, educational opportunities for people varied. The Melanesian Mission's idea was to teach in Mota language and for students at the schools, mostly men, to learn 'industry, regularity and responsibility rather than learning' (Boutilier 1974:

37). The Methodists at their large profitable industrial mission at Kokeqelo on the Munda coast in Roviana Lagoon stressed the 'importance and the reward of honest labour'. Kokeqelo—meaning sweet-smelling flowers—may have seemed a prophetic name for the Methodists but it was a place of spirits for the local people. When local *banara* sold the land to the mission it may have been to test the quality of Christian efficacy and power (Bennett 2000a: 50). Adherents of the mission could learn boat building, carpentry, timber milling and plantation work—all employment that supported the mission while contributing to personal and village prosperity. They thereby gained access to medical services, recreational facilities and ministry, but access to good education was late in coming. The fundamentals of mission doctrine are clearly illustrated in the film *The Transformed Isle: Barbarism to Christianity* with its subtext that there is no such thing as a lazy Christian (Boutilier 1974: 39–40; Bennett 2000a: 51–53 for photographs of Kokeqelo circa 1905).

The Catholics saw their main task as conversion, an 'activity which achieved its purpose when the convert was baptised, safely ensconced in a Christian marriage, and beyond the reach of Protestantism' (Boutilier 1974: 41 quoting Laracy 1969: 195). The Society of Mary had established missions at Rua Sura under Father Bertreaux and at Poporang in the Shortland Islands supervised by Fathers Forestier and Hausch (British Solomon Islands Protectorate 1909: 13; *The Queenslander* 22 December 1906: 25). The Catholics had purchased land at Rere on the north coast of Guadalcanal and Bertreaux used this land, mostly sago swamp on the coast, for leaf material used for the construction of houses on Rua Sura. He repeatedly complained to Woodford that thatch and ivory nuts were being stolen by local people from inland villages (Bertreaux to Woodford 20 March 1911 WPHC 4/IV 134/1899). Arguments over ownership of the Rere land continued and the Catholics wished to sell it to Lever's Pacific Plantations. This was refused on the grounds that Lever's already had more land than they could use. When the Malayta Company made tentative interest in the land Woodford wrote: 'the whole question [land ownership] hinges upon keen competition and bitter animosity existing between Lever and the Malayta Company and between the Catholic and Evangelical Missions' (Woodford to Major 27 September 1910 WPHC 134/1899). His final recommendation to Major was that the Rere plantation 'land should revert to the natives and should not be permitted to be sold again to anyone at present'.

The South Seas Evangelical Mission was even more rigid in its perception of the value of a good education. In 1909 the Malayta Company established a training school for workers at Baunani plantation north of Onepusu, but the level of education was basic. Students were instructed in reading and writing in English and Pijin. They were also given religious instruction. Missionaries there believed that the 'main objective, which is to preach the gospel and establish an indigenous church on a knowledge of the word of God' was the sole criterion for the establishment of schools. The aim of basic education was for the students to be able to read the Bible. Norman Deck, nephew of Florence Young and a leading missionary, stated categorically that he was 'afraid ... of a secular education which lifts a considerable proportion of natives out of their natural environment unless such natives can be usefully absorbed, lest such natives may form a disloyal and dissatisfied class' (Boutiler 1974: 49 quoting Norman Deck to Ashley 29 October 1931 WPHC 4/IV 2594/1931). Village teachers sent out by the South Seas Evangelical Mission were to teach Godliness, cleanliness and industry. The motto of the mission remained staunchly 'salvation before education or civilisation' (Boutilier 1974: 50).

By the end of the 1930s there was little real educational progress in the Protectorate. As a result of parsimony, other priorities, the vagaries in copra prices, and a low regard for the intellectual qualities of islanders generally, official indifference left the Solomon Islands far behind even other colonies in the Western Pacific. 'The failure of the Administration and the missions to provide adequate education and medical services was in many ways a tragedy' (Boutilier 1974: 64). It was a tragedy for the many islanders who saw Christianity as a new beginning and a secular and useful education as a way into the European-dominated world. The various Christian churches and missions with their array of beliefs and attitudes, often in competition for the souls of the people but most often in conflict with each other, also served to confuse people at a time of great change.

Personal health crisis

In 1907, Woodford's health failed. Memos to im Thurn indicated that he may have had a severe case of cerebral malaria and anaemia. Woodford wrote: 'For the last ten days I have been in bed with a shaved head suffering from inflammation of the brain, brought on by anxiety and worry occasioned by the continuous and repeated mistakes and delays which have arisen in the Fiji Office' (Heath 1974: 102). The health crisis was exacerbated by errors made in Suva when the High Commissioner's office procrastinated in preparing new customs regulations (WPHC 10/V Item 132). While the *Solomons (Customs) Regulations of 1907* (King's Regulation no 2 of 1907) were being prepared and the *Solomons (Tobacco) Import Duty Regulations of 1906* were being repealed, matters came to a head. Officials in Tulagi watched as large qualities of dutiable goods, mostly tobacco and alcohol, landed at various parts of the Protectorate. The customs duties levied for imported alcohol were particularly heavy and it is likely that attempts to circumvent the charges were frequent (*The Argus* 9 September 1908: 9). To make matters worse some of the tax evaders were German merchants.

When the customs regulations were finally issued, an incorrect port of call for customs had been entered. In hindsight, a minor bureaucratic error meant that there were no customs regulations in place for about six months. The cost to the Protectorate was about £1,900 (Woodford to im Thurn 3 May 1907 WPHC 4/IV 59/1907).

Lacking caution, no doubt when he was ill, Woodford told im Thurn and Merton King that it was impossible for the High Commissioner to exercise control over the British Solomon Islands Protectorate from Fiji. To compound this he added that the High Commission was unable to manage the affairs of the entire Western Pacific. He then sent a copy of his complaint to the Colonial Office in London. This was not the first intemperate letter to pass between Woodford and im Thurn. When stranded in Albany on the way to London in May 1905, Woodford unwisely voiced his complaint that the High Commission in Suva had lost touch with the affairs in the Western Pacific following the death of Thurston and the retirement of Collet. Instead of a series of short requests for action on a number of separate points, Woodford harangued im Thurn on a wide ranging series of issues—land regulations, labour recruitment, house, pay and staffing problems, the use of private money for entertainment of visitors, and personal family concerns. Individually most were legitimate complaints at the time but im Thurn could not have solved them without direction and money from London (Woodford to im Thurn 24 May 1905 WPHC 4/IV 82/1898). They sowed the seeds of distrust, but it should have been clear to Suva that Woodford had health problems.

Personal antagonism between the two men became clear in correspondence after Woodford was admitted to St Malo Private Hospital in North Sydney in April 1907. Florence Woodford, living in Silverleigh at Tonbridge in Kent where her sons were being educated, appealed to the Colonial Office for information on her husband's medical condition only to be told that any telegram sent to Sydney had to be at full rates and at her own expense. Once again the Colonial Office illustrated its famous parsimonious attitude (Florence Woodford to Colonial Office 2 May 1909 CO 225 80 15710). On the other hand, im Thurn was anxious to have evidence Woodford was suffering mental health problems. He only received assurances from Dr Clarence Read, Woodford's specialist, that he was experiencing physical problems caused by overwork and climate. The High Commissioner then contacted the office of the Governor General Lord Northcote. Northcote's personal physical, Dr Thomas Fiaschi, interviewed Woodford in hospital. He too stated the conditions were physical and not mental. Northcote's Private Secretary, H. H. Share, also interviewed Woodford in hospital and wrote to Merton King that Woodford's health was improving. All this was again supported by correspondence from Robert Gemmell-Smith, a former manager with Colonial Sugar Refining in Fiji, now retired to Sydney.

From his home in Parramatta James Burns wrote to Atlee Hunt, the Permanent Head of the Department of External Affairs, on 23 July 1908 that 'accounts from the Solomons say that Mr Woodford is far from well, and unless he goes away for a change things may be serious' (AU NBAC N115/601). Woodford's health crisis was becoming a matter of some high level correspondence in Australia. But im Thurn continued to press for a medical certificate before allowing Woodford to return to Tulagi.

While in hospital, Woodford received a curt letter from im Thurn acknowledging that the High Commission had been in error over the customs regulations. This passage of memos between Suva and Woodford in hospital further inflamed passions. The result was that im Thurn wrote to the Colonial Office suggesting Woodford be retired on a pension. Im Thurn used the opportunity provided by the enforced hospitalisation to send a message to the Colonial Office detailing calculations for a pension entitlement. Im Thurn's estimates of a lowly £233/6/8 a year, increased to a possible £250 or even £300 were duly noted but not actioned (im Thurn to Colonial Office 7 March 1908 CO 225 81 14096).

Woodford lied to London and stated that his age was 54—he was actually 55, the recommended retiring age. From then on, once he was back in Tulagi, relations between Suva and Tulagi could never be mended. The Colonial Office made Woodford apologise to im Thurn conditional to an enforced retirement. This formal apology was forwarded on 18 May after which im Thurn informed the Secretary of State for the Colonies that Woodford, in a private letter, had written: 'I desire therefore to apologize in the fullest and most unreserved way for any improper expressions that I may have made use of any to beg you to accept my most solemn assurances that nothing of the sort shall occur again'. Nevertheless im Thurn made it clear to the Colonial Office that only official correspondence was now undertaken between Tulagi and Suva. Woodford, it appears, had also written to London requesting that administration of the Solomon Islands be transferred to Tulagi but this would have meant the Solomon Islands becoming a Crown Colony. Woodford was accused of a lack of discipline (im Thurn to Colonial Office 11 June 1907 WPHC 4/IV 65/1907).

The Bernays incident

During his hospitalisation in Sydney Woodford was replaced by Claude Lewis Bernays, a clerk in the Tulagi office. This in itself would have caused further questions to be asked in London for Bernays, a young Queenslander whose father was a highly regarded clerk of Parliament in Brisbane, was only 23 at the time. Like many Pacific adventurers, Bernays had a short but interesting life. He went to the Solomons at age 16 and worked for Oscar Svensen at Marau. He then became a manager for Levers at the Gavutu station and later joined the colonial service on Tulagi. He read a paper on developments in the Solomon Islands before the Royal Geographical Society in Queensland that promoted a bright future for the islands (Woodford papers PMB 1290 Item 7/44; *The Queenslander* 5 June 1909: 32). Unfortunately, Bernays himself would not have a bright future there. He was Acting Resident Commissioner when Zito attacked the Binskin family on Mbava Island. Panicked by the incident, pressured by traders and planters and guided by Edge-Partington on Gizo, the inexperienced officer launched the second failed attempt to arrest Zito. It appears he worked for the administration for about 5 years.

After relieving Woodford on emergency leave, he applied for a Certificate of Occupation for Mandoliana Island off Nggela Pile which had been the site of the massacre of Lt Bowers and the HMS *Sandfly* crew. His application was supported by Woodford on the grounds that the Gaeta people had given the island to the government (Woodford to High Commission 13 April 1908 CO 225 82 32932). It is most likely that the villagers were glad to dispose of an island with such a bad reputation. Bernays subsequently went into partnership with Norman Wheatley in a coconut plantation near Ilaroo (Ilemi) in Viru Harbour. He was killed by his own rifle which discharged when he was seated on a log during a hunting trip in the bush in June 1911 (*The Sydney Morning Herald* 6 June 1911: 7, *Cairns Post* 12 June 1911: 7). Fortunately for Woodford, no more questions about being replaced by incompetent newcomers or junior officials would be asked. Everard im Thurn retired in August 1910. Relief in the release from control by im Thrun was considerable with Woodford writing to his brother-in-law Dr Harold Hodgson: 'My bugbear Everard im Thurn, Judas as we call him, has retired thank goodness. The Colonial Office has accepted my Land policy and rejected his proposals and I believe that after years of misrepresentation, they are realising that I am right after all' (Woodford papers PMB 1381/004 Letter to Harold Hodgson 12 March 1911).

Im Thurn was succeeded by the more accommodating Sir Francis Henry May who was more willing to permit Woodford's foibles. Under May's successor, Sir Ernest Bickham Sweet-Escott, relations improved further. In 1911, almost 14 years after establishment of the Protectorate, the first audit of the financial affairs was undertaken. This audit document, dated 6 May 1911, has survived (BSIP 3/1/1) and is a historically important file. It is comprehensive and detailed. The first entry is for 29 July 1897. The Colonial Auditor commented that he 'found them [the financial records] on the whole accurately kept' and that 'Mr Woodford's own accuracy is well known'. A comment that surely shows criticism of Woodford's accounting practices is mistaken. The audit found that the Protectorate was in debt to the High Commission for £68/8/11. On 1 September 1911 Woodford wrote requesting an explanation of figures held in the Deceased Estates ledgers. These were divided into two sets of figures: the deceased estates of Europeans, and the records of unpaid wages owed to the estates of deceased labourers and other locally employed indentured workers. Woodford wrote correcting the audit figures and supplied long pages of accounts, many countersigned by the Treasurer, Richard Russell Pugh. His opinion was that 'instead of money being owing to the High Commission office, I have, on the contrary overpaid the amount'. The difference was over the supply of 75 Martini-Enfield rifles for the police to be supplied by the Crown Agents through the Fiji government. These guns, costing £197/13/7, were paid for but never received. In their place Woodford received guns costing £60/19/- but had not paid for them, a difference owing to the Protectorate of £136/14/7. This, after some time, was accepted by the Colonial Auditor with criticism being directed at the Treasurer instead of the Resident Commissioner. The Crown Auditor found that the Treasurer showed a 'lack of financial management' when the Protectorate owed money to the Crown Agents in London but held money in the Bank of New Zealand in Sydney and nearly £6,000 in interest earning fixed trusts (Colonial Auditor 22 November 1915 BSIP 3/1/1/).

These seemingly pedantic comments over small financial matters and clashes of personality were not uncommon in small colonial states. The hot-house nature of small administrative units and the constant demands made by financial restrictions, bureaucratic entanglements and settler aspirations led to many conflicts that resulted in bitterness and enmity. This was not just confined to Woodford and his relations with im Thurn and his Secretary, Merton King. A copy of the Merton King/Woodford enmity almost occurred in the 1930s with the Secretary to the High Commissioner H. Vaskess and the then Resident Commissioner F. Ashley actively disliking each other: 'Vaskess was a very meticulous and pedantic civil servant ... he seems to have entertained a deep and abiding anti-pathy towards Ashley and his scant regard for the Resident Commissioner is constant source of bias in W.P.H.C. material during the 1930s' (Boutilier 1974: 36 fn104).

Honours and recognition

In the King's Birthday Honours list of 14 June 1912, and in recognition of his services first as Deputy Commissioner and the as Resident Commissioner of the British Solomon Islands Protectorate, Charles Morris Woodford was made an Ordinary Member of the Third Class, a Companion of the Order of St Michael and St George (*The Supplement to the London Gazette* of Tuesday, the 11th of June 1912: 4299; *The Manchester Guardian* 14 June 1912). The announcement was also published in New Zealand and Australian papers (*Evening Post* [Wellington] 83 (141), 14 June 1912: 8; *The Sydney Morning Herald* 15 June 1912: 15). Woodford was recommended for the order by Sir Francis May who was mindful that, during the stormy period under im Thurn, many of Woodford's recommendations for the Solomon Islands went no further than Suva (May to Harcourt 8 December 1911 WPHC 4/IV 2161/1911; Heath 1974a: 106). May was one of the very few High Commissioners to ever visit the Solomon Islands.

On 13 June 1912 John Campbell, the Duke of Argyle and Chancellor of the Order, wrote to Woodford to inform him that the King had appointed him a Companion to the Order of St Michael and St George. From other correspondence it appears that Woodford's name had been proposed to the King by Lewis, Viscount Harcourt, the Secretary of State for the Colonies in the Asquith government (Woodford papers PMB 1381/008i–j). Woodford was notified by May's successor, Sir Ernest Bickham Sweet-Escott, that he would invest Woodford with the Order on a personal visit to Tulagi (Woodford papers PMB 1381/008). Appointment to the Order, and mention in the Colonial Office honours list, allowed Woodford to put CMG after his name. The Order was traditionally awarded to members of the colonial service. It continues to be awarded to former ambassadors and senior consular officials from the Foreign Office. Membership remains limited by the number who can be appointed at the different levels and so Woodford joined a select group of highly regarded officials.

Recognition came late in his career. The Rev George Brown, who had a warm personal relationship with Woodford, had even written to Lord Stanmore on 26 April 1911 suggesting Woodford be given the CMG, but considering Stanmore's role in the failed Pacific Islands Company fiasco and Woodford's anger over the dealings on Banaba, it is not surprising that Brown received a pessimistic reply (Woodford papers PMB 1381/004 and 1381/008i). Just prior to the announcement, Woodford had been the subject of a brief, and decidedly uncritical, article in *The Lone Hand* on 1 March 1911. Under the title 'Good Australians' it reported that although Woodford had been born in Kent, and remained staunchly English all his life, the magazine felt that his successful work in the Solomon Islands meant 'that there would seem to be rather more than mere justification for our claim to him as a Good Australian' (Anon 1911b: 378; Woodford papers PMB 1381/018d). The readers were told that with staff of not more than four white assistants he ruled over 400,000 natives—a gross exaggeration—'who have for many years borne an unenviable reputation for savagery and bloodthirstiness'. The population figure was a complete guess and by 1911 head hunting was a fading memory. Woodford was 'the man who, literally almost single-handed, has won the Islands for the Empire'. The article is not signed but Arthur Jose, collaborator with Walter Henry Lucas in the articles *British Mismanagement in the Pacific* (1907), was an occasional contributor to *The Lone Hand*, a sister magazine to *The Bulletin*. Both journals followed common themes of aggressive Australian nationalism, mateship, the cause of labour politics, and the White

Australian Policy. *The Lone Hand* was a popular newsy magazine containing literature and poetry designed to appeal to readers who did not subscribe to *The Bulletin*. Articles were solicited and authors paid for their stories. Some who contributed were C. J. Dennis, Steele Rudd, Henry Lawson and Norman Lindsay. *The Lone Hand* also printed articles on working class social conditions in the cities—such as scandals about illegal sweatshops in Sydney. Much later, a more balanced article in the *Pacific Islands Monthly* noted that a bronze memorial plate had been placed on a lamp standard on Tulagi waterfront in Woodford's memory by J. C. Barley. This presumably was between 1919 and 1921 when Barley was Acting Resident Commissioner (Lever 1974: 59, 101). The plaque is unlikely to have survived the Second World War.

Legacy

Two themes are evident in examining Woodford and his vision for the Solomon Islands. First, he saw a prosperous future for the islands and sought to encourage that goal by pacifying head hunting and advancing a plantation economy. These goals can be easily criticised today. Pacification was often heavy-handed and much property was destroyed. The goal was achieved when European military, naval and policing actions intersected with the local people's perceptions of that power and with the new social, religious and economic forces that grew up around colonialisation. The plantation economy certainly deprived Melanesians of much land. On Guadalcanal especially that land still remains alienated from customary owners. Much of the land was also neglected and degraded, for the copra industry did not provide the promised economic blessings. In the period before the First World War when tropical products like rubber and copra were used for important industrial purposes, the plantation economy supplied those resources. Large-scale European dominated companies that employed contracted or indentured agricultural labour were not considered exploitative. The theory was that they provided employment for semi-illiterate, semi-skilled people who, when necessary, had the village to fall back upon in cases of economic downturn. The fallacy of this thesis is that the subsistence economy is not an economic safety net. In times of high population growth and poor governmental services people do not return to their villages. Rather, they make a poor life in squatter camps around regional towns and cities. This is now evident in both the Solomon Islands and Papua New Guinea.

Secondly, Woodford saw himself as the creator of that glowing future. After all, he had written his own job description in 1890 when he stated: 'I know of no place where firm and paternal government would sooner produce beneficial results than in the Solomons' (Woodford 1890b: 23fn). His ownership of the future of the islands was understandable. But even for Woodford the Solomon

Islands was not a stepping-stone to career success. Men like Mahaffy, with well-established family backgrounds and a solid university education, more often ended their life in small outposts of civilisation. They too rarely made it to the top echelons. Mahaffy died early in the West Indies. Thomas Edge-Partington, an able man from an old establishment family, died in 1920 at the age of 36 in Ceylon (Sri Lanka). Woodford spent a large part of his life in the islands, his health suffered and he was forced to spend long periods away from his wife and two sons. When he left the islands for the last time in July 1914 he was heading for a quiet retirement in rural England.

Woodford received notification from the Colonial Office on 8 January 1915 that his resignation from the post of Resident Commissioner had been officially accepted. In January 1914, communicating with Lewis Harcourt, the Secretary of State for the Colonies, the High Commissioner Bickham Sweet-Escott acknowledged that Woodford's original pension estimate may be raised due to 'service of particular and extraordinary merit'. However he rejected this. He contended that Woodford was adequately compensated for his service in the islands but wrote: 'Mr Woodford is on safer grounds in urging the climate of the Solomon Islands as a reason for his being granted a higher pension'. Based on Woodford's final salary of £1,000 a year the pension was minutely, even pedantically, calculated at £466/13/4 a year (Sweet-Escott to Colonial Office 30 January 1914 WPHC 4/IV 183/1914). With less than extraordinary generosity it was raised by £33/6/8 a year to £500 a year (£140,000 a year in current values). This was considered to be higher than the rate originally proposed but one that Harcourt approved 'to recognize the value of the special services which you have rendered in connection with the administration of the Protectorate from the first days of its establishment'. It was exactly half Woodford's annual salary (Woodford papers PMB 1381/008k). Harcourt rejected the difficult and dangerous climate as justification for a pension increase and chose the recognition of special services option instead (Lambert to Woodford 8 January 1915 Woodford papers PMB 1381/008k). It had been a long, often arduous career.

Figure 41. Charles Morris Woodford wearing dress uniform and insignia of the Companion to the Order of St Michael and St George, July 1916.

Source: PMB Photo 56–014.

Figure 42. *The Grinstead*, home of Charles Morris and Florence Woodford, Partridge Green, Sussex.

Source: Courtesy of Herbie Whitmore, 2013.

Woodford and his wife settled on a substantial country estate of 22 acres of pasture, gardens and woodlands called 'The Grinstead' (now known as 'The Grinstead House Farm') in Littleworth Lane near the village of Partridge Green in Horsham, West Sussex. Woodford purchased the house for £1,400 from the deceased estate of James Andrew Mack at auction in 1914 (Woodford papers PMB 1381/013; *The London Gazette* 12 December 1913: 9209). It is a fine country house with five bedrooms located at the end of a long carriage drive surrounded by gardens, an orchard and a small wood with ponds. From there he continued his interest in natural history (Woodford papers PMB 1381/021e). Along with other former colonial administrators he served for a period as Vice-President of the English Committee of the Melanesian Mission (Woodford papers PMB 1381/01, 1381/021e and 1381/032; Hilliard 1978: 256 fn84)). He was not an uncritical representative of the mission, for he decried its neglect of young missionaries who had to face overwork, poor housing, a difficult climate and ill-health (Hillard 1978: 149). He contributed articles on ethnographic interest to noted anthropological journals and planned a book on Solomon Islands history that never materialised. His contribution to the early development years in the Solomon Islands was significant. Heath (1979: 146–147), commenting on that period, wrote:

The Woodford years had seen the growth of European control from a one man symbol of empire to a flourishing, albeit small, colonial administration. Under Woodford's direction, the Solomons had been largely pacified. Head hunting had disappeared and it was generally safe on most islands for Europeans to engage in trading or agriculture. By 1914 Woodford's vision of a prosperous and growing plantation economy had been realised … However, the seeds of future difficulties had been planted in the generally prosperous and peaceful Protectorate … In one sense, the uncertainty of European titles was the result, ironically, of the shift in colonial policy away from protecting 'native interests' towards supporting European enterprise.

At the end of Woodford's career as Resident Commissioner in 1915, the Solomon Islands remained a minor part of the wider British Empire. It had never been seriously considered for Crown Colony status. Economically it had not prospered. Socially it remained a small outpost of expatriate white colonial officials who ruled over a population of less than 90,000 people. Following the expansiveness of the Victorian era, the Edwardian period from 1901 to 1910 was one of consolidation leading to the devastating First World War. From the early-Victorian period Britain had climbed steadily to the pinnacle of Imperial power. By the early-20th century Britain had reached that apex of economic and political domination. Imperialism and expansionism had changed the entire social and economic fabric of the 'Motherland'. For the national government, the main sources of income were income tax, property tax, legacy and succession duties, and post office receipts, including postage and telegraph services. The late-Victorian and Edwardian eras in England saw increases in real incomes and enfranchisement for all middle class men and many working class males, but not for women. The rising population only served to emphasise the inherent problems of social class and inequality. Nearly 87 per cent of the British people were classed as 'struggling and poor', ten per cent were comfortably middle-class and only 3 per cent rich or very rich (McGowan and Kordan 1981: 52). The population in England and Wales had increased to over 30 million, Scotland had about four million people but Ireland had lost nearly 80 per cent of its people to overseas migration. In the 50 colonies of the British Empire there was a staggering 345 million people (Butlin 2009: 50).

In the early-19th century Britain was an agricultural land that raised its own food. There were few large towns outside the main capital areas. By the turn of the 20th century Britain was industrialised, imported much of its food, and large cities had grown up, especially across the industrialised north. The main increases in national expenditure were on a more professional civil service and on an increasingly large army and navy serving in foreign regions. British colonies were important sources of raw materials but food imports were mostly sourced from France, Germany, Russia and the United States rather than the colonies. Public transportation, especially the railway, had changed the landscape and steamers slowly replaced most sailing ships (Ireland 1901). By the latter part of the 19th century, long distance postal and telegraphic communications and the expansion of trade were the most obvious embodiments of the spirit of Western science in the powerful British Empire (Macleod 1993: 131).

Better transportation resulted in a dramatic fall in freight costs. Industrialisation at the centre of the Empire meant that raw products from the periphery states could now be imported more cheaply. Imperialism was partly generated by economic forces from within the metropole. The colonial empire served as an outlet for the surplus capital and produce that capitalism generated. This wage-labour based European capitalism led to the full development and economic predominance of market trade. The late-19th century saw the escalating volume, speed and intensity by which capital, knowledge, commodities, technology and people moved about the globe. The power of the Imperial government in London travelled outwards and downwards and supported the paramountcy of the West (Wolfe 1997). The numerous British colonies were socially, economically and psychologically tied to the apron strings of mother England.

The Australian colonies benefited from this economic expansionism. Australia was caught up in this rapid growth when trade increased and overseas finance was invested in service industries and the development of regional towns. It was in this period that the Queensland sugar plantation economy emerged (Graves 1993: 10). But to support this growth, capitalism required the necessary relationship between development and underdevelopment. Where did this geopolitical structure leave small, obscure protectorates like the Solomon Islands? When Britain and Australia industrialised, these Western economies changed socially and politically, but the marginalised tropical colonies remained non-industrial and producers of primary products where people remained poorly educated, contract labourers in unskilled or semi-skilled plantation employment. The Solomon Islands, like other colonies in the Caribbean, Africa and the Pacific, were left with a colonial legacy of poor infrastructure and an urgent need for land reform. Inadequate health and education services were maintained by the missions. Internal migrant labour and a rising population created many social problems. Today, more than 30 years after independence, the Solomon Islands is still struggling to overcome with many of these problems. But despite its many problems, the Solomon Islands remain, in Woodford's words, 'these beautiful islands'.

Museum collections

Aoife O'Brien (2011) has made a comprehensive study of the collections made by Woodford and Mahaffy during their time in the Western Pacific. Her thesis also contains a valuable photographic catalogue of museum objects examined. In all, 545 objects in the British Museum provenanced to the Solomon Islands, Fiji and Samoa can be associated with Charles Morris Woodford (O'Brien 2011: 74, 113–176). One object in the British Museum has not been positively identified. Of these, 516 objects are from the Solomon Islands, the remaining 29 are from New Guinea, Fiji, The Ellice Islands (Tuvalu), Samoa, New Britain, Manus and the New Hebrides (Vanuatu). Woodford collected ethnographic material as supplementary to his original natural history collecting and this is evident in the range of objects that he donated or sold to museums.

It is interesting to note the geographical distribution of the 516 objects from the Solomon Islands collections made by Woodford. He visited Rennell and Bellona Islands in 1906 at a time when little ethnological or natural history collecting had been done there. He later contributed a short paper on the islands (Woodford 1907) and one on the use of a ceremonial mace (Woodford 1910). His largest collection of artefacts from the Solomons comprises 94 objects from Rennell and 11 from Bellona. During the visit he made notes on a new species of Honey-eater endemic to the islands that he called *Woodfordia superciliosa* (North)(Woodford papers PMB 1290 Items 3/14, 5/4, 7/12, 2/13 and 6/1; Woodford 1916). It is not so surprising that he collected 72 objects from New Georgia considering his two trips to Roviana in 1886 and 1887 and the time spent during the punitive expeditions when objects were removed from raided villages. Woodford obtained 46 objects from Malaita, 25 from Ontong Java, 25 from Guadalcanal—most likely concentrated on the Aola district—and 23 from the Shortland Islands where he spent considerable time in 1886. He collected 15 objects from Bougainville that may have been obtained from Shortland Islanders, 15 from Sikiana that he visited in 1906 and the rest from Santa Cruz, Makira and Vella Lavella (O'Brien 2011: 74, 80).

The Woodford collection in the British Museum comprises 483 objects, mostly donated, to the museum although 10 objects were sold to the museum by a solicitor in 1906 for £10, and Mary Jane Woodford, his sister, sold 92 items to the British Museum in 1908 for £25. Prior to leaving the islands for retirement in 1914, Woodford dispatched a collection of artefacts from Tulagi to Charles Hercules Read at the British Museum (Woodford papers PMB 1290 Item 2/110). In 1915, now in retirement in Sussex, Woodford sold the Museum 44 items for £95. Harry Beasley was a private collector who established the Cranmore Ethnological Museum in Chislehurst, Kent in 1928 and a substantial collection of 118 objects collected by Woodford, but part of the Harry Beasley museum, was sold to the British Museum for £100 in 1929 (O'Brien 2011: 80). Beasley's museum collection was further sold off or donated on his death in 1939 (O'Brien 2011: 343; Carreau 2009). Woodford also sent 30 objects to the World Museum in Liverpool, 12 to the Pitt Rivers Museum in Oxford, 12 to the Australian Museum in Sydney, seven to the Cambridge Museum of Archaeology and Anthropology, and two objects to the Royal Geographical Society in London (O'Brien 2011: 74).

Mahaffy also made a valuable collection of ethnographic objects from the Solomon Islands and his collection is especially important for the association between Mahaffy and Graham Officer (Richards 2012). Their time spent together in the New Georgia area in 1901, documented in the Officer diaries, serves to emphasise the link between the Mahaffy collection in Dublin and the Officer collection in Melbourne. Mahaffy collected 530 objects according to O'Brien (2011: 95) although this includes the war canoe (*tomoko*) in the Museum of Victoria (MV X8042). O'Brien states this was donated to the museum, presumably through Officer, by Mahaffy. As this is one of the 600 objects brought back to Melbourne by Graham Officer it may more correctly be called part of his collection rather than from the Mahaffy collection. Apart from this war canoe, 519 objects were donated to the National Museum of Ireland, Dublin and 10 were sent to the Pitt Rivers Museum in Oxford. Of this collection, 341 came from the Solomon Islands although 49 have no accurate provenance. The Solomon Islands collection comprises 98 objects from New Georgia, understandable given Mahaffy's work centred on Gizo, but 32 have not been provenance to any specific island or area of the western Solomons. 52 objects come from Santa Cruz, 43 objects are from Bougainville and the Shortland Islands, 20 from Malaita, 18 are from Vella Lavella, and 10 from Ontong Java. The rest are smaller collections from other districts (O'Brien 2011: 101). Rhys Richards has recently published a new study of the collecting habits of Mahaffy and Officer, and an examination of the work undertaken by Arthur Hocart on Simbo. His provenancing of the canoe collected by Officer and housed in Museum Victoria to the village of Kumbokota, now Pienuna, on Ranongga establishes its origins and maker (Richards 2012).

Collections like those made by Woodford, Mahaffy and Officer grew out of the attitudes of the time that considered it the duty of colonial administrators, and officially sanctioned museum curators like Graham Officer, to engage in sourcing material culture objects. It was what men of science and education undertook. The concept of 'salvage' ethnology encouraged collecting from indigenous communities that were considered to be rapidly disappearing. For men like Woodford and Mahaffy collecting material culture was a way of having greater knowledge of the people (Schaffarczyk n.d.). Collecting and displaying objects promoted the idea that pacification and control of new territories was largely completed. With the removal of traditional weapons, charms and objects of ritual newly pacified peoples were now part of a new regime, a new civilised Christianised colony. The display of traditional material culture emphasised the success of the economic and political mission.

The British Museum in particular was the exemplar institution where ethnographic materials of the colonial areas were displayed by geographical regions. The public visitors to these galleries were attracted by the exoticism of difference represented by these artefacts. Visitors defined their own European identity through contrast. The public was little interested in deeper understandings of the cultures that had created the objects (Owen 2006: 14). Artefacts illustrated the 'dualistic perceptions of human nature'—them and us, superior and inferior—that underpinned ideas of Empire and Western progress. Ethnographic collections and displays in major museums supported the liberal progressivist philosophies of the West. These gradual social, political, and economic ideals emphasised that European cultures, with greater technological advancements, higher cultural values and moral structures, were moving towards Utopian states of perfection. Museum displays served both to support evolutionary typologies that promoted this progressive ideology as a scientific fact while educating the wider population about their place in society and nature (Owen 2006: 21). From these amassed displays it was possible for the British public to feel economically, culturally, politically, morally and socially superior to the peoples they colonised (Stanley 1989: 119). Now the very value of those collections, both artefact and photographic, is that they relate not only to the past, but to the present and, hopefully, to the future of the peoples of the Solomon Islands. Perhaps, the common humanity of mankind is best described by Barthes (1973 quoted in Eves 2006: 738): 'Any classic humanism postulates that in scratching the history of men a little, the relativity of their institutions or the superficial diversity of their skins ... one very quickly reaches the solid rock of a universal human nature'.

Published papers on the Solomon Islands

In addition to the popular account of life in the Solomon Islands published in the *Popular Science Monthly* (Woodford 1889) and his book on the expeditions to the Solomon Islands made between 1886 and 1889 (Woodford 1890b) Charles Woodford published two important articles on his explorations. The first describes those made between 1886 and 1887 and the second details his travels in search of the landing places of the Spanish fleets under Mendaña. This expedition was undertaken in 1888. These articles were published in *The Proceedings of the Royal Geographic Society* (Woodford 1888a, 1890c). As a result of these expeditions and their findings Woodford was awarded the Gill Memorial in 1890. He continued to contribute to scholarly journals until after retirement in 1915. Following the publication of *A Naturalist Among the Head-hunters*, the first article published was his account of the voyage to the Gilbert Islands on the labour vessel returning labourers to the northern islands (Woodford 1895).

Many articles contributed during his tenure as Resident Commissioner were short papers describing material culture published in *Man*, the Journal of the Royal Anthropological Institute of Great Britain and Ireland. They are useful descriptive accounts of artefacts and cultural practices that would have informed museum curators in London. Woodford forwarded artefacts to the British Museum during his years in the islands and these pieces would have been useful background information (Woodford 1905, 1908a, 1908b, 1910, 1911, 1912, 1918, 1921 and 1922a). His account on the manufacture of shell money by women from the Langa-Langa lagoonal villages of northern Malaita was one of the first articles to examine this practice (Woodford 1908b; Woodford papers PMB 1290 Item 4/38). It is particularly important for Woodford sketched all the implements used for the manufacture of shell beads used in *Tafuli'ae* (*Bata*: Solomons Pijin). Lengths of 1.5 metres of shell money are still made today especially for bride wealth payment, compensation, or for general presentations to dignitaries. Woodford was particularly interested in Polynesian *tatu* patterns on Ontong Java (Woodford 1901), the manufacture of stone clubs (Woodford 1908a and 1910) and the use of bone for spear heads (Woodford 1918). He collected details of social customs such as totemism, witchcraft and magic (Woodford papers PMB 1290 Items 4/29–4/34). Using photographs published in *Man*, Woodford was able to get Hiqava to identify artefacts taken from Kolokongo (Kolikongo or Kalikoqu) on Nusa Roviana by Captain Edward Davis of HMS *Royalist* in 1891 and now housed in the British Museum (Woodford 1905).

Occasionally, Woodford had time to write a more personal descriptive piece on the geography or natural history of more isolated islands in the region such as Leueneuwa (Ontong Java) (Woodford 1906a and 1909a; Woodford papers PMB 1290 Item 3/34) and Sikaiana (Woodford 1906b and 1912; Woodford papers PMB 1290 Item 3/27, 2/121) and Rennell Island (Woodford 1907, 1910 and 1916a). He was in a position to be able to visit these outlying islands and fortunate to be senior enough for local people to be polite and respectful around him. In this way he was able to have people willingly recount origin stories, language and customs to him. A substantial paper on the canoes of the Solomon Islands was written for *The Journal of the Royal Anthropological Institute of Great Britain and Ireland* (Woodford 1909b) and very brief notes on the names for the parts of a canoe on Sikaiana (Woodford 1912; Woodford papers PMB 1290 Item 4/25). Like all early visitors to the islands, Woodford was impressed with the elegance and grace of the large canoes, especially of those from New Georgia and Makira, made from planks rather than dug-outs, neatly joined and beautifully decorated with nautilus, cowries and pearl shell. Woodford considered the construction of the canoes of the Shortland Islands to be the neatest but gave the prize for decoration to those of New Georgia. He wrote: 'It is difficult to understand how the natives were able, before they became acquainted with iron tools, to adze down the canoe plants to the requisite degree of thinness and shape them with the aid of only stone implements, but it appears from the descriptions ... that they undoubtedly did so, and that the canoes have changed [in 1909] but little in type since the days of Mendaña' (Woodford 1909b: 508).

It appears from this article that the *tomoko* confiscated in 1900 and used as a 'police boat', came from 'an island near Oneavisi' (Honiavasa Island next to Nusa Roviana) in the Roviana Lagoon. It was captured during the suppression of head hunting and in retaliation for a raid made at Pirihadi Bay in the southern Bugotu district of Isabel (Woodford 1909b: 511). The raid on Honiavasa was also part of a larger raid on the Kolokongo area (Kolikongo or Kalikoqu) of Nusa Roviana Lagoon led by Woodford, Mahaffy and his police. The raid on Kalikoqu was made on 21 January 1900. Mahaffy, Woodford and 20 police attacked the village at 5 o'clock in the morning in heavy rain. One man was killed and five wounded. The man killed was presumed to be the one who led the raid on Isabel Island, 'and the canoe in which the raid was made was captured. It was a very fine specimen of a head hunting canoe, being nearly new, with a capacity of forty men' (*The Morning Bulletin* [Rockhampton] 3 March 1900: 6). Perhaps because of the association with the earlier head hunting raid at Pirihadi, the illustrations in Woodford's article drawn by Thomas Edge-Partington incorrectly call it a canoe from 'Ysabel' rather than from New Georgia (Woodford 1909: plates 41–44). Woodford wrote that the police canoe was captured from Kalikoqu and 'after its capture it was used at the Government Station at Gizo, but having become leaky and almost beyond repair, I offered to pack it and to deliver it in Sydney at my own expense, if it could be conveyed home from there to London for the British Museum'. Funds were not forthcoming and the canoe, with a good provenance and history, was bought by a dealer for a German museum collection (Woodford 1909b: 511; Jackson 1975: 77; *The Morning Bulletin* [Rockhampton] 3 March 1900: 6; *The Brisbane Courier* 27 February 1900: 6; O'Brien 2011: 88). Honiavasa was again raided in March 1901 and another *tomoko* confiscated (Jackson 1978: 127). Certainly the sight of numerous confiscated, and decaying, war canoes on the front beach at Gizo would have given the impression that the government was powerful, and that power was moving away from the chiefs towards the police and the administration.

The more substantial paper on Polynesian settlements in the southern islands was published by *The Geographical Journal* (Woodford 1916b; Woodford papers PMB 1381/031r) with a long discussion between contributing authors including Sir Basil Thomson, Alfred Cort Haddon, C. G. Seligman and Sidney Ray published following the paper (Thomson *et al.* 1916). Woodford maintained a close relationship with Ray and they corresponded for many years on topics relating to Polynesian linguistics (Woodford papers PMB 1381/031). The paper on Polynesian settlements was presented at a meeting of the Royal Geographical Society on 6 March 1916 and published following Woodford's retirement in England. The paper was a more substantial contribution that included detailed accounts of European discovery of Ontong Java, Sikaiana and a shorter account of Rennell and Bellona Islands, as well as including photographs taken by missionaries George Brown, the Methodist, and Northcote Deck from the South Seas Evangelical Mission. Woodford (1922b) also contributed to the volume published by William Rivers on depopulation in Melanesia. His final paper (Woodford 1926) published in *The Geographical Journal* was a short piece containing notes on the Solomon Islands that were really only annotations to a paper on Spanish discoveries published in the journal by Rev W. G. Ivens (1926). This was the last paper published by Woodford, who died the following year. In all, he published 24 papers and one book on the material culture and cultural life of the Solomon Island people and the geography of the region.

Conclusion

When Woodford died at 'Bramley', his home in Goring Road, Steyning, on 4 October 1927, he was 75. He had sold his large country house 'The Grinstead' in the same year and moved to the nearby town. He was buried at St Peter's Church, Cowfold on 8 October. His headstone reads:

CHARLES MORRIS WOODFORD C.M.G

First Resident Commissioner of the

British Solomon Islands

Loved husband of Florence Margaret

Died October 4th 1927

Aged 75 years.

Figure 43. Headstone of Charles Morris Woodford, St Peter's Church, Cowfold, Sussex.

Source: Courtesy of Herbie Whitmore, 2013.

His estate was valued at £5,245 (£750,000 in current values). His two sons were educated at Tonbridge School and in 1914 they enlisted in the British Army. The youngest son, Harold Vivian, the favourite of Florence Woodford, commissioned in the 8th Battalion of the Royal Berkshire Regiment, was killed on 13 October 1915, early in the war, and buried in France. He is listed on the memorial plaque at Loos-en-Gohelle cemetery in Pas-de-Calais and on memorials in Cowfold, West Grinstead, at Tonbridge School and at the Hawkesbury Agricultural College in New South Wales where he had been a student (Woodford papers PMB 1381/006; H. Whitmore, West Grinstead Local History Group, pers. comm. 2013). It is perhaps befitting that the Loos memorial was designed by the noted architect, and fellow Tonbridgian, Sir Herbert Baker. Surprisingly, given the antipathy between the two men, im Thurn wrote Woodford and his wife a kind, sympathetic and warm personal letter in July 1916 when he heard of the death of Harold during the war (Woodford papers PMB 1381/017). It appears that im Thurn had heard much about Woodford's son from Mahaffy in Suva. Their working relationship cannot have been too acrimonious if they could discuss other men's children. The eldest son, Charles Edward Montgomery, went to Oxford and then worked on rubber plantations in Malaya. During the First World War he became a Captain in the 1st Battalion of the Sherwood Foresters. Later he bought 'Bowshot's Farm' in West Grinstead not far from the family home outside Partridge Green. In 1929 he returned to Australia with his mother and settled at Denman near Sydney. He subsequently bought the family property, 'Gowan Brae', at Bundanoon, north of Canberra. He also served in the Australian Army in the Second World War (Woodford papers PMB 1381/017). The only daughter of Charles Morris and Florence Woodford, Sylvia Margaret, was born on 16 February 1900 but died in Sydney at 10 months from a fever caught in Tulagi (*The Sydney Morning Herald* 20 February 1900).

In 1928, Woodford's obituary in *The Geographical Journal* made some mention of his explorations, his publication and journal articles but largely overlooked his many years of administrative experience in the Solomon Islands. Again reference was made to the 'firm but benevolent administration [that] was to effect a complete transformation in the conditions of the group, which settled down to a flourishing and in the main peaceable British Protectorate' (Anon 1928: 206–207). The *Ibis*, the journal of the Ornithological Society, reported on the valuable collections of birds sent to the British Museum and to the chapter on birds in Woodford's 1890 monograph (Sclater 1928: 140–141). His death was quickly noted by the *Sydney Morning Herald* on 8 October 1927 and the *Brisbane Courier* on 11 October 1927: 21) but the Sydney paper followed this brief notice with a much longer obituary in December written by R. F. Thomson, the chief inspector of native labour at Tulagi from 1925 to 1931 (*The Sydney Morning Herald* 12 December 1927: 10). The obituary title 'A remarkable man' covered Woodford's personal life, his collecting and explorations and his official life. It is a remarkably sympathetic and affectionate report on Woodford's life. In it Thomson again repeats the lines that bringing peace and security to the islands 'is an object worthy indeed the devotion of one's life'. Thomson accurately summarised Woodford's early collecting career and his official life in Tulagi. Thomson also stated the long held belief that it was well known in days when access to the High Commissioner's court in Suva was long and costly '[a] nod by him in the direction of the Burns Philp steamer to a rough diamond meant to German Charlie or Russian Harry', or any other itinerant in the islands, that if they could get an accursed man out of the islands it was best for all. Court cases were not only long and costly but guaranteeing the attendance of witnesses in Suva was almost impossible. Securing a conviction was likewise near impossible. There remained one rule for the coloniser and another for the colonised. Woodford undoubtedly ruled with paternalism. Even Thomson remarked: 'He governed the Islands in a strong fatherly way and was greatly assisted by his good wife who accompanied him nearly everywhere in the Government vessel'. Such action, and similar comments made today, would be taken as condescending. This paternalism was not unique to Woodford. Sir William MacGregor, a close associate, describing the best method of government for Papua wrote 'the paternal form [of rule] is the most suitable for a native population in the act of stepping out of savagery into civilisation' (Joyce 1971: 36 quoting MacGregor to Lamington 3 June 1898 in Lamington to Colonial Office 13 August 1898 CO 422 12). Both men were supported by a strong Victorian morality that saw British civilisation as infinitely preferable to any other.

Woodford's death in 1927 came at the same time as the murder of William Bell, then District Officer on Malaita, along with Bell's European cadet, Kenneth Lilies, and 13 Solomon Islander police and servants on 4 October at Sinarango (Sinalanggu) Harbour on the east coast of Malaita (Keesing 1990: 279). In fact R. F. Thomson, who paid tribute to Woodford in a long obituary, had only that October given warm praise to the work of Bell on Malaita after news of the murders had been received (*The Sydney Morning Herald* 11 October 1927: 11). The comparison in the obituary between Woodford and Bell was not lost on old Solomon hands. Thomson began and ended his obituary to Woodford with tributes to both men. It is worth briefly comparing the two. William Bell was a Boer War veteran born in Victoria who first went to the Solomon Islands as a Government Agent aboard the Fijian labour schooner, *Clansman* (Chapelle 1976: 387; Giles and Scarr 1968: 121). He worked on the schooner for about three years before applying for the position as Labour Inspector in 1911. He clashed with Woodford over what Bell considered to be the inadequacies of the labour regulations of 1910. Bell was a complex loner with a commanding physical presence. Despite his size, heavy-handedness and apparent ruthlessness, Bell was considered a remarkably good local administrator (Keesing 1967: 86). Bell was sent to Malaita as relieving officer but Edge-Partington wrote to Woodford in 1913 to say: 'There is too much Mr Bell over here [Malaita], what I mean to infer is that a lot of natives think because Mr Bell was Government Agent of the "Clansmen" that he is the Resident Commissioner at Tulagi' (BSIP 14/41).

When the First World War resulted in many young men enlisting for the services, Bell, who had been wounded in the arm, was made the District Officer on Malaita. Bell had respect for Malaitan customs but he opposed the role of the *ramo*, the culturally sanctioned paid killer used in ritual 'pay-back' and he wrote angrily to Barnett that the 'blood-lust of a few professional murderers' did not deserve sympathy and attention (BSIP 14/44). In 1916, he even requested permission to return to his former post as Inspector of Labour because he disagreed with policy concerning police action on Malaita. The Kwaio warriors from central Malaita had long-standing grievances relating to taxation, the confiscation of firearms and were antagonised by Bell's heavy-handed strongman approach (Keesing 1990: 282). The Kwaio had also been the victims of the punitive action in 1911 when the HMS *Torch* bombarded coastal villages. To the hill tribes, taxation represented tribute and being forced to disarm meant surrender to British law. By this time, local men could only carry a firearm if they were in the employment of a white man (King's Regulation no 5 of 1910). While this would have been seen as a minor issue among whites, among the local men this was a further act of surrender and a sign of subservience.

Many young men from the Kwaio, and the 'Are'are peoples from the south, had been recruited into the Pacific labour trade. When the local plantation economy expanded and Malaitan migrant workers were again recruited, they were juxtaposed against the more prosperous land owners in Guadalcanal and the New Georgia group. Their resentments were long and deep. In the inquiry into the Bell massacre, Commissioner Harry Moorhouse could not lay the cause of Kwaio resentment to any single issue and concluded that 'no single act or administrative measure of the Government ... led to the murder, but the combination of circumstances', as he set out in his report. These included government interference in Malaita customs, the penalty of a fine or short imprisonment for adultery, a grievous crime on Malaita, the insistence on village rules of health and hygiene and finally the order to surrender firearms (British Solomon Islands Protectorate 1929: 12–13). The massacre was, in Kwaio eyes at least, a symbol of the struggle for autonomy, a challenge to colonial power and the assertion of cultural status. In the eyes of the colonial government it was an outrage caused by primitivism and fanaticism. HMAS *Adelaide* was sent to Malaita and a defence force of traders, government officials and police attacked the Sinalanggu area. Both missionaries and planters supported the retaliation campaigns that included Malaitan police, notably from the northern Lau and To'aba'ita regions that Bell had favoured. These northerners had been Christianised by men like Walter Ivens. These coastal lagoon dwellers now saw the Kwaio as pagans and sought to avenge the deaths of kinsmen who had been murdered by them. In the retaliation campaigns Kwaio men, women and children were shot by police, many in cold blood (Keesing 1967). 198 Kwaio men were arrested in all and removed to Tulagi. 28 died there, 16 during a dysentery epidemic in the jail. 18 men were sentenced to longer imprisonment terms in Tulagi and six warriors, including Basiana who instigated the attack, were executed. Eventually, on Moorhouse's recommendation, the remaining 134 men were returned to their homes (Boutilier 1983: 71; Keesing 1990: 282; British Solomon Islands Protectorate 1929: 14). After more than 30 years of direct colonial rule the administration was still focussed on punitive police actions, the suppression of armed insurrection and the maintenance of an economically sub-standard copra industry.

The Bell massacre and the retribution signalled the start of peace in the short term. The administration had to realise that punitive measures and extractive policies—seeing Malaitans as wage labourers on other people's lands—was not conducive to peace. Malaitans learnt that access to government services, however poor, required the grudging acceptance of colonial law and order. In local terms, being given peace required a reciprocal gift of submission. But Malaitans would not accept submission except on their own terms. Kessing's account of the rebellion and his not 'quite standard colonial history' still resonates within any truthful examination of the British colonial period in the Western Pacific. Keesing (1990: 287) wrote:

Not once did the British authorities concede that Solomon Islanders had ever had sovereign rights to their islands. The Solomons were simply there waiting to be 'discovered' and colonized by the Europeans. Not once did the government recognize … that colonization was a process of armed invasion and conquest … To resist the recruiters who trafficked in human cargo, to resist the missionaries, to resist the government, was to commit 'outrages' and 'murders'. To violate colonial statutes and follow old customs was 'lawless'. Not once did the administrators of the Protectorate doubt that it was their right, indeed their duty, to pacify, to civilize and to uplift 'the natives'.

Moorhouse echoed these words in his official report on the massacre and the following actions when he wrote: 'In the early stages the relations between the Administration and the natives were necessarily in the main punitive; head hunting and inter-island and inter-tribal wars were rife and murder was almost a feature of daily life; their repression was essential before any settled form of administration could be introduced' (British Solomon Islands Protectorate 1929: 19). But Moorhouse also laid some of the blame for the disparity in fortunes between islanders and settlers when he criticised the woeful education services provided by the administration and the poor quality teaching at the mission schools where the more than 7,000 children learnt little apart from Christianising, and good habits of discipline, order and hygiene.

When Woodford died in 1927 the Solomon Islanders had been British protected persons for more than 30 years. Contact with the Royal Navy, traders and missionaries predated that. By 1927 the islanders had little to show for this colonial benevolence in the way of meaningful social progress, economic development and political unity. The colonial administrations of the British Solomon Islands were concerned with the administration of justice and the plantation economy. A 'dual economy' was taken for granted. The villagers lived in small communities where they grew their own produce, raised pigs and chickens, and caught fish. Surplus labour circulated through the plantations and colonial workplaces such as on the wharves, on small ships and some as domestics in the homes of expatriates. The indentured labour system was 'invidious, inefficient and expensive, existing solely to make plantations viable as the only possible form of economic development in remote, tropical places' (Campbell 2007: 56). Private capital had not been able to develop any more than 14 per cent of the land alienated despite the exaggerated claims of access to abundant land and a willing labour force. Before the First World War, the annual reports of the administration discuss native affairs only in relation to pacification and the labour supply, either the external Pacific labour trade before 1911 or the internal labour force after that date. In comparison with the annual reports of British New Guinea and Papua which contain substantial ethnographic, linguistic and cultural notes, exploration maps and patrol reports, they are rather dreary affairs.

Campbell (2007: 59) stated: 'Economic viability of the government was understandably the highest priority, and it is difficult to be sure whether development was the means to achieve the morally higher objective of pacification, or whether pacification was the means to achieve the morally higher purpose of commercial agriculture'. The British government saw costly, uneconomic protectorates as a burden. The proviso for accepting them as colonies or protectorates, under whatever name they were called, was that they should come at no cost to the British taxpayer. While the proviso was that these overseas territories should come at no cost to the British taxpayer, there were few if any that did not receive subsidies, support funds or Imperial Treasury grants (Campbell 2007: 57). This self-sufficiency policy was hostage to fluctuating copra prices. With the Solomon Islands producing poor quality copra the fluctuations in price were even greater, with marked economic consequences. The penury of the Protectorate and the parsimony of the Treasury led to the postponement of advances in social services. It was only just before the First World War that a formal cadet scheme was implemented, with young male university graduates being appointed to the colonial administration. They faced isolation, illness and physical discomfort. By contrast the Kiap system in the Territories of Papua and New Guinea held greater prospects for career advancement within a wider social circle of expatriates in a climate not too unlike that of northern Australia. The history of British colonial policy in the Solomon Islands is marked by Colonial Office conservatism, Treasury restraint, an antagonistic Western Pacific High Commission, and an isolated administration in Tulagi. It is little wonder that Woodford was often judged critically by his superiors.

When Woodford (1890b: 23fn) wrote, 'I know of no place where firm and paternal government would sooner produce beneficial results than in the Solomons. The numerous small tribes into which the population is split up would render any organised resistance to properly constituted authority quite futile, while I believe that the natives themselves would not be slow to recognise the advantages of increased security to life and property. Here is an object worthy indeed the devotion of one's life', the Solomon Islands were a loose collection of islands inhabited by small tribal communities living largely, but not wholly, independent from each other. The only whites were the itinerant trader, often living on a small offshore island for self-protection and security of property and the occasional missionary supported by regular visits from the home mission base. The islands were visited annually by Royal Navy ships administering 'Commodore Justice' to communities that had broken the English laws of which they had no knowledge. Socially and culturally the colonial structure of the British Solomon Islands Protectorate had little real contact with the people. This was true for most colonial situations in the Pacific. After 18 years as Resident Commissioner, the Protectorate was largely Woodford's creation. For many years it was almost wholly under his supervision and '[i]n a very real sense the administration was his' (Heath 1974a: 8). The history of the Solomon Islands from 1896 to 1915 was fundamentally determined by Charles Morris Woodford but the dilemma that faced him and his successors was how to reconcile the tension between conserving traditional society and modernising it. This tension still exists.

Bibliography

Adam, Leonhard (1950/1951). 'In Memoriam Felix Speiser', *Oceania*, 21: 66–72.

Adams, Emma H. (1890). *Two Cannibal Archipelagoes: New Hebrides and Solomon groups*. Oakland, CA, Pacific Press.

Allan, Colin H. (1957). *Customary land tenure in the British Solomon Islands Protectorate: report of the Special Lands Commission*. Honiara, High Commissioner for the Western Pacific.

Allen, Jim (1976). 'New Light on the Spanish Settlement of the Southeast Solomons', In: Green, R. C. and Cresswell, M. M. (eds). *Southeast Solomon Islands cultural history: a preliminary survey*. Wellington, The Royal Society of New Zealand: 19–29.

Allen, Matthew (2005). 'Greed and Grievance: The role of economic agendas in the conflict in Solomon Islands', *Pacific Economic Bulletin*, 20 (2): 56–71.

Allen, Matthew (2009). 'Resisting RAMSI: Intervention, identity and symbolism in Solomon Islands', *Oceania*, 79 (1): 1–17.

Allen, Matthew (2011). 'Long-term Engagement: The future of the Regional Assistance Mission to Solomon Islands', *ASPI Strategic Insights*, 51: 1–17.

Allen, M. G., Bourke, R. M., *et al.* (2005). *Solomon Islands Smallholder Agriculture Study*. Volume 1: Main finding and recommendations; Volume 2: Subsistence production, livestock and social analysis; Volume 3: Markets and marketing issues; Volume 4. Provincial reports; Volume 5: Literature review: A brief national assessment of the agricultural sector. Canberra, AusAID.

Allen, Matthew and Dinnen, Sinclair (2010). 'The North Down Under: Antinomies of conflict and intervention in Solomon Islands', *Conflict, Security and Development*, 10 (3): 299–327.

Allen, Percy S. (1919). *Stewart's Hand-book of the Pacific Islands: A reliable guide to all the inhabited islands of the Pacific Ocean for traders, tourists and settlers*. Sydney, McCarron, Stewart.

Amadon, Dean (1943). 'Birds Collected During the Whitney South Sea Expedition, 52: Notes on some non-passerine genera, 3, *American Museum Novitates*, 1237: 1–22.

Amherst, William Amhurst Tyssen (1ˢᵗ Baron Amherst of Hackney) and Thomson, Basil (eds) (1901). *The Discovery of the Solomon Islands by Alvaro de Mendaña in 1568*. Translated from the original Spanish manuscripts, edited with introduction and notes. 2 volumes. London, Hakluyt Society.

Anderson, Atholl (2002). 'Faunal Collapse, Landscape Change and Settlement History in Remote Oceania', *World Archaeology*, 33 (3): 375–390.

Anderson, Stuart (1978). '"Pacific Destiny" and American Policy in Samoa, 1872–1899', *The Hawaiian Journal of History*, 12: 45–60.

Anon. (1854). 'A Manual of Ethnological Inquiry: Review', *Journal of the Ethnological Society of London*, 3: 193–208.

Anon. (1869). *The Island Mission: Being a history of the Melanesian Mission from its commencement*. London, Macintosh

Anon. (1887). 'Review: Guppy, H. B. The Solomon Islands and their Natives, The Solomon Islands: Their Geology, General Features and Suitability for Colonisation', *Proceedings of the Royal Geographical Society and Monthly Record of Geography*, 9 (12): 782–783.

Anon. (1888a). 'The Natives of the Solomon Islands', *The Westminster Review*, 29: 552–572.

Anon. (1888b). 'The Discovery of the Solomon Islands', *The Westminster Review*, 29: 457–476.

Anon. (1888c). 'The Discovery of the Solomon Islands', *Littell's Living Age*, 177 (5ᵗʰ series, 62) (2289): 321–340.

Anon. (1889a). 'The Situation in Samoa', *Science*, 13 (313): 85–86.

Anon. (1889b). 'The Solomon Islands', *Illustrated London News*, February 23, 1889, 246–247.

Anon. (1892). *Queensland: Imperial and Colonial Acts relating to the recruiting etc of Pacific Island labourers*. Brisbane, James Beal, Government Printer.

Anon. (1896). 'The Island Voyage', In: *The Southern Cross Log*, 2 (22), Auckland: 1–30. (http://anglicanhistory.org/island_voyage1896).

Anon. (1900). 'The Solomon Islands (British)', *The Sydney Mail and New South Wales Advertiser*, November 1900: 1040, 1051. [Illustrations by Walter H. Lucas and Charles Morris Woodford, article most likely by Walter H. Lucas].

Anon. (1906). 'Obituary: Coutts Trotter', *The Geographical Journal*, 27 (5): 512–513.

Anon. (1908). 'Obituary: A. J. Mounteney Jephson', *The Geographical Journal*, 32 (6): 630.

Anon. (1911a). Album presented to Walter H. Lucas Esq. by the members of the Federal party visiting Papua in June 1911. Album 782. Canberra, National Library of Australia.

Anon. (1911b). 'Good Australians: CM Woodford CMG', *The Lone Hand*, March 1, 1911: 378–380.

Anon. (1926). *Melanesia: The story of the Melanesian Mission*. Westminster, The Melanesian Mission. (http://anglicanhistory.org/oceania/story_melanesia1926).

Anon. (1928). 'Obituary: Charles Morris Woodford, CMG', *The Geographical Journal*, 71(2): 206–207.

Anon. (1934). 'The Templeton Crocker Expedition to the Solomon Islands', *Science*, 79 (2050): 344–345.

Anon. (1978). 'Miscellaneous: Solomon Islands achieves independence', *Commonwealth Law Bulletin*, 4: 659–663.

Armstrong, E. S. (1900). *The History of the Melanesian Mission*. London, Isbister and Company.

Ashton, Rosemary (2006). *142 Strand: A radical address in Victorian London*. London, Chatto & Windus.

Asian Development Bank (1998). *Solomon Islands: Country economic review*. Mandaluyong City, Philippines, Asian Development Bank.

Asian Development Bank (2004). *Solomon Islands: Country strategy and program update 2005–2006*. Mandaluyong City, Philippines, Asian Development Bank.

Asian Development Bank (2012). *Key Indicators for Asia and the Pacific 2012*. 43rd edition. Mandaluyong City, Philippines, Asian Development Bank.

Aswani, Shankar (2000) 'Changing Identities: The ethnohistory of Roviana predatory head-hunting', *The Journal of the Polynesian Society*, 109 (1): 39–70.

Aswani, Shankar (2008). 'Forms of Leadership and Violence in Malaita and in the New Georgia Group, Solomon Islands', In: Stewart, Pamela J. and Strathern, Andrew (eds). *Exchange and Sacrifice*. Durham, NC, Carolina Academic Press: 171–194.

Aswani, Shankar and Sheppard, Peter (2003). 'The Archaeology and Ethnohistory of Exchange in Precolonial and Colonial Roviana', *Current Anthropology*, 44 (Special Issue: Multiple methodologies in anthropological research): 51–78.

Atmore, Anthony and Sanders, Peter (1971). 'Sotho Arms and Ammunition in the Nineteenth Century', *The Journal of African History*, 12 (4): 535–544.

Australia. Custodian of Expropriated Property (1925). *Sale of Expropriated Properties (First Group) in the Territories of New Guinea and Papua*. Melbourne, Government Printer. (AU NBAC Z385/433)

Australia. Department of Foreign Affairs and Trade. Economic Analytical Unit (2004). *Solomon Islands: Rebuilding an island economy*. Canberra, Department of Foreign Affairs and Trade.

Australia. Parliament (1904). *Royal Commission on the Affray at Goaribari Island, British New Guinea on the 6th March 1904*. Sydney, Government Printer.

Australia. Parliament (1907). *British New Guinea: Report of the Royal Commission of Inquiry into present conditions, including the method of Government, of the Territory of Papua, and the best means for their improvement*. Melbourne, J. Kemp, Acting Government Printer for Victoria.

Australian Agency for International Development (AusAID) (2006a). *Pacific 2020*. Canberra, AusAID.

Australian Agency for International Development (AusAID) (2006b). *Solomon Islands Transitional Country Strategy, 2006 to mid-2007*. Canberra, AusAID.

The Australian Museum (1890–1910). Album of photographs taken in the Solomon Islands, Vanuatu, Papua New Guinea and Australia, donated by Harry Beran. Sydney, The Australian Museum.

The Australian Museum (c.1900). Solomon Islands Photographs c.1900 donated by Rev. Arthur Capell. Sydney, The Australian Museum. (Collection of photographs of the Solomon Islands by Walter Henry Lucas).

Awdry, Frances (1902). *In the Isles of the Sea*. London, Bemrose & Sons. (http://anglicanhistory.org/oceania/awdry1902/14.html).

Bach, John (1968). 'The Royal Navy in the Pacific Islands', *The Journal of Pacific History*, 3: 3–20.

Bach, John (1983). 'The Royal Navy in the South West Pacific: The Australia Station, 1859–1913', *The Great Circle*, 5 (2): 116–132.

Baker, John (1996). '"Way back in Papua": Representing society and change in the publications of the London Missionary Society in New Guinea, 1871–1932', *Pacific Studies*, 19 (3): 107–142.

Baker, John R. (1928). 'Depopulation in Espiritu Santo, New Hebrides', *Journal of the Royal Anthropological Institute of Great Britain and Ireland*, 58: 279–303.

Ballantyne, Tony (ed.) (2004). *Science, Empire and the European exploration of the Pacific*. Aldershot, UK, Ashgate.

Ballard, Charles (1986). 'Drought and Economic Distress: South Africa in the 1880s', *The Journal of Interdisciplinary History*, 17 (2): 359–378.

Barrow, Mark V. (2000). 'The Specimen Dealer: Entrepreneurial natural history in America's Gilded Age', *Journal of the History of Biology*, 33 (3): 493–534.

Barraud, Cécile (1972). 'De la chasse aux têtes a la pêche a la bonite: Essai sur la chefferie à Eddystone', *L'Homme*, 12 (1): 67–104.

Barthes, Roland (1973). *Mythologies*. Frogmore, UK, Paladin.

Barthes, Roland (1981). *Camera Lucida*. New York, Hill & Wang.

Barthorp, Michael (2002). *Slogging Over Africa: The Boer wars, 1815–1902*. London, Cassell.

Bartlett, Frederic C. (1923). *Psychology and Primitive Culture*. Cambridge, Cambridge University Press.

Bassett, Marnie (1969). *Letters from New Guinea, 1921*. Melbourne, The Hawthorn Press.

Bayliss-Smith, Tim (2006). 'Fertility and the Depopulation of Melanesia: Childlessness, abortion and introduced disease in Simbo and Ontong Java, Solomon Islands', In: Ulijaszek, Stanley J. (ed.). *Population, Reproduction and Fertility in Melanesia*. New York, Berghahn Books: 13–52.

Bayliss-Smith, Tim, Hviding, Edvard and Whitmore, Tim (2003). 'Rainforest Composition and Histories of Human Disturbance in Solomon Islands', *Ambio*, 32 (5): 346–352.

Beattie, J. W. (1900). *Catalogue of a Series of Photographs Illustrating the Scenery and Peoples of the Islands in the South and Western Pacific*. Hobart, the Mercury Print.

Beattie, J. W. (1906). 'Journal of a Voyage to the Western Pacific in the Melanesian Mission Yacht "Southern Cross", 25 August–10 November 1906'. Royal Society of Tasmania MSS RS.29/3. (http://anglicanhistory.org/oceania/beattie_journal1906.html).

Beck, Stephen (2009). 'Maritime Mechanisms of Contact and Change: Archaeological perspectives on the history and conduct of the Queensland labour trade'. Unpublished PhD thesis, James Cook University. (http://eprints.jcu.edu.au/8113).

Beckett, John and Watkins, Charles (2011). 'Natural History and Local History in Late Victorian and Edwardian England: The contribution of the Victoria County History', *Rural History*, 22 (1): 59–87.

Bedford, Richard, Macdonald, Barrie and Munro, Doug (1980). 'Population Estimates for Kiribati and Tuvalu, 1850–1900: Review and speculation', *The Journal of the Polynesian Society*, 89 (2): 199–246.

Beecher, W. J. (1945). 'A Bird Collection from the Solomon Islands', *Fieldiana.Zoology*, 31 (4): 31–38.

Bell, Duncan (2007). *The Idea of Greater Britain: Empire, nation, and the future of global order, 1860–1900*. Princeton, Princeton University Press.

Bell, Joshua A. (2009). '"For scientific purposes a stand camera is essential": Salvaging photographic histories in Papua', In: Morton, Christopher and Edwards, Elizabeth (eds). *Photography, Anthropology and History: Expanding the frame*. Farnham, UK, Ashgate: 143–169.

Bell, Joshua A. and Geismar, Haidy (2009). 'Materialising Oceania: New ethnographies of things in Melanesia and Polynesia', *The Australian Journal of Anthropology*, 20 (1): 3–27.

Bellwood, Peter, Fox, James J. and Tryon, Darrell (eds) (1995). *The Austronesians: Historical and comparative perspectives*. Canberra, Comparative Austronesian Project, Department of Anthropology, The Australian National University.

Ben, Waita *et al.* (1979). *Land in Solomon Islands*. Honiara, Solomon Islands, Institute of Pacific Studies, University of the South Pacific and the Ministry of Agriculture and Lands.

Bennett, George (1962). *The Concept of Empire: Burke to Attlee, 1774–1947*. 2nd edition. London, Adam and Charles Black.

Bennett, Judith A. (1981). 'Oscar Svensen: A Solomons trader among "The Few"', *The Journal of Pacific History*, 16 (4): 170–189.

Bennett, Judith A. (1987). *The Wealth of the Solomons: A history of a Pacific archipelago, 1800–1978*. Honolulu, University of Hawai'i Press.

Bennett, Judith A. (1995). 'Forestry, Public land, and the Colonial Legacy in Solomon Islands', *The Contemporary Pacific*, 7(2): 243–275.

Bennett, Judith A. (2000a). *Pacific Forest: A history of resource control and contest in Solomon Islands, c. 1800–1997*. Leiden, Brill.

Bennett, Judith A. (2000b). '"The grievous mistakes of the Vanikoro concession": The Vanikoro Kauri Timber Company, Solomon Islands, 1926–1964', *Environment and History*, 6: 317–347.

Bennett, Judith A. (2006). 'Gorai and Population Decline in the Shortlands: A reply to Peter Sack', *The Journal of Pacific History*, 41 (1): 97–102.

Bernatzik, Hugo Adolphe (1952). *Canaques et Papous (Sudsee)*. Traduit de l'allemand par Henri Daussy. Paris, Société Nouvelle des Éditions Self.

Bevans, Charles I. (1968). *Treaties and Other International Agreements of the United States of America 1776–1949: Volume 1, Multilateral 1776–1917*. Washington, U. S. Printing Office.

Binder, Pearl (1978). *Treasure Islands: The trials of the Ocean Islanders*. Sydney, Angus & Robertson.

Binskin, Joseph Kitney (1909). Unpublished diary concerning murder of his wife and children at Mbava in 1909 and subsequent police action. National Library of Australia MS Acc09/031.

Biskup, Peter (1971). 'Hahl at Herbertshoehe, 1896–1898: The genesis of German native administration in New Guinea', In: Inglis, K. S. (ed.). *The History of Melanesia, 2nd Waigani Seminar, 1968*. Canberra, Research School of Pacific Studies, The Australian National University and the University of Papua New Guinea: 77–99.

Blain, Michael and Brown, Terry (n.d.). 'Historical Note on the Diocese of Melanesia and the Mandated Territory of New Guinea (1885–1949)'. (http://anglicanhistory.org/oceania/blain_mandated_territory.pdf).

Blain, Michael and Brown, Terry (2008). 'Anglicism in Oceania: Polynesia, Melanesia and Papua New Guinea'. (http://anglicanhistory.org/oceania/).

Blakeslee, George H. (1928). 'The Future of American Samoa', *Foreign Affairs*, 7 (1): 139–143.

Bollard, A. E. (1981). 'The Financial Adventures of J. C. Godeffroy and Son in the Pacific', *The Journal of Pacific History*, 16 (1): 3–19.

Bonshek, Elizabeth (1999). 'Objects Mediating Relationships in Changing Contexts: The Firth collection from Tikopia, Solomon Islands'. Unpublished MA thesis, The Australian National University.

Bonshek, Elizabeth (2004). 'Ownership and a Peripatetic Collection: Raymond Firth's collection from Tikopia, Solomon Islands', *Records of the Australian Museum*, Supplement 29: 37–45.

Booth, Charles (1887). 'The Inhabitants of Tower Hamlets (School Board Division), Their Condition and Occupations', *Journal of the Royal Statistical Society*, 50 (2): 326–401.

Borrie, W. D., Firth, Raymond and Spillius, James (1957). 'The Population of Tikopia, 1929 and 1952', *Population Studies*, 10 (3): 229–252.

Boulay, Roger (2007). *"The Aristocrat and his Cannibals": Count Festetics von Tolna's travels in Oceania, 1893–1896*. Paris, Musée du Quai Branly.

Boulenger, G. A. (1887). 'Second Contribution to the Herpetology of the Solomon Islands', *Proceedings of the Zoological Society of London*, 55 (2): 333–338. (Woodford papers, PMB 1290 Item 7/21/3).

Boulenger, G. A. (1888). 'Third Contribution to the Herpetology of the Solomon Islands', *Proceedings of the Zoological Society of London*, 56 (1): 88–90.

Boulenger, G. A. (1890a). 'Fourth Contribution to the Herpetology of the Solomon Islands', *Proceedings of the Zoological Society of London*, 58: 30–31.

Boulenger, G. A. (1890b). 'On the Reptiles and Batrachians of the Solomon Islands', *Transactions of the Zoological Society of London*, 12: 35–62.

Boutilier, James A. (1969). 'The Western Pacific High Commission, 1877–1888: Its creation and problems of administration'. Unpublished PhD thesis, University of London.

Boutilier, James A. (1974). 'The Role of the Administration and the Missions in the Provision of Medical and Educational Services in the British Solomon Islands Protectorate, 1893–1942'. Ms. Church House Library, Canada. [Later published as 'Missions, Administration, and Education in the Solomon Islands, 1893–1942', In: Boutilier, James A. *et al.Mission, Church and Sect in Oceania*, Ann Arbor, University of Michigan Press, 1978].

Boutilier, James A. (1975). 'The New Georgia Days of Norman Wheatley', *Journal of the Solomon Islands Cultural Association*, 3: 29–41.

Boutilier, James A. (1983). 'Killing the Government: Imperial policy and the pacification of Melanesia', In: Rodman, Margaret and Cooper, Matthew (eds). *The Pacification of Melanesia*. Lanham MD, University Press of America: 43–87.

Braithwaite, John *et al.* (2010). *Pillars and Shadows: Statebuilding as peacekeeping in Solomon Islands*. Canberra, ANU E Press.

Brenchley, Julius L. (1873). *Jottings During the Cruise of HMS Curaçoa Among the South Sea Islands in 1865*. London, Longmans, Green and Co.

Bridge, Cyprian (1886) 'Cruises in Melanesia, Micronesia and Western Polynesia in 1882, 1883 and 1884 and visits to New Guinea and the Louisiades in 1884 and 1885', *Proceedings of the Royal Geographical Society and Monthly Record of Geography*, new monthly series 8 (9): 545–567.

British New Guinea (1886–1906). *Annual Reports*. (PMB DOC 312, Reels 1 and 2).

British Solomon Islands Protectorate (1909). *Statistics to 31st March 1909 compiled by the Resident Commissioner*. Sydney, Turner & Henderson Printers.

British Solomon Islands Protectorate (1911). *Handbook of the British Solomon Islands Protectorate*. Tulagi.

British Solomon Islands Protectorate (1915). *Estimates of Revenue and Expenditure for the year 1st April 1915 to 31st March 1916*. Suva, S. Bach.

British Solomon Islands Protectorate (1929). *Report of Commissioner appointed by the Secretary of State for the Colonies to Inquire into the Circumstances in Which Murderous Attacks Took Place in 1927 on Government Officials on Guadalcanal and Malaita*. London, HMSO. C.3248. [Report by Sir Harry C. Moorhouse].

Brockway, Lucile H. (1979). 'Science and Colonial Expansion: The role of British Royal Botanic Gardens', *American Ethnologist*, 6 (3), Interdisciplinary Anthropology: 449–465.

Brooke, C. H. (1872). 'The Death of Bishop Patteson', In: Halcombe, J. J. (ed.). *Mission Life: An illustrated magazine of home and foreign church work*, Volume III, Part I. London, W. Wells Gardner: 1–23. (anglicanhistory.org/oceania/brooke_patteson1872.html).

Brooke, C. H. (1873–1874). 'Last cruise of the Second "Southern Cross"', *Mission Life*, IV (new series): 593–602; V (New series): 190–196; 256–264; 289–298. (http://anglicanhistory.org/oceania/brooke_last.html).

Brown, George (1908). *George Brown, DD: Pioneer-missionary and explorer: An autobiography*. London, Hodder and Stroughton.

Brown, George (1910). *Melanesians and Polynesians: Their life-histories described and compared*. London, Macmillan & Co.

Brown, Kenneth (2000). 'The Language of Land: Look before you leap', *Journal of South Pacific Law*, 4: 1–13. (http://www.paclii.org/journals/fJSPL/vol04/2.shtml).

Brunt, Peter and Thomas, Nicholas (eds) (2012). *Art in Oceania: A new history*. London, Thames & Hudson.

Buckley, Kenneth D. and Klugman, K. (1981). *The History of Burns Philp: The Australian company in the South Pacific*. Sydney, Burns, Philp & Co.

Burman, Rickie (1981). 'Time and Socioeconomic Change on Simbo, Solomon Islands', *Man*, 16 (2): 251–267.

Burnett, Frank (1911). *Through Polynesia and Papua: Wanderings with a camera in Southern Seas*. London, Francis Griffith.

Burns, Philp & Co (1883–1983). Burns, Philp & Co Sydney Office and branches. (AU NBAC N115).

Burns, Philp & Co (1883–1996). Burns, Philp & Co holding deposit. (AU NBAC Z385).

Burns, Philp & Co (1911). *Picturesque Travel Under the Auspices of Burns, Philp & Company Limited*. Sydney, Burns, Philp & Co.

Burns, Philp & Co (1913). *Picturesque Travel Under the Auspices of Burns, Philp & Company Limited*. Sydney, Burns, Philp & Co.

Burt, Ben and Kwa'ioloa, Michael (eds). (2001). *A Solomon Islands Chronicle: As told by Samuel Alasa'a*. London, The British Museum Press. [With contributions from the Kwara'ae chiefs].

Buschmann, Rainer (2000). 'Exploring Tensions in Material Culture: Commercialising ethnography in German New Guinea, 1870–1904', In: O'Hanlon, Michael and Welsch, Robert L. (eds). *Hunting the Gatherers: Ethnographic collectors, agents and agency in Melanesia, 1870s–1930s*. New York, Berghahn Books: 55–80.

Butler, Arthur G. (1884). 'A Collection of Butterflies from the Fiji Islands', *The Annals and Magazine of Natural History*, 5th series, 13: 343–348. (Woodford papers PMB 1290 Item 7/20/1).

Butler, Arthur G. (1885). 'Lepidoptera Collected by Mr C. M. Woodford in the Ellice and Gilbert Islands', *The Annals and Magazine of Natural History*, 5th series, 15: 238–242. (Woodford papers PMB 1290 Item 7/20/3).

Butler, Arthur G. (1887a). 'Descriptions of New Species of Bombycid Lepidoptera From the Solomon Islands', *The Annals and Magazine of Natural History*, 5th series, 19: 214–225. (Woodford papers PMB 1290 Item 7/20/4).

Butler, Arthur G. (1887b). 'Descriptions of New Species of Moths (*Noctuites*) From the Solomon Islands', *The Annals and Magazine of Natural History*, 5th series,19: 432–439. (Woodford papers PMB 1290 Item 7/20/6).

Butler, Arthur G. (1887c). 'Descriptions of New Species of Heterocerous Lepidoptera (*Pyralites*) From the Solomon Islands', *The Annals and Magazine of Natural History*, 5th series, 20: 114–124. (Woodford papers PMB 1290 Item 7/20/7).

Butler, Arthur G. (1887d). 'Descriptions of New Species of Lepidoptera From the Solomon Islands', *The Annals and Magazine of Natural History*, 5th series, 20: 240–247.

Butler, Arthur G. (1887e). 'Descriptions of Two New Species of *Hyponomeutidae* From the Solomon Islands', *The Annals and Magazine of Natural History*, 5th series, 20: 414–415.

Butlin, Robin A. (2009). *Geographies of Empire: European empires and colonies c.1880–1960*. Cambridge, Cambridge University Press.

Butterworth, A. R. *et al.* (1897). 'Australasia', *Journal of the Society of Comparative Legislation*, 2: 158–203.

Butterworth, A. R. *et al.* (1902). 'Australasia', *Journal of the Society of Comparative Legislation*, New series, 4 (2): 250–299.

Cahill, Peter (1997). '"A prodigy of wastefulness, corruption, ignorance and indolence": The Expropriation Board in New Guinea 1920–1927', *The Journal of Pacific History*, 32 (1): 3–28.

Cain, P. J. and Hopkins, A. G. (1980). 'The Political Economy of British Expansion Overseas, 1750–1914', *The Economic History Review*, 33 (4): 463–490.

Cain, P. J. and Hopkins, A. G. (1987). 'Gentlemanly Capitalism and British Expansion Overseas II: New Imperialism, 1850–1945', *The Economic History Review*, 40 (1): 1–26.

Campbell, I. C. (2003). 'The Culture of Culture Contact: Refractions from Polynesia', *Journal of World History*, 14 (1): 63–86.

Campbell, I. C. (2005). 'Resistance and Colonial Government: A comparative study of Samoa', *The Journal of Pacific History*, 40 (1): 45–69.

Campbell, I. C. (2007). 'To Not Reinstate the Past: Wartime optimism and planning for the British Solomon Islands Protectorate', *The Journal of Pacific History*, 42 (1): 55–72.

Capell, Arthur (c.1900). Album of Solomon Island photographs donated to the Australian Museum in 1944 by Rev. Arthur Capell. Sydney, The Australian Museum.

Carreau, Lucie (2009). 'Collecting the Collector: Being an exploration of Harry Geoffrey Beasley's collection of Pacific artefacts made in the years 1895–1939'. 2 volumes. Unpublished PhD thesis, Sainsbury Research Unit for the Arts of Africa, Oceania and the Americas, University of East Anglia.

C. B. (1889). *My Diary of a Trip to Australia in the S.S. "Ormuz" and Back to England*. Henley-on-Thames, Thomas Higgs.

Chamberlain, Joseph (1897). 'The True Conception of Empire: Speech of the British Secretary of State for the Colonies at the annual dinner of the Royal Colonial Institute on March 31, 1897', *Proceedings of the Royal Colonial Institute*, 28: 235–239.

Chapelle, Tony (1976). 'Land and Race in Fiji: The administration of Sir Edvard im Thurn, 1904–1910'. Unpublished PhD thesis, University of the South Pacific.

Chapman, J. K. (1964). *The Career of Arthur Hamilton Gordon*. Toronto, University of Toronto Press.

Cheyne, Andrew (1852). *A description of the Islands in the Western Pacific Ocean, North and South of the Equator, Together With Their Productions: Manners and customs of the natives, and vocabularies of their various languages*. London, Potter.

Christiansen, Sofus (1975). *Subsistence on Bellona Island (Mungiki)*. København, Reitzels Forlag and Bianco Lunos Bogtrykkeri.

Christopher, A. J. (2008). 'The Quest for a Census of the British Empire c.1840–1940', *Journal of Historical Geography*, 34: 268–285.

Chung, Margaret (1993). 'Population, Politics and the Paradigm of Social Evolution', *Asian Geographer*, 12 (1–2): 67–81.

Church, Roy and Clark, Christine (2001). 'Product Development of Branded, Packaged Household Goods in Britain, 1870–1914: Colman's, Reckitt's, and Lever Brothers', *Enterprise and Society*, 2: 503–530.

Churchward, W. B. (1888). *"Blackbirding" in the South Pacific or The First White Man on the Beach*. London, Swan Sonnenschein & Co.

Clay, Brenda Johnson (2005). *Unstable Images: Colonial discourse on New Ireland, Papua New Guinea, 1875–1935*. Honolulu, University of Hawai'i Press.

Clay, Diskin (1988). 'The Archaeology of the Temple of Juno in Carthage (Aen. 1 446–493)', *Classical Philology*, 83 (3): 195–205.

Coates, Austin (1970). *Western Pacific Islands*. London, HMSO.

Codrington, Robert Henry (1863). 'Lecture on the Melanesian Mission', delivered at Nelson, September 25, 1863. (http://anglicanhistory.org/oceania/codrington_lecture1863.pdf).

Codrington, Robert Henry (1915). 'Melanesians', In: Hastings, James (ed.). *Encyclopedia of Religion and Ethics*, Volume III. Edinburgh, T. & T. Clark: 529–538. (http://anglicanhistory.org/oceania/codrington/melanesians1915.html).

Colley, Linda (1992). 'Britishness and Otherness: An argument', *Journal of British Studies*, 31 (4): 309–329.

Colony of Fiji (1896). *Commission Appointed to Inquire into the Decrease of the Native Population: Report*. Suva, Edward John March, Government Printer.

Comaroff, John L. (1989). 'Images of Empire: Contests of conscience: Models of colonial domination in South Africa', *American Ethnologist*, 16 (4): 661–685.

Conington, John (1903). *The Aeneid of Virgil*. Translated into English verse by John Conington. New York, A. L. Burt.

Connell, J. (1983). *Migration, Employment and Development in the South Pacific: Country report, 16: Solomon Islands*. Noumea, South Pacific Commission.

Connell, J. (2006). '"Saving the Solomons": A new geopolitics in the "Arc of Instability"', *Geographical Review*, 44 (2): 111–122.

Cooper, Frederick and Stoler, Ann L. (1989). 'Introduction: Tensions of Empire: Colonial control and visions of rule', *American Ethnologist*, 16 (4): 609–621.

Cooper, H. Stonehewer (1879). *Fiji: Its resources and prospects*. London, G. Street and Co.

Cooper, Matthew (1983). 'On the Beginnings of Colonialism in Melanesia', In: Rodman, Margaret and Cooper, Matthew (eds). *The Pacification of Melanesia*. Lanham MD, University Press of America: 25–41.

Coote, Jeremy and Edwards, Elizabeth (1997). 'Images of Benin at the Pitt Rivers Museum', *African Arts*, 30 (4) (Special issue: the Benin Centenary (Part 2)): 26–35, 93.

Coote, Walter (1882). *Wanderings, South and East*. London, Sampson Low, Marston, Searle and Rivington.

Coote, Walter (1883). *The Western Pacific: Being a description of the groups of islands to the north and east of the Australian continent*. London, Sampson Low, Marston, Searle and Rivington.

Coriale, Danielle (2008). 'Gaskell's Naturalist', *Nineteenth-Century Literature*, 63 (3): 346–375.

Corner, E. J. H. (1969a). 'Introduction', *Philosophical Transactions of the Royal Society of London. Series B. Biological sciences*, 255 (800): 187–188. [A discussion of the results of the Royal Society Expedition to the British Solomon Islands Protectorate, 1965].

Corner, E. J. H. (1969b). 'Mountain Flora of Popomanaseu, Guadalcanal', *Philosophical Transactions of the Royal Society of London. Series B. Biological sciences*, 255 (800): 575–577. [A discussion of the results of the Royal Society Expedition to the British Solomon Islands Protectorate, 1965].

Corris, Peter (1968). '"Blackbirding" in New Guinea Waters, 1883–84', *The Journal of Pacific History*, 3: 85–105.

Corris, Peter (1973). *Passage, Port and Plantation: A history of Solomon Islands Labour Migration 1870–1914*. Melbourne, Melbourne University Press.

Croom–Johnson, R. P. (1928). *The Stamps of the British Solomon Islands (Les timbres-postes des Îsles Salomon)*. Torino, Editrice Filatelica. (Woodford papers PMB 1381/007).

Cruden, Robert Peirce (1843). *The History of the Town of Gravesend in the County of Kent and of the Port of London*. London, William Pickering.

Czarkowska Starzecka, Dorota and Cranstone, B. A. L. (1974) *The Solomon Islanders*. London, British Museum.

Dalziell, Rosamund (2007). 'Everard im Thurn in British Guiana and the Western Pacific', In: Hulme, Peter and McDougall, Russell (eds). *Writing, Travel and Empire: In the margins of anthropology*. London, I. B. Tauris & Co: 97–116.

D'Arcy, Paul (1987). 'Firearms on Malaita, 1870–1900', In: Lal, Brij (ed.). *Wansalawara: Soundings in Melanesian history*. Honolulu, Pacific Studies Program, University of Hawai'i at Manoa: 50–87.

Darwin, Charles (1859). *On the Origin of the Species by Means of Natural Selection*. London, John Murray.

Davidson, Allan K. (ed.) (2000). *The Church of Melanesia 1849–1999*. Auckland, College of St John the Evangelist. [1999 Selwyn Lectures marking the 150th Anniversary of the Founding of The Melanesian Mission].

Davis, Richard (ed.) (2004). *Woven Histories, Dancing Lives: Torres Strait Islander identity, culture and history*. Canberra, Aboriginal Studies Press.

de Bruijn, B. *et al.* (2000). *Report on the 1999 Population and Housing Census: Basic tables and census description*. Honiara, Statistics Office, Solomon Islands Government.

de Bruijn, B. *et al.* (2002). *Report on the 1999 Population and Housing Census: Analysis*. Honiara, Statistics Office, Solomon Islands Government.

Dennis, Alfred L. P. (1909). 'Tendencies in British Foreign Policy since Disraeli', *Proceedings of the American Political Science Association*, 6, 6th annual meeting: 109–120.

Diamond, Jared (1997). *Guns, Germs and Steel: The fates of human societies*. London, Jonathan Cape.

Dillane, Fionnuala (2009). 'Re-reading George Eliot's "Natural History": Marian Evans, "the People," and the periodical', *Victorian Periodicals Review*, 42 (3): 244–266.

Dinnen, Sinclair (2002). 'Winners and Losers: Politics and disorder in the Solomon Islands 2000–2002', *The Journal of Pacific History*, 37 (3): 285–298.

Dinnen, Sinclair and Firth, Stewart (eds) (2008). *Politics and State Building in Solomon Islands*. Canberra, Asia Pacific Press, The Australian National University.

Dobyns, Henry F. (1993). 'Disease Transfer at Contact', *Annual Review of Anthropology*, 22: 273–291.

Docker, Edward Wyberg (1970). *The Blackbirders: The recruiting of South Seas labour for Queensland, 1863–1907*. Sydney, Angus and Robertson. [Later published as *The Blackbirders: A brutal story of the Kanaka slave-trade*, Sydney, Angus and Robertson, 1981].

Douglas, Bronwen (2001). 'Encounters with the Enemy?: Academic readings of missionary narratives on Melanesians', *Comparative Studies in Society and History*, 43 (1): 37–64.

Douglas, Ngaire (1997). 'The Fearful and the Fanciful: Early tourists' perceptions of Western Melanesia', *The Journal of Tourism Studies*, 8 (1): 52–61.

Driver, Felix (1991). 'Henry Morton Stanley and His Critics: Geography, exploration and empire', *Past and Present*, 133: 134–166.

Driver, Felix (1998). 'Scientific Exploration and the Construction of Geographical Knowledge: Hints to travellers', *Finisterra*, 33 (65): 21–30.

Driver, Felix (2004). 'Distance and Disturbance: Travel, exploration and knowledge in the Nineteenth Century', *Transactions of the Royal Historical Society*, 6th series, 14: 73–92.

Druce, Hamilton H. (1890). 'Descriptions of Twelve New Species of *Lycaenidae* from West Africa and One From the Solomon Islands in the Collection of Herbert Druce', *The Annals and Magazine of Natural History*, 6th series, 5: 24–31.

Druce, Herbert (1888a). 'List of Lepidoptera Heterocera Collected by Mr. C. M. Woodford at Suva, Viti Levu, Fiji Islands, With Descriptions of Some New Species', *Proceedings of the Zoological Society of London*, 56 (1): 219–231.

Druce, Herbert (1888b). 'List of Lepidoptera Heterocera, With Descriptions of the New Species, Collected by Mr. C. M. Woodford at Aola, Guadalcanar Island, Solomon Islands', *Proceedings of the Zoological Society of London*, 56 (1): 570–580.

Drus, Ethel (1950). 'The Colonial Office and the Annexation of Fiji: The Alexander Prize essay', *Transactions of the Royal Historical Society*, 4th series, 32: 87–110.

Dureau, Christine (1998). 'Decreed Affinities: Nationhood and the Western Solomon Islands', *The Journal of Pacific History*, 33 (2): 197–220.

Dureau, Christine (2000). 'Skulls, *Mana* and Causality', *The Journal of the Polynesian Society*, 109 (1): 71–98.

Durrad, W. J. (1922). 'The Depopulation of Melanesia', In: Rivers, William Halse Rivers (ed.). *Essays on the Depopulation of Melanesia*. Cambridge, Cambridge University Press: 3–24.

Eckstein, A. M. (1991). 'Is There a "Hobson-Lenin Thesis" on Late Nineteenth-Century Colonial Expansion', *The Economic History Review*, 44 (2): 297–318.

Economist Intelligence Unit (2004). *Solomon Islands: Country profile*. London, The Economist.

Edge-Partington, J. (1903). 'Food Trough from Rubiana, New Georgia', *Man*, 3: 161–162.

Edge-Partington, J. and Woodford, C. M. (1901). 'Native Ornaments from the Solomon Islands, Recently Presented to the British Museum by Mr. C. M. Woodford'. *Man*, 1: 100–101.

Edge-Partington, T. W. (1906). 'Note on the Food Bowl from Rubiana, New Georgia', *Man*, 6: 121.

Edge-Partington, T. W. (1907). 'Ingava: Chief of Rubiana, Solomon Islands: Died 1906', *Man*, 7: 22–23.

Edwards, Elizabeth (1998). 'Performing Science: Still photography and the Torres Strait expedition', In: Herle, Anita and Rouse, Sandra (eds). *Cambridge and the Torres Strait: Centenary essays on the 1898 Anthropological Expedition*. Cambridge, University of Cambridge Press: 106–135.

Edwards, Elizabeth (2000). 'Surveying Culture: Photography, collecting and material culture in British New Guinea, 1898', In: O'Hanlon, Michael and Welsch, Robert L. (eds). *Hunting the Gatherers: Ethnographic collectors, agents and agency in Melanesia, 1870s–1930s*. New York, Berghahn Books: 103–126.

Edwards, Elizabeth (2008). 'Straightforward and Ordered: Amateur photographic surveys and scientific aspiration, 1885–1914', *Photography and Culture*, 1 (2): 185–210.

Edwards, Elizabeth (2012). 'Objects of Affect: Photography beyond the image', *Annual Review of Anthropology*, 41: 221–234.

Eggert, Paul (2003). 'Robbery Under Arms: The colonial market, imperial publishers, and the demise of the three-decker vovel', *Book History*, 6: 127–146.

Eldridge, Elizabeth A. (1992). 'Sources of Conflict in Southern Africa, c.1800–30: The "Mfecane" reconsidered', *The Journal of African History*, 33 (1): 1–35.

Eliot, George (1872). *Middlemarch: A study of provincial life*. New York, Signet Classics

Elkington, E. Way and Hardy, Norman H. (1907). *The Savage South Seas*. London, A & C Black.

Elliot Smith, Grafton (1911). *The Ancient Egyptians and Their Influence Upon the Civilization of Europe.* London, Harper & Brothers. [A revised edition was published in 1923 as *The Ancient Egyptians and the Origin of Civilization*].

Elliott, Paul (2003). 'The Origins of the "Creative Class": Provincial urban society, scientific culture and socio-political marginality in Britain in the Eighteenth and Nineteenth Centuries', *Social History*, 28(3): 361–387.

Ellison, Joseph Waldo (1939). 'The Partition of Samoa: A study in imperialism and diplomacy', *Pacific Historical Review*, 8 (3): 259–288.

Elton, F. (1888). 'Notes on the Natives of the Solomon Islands', *The Journal of the Anthropological Institute of Great Britain and Ireland,* 17: 90–99.

Etherington, Norman (2004). 'A Tempest in a Teapot?: Nineteenth-Century contests for land in South Arica's Caledon Valley and the invention of the "Mfecane"', *The Journal of African History*, 45 (2): 203–219.

Evans, E. B. (1908). 'The Stamps of British New Guinea', *Gibbons Stamp Weekly*, 25 July, 1908: 59–60. (Woodford papers PMB 1290 Item 7/39).

Everill, Henry Charles (1886). *Official Report of Capt. H.C. Everill, Leader of the New Guinea Exploring Expedition.* Sydney.

Eves, Richard (2005). 'Unsettling Settler Colonialism: Debates over climate and colonization in New Guinea, 1875–1914', *Ethnic and Racial Studies*, 28 (2): 304–330.

Eves, Richard (2006). '"Black and white: a significant contrast": Race, humanism and missionary photography in the Pacific', *Ethnic and Racial Studies*, 29 (4): 725–748.

Fagan, Melinda B. (2007). 'Wallace, Darwin, and the Practice of Natural History', *Journal of the History of Biology*, 40 (4): 601–635.

Fairbairn, I. J. (1971). 'Pacific Island Economies', *The Journal of the Polynesian Society*, 80 (1): 74–118.

Fairclough, H. R. and Brown, Sheldon L. (1920). *Virgil's Aeneid: Books I–VI.* Chicago, Sanborn & Co.

Fairley, Rigby and Co Ltd (1912–1941). Documents and papers of Fairley, Rigby & Co and the Vanikoro Kauri Timber Company. Melbourne, University of Melbourne Archives.

Favenc, Ernest and Taylor, Cheryl (eds) (1997). *Tales of the Austral Tropics.* Sydney, UNSW Press.

Feinstein, Charles (1990a). 'What Really Happened to Real Wages?: Trends in wages, prices and productivity in the United Kingdom, 1860–1913', *The Economic History Review*, 43 (3): 329–355.

Feinstein, Charles (1990b). 'New Estimates of Average Earnings in the United Kingdom, 1880–1913', *The Economic History Review*, 43 (4): 595–632.

Festetics de Tolna, Le Comte Rodolphe (1903). *Chez les Cannibales: Huit ans de croisière dans L'Océan Pacifique à bord du yacht 'Le Tolna'*. Paris, Librairie Plon, Plon-Nourrit.

Firth, Raymond (1940). 'The Analysis of *Mana*: An empirical approach', *The Journal of the Polynesian Society*, 49 (196): 482–510.

Firth, Raymond (1965). *Primitive Polynesian Economy*. 2nd edition. London, Routledge & Kegan Paul.

Firth, Raymond (1969). 'Extraterritoriality and the Tikopia chiefs', *Man*, 4 (3): 354–378.

Firth, Raymond (1983, c.1957). *We, the Tikopia: A sociological study of kinship in primitive Polynesia*. 2nd edition. Stanford, Stanford University Press.

Firth, Stewart (1972). 'The New Guinea Company, 1885–1899: A case of unprofitable Imperialism', *Australian Historical Studies*, 15: 361–377.

Firth, Stewart (1973). 'German Firms in the Western Pacific Islands, 1857–1914', *The Journal of Pacific History*, 8: 10–28.

Firth, Stewart (1976). 'The Transformation of the Labour Trade in German New Guinea, 1899–1914', *The Journal of Pacific History*, 11 (1): 51–65.

Firth, Stewart (2000). 'The Pacific Islands and the Globalization Agenda', *Contemporary Pacific*, 12 (1): 178–192.

Flannery, Tim (1995). *The Future Eaters: An ecological history of the Australasian lands and peoples*. Sydney, Reed.

Flannery, Tim (2011). *Among the Islands*. Melbourne, Text Publishing Co.

Foster, Joseph (1893). *Oxford Men: 1880–1892 with a record of their schools, honours and degrees*. Oxford, James Parker.

Foukona, Joseph D. (2007). 'Legal Aspects of Customary Land Administration in Solomon Islands', *Journal of South Pacific Law*, 11 (1): 64–72.

Fox, A. Wilson (1903). 'Agricultural Wages in England and Wales During the Last Fifty Years', *Journal of the Royal Statistical Society*, 66 (2): 273–359.

Fox, Charles E. (1967). *The Story of the Solomons*. Taroaniara, Nggela, Diocese of Melanesia Press.

Fraenkel, J (2004). *The Manipulation of Custom: From uprising to intervention in the Solomon Islands*. Canberra, Pandanus Books.

Franks, Don (2000a). 'Woodford's Large Canoe Adhesive Stamp Design', *Pacifica: The Pacific Islands Study Circle*, 38.

Franks, Don (2000b). 'Solomons: 1907–8 large canoe "Tomako" adhesives: Their design and usage: Part II', *Pacifica: The Pacific Islands Study Circle*, 179.

Franks, Don and Forrestier Smith, Peter (2001). *The Stamps and Postal History of the Solomon Islands: Illustrated check list of postal history items of the pre-Protectorate and the 'Woodford' eras*. London, The Pacific Islands Study Circle UK.

Frazer, J. G. and Holmes, T. V. (1889).'Questions on the Manners, Customs, Religion, Superstitions, &c of Uncivilized or Semi-Civilized Peoples', *The Journal of the Anthropological Institute of Great Britain and Ireland*, 18: 431–440. [Published in three editions: 1887, 1889 and 1907].

Gahan, Charles J. (1888). 'Descriptions of a New Genus and of Some New Species of Longicorn Coleoptera in the Family *Lamiidae* obtained by Mr. C. M. Woodford in the Solomon Islands', *The Annals and Magazine of Natural History*, 6th series, 1: 190–193.

Galton, Francis (1878). *Hints to Travellers*. London, Edward Stanford for the Royal Geographical Society. [Edited by a committee of council of the Royal Geographical Society. 4th edition edited by Francis Galton. 5th edition edited by John Laughton. Published in at least 11 editions: 1865 (2nd), 1871 (3rd), 1878 (4th), 1883 (5th), 1889 (6th), 1893 (7th), 1906 (9th) and 1935 (11th)].

Ganter, Regina (1994). *The Pearl-Shellers of Torres Strait: Resource use, development and decline, 1860s–1960s*. Melbourne, Melbourne University Press.

Gardner, Helen B. (2006). *Gathering for God: George Brown in Oceania*. Dunedin, Otago University Press.

Gardner, Helen and Philp, Jude (2006). 'Photography and the Christian Mission', *The Journal of Pacific History*, 41(2): 175–190.

Garran, A. (ed.) (1868–88). *Picturesque Atlas of Australasia*. 3 volumes. Sydney, Picturesque Atlas Publishing Co.

Garran, R. R. et al. (1912). 'Australasia', *Journal of the Society of Comparative Legislation*, New series, 12 (2): 388–447.

Garran, R. R. et al. (1915). 'Australasia', *Journal of the Society of Comparative Legislation*, New series, 15: 27–78.

Garson, John George and Read, Charles Hercules (1892). *Notes and Queries on Anthropology*. London, The Anthropological Institute. [Published in six editions: 1874, 1892, 1899, 1912, 1929 and 1951].

Gash, Noel and Whittaker, June (1975). *A Pictorial History of New Guinea*. Milton, Jacaranda Press.

Gazeley, Ian (1989). 'The Cost of Living for Urban Workers in Late Victorian and Edwardian Britain', *The Economic History Review*, 42 (2): 207–221.

Gibbney, H. J. (1966). 'The Interregnum in the Government of Papua, 1901–1906', *Australian Journal of Politics and History*, 12 (3): 341–359.

Gilding, Michael (1982). 'The Massacre of the *Mystery*: A case study in contact relations', *The Journal of Pacific History*, 17 (1): 66–85.

Giles, W. E. and Scarr, Deryck (eds) (1968). *A Cruize in a Queensland Labour Vessel to the South Seas*. Canberra, Australian National University Press.

Gisburn, Harold G. D. (1956). *British Solomon Islands Protectorate: Its postage stamps and postal history*. Southampton, J. Sanders (Philatelist) Ltd.

Godman, F. D. and Salvin, O. (1888a). 'New Species of Butterflies Collected by Mr. C. M. Woodford in the Solomon Islands', *The Annals and Magazine of Natural History*, 6th series, 1: 90–101.

Godman, F. D. and Salvin, O. (1888b). 'New Species of Butterflies Collected by Mr. C. M. Woodford in the Solomon Islands', *The Annals and Magazine of Natural History*, 6th series, 1: 209–214.

Golden, Graeme A. (1993). *The Early European settlers of the Solomon Islands*. Melbourne, G. Golden.

Goldenweiser, A. A. (1916). 'The History of Melanesian Society by W. H. R. Rivers', *The American Historical Review*, 21 (2): 336–339.

Goldie, John F. (1908) 'The People of New Georgia, Their Manners and Customs and Religious beliefs', *Proceedings of the Royal Society of Queensland*, 22: 23–30.

Goldie, John F. (1932). 'Letter to the Editors, Journal of the Polynesian Society', *The Journal of the Polynesian Society*, 41 (163): 232–233.

Gordon, Sir Arthur Hamilton (Lord Stanmore) (1901–1904). *Fiji: records of private and public life, 1875–1880*. Edinburgh, R&R Clark.

Gordon Cumming, C. F. (1882). *At Home in Fiji*. New York, Armstrong and Son.

Government of Solomon Islands (2002). *Solomon Islands Human Development Report: Building a Nation, Vol. 1*. Honiara, Government of Solomon Islands.

Graves, Adrian (1983). 'Truck and Gifts: Melanesian immigrants and the trade box system in colonial Queensland', *Past & Present*, 101: 87–124.

Graves, Adrian (1993). *Cane and Labour: The political economy of the Queensland sugar industry, 1862–1906*. Edinburgh, Edinburgh University Press.

Gray, Geoffrey (1999). '"Being honest to my science": Reo Fortune and J. H. P. Murray, 1927–30', *The Australian Journal of Anthropology*, 10 (1): 56–76.

Greasley, David (1986). 'British Economic Growth: The paradox of the 1880s and the timing of the climacteric', *Explorations in Economic History*, 23: 416–444.

Great Britain. Admiralty. (1871). *A Manual of Scientific Enquiry Prepared for the Uuse of Officers in Her Majesty's Navy and Travellers in General*. London, John Murray for the Admiralty. [Originally edited by Sir John Herschel. 3th edition by Robert Main. 5th edition by Robert Ball. ublished in five editions: 1849, 1851, 1859, 1871 and 1886].

Great Britain. Admiralty. Hydrographic Department (1956). *Pacific Islands Pilot: Volume 1*. 8th edition. London, Hydrographic Department, Admiralty.

Great Britain. Admiralty, Naval Intelligence Bureau (1943–1945). *Pacific Islands: Volume 1: General Survey. Volume II: Eastern Pacific. Volume III: Western Pacific*. London, Naval Intelligence Bureau.

Great Britain. Colonial Office (1878–1951). *Western Pacific: Original correspondence*. London, Colonial Office. (CO 225).

Great Britain. Colonial Office (1878–1908). *Western Pacific: Register of correspondence*. London, Colonial Office. (CO 492).

Great Britain. Colonial Office (1879–1900). *Western Pacific: Register of out-letters*. London, Colonial Office. (CO 493)

Great Britain. Colonial Office (1923). *Handbook of the British Solomon Islands Protectorate*. Suva, S. Bach printer to HM High Commissioner for the Western Pacific.

Great Britain. Foreign Office (1895). *Western Pacific: Report for the year 1894 on the trade of Samoa.* London, H.M.S.O. (Diplomatic and Consular Reports on Trade and Finance, no. 1587). (Pacific Manuscript Bureau, Woodford papers PMB 1290 Item 8/22). [Report by Acting-Consul Woodford to the Earl of Kimberley].

Great Britain. Foreign and Commonwealth Office (2002). *The Western Pacific Archive: Selected documents.* London, Foreign and Commonwealth Office.

Great Britain. High Commission for the Western Pacific (1875–1941). *Records of the Office of the High Commissioner for the Western Pacific: Inwards correspondence, MP series.* Suva, Western Pacific Archives. (WPHC).

Great Britain. High Commission for Western Pacific Islands (1893–1912). *King's Regulations Made by His Britannic Majesty's High Commissioner for the Western Pacific Ender the Provisions of the Pacific Order in Council, 1893.* Suva, S. Bach, Government Printer. [Regulations made for 1893–1901 issued as Queen's Regulations].

Great Britain. High Commission for Western Pacific Islands (1912). *British Solomon Islands Protectorate: Labour regulations.* Suva, Edward John March Printer to the Government of His Britannic Majesty's High Commission for the Western Pacific.

Great Britain. House of Commons. Parliamentary Papers (1872). *Report of the Proceedings of HM ship 'Rosario' during her cruise among the South Sea Islands between 1stNovember 1871 and 12th February 1872.* London, Eyre and Spottiswoode. (C.542). [Report by A. H. Markham].

Great Britain. House of Commons. Parliamentary Papers (1873). *South Sea Islands: Copies or extracts of any communication of importance respecting outrages committed upon natives of the south sea islands etc.* London, by order of The House of Commons. (C.244).

Great Britain. House of Commons. Parliamentary Papers (1874a). *Report of Commodore Goodenough and Mr. Consul Layard on the Offers of the Cession of the Fiji Islands to the British Crown.* London, Harrison and Sons (C.1011).

Great Britain. House of Commons. Parliamentary Papers (1874b). *Fiji Islands: Copy of a letter addressed to Commodore Goodenough, RN and E. L. Layard instructing them to report upon various questions connected with the Fiji Islands: With enclosures.* London, William Clowes & Sons (C.983).

Great Britain. House of Commons. Parliamentary Papers (1881). *Solomon Islands &c (Punishment of Natives): Copy of papers relating to punishment of batives for outrages committed by them in the Solomon Island and other groups of the Western Pacific*. London, Admiralty. (C.284).

Great Britain. House of Commons. Parliamentary Papers (1883a). *Western Pacific: Correspondence respecting the natives of the Western Pacific and the labour trade*. London, Eyre and Spottiswoode. (C.3641).

Great Britain. House of Commons. Parliamentary Papers (1883b). *Western Pacific Islands: Correspondence respecting New Guinea, the New Hebrides and other islands in the Pacific*. London, Eyre and Spottiswoode. (C.3814).

Great Britain. House of Commons. Parliamentary Papers (1884a). *Reports Concerning the State of Affairs in the Western Pacific Received from Deputy Commissioner Romilly*. London, H.M.S.O. (C.4126).

Great Britain. House of Commons. Parliamentary Papers (1884b). *Western Pacific: Report of a commission appointed to inquire into the working of the western Pacific orders in council, and the nature of the measures requisite to secure the attainment of the object for which those orders in council were issued*. London, Eyre and Spottiswoode. (C.3905).

Great Britain. House of Commons. Parliamentary Papers (1884–5). *Further Correspondence Respecting New Guinea and Other Islands and the Convention at Sydney of Representatives of the Australasian Colonies*. London, Eyre and Spottiswoode. (C.4217).

Great Britain. House of Commons. Parliamentary Papers (1885). *Correspondence Relating to the Native Population of Fiji*. London, Eyre and Spottiswoode. (C.4434).

Great Britain. House of Commons. Parliamentary Papers (1886a). *Declarations Between the Governments of Great Britain and the German Empire Relating to the Demarcation of the British and German Spheres of Influence in the Western Pacific*. London, H.M.S.O. (C.4656).

Great Britain. House of Commons. Parliamentary Papers (1886b). *Papers Relative to Armed Reprisals Inflicted Upon Natives of Various Islands in the Western Pacific by HMS 'Diamond'*, London, Henry Hansard & Sons. (51–sess.2 25 September 1886).

Great Britain. House of Commons. Parliamentary Papers (1887a). *Correspondence Relating to Proposals for an International Agreement Regulating the Supply of Arms, Ammunition, Alcohol and Dynamite to Natives of the Western Pacific*. London, H.M.S.O. (C.5240).

Great Britain. House of Commons. Parliamentary Papers (1887b). *HMS "Opal": Papers relating to the recent operations of HMS "Opal" against natives of the Solomon Islands*. London, Henry Hansard and Son. (C.58).

Great Britain. House of Commons. Parliamentary Papers (1889). *Correspondence Respecting the Affairs of Samoa: Samoa No. 1 (1889)*. London, H.M.S.O. (C.5629).

Great Britain. House of Commons. Parliamentary Papers (1890). *Final Act of the Conference on the Affairs of Samoa, Signed at Berlin, June 14, 1889*. London, H.M.S.O. (The Berlin Act 1889, C.5911).

Great Britain. House of Commons. Parliamentary Papers (1893). *Pacific Orders in Council: Schedule of rules and forms*. London, H.M.S.O. [*The Pacific Order, 1893* also known as *The Pacific Order, 1893, no. 78*].

Great Britain. House of Commons. Parliamentary Papers (1893–94). *Further Correspondence Respecting the Affairs of Samoa: Samoa no.1 (1893)*. London, H.M.S.O. (C.6973).

Great Britain. House of Commons. Parliamentary Papers (1897a). *Papers Relating to the Massacre of British Officials Near Benin, and the Consequent Punitive Expedition*. London, H.M.S.O. (Africa no. 6 (1897), C.8677).

Great Britain. House of Commons. Parliamentary Papers (1897b). *Western Pacific: Report on the British Solomon Islands by Mr C. M. Woodford*. London, H.M.S.O. (Colonial Reports–Miscellaneous No. 8, C.8457).

Great Britain. House of Commons. Parliamentary Papers (1898). *British Solomon Islands: Annual report for 1897–8*. London, Eyre and Spottiswoode. (Colonial Reports–Annual, no. 251, C.9046–19).

Great Britain. House of Commons. Parliamentary Papers (1899a). *British Solomon Islands: Annual report for 1898–9*. London, Eyre and Spottiswoode. (Colonial Reports–Annual, no. 275, C.9498–9).

Great Britain. House of Commons. Parliamentary Papers (1899b). *Correspondence Respecting the Affairs of Samoa: Report of the Joint Commission*. (Samoa No. 1, 1899, C.9506).

Great Britain. House of Commons. Parliamentary Papers (1900a). *Convention and Declaration Between the United Kingdom and Germany for the Settlement of the Samoan and Other Questions, Signed at London, November 14, 1899*. London, H.M.S.O. (Treaty series no. 7 1900, C.38). [Also available at WPHC 4/IV, 218/1900].

Great Britain. House of Commons.Parliamentary Papers (1900b). *Convention Between the United Kingdom, Germany, and the United States of America Relating to the Settlement of Certain Claims in Samoa by Arbitration, Signed at Washington, November 7, 1899.* London, H.M.S.O. (Treaty series no. 10, 1900, C.98).

Great Britain. House of Commons. Parliamentary Papers (1900c). *Convention Between the United Kingdom, Germany, and the United States of America for the Adjustment of Questions Relating to Samoa, Signed at Washington, December 2, 1899.* London, H.M.S.O. (The Tripartite Convention of 1899, C.39).

Great Britain. House of Commons. Parliamentary Papers (1901). *British Solomon Islands: Annual report for 1899–1900.* London, Eyre and Spottiswoode. (Colonial Reports–Annual, no. 320, C.431–12).

Great Britain. House of Commons. Parliamentary Papers (1902a). *British Solomon Islands: Annual report for 1900–1901.* London, Eyre and Spottiswoode. (Colonial Reports–Annual, no. 347, C.788–17).

Great Britain. House of Commons. Parliamentary Papers (1902b). *British Solomon Islands: Annual report for 1901–1902.* London, Eyre and Spottiswoode. (Colonial Reports–Annual, no. 372, C.788–42).

Great Britain. House of Commons. Parliamentary Papers (1903). *British Solomon Islands: Annual report for 1902–1903.* London, Eyre and Spottiswoode. (Colonial Reports–Annual, no. 401, C.168–6).

Great Britain. House of Commons. Parliamentary Papers (1905). *British Solomon Islands: Annual report for 1903–4 and 1904–5.* London, Eyre and Spottiswoode. (Colonial Reports–Annual, no. 461, C.2634–7).

Great Britain. House of Commons. Parliamentary Papers (1908). *Correspondence Relating to the Administration of the Gilbert and Ellice Islands Protectorate.* London, H.M.S.O. (C.4356).

Great Britain. House of Commons. Parliamentary Papers (1910). *Report by Mr Arthur Mahaffy on a Visit to the Gilbert and Ellice Islands, 1909.* London, H.M.S.O. (C.4992).

Great Britain. House of Commons. Parliamentary Papers (1913). *British Solomon Islands: Annual report to 30 June 1913.* London, Eyre and Spottiswoode. (Colonial Reports–Annual, no. 774).

Great Britain. Laws etc (1877–1893). *Western Pacific Order in Council of 13 August 1877, 14 August 1879 and 15 March 1893.* London, H.M.S.O. [See Whittaker et al. 1975: document D39. http://vanuatu.usp.ac.fj/library/online/texts/Pacific_archive].

Green, Kaye (1976). 'The History of Post-Spanish European Contact in the Eastern District Before 1939', In; Green, R. C. and Cresswell, M. M. (eds) (1976). *Southeast Solomon Islands Cultural History: A preliminary survey.* Wellington, The Royal Society of New Zealand: 31–46.

Green, R. C. and Cresswell, M. M. (eds) (1976). *Southeast Solomon Islands Cultural History: A preliminary survey.* Wellington, The Royal Society of New Zealand.

Grimble, Arthur (1921). 'From Birth to Death in the Gilbert Islands', *The Journal of the Royal Anthropological Institute of Great Britain and Ireland*, 51: 25–54.

Groenewegen, K. (1970). *Report on the Census of the Population, 1970: Western Pacific High Commission, British Solomon Islands Protectorate.* Southampton, Hobbs the Printers.

Grose Smith, H. (1888–1889). 'Descriptions of New Species of Butterflies Captured by Mr. C. M. Woodford in the Solomon Islands', *The Entomologist's Monthly Magazine*, 25: 299–303.

Grover, J. C. (1957). 'Some Geographical Aspects of the British Solomon Islands in the Western Pacific', *The Geographical Journal*, 123: 298–314.

Gunson, Niel (1968). 'Melanesian Unity: The church example', *The Journal of Pacific History*, 3: 159–161.

Guppy, Henry Brougham (1887a). *The Solomon Islands: Their geology, general features and suitability for colonization.* London, Swan Sonnenschein, Lowrey.

Guppy, Henry Brougham (1887b). *The Solomon Islands and Their Natives.* London, Swan Sonnenschein.

Guppy, Henry Brougham (1903–1906). *Observations of a Naturalist in the Pacific Between 1896 and 1899.* 2 volumes. London, Macmillan.

Haddon, A. C. (ed.) (1901–1935). *Reports of the Cambridge Anthropological Expedition to Torres Straits.* 6 Volumes. Cambridge, Cambridge University Press. (https://archive.org/details/reportsofcambrid02hadd).

Haddon, A. C., Bartlett, F. C. and Fegan, Ethel S. (1922). 'William Halse Rivers Rivers, MD, FRS, President of the Royal Anthropological Institute, Born 1864, Died June 4th 1922 [obituary]', *Man*, 22: 97–104.

Hastings, Peter (1969). *New Guinea: Problems and prospects*. Melbourne, Cheshire for the Australian Institute of International Affairs.

Haque, Tobias A. (2012). 'The Influence of Culture on Economic Development in Solomon Islands: A political-economy perspective', SSGM discussion paper 2012/1, Canberra, State Society and Governance in Melanesia, The Australian National University.

Haines, Robin (2003). '"The idle and the drunken won't do there": Poverty, the New Poor Law and Nineteenth-Century government-assisted emigration to Australia from the United Kingdom', In: Samson, Jane (ed.) *British Imperial Strategies in the Pacific, 1750–1900*. Aldershot, Hampshire, Ashgate Variorum: 183–203. [Reprinted from *Australian Historical Studies*, 108 (1997): 1–21].

Hall, Russell E. (1938). 'Outposts of Empire in Southern Pacific', *Far Eastern Survey*, 7 (4): 35–43.

Hansell, J. R. F. and Wall, J. R. D. (1976). *Land Resources of the Solomon Islands. Volume 1: Introduction and recommendations. Volume 2: Guadalcanal and the Florida Islands. Volume 3: Malaita and Ulawa. Volume 4: New Georgia Group and the Russell Islands. Volume 5: Santa Isabel. Volume 6: Choiseul and the Shortland Islands. Volume 7: San Cristobal and adjacent islands. Volume 8: Outer islands*. Surbiton, Surrey, Land Resources Division, Ministry of Overseas Development.

Harrison, Mark (2005). 'Science and the British Empire', *Isis*, 96 (1): 56–63.

Hays, Terence E. (1991). '"No tobacco, no Hallelujah": Missions and the early history of tobacco in Eastern Papua', *Pacific Studies*, 14 (4): 91–112.

Healy, A. M. (1967). 'Paternalism and Consultation in Papua, 1880–1960', *ANU Historical Journal*, 4: 19–27.

Hearnshaw, F. J. C. (ed.) (1913). *King's College Lectures on Colonial Problems*. London, G. Bell & Sons.

Heath, Ian (1974a). 'Charles Morris Woodford of the Solomon Islands: A biographical note, 1852–1927'. Unpublished MA thesis, The Australian National University (PMB 1368).

Heath, Ian (1974b). 'Toward a Reassessment of Gordon of Fiji', *The Journal of Pacific History*, 9: 81–92.

Heath, Ian (1978). 'Charles Morris Woodford: Adventurer, naturalist, administrator', In: Scarr, Deryck (ed.). *More Pacific Islands Portraits*. Canberra, Australian National University Press: 193–209.

Heath, Ian (1979). 'Land Policy in Solomon Islands'. Unpublished PhD thesis, Department of History, La Trobe University.

Heath, Ian (1981). 'Solomon Islands: Land policy and independence', *Kabar Seberang/Saluting Maphilindo*, 8/9: 62–77.

Hegarty, D *et al*. (2004). 'Rebuilding State and Nation in Solomon Islands: Policy options for the Regional Assistance Mission', SSGM discussion paper 2004/2, Canberra, State Society and Governance in Melanesia, The Australian National University.

Helgen, Kristofer M. (2005). 'Systematics of the Pacific Monkey-faced Bats (Chiroptera: Pteropodidae), With a New Species of *Pteralopex* and a New Fijian Species', *Systematics and Biodiversity*, 3 (4): 433–453.

Hemmen, George R. (2010). 'Royal Society Expeditions in the Second Half of the Twentieth Century', *Notes and Records of the Royal Society*, 64: S89–S99.

Hemsley William Botting (1891). 'New Solomon Island Plants', *Annals of Botany*, os–5 (4): 501–508.

Hemsley, William Botting (1895). 'The Flora of the Tonga or Friendly Islands: With descriptions of and notes on some new or remarkable plants, partly from the Solomon Islands', *The Journal of the Linnean Society of London. Botany*, 30: 158–217.

Henderson, W. O. (1938). 'Germany's Trade With Her Colonies, 1884–1914', *The Economic History Review*, 9 (1): 1–16.

Herle, Anita (2009). 'John Layard *long* Malakula 1914–1915: The potency of field photography', In: Morton, Christopher and Edwards, Elizabeth (eds). *Photography, Anthropology and History: Expanding the frame*. Farnham, UK, Ashgate: 241–263.

Herle, Anita and Rouse, Sandra (eds). (1998). *Cambridge and the Torres Strait: Centenary essays on the 1898 anthropological expedition*. Cambridge, University of Cambridge Press.

Hertslet, Lewis (1880–1905). *Hertslet's Commercial Treaties: A collection of treaties and conventions between Great Britain and foreign powers*. London, HMSO. [Volume 14, 1880; Volume 15, 1885; Volume 17, 1890; Volume 19, 1895; Volume 21, 1901; Volume 23, 1905].

Hess, Mona *et al*. (2009). 'Niabara: The Western Solomon Islands war canoe at the British Museum: 3D documentation, virtual reconstruction and digital repatriation', In: Sablatnig, Robert, Kempel, Martin and Lettner, Martin (eds). *2009 15th International Conference on Virtual Systems and Multimedia, proceedings*. Los Alamitos, CA, IEEE Computer Society: 41–46. (http://espace.library.uq.edu.au/view/UQ:228767).

Hilliard, David (1966). 'Protestant Missions in the Solomon Islands, 1849–1942'. Unpublished PhD thesis, The Australian National University.

Hilliard, David (1969). 'The South Sea Evangelical Mission in the Solomon Islands: The foundation years', *The Journal of Pacific History*, 4: 41–64.

Hilliard, David (1974). 'Colonialism and Christianity: The Melanesian Mission in the Solomon Islands', *The Journal of Pacific History*, 9: 93–116.

Hilliard, David (1978). *God's Gentlemen: A history of the Melanesian Mission, 1849–1942*. St Lucia, University of Queensland Press.

Hocart, A. M. (1922). 'The Cult of the Dead in Eddystone of the Solomons', *The Journal of the Royal Anthropological Institute of Great Britain and Ireland*, 55: 71–112, 259–305.

Hocart, A. M. (1931). 'Warfare in Eddystone of the Solomon Islands', *The Journal of the Royal Anthropological Institute of Great Britain and Ireland*, 61: 301–324.

Hocart, A. M. (1932). '*The Island Builders of the Pacific* by W. G. Ivens: [review]', *Man*, 32: 268–269.

Hogbin, H. Ian (1930). 'The Problem of Depopulation in Melanesia as Applied to Ongtong Java (Solomon Islands)', *Oceania*, 39 (153): 43–66.

Hogbin, H. Ian (1932). 'Letter to the Editors, Journal of the Polynesian Society', *The Journal of the Polynesian Society*, 41 (163): 233–234.

Hogg, S. N. (1911). 'A Trip to the Solomons or Two Months on an Island Schooner', *The Queanbeyan Age*, Friday 28 April–Friday 30 June, 1911. [8 articles].

Hole, H. Marshall (1936). 'Pioneer Days in Southern Rhodesia', *Journal of the Royal African Society*, 35 (138): 37–47.

Hook, Milton (n.d.). *Vina Juapa Rane: Early Adventism in the Solomon Islands*. Wahroonga, NSW, Adventist Education, South Pacific Division, Department of Education. [SDA Heritage Series: booklet 29].

Hookey, J. F. (1971). 'The Establishment of a Plantation Economy in the British Solomon Islands Protectorate', In: Inglis, K. S. (ed.). *The History of Melanesia,*

2nd Waigani Seminar, 1968. Canberra, Research School of Pacific Studies, The Australian National University and the University of Papua New Guinea: 229–238.

Hooper, Steven (2006). *Pacific Encounters: Art and divinity in Polynesia, 1760–1860*. London, The British Museum Press.

Hopkins, Arthur Innes (1922). 'Depopulation in the Solomon Islands', In: Rivers, William Halse Rivers (ed.). *Essays on the Depopulation of Melanesia*. Cambridge, Cambridge University Press: 62–66.

Hopkins, Arthur Innes (1927). *Melanesia To-day: A study circle book*. London, Society for Promoting Christian Knowledge. (http://anglicanhistory.org/oceania/hopkins_today1927).

Hopkins, Arthur Innes (1934). 'Manuscript autobiography of the Reverend Arthur Hopkins.' Transcription of copy of typescript from Church of Melanesia deposited at National Archives in Honiara, Solomon Islands. Submitted to Project Canterbury by Dr David Akin. (http://anglicanhistory.org/oceania/aihopkins/ms1934.html).

Horthy, Nicholas (2000). *Admiral Nicholas Horthy: Memoirs*. Safety Harbour, FL, Simon Publications.

Howard-White, F. B. (1972). 'British Solomon Islands', *The London Philatelist*, 81 (959): 216–223. (Pacific Manuscript Bureau, PMB 1381/007).

Hughes, Ian (1978). 'Good Money and Bad: Inflation and devaluation in the colonial process', *Mankind*, 11: 308–318.

Hughes-D'Aeth, Tony (2001). *Paper Nation: The story of the Picturesque Atlas of Australasia, 1886–1888*. Melbourne, Melbourne University Press.

Hughes-Hughes, Walter Oldham (ed.) (1893). *The Register of Tonbridge School from 1820 to 1893*. London, Richard Bentley & Son. [Facsimile edition by Bibliolife, 2011].

Hulme, Peter and McDougall, Russell (eds) (2007). *Writing, Travel, and Empire: In the margins of anthropology*. London, I. B. Tauris.

Hviding, Edvard (1996). *Guardians of Marovo Lagoon: Practice, place, and politics in maritime Melanesia*. Honolulu, University of Hawai'i Press.

Hyam, Ronald (2002). *Britain's Imperial Century, 1815–1914: A study of empire and expansion*. 3rd edition. Basingstoke, Hampshire, Palgrave Macmilllan.

Ide, Henry C. (1899). 'The Imbroglio in Samoa', *The North American Review*, 168 (511): 679–693.

Ilbert, Courtenay (1899). 'Introduction to the Review of the Legislation of the Empire', *Journal of the Society of Comparative Legislation*, New series, 1 (1): xiii–xvi.

im Thurn, Everard Ferdinand (1967). *Among the Indians of Guiana: Being sketches chiefly anthropologic from the interior of British Guiana*. London, Dover Publications. [Unabridged re-publication of original 1883 edition].

im Thurn Everard Ferdinand (1887). 'The Botany of the Roraima Expedition of 1884', *The Transactions of the Linnean Society of London, 2nd Ser, Botany*, 2 (13).

im Thurn, Everard Ferdinand (1893). 'Anthropological Uses of the Camera', *The Journal of the Anthropological Institute of Great Britain and Ireland*, 22: 184–203.

im Thurn, Everard Ferdinand. (1909). 'The Western Pacific: Its history and present condition', *The Geographical Journal*, 34 (43): 271–288.

im Thurn, Everard Ferdinand (1913). 'Native Land and Labour in the South Seas', In: Hearnshaw, F. J. C. (ed.). *King's College Lectures on Colonial Problems*. London, G. Bell & Sons: 35–71.

im Thurn, Everard Ferdinand (1922).'Preface', In: Rivers, William Halse Rivers (ed.). *Essays on the Depopulation of Melanesia*. Cambridge, Cambridge University Press: v–xviii.

im Thurn, Everard Ferdinand (1934). *Thoughts, Talks and Tramps: A collection of papers*. Edited with a memoir by R. R. Marett. London, Oxford University Press.

Ingham, Kenneth (1969). 'New Light on the Emin Pasha Relief Expedition: Review: The Diary of A. J. Mounteney Jephson by Dorothy Middleton: A. J. Mounteney Jephson', *The Geographical Journal*, 135 (3): 408–409.

Inglis, K. S. (ed.) (1971). *The History of Melanesia, 2nd Waigani Seminar, 1968*. Canberra, Research School of Pacific Studies, The Australian National University and the University of Papua New Guinea.

Innes, Stephen (2007). 'From the Archives: Western Pacific Archives in their new home', *The Journal of Pacific History*, 42 (2): 265–273.

International Federation of Red Cross and Red Crescent Societies (2005). *Solomon Islands: From risk assessment to community actions*. Geneva, International Federation.

Ireland, Alleyne (1901). 'The Victorian Era of British expansion', *The North American Review*, 172 (533): 560–572.

Irvine, H. J. (2004). 'Sweet and Sour: Accounting for South Sea Islanders labour at a North Queensland sugar mill in the late 1800s', In: *Proceedings of the 10th World Congress of Accounting Historians, St Louis, Missouri and Oxford, Mississippi, USA, 1–5 August, 2004*. (http://ro.uow.edu.au/commpapers/126).

Irwin, Geoffrey (1973). 'Man–Land Relationships in Melanesia: An investigation of prehistoric settlement in the islands of the Bougainville Strait', *Archaeology in Oceania*, 8: 226–252.

Ivens, Walter G. (1918). *Dictionary and Grammar of the Ganguage of Sa'a and Ulawa, Solomon Islands*. Washington, Carnegie Institution of Washington.

Ivens, Walter G. (1926) 'Notes on the Spanish Account of the Solomon Islands, 1568', *The Geographical Journal*, 67 (4): 342–351.

Ivens, Walter G. (1930). *The Island Builders of the Pacific: How and why the people of Mala construct their artificial islands, the antiquity & doubtful origin of the practice, with a description of the social organization, magic, & religion of the inhabitants*. London, Seeley Service & Co.

Jack-Hinton, Colin (1962). 'The European Discovery, Rediscovery and Exploration of the Solomon Islands, 1568–1838'. Unpublished PhD thesis, The Australian National University.

Jackson, K. B. (1975). 'Head-hunting in the Christianization of Bugotu 1861–1900', *The Journal of Pacific History*, 10 (1): 65–78.

Jackson, K. B. (1978). 'Tie Hokara, Tie Vaka: Black man, White man: A study of the New Georgia group to 1925'. Unpublished PhD thesis, The Australian National University.

Jephson, A. J. Mounteney (1890). *Emin Pasha and the Rebellion at the Equator: A story of nine months' experiences in the last of the Soudan Provinces*. 3rd edition. London, Sampson Low, Marston, Searle and Rivington.

Jephson, A. J. Mounteney (1969). *The Diary of A. J. Mounteney Jephson: Emin Pasha Relief Expedition 1887–1889*. Edited by Dorothy Middleton. Cambridge, Cambridge University Press

Johanson, Kristiina (2006). 'The Contribution of Stray Finds for Studying Everyday Practices: The example of stone axes', *Estonian Journal of Archaeology*, 10 (2): 99–131.

Johnson, Niall P. A. S. and Mueller, Juergen (2002). 'Updating the Accounts: Global mortality of the 1918–1920 "Spanish" influenza pandemic', *Bulletin of Medical History*, 76: 105–115.

Johnston, Ewan (2005). 'Reinventing Fiji at 19th Century and Early 20th Century Exhibitions', *The Journal of Pacific History*, 40 (1): 23–44.

Johnston, W. Ross (1980). 'Captain Hamilton and the Labour Trade', *Journal of the Royal Society of Queensland*, 11(1): 48–61.

Jose, Arthur W. and Lucas, Walter Henry (1907). *'British Mismanagement in the Pacific Islands': Being a series of articles reprinted from the 'Sydney Morning Herald' October–November 1907*. Sydney, Websdale, Shoosmith & Co. [A second series of articles appeared in *The Sydney Morning Herald* in May–June 1915, titled *British Mismanagement in the Pacific No. 2*].

Joseph, Keith and Beu, Charles Browne (2008). 'Church and State in Solomon Islands', SSGM discussion paper 2008/11, Canberra, State Society and Governance in Melanesia, The Australian National University.

Joyce, R. B. (1971). 'William MacGregor: The role of the individual' In: Inglis, K. S. (ed.). *The History of Melanesia, 2nd Waigani Seminar, 1968*. Canberra, Research School of Pacific Studies, The Australian National University and the University of Papua New Guinea: 33–44.

Joynes, Sara and Powell, Graeme (2000). 'Pacific Sources Filmed in 1983–98 by the Australian Joint Copying Project', *The Journal of Pacific History*, 35(2): 219–231.

Kabui, Frank (1997). 'Crown Ownership of Foreshores and Seabed in Solomon Islands', *The Journal of Pacific Studies*, 21: 123–144.

Kabutaulaka, T. (2001). 'Beyond Ethnicity: The political economy of the Guadalcanal crisis in Solomon Islands', SSGM working paper 01/1, Canberra, State Society and Governance in Melanesia, The Australian National University.

Keesing, Roger M. (1967). 'Christians and Pagans in Kwaio, Malaita', *The Journal of the Polynesian Society*, 76: 82–100.

Keesing, Roger M. (1984). 'Rethinking "Mana"', *Journal of Anthropological Research*, 40 (1) (40th anniversary issue, 1944–1984): 137–156.

Keesing, Roger M. (1986). 'The *Young Dick* Attack: Oral and documentary history on the colonial frontier', *Ethnohistory*, 33 (3): 268–292.

Keesing, Roger M. (1990), 'Colonial history as Contested Ground: The Bell Massacre in the Solomons', *History and Anthropology*, 4: 279–301.

Keighren, Innes M. and Withers, Charles W. J. (2012). 'The Spectacular and the Sacred: Narrating landscape in works of travel', *Cultural Geographies*, 19 (1): 11–30.

Kelly's Directories Ltd (1903). *Kelly's Directory of Kent for 1903*. London, Kelly's Directories Ltd.

Kennedy, P. M. (1972). 'Bismarck's Imperialism: The case of Samoa, 1880–1890', *The Historical Journal*, 15 (2): 261–283.

Kirch, Patrick Vinton and Yen, D. E. (1982). *Tikopia: The prehistory and ecology of a Polynesian outlier*. Honolulu, Bishop Museum Press.

Kirsch, Stuart (2006). *Reverse Anthropology: Indigenous analysis of social and environmental relations in New Guinea*. Stanford, CA, Stanford University Press.

Klug, Heinz (1995). 'Defining the Property Rights of Others: Political power, Indigenous tenure and the construction of customary land law', *Journal of Legal Pluralism and Unofficial Law*, 35: 119–148.

Knapman, B. (1985). 'The Rise and Fall of the White Sugar Planter in Fiji 1880–1925', *Pacific Studies*, 9(1): 53–82.

Knauft, Bruce M. (1999). *From Primitive to Postcolonial in Melanesia and Anthropology*. Ann Arbor, University of Michigan Press.

Knibbs, S. G. C. (1929). *The Savage Solomons As They Were & Are: A record of a head-hunting people gradually emerging from a life of savage cruelty & bloody customs, with a description of their manners & ways & of the beauties & potentialities of the islands*. London, Seeley, Service & Co.

Kolshus, Thorgeir and Hovdhaugen, Even (2010), 'Reassessing the Death of Bishop John Coleridge Patteson', *The Journal of Pacific History*, 45 (3): 331–355.

Kuklick, Henrika (1996). 'Islands in the Pacific: Darwinian biogeography and British anthropology', *American Ethnologist*, 23 (3): 611–638.

Kupiainen, Jari (n.d.) 'The Stolen Museum: The Stolen Heritage: Issues of protecting cultural heritage in the Solomon Islands'. Unpublished translation by author. [Originally published as 'Varastettu museo, varastettu perinne- kysymyksiä kulttuuriperinnön suojaamisesta Melanesiassa' with the film, 'The Stolen Museum'. *EloreJournal of the Finnish Folklore Society.* 1/2009. 1–15.] (http://www.elore.fi/arkisto/1_09/art_kupiainen_1_09.pdf; http://www.elore.fi/arkisto/1_09/kupiainen.mov).

Kupiainen, Jari (2000). *Tradition, trade and woodcarving in Solomon Islands.* Transactions of the Finnish Anthropological Society 45. Helsinki, Finland & Højberg, Denmark, The Finnish Anthropological Society and Intervention Press.

Lamour, Peter (1984). 'Alienated Land and Independence in Melanesia', *Pacific Studies*, 8 (1): 1–47.

Laracy, Hugh (1976). *Marists and Melanesians: A history of Catholic missions in the Solomon Islands.* Canberra, Australian National University Press.

Laracy, Hugh (2000). 'Niels Peter Sorensen: The story of a criminal adventurer', *The Journal of Pacific History*, 35: 147–162.

Laracy, Hugh (2001). '"Quixotic and Utopian": American adventurers in the southwest Pacific, 1897–1898', *Pacific Studies*, 24 (1–2): 39–62.

Laracy, Hugh (ed.), Alasia, Sam *et al.* (1989). *Ples Blong Iumi: Solomon Islands, the past four thousand years.* Suva, Fiji, Institute of Pacific Studies of the University of the South Pacific.

Laracy, Hugh and Laracy, Eugénie (1980). 'Custom, Conjugality and Colonial rule in the Solomon Islands', *Oceania*, 51 (2): 133–147.

Larson, Eric H. (1968). 'Tikopian Labour Migration to the Russell Islands', *The Journal of the Polynesian Society*, 77 (2): 163–176.

Larson, Eric H. (1970). 'Tikopia Plantation Labour and Company Management Relations', *Oceania*, 40 (3): 195–209.

Lascelles, A. G. *et al.*(1900). 'Modes of Legislation in the British Colonies', *Journal of the Society of Comparative Legislation*, New series, 2 (1): 86–117.

Lattas, Andrew (1996). 'Humanitarianism and Australian Nationalism in Colonial Papua: Hubert Murray and the project of caring for the self of the coloniser and colonised', *The Australian Journal of Anthropology*, 7 (2): 141–164.

Lattas, Andrew and Rio, Knut M. (2011). 'Securing Modernity: Towards an ethnography of power in contemporary Melanesia', *Oceania*, 81(1): 1–21.

Lātūkefu, Sione (1971). 'The Methodist Mission and Modernization in the Solomon Islands', In: Inglis, K. S. (ed.). *The History of Melanesia, 2ⁿᵈ Waigani Seminar, 1968*. Canberra, Research School of Pacific Studies, The Australian National University and the University of Papua New Guinea: 305–318.

Lātūkefu, Sione (ed.) (1989). *Papua New Guinea: A century of colonial impact, 1884–1984*. Port Moresby, The National Research Institute and the University of Papua New Guinea.

Law, Gwillim (2011). 'Provinces of Solomon Islands' [Statistics]. (http://www.statoids.com/usb.html).

Lawrence, David Russell (1994). 'Customary Exchange Across Torres Strait', *Memoirs of the Queensland Museum*, 34 (2): 241–446.

Lawrence, David Russell (2000). *Kakadu: The making of a national park*. Melbourne, Melbourne University Press/Miegunyah Press.

Lawrence, David Russell (2005). 'The Early Ethnographic Writings of E. W. Pearson Chinnery: Government anthropologist of New Guinea', 2005 Frederick Watson Fellowship Paper, National Archives of Australia. (http://www.naa.gov.au/Images/Lawrence_tcm16-35760.pdf).

Lawrence, David Russell (2010a). *Gunnar Landtman in Papua: 1910 to 1912*. Canberra, ANU E Press. (http://press.anu.edu.au/titles/gunnar_citation/).

Lawrence, David Russell (2010b). 'Completing the Circle: "Reading" the story behind a century of images from the Torres Strait and the Fly River 1898–1998', 2010 scholar-in-residence paper, National Film and Sound Archive.

Lawrence, David Russell, Allen, Matthew, et al. (2006–2007) *Hem nao, Solomon Islands, tis taem: Reports of the CSP Community Snapshot, Honiara, Solomon Islands*. Volume 1: Provincial Profiles; Volume 2: Main Report; Volume 3: Provincial Perspectives. Canberra, AusAID.

Lawrence, David Russell, Kenchington, Richard and Woodley, Simon (2002). *The Great Barrier Reef: Finding the right balance*. Melbourne, Melbourne University Press.

Layton, W. T. (1908). 'Changes in the Wages of Domestic Servants During Fifty Years', *Journal of the Royal Statistical Society*, 71 (3): 515–524.

Leavesley, Matthew G. (2007). 'A Shark-tooth Ornament from Pleistocene Sahul', *Antiquity*, 81 (312): 308–315.

Lett, Lewis (1944). *The Papuan Achievement*. 2ⁿᵈ edition. Melbourne, Melbourne University Press.

Lett, Lewis (1949). *Sir Hubert Murray of Papua*. London, Collins.

Lever, R. A. (1974). 'Nature Lover Who Ruled the Solomons', *Pacific Islands Monthly*, September 1974: 59, 101.

Lewis, David (1977). *From Maui to Cook: The discovery and settlement of the Pacific*. Sydney, Doubleday.

Lindt, J. W. (1887). *Picturesque New Guinea*. London, Longmans, Green and Co. [Photographs held at Mitchell Library Q988 4/L].

London, Jack (1911). *Adventure*. New York, Macmillan.

Lord Amherst of Hackney and Thomson, Basil (eds) (1901). *The Discovery of the Solomon Islands by Alvaro de Mendaña in 1568*. 2 volumes. London, Hakluyt Society. [Translated from the original Spanish manuscripts].

Lorimer, Douglas (1988). 'Theoretical Racism in Late-Victorian Anthropology, 1870–1900', *Victorian Studies*, 31 (3): 405–430.

Lowie, Robert H. (1915). 'Oceania: The History of Melanesian Society [review]', *American Anthropologist*, New series, 17: 588–591.

Lucas, C. P. (1913). 'The Influence of Science of Empire', In: Hearnshaw, F. J. C. (ed.). *King's College Lectures on Colonial Problems*. London, G. Bell & Sons: 109–139.

Lucas, Walter Henry (1911). Album of photographs of British and German New Guinea and New Britain [Album 783]. Canberra, National Library of Australia.

Ludlow, Peter (2009). 'A brief history of Peel Island'. (http://historianludlow.com/Historian_Ludlow/Peel_Island_Quest.html).

Lye, William F. (1967). 'The Difaqane: The Mfecane in the Southern Sotho area, 1822–24', *The Journal of African History*, 8 (1): 107–131.

McArthur, Norma (1970). 'The Demography of Primitive Populations', *Science*, New series, 167 (3921): 1097–1101.

Macdonald, Barrie (1972). 'Te Reitaki n Nonouti: A survival of traditional authority in the Gilbert Islands', *The Journal of Pacific History*, 7: 137–150.

Macdonald, Barrie (1978). 'Grimble of the Gilbert Islands: Myth and man', In: Scarr, Deryck (ed.). *More Pacific Islands Portraits*. Canberra, Australian National University Press: 193–209.

Macdonald, Barrie (2001). *Cinderellas of the Empire: Towards a history of Kiribati and Tuvalu*. Suva, Institute of Pacific Studies, University of the South Pacific. [First published by The Australian National University Press in 1982].

McDougall, Russell (2007). 'Henry Ling Roth in Tasmania', In: Hulme, Peter and McDougall, Russell (eds). *Writing, Travel and Empire: In the margins of anthropology*. London, I. B. Tauris & Co: 43–68.

MacGillivray, John (1852–1854). *Voyage of HMS Herald under the command of Captain H. Mangles Denham (RN)*. London, Faber Microfilms Library. (http://trove.nla.gov.au/work/18910776).

McGowan, Patrick J. and Kordan, Bohdan (1981). 'Imperialism in World-system Perspective: Britain 1870–1914', *International Studies Quarterly*, 25 (1), World System Debates: 43–68.

Macintyre, Martha and Mackenzie, Maureen (1992). 'Focal Length as an Analogue of Colonial Distance', In: Edwards, Elizabeth (ed.). *Anthropology and Photography: 1860–1920*. New Haven, Yale University Press: 158–164.

MacIver, Henry Ronald H. Douglas (1885) *Rivals for Supremacy in the Pacific: a book for every British subject*. Sydney, Gibbs, Shallard & Co. (Pacific Manuscript Bureau, Woodford papers PMB 1381/035).

McKinnon, J. M. (1975), 'Tomahawks, Turtles and Traders: A reconstruction in the circular causation of warfare in the New Georgia Group', *Oceania*, 45 (4): 290–307.

McLaren, Jack (1923). *My Odyssey*. London, Jonathon Cape.

McLaren, Jack (1940). *Gentlemen of the Empire: The colourful and remarkable experiences of District Commissioners, Patrol Officers and other officials in some of the British Empire's tropical outposts*. London, Hutchinson.

McLaren, Jack (1940). *Gentlemen of the Empire*. London, Hutchinson & Co.

Maclean, Neil (1998). 'Mimesis and Pacification: The colonial legacy in Papua New Guinea', *History and Anthropology*, 11 (1): 75–118.

Macleod, Roy (1993). 'Passages in Imperial Science: From Empire to Commonwealth', *Journal of World History*, 4(1): 117–150.

McMahon, Thomas J. (1918). '"Some" Plates: What can be done with Austral "Anti-therm plates"', *The Australasian Photo-Review*, March 15, 1918: 157. (State Library of Victoria, Officer 1901 MS 9321).

Macmillan, David S. (1957). *A Squatter Went to Sea: The story of Sir William Macleay's New Guinea Expedition (1875) and his life in Sydney.* Sydney, Currawong Publishing Co.

Mahaffy, Arthur (1902). 'The Solomon Islands', *The Empire Review*, September 1902: 190–196.

Mahaffy, Arthur (1910a). 'Ocean Island', *Blackwood's Magazine*, 188 (1141): 569–585.

Mahaffy, Arthur (1910b). *Western Pacific: Report by Mr Arthur Mahaffy on a visit to the Gilbert and Ellice Islands, 1909.* London, HMSO. (C.4992). [Cited as Great Britain. House of Commons. Parliamentary Papers 1910].

Maiden, Peter (2003). *Missionaries, Headhunters and Colonial Officers.* Rockhampton, Central Queensland University Press.

Mair, L. P. (1970). *Australia in New Guinea.* 2nd edition. Melbourne, Melbourne University Press.

Marett, R. R. (1932). 'Sir Everard im Thurn', *Folklore*, 43 (4): 455–456.

Markham, A. H. (1871–1872). 'The New Hebrides and Santa Cruz Groups, South-West Pacific', *Proceedings of the Royal Geographical Society of London*, 16 (5): 388–395.

Markham, A. H. (1872). 'The New Hebrides and Santa Cruz Groups', *Journal of the Royal Geographical Society of London*, 48: 213–243.

Markham, Sir Clements (1904). *The Voyages of Pedro Fernandez de Quiros, 1595 to 1606.* 2 volumes. London, Hakluyt Society.

Mather, Patricia (1986). *A Time for a Museum: The history of the Queensland Museum, 1862–1986.* Brisbane, Queensland Museum.

Mathew, Gervase F. (1887). 'Descriptions of Some New Species of Rhopalocera from the Solomon Islands', *Transactions of the Entomological Society of London*, 1887: 37–50.

Maude, H. C. and Maude, H. E. (1932). 'The Social Organization of Banaba or Ocean Island, Central Pacific', *The Journal of the Polynesian Society*, 41 (164): 262–301.

Maude, H. E. and Leeson, Ida (1965). 'The Coconut Oil Trade of the Gilbert Islands', *The Journal of the Polynesian Society*, 74 (4): 396–437.

May, R. J. and Nelson, Hank (1982). *Melanesia: Beyond diversity*. 2 volumes. Canberra, Research School of Pacific Studies, The Australian National University.

Mayer, Carol E. (2006). 'The Traveller and the Island Belle: Frank Burnett's photography in the Pacific', *The Journal of Pacific Studies*, 29 (2): 217–242.

Mayo, John (1973). 'A Punitive Expedition in British New Guinea, 1886', *The Journal of Pacific History*, 8: 89–99.

Mayr, Ernst (1932). 'Birds Collected During the Whitney South Sea Expedition XIX: Notes on the bronze Cuckoo *Chalcites lucidus* and its subspecies', *American Museum Novitates*, 520: 1–9.

Megarrity, Lyndon (2006). '"White Queensland": The Queensland Government's ideological position on the use of Pacific Island labourers in the sugar sector 1880–1901', *Australian Journal of Politics and History*, 52(1): 1–12.

Mercer, P. M. and Moore, C. R. (1976). 'Melanesians in North Queensland: The retention of indigenous religious and magical practices', *The Journal of Pacific History*, 11 (1), Labour Trade, Part 1: 66–88.

Middleton, Dorothy (1972). 'The Search for the Nile Sources', *The Geographical Journal*, 138 (2): 209–221.

Miller, Daniel (1978). 'An Organizational Approach to Exchange Media: An example from the Western Solomons', *Mankind*, 11: 288–295.

Miller, Daniel (1980). 'Settlement and Diversity in the Solomon Islands', *Man*, New series, 15(3): 451–466.

Molesworth, B. H. (1917). 'Kanaka Labour in Queensland', *Journal of the Royal Historical Society of Queensland*, 1 (3): 140–154.

Monckton, H. & Monckton, E. P; Woodford, C. M. & Woodford, F. M. (1909–1928). *Correspondence, British Solomon Islands, 1909–1928*. (Pacific Manuscrips Bureau, PMB 1021).

Montgomery, H. H. (1904). *The Light of Melanesia: A record of fifty years mission work in the South Seas*. New York, E. S. Gorham. (http://anglicanhistory.org/aus/melanesia/montgomery1904).

Moore, Clive (1981). 'Kanakas, Kidnapping and Slavery: Myths from the Nineteenth Century Labour Trade and their relevance to Australian Melanesians', *Kabar Seberang/Sulating Maphilindo*, 8–9: 78–92.

Moore, Clive (1985). *Kanaka: A history of Melanesian Mackay*. Port Moresby, Institute of Papua New Guinea Studies and University of Papua New Guinea Press.

Moore, Clive (2000). '"Good-bye Queensland, good-bye White Australia; Good-bye Christians": Australia's South Sea Islander community and deportation, 1901–1908', *The New Federalist*, 4: 22–29.

Moore, Clive (2004). *Happy Isles in Crisis: The historical causes for a failing state in Solomon Islands, 1998–2004*. Canberra, Asia Pacific Press.

Moore, Clive (2007). 'The Misappropriation of Malaitan Labour', *The Journal of Pacific History*, 42(2): 211–232.

Moore, Clive (2008a). 'Anglican Missions to South Sea Islanders in Queensland, 1880s–1900s', *Journal of the Royal Historical Society of Queensland*, 20 (7): 296–320.

Moore, Clive (2008b). 'Biography of a Nation: Compiling a historical dictionary of the Solomon Islands', In: Lal, Brij V. and Luker, Vicki (eds). *Telling Pacific Lives: Prisms of process*. Canberra, ANU E Press: 277–292.

Moore, Clive (2009a). *Florence Young and the Queensland Kanaka Mission, 1886–1906: Beginnings of an Indigenous Pacific church*, Solomon Islands Museum Occasional Paper No. 2, December 2009, Honiara, Solomon Islands Museum.

Moore, Clive (2009b). 'Tulagi: Imagining the British Empire in the Pacific', unpublished paper presented at the Pacific History Association Conference, Suva, Fiji, December 2009.

Moore, Clive (2010). *Decolonising the Solomon Islands: British theory and Melanesian practice*. Melbourne, Alfred Deakin Research Institute, Deakin University.

Moore, Clive (2013a). 'Peter Ambu'ofa and the Founding of the South Sea Evangelical Mission in the Solomon Islands, 1894–1904', *Journal of Pacific History*: 1–20.

Moore, Clive (2013b). 'The Pacific Islanders' Fund and the Misappropriation of the Wages of Deceased Pacific Islanders by the Queensland Government', HPRC Public Lecture, University of Queensland. (http://www.uq.edu.au/hprc/docs/ASSI-Pacific-Islanders-Fund-Moore-15-August-2013.pdf).

Moore, H. E. (1969). 'A Preliminary Analysis of the Palm Flora of the Solomon Islands', *Philosophical Transactions of the Royal Society of London, Series B, Biological sciences*, 255 (800): 589–593. [A discussion of the results of the Royal Society Expedition to the British Solomon Islands Protectorate, 1965].

Moorhouse, Harry C. (1929) *Report of Commissioner Appointed by the Secretary of State for the Colonies to Inquire into the Circumstances in Which Murderous Attacks Took Place in 1927 on Government Officials on Guadalcanal and Malaita*. London, HMSO. (C.3248). [Report by Sir Harry C. Moorhouse. Cited as British Solomon Islands Protectorate (1929)].

Moresby, John (1876). *New Guinea and Polynesia: Discoveries and surveys in New Guinea and the D'Entrecasteaux Islands: A cruise in Polynesia and visits to the pearl-shelling stations of HMS Basilisk*. London, John Murray. [Facsimile edition by Adamant Media Corporation, 2005].

Morrell, W. P. (1960). *Britain in the Pacific Islands*. Oxford, Clarendon Press.

Mortensen, Reid (2000). 'Slaving in Australian Courts: Blackbirding cases, 1869–1871', *Journal of South Pacific Law*, 4: 1–19.

Morton, Alexander (1883). 'Notes on a Cruise to the Solomon Islands', *Proceedings of the Linnean Society of New South Wales*, Series 1, 7: 59–66.

Morton, Christopher and Edwards, Elizabeth (eds) (2009). *Photography, Anthropology and History: Expanding the frame*. Farnham, UK, Ashgate.

Morus, Iwan Rhys (1996). 'Manufacturing Nature: Science, technology and the Victorian consumer culture', *The British Journal for the History of Science*, 29 (4): 403–434.

Mosby, Tom and Robinson, Brian (1998). *Ilan pasin (This Is Our Way): Torres Strait art*. Cairns, Cairns Regional Gallery.

Mullins, Steve (2012). 'The Andrew Goldie Manuscript', *Memoirs of the Queensland Museum—Culture*, 6: 1–5.

Mullins, Steve and Bellamy, Martin (2012). 'Andrew Goldie: The experience of empire', *Memoirs of the Queensland Museum—Culture*, 6: 7–38.

Mullins, Steve, Bellamy, Martin and Moore, Clive (eds) (2012). 'Andrew Goldie in New Guinea 1875–1879: Memoir of a natural history collector', *Memoirs of the Queensland Museum—Culture*, 6: iii–216.

Munro, Doug (1992). 'Gilbert and Ellice Islanders on Queensland Canefields, 1884–1899', *Royal Queensland Historical Society Journal*, 14 (11): 449–465. [Paper presented to the monthly meeting of the Royal Historical Society of Queensland, September 26, 1991].

Munro, Doug (1995a). 'The Labor Trade in Melanesian to Queensland: An historiographic essay', *Journal of Social History*, 28(3): 609–627.

Munro, Doug (1995b). 'Review: Revisionism and its enemies: Debating the Queensland labour trade', *The Journal of Pacific History*, 30(2): 240–249.

Munro, Doug and Firth, Stewart (1987). 'From Company Rule to Consular Control: Gilbert Island labourers on German plantations in Samoa, 1867–96', *Journal of Imperial and Commonwealth History*, 16: 24–44.

Munro, Doug and Firth, Stewart (1990). 'German Labour Policy and the Partition of the Western Pacific: The view from Samoa', *The Journal of Pacific History*, 25 (1): 85–102.

Munro, Doug and Firth, Stewart (2003). 'Towards Colonial Protectorates: The case of the Gilbert and Ellice Islands', In: Samson, Jane (ed.). *British Imperial Strategies in the Pacific, 1750–1900*. Aldershot, Hampshire, Ashgate Variorum: 233–241. [Reprinted from *The Australian Journal of Politics and History*, 32 (1986): 63–71].

Munro, Doug, McCreery, David and Firth, Stewart (2004). 'Migrant Labourers as British Protected Persons', *The Journal of Pacific Studies*, 27 (2): 141–160.

Murray, J. H. P. (1912). *Papua or British New Guinea*. London, Fisher Unwin.

Murray, J. H.P. (1932). *The Scientific Aspect of Pacification of Papua*. Port Moresby, Government Printer.

Murray, J. H. P. (1933). 'Depopulation in Papua', *Oceania*, 3 (2): 207–213.

Musgrove, F. (1959). 'Middle-class Education and Employment in the Nineteenth Century', *The Economic History Review*, New series, 12 (1): 99–111.

Mühlhäusler, Peter (1976). 'Samoan Plantation English and the Origins of New Guinea Pidgin: An introduction', *The Journal of Pacific History*, 11(2), Labour Trade, Part 2: 122–125.

Mytinger, Caroline (1942). *Headhunting in the Solomon Islands: Around the Coral Sea*. New York, Macmillan.

Nagaoka, Takuya (2000). 'Hope and Other Sacred Places in Kokopara'. Auckland, University of Auckland. (http://westernsolomons.uib.no/docs/Nagaoka,%20 Takuya/Nagaoka_2000.pdf).

Nagaoka, Takuya (2011). 'Late Prehistoric–Early Historic Houses and Settlement Space on Nusa Roviana, New Georgia group, Solomon Islands'. Unpublished PhD thesis, University of Auckland. (https://researchspace.auckland.ac.nz/handle/2292/9507).

Naitoro, John Houainamo (2000). 'Solomon Islands Conflict: Demands for historical rectification and restorative justice', Asia Pacific School of Economics and Management Update Paper, June 2000, Canberra, Asia Pacific School of Economics and Management, The Australian National University.

National Archives of Australia (1904–1907). Reports and papers presented to the Papua Royal Commission. (A1, 1904/6164; A1, 1905/3780 Parts 1–19; A1 1907/1457, 1458, 1459, 1995, 3042, 4458 and 4653).

National Archives of Australia (1911a). 'Visit of Members of Parliament to Papua'. (A1, 1911/16361).

National Archives of Australia (1911b). 'Miscellaneous correspondence re visit Federal Members of Parlt [Parliament] to Papua'. (A1, 1911/3212).

National Archives of Australia (1911c). 'Replies from members of Parliament re visit to Papua'. (A1, 1911/3513).

Nelson, Hank (1971). 'Hubert Murray: Private letters and public reputation', *Australian Historical Studies*, 14: 612–621.

Nelson, Hank (1982). *Taim bilong Masta: The Australian involvement with Papua New Guinea*. Sydney, Australian Broadcasting Commission.

Newbury, Colin (1981). 'The Melanesian Labour Reserve: Some reflections on Pacific labor markets in the Nineteenth Century', *Pacific Studies*, 4 (1): 1–25.

Newbury, Colin (2010). *Patronage and Politics in the Victorian Empire: The personal governance of Sir Arthur Gordon (Lord Stanmore)*. Amherst, NY, Cambria Press.

Norris, Rachel M. (2002). 'Morphology and Systematics of the Solomon Island *Ranid* Frogs'. Unpublished PhD thesis, University of Adelaide.

North, Alfred J. (1906–1907). 'Description of a New Genus and Species of Honey-eater from Rennell Island, Solomon Group', *The Victorian Naturalist*, 23: 104–105.

O'Brien, Aoife (2011). 'Collecting the Solomon Islands: Colonial encounters and Indigenous experiences in the Solomon Island collections of Charles Morris Woodford and Arthur Mahaffy (1886–1915)'. Unpublished PhD thesis, University of East Anglia, School of World Art Studies and Museology, Sainsbury Research Unit for the Arts of Africa, Oceania and the Americas.

O'Brien, Patricia (2009). 'Remaking Australia's Colonial Culture?: White Australia and its Papuan frontier, 1901–1940', *Australian Historical Studies*, 40 (1): 96–112.

O'Ferrall, W. C. (1908). *Santa Cruz and the Reef Islands*. Westminster, The Melanesian Mission. (http://anglicanhistory.org/oceania/oferrall_santacruz1908). [Photos by J. W. Beattie].

O'Ferrall, W. C. (1922). 'The Depopulation of Santa Cruz and the Reef Islands', In: Rivers, William Halse Rivers (ed.). *Essays on the Depopulation of Melanesia*. Cambridge, Cambridge University Press: 67–68.

Officer, Graham (1901–). Diaries, papers and reprints. (State Library of Victoria, MS 9321, Box sequence 4332/1–6).

Ogilvie-Grant, W. R. (1887). 'A List of the Birds Collected by Mr. Charles Morris Woodford in the Solomon Archipelago', *Proceedings of the Zoological Society of London*, 55 (2): 328–333. (Woodford papers PMB 1290 Item 7/21/3).

Ogilvie-Grant, W. R. (1888). 'Second List of the Birds Collected by Mr. C. M. Woodford in the Solomon Islands', *Proceedings of the Zoological Society of London*, 56: 185–204.

O'Hanlon, Michael (2000). 'Introduction', In: O'Hanlon, Michael and Welsch, Robert L. (eds). *Hunting the Gatherers: Ethnographic collectors, agents and agency in Melanesia, 1870s–1930s*. New York, Berghahn Books: 1–34.

O'Hanlon, Michael and Welsch, Robert L. (eds). (2000). *Hunting the Gatherers: Ethnographic collectors, agents and agency in Melanesia, 1870s–1930s*. New York, Berghahn Books.

Ohff, Hans-Jürgen (2008). 'Empires of Enterprise: German and English commercial interests in east New Guinea, 1884 to 1914'. Unpublished PhD thesis, University of Adelaide. (http://digital.library.adelaide.edu.au/dspace/handle/2440/48479).

Oliver, Douglas (1973). *Bougainville: A personal history*. Melbourne, Melbourne University Press.

Oliver, Roland and Atmore, Anthony (2001). *Medieval Africa, 1250–1800*. Cambridge, Cambridge University Press.

O'Neill, Sally (1969), 'Coote, Audley (1839–1915)', In *Australian Dictionary of Biography*, Volume 3, Melbourne, Melbourne University Press. (http://adb.anu.edu.au/biography/coote-audley-3256).

Orchard, Barry (1991). *A Look at the Head and the Fifty: A history of Tonbridge School*. London, James & James.

Overlack, Peter (1973). 'German New Guinea: A diplomatic, economic and political survey', *Journal of the Royal Historical Society of Queensland*, 9 (4): 128–152.

Overlack, Peter (1998). '"Bless the Queen and curse the Colonial Office": Australasian reaction to German consolidation in the Pacific 1871–99', *The Journal of Pacific History*, 33 (2): 133–152.

Owen, Janet (2006). 'Collecting Artefacts, Acquiring Empire', *Journal of the History of Collections*, 18 (1): 9–25.

Pacific Islands Company Ltd (1840–1914). Legal papers, agreements, reports, notes and press cuttings on islands. (PMB 1205 MP1174/1/172–MP1174 1/323).

Pacific Islands Company Ltd and Pacific Phosphate Company Ltd (1897–1909). Australian office, correspondence files. (PMB 1176).

Pacific Phosphate Company Ltd (1900–1921). Sydney and Melbourne offices, Ocean Island and Nauru correspondence. (PMB 1206).

Palmer, George (1871). *Kidnapping in the South Seas: Being a narrative of a three months cruise of HM Ship "Rosario"*. Harmondsworth, Penguin. [Facsimile edition published in 1973].

Papua (1906/07–1940/41). Reels 1–3. *Annual reports*. (PMB DOC 313).

Parkinson, Richard (1887–1888). 'Beiträge zur Kenntnis des deutschen Schutzgebietes in der Südsee', *Geographische Gesellschaft Hamburg, Mitteilungen*: 201–283. [Contribution to the knowledge of the German protectorates in the South Seas].

Parkinson, Richard (1999). *Thirty Years in the South Seas*. Honolulu and Bathurst, University of Hawai'i Press and Crawford House. [Translation of *Dreißig Jahre in der Südsee* 1907].

Parnaby, Owen W. (1972). 'The Labour Trade', In: Ward, R. Gerard (ed.). *Man in the Pacific Islands*. Oxford, Clarendon Press: 124–144.

Parsonson, G. S. (2010). 'Inglis, John', *Te Ara: The Encyclopaedia of New Zealand*. (http://www.teara.govt.nz/en/biographies/1i1).

Patterson, K. David (1975). 'The Vanishing Mpongwe: European contact and demographic change in the Gabon River', *The Journal of African History*, 16 (2): 217–238.

Patteson, J. C. (1871). 'South Sea Island Labour Traffic', In: *Appendices to the Journals of the New Zealand House of Representatives*, 1871, G-35. (http://anglicanhistory.org/nz/patteson/traffic1871.html).

Pels, Peter (1997). 'The Anthropology of Colonialism: Culture, history, and the emergence of Western governmentality', *Annual Review of Anthropology*, 26: 163–183.

Penny, Alfred (1888). *Ten Years in Melanesia*. London, W. Gardner, Darton & Co. (http://anglicanhistory.org/oceania/penny1888/).

Pentony, B. (1954). 'Psychological Causes of Depopulation of Primitive Groups', *Oceania*, 24: 142–145.

Perkins, Hannah and Quanchi, Max (2010). 'To the Islands: Photographs of tropical colonies in *The Queenslander*', *History Compass*, 8 (1): 11–31.

Perry, W. J. (1923). *The Children of the Sun: A study in the early history of civilization*. London, Methuen.

Petch, A. (2007). 'Notes and Queries and the Pitt Rivers Museum', *Museum Anthropology*, 30: 21–39.

Petterson, M. G. et al. (2003). 'The Eruptive History and Volcanic Hazards of Savo, Solomon Islands', *Bulletin of Volcanology*, 65 (2–3): 165–181.

Philp, Jude (2001). *Past Time: Torres Strait Islander material from the Haddon Collection, 1888–1905*. Canberra, National Museum of Australia.

Philp, Jude (2004). '"Embryonic science": The 1898 Torres Strait photographic collection of A. C. Haddon', In: Davis, Richard (ed.). *Woven Histories, Dancing Lives: Torres Strait Islander identity, culture and history*. Canberra, Aboriginal Studies Press: 90–106.

Phimister, I. R. (1974). 'Rhodes, Rhodesia and the Rand', *Journal of Southern African Studies*, 1 (1): 74–90.

Poignant, Roslyn (1992). 'Surveying the Field of View: The making of the RAI Photographic Collection', In: Edwards, Elizabeth (ed.). *Anthropology and Photography: 1860–1920*. New Haven, Yale University Press: 42–73.

Price, Charles A. and Baker, Elizabeth (1976). 'Origins of Pacific Island Labourers in Queensland, 1863–1904: A research note', *The Journal of Pacific History*, 11 (2), Labour Trade, Part 2: 106–121.

Pringle, Thomas (1835). *Narrative of a Residence in South Africa*. London, Edward Moxon.

Protectorate of British Solomon Islands (1909). *Statistics to 31st March, 1909 complied by the Resident Commissioner*. Sydney, Turner and Henderson. (Woodford papers PMB 1290 Item 8/16).

Quanchi, Max (2003). 'Contrary Images: Photographing the new Pacific in "Walkabout" magazine', *Journal of Australian Studies*, 27 (79): 77–92.

Quanchi, Max (2004). 'Jewel of the Pacific and Planter's Paradise: The visual argument for Australian sub-Imperialism in the Solomon Islands', *The Journal of Pacific History*, 39 (1): 43–58.

Quanchi, Max (2006). 'Photography and History in the Pacific Islands', *The Journal of Pacific History*, 41 (2): 165–173.

Quanchi, Max (2007). *Photographing Papua: Representation, colonial encounters and imaging in the public domain*. Newcastle UK, Cambridge Scholars Publishing.

Quanchi, Max (2008). 'To the Islands: Photographs of tropical colonies in *The Queenslander*'. Paper presented to the 18th Pacific History Association Conference, December 2008, University of the South Pacific, Suva.

Queensland Art Gallery/Gallery of Modern Art (2011). *The Torres Strait Islands: A celebration*. Brisbane, Queensland Art Gallery/Gallery of Modern Art.

Queensland. Department of Immigration. Pacific Island Labour Branch (1900). 'Vessels engaged in Pacific Island Trade since the 31st May 1838'. (Woodford papers PMB 1290 Item 8/26).

Queensland. Royal Commission appointed to inquire into the circumstances under which labourers have been introduced into Queensland from New Guinea and other islands etc. (1885) *Recruiting Polynesian labourers in New Guinea and adjacent islands: Report with minutes of evidence*. Commissioners: John F. Buckland, W Kinniard Rose, Hugh M. Milman, W. C. Lawrie, Secretary. Brisbane, Government Printer. [Also known as the Polynesian Labour Commission, 1885. The report of the Royal Commission was subsequently published in the *Brisbane Courier*, Monday 4 May 1885: 2–3 under the title *The Labour Trade*].

Queensland. Sugar Industry Labour Commission (1906). *Report with Minutes of Proceedings and Appendices*. Chairman: RA Ranking. Brisbane, Government Printer.

Quinnell, Michael (2000). '"Before it has become too late": The making and repatriation of Sir William MacGregor's official collection from British New Guinea', In: O'Hanlon, Michael and Welsch, Robert L. (eds). *Hunting the Gatherers: Ethnographic collectors, agents and agency in Melanesia, 1870s–1930s*. New York, Berghahn Books: 81–102.

Quiggin, A. Hingston (1949). *A Survey of Primitive Money: The beginnings of currency*. Strand, Methuen & Co.

Raffles, Hugh (2001). 'The Uses of Butterflies', *American Ethnologist*, 26 (3): 513–548.

Rainbow, W. J. (1913). 'Arachnida from the Solomon Islands, *Records of the Australian Museum*, 10 (1): 1–16.

Ramsay, E. P. (1879a). 'Contributions to the Zoology of New Guinea, Parts I and II', *Proceedings of the Linnean Society of New South Wales*, Series 1, 3: 241–305.

Ramsay, E. P. (1879b). 'Contributions to the Zoology of New Guinea, Part III', *Proceedings of the Linnean Society of New South Wales*, Series 1, 3: 402–405.

Ramsay, E. P. (1880a). 'Notes on Birds from the Solomon Islands', *Proceedings of the Linnean Society of New South Wales*, Series 1, 4: 313–318.

Ramsay, E. P. (1880b). 'Notes on the Zoology of the Solomon Islands, Part I. Aves', *Proceedings of the Linnean Society of New South Wales*, Series 1, 4: 65–84.

Ramsay, E. P. (1882a). 'Description of Two New Birds from the Solomon Islands', *Proceedings of the Linnean Society of New South Wales*, Series 1, 6: 833–834.

Ramsay, E. P. (1882b). 'Notes on the Zoology of the Solomon Islands with Descriptions of Some New Birds: Part II', *Proceedings of the Linnean Society of New South Wales*, Series 1, 6: 176–180.

Ramsay, E. P. (1882c). 'Notes on the Zoology of the Solomon Islands with Descriptions of Some New Birds, Part III', *Proceedings of the Linnean Society of New South Wales*, Series 1, 6: 718–726.

Ramsay, E. P. and Ogilby, J. Douglas (1890). 'Report on the Zoological Collection from the Solomon Islands. Part 1 by E. P. Ramsay; Part II by J. Douglas Ogilby', *Records of the Australian Museum*, 1: 3–7.

Rapaport, Moshe (2006). 'Eden in Peril: Impact of humans on Pacific Island ecosystems', *Island Studies Journal*, 1 (1): 109–124.

Ravenstein, E. G. (1904). 'Obituary: Henry Morton Stanley', *The Geographical Journal*, 24 (1): 103–106.

Rechinger, Karl (1907–1914). *Botanische und zoologische Ergebnisse einer wissenschaftlichen Forschungsreise nach den Samoainseln, dem Neuguinea-Archipel und den Salomonsinseln von März bis Dezember 1905*. Wien, A. Hölder. [Botanical and zoological results of a scientific expedition to the Samoan Islands, the New Guinea archipelago and the Solomon Islands].

Rechinger-Favarger, Lily and Rechinger, Karl (1908). *Streifzüge in Deutsch-Neu-Guinea und auf den Salomons-Inseln*. Berlin, Dietrich Reimer (Ernst Vohsen). [Forays into German New Guinea and the Solomon Islands].

Reeson, Margaret (2013). *Pacific Missionary: George Brown, 1835–1917: Wesleyan Methodist Church*. Canberra, ANU E Press. (http://press.anu.edu.au/titles/pacific-missionary-george-brown/).

Regan, A (2005). 'Clever People Solving Difficult Problems: Perspectives on the weakness of state and nation in Papua New Guinea', SSGM working paper 2005/2, Canberra, State Society and Governance in Melanesia, The Australian National University.

Reilly, B (2004). 'State Functioning and State Failure in the South Pacific', *Australian Journal of International Affairs*, 58 (4): 479–493.

Ribbe, Carl (1903). *Zwei Jahre unter den Kannibalen der Salomo-Inseln: Reiseerlebnisse und Schilderungen von Land und Leuten*. Dresden-Blasewitz, Elbgau-Buchdruckerei, Herman Beyer. [Two Years with the Cannibals of the Solomon Islands: Travel experiences and descriptions of the land and people].

Richards, Rhys (2012). *Head Hunters Black and White: Three collectors in the western Solomon Islands 1893 to 1914: And the diary of Graham Officer, collector of museum objects in the Solomon Islands in 1901 for Museum Victoria in Melbourne*. Wellington, Paremata Press.

Richards, Rhys and Roga, Kenneth (2004). 'Barava: Land title deeds in fossil shell from the western Solomon Islands', *Tuhinga*, 15: 17–26.

Rideing, William H. (1874). 'The South Sea Islands', *Harper's New Monthly Magazine*, 49 (292): 488–500.

Riesenfeld, Alphonse (1950). *The Megalithic Cultures of Melanesia*. Leiden, Brill.

Rivers, William Halse Rivers (1906). *The Todas*. London, Macmillan.

Rivers, William Halse Rivers (1910). 'Speech by Dr Rivers at the Annual Meeting [Melanesian Mission] in England', In: *The Southern Cross Log*, Australia/New Zealand edition, February 5, 1910: 1401–144. (http://anglicanhistory.org/oceania/rivers_speech1910.html).

Rivers, William Halse Rivers (1914). *The History of Melanesian Society*. Cambridge, Cambridge University Press.

Rivers, William Halse Rivers (1915). 'Sun-cult and Megaliths in Oceania', *American Anthropologist*, New series, 17 (3): 431–445.

Rivers, William Halse Rivers (ed.) (1922). *Essays on the Depopulation of Melanesia*. Cambridge, Cambridge University Press.

Roberts, Stephen H. (1927). *Population Problems of the Pacific*. London, Routledge & Sons.

Robson, Andrew E. (1995). 'The Trial of Consul Pritchard', *The Journal of Pacific History*, 30 (2): 173–193.

Rockel, Stephen J. (2000). '"A Nation of Porters": The Nyamwezi and the labour market in nineteenth-century Tanzania', *The Journal of African History*, 41 (2): 173–195.

Rodman, Margaret and Cooper, Matthew (eds) (1983). *The Pacification of Melanesia*. Lanham MD, University Press of America.

Romilly, Hugh Hastings (1882). *A True Story of the Western Pacific in 1879–80*. London, Longmans, Green, & Co.

Romilly, Hugh Hastings (1886). *The Western Pacific and New Guinea: Notes on the natives, Christian and cannibal with some account of the old Labour Trade*. London, John Murray.

Romilly, Hugh Hastings (1889). *From My verandah in New Guinea: Sketches and traditions*. London, David Nutt.

Romilly, Hugh Hastings (1893). *Letters from the Western Pacific and Mashonaland 1878–1891*. Edited with a memoir by Samuel H. Romilly. Introduction by Lord Stanmore. London, David Nutt.

Rosenberg, Sheila (2000). 'The "Wicked Westminster": John Chapman, his contributors ad promises fulfilled', *Victorian Periodicals Review*, 33 (3): 225–246.

Rothschild, Walter and Hertert, Ernst (1905). 'Further Contributions to Our Knowledge of the Ornis of the Solomon Islands', *Novitates Zoologicae*, 12 (2): 242–268.

Rowan, Jeremy David (2003). 'Imagining Corporate Culture: The industrial paternalism of William Hesketh Lever at Port Sunlight, 1888–1925'. Unpublished PhD thesis, Louisiana State University and Agricultural and Mechanical College.

Royal Navy (1886–1896). *Australia Station: New Guinea and Solomon Islands: Correspondence respecting outrages by natives on British subjects.* (Woodford papers PMB 1290 Items 8/21/1–12).

Royal Society of London (1969). 'A Discussion of the Results of the Royal Society Expedition to the British Solomon Islands Protectorate, 1965', *Philosophical Transactions of the Royal Society of London. Series B. Biological sciences*, 255 (800): 185–631. [Organized by E. J. H. Corner].

Ruby, Jay (1996). 'Visual Anthropology', In: Levinson, David and Ember, Melvin (eds). *Encyclopedia of Cultural Anthropology*. Volume 4. New York, Henry Holt & Co, 1345–1351.

Rukavina, Alison (2010). 'A Victorian Amazon.com: Edward Petherick and his colonial booksellers' agency', *Book History*, 13: 104–121.

Russell, T. (1948). 'The Culture of Marovo, British Solomon Islands', *The Journal of the Polynesian Society*, 57: 306–329.

Ryan, James R. (1997). *Picturing Empire: Photography and the visualization of the British Empire*. Chicago, University of Chicago Press.

Sack, Peter (1981–1983). 'Protectorates and Twists: Law, history and the annexation of German New Guinea', *1983 Australian Year Book of International Law*, 10: 1–66.

Sack, Peter (2005). 'Who Wants to Know What "Really" Happened?: "King" Gorai and the population decline in the Shortland Islands', *The Journal of Pacific History*, 40 (3): 339–351.

Sahlins, Marshall D. (1963). 'Poor Man, Rich Man, Big-man, Chief: Political types in Melanesia and Polynesia', *Comparative Studies in Society and History*, 5 (3): 285–303.

Salisbury, Richard F. (1970). *Vunamami: Economic transformation in a traditional society*. Melbourne, Melbourne University Press.

Salvin, Osbert (1888). 'A Note on *Ornithoptera Victoriae*, Gray', *Proceedings of the Zoological Society of London*, 56 (1): 116–122.

Samson, Jane (ed.) (2003a). *British Imperial Strategies in the Pacific, 1750–1900*. Aldershot, Hampshire, Ashgate Variorum.

Samson, Jane (2003b). 'Imperial Benevolence: The Royal Navy and the South Pacific labour trade, 1867–72', In: Samson, Jane (ed.). *British Imperial Strategies in the Pacific, 1750–1900*. Aldershot, Hampshire, Ashgate Variorum: 283–298. [Reprinted from *Great Circle*, 18 (1996): 14–29].

Samuel, Herbert (1919). 'The Taxation of the Various Classes of the People', *Journal of the Royal Statistical Society*, 82 (2): 143–182.

Sanborn, Colin Campbell and Nicholson, A. J. (1950). 'Bats from New Caledonia, the Solomon Island, and New Hebrides', *Fieldiana. Zoology*, 31 (36): 313–338.

Sapir, J. David (1994). 'On Fixing Ethnographic shadows: Review', *American Ethnologist*, 21 (4): 867–885.

Saunders, Kay (1976). 'The Pacific Islander Hospitals in Colonial Queensland: The failure of liberal principals', *The Journal of Pacific History*, 11 (1), Labour Trade, Part 1: 28–50.

Scarr, Deryck (1967a). *Fragments of Empire: A history of the Western Pacific High Commission 1877–1914*. Canberra, Australian National University Press.

Scarr, Deryck (1967b). 'Recruits and Recruiters: A portrait of the Pacific Islands Labour Trade', *The Journal of Pacific History*, 2: 5–24. [A shorter version of Scarr 1970].

Scarr, Deryck (1970). 'Recruits and Recruiters: A portrait of the labour trade', In: Davidson, J. W. and Scarr, Deryck (eds). *Pacific Islands Portraits*. Canberra, Australian National University Press: 225–251.

Scarr, Deryck (1973). *The Majesty of Colour: A life of Sir John Bates Thurston, Volume 1: I, the very bayonet*. Canberra, Australian National University Press.

Scarr, Deryck (1980). *The Majesty of Colour: A life of Sir John Bates Thurston, Volume 2: Viceroy of the Pacific*. Canberra, The Australian National University.

Schaffarczyk, Sylvia (n.d.). 'Australia's Official Papuan Collection: Sir Hubert Murray and the how and why of a colonial collection'. Canberra, National Museum of Australia. (http://recollections.nma.gov.au/issues/vol_1no_1/papers/the_papuan_collection).

Schaller, Georg (2005). 'Das Kreuz auf Guadalcanar ein Reisebrief von Georg Schaller'. (www.doppeladler.com/kuk/guadalcanar).

Scheffler, Harold W. (1962). 'Kindred and Kin groups in Simbo Island Social Structure', *Ethnology*, 1 (2): 135–157.

Scheffler, Harold W. (1964). 'The Social Consequence of Peace on Choiseul Island', *Ethnology*, 3 (4): 398–404.

Scheps, Birgit (2005). *Das verkaufte Museum: die Südsee-Unternehmungen des Handelshauses Joh. Ces. Godeffroy & Sohn, Hamburg, und die Sammlungen Museum Godeffroy*. Keltern-Weiler, Germany, Goecke & Evers. [The Museum Sold Off: The South Sea enterprises of the trading house Joh. Ces. Godeffroy & Son, Hamburg, and the collections of the Godeffroy Museum].

Schieffelin, Edward L. and Crittenden, Robert (1991). *Like People You See in the Dream: First contact in six Papuan societies*. Stanford, CA, Stanford University Press.

Schmidt, Karl P. (1932). 'Reptiles and Amphibians from the Solomon Islands', *Field Museum of Natural History, Zoological Series*, 18 (9): 175–190. [Reports on the results of the Crane Pacific Expedition].

Schneider, Gerhard (1996). 'Land Dispute and Tradition in Munda, Roviana Lagoon, New Georgia Island, Solomon Islands: From headhunting to the quest for the control of land'. Unpublished PhD thesis, Churchill College, University of Cambridge.

Scholefield, Guy H. (1919). *The Pacific: Its past and future and the policy of the Great Powers from the eighteenth century*. New York, Charles Scribner's Sons.

Sclater, W. L. (1928).'Charles Morris Woodford: Obituary', *Ibis*, 12th series, 4: 140–141.

Scragg, Roy (2010). 'Science and Survival in Paradise', *Health and History*, 12 (2): 57–78.

Seeman, Berthold (1853). *Narrative of the Voyage of HMS Herald During the Years 1845–51 Under the Command of Captain Henry Kellett*. 2 volumes. London, Reeve and Co.

Selwyn, John Richardson (1894). 'The Islands of the Western Pacific', *Proceedings of the Royal Colonial Institute*, 25, 1893–1894: 361–393.

Selwyn, John Richardson (1896). 'Occasional Paper of the Melanesian Mission: Christmas 1896'. Ludlow, CA Partridge. (http://anglicanhistory.org/oceania/occasional1896christmas.html).

Sewell, William H. (1992). 'A Theory of Structures: Duality, agency, and transformation', *American Journal of Sociology*, 98 (1): 1–29.

Sheppard, Peter J. (2011). 'Lapita Colonization across the Near/Remote Oceania Boundary', *Current Anthropology*, 52 (6): 799–840.

Sheppard, Peter J. and Walker, Richard (2006). 'A Revised Model of Solomon Islands Culture History', *The Journal of the Polynesian Society*, 115 (1): 47–76.

Sheppard, Peter J., Walter, Richard and Aswani, Shankar (2004). 'Oral Tradition and the Creation of Late Prehistory in Roviana Lagoon, Solomon Islands'. In: Attenbrow, Val and Fullagar, Richard (eds). *A Pacific Odyssey: Archaeology and anthropology in the Western Pacific: Papers in honour of Jim Specht*. Sydney, Australian Museum: 123–132.

Sheppard, Peter J., Walker, Richard and Nagaoka, Takuya (2000). 'The Archaeology of Head-hunting in Roviana Lagoon, New Georgia', *The Journal of the Polynesian Society*, 109 (1): 9–38.

Sharpe, R. Bowdler (1888). 'Descriptions of Some New Species of Birds From the Island of Guadalcanar in the Solomon Islands, Discovered by Mr. C. M. Woodford', *Proceedings of the Zoological Society of London*, 56 (1): 182–185.

Sherlock, S (2003). 'Behind the Solomons Crisis: A problem of development', *Department of the Parliamentary Library. Research note*, 2, 2003–04.

Shineberg, Dorothy (ed.) (1971). *The Trading Voyages of Andrew Cheyne, 1841–1844*. Canberra, Australian National University Press.

Shlomowitz, Ralph (1981). 'Markets for Indentured and Time–expired Melanesian Labour in Queensland, 1863–1906', *The Journal of Pacific History*, 16 (2): 70–91.

Shlomowitz, Ralph (1986). 'The Fiji Labour Trade in Comparative Perspective, 1864–1914', *Pacific Studies*, 9 (3): 107–152.

Shlomowitz, Ralph (1989). 'Epidemiology and the Pacific Labor Trade', *Journal of Interdisciplinary History*, 19(4): 585–610.

Shlomowitz, Ralph and Bedford, Richard D. (1988). 'The Internal Labor Trade in New Hebrides and Solomon Islands c.1900–1941', *Journal de la Société des Océanistes*, 86 (1): 61–85.

Shlomowitz, Ralph and Munro, Doug (1992). 'The Ocean Islands (Banaba) and Nauru Labour Trade 1900–1940', *Journal de la Société des Océanistes*, 94 (1): 103–117.

Siegel, Jeff (1985). 'Origins of Pacific Labourers in Fiji', *The Journal of Pacific History*, 20 (1): 42–54.

Silverman, Martin G. (1962). 'The Resettled Banaban (Ocean Island) Community in Fiji: A preliminary report', *Current Anthropology*, 3 (4): 429–431.

Sinclair, Keith (2011). 'Grey, George', *Te Ara: the Encyclopaedia of New Zealand*. (http://www.teara.govt.nz/en/biographies/1g21).

Sinker, William (1907). *By Reef and Shoal: Being an account of a voyage amongst the islands in the South-West Pacific*. London, Society for Promoting Christian Knowledge. (http://anglicanhistory.org/oceania/sinker_reef1907.html).

Smith, H. Hamel and Pape, F. A. G. (1917). *Coconuts: The consols of the East*. 2nd edition. London, "Tropical Life" Publishing Dept.

Smith, Iain R. (1972). *The Emin Pasha Relief Expedition, 1886–1890*. Oxford, Clarendon Press.

Smith, Jim (1971) 'Island of Dreams', *The Australian Woman's Weekly*, April 14, 1971: 1–10.

Sohmer, Sara H. (1984). 'Idealism and Pragmatism in Colonial Fiji: Sir Arthur Gordon's native rule policy and the introduction of Indian contract labor', *The Hawaiian Journal of History*, 18: 140–155.

Solomon Islands Government. Commission of Inquiry into the Land Dealings and Abandoned Properties on Guadalcanal (2012). *A Review of the Literature*. Honiara, the Commission. (http://www.comofinquiry.gov.sb/Articles/1891-codrington%20RH.pdf).

Solomon Islands Government. Department of Lands and Survey. Geographic Information Unit (2004). *Solomon Islands National Gazetteer of Place Names for 1:50,000 scale mapping*. Honiara, Department of Lands and Survey.

Solomon Islands Government. Ministry of Finance, Statistics Office (1995). *Statistical Bulletin No. 18/95, Income and Expenditure Survey 1993*. Honiara, Statistics Office.

Solomon Islands Government. Ministry of Finance, Statistics Office (1997). *Statistical Bulletin No. 10/97. Report 2: Village Resources Survey, 1995/96*. Honiara, Statistics Office.

Solomon Islands Government. Ministry of Provincial Government and Rural Development (2001a). *Malaita Province Development Profile*. Rural Development Division, Ministry of Provincial Government and Rural Development, with technical assistance from UNDP/UNOPS Solomon Islands Development Administration and Participatory Planning Program, Honiara.

Solomon Islands Government. Ministry of Provincial Government and Rural Development (2001b). *Rennell Bellona Province Development Profile*, Rural Development Division, Ministry of Provincial Government and Rural Development, with technical assistance from UNDP/UNOPS Solomon Islands Development Administration and Participatory Planning Program, Honiara.

Solomon Islands Government. National Statistics Office (2011). *Report on 2009 Population and Housing Census*. Honiara, Solomon Islands Government.

Solomon Islands Government. Truth and Reconciliation Commission (2012). *Truth and Reconciliation Commission: Reports*. 5 volumes. Honiara, TRC.

Somerville, Boyle T. (1897). 'Ethnological Notes in New Georgia, Solomon Islands', *The Journal of the Anthropological Institute of Great Britain and Ireland*, 26: 357–412.

Specht, Jim and Fields, John (1984). *Frank Hurley in Papua: Photographs of the 1920–1923 expeditions*. Bathurst, Robert Brown in association with the Australian Museum Trust.

Speiser, Felix (1913). *Two Years with the Natives in the Western Pacific*. London, Mills and Boon.

Speiser, Felix (1922). 'Decadence and Preservation in the New Hebrides', In: Rivers, William Halse Rivers (ed.). *Essays on the Depopulation of Melanesia*. Cambridge, Cambridge University Press: 25–61.

Staniforth-Smith, Miles (1903). *British New Guinea: With a preface on Australia's policy in the Pacific*. Melbourne, F. W. Niven & Co.

Stanley, Henry Morton (1885). *The Congo and the Founding of its Free State: A story of work and exploration*. 2 volumes. London, Sampson Low, Marston.

Stanley, Henry Morton (1890) 'Geographical results of the Emin Pasha Relief Expedition', *Proceedings of the Royal Geographical Society and Monthly Record of Geography*, new monthly series, 12 (6): 313–331.

Stanley, Nick (1989). 'The Unstable Object: Reviewing the status of ethnographic artefacts', *Journal of Design History*, 2 (2–3): 107–122.

Stawell, W. (1910). 'Letter to W. Stawell from [Austral Chambers] located at 99 Queen Street, Melbourne [possibly office of John Goodall, Stockbroker] dated 4 May 1910'. (State Library of Victoria, MS 9273).

Stephens, Geoffrey (1985). 'H.H. Montgomery: The Mutton Bird Bishop', University of Tasmania Occasional Paper 39, Hobart, University of Tasmania.

Stevens, E. V. (1950). 'Blackbirding: A brief history of the South Sea Island Labour Trade and the vessels engaged in it'. Unpublished paper read at the meeting of the Historical Society of Queensland, March 23, 1950.

Stoler, Ann Laura (1989). 'Rethinking Colonial Categories: European communities and the boundaries of rule', *Comparative Studies in Society and History*, 31 (1): 134–161.

Straatman, R, (1969). 'Notes on the Biology and Hostplant Associations of *Ornithoptera Priamus Urvilleanus* and *O. Victoriae* (Papilionidae)', *Journal of the Lepidopterists' Society*, 23 (2): 76.

Sullivan, Eileen P. (1983). 'Liberalism and Imperialism: J. S. Mill's defence of the British Empire', *Journal of the History of Ideas*, 44 (4): 599–617.

Sullivan, Marjorie (2007). 'Recognition of Customary land in the Solomon Islands: Status, issues and options', Resource Management in Asia Pacific working paper 66, Canberra, Resource Management in Asia Pacific, The Australian National University.

Summers, John (2000). 'The Parliament of the Commonwealth of Australia and Indigenous peoples 1901–1967', Research Paper 10 2000-01, Canberra, Parliament of Australia. (http://www.aph.gov.au/About_Parliament/Parliamentary_Departments/Parliamentary_Library/pubs/rp/rp0001/01RP10).

Swadling, Pamela (1996). *Plumes from Paradise: Trade cycles in outer Southeast Asia and their impact on New Guinea and nearby islands until 1920*. Port Moresby, Papua New Guinea National Museum in association with Robert Brown & Associates (Qld).

Tagini, Phillip (2001). 'The Effect of Land Policy on Foreign Direct Investment in the Solomon Islands', *Journal of South Pacific Law*, 5: 1–9. (http://www.paclii.org/journals/fJSPL/vol05/5.shtml).

Taylor, Jacqueline (1975). 'Violence in Melanesia: Case study: Acts of violence by indigenes towards European traders and settlers in the Solomon Islands 1878–1893'. Unpublished PhD thesis, University of Auckland.

Tedder, James L. O. (2008). *Solomon Island Years: A district administrator in the islands 1952–1974*. Stuarts Point, NSW, Tuatu Studies.

Tennant, W. John (1997). 'The Type locality of *Ornithoptera Victoriae* Gray, 1856, and the Circumstance of the Capture of the Holotype Female (Lepidoptera, Rhopalocera)', *Archives of Natural History*, 24 (2): 163–173.

Tennant, W. John (1999). 'Charles Morris Woodford (CMG): Pacific adventurer and forgotten Solomon Islands naturalist', *Archives of Natural History*, 26(3): 419–432.

Terrell, J. E. and Irwin, G. J. (1972). 'History and Tradition in the Northern Solomons: An analytical study of the Torau migration to southern Bougainville in the 1860s', *The Journal of the Polynesian Society*, 81 (3): 317–349.

Terrell, John (1977). 'Human Biogeography in the Solomon Islands', *Fieldiana. Anthropology*, 68 (1): 1–47.

Thomas, Nicholas (1989), 'Material Culture and Colonial Power: Ethnological collecting and the establishment of colonial rule in Fiji', *Man,* New series, 24 (1): 41–56.

Thomas, Nicholas (1990). 'Partial Texts: Representation, colonialism and agency in Pacific history', *The Journal of Pacific History*, 25 (2): 139–158.

Thomas, Nicholas (1992). 'Colonial Conversions: Difference, hierarchy, and history in early Twentieth-Century evangelical propaganda', *Comparative Studies in Society and History*, 34 (2): 366–389.

Thomas, Nicholas (1999). *Possessions: Indigenous art/colonial culture.* London, Thames and Hudson.

Thomas, Oldfield (1887a). 'Diagnoses of Two New Fruit-eating Bats from the Solomon Islands', *The Annals and Magazine of Natural History*, 5th series, 19: 147.

Thomas, Oldfield (1887b). 'On the Bats Collected by Mr. C. M. Woodford in the Solomon Islands', *Proceedings of the Zoological Society of London*, 55 (2): 320–328. (Woodford papers PMB 1290 Item 7/21/3).

Thomas, Oldfield (1888a). 'Diagnoses of Six New Mammals from the Solomon Islands', *The Annals and Magazine of Natural History*, 6th series, 1: 155–158. (Woodford papers PMB 1290 Item 7/20/8).

Thomas, Oldfield (1888b). 'The Mammals of the Solomon Islands, Based on the Collections Made by Mr. C. M. Woodford During His Second Expedition to the Archipelago', *Proceedings of the Zoological Society of London*, 56 (1): 470–484.

Thomas, Tim, Sheppard, Peter and Walter, Richard (2001). 'Landscape, Violence and Social Bodies: Ritualized architecture in a Solomon Islands society', *The Journal of the Royal Anthropological Institute*, 7 (3): 545–572.

Thompson, Roger C. (1986). 'Hubert Murray and the Historians', *Pacific Studies*, 10 (1): 79–96.

Thomson, Basil (1899) 'Curiosities of the South Seas', *Wide World Magazine*, 3: 509–516. (Woodford papers PMB 1290 Item 7/46).

Thomson, Basil, Haddon, Alfred Cort, Seligman, C. G., Woodford, Charles Morris and Ray, Sidney H. (1916). 'On Some Little-Known Polynesian Settlements in the Neighbourhood of the Solomon Islands: Discussion', *The Geographical Journal*, 48 (1): 49–54.

Thurnwald, Richard C. (1936) 'The Price of White Man's Peace', *Pacific Affairs*, 9 (3): 347–357.

Thurston, John Bates (1886). *Catalogue of Trees, Shrubs, and Foliage Plants at Thornbury, Suva and St Helier's, Taviuni, Fiji*. Suva, E. J. March, Government Printer.

Townsend, Mary Evelyn (1921). *Origins of Modern German Colonialism: 1871–1885*. New York, Columbia University.

The Transformed Isle: Barbarism to Christianity: A genuine portrayal of yesterday to to-day, the story of fifteen years among the head-hunters of the island of Vella Lavella. (1920). Sydney, Australian Religious Tract Society.

Treadaway, Julian (2007). *Dancing, Dying, Crawling, Crying: Stories of continuity and change in the Polynesian community of Tikopia*. Suva, IPS Publications, University of the South Pacific.

Trotter, Coutts (1884). 'New Guinea: A summary of our present knowledge with regard to the island', *Proceedings of the Royal Geographical Society and Monthly Record of Geography*, 6 (4): 195–216.

Trotter, Coutts (1888). 'Notes on the Natives of the Polynesian Islands', *The Journal of the Anthropological Institute o Great Britain and Ireland*, 17: 74–78.

Turner, Frank M. (1978). 'The Victorian Conflict Between Science and Religion: A professional dimension', *Isis*, 69 (3): 356–376.

Turner, Mark (2000). 'Defining Discourses: The "Westminster Review", "Fortnightly Review", and Comte's positivism', *Victorian Periodicals Review*, 33 (3): 273–282.

Turner, Michael J. (2005). '"Raising up Dark Englishmen": Thomas Perronet Thompson, colonies, race, and the Indian Mutiny', *Journal of Colonialism and Colonial History*, 6 (1).

UNESCAP, UNDP and ADB (2005). *A Future Within Reach: Reshaping institutions in a region of disparities to meet the Millennium Development Goals in Asia and the Pacific*. New York, United Nations.

UNICEF (1993). *A Situation Analysis of Women and Children in the Solomon Islands*. Honiara, UNICEF.

UNICEF [with the Government of the Solomon Islands] (2005). *Solomon Islands: A situation analysis of children, youth and women*. Honiara, UNICEF.

United States. Defense Mapping Agency (1974). *British Solomon Islands Protectorate and Gilbert and Ellice Islands Colony: Official standard names*. Washington, Defense Mapping Agency.

Urry, James (1972). '"Notes and Queries on Anthropology" and the Development of Field Methods in British Anthropology, 1870–1920', *Proceedings of the Royal Anthropological Institute of Great Britain and Ireland*, 1972: 45–57.

The Vagabond [Julian Thomas] (1876–1878). *The Vagabond Papers: Sketches of Melbourne life in light and shade*. 5 volumes. Melbourne, George Robertson.

The Vagabond [Julian Thomas] (1881). *South Sea Massacres*. Sydney, *The Australian*. [Reprints, edited, from articles published in *The Sydney Morning Herald*, 2 April 1881: 7, 19 April 1881: 7, 24 October 1881: 9 and *The Sydney Daily Telegraph*, see also *The Argus*, 22 March 1881: 6].

The Vagabond [Julian Thomas] (1886). *Cannibals and Convicts: Notes of personal experiences in the Western Pacific*. London, Cassell & Company.

VanArsdel, Rosemary T. (1968). 'Notes on Westminster Review Research', *Victorian Periodicals Newsletter*, 1 (1): 20–23.

Vanderwal, R. (2001). 'Graham Officer in the Solomon Islands, 1901', In: Rasmussen, Carolyn (ed.). *A Museum for the People: A history of* Museum Victoria *and its predecessors, 1854–2000*. Melbourne, Scribe Publications: 108–112.

Veperdi, András (n.d.). 'The journey of SMS "Albatros" in the Solomons'. (http://mateinfo.hu/a-albatros.htm).

Victoria. Parliament (1879). *Government Gazette*, no. 117, December 5, 1879.

Virgil (2007). *The Aeneid*. Translated with notes by Frederick Ahl, with an introduction by Elaine Fantham. New York, Oxford University Press.

Vogt, Evon Z. (1954). 'Notes and Queries on Anthropology [review]', *American Anthropologist*, 56: 1154–1156.

Voigt, J. C. (1900). 'The Afrikanders in Natal', *The North American Review*, 170 (519): 212–224.

Wainright, E. (2003). *Our Failing Neighbour: Australia and the failure of Solomon Islands*. Canberra, Australian Strategic Policy Institute.

Wairiu, M. (n.d.). 'Solomon Islands Livelihood Realities', Unpublished paper.

Waite, Deborah (2000). 'An Artefact/Image Text of Head-hunting Motifs', *The Journal of the Polynesian Society*, 109 (1): 115–144.

Waite, Deborah and Conru, Kevin (2008). *Solomon Islands Art: The Conru Collection*. 5 Continents.

Wallace, Alfred Russel (1853). *Palm Trees of the Amazon and Their Uses*. London, John van Voorse.

Wallace, Alfred Russel (1855). 'On the Law Which has Regulated the Introduction of New Species', *Annals and Magazine of Natural History*, 2nd series, 16: 184–196.

Wallace, Alfred Russel (1869). *The Malay Archipelago: The land of the orang-utan and the bird of paradise: A narrative of travel, with studies of man and nature*. 2 volumes. London, Macmillan.

Wallace, Alfred Russel (1876). *The Geographical Distribution of Animals: With a study of the relations of living and extinct faunas as elucidating the past changes of the earth's surface*. 2 volumes. London, Macmillan.

Wallace, Alfred Russel (1880). *Islands Life: Or, the phenomena and causes of insular faunas and floras: including a revision and attempted solution of the problem of geological climates*. London, Macmillan.

Wallace, Alfred Russel (1890). 'A Naturalist Among the Head-hunters [Review]', *Nature*, April 24, 1890: 582–583.

Walter, Richard and Sheppard, Peter (2000). 'Nusa Roviana: The archaeology of a Melanesian chiefdom', *Journal of Field Archaeology*, 27 (3): 295–318.

Ward, John Manning (1948). *British Policy in the South Pacific, 1786–1893: A study in British policy towards the South Pacific islands prior to the establishment of government by the Great Powers*. Sydney, Australasian Publishing Co.

Ware, Helen (2005). 'Demography, Migration and Conflict in the Pacific', *Journal of Peace Research*, 42 (2) (Special issue on the Demography of Conflict and Violence): 435–454.

Wawn, William Twizell (1893). *The South Sea Islanders and the Queensland Labour Trade: A record of voyages and experiences in the Western Pacific from 1875 to 1891*. London, Swan Sonnerschei & Co.

Wawn, William Twizell and Corris, Peter (ed.) (1973). *The South Sea Islanders and the Queensland Labour Trade*. Honolulu, University Press of Hawai'i.

Welsch, Robert L. (1996). 'Collaborative Regional Anthropology in New Guinea: From the New Guinea Micro-evolution Project to the A. B. Lewis Project and beyond', *Pacific Studies*, 19 (3): 143–186.

Welsch, Robert L. and Lewis, A. B. (1998). *An American Anthropologist in Melanesia: A. B. Lewis and the Joseph N. Field South Pacific Expedition, 1909–1913*. Honolulu, University of Hawai'i Press.

Wesley-Smith, Terence (2007).'Self-determination in Oceania', *Race & Class*, 48 (3): 29–46.

West, Andrew (1992). 'The History of the Ethnography Collections of W. H. Lever', *Journal of the History of Collections*, 4 (2): 273–283.

Western Pacific Archives (c.1977). Solomon Island National Archives. British Solomon Islands Protectorate. Records control list numbers BSIP 1–32. Suva, WPA. (BSIP 14/II). [These record control lists and files are located in the National Archives Solomon Islands, Honiara].

Western Pacific High Commission. (1875–1941). *Inward Correspondence: Minute Papers (MP) series*. 4/IV. Suva. (WPHC 4/IV).

Wetherell, David (1996). *Charles Abel and the Kwato Mission of Papua New Guinea 1891–1975*. Melbourne, Melbourne University Press.

Wheeler, Gerard C. (1926). *Mono-Alu Folklore (Bougainville Strait, Western Solomon Islands)*. London, Routledge.

W. H. H. (1888). 'The Solomon Islands, their Geology etc by H. B. Guppy [Review]', *Geographical Magazine*, Decade III, 5 (4): 168–171.

White, Geoffrey (1983). 'War, Peace, and Piety in Santa Isabel, Solomon Islands', In: Rodman, Margaret and Cooper, Matthew (eds). *The Pacification of Melanesia*. Lanham MD, University Press of America: 109–139.

White, Geoffrey (1991). *Identity Through History: Living stories in a Solomon Islands society*. Cambridge, Cambridge University Press.

Whittaker, J. L. *et al*. (1975). *Documents and Readings in New Guinea history: Prehistory to 1889*. Milton, The Jacaranda Press.

Wickler, Stephen (2001). *The Prehistory of Buka: A stepping stone in the Northern Solomons*. Canberra, Department of Archaeology and Natural History and Centre for Archaeological Research, The Australian National University.

Wilkinson. Rupert H. (1963). 'The Gentleman Ideal and the Maintenance of a Political Elite: Two case studies: Confucian education in the Tang, Sung, Ming and Ching Dynasties: And the Late Victorian Public Schools (1870–1914)', *Sociology of Education*, 37 (1): 9–26.

Williams, Francis Edgar (1923). *The Collection of Curios and the Preservation of Native Culture*. Port Moresby, Government Printer.

Williams, Francis Edgar (1933). *Depopulation of the Suau District*. Port Moresby, Government Printer.

Williams, Shaun (2011). 'Public Land Governance in Solomon Islands', *Justice for the Poor Briefing Note*, 6 (1), February 2011.

Williamson, Jeffrey G. (1980).'Earnings Inequality in Nineteenth-Century Britain', *The Journal of Economic History*, 40 (3): 457–475.

Williamson, Robert W. (1912). *The Mafulu: Mountain people of British New Guinea*. London, Macmillan. (http://www.gutenberg.org/files/17910/17910-h/17910-h.htm).

Williamson, Robert W. (1914). *The Ways of the South Sea Savage: A record of travel and observation amongst the savages of the Solomon Islands & primitive coast & mountain peoples of New Guinea*. Philadelphia, J. B. Lippincott Co.

Wilson, Cecil (1900). 'Island Voyage, 1900', In: *The Island Voyage & Report*, Auckland, June 1901: 1–6. (http://anglicanhistory.org/oceania/cwilson/report1900.html).

Wilson, Cecil (1932). *The Wake of the "Southern Cross": Work and adventures in the South Seas*. London, John Murray. (http://anglicanhistory.org/oceania/wilson_wake1932).

Wilson, Ellen (1911). *The Isles That Wait*. London, Society for Promoting Christian Knowledge. (http://anglicanhistory.org/oceania/wilson_isles1911).

Wilson, Ellen (1935). *Dr Welchman of Bugotu*. London, Society for Promoting Christian Knowledge. (http://anglicanhistory.org/oceania/wilson_welchman1935).

Wilson, Nick *et al*. (2005). 'Modelling the Impact of Pandemic Influenza on Pacific Islands', *Emerging Infectious Diseases*, 11 (2): 347–349.

Withers, Charles W. J. and Finnegan, Diarmid A. (2003). 'Natural History Societies, Fieldwork and Local Knowledge in Nineteenth-Century Scotland: Towards a historical geography of civic science', *Cultural Geographies*, 10: 334–353.

Wolfe, Patrick (1997). 'History and Imperialism: A century of theory, from Marx to Postcolonialism', *The American Historical Review*, 102 (2): 388–420.

Wood, George H. (1909). 'Real Wages and the Standard of Comfort Since 1850', *Journal of the Royal Statistical Society*, 72 (1): 91–103.

Woodford, Charles Morris (1852–1927). 'Charles Morris Woodford collection'. (ANU Archives, Woodford papers AU ANUA 481). [6m; 1 album; 9 large framed photographs].

Woodford, Charles Morris (1852–1927). 'C. M. Woodford (1852–1927). Papers on the Solomon Islands and other Pacific Islands, 1872–1927'. (Woodford papers PMB 1290).

Woodford, Charles Morris (1852–1927). 'C. M. Woodford (1852–1927) Papers on the Solomon Islands and other Pacific Islands, 1864–2003'. (Woodford papers PMB 1381).

Woodford, Charles Morris (1852–1927). 'Woodford, C. M. Two albums of photographs taken during a voyage to and residence in the Solomon Islands from April to October 1886, and additional loose photographs'. (PMB Photo 56/1–240).

Woodford, Charles Morris (1852–1927). 'Woodford, C. M. Solomon Islands photographs c.1890s–c.1920'. (Woodford papers PMB Photo 58/1–233).

Woodford, Charles Morris (1884–1896). Diaries.

PMB 1290 1/1: Gilbert Islands 4 March–22 June 1884;

PMB 1381/022a 20 October 1885–8 April 1886;

PMB 1290 1/2: 16 April–5 July 1886;

PMB 1290 1/3: 6 July–3 August 1886;

PMB 1290 1/4: 4 August–10 November 1886 [also at PMB 1381/022b];

PMB 1290 1/5: Revised diary 16 April–5 July 1886 [see also 1/2];

PMB 1290 1/6: 24 January–5 June 1887;

PMB 1290 1/7: 7 June–25 September 1887;

PMB 1290 1/8: 16 August 1888–3 January 1889;

PMB 1290 1/9: Voyage on the HMS *Pylades* 30 May–10 August 1896.

Woodford, Charles Morris (1885). 'Remarks Upon Lepidoptera Collected in the Ellice and Gilbert Islands', *The Annals and Magazine of Natural History*, 5th series, 15: 414–416. (Woodford papers PMB 1290 Item 6/10).

Woodford, Charles Morris (1888a). 'Exploration of the Solomon Islands', *The Proceedings of the Royal Geographical Society and Monthly Record of Geography*, New Monthly Series, 10 (6): 351–376.

Woodford, Charles Morris (1888b). 'General Remarks on the Zoology of the Solomon Islands, and Notes on Brenchley's Megapode', *Proceedings of the Zoological Society of London*, 56 (1): 248–250. (Woodford papers PMB 1290 Item 6/2).

Woodford, Charles Morris (1889). 'Life in the Solomon Islands', *The Popular Science Monthly*, 35: 476–487.

Woodford, Charles Morris (1890a). 'Report on a Photographic Exhibition at the Zoological Society', *Proceedings of the Zoological Society of London*, 58: 148.

Woodford, Charles Morris (1890b). *A Naturalist Among the Head-hunters: Being an account of three visits to the Solomon Islands in the years, 1886, 1887, and 1888*. 2nd edition. London, George Phillip & Sons.

Woodford, Charles Morris (1890c). 'Further Explorations in the Solomon Islands', *Proceedings of the Royal Geographical Society and Monthly Record of Geography*, New Monthly Series, 12 (7): 393–418.

Woodford, Charles Morris (1895) 'The Gilbert Islands', *The Geographical Journal*, 6 (4): 325–350.

Woodford, Charles Morris (1897). *Western Pacific: Report on the British Solomon Islands*. London, Eyre and Spottiswoode. (Colonial Reports—Miscellaneous no. 8, C.8457). [Cited as: Great Britain. House of Commons. Parliamentary Papers (1897)].

Woodford, Charles Morris (1901). 'Note on Tatu-Patterns Employed in Lord Howe's Island', *Man*, 1: 40.

Woodford, Charles Morris (1905). 'Further Note on Funerary Ornaments from the Solomon Islands', *Man*, 5: 38–39.

Woodford, Charles Morris (1906a). 'Notes on Leueneuwa, or Lord Howe's Group', *Man*, 6: 133–135.

Woodford, Charles Morris (1906b) 'Some Account of Sikaiana or Stewart's Island in the British Solomon Islands Protectorate', *Man*, 6: 164–169.

Woodford, Charles Morris (1907). 'Notes on Rennell Island', *Man*, 7: 33–37.

Woodford, Charles Morris (1908a). 'Note on Stone-Headed Clubs from Malaita, Solomon Islands', *Man*, 8: 165–166.

Woodford, Charles Morris (1908b). 'Notes on the Manufacture of the Malaita Shell Bead Money of the Solomon Group', *Man*, 8: 81–84.

Woodford, Charles Morris (1909a). 'Note on the Atoll of Ongtong Java or Lord Howe's Group in the Western Pacific', *The Geographical Journal*, 34 (5): 544–549.

Woodford, Charles Morris (1909b). 'The Canoes of the British Solomon Islands', *The Journal of the Royal Anthropological Institute of Great Britain and Ireland*, 39 (July–December): 505–516.

Woodford, Charles Morris (1910). 'Stone-headed Mace from Rennell Island', *Man*, 10: 121–122.

Woodford, Charles Morris (1911). 'Note on Bone Spear-Heads from the New Georgia Group, British Solomon Islands', *Man*, 11: 120–122.

Woodford, Charles Morris (1912). 'Description and Names of Various Parts of a Canoe of Sikaiana or Stewart's Island', *Man*, 12:185.

Woodford, Charles Morris (1916a). 'Note on a Remarkable Honey-eater (*Woodfordia Superciliosa* North) from Rennell Island in the Western Pacific', *Ibis*, series 10, 4: 118–122.

Woodford, Charles Morris (1916b). 'On Some Little-Known Polynesian Settlements in the Neighbourhood of the Solomon Islands', *The Geographical Journal*, 48(1): 26–49.

Woodford, Charles Morris (1918). 'Fish-hooks from the Solomon Islands', *Man*, 18: 130–132.

Woodford, Charles Morris (1921). 'Note on the Use of Spider's Web for Fishing and Other Purposes in the Solomon Islands and the New Hebrides', *Man*, 21: 187.

Woodford, Charles Morris (1922a). 'A Singular Method of Catching Prawns', *Man*, 22: 78.

Woodford, Charles Morris (1922b). 'The Solomon Islands', In: Rivers, William Halse Rivers (ed.). *Essays on the Depopulation of Melanesia*. Cambridge, Cambridge University Press: 69–77.

Woodford, Charles Morris (1926). 'Notes on the Solomon Islands', *The Geographical Journal*, 68 (6): 481–487.

Worboys, Michael (2000). 'The Colonial World as Mission and Mandate: Leprosy and Empire, 1900–1940', *Osiris*, 2nd series, 15, (Nature and Empire: Science and the colonial enterprise): 207–218.

World Bank (2010). *Solomon Islands Growth Prospects: Constraints and policy priorities*. Sydney, World Bank's Pacific Department.

World Bank. Pacific Department (2011). 'Discussion Note: Pacific futures'. Sydney, World Bank's Pacific Department.

Worster, Donald (1994). *Nature's Economy: The history of ecological ideas*. 2nd edition. Cambridge, Cambridge University Press.

Wright, Christopher (2004). 'Material and Memory: Photography in the Western Solomon Islands', *Journal of Material Culture*, 9 (1): 73–85.

Wright, Christopher (2005). 'The Echo of Things: Photography in Roviana Lagoon, Solomon Islands'. Unpublished PhD thesis, University College, London.

Wright, Christopher (2009). 'Faletau's Photocopy: Or the mutability of visual history in Roviana', In: Morton, Christopher and Edwards, Elizabeth (eds). *Photography, Anthropology and History: Expanding the frame*. Farnham, UK, Ashgate: 223–239.

Wright, D. (1969). 'The Expulsion of the Kanakas from Queensland: An early issue in Commonwealth–State relations', *Queensland Heritage*, 1 (10): 9–15.

Yen, D. E. (1973). 'Ethnobotany from the Voyages of Mendaña and Quiros in the Pacific', *World Archaeology*, 5 (1): 32–43.

Young, Michael W. (1998). *Malinowski's Kiriwina: Fieldwork photographs, 1915–1918*. Chicago, University of Chicago Press.

Young, Michael W. (2000). 'The Careless Collector: Malinowski and the Antiquarians', In: O'Hanlon, Michael and Welsch, Robert L. (eds). *Hunting the Gatherers: Ethnographic collectors, agents and agency in Melanesia, 1870s–1930s*. New York, Berghahn Books: 181–202.

Young, Michael W. and Clark, Julia (2001). *An Anthropologist in Papua: The photography of F. E. Williams, 1922–39*. Adelaide, Crawford House in association with the National Archives of Australia.

Zelenietz, Martin (1983). 'The End of Headhunting in New Georgia', In: Rodman, Margaret and Cooper, Matthew (eds). *The Pacification of Melanesia*. Lanham MD, University Press of America: 91–108.

Zoological Society of London (1888). *Proceedings of the Scientific Meetings of the Society for the Year 1888*. London, Longmans, Green and Co.

www.ingramcontent.com/pod-product-compliance
Lightning Source LLC
Chambersburg PA
CBHW041244240426
43670CB00025B/2972